THE CAMBRIDGE ECONOMIC HISTORY OF
THE MODERN WORLD

The first volume of *The Cambridge Economic History of the Modern World* traces the emergence of modern economic growth in eighteenth-century Britain and its spread across the globe. Focusing on the period from 1700 to 1870, a team of leading experts in economic history offer a series of regional studies from around the world, as well as thematic analyses of key factors governing the differential outcomes in different parts of the global economy. Topics covered include population and human development, capital and technology, geography and institutions, living standards and inequality, international flows of trade and labour, the international monetary system, and warfare and empire.

STEPHEN BROADBERRY is Professor of Economic History at the University of Oxford and a Fellow of the British Academy. He has been Managing Editor of the *Economic History Review* and also the *European Review of Economic History*, and President of the Economic History Society and the European Historical Economics Society.

KYOJI FUKAO is President of the Institute of Developing Economies, Japan External Trade Organization (IDE-JETRO) and Specially Appointed Professor at the Institute of Economic Research, Hitotsubashi University. He has been President of the Asian Historical Economics Society and has published widely on Japanese and global economic history.

THE CAMBRIDGE ECONOMIC HISTORY OF

THE MODERN WORLD

The Cambridge Economic History of the Modern World offers an unprecedented global account of the emergence of modern economic growth and its spread across the world since 1700. Each volume provides a series of regional studies from across the globe, as well as thematic analyses of key factors governing differential outcomes in different parts of the global economy. Written by leading experts in economic history and covering topics such as demography and human development, capital and technology, living standards and inequality, geography and institutions, trade and migration, international finance, and warfare and empire, these volumes offer the most authoritative account to date of modern economic growth.

VOLUME I

1700 to 1870

EDITED BY STEPHEN BROADBERRY AND KYOJI FUKAO

VOLUME II

1870 to the Present

EDITED BY STEPHEN BROADBERRY AND KYOJI FUKAO

THE CAMBRIDGE ECONOMIC HISTORY OF THE MODERN WORLD

*

VOLUME I

1700 to 1870

*

Edited by
STEPHEN BROADBERRY
University of Oxford
KYOJI FUKAO
Hitotsubashi University, Tokyo

CAMBRIDGE
UNIVERSITY PRESS

CAMBRIDGE
UNIVERSITY PRESS

Shaftesbury Road, Cambridge CB2 8EA, United Kingdom

One Liberty Plaza, 20th Floor, New York, NY 10006, USA

477 Williamstown Road, Port Melbourne, VIC 3207, Australia

314–321, 3rd Floor, Plot 3, Splendor Forum, Jasola District Centre, New Delhi – 110025, India

103 Penang Road, #05–06/07, Visioncrest Commercial, Singapore 238467

Cambridge University Press is part of Cambridge University Press & Assessment,
a department of the University of Cambridge.

We share the University's mission to contribute to society through the pursuit of education, learning and research at the highest international levels of excellence.

www.cambridge.org
Information on this title: www.cambridge.org/9781316612248

DOI: 10.1017/9781316671566

First published 2021
First paperback edition 2025

A catalogue record for this publication is available from the British Library

Two-Volume Set ISBN 978-1-108-95377-1 Hardback
Volume I ISBN 978-1-107-15945-7 Hardback
Volume II ISBN 978-1-107-15948-8 Hardback
ISBN 978-1-316-61224-8 Paperback

Contents

Figures

Tables

Contributors to Volume I

Jean-Pascal Bassino, Department of Social Sciences, École Normale Supérieure, Lyon
Stephen Broadberry, Department of Economics, University of Oxford
Paul Caruana-Galizia, Department of Economic History, London School of Economics
Romola Davenport, Department of Geography, University of Cambridge
Rui Pedro Esteves, Departments of International Economics and International History, The Graduate Institute, Geneva
Giovanni Federico, Social Science Division, NYU Abu Dhabi
Kyoji Fukao, Institute of Economic Research, Hitotsubashi University
Regina Grafe, Department of History and Civilization, European University Institute
Tomoko Hashino, Graduate School of Economics, Kobe University
Philip T. Hoffman, Division of the Humanities and Social Sciences, California Institute of Technology
Christopher Isett, College of Liberal Arts, University of Minnesota
Wolfgang Keller, Department of Economics, University of Colorado
Markus Lampe, Institute for Economic and Social History, Vienna University of Economics and Business
Patrick Manning, Department of History, University of Pittsburgh
Andrei Markevich, New Economic School, Moscow
David Meredith, Faculty of History, University of Oxford
Masaki Nakabayashi, Institute of Social Science, University of Tokyo
Pilar Nogues-Marco, Department of History, Economics and Society, University of Geneva
Alessandro Nuvolari, Institute of Economics, Sant'Anna School of Advanced Studies, Pisa
Şevket Pamuk, Ataturk Institute for Modern Turkish History, Bogazici University
Joshua L. Rosenbloom, Department of Economics, Iowa State University
Tirthankar Roy, Department of Economic History, London School of Economics
Osamu Saito, Institute of Economic Research, Hitotsubashi University
Max-Stephan Schulze, Department of Economic History, London School of Economics
Carol Shiue, Department of Economics, University of Colorado
Anand V. Swamy, Department of Economics, Williams College

Contributors to Volume I

Masayuki Tanimoto, Graduate School of Economics, University of Tokyo
Bas van Leeuwen, International Institute of Social History, Amsterdam
Jan Luiten van Zanden, Department of History, Utrecht University
John Joseph Wallis, Department of Economics, University of Maryland
Yi Xu, Historical Culture and Tourism College, Guangxi Normal University

Preface and Acknowledgements

Within a generation, economic history has globalized. Forty years ago, most economic history research and teaching focused on national trends, and was conducted by local scholars in their own language. International travel was expensive and communication difficult, with international conferences few and far between. Today, there is a large literature on most regions of the world written in English, and a growing trend in co-authorship has facilitated a comparative approach, and encouraged researchers to present their findings within a global framework. These trends are most advanced in the period from around 1700, which led us to the idea of producing a *Cambridge Economic History of the Modern World.*

A traditional strength of economic history has always been its firm grounding in the local context, and we believe that the embracing of the global must not come at the expense of the institutional details of national and regional history. Here, we are fortunate in being able to draw on other volumes in the Cambridge Economic History series, which at the time of writing covers Europe, Modern Britain, Modern Europe, the United States, India, Australia, Latin America and the Greco-Roman World, with other titles in preparation. As a result, we made a decision to start each volume with a series of regional chapters before moving on to a consideration of the key themes within a global context. Here, we have been able to draw on the growing use of quantitative data and accessible economic analysis that has occurred in recent years. We have also chosen to focus on the issue of economic growth and development, to provide a unifying framework and keep the project down to a manageable length.

The large number of authors needed for the two volumes are drawn from international networks straddling the major regions of the world. The editors have been deeply involved in the Asian Historical Economics Conference (AHEC), the European Historical Economics Society (EHES), the Economic History Society (EHS), the Economic History Association (EHA), the

International Economic History Association (IEHA), the Maddison Project, the Economic History Programme of the Centre for Economic Policy Research (CEPR) and the Centre for Competitive Advantage in the Global Economy (CAGE) at the University of Warwick. Authors were also recruited through relations with a number of other organizations, including the African Economic History Network (AEHN), the Economic History Society of Australia and New Zealand (EHSANZ) and *Revista de Historia Económica – Journal of Iberian and Latin American Economic History* (RHE-JILAEH). The cohesion provided by these informal networks has been crucial in ensuring that the project could be completed in a timely fashion.

We put our authors through two gruelling conferences at which we discussed chapter drafts, held at Oxford in 2017 and Tokyo in 2018. We are extremely grateful to the Hitotsubashi University Institute of Economic Research, the Oxford University Department of Economics and Nuffield College for their financial and organizational support of these conferences. Additional funding was provided by Hitotsubashi Institute for Advanced Study (HIAS), Hitotsubashi University and Grant-in-Aid for Scientific Research (S) Grant Number 16H06322 Project 'Service Sector Productivity in Japan (SSPJ): Determinants and Policies'. We would also like to thank all the contributors for their enthusiasm and stamina.

Introduction to Volume I

STEPHEN BROADBERRY AND KYOJI FUKAO

This book tells the story of the beginnings of modern economic growth, or the sustained increase of per capita incomes together with population growth, surely one of the most important developments in world history. Part I on regional developments documents how modern economic growth first emerged in eighteenth-century Britain, and follows its spread to other parts of the world. Its origins can be traced back to earlier developments in north-west Europe, which began to break free from the Malthusian cycle of alternating periods of positive and negative growth after the arrival of the Black Death in the mid-fourteenth century. Europe thus experienced a Little Divergence as the rest of the continent continued to experience periods of shrinking as well as growing. Within Asia, there was also regional variation, with China and India experiencing negative growth during the eighteenth century while Tokugawa Japan caught up with China and then forged ahead, creating an Asian Little Divergence. Pinning down the timing of the Great Divergence between Europe and Asia in the face of such regional variation requires taking account of the richest economies in both continents, as well as the continent-wide averages, and this suggests that Asia fell behind decisively only during the eighteenth century. A further reversal of fortune also occurred in the Americas, with North America overtaking the previously richer Latin America. The United States had already made the transition to modern economic growth by the early nineteenth century, and by 1870 Japan was poised to become the first Asian economy to experience modern economic growth, following the Meiji Restoration of 1868.

Part II examines the factors governing the differential outcomes of the economies described in Part I. One approach is to focus on the proximate factors that explain the different outcomes, such as investment in physical and human capital and the development of better technology. These factors unquestionably played an important role. However, this merely raises further questions about why the economies that innovated in these areas did so, and even more puzzlingly, why the lagging economies did not follow them. This leads naturally to the consideration of more fundamental factors, which can be broken down into geography and institutions. Most historical accounts of economic growth and development discuss the importance of first nature geography, including factors such as natural resources and climate. This book is unusual in also discussing second nature geography, focusing on agglomeration economies and location near to buoyant markets, drawing on recent research in 'new economic geography'. These agglomeration effects can help to understand how peripheral economies remain locked out of economic development. Perhaps one of the biggest changes in economic history over the last two or three decades has been the growing influence of research on institutions. Defined as the 'rules of the game', institutions can be seen as setting incentives for socially productive activities such as trade, investment, and innovation. Since these incentives need to be stable over time to have a significant effect on growth and are widely perceived to be difficult to change, they are also helpful in understanding differential economic performance in history.

The book thus seeks to provide an overview of the modern world economy from around 1700 to 1870, dealing with the material in such a way as to give due weight to chronology, regional balance, and coverage of the main topics. It forms part of a two-volume publication, with the second volume taking the story from 1870 to the present. It draws on the upsurge of literature on the economic history of most regions of the world that has occurred in recent years, much of it available in the English language, but also firmly grounded in national literatures written in other languages. Much of this literature has also been based on quantitative data and makes explicit use of economic analysis, but in an accessible way. The book is aimed at a wide audience of historians and social scientists.

Part I: Regional Developments

Traditionally, economic historians have seen the world as stuck in a Malthusian trap until the eighteenth century, where any short-term gain in living standards led to an increase in the population, which resulted in the temporary gains being eaten away by the expanded population (Clark 2007). Fluctuations in living standards could thus occur, but without any long-term trend until the Industrial Revolution of the eighteenth century broke this mould. Following its beginnings in Britain, modern economic growth spread quickly to other parts of Europe and the British offshoots in the New World (Landes 1969; North and Thomas 1973; Landes 1998). On this view, the Great Divergence thus occurred largely as a result of the emergence of sustained growth in the West and continued stagnation in the rest of the world. Furthermore the breakthrough in the West is often portrayed as building upon institutional foundations laid during the early modern period, or even reaching back to the medieval period (Weber 1930; Pirenne 1936).

This traditional view requires some modification in the light of recent research to quantify long run trends in income within a national accounting framework. Table i.1 sets out trends in the level of average per capita income in the world economy between 1500 and 1870, as measured by per capita gross domestic product (GDP). The process of quantifying global economic performance in this way was begun by Maddison (2001), who had to rely on conjectures for many of his pre-nineteenth century estimates. Since then, much work has been done to build up a more complete picture based on hard data, although the project continues (Bolt and van Zanden 2014). Following Maddison, GDP per capita estimates for each country are presented in terms of a common currency unit, 1990 international dollars, so that they can be compared across both space and time. Although this clearly creates index number problems, it is likely that these are dwarfed by measurement errors, and the exercise should be treated as indicating broad trends rather than being correct to the second decimal point. To fix orders of magnitude, it is worth bearing in mind that in 1990 the World Bank regarded anyone existing on less than $1 per day as living in poverty. This means that the minimum GDP per capita consistent with a society being able to support itself and reproduce should be around $400, with most people living on $1 per day and a small elite who may have been much richer but had only a small impact on the average income.

Table i.1 shows that there was no simple story of per capita incomes rising slowly from 1500 in Europe and the British offshoots and then accelerating from the eighteenth century while incomes continued to stagnate in Asia, Latin America, and Africa throughout the period. Clearly, there was not just considerable variation in outcomes between the main regions, as would be consistent with the traditional view, but also systematic variation in outcomes within regions. First, the strong upward trend in per capita income within Europe was confined to the North Sea area economies of Britain and the Low Countries (van Zanden and van Leeuwen 2012; Broadberry et al. 2015a). The North Sea area forged ahead of the previously richer Mediterranean economies of southern Europe, particularly Italy, in what

Table i.1 GDP per capita by region, 1500–1870 (1990 international dollars)

	1500	1600	1700	1750	1800	1870
Great Britain	1,041	1,037	1,513	1,695	2,097	3,657
Netherlands	1,119	2,049	1,620	1,812	2,008	2,744
Belgium	1,467	1,589	1,375	1,361	1,479	2,692
Sweden	1,086	761	1,340	973	857	1,345
NW EUROPE	1,149	1,201	1,471	1,487	1,684	2,953
France	1,063	1,010	1,063	1,052	1,126	1,876
Italy	1,533	1,363	1,476	1,533	1,363	1,542
Spain	846	892	814	783	916	1,207
Portugal	724	665	957	1,331	775	809
SOUTHERN EUROPE	1,154	1,096	1,142	1,161	1,144	1,590
Germany	1,146	807	939	1,050	986	1,839
Poland	702	810	569	602	634	946
CENTRAL & EASTERN EUROPE	880	809	728	786	795	1,333
EUROPE	1,050	996	1,040	1,060	1,087	1,741
China	852	859	1,089	749	654	530
Japan	545	667	675	675	828	1,011
India	600	682	622	573	569	533
Java					507	517
Ottoman Empire	620	620	640	720	700	850
ASIA	715	766	817	676	634	540
US (settlers only)			1,238	1,277	1,296	2,445
US (multicultural)	400	400	480	747	1,164	2,415
Australia					518	3,273
BRITISH OFFSHOOTS	400	400	480	747	1,143	2,419
Mexico	400	497	919	807	813	651
Peru	400	579	727	694	665	694
LATIN AMERICA	400	525	876	785	788	794
Cape Colony / S. Africa			1,703	1,692	959	807
AFRICA	440	440	440	460	460	613
WORLD	717	763	812	719	702	884

Sources: Adapted from Maddison (2001: 264) and the Maddison Project Database, version 2013 (Bolt and van Zanden 2014), incorporating new long run series as follows: GB: Broadberry et al. (2015a); Netherlands: van Zanden and van Leeuwen (2012); Belgium: Buyst (2011); Sweden: Schön and Krantz (2012); Krantz (2017); France: Ridolfi (2016); Italy: Malanima (2011); Spain: Álvarez-Nogal and Prados de la Escosura (2013); Portugal: Palma and Reis (2017); Germany: Pfister (2011); Poland: Malinowski and van Zanden (2017); China: Broadberry et al. (2018); Japan: Bassino et al. (2019); India: Broadberry et al. (2015b); Java: van Zanden (2012); Ottoman Empire: Pamuk (2006; 2009); United States: data for US settlers from Sutch (2006) for 1800–70 and Mancall and Weiss (1999) for 1700–1800; multicultural estimates derived using information on Native American Indian population from Ubelaker (1992); Mexico and Peru: Arroyo Abad and van Zanden (2016); Cape Colony / South Africa: Fourie and van Zanden (2013).

has come to be known as the European Little Divergence, to set against the backdrop of the Great Divergence between Europe and Asia. Although less quantitative information is available for central and eastern Europe, the data that we do have for Poland suggest that the region continued to lag behind the rest of the European continent (Malinowski and van Zanden 2017). These trends are discussed in Chapters 1 and 2.

Second, within large parts of Asia, incomes did not just stagnate but actually trended downwards significantly. Of most significance here is the decline in Chinese GDP per capita during the Qing dynasty, but there was also a downward trend in India from the high point of the Mughal Empire under Akbar (Broadberry et al. 2015b; 2018). These trends are examined here in Chapters 4 and 5, respectively. At the same time, however, Chapter 3 shows that there was a clear upward trend in Japan, which went on to be the first non-Western economy to achieve modern economic growth after the Meiji Restoration of 1868 (Bassino et al. 2019). This reversal of fortunes between Japan and China represents an Asian Little Divergence to set alongside the European Little Divergence (Broadberry 2013). In west Asia, incomes continued to increase within the Ottoman Empire, but more slowly than in Japan (Pamuk 2009). There is less quantitative information available for South East Asia, but for Java, where we do have data for the nineteenth century thanks to the work of van Zanden (2012), incomes stagnated. Developments in South East Asia and the Ottoman Empire are outlined in Chapters 6 and 7, respectively.

Third, the European settlers who arrived in the New World from the sixteenth century experienced varying fortunes, with the British offshoots achieving better outcomes for living standards than the Latin American economies in the long run. However, the national accounting data suggest that until the eighteenth century Mexico and Peru outperformed the British American Colonies that later formed the United States (Arroyo Abad and van Zanden 2016). This is consistent with a third reversal of fortunes between the British offshoots and Latin America (Engerman and Sokoloff 1997). Before the arrival of permanent settlers from Europe in North America from the early seventeenth century and in Australia from the late eighteenth century, the lands were inhabited by tribes who are normally assumed to have lived close to subsistence income of $400 per year. It should be noted that the incomes of indigenous peoples are included in Maddison's per capita GDP estimates for Australia, in the multicultural estimates for the United States and also in the estimates for Mexico and Peru, which therefore remained relatively low for some time after colonization until the growing settler communities

Table i.2 Growth rates of GDP per capita by region (percentage per annum)

	1500–1700	1700–1750	1750–1800	1800–1870
North-west Europe	0.12	0.02	0.25	0.80
Southern Europe	0.00	0.03	−0.03	0.47
Central-eastern Europe	−0.09	0.15	0.02	0.74
Total Europe	0.00	0.04	0.05	0.67
Asia	0.07	−0.38	−0.12	−0.17
British offshoots	0.09	0.88	0.85	1.09
Latin America	0.39	−0.22	0.01	−0.25
Africa	0.00	0.09	0.00	0.41
World	0.06	−0.24	−0.05	0.33

Source and notes: Derived from Table i.1. North-west Europe = GB, NL, Belgium, Sweden; Southern Europe = France, Italy, Spain, Portugal; central-eastern Europe = Germany, Poland.

outnumbered the declining native populations.[1] North America and Latin America are covered in Chapters 8 and 9, respectively, while Australia is discussed in Chapter 11.

Fourth, there are also signs of substantial regional variation in economic outcomes within Africa, as noted in Chapter 10. In addition to the data for the whole of Africa in Table i.1, we have included estimates of per capita income in South Africa, based on available data for the Cape Colony, which clearly generated high incomes for its Dutch settler population in the eighteenth century (Fourie and van Zanden 2013).[2] Furthermore, the data on African exports presented in Chapter 10 are also suggestive of substantial fluctuations in income, with significant phases of shrinking (or negative growth) as well as positive growing.

The data from Table i.1 can be used to calculate the annual growth rates of per capita GDP in Table i.2. This reveals the generally low rates of growth achieved even in the successful north-west European economies, at just 0.8 per cent in the period 1800–70. Note that the growth rate was faster in the British offshoots from the eighteenth century, but because they were starting from a lower level of per capita income, they had still not forged ahead of Great Britain by 1870. Asia experienced negative growth (or

1 The incomes of the colonists considered alone were substantially higher, as shown in the US (settlers only) estimates, and the issue of their level relative to the Old World will be addressed below.

2 Note, however, that Fourie and van Zanden (2013) make no allowance for the indigenous African population.

shrinking) in three out of the four periods, while Latin America also shrank in the first half of the eighteenth century and stagnated during the nineteenth century. Africa experienced the most stagnant long run economic performance, but it is likely that better data would reveal greater volatility with more significant periods of shrinking interspersed between periods of growing.

One striking feature of Table i.2 is that most regions experienced negative per capita income growth over periods of half a century or more as well as periods of positive growth. This points to an important role for changes in the extent of shrinking (or periods of negative growth) as well as positive growing. Where annual information is available back as far as the late thirteenth century, the new data reveal that what makes the difference between a successful economy with an upward trend in per capita income and an economy that stagnates over the long run lies largely on the shrinking rather than the growing side. In other words, successful North Sea area economies like Britain and the Netherlands overtook Mediterranean economies like Italy and Spain not by growing faster when they grew, but rather by shrinking more slowly when they shrank and by experiencing fewer years of shrinking (Broadberry and Wallis 2017). This can be seen in Figure i.1, which plots the annual observations of GDP per capita for these four economies between the late thirteenth and the late nineteenth centuries. Of particular importance was the fact that the gains in per capita income after the mortality crisis of the Black Death in the mid-fourteenth century were never reversed in Britain and the Netherlands as population recovered from the mid-fifteenth century.

Two major issues that continue to be debated by economic historians can be addressed with the data from Table i.1: the timing of the Great Divergence and comparative living standards in the New World and the Old World before the twentieth century. The data on average incomes in Table i.1 suggest that Europe was already ahead of Asia during the early modern period, with a European advantage of around 25 per cent in 1700. However, before concluding that the Great Divergence was already under way by 1500, it is worth bearing in mind that Asia had a population four times the size of Europe's. Pomeranz (2000) claimed that Europe-Asia comparisons should be made on the basis of similarly sized units and set out to show that the leading regions of Asia, such as the Yangzi Delta in China, were on a par with the leading regions of Europe as late as 1800. Figure i.2 addresses this issue by comparing GDP per capita in the leading regions of Europe and China. The income of the European leader is based on Italy until the 1540s, followed by the Netherlands until the 1800s and then Great Britain. For China, we know

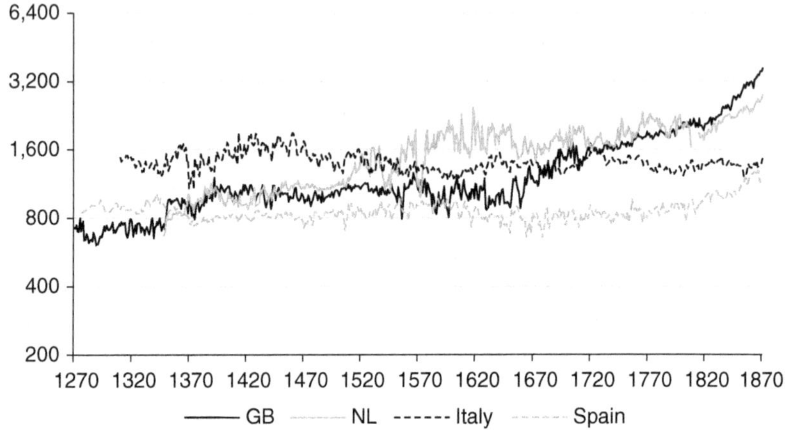

Figure i.1 Real GDP per capita in Britain, the Netherlands, Italy, and Spain 1270–1870 (1990 international dollars, log scale)
Sources: GB: Broadberry et al. (2015a); Netherlands: van Zanden and van Leeuwen (2012); Italy: Malanima (2011); Spain: Álvarez-Nogal and Prados de la Escosura (2013).

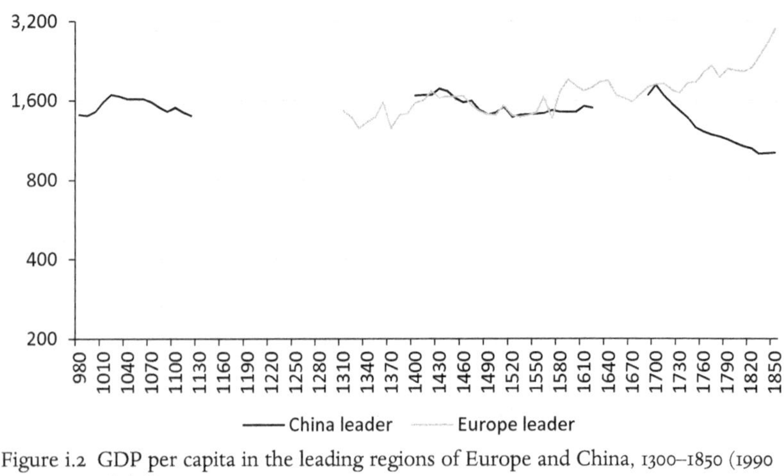

Figure i.2 GDP per capita in the leading regions of Europe and China, 1300–1850 (1990 international dollars)
Source: Broadberry et al. (2018).

that the income level in the Yangzi Delta in the 1820s was 75 per cent higher than in China as a whole (Li and van Zanden 2012). The China leader series is obtained by projecting this ratio back in time. Note that this does not require that the Yangzi Delta was always the richest region, just that there was always at least one region that was around 1.75 times the average for China as a whole. It is clear that a substantial gap opened up between the leading regions of Europe and China during the eighteenth rather than the nineteenth century. Pomeranz (2011; 2017) now accepts that his early claim that the Great Divergence began only in the nineteenth century was exaggerated, and agrees that the eighteenth century was more likely, but notes that this is still a lot later than traditionally assumed.

Turning to the issue of living standards in the New World compared with Europe, Maddison's (2010) estimates of GDP per capita for the territory of the modern United States show a continued British advantage until the late nineteenth century, and this is also reflected here in the estimates of Table i.1. This has been the subject of some controversy, with Prados de la Escosura (2000) and Ward and Devereux (2003) claiming that the United States was already ahead by the mid-nineteenth century, while Broadberry (2003) and Broadberry and Irwin (2006) continued to support Maddison's view. The first point to note is that the multicultural estimates include Native American Indians living at subsistence, which substantially lowers average income in the seventeenth and eighteenth centuries, and continues to have an impact during the nineteenth century, although the British advantage remains if attention is confined to the living standards of the US settlers in Table i.1. A second factor to consider is the existence of slavery, which serves as another reminder that until the 1860s the southern United States could not be considered a modern economy. Slaves accounted for 12.6 per cent of the US population in 1860 (Haines 2006).

Confining attention to free members of the settler population, it seems likely that for many, per capita incomes were at least as high as those in the countries from which immigrants were attracted. Indeed, Allen et al. (2012) demonstrate higher real wages in the American colonies than in Britain all the way back to the mid-seventeenth century. Nevertheless, even here it is worth noting that although staple commodities were available in greater abundance in the New World than in Europe as a result of the easy availability of land, manufactured goods and services were much harder to come by before the late nineteenth century. In these circumstances, living standards appear higher in the New World if incomes are compared using the prices of a basket of staple commodities, but this advantage disappears as more manufactured items or services are included. A suggestive study by Geloso (2015) demonstrates this for a comparison between New France (the current Canadian province of Quebec) and France during the period 1688–1760, using Allen's (2009) 'bare bones' and 'respectability' baskets. Geloso (2015: 99) concludes that 'the inhabitants of New France could more easily satisfy their basic needs. However, rising beyond that point was harder. Any advantage enjoyed at the bare bones level disappears at the respectable level.' A further point worth remembering in the US case is that warfare took its toll on two occasions, during the War of Independence (1776–83) and the Civil War (1861–65). A recent contribution by Lindert and Williamson (2016) argues that the thirteen colonies were ahead of Britain in the eighteenth century, but fell back behind by 1800 as a result of destruction wrought during the War of Independence. Lindert and Williamson then see the United States as regaining the lead by 1850, but suffering another setback during the 1860s due to the Civil War, and then finally forging ahead permanently after 1870, as in the conventional Maddison chronology.

Although GDP per capita is widely used as a measure of living standards, it is at best an incomplete measure, and needs to be supplemented by additional information. Two important variables widely monitored are life expectancy and education, which tend to show smaller differences between nations than GDP per capita. The human development index (HDI), which combines GDP per capita with measures of life expectancy and education is sometimes used as a composite measure of the standard of living (UNDP 1990). In its standard form, however, the HDI is still subject to the shortcoming that it is based on mean values and therefore cannot say anything about the distribution of welfare across individuals. To take account of distributional issues, it is necessary to incorporate measures of inequality such as the Gini coefficient or the Atkinson inequality index. These issues are considered in Chapter 16.

Part II: Factors Governing Differential Outcomes in the Global Economy

Part II explores the factors governing differential outcomes in the various regions that are examined in Part I. An important distinction is made between the proximate and fundamental sources of growth, while a final section analyses the world economy as a system.

The Proximate Sources of Growth

Growth accounting helps us to assess whether economic growth came from the use of more factor inputs or from the more effective use of existing inputs (Solow 1957). In the simplest formulation, aggregate output is produced using factor inputs of capital and labour. The growth rate of output can then be related to the growth rates of the inputs of capital and labour and a residual factor representing any change in the efficiency with which the factors are used. Each factor is weighted by its relative importance in the production process, measured by its share in the costs of production. For labour this is the share of wages in the value of output, while for capital it is the share of profits. The residual factor, known as total factor productivity (TFP) is often associated with technological progress, but it can also reflect changes in organization, such as the introduction of the factory system.

Labour, which is considered in Chapter 12, has always been an important factor input. In addition to the increase in the number of workers as population grows, it is necessary to consider the quality of workers, particularly as a result of investment in human capital. More educated workers should be able to produce more output, so an increase in education should raise the growth rate, other things being equal. However, education is costly to provide, so as production becomes more complex with economic development, parents may face a choice between having a small number of well-educated children or a larger number of poorly educated children. Such considerations must inevitably impact on decisions about fertility, and are now considered by many economists to be central to understanding the demographic transition from a poor economy with high rates of fertility and mortality to a rich economy with low rates of fertility and mortality (Galor 2005).

Capital and technology accounted for an increasing share of growth between 1700 and 1870, and are considered here in Chapter 13. The growing importance of capital reflected in turn the growing importance of fixed capital relative to working capital, while the growing importance of technological progress reflected the growth of mechanization and the use of the steam engine as a major source of power.

The Ultimate Sources of Growth

Even if we had perfect information on the proximate sources of growth, however, this would only tell us *how* the transition to modern economic growth occurred, rather than *why* it occurred. If some economies grew faster than others because of more investment or faster technological progress, we would want to know why investment and technological progress were faster in those economies. Economists divide the more fundamental underlying sources of growth into two categories: geography and institutions.

The role of geography can be analysed using the distinction between first and second nature geography. First nature geography covers natural endowments such as mineral deposits or climate, while second nature geography covers man-made factors such as access to markets and agglomeration economies. First nature geography has traditionally featured heavily in explanations of differential performance during the Industrial Revolution, with coal deposits playing an important role in the location of industry. Recently, however, a new literature has arisen, emphasizing the importance of second nature geography (Krugman and Venables 1995). The basic idea here is that exogenously given first nature geography advantages or disadvantages become amplified rather than reduced by forces of economic integration. Favourable locations with high productivity are seen as attracting people and investment, which further raises productivity. Unfavourable locations with low productivity attract fewer people and investment, thus falling further behind. Reductions in the cost of trade may thus have asymmetric effects on different regions, with industry clustering in a few favourable locations rather than being dispersed evenly around the world. Building on the approach of Crafts and Venables (2003), Chapter 14 assesses to what extent the differential outcomes in the global economy over the period 1700–1870 can be explained using this new approach.

One of the key developments in economic history in recent decades has been the systematic analysis of institutions as a fundamental determinant of economic performance. A key player in the development of this analysis was the Nobel laureate Douglass North, who defined institutions as 'the rules of the game and the means of enforcement' (North 1990: 3). John Wallis draws an important distinction in Chapter 15 between primary and secondary rules. Primary rules are the rules that directly govern behaviour, such as traffic laws, property laws, and criminal laws, while secondary rules are the rules that govern the formation or alteration of the primary rules. Primary rules can be seen as structuring the economic system and secondary rules the political system. Understanding the role of institutions in explaining differential outcomes in the global economy therefore requires more than considering primary institutions such as property rights, but also requires an analysis of secondary institutions such as democracy or dictatorship, and how primary and secondary rules interact. Wallis contrasts the case of British North America, where modern economic growth began in this period, with Latin America, where it did not. He also considers the case of Japan, which underwent a radical institutional change with the Meiji Restoration of 1868.

The Global Economy

The world economy can clearly be broken down into its regional components as in Part I of this volume. However, it is also helpful to think of the world economy as a global system, governing international transactions, such as international trade and migration and international finance. It is also important to stand back and assess the roles of warfare and empire. This can be useful in guarding against a tendency of earlier generations of economic historians to focus only on the effects of European developments on the rest of the world, without paying much attention to the impact of developments flowing in the opposite direction. Whilst the two-way nature of these reciprocal flows became too obvious to ignore in the second half of the twentieth century, they also need to be borne in mind when considering earlier eras.

The real flows of goods (via international trade) and labour (via migration) between 1700 and 1870 tell the story in Chapter 17 of the integration of product and factor markets in different parts of the world. There is overwhelming evidence of a greater trend towards market integration after 1820 than before, as the global economy was transformed by a host of revolutionary technologies in transportation and communications (O'Rourke and Williamson 2002). Warfare can be seen as a major barrier to integration during the eighteenth century, culminating in the disruption of the French Revolutionary and Napoleonic Wars (1792–1815), which were fought not just in Europe, but also in the Middle East, North America, the Caribbean, India, and South East Asia. After about 1820, market integration received a boost not just from declining transport costs as a result of technological progress but also from a shift in trade policy away from mercantilism towards free trade.

The international monetary system, analysed in Chapter 18, was based largely on silver and gold during the early modern period. With well-integrated bullion markets, countries were forced to coordinate legal ratios to preserve bimetallism. An important exception here was England, which was effectively on a gold standard *de facto* from 1717 and *de jure* from 1816. During the third quarter of the nineteenth century, many other nations switched away from a bimetallic standard and the gold standard emerged at the heart of the international monetary system. Early modern intercontinental trade occurred with a steady flow of silver from the Americas in the West to Asia in the East, mainly via Europe, although there were also some direct flows from the Americas to Asia via the Philippines. Commodity money was replaced by bills of exchange to transfer funds for long-distance trade and finance, with the bills of exchange market being progressively enlarged from a European system in the mid-eighteenth century to a global system by the mid-nineteenth century.

Economic historians often focus on pre-war, post-war, and interwar periods, as if warfare was some kind of anomaly and minor disruption to normal events rather than a common occurrence that could sometimes lead to major turning points in history. Yet China as well as the major European powers spent more than half the time between 1500 and 1799 at war with foreign enemies, and by 1914, as much as 84 per cent of the world was under European control, either directly or as a now independent colony dominated by Europeans. Chapter 19 therefore considers warfare and empire as a separate topic within the framework of international transactions. How did Europeans come to so dominate the world? Part of the answer must lie in the higher incomes and better technology afforded by their earlier transition to modern economic growth, which provided more resources for warfare. However, European states also raised more tax revenue per head, formed credible alliances and designed effective armies.

Although there is a minority view that sees colonizers as helping to lay the foundations for later development, empire is usually seen as bad for the people that were colonized (Ferguson 2003). However, one of the most controversial debates in economic history concerns the costs and benefits of empire for the colonizers. It is easy to point to large fortunes accumulated by individual merchants through colonial investments, but there were costs as well as benefits to maintaining an empire. Retrospective cost-benefit analysis suggests that the colonial powers earned a social rate of return that was below the risk-free rate (Davis and Huttenback 1986). In other words, they would have reaped a higher rate of return by holding government bonds. Why, then, were the empires held? It is important to remember that the benefits were concentrated in the hands of a few, who were able to mobilize and influence governments, whereas the costs were spread across all taxpayers, who were less able to mobilize effectively.

Concluding Comments

This book provides an overview of the modern world economy from around 1700 to 1870, focusing on the issues of economic growth and development. We examine the beginnings of modern economic growth, giving due weight to chronology, regional balance, and coverage of the main factors governing differential outcomes in different parts of the global economy.

Part I on regional developments covers the first emergence of modern economic growth in eighteenth-century Britain, and follows its spread to other parts of the world. The forging ahead of economies making the transition to modern economic growth led to reversals of fortune within and between continents. Within Europe, the first transition to modern economic growth in Britain led to a reversal of fortunes between the North Sea area and the Mediterranean region. The drive of Japan towards modern economic growth during the Tokugawa Shogunate, combined with declining per capita incomes in Qing dynasty China, led to a reversal of fortunes within Asia. A reversal of fortunes also occurred within the Americas between North America and Latin America.

Part II on the factors governing differential outcomes covers both the proximate and ultimate sources of growth. Dealing first with the proximate factors, investment in physical and human capital and the development of better technology undoubtedly played an important role. However, they can only tell us how rather than why the transition to modern economic growth occurred. To get at the ultimate sources of growth, we need to examine the roles of geography and institutions. First nature geography has always been seen as playing a role in the location of the Industrial Revolution in Britain and its spread to other parts of the world through the location of coal. However, recent work has also highlighted the role of second nature geography through agglomeration economies and access to nearby buoyant markets. Institutions matter because they provide the incentives for socially productive activities such as trade, investment and innovation.

References

Allen, R. C. (2009). *The British Industrial Revolution in Global Perspective*, Cambridge University Press.

Allen, R. C., Murphy, T. E. and Schneider, E. B. (2012). 'The Colonial Origins of Divergence in the Americas: A Labor Market Approach', *Journal of Economic History*, 72, 863–94.

Álvarez-Nogal, C. and Prados de la Escosura, L. (2013). 'The Rise and Fall of Spain (1270–1850)', *Economic History Review*, 66, 1–37.

Arroyo Abad, L. and van Zanden, J. L. (2016). 'Growth under Extractive Institutions? Latin American per capita GDP in Colonial Times', *Journal of Economic History*, 76, 1182–1215.

Bassino, J.-P., Broadberry, S., Fukao, K., Gupta, B. and Takashima, M. (2019). 'Japan and the Great Divergence, 730–1870', *Explorations in Economic History*, 72, 1–22.

Bolt, J. and van Zanden, J. L. (2014). 'The Maddison Project: Collaborative Research on Historical National Accounts'. *Economic History Review*, 67, 627–651.

Broadberry, S. (2003). 'Relative per Capita Income Levels in the United Kingdom and the United States since 1870: Reconciling Time-Series Projections and Direct-Benchmark Estimates', *Journal of Economic History*, 63, 852–863.

(2013). 'Accounting for the Great Divergence', LSE Economic History Working Papers, No. 184/2013, http://eprints.lse.ac.uk/54573/1/WP184.pdf.

Broadberry, S. and Irwin, D. (2006). 'Labor Productivity in the United States and the United Kingdom During the Nineteenth Century', *Explorations in Economic History*, 43, 257–279.

Broadberry, S. and Wallis, J. (2017). 'Growing, Shrinking and Long Run Economic Performance: Historical Perspectives on Economic Development', National Bureau of Economic Research Working Paper No. 23343, www.nber.org/papers/w23343 (accessed 29 September 2020).

Broadberry, S., Campbell, B., Klein, A., Overton, M. and van Leeuwen, B. (2015a). *British Economic Growth, 1270–1870*, Cambridge University Press.

Broadberry, S., Custodis, J. and Gupta, B. (2015b). 'India and the Great Divergence: An Anglo-Indian Comparison of GDP per capita, 1600–1871', *Explorations in Economic History*, 55, 58–75.

Broadberry, S., Guan, H. and Li, D. (2018). 'China, Europe and the Great Divergence: A Study in Historical National Accounting', *Journal of Economic History*, 78, 955–1000.

Buyst, E. (2011). 'Towards Estimates of Long Term Growth in the Southern Low Countries, ca.1500–1846', paper for the 'Quantifying Long Run Economic Development' conference at the University of Warwick in Venice, March 22–24, www2.warwick.ac.uk/fac/soc/economics/events/seminars-workshops-conferences/conferences/venice3/programme/buyst.pdf (accessed 29 September 2020).

Clark, G. (2007). *A Farewell to Alms: A Brief Economic History of the World*, Princeton University Press.

Crafts, N. F. R. and Venables, A. J. (2003). 'Globalization in History: A Geographical Perspective', in Bordo, M., Taylor, A. M. and Williamson, J. G. (eds.), *Globalization in Historical Perspective*, Chicago: Chicago University Press, 323–364.

Davis, L. E. and Huttenback, R. A. (1986). *Mammon and the Pursuit of Empire: The Political Economy of British Imperialism, 1860–1912*, New York: Cambridge University Press.

Engerman, S. L. and Sokoloff, K. L. (1997). 'Factor Endowments, Institutions, and Differential Paths of Growth Among New World Economies: A View from Economic Historians of the United States', in Haber, S. (ed.), *How Latin America Fell Behind: Essays on the Economic History of Brazil and Mexico, 1800–1914*, Stanford University Press, 260–304.

Ferguson, N. (2003). *Empire: How Britain made the Modern World*, London: Allen Lane.

Fourie, J. and van Zanden, J. L. (2013). 'GDP in the Dutch Cape Colony: The National Accounts of a Slave-Based Society', *South African Journal of Economics*, 81, 467–490.

Galor, O. (2005). 'From Stagnation to Growth: Unified Growth Theory', in Aghion, P. and Durlauf, S. N. (eds.), *Handbook of Economic Growth, Volume 1A*, Amsterdam: Elsevier, 171–285.

Geloso, V. (2015). 'The Seeds of Divergence: The Economy of French America, 1688 to 1760', Unpublished PhD thesis, London School of Economics and Political Science, etheses.lse.ac.uk/3442/1/Geloso_seeds_of_divergence.pdf.

Haines, M. R. (2006). 'Population Characteristics', in Historical Statistics of the United States Database, hsus.cambridge.org/HSUSWeb/HSUSEntryServlet.

Krantz, O. (2017). 'Swedish GDP 1300–1560: A Tentative Estimate', Lund Papers in Economic History; No. 152, Department of Economic History, Lund University.

Krugman, P. and Venables, A. (1995). 'Globalization and the Inequality of Nations', *Quarterly Journal of Economics*, 110, 857–880.

Landes, D. S. (1969). *The Unbound Prometheus. Technological Change and Industrial Development in Western Europe from 1750 to the Present*, Cambridge University Press.

(1998). *The Wealth and Poverty of Nations: Why Some are So Rich and Some So Poor*, London: Little, Brown.

Li, B. and van Zanden, J. L. (2012). 'Before the Great Divergence? Comparing the Yangzi Delta and the Netherlands at the Beginning of the Nineteenth Century', *Journal of Economic History*, 72, 956–989.

Lindert, P. H. and Williamson, J. G. (2016). *Unequal Gains: American Growth and Inequality since 1700*, Princeton University Press.

Maddison, A. (2001). *The World Economy: A Millennial Perspective*, Paris: Organisation for Economic Co-operation and Development.

(2010). 'Statistics on World Population, GDP and Per Capita GDP, 1–2008 AD', Groningen Growth and Development Centre, www.ggdc.net/MADDISON/oriindex.htm (accessed 29 September 2020).

Malanima, P. (2011). 'The Long Decline of a Leading Economy: GDP in Central and Northern Italy, 1300–1913', *European Review of Economic History*, 15, 169–219.

Malinowski, M. and van Zanden, J. L. (2017). 'Income and its Distribution in Pre-Industrial Poland', *Cliometrica*, 11, 375–404.

Mancall, P. C. and Weiss, T. (1999). 'Was Economic Growth Likely in Colonial British North America?', *Journal of Economic History*, 59(1), 17–40.

North, D. C. (1990). *Institutions, Institutional Change, and Economic Performance*, Cambridge University Press.

North, D. C. and Thomas, R. P. (1973). *The Rise of the Western World: A New Economic History*, Cambridge University Press.

O'Rourke, K. H. and Williamson, J. G. (2002). 'When did Globalisation Begin?', *European Review of Economic History*, 6, 23–50.

Palma, N. and Reis, J. (2017). 'From Convergence to Divergence: Portuguese Economic Growth, 1527–1850', Unpublished manuscript, University of Manchester.

Pamuk, S. (2006). 'Estimating Economic Growth in the Middle East since 1820', *Journal of Economic History*, 66, 809–828.

(2009), 'Estimating GDP per capita for the Ottoman Empire in a European Comparative Framework, 1500–1820', paper presented at the XVth World Economic History Congress, August 2009, Utrecht.

Pfister, U. (2011). 'Economic Growth in Germany, 1500–1850', paper for the 'Quantifying Long Run Economic Development' conference at the University of Warwick in Venice, March 22–24, warwick.ac.uk/fac/soc/economics/seminars/seminars/conferences/venice3/programme/pfister_growth_venice_2011.pdf (accessed 5 October 2020).

Pirenne, H. (1936). *Economic and Social History of Medieval Europe*, London: Routledge & Kegan Paul.

Pomeranz, K. (2000). *The Great Divergence: China, Europe, and the Making of the Modern World Economy*, Princeton University Press.

(2011). 'Ten Years After: Responses and Reconsiderations', *Historically Speaking*, 12(4), 20–25. Project Muse.

(2017). 'The Data We Have vs. the Data We Need: A Comment on the State of the "Divergence" Debate (Part I)', The NEP-HIS Blog, nephist.wordpress.com/2017/06/06/the-data-we-have-vs-the-data-we-need-a-comment-on-the-state-of-the-divergence-debate-parti/#comments">nephist.wordpress.com">nephist.wordpress.com/2017/06/06/the-data-we-have-vs-the-data-we-need-a-comment-on-the-state-of-the-divergence-debate-parti/#comments (accessed 5 October 2020).

Prados de la Escosura, L. (2000). 'International Comparisons of Real Product, 1820–1990', *Explorations in Economic History*, 37, 1–41.

Ridolfi, L. (2016). 'The French Economy in the Longue Durée. A Study on Real Wages, Working Days and Economic Performance from Louis IX to the Revolution (1250–1789)", Unpublished PhD thesis, IMT School for Advanced Studies, Lucca.

Schön, L. and Krantz, O. (2012). 'The Swedish Economy in the Early Modern Period: Constructing Historical National Accounts', *European Review of Economic History*, 16, 529–549.

Solow, R. (1957). 'Technical Change and the Aggregate Production Function', *Review of Economics and Statistics*, 39, 312–320.

Sutch, R. (2006). 'National Income and Product', in Historical Statistics of the United States Database, hsus.cambridge.org/HSUSWeb/HSUSEntryServlet (accessed 29 September 2020).

Ubelaker, D. H. (1992). 'North American Indian Population Size: Changing Perspectives', in Verano, J. W. and Ubelaker, D. H. (eds.), *Disease and Demography in the Americas*, Washington, DC: Smithsonian Institution Press, 169–176.

United Nations Development Program [UNDP] (1990). World Development Report, Oxford University Press.

Ward, M. and Devereux, J. (2003). 'Measuring British Decline: Direct Versus Long-Span Income Measures', *Journal of Economic History*, 63, 826–851.

Weber, M. (1930). *The Protestant Ethic and the Spirit of Capitalism*. London: Allen & Unwin.

van Zanden, J. L. (2012). 'Economic Growth in Java 1815–1939: The Reconstruction of the Historical National Accounts of a Colonial Economy', Maddison-Project Working Paper WP-3, www.rug.nl/ggdc/historicaldevelopment/maddison/publications/wp3.pdf (accessed 29 September 2020).

van Zanden, J. L. and van Leeuwen, B. (2012). 'Persistent but not Consistent: The Growth of National Income in Holland, 1347–1807', *Explorations in Economic History*, 49, 119–130.

PART I

★

REGIONAL DEVELOPMENTS

I

Britain, the Industrial Revolution, and Modern Economic Growth

STEPHEN BROADBERRY

Introduction

Economic historians have traditionally seen the Industrial Revolution as marking the beginning of the modern world. Early work in the subject tended to see living standards before the Industrial Revolution as uniformly low, with little if any progress from the ancient world through the medieval period to the early modern era. The transition to modern economic growth was characterized as occurring first in Britain from the mid-eighteenth century, with the Industrial Revolution initiating an increase in the rate of growth of population and production, but with production growth outstripping population growth. Eventually population growth slowed down as the economy went through a demographic transition, but output per head continued to grow and even accelerated from the late nineteenth century. For the first time, it seemed that a society was able to improve the material living standards of virtually all of its members, rather than just a small elite.

A new generation of researchers has challenged aspects of this simple account, but without dethroning the British Industrial Revolution from its central role in the transition to modern economic growth. First, new estimates of gross domestic product (GDP) per head show that there were several episodes of pre-industrial growth in Britain, interspersed with episodes of stagnation rather than decline, so that the Industrial Revolution built upon prior developments. Second, international comparisons have clarified the extent to which the Industrial Revolution was a purely British phenomenon, placing it within the context of both a Little Divergence within Europe and a Great Divergence between Europe and Asia. Third, with long time series of output and population, researchers have questioned the extent to which the pre-industrial economy conformed to the Malthusian model.

Fourth, new work on real wages in Britain and a wide range of European and Asian economies has established that living standards were not uniformly low before the mid-eighteenth century, but rather that the Industrial Revolution occurred in Britain at least partly in response to high wages, which stimulated the substitution of capital for labour, the accumulation of human capital and labour-saving changes in technology.

British Economic Performance, 1700–1870

British Economic Growth in Long Run Perspective

Although there has been broad agreement about the quantitative dimensions of British economic growth during the period 1700–1870 since the work of Crafts and Harley (1992), recent work by Broadberry et al. (2015) sheds new light on this work by providing historical national accounts for Britain reaching back to the late thirteenth century. An important result of the Crafts-Harley work was to demonstrate that economic growth during the Industrial Revolution was much slower than had originally been suggested by Deane and Cole (1967). This meant that Britain must have entered the Industrial Revolution already richer and more developed than earlier economic historians had assumed. To understand Britain's transition to modern economic growth, it is therefore necessary to examine what happened further back in time.

Broadberry et al. (2015) reconstruct the path of GDP for Britain from series for the output of the agricultural, industrial and service sectors, combined with a set of sectoral weights that capture the changing structure of the economy. To estimate GDP per head, this aggregate GDP series is divided by population. Figure 1.1 shows the long run evolution of real GDP, population and real GDP per head over the long period 1270–1870. GDP per head stagnated during 1270–1348, before increasing sharply between 1348 and 1400, as population declined more sharply than GDP following the shock of the Black Death. GDP per head then remained on a plateau between *c.*1400 and 1650 as population at first continued to fall and then began to recover from the late fifteenth century. A new GDP per head growth phase started around 1650, as population stagnated and then declined slightly. Although GDP per head growth slowed down after 1700 as population growth resumed, it remained positive and became increasingly stable, with fewer and fewer years of negative GDP per head growth. It seems, then, that the Industrial Revolution was more about shrinking less frequently than about growing faster (Broadberry and Wallis 2017).

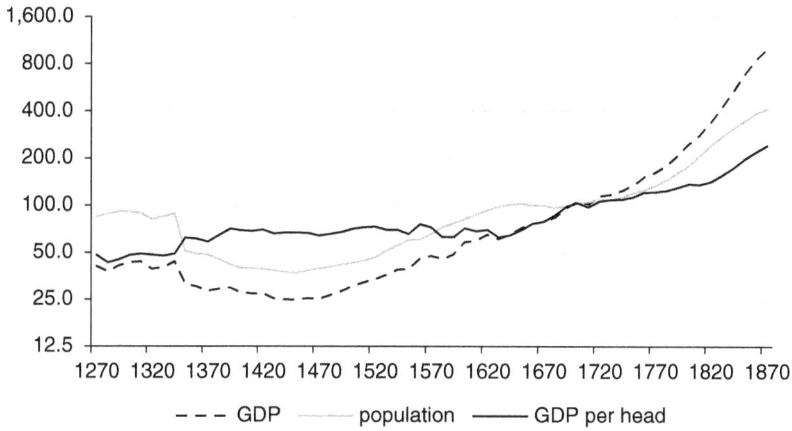

Figure 1.1 Real GDP, population, and real GDP per head, England 1270–1700 and Great Britain 1700–1870 (averages per decade, log scale, 1700 = 100)
Source: Broadberry et al. (2015: 204).

Table 1.1 presents the average annual growth rates for the same three series: GDP, population and GDP per head. Notice how the growth rate of GDP per head after 1800 was actually slightly slower than after the Black Death (1350s–1400s) and after the Civil War (1650s–1700), despite the fact that GDP growth was much faster. The reason for this was the very different paths of population in these three periods. Whereas population declined very sharply after the Black Death, and still declined slightly after the Civil War, it grew very rapidly during the first two-thirds of the nineteenth century. This points to a major difference between modern economic growth and pre-industrial growth, as highlighted by Kuznets (1966). Pre-industrial growth required falling population, and this led to an increase in land per head and capital per head, which in turn led to higher output per head. However, this was clearly not a route to sustained growth. For Kuznets, sustained or modern economic growth required rising output per head together with a growing population.

Structural Change in Britain

Another important aspect of modern economic growth is structural change. It has long been noted that economic development is associated with a shift in the structure of the economy away from dependence on agriculture. This has traditionally been seen as a process of industrialization, although recent research suggests that this understates the role of services. Broadberry et al.

Table 1.1 Annual growth rates of real GDP, population, and real GDP per head, Great Britain 1700–1870 (percentage)

	Real GDP	Population	Real GDP per head
A. England			
1270s–1300s	−0.02	0.27	−0.29
1300s–1350s	−0.64	−0.52	−0.12
1350s–1400s	−0.30	−1.06	0.76
1400s–1450s	−0.06	−0.21	0.15
1450s–1500s	0.40	0.25	0.15
1500s–1550s	0.51	0.65	−0.14
1550s–1600s	0.81	0.62	0.19
1600s–1650s	0.41	0.51	−0.10
1650s–1700	0.78	−0.04	0.82
1270s–1700	0.22	0.04	0.18
B. Great Britain			
1700–1750s	0.49	0.30	0.19
1750s–1800s	1.21	0.77	0.44
1800s–1850s	2.08	1.34	0.74
1850s–1870	0.12	1.54	0.58
1700–1870	1.31	0.84	0.48

Source: Broadberry et al. (2015: 208).

(2015) note that the British economy diversified away from agriculture over a longer time span than was once believed by economic historians. Agriculture was less important and services more important earlier than widely perceived, with important consequences for sectoral productivity performance. Labour productivity growth was faster in industry than in agriculture during the Industrial Revolution rather than the reverse, as early quantification of the Industrial Revolution had appeared to suggest.

The quantitative dimensions of the structural shift away from agriculture in the British economy are set out in Table 1.2. The first point to note is that agriculture's share of output and employment declined in importance over time, while the shares of industry and services increased, as would be expected for a developing nation. Second, however, note that even as early as 1381, agriculture accounted for less than 60 per cent of employment and less than 50 per cent of nominal GDP, so that even in the fourteenth century, industry and services accounted for a substantial share of economic activity. Third, although agriculture accounted for a smaller share of output than employment for most of the period under consideration here, thus making

Table 1.2 Sectoral shares in nominal GDP and the labour force, England 1381–1700 and Great Britain 1700–1870 (percentage)

A. Nominal GDP shares

Year	Region	Agriculture	Industry	Services	Total
1381	England	45.5	28.8	25.7	100.0
1522	England	39.7	38.7	21.6	100.0
1700	England and Britain	26.7	41.3	32.0	100.0
1759	Britain	29.7	35.2	35.1	100.0
1801	Britain	31.3	32.7	36.0	100.0
1841	Britain	22.1	36.4	41.5	100.0

B. Labour force shares

Year	Region	Agriculture	Industry	Services	Total
1381	England	57.2	19.2	23.6	100.0
1522	England	58.1	22.7	19.2	100.0
1700	England and Britain	38.9	34.0	27.2	100.0
1759	Britain	36.8	33.9	29.3	100.0
1801	Britain	31.7	36.4	31.9	100.0
1841	Britain	23.5	45.6	30.9	100.0

Source: Broadberry et al. (2015: 344).

agriculture a low productivity sector, this had ceased to be the case by 1801, a point first noted by Crafts (1985). Fourth, although industry increased its share of nominal GDP more rapidly than services until 1700, this ceased to be the case during the Industrial Revolution period. This may at first sight seem surprising but can be explained by a decline in the relative price of industrial goods, as technological progress increased productivity and drove down prices. By contrast, the more modest productivity improvement in services led to an increase in their relative price, so that the share of services in nominal GDP increased more rapidly than the share of industry after 1700.

A fifth striking feature of Table 1.2 is that much of the shift of labour from agriculture to industry occurred before 1759, which has important implications for the pattern of labour productivity growth before and during the Industrial Revolution. If, as was once believed, the shift of labour from agriculture to industry had taken place at the same time as the Industrial Revolution, then much of the growth of industrial output could be explained by increased labour input rather than by productivity growth. This counter-intuitive result

Table 1.3 Sectoral annual growth rates of output, labour force, and labour productivity, England 1381–1700 and Great Britain 1700–1851

	Annual % growth:					
	Agriculture			Industry		
Period	Output	Labour force	Labour productivity	Output	Labour force	Labour productivity
1381–1522	0.01	−0.01	0.02	0.27	0.10	0.17
1522–1700	0.38	0.25	0.13	0.73	0.66	0.07
1700–59	0.79	0.22	0.57	0.63	0.31	0.32
1759–1801	0.85	0.44	0.41	1.54	0.97	0.57
1801–51	0.74	0.64	0.10	3.00	1.74	1.23
1381–1759	0.30	0.13	0.17	0.54	0.40	0.14
1759–1851	0.79	0.54	0.24	2.33	1.39	0.93
	Services			GDP		
	Output	Labour force	Labour productivity	Output	Labour force	Labour productivity
1381–1522	0.06	−0.16	0.23	0.11	−0.02	0.14
1522–1700	0.74	0.60	0.14	0.60	0.45	0.16
1700–59	0.70	0.44	0.26	0.69	0.32	0.38
1759–1801	1.36	1.00	0.36	1.23	0.79	0.44
1801–51	2.16	1.45	0.71	2.10	1.35	0.74
1381–1759	0.48	0.31	0.17	0.43	0.25	0.18
1759–1851	1.80	1.24	0.55	1.70	1.09	0.60

Source: Broadberry et al. (2015: 367).

was implicit in the work of Deane and Cole (1967), and also confronted more explicitly by Crafts and Harley (1992). With much of the shift of labour from agriculture to industry occurring between 1522 and 1759, there was a period of labour-intensive industrialization (or proto-industrialization) without dramatic industrial productivity growth, which can be tracked in Table 1.3. This was then followed by the Industrial Revolution, where capital deepening and technological progress raised industrial labour productivity rapidly after 1759.

Britain in the Global Economy

Britain's rise to income leadership can be seen as part of a Little Divergence within Europe as the North Sea area economies of Britain and the Netherlands overtook the Mediterranean economies of Italy and Spain. This occurred in parallel with a Little Divergence within Asia as Japan

Table 1.4 Levels of GDP per head in Europe and Asia (1990 international dollars)

	GB	NL	Italy	Spain	Japan	China	India
1300	724	674	1,466	889	531	833	
1400	1,045	958	1,570	822	548	991	
1500	1,068	1,141	1,408	826	548	852	
1600	1,077	1,825	1,224	876	667	859	682
1650	1,055	1,671	1,372	838	667	859	638
1700	1,563	1,849	1,344	817	676	1,089	622
1750	1,710	1,877	1,446	845	752	749	573
1800	2,080	1,974	1,327	893	828	654	569
1850	2,997	2,397	1,306	1,144	904	600	556

Source: Broadberry et al. (2018).

overtook China. The Great Divergence between the two continents was the net result of these regional developments within both Europe and Asia, as north-west Europe forged ahead of the rest of Europe and Asia.

These developments are shown in Table 1.4, where levels of GDP per head are shown in a common unit, 1990 international dollars, so that average living standards can be compared across both space and time. The Little Divergence within Europe can be seen in the first four columns of Table 1.4. In 1300, GDP per head was higher in Italy and Spain, reflecting the dominant position of the Mediterranean region in the European economy. After 1500, however, with the opening of new trade routes between Europe and Asia around the south of Africa and between Europe and the New World across the Atlantic, the Mediterranean lost its role as the centre of economic activity in Europe. In these changed circumstances, access to the Atlantic became more important, and the North Sea area economies of the Netherlands and Britain became the leading European economies. The Netherlands was the first north-west European economy to forge ahead during its Golden Age between 1570 and 1650, but Great Britain grew more rapidly after 1650 and ultimately emerged as the first economy to achieve modern economic growth, with sustained growth of GDP per head accompanied by rapid population growth.

Within Asia, another Little Divergence was occurring as Japan forged ahead of China in the eighteenth century. Although Japan experienced positive growth during the sixteenth century, and again in the eighteenth and nineteenth centuries under the Tokugawa Shogunate, growth was slower than in Britain, so that Japan's rise to economic leadership within Asia depended also on the decline of GDP per head that occurred in Qing dynasty China during the eighteenth century. Japan achieved modern economic growth after the Meiji Restoration of 1868, but until then the slower rate of growth in the leading Asian economy compared to the leading parts of Europe meant that the gap in living standards between the two continents continued to widen in the phenomenon known as the Great Divergence.

Accounting for British Economic Growth: Proximate Sources

Growth accounting helps us to assess whether economic growth came from the use of more factor inputs or from the more effective use of existing inputs. In the simplest formulation, as set out in the Introduction to this volume, the growth rate of output can be related to the growth rates of the inputs of capital and labour and the growth rate of total factor productivity. Each factor is weighted by its share of national income, which is wages in the case of labour and profits in the case of capital.

Growth Accounting with Physical Capital and Raw Labour

Crafts and Harley (1992) conducted a growth accounting exercise for Great Britain in the period 1700–1860 using this simple two-factor approach, based on their own estimates of output growth, the growth of population from Wrigley and Schofield (1981) as the labour input, and Feinstein's (1988) capital stock data. Crafts and Harley's estimates, reproduced here in Table 1.5, show that about two-thirds of the increase in output growth from 0.70 per cent during 1700–1760 to 2.5 per cent during 1831–1860 was due to faster growth of factor inputs, and only one-third due to faster growth of total factor productivity (TFP). McCloskey's (1981: 108) claim that 'ingenuity rather than abstention governed the industrial revolution' does not seem to be borne out by this simple exercise in growth accounting. Rather than being the result of ingenious new ways of combining inputs (hence raising TFP growth), higher output growth seems to have been due primarily to abstention from leisure (hence more labour inputs) and abstention from consumption (hence more savings to invest in capital inputs). Furthermore, a good part of the increased input growth was due to labour rather than capital, as a result of the rapid rate of population growth, hence leading to a relatively modest rate of growth of GDP per head. And to the extent that TFP growth did increase, it was largely delayed until after 1830.

Growth Accounting with Human Capital

In a more sophisticated formulation of growth accounting, a distinction can be made between skilled and unskilled labour, so that there are three factors of production, including human capital as well as physical capital and raw labour. Crafts (1995) conducted a growth accounting exercise on this basis for Great Britain in the period 1760–1913, shown here in Table 1.6. Human capital seems not to have been very important during the early stages of the Industrial Revolution, with literacy rates stagnating during the second half of the eighteenth century (Schofield 1973). Although the periodization is slightly different between Tables 1.5 and 1.6, it is nevertheless clear that the inclusion of human capital results in even lower rates of TFP growth during the Industrial Revolution than in the simple two-factor growth accounting exercise. This strengthens the finding that the increase in output growth owed more to the faster growth of factor inputs than to greater efficiency in their use.

The 'Industrious Revolution' and the Labour Input

The growth accounting exercise in Table 1.5 assumes that the labour input grew in line with population. However, this assumes that the number of days worked per year remained unchanged, which has always been disputed by those who see the Industrial Revolution as leading to an intensification of work effort, as people worked harder to obtain the new goods made available by long-distance trade and new technology (de Vries 1994). Although

Table 1.5 Accounting for British GDP growth, 1700–1860, two-factor model (percentage per annum)

	Output growth	Due to capital	Due to labour	TFP growth
1700–60	0.70	0.35	0.15	0.20
1760–1801	1.00	0.50	0.40	0.10
1801–31	1.90	0.85	0.70	0.35
1831–60	2.50	1.00	0.70	0.80

Sources and notes: Derived from Crafts (1985: 81); Crafts and Harley (1992: 718); Harley (1993: 198). All calculations are on a two-factor basis, with capital and labour weighted equally.

Table 1.6 Accounting for British GDP growth, 1760–1913, three-factor model (percentage per annum)

	Output growth	Due to capital	Due to labour	Due to human capital	TFP growth
1760–80	0.60	0.25	0.20	0.10	0.05
1780–1831	1.70	0.60	0.45	0.45	0.20
1831–73	2.40	0.90	0.45	0.70	0.35
1873–99	2.10	0.80	0.30	0.50	0.50
1899–1913	1.40	0.80	0.30	0.50	−0.20

Sources and notes: Crafts (1995: 752). Weights are 0.4 for capital, 0.35 for labour and 0.25 for human capital.

evidence for the idea of an 'industrious revolution' initially proved elusive, quantitative information has recently emerged to suggest that it played quite an important role. Voth (2001) uses court records from London and the north of England to infer the decline of the pre-industrial practice of not working on Mondays (known colloquially as St Monday). His estimates suggest that annual hours worked per person increased from 2,576 in 1760 to 3,328 by 1800 and 3,356 by 1830, so that labour input grew at an annual rate of 1.4 per cent between 1760 and 1801, rather than at the 0.8 per cent rate suggested by population growth. This would reduce TFP growth during this period by 0.3 per cent per year, which would be sufficient to make TFP growth slightly negative rather than positive for the period 1760–1801 in Table 1.5. Abstention rather than ingenuity seems to have governed the Industrial Revolution by a considerably greater margin than contemplated even by Crafts and Harley (1992), let alone by McCloskey (1981).

The idea of a significant increase in annual working hours during the Industrial Revolution has recently received further quantitative support from Humphries and Weisdorf (2016), who contrast the real wages of workers employed on annual contracts with those of workers paid on daily rates. The difference between the two series can be taken as representing the change in the number of days worked per year. The path of real wages shown by their 'annual' series tracks quite closely the path of real GDP per head as estimated by Broadberry et al. (2015), and is thus consistent with their claim that the daily real wage series can be reconciled with the GDP per head data during the period 1700–1870 largely through an increase in days worked per year, with smaller contributions from a reduction in the share of GDP going to labour and an increase in the relative price of food. The number of days

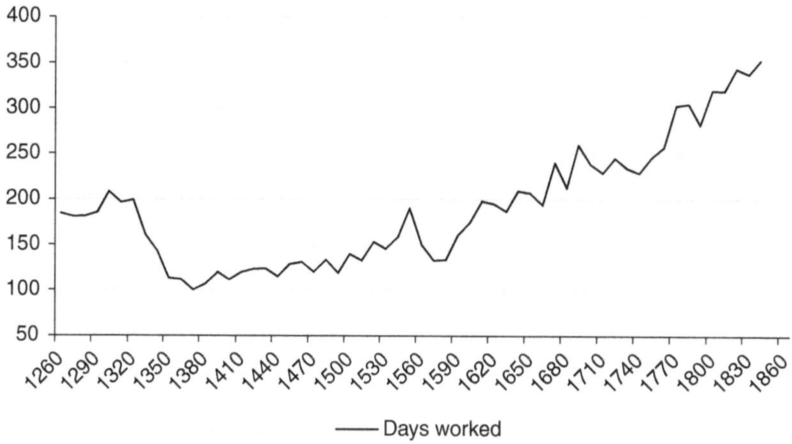

Figure 1.2 The implied working year of day workers, 1260s–1840s
Source: Humphries and Weisdorf (2016).

worked per year implied by the Humphries and Weisdorf data over the period from the 1260s to the 1840s is shown in Figure 1.2.

The Role of Technology

Growth accounting was introduced by Solow (1957) and is often associated with his one-sector neoclassical growth model, in which total factor productivity growth is treated as an exogenous variable and equated with technological progress (Solow 1956). In fact, this is not strictly necessary and Barro (1999) shows within a growth accounting framework how TFP growth can be seen as reflecting endogenous technological progress or spillover effects from accumulation. These findings were anticipated by Crafts (1995) in an early attempt to reconsider the Industrial Revolution in the light of endogenous growth theory. The strongest result of Crafts (1995: 754) was that spillover effects from accumulation were unlikely to have played a major role in the British Industrial Revolution, since Britain was characterized by relatively low rates of investment in both physical and human capital. Crafts (1995: 761–767) thus saw the endogenization of innovation as a more promising line of enquiry, but pointed to relatively low levels of spending on research and development compared with later periods, and placed more emphasis on wider growth-promoting characteristics of British society such as incentives for wealth creation rather than rent-seeking, a low share of direct taxes in overall taxes and high rates of urbanization.

The Industrial Revolution is rightly remembered as a period of innovation in manufacturing. Museums continue to celebrate the spinning jenny, the water frame, the mule and the power loom in cotton textiles, coke smelting and the reverberatory furnace in iron, and the use of the steam engine to power machinery across all branches of manufacturing. However, it is worth bearing in mind that the first industrial use of the steam engine occurred in mining, and that it soon spread beyond industry to the agricultural and service sectors. Indeed, some of the most important applications of the steam engine lay in transport, with the development of the steam locomotive on the railways revolutionizing inland transport and the steamship having a similar effect on overseas transport.

Recent work by Allen (2009) and Mokyr (2009) has sought to place technological progress at the heart of explaining the Industrial Revolution, but with quite different emphases. Whereas Allen (2009) sees technological progress in Britain as a response to a unique set of factor prices, Mokyr (2009) emphasizes a wider 'industrial enlightenment'. Before examining these two approaches in detail, however, it is worth emphasizing once again the key result of this section, which has established that growth of factor inputs accounted for two-thirds of the increase in the rate of output growth, leaving the other third to be explained by TFP growth, which includes all other efficiency gains as well as technological progress.

Explaining the Industrial Revolution and the Transition to Modern Economic Growth

Growth accounting is useful in identifying the proximate sources of growth, but cannot really explain why the Industrial Revolution occurred in Britain rather than elsewhere. If an industrious revolution and capital accumulation were the proximate sources, why did they happen in Britain rather than in France or the Netherlands? And to the extent that technological progress was responsible, why again did the key innovations occur in Britain? In this section we therefore turn to the more fundamental causes of economic growth. Economists tend to divide the fundamental causes of economic growth into two categories: geography and institutions.

Geography

Economic geographers make an important distinction between first nature and second nature geography. First nature geography covers natural endowments such as mineral deposits or climate, while second nature geography covers man-made factors such as access to markets and agglomeration economies. Allen (2009) emphasizes both aspects of economic geography in his explanation of Britain's primacy during the Industrial Revolution. First nature geography played an important role because of Britain's large reserves of coal. However, it is clear that this would not be sufficient on its own, since the coal deposits were always there and did not suddenly materialize during the eighteenth century. Rather, their utilization depended on a number of factors that can be seen as reflecting second nature geography. Allen places particular emphasis on the growth of London, which stimulated the coal industry in the north of England to satisfy London's growing demand for fuel as wood became scarce and was increasingly replaced by coal shipped from Newcastle. This resulted in the first element of what Allen sees as Britain's unique factor-price combination of low coal prices and high wages. The high wages resulted from agglomeration economies associated with the growth of London, combined with the effects of Britain's growing success in international trade, following the shift of Europe's trading focus from the Mediterranean to the Atlantic from around 1500.

Allen sees the key innovations of the Industrial Revolution as a response to high wages and low coal prices in Britain, with the new technology characterized as labour-saving and coal-using. This framework is also useful in understanding why the key innovations of steam-driven machinery in industries such as cotton textiles, iron and engineering were not immediately adopted elsewhere, since they were designed to be profitable in the circumstances of Britain's unique factor-price combination. But Britain's advantage did not last forever, as further technological change adapted the new technologies to other factor-price combinations, and eventually made them dominate the old technologies over a much wider range of factor prices.

Institutions

Allen (2009) sees technological change as a response to the incentives faced by entrepreneurs, which can be seen ultimately as shaped by both first and second nature geography. Although Allen (2009: 4–5, 14–15, 125–126) explicitly seeks to distance himself from the idea of institutions playing an important role, it seems but a small step from the characterization of entrepreneurs as responding to factor-price incentives to a consideration of how individuals respond to the incentives provided by the 'rules of the game' embodied in the wider institutional framework (North 1990). North defined institutions as the rules of the game, both formal and informal, which define and limit the set of choices that individuals make. He saw institutions as affecting economic performance by providing incentives for individuals to engage in socially productive activities such as exchange and production, invention and innovation, saving and investment. Although North and Weingast (1989) sought to 'explain' the Industrial Revolution as a response to the institutional changes introduced by the Glorious Revolution of 1688, the lag of around a century between the two developments makes it hard to draw a firm link between the 'credible commitment' supposedly secured by the constitutional settlement and the later economic development. To be convincing, a clearer link is needed between the institutional change and the innovations of the Industrial Revolution.

Like Allen, Mokyr (2009) places the explanation of a sustained acceleration in the rate of technological progress at the heart of understanding the Industrial Revolution. Unlike Allen, however, Mokyr (2009: 40) embeds his explanation firmly within the wider institutional framework, drawing on his idea of a European 'industrial enlightenment', with scientists, engineers and inventors engaged on a Baconian programme of research based on experimentation and scientific method, directed at solving practical problems to produce 'useful knowledge'. In the British case, however, Mokyr (2009: 120) sees it as important that these scientists, engineers and inventors were able to engage with a supply of skilled craftsmen, which existed partly as a result of historical contingency from past industrial developments, and partly as a result of a flexible institution in the form of the apprenticeship system. Mokyr (2009: 63–78) also emphasizes the effects of the Enlightenment on the wider institutional structure of society, although this part of the argument, with its emphasis on ideology increasingly coming to dominate vested interests, is necessarily more speculative.

As Crafts (2011: 166) notes, although Allen (2009) and Mokyr (2009) see themselves as offering competing explanations of the Industrial Revolution, their arguments are not mutually exclusive and could indeed be characterized as complementary. It would not be unreasonable to see British innovators as responding to the factor-price combination that they faced within an environment shaped by the Enlightenment.

The Standard of Living

What were the consequences of the Industrial Revolution for the living standards of the British people? This has been a controversial issue that has divided economic historians for as long as the subject has been studied. To understand the enduring nature of this controversy, it is helpful to see a single fault line dividing most economic historians, with the debate evolving over time. Coleman (1987: 63–92) labelled the two sides 'reformists' and 'neutralists', characterizing reformists as hostile to capitalism and market forces, and supportive of government intervention capable of reforming the system, while seeing neutralists as more favourably disposed towards market forces and sceptical of the ability of interventionist governments to improve the situation. Sometimes reformists have been called 'pessimists' on account of their stance over what happened to the living standards of workers during the Industrial Revolution, while neutralists have been called 'optimists'.

In a complex debate, Hartwell and Engerman (1975) identified three questions. First, there is the factual question of what happened to workers' real incomes during the Industrial Revolution. This may not be enough to settle the debate over the consequences of industrialization for living standards, however, because there may have been other developments besides industrialization that had a substantial impact on the trend in living standards at this time. Second, therefore, Hartwell and Engerman identified a counterfactual question: were workers better off than they would have been in the absence of industrialization? This admits the possibility that because of, say, an exogenously given increase in population growth, living standards might have deteriorated substantially without industrialization, so that stagnation of living standards in the face of such demographic pressure should be seen as a considerable achievement. Third, however, reformists might want to know if there was some set of policies that could have made workers better off than they actually were during industrialization. Mokyr (1993: 119) calls this the hypercounterfactual question.

What Happened to Living Standards?

On the factual question, a consensus remains elusive. Although there is now broad agreement on the path of nominal wages, there remain substantial differences over the path of consumer prices, so that different real wage series continue to show very different trends. Figure 1.3 plots the most widely used series in the current debates, with unskilled building labourers' wages deflated by different consumer price indices. Although Clark's (2005) real wage series doubles over the period 1700–1870, more or less in line with GDP per head, Allen's (2001) series exhibits almost no long run gain, as the rising real wage from the 1820s follows an absolute decline during the 1760s followed by a long period of stagnation. Allen's pessimistic position in the standard of living debate is worth noting because he is criticized by

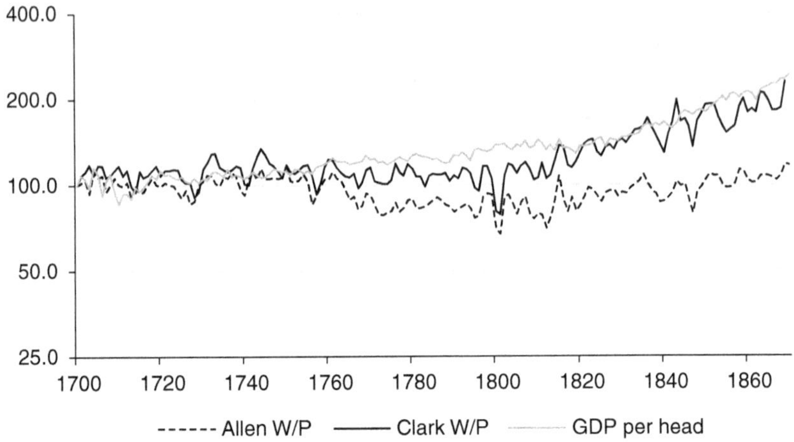

Figure 1.3 Real wages and GDP per head in Britain, 1700–1870 (log scale, 1700=100)
Sources: Allen (2001); Clark (2005); Broadberry et al. (2015).

Humphries (2013) for his characterization of Britain as a high-wage economy. It is important to keep in mind that however low British living standards were compared with later periods, they were nevertheless relatively high compared with other countries at the time of the Industrial Revolution.

A number of other indicators of the standard of living have been deployed in seeking to answer the factual question, but without decisively resolving the debate. Pessimists can point to the increase in hours worked per year as evidence of workplace intensification imposed on the workers by hard-driving factory owners determined to keep their capital fully utilized, while optimists can see the same change as allowing workers the freedom to enjoy higher consumption of the new goods being made available by technological progress and long-distance trade. Optimists can point to rising life expectancy, while pessimists can see the same gains as painfully slow to arrive due to the urban disamenities of industrializing Britain. The introduction of anthropometric data into the debate promised a way out of the deadlock, but initially optimistic evidence of rising heights provided by Floud et al. (1990) was soon countered by Nicholas and Steckel (1991) and Komlos (1993) with evidence of declining heights obtained from different samples. Given the range of possible outcomes available for each individual indicator, it is no surprise that composite indicators such as the human development index also give an ambiguous answer to the factual question of what happened to workers' living standards (Crafts 1997; Voth 2004: 289).

Were Workers Better Off Than They Would Have Been Without Industrialization?

An unambiguous answer to the factual question would still not settle the standard of living debate, because there may have been developments occurring at the time that made it harder to achieve rising living standards. The obvious counterfactual question to ask is: how would Britain have fared if it had been forced to cope with the rapidly rising population of the Industrial Revolution period without the gains of industrialization? In a standard Malthusian model, rapid population growth leads to declining real wages, so even stable real wages in a period of rapid population growth could be seen as an achievement. As Mokyr (1993: 119–121) notes, the case of Ireland provides a stark warning of what could have happened to Britain. Ireland had a similar history to Britain in terms of population growth and supply shocks, but without industrialization. Ireland's continued vulnerability to famine, with catastrophic consequences when the potato blight struck in 1845–46, suggests that even if living standards were slow to rise in Britain, the economy performed well enough to avoid a Malthusian crisis.

Could a Reformist Government Have Improved Workers' Living Standards Without Blocking Industrialization?

The hypercounterfactual question is more subtle still, and addresses the concerns of reformists to smooth the pains of industrialization, but without undermining the whole process of economic development. Could an enlightened state have intervened to avoid some of the worst consequences of industrialization, but without preventing the Industrial Revolution? Williamson (1990) argues that Britain underinvested in social overhead capital during the Industrial Revolution, especially in urban areas, because although rates of return on such projects were high, an unfair and inefficient tax system led to 'public-sector failure'. As a result, overhead projects such as sewage, water supply, fire protection and public health were undersupplied, leading to the squalid conditions noted by social reformers.

Williamson goes on to note that without sufficient investment in infrastructure, rates of return may have been depressed in the private sector, slowing down industrialization. The reason for this is that dirty, unhealthy cities drive up the effective cost of labour, by creating a disamenities premium that firms have to pay to attract workers. The situation improved only after 1830, as social reformers pointed to the terrible conditions. Chadwick's (1842) *Report from the Poor Law Commissioners on an Inquiry into the Sanitary*

Conditions of the Labouring Population of Great Britain, with its early use of cost-benefit analysis and demonstration of the high social rate of return to investment in urban social overhead capital, is often seen as a turning point. However, Williamson argues that it would be a mistake to see progress in this area as held up before 1842 simply by lack of knowledge. Part of the blame can be put on government war expenditure during the Napoleonic Wars, which crowded out investment in infrastructure. But most blame is placed by Williamson on the system of taxation.

Local taxes, known as 'the rates', were assessed on the rental value of property, a very narrow base, and property owners were also the voters, with a big influence over how the rates were spent. These property owners were reluctant to increase spending on drainage and sanitation, because it meant higher rates, which they had to pay. They were also reluctant to close squalid dwellings, which meant losing rental income. Two developments helped to overcome these problems in the 1860s: first, general economic growth in cities augmented the local tax base and thus lowered the effective rate of tax; and second, central government action led to subsidized loans for town improvements.

Williamson thus identifies a set of reformist government policies that, had they been implemented earlier, would not have hindered the process of industrialization, but might even have speeded it up by raising the rate of return in the private sector, as well as relieving the squalid conditions that pessimists in the standard of living debate have pointed to as the unacceptable face of unconstrained capitalist development. Williamson's conclusion reminds us of the importance of the institutional framework in aligning private and social returns so as to bring about good social outcomes.

Trade and Empire

Trade: Demand and Supply Factors

Pessimists in the standard of living debate like to stress the importance for growth of export demand, with home demand seen as playing a subsidiary role on account of the squeeze on workers' incomes. As Hobsbawm (1968: 32) famously put it: 'home demand increased but foreign demand multiplied . . . If a spark was needed, this is where it came from.' However, although the increase in exports in Table 1.7 accounted for up to 30 per cent of the increase in national output in some periods, the level of exports as a share of national output remained below 20 per cent, and at times below 10 per cent. Indeed,

Table 1.7 Exports as a share of national output and its growth (percentage)

	Exports as a share of national output		Increase in exports as a proportion of the increase in national output
1700	8.4	1700–60	30.4
1760	14.6	1760–80	5.1
1780	9.4	1780–1801	21.0
1801	15.7	1801–31	11.3
1831	14.3	1831–51	29.4
1851	19.6		

Source: Crafts (1985: 131).

the most rapid growth came at times when the share of exports was at its lowest. However, of more significance is the path of the terms of trade, for if export demand was the prime mover, as Hobsbawm believed, we should expect to see an improvement in Britain's terms of trade when exports were growing fast. Yet, as Findlay and O'Rourke (2007: 332) note, Britain's terms of trade deteriorated substantially during the first half of the nineteenth century. The benefits of technological change in Britain were therefore shared with global consumers rather than being retained purely by British workers, which helps to explain the enduring controversy of the standard of living debate.

Trade and Exploitation

To what extent were Britain's gains from participating in the world economy obtained at the expense of other countries? This issue has been addressed by O'Brien (1982) in a critical appraisal of Wallerstein's (1974) *Modern World System*, which sought to establish that international trade was very important for Western development, created huge supernormal profits that financed the investment needed for the Industrial Revolution and created other spin-offs and externalities that further promoted Western growth. O'Brien shows, rather, that commerce between Europe and the rest of the world during the early modern period was on a small scale, was not a uniquely profitable field of enterprise, did not contribute much to Western industrial investment and generated few externalities that were beneficial for Western growth. An upper bound measure of trade between the core and periphery would be 4 per cent of core GDP, so that even allowing an unthinkably high profit rate of 50 per cent and an astonishingly high reinvestment rate of 50 per cent of profits would only produce a contribution of long-distance trade to core investment of 1 per cent of GDP.

O'Brien's (1982) findings fit well with the trend in the terms of trade noted in the last section. British exporters were forced to accept lower prices for their manufactures, thus sharing the gains of British technological progress with consumers overseas. These findings also fit well with the high price of imported goods established as a result of the mercantilist restrictions on trade within the British Empire, to which we turn in the next section.

Costs and Benefits of Empire

Britain and a number of other West European states did not just trade with Africa, Asia and the Americas, but also acquired colonies. Was this perhaps the way in which Britain was able to exploit the periphery? Individuals clearly made fortunes out of their colonial investments, but this does not necessarily mean that colonies were a net economic benefit for the country as a whole. Sugar producers from the British West Indies (BWI) were given a monopoly of the British market and were able to charge high prices, while acquiring and maintaining an empire had costs as well as benefits. Conducting a retrospective cost-benefit analysis of Britain's colonies, Thomas (1968) estimates the social rate of return on capital invested in the BWI as about 2 per cent, which compares with a rate of return on British government bonds of 3.5 per cent. This implies that Britain would have been better off without colonies and just investing the same money in risk-free assets.

If colonies were an economic loss, then this raises the question of why they were widely held. The answer lies in the fact that writers such as Thomas are measuring the social return to the country as a whole, but private returns to individual plantation and farm owners were often much higher. These private benefits accrued to a small number of plantation owners and investors, who were well represented in Parliament. On the other hand, the costs took the form of higher prices, which were borne by consumers, and administrative costs, which were borne by taxpayers. These costs were widely diffused and therefore less effective in mobilizing against the interests of the plantation owners and investors. Governments were content to go along with the mercantilist system that underpinned the empire because it generated revenue that allowed the expansion of state capacity. As the nineteenth century unfolded, however, criticism of the mercantilist system mounted, and British governments began a movement towards free trade, which combined with declining transport costs to produce an unprecedented wave of globalization and convergence of incomes in the last third of the century (O'Rourke and Williamson 1999).

Conclusions

Eighteenth-century Britain was the first economy to make the transition to modern economic growth, with sustained growth of GDP per head while population was growing rapidly. However, this breakthrough built upon earlier episodes of GDP per head growth following the Black Death in the fourteenth century and the Civil War during the seventeenth. Between these two episodes, the economy remained on a plateau rather than sinking back to Malthusian subsistence as population recovered. As a result, Britain, together with other dynamic economies in the North Sea area, improved its position relative to the rest of Europe and Asia.

The proximate sources behind economic growth in Britain during the Industrial Revolution included capital accumulation and the growth in the number and quality of workers. Factor inputs accounted for about two-thirds of the increase in output growth, leaving the other third to be explained by technological progress. Turning to the ultimate sources of Britain's Industrial Revolution growth, there is surely a role for first nature geography in the form of coal reserves, and second nature geography, with the growth of London leading to high wages through agglomeration economies and stimulating the northern coal industry through the demand for fuel. The resulting high wages and low coal prices can then be seen as stimulating the labour-saving and coal-using technology of the Industrial Revolution. However, it is difficult not to see also an important role for the institutional framework, enabling scientists, engineers and inventors working in Britain to engage with the supply of skilled craftsmen that existed there due to the flexible apprenticeship system, to produce 'useful knowledge'.

The impact of the Industrial Revolution on the living standards of the British people has been the subject of major controversy. The simple factual question of whether living standards rose or fell cannot settle the debate because of the counterfactual question of whether living standards were better than they would have been in the absence of industrialization. Here, optimists can point to the example of Ireland, which highlights the fragility of an economy subject to strong population growth and supply shocks but without industrialization. Also, it is possible to ask the hypercounterfactual question of whether a reformist government could have improved workers' living standards without blocking industrialization. Here, pessimists see the underinvestment in social overhead capital with a high rate of social return as a significant public-sector failure.

Finally, this chapter has addressed issues of trade and empire. Although exports grew more rapidly than output, this does not mean that the British economy was merely responding to demand from overseas, since the terms of trade deteriorated. This suggests that far from Britain gaining through unequal trade, the benefits of technological change in Britain were shared with global consumers. Furthermore, cost-benefit analysis indicates that although a number of individuals made large fortunes from the colonies, the social rate of return on the colonies for Britain as a whole was less than the risk-free rate of return. This means that plantation owners and investors benefited at the expense of British consumers and taxpayers.

References

Allen, R. C. (2001). 'The Great Divergence in European Wages and Prices from the Middle Ages to the First World War', *Explorations in Economic History*, 38, 411–447.

—— (2009). *The British Industrial Revolution in Global Perspective*, Cambridge University Press.

Barro, R. J. (1999). 'Notes on Growth Accounting', *Journal of Economic Growth*, 4, 119–137.

Broadberry, S. and Wallis, J. (2017). 'Growing, Shrinking and Long Run Economic Performance: Historical Perspectives on Economic Development', National Bureau of Economic Research Discussion Paper No. 23343, www.nber.org/papers/w23343 (accessed 29 September 2020).

Broadberry, S., Campbell, B., Klein, A., Overton, M. and van Leeuwen, B. (2015). *British Economic Growth, 1270–1870*, Cambridge University Press.

Broadberry, S., Guan, H. and Li, D. (2018). 'China, Europe and the Great Divergence: A Study in Historical National Accounting', *Journal of Economic History*, 78, 955–1000.

Chadwick, E. (1842). *Report from the Poor Law Commissioners on an Inquiry into the Sanitary Conditions of the Labouring Population of Great Britain*, London: HMSO.

Clark, G. (2005). 'The Condition of the Working Class in England, 1209–2004', *Journal of Political Economy*, 113, 1307–1340.

Coleman, D. C. (1987). *History and the Economic Past: An Account of the Rise and Decline of Economic History in Britain*, Oxford: Clarendon Press.

Crafts, N. F. R. (1985). *British Economic Growth during the Industrial Revolution*, Oxford: Clarendon Press.

—— (1995). 'Exogenous or Endogenous Growth? The Industrial Revolution Reconsidered', *Journal of Economic History*, 55, 745–772.

—— (1997). 'Some Dimensions of the "Quality of Life" During the British Industrial Revolution', *Economic History Review*, 50, 617–639.

—— (2011). 'Explaining the First Industrial Revolution: Two Views', *European Review of Economic History*, 15, 153–168.

Crafts, N. F. R. and Harley, C. K. (1992). 'Output Growth and the Industrial Revolution: A Restatement of the Crafts-Harley View', *Economic History Review*, 45, 703–730.

Deane, P. and Cole, W. A. (1967). *British Economic Growth, 1688–1959: Trends and Structure*, 2nd edition, Cambridge University Press.

de Vries, J. (1994). 'The Industrial Revolution and the Industrious Revolution', *Journal of Economic History*, 54, 249–270.

Feinstein, C. H. (1988). 'National Statistics 1760–1920', in Feinstein, C. H. and Pollard, S. (eds.), *Studies in Capital Formation in the United Kingdom, 1750–1920*, Oxford: Clarendon Press, 257–471.

Findlay, R. and O'Rourke, K. H. (2007). *Power and Plenty: Trade, War, and the World Economy in the Second Millennium*, Princeton University Press.

Floud, R., Wachter, K. and Gregory, A. (1990). *Height, Health and History: Nutritional Status in the United Kingdom, 1750–1980*, Cambridge University Press.

Harley, C. K. (1993). 'Reassessing the Industrial Revolution: A Macro View', in Mokyr, J. (ed.), *The British Industrial Revolution: An Economic Perspective*, Boulder: Westview, 171–226.

Hartwell, R. M. and Engerman, S. (1975). Models of Immiserisation: The Theoretical Basis of Pessimism', in Taylor, A. J. (ed.), *The Standard of Living in Britain in the Industrial Revolution*, London: Methuen, 189–213.

Hobsbawm, E. (1968). *Industry and Empire*, London: Weidenfeld & Nicolson.

Humphries, J. (2013). 'The Lure of Aggregates and the Pitfalls of the Patriarchal Perspective: A Critique of the High Wage Economy Interpretation of the British Industrial Revolution', *Economic History Review*, 66, 693–714.

Humphries, J. and Weisdorf, J. (2016). 'Unreal Wages? A New Empirical Foundation for the Study of Living Standards and Economic Growth, 1260–1860', Oxford Economic and Social History Working Papers No. 147, www.economics.ox.ac.uk/materials/papers/14729/147.pdf (accessed 29 September 2020).

Komlos, J. (1993). 'The Secular Trend in the Biological Standard of Living in the United Kingdom, 1730–1860', *Economic History Review*, 46, 115–144.

Kuznets, S. (1966). *Modern Economic Growth: Rate, Structure and Spread*, New Haven: Yale University Press.

McCloskey, D. N. (1981). 'The Industrial Revolution 1780–1860: A Survey', in Floud, R. and McCloskey, D. N. (eds.), *The Economic History of Britain since 1700, vol. 1: 1700–1860*, Cambridge University Press, 103–127.

Mokyr, J. (1993). 'Editor's Introduction: The New Economic History and the Industrial Revolution', in Mokyr, J. (ed.). *The British Industrial Revolution: An Economic Perspective*, Boulder: Westview, 118–130.

(2009). *The Enlightened Economy: An Economic History of Britain 1700–1850*, New Haven: Yale University Press.

Nicholas, S. and Steckel, R. H. (1991). 'Heights and Living Standards of English Workers During the Early Years of Industrialization, 1770–1815', *Journal of Economic History*, 51, 937–957.

North, D. C. (1990). *Institutions, Institutional Change and Economic Performance*, Cambridge University Press.

North, D. C. and Weingast, B. R. (1989). 'Constitutions and Commitment: The Evolution of Institutions Governing Public Choice in Seventeenth-Century England', *Journal of Economic History*, 49, 803–832.

O'Brien, P. K. (1982). 'European Economic Development: The Contribution of the Periphery', *Economic History Review*, 35, 1–18.

O'Rourke, K. H. and Williamson, J. G. (1999). *Globalization and History: The Evolution of a Nineteenth-Century Atlantic Economy*, Cambridge, MA: MIT Press.

Schofield, R. S. (1973). 'Dimensions of Illiteracy, 1750–1850', *Explorations in Economic History*, 10, 437–454.

Solow, R. M. (1956). 'A Contribution to the Theory of Economic Growth', *Quarterly Journal of Economics*, 70, 65–94.

(1957). 'Technical Change and the Aggregate Production Function', *Review of Economics and Statistics*, 39, 312–320.

Thomas, R. P. (1968). 'The Sugar Colonies of the Old Empire: Profit or Loss for Great Britain?', *Economic History Review*, 21, 30–45.

Voth, H.-J. (2001). 'The Longest Years: New Estimates of Labor Input in England, 1760–1830', *Journal of Economic History*, 61, 1065–1082.

(2004). 'Living Standards and the Urban Environment', in Floud, R. and Johnson, P. A. (eds.), *The Cambridge Economic History of Modern Britain, vol. 1: Industrialisation, 1700–1860*, Cambridge University Press.

Wallerstein, I. (1974). *The Modern World-System, Volume I: Capitalist Agriculture and the Origins of the European World-Economy in the Sixteenth Century*, New York: Academic Press.

Williamson, J. G. (1990). *Coping with City Growth During the British Industrial Revolution*, Cambridge University Press.

Wrigley, E. A. and Schofield, R. S. (1981). *The Population History of England, 1541–1871, A Reconstruction*, Cambridge University Press.

2

Continental Europe

GIOVANNI FEDERICO AND ANDREI MARKEVICH

Introduction: Continental Europe Around 1700

In 1700 Europe was just starting its bid for world economic and political hegemony. Europeans were comparatively few, were poor, and in many cases malnourished. Outside England and the Netherlands, traditional agriculture still employed the overwhelming majority of the population. In most of the continent manufacturing was still organized by guilds, markets were heavily regulated, and in large parts of the East peasants were trapped in serfdom. In the West, people had more freedom and rights, but the distribution of income was very unequal. Arguably, Europe enjoyed a clear technological leadership only in warfare, and indeed England, France, and the Netherlands were starting to build their colonial empires, joining Spain and Portugal. Yet the last Ottoman invasion had been defeated only seventeen years before.

In the next 170 years, much changed, mostly as a consequence of the Industrial Revolution in Britain. It challenged first the areas close to the Channel, and industries competing with British ones, but ultimately it affected the whole economy of all continental countries. The difference in impact deepened the divergence between the core, including Belgium, the Netherlands, northern France and western Germany and the periphery (the rest of the continent).

We outline the macroeconomic changes in the next two sections of the chapter, dealing first with population growth and its causes and with gross domestic product (GDP), structural change, and inequality. We then discuss the causes of economic growth in the next three sections, covering both proximate and ultimate sources. For the proximate sources, we focus on technical progress and trade and market integration, which lead to a more efficient use of factors of production. This is followed by discussion of institutional change and the state as the ultimate sources of growth.

Many More Europeans

From 1700 to 1870, the European population, including the United Kingdom, Russia and the European part of the Ottoman Empire, increased by two and a half times, from 122 million to 310 million, and the density from 11.1 to 29.9 per km^2 (Malanima 2009: Table 1). Europeans accounted for 19.5 per cent of the world population in 1700 and for 27.5 per cent in 1900 (Maddison 2001). Population growth accelerated from 0.32 per cent per annum in 1700–50, to 0.55 per cent in 1750–1800 and eventually to 0.71 per cent in 1800–70. Clearly, Europe escaped from the Malthusian regime of slow-growing or stable population, if it had ever been in it. The rates differed between countries, from a maximum of 0.70% in Scandinavia over the whole period 1700–1870 to a minimum of 0.33% in France. As a consequence, the distribution of European population changed, shifting northwards and eastwards away from the Mediterranean basin.

The standard narrative interprets this population growth as a temporary disequilibrium during the transition from a traditional regime of high mortality/high fertility to a modern one of low mortality and low fertility (Chesnais 1992). Before 1870, this transition had started only in north-western Europe and was well advanced only in France. French death rates declined steadily from the mid-eighteenth century onwards while birth rates declined mostly after Waterloo, down to less than 30 per cent after 1870. Elsewhere in north-western Europe, mortality started to decline in the late eighteenth century and fertility from the 1830s. In the periphery, the transition began only in the second half of the nineteenth century or even the early twentieth century. Fertility rates in eastern European countries, Russia, and the Balkans remained extremely high – around 50‰. This difference in the timing of the demographic transition mirrors to some extent a difference in marriage patterns across Europe that had emerged in the Middle Ages. Women in north-western Europe married later, or did not marry at all – so that fertility was low and people lived in nuclear families as opposed to extended ones in the east and south. This European marriage pattern (EMP) has been deemed a major factor of economic development in north-western Europe, but this statement is still controversial (Dennison and Ogilvie 2014).

The contributions of advances in medical practice and of economic growth to the fall in mortality have long been debated (Alter and Clark 2010), but there seems to be a consensus on the key role of public policies (most notably the construction of sewers and the provision of clean water), jointly with the, albeit slow, diffusion of best practice of personal and house cleanliness. On top of this, mortality declined because three traditional sources of demographic shocks (almost) disappeared. A century of bloody warfare culminated in the Napoleonic Wars, but after Waterloo the continent remained comparatively peaceful. Famines disappeared from western (but not eastern) Europe in the eighteenth century, with the awful exception of the Great Irish famine from 1845 to 1849 (Ó Gráda 2009), thanks to the growth in agricultural production and to market integration. The bubonic plague disappeared in the early eighteenth century, and deaths from other transmissible diseases, especially affecting children, declined sizably (Riley 2001). Indeed, inoculation against smallpox was by far the major success of medical science. In the long run, the decline in mortality brought about a parallel trend in fertility, as households realized that fewer births were necessary to have the desired number of surviving children.

The growth of European population was dampened by the start of mass emigration. The overseas empires had always attracted soldiers, civil servants, merchants, and adventurers from the mother countries, but their number was small. The majority of the European population could not afford the transatlantic passage: from the eighteenth century onwards, immigrants were subsidized by prospective employers, which the emigrants repaid with a sort of temporary serfdom (indentured service). Free migration started in the nineteenth century, first from the British Isles, with a massive wave from Ireland after the famine, and then from Scandinavia and Germany (Hatton and Williamson 1998). The low fertility rate prevented massive emigration from France, while southern Europeans were still too poor and eastern Europeans were poor and had enough land for internal colonization.

By definition, population growth increased the potential supply of labour, but the actual supply depended on workers' choices. In north-western Europe from the late seventeenth century onwards, actual labour supply increased faster than population once more women and children started to work for the market, and all workers worked longer hours to afford a (modestly) better standard of living (de Vries 2008). There is no strong evidence of such an 'industrious revolution' in the periphery. The spread of the factory system reduced the demand for household work for women and children, but not necessarily their employment. The supply of child labour was hardly affected by the approval of the early protective legislation in some countries (Huberman and Lewchuck 2003), while it was somewhat reduced by the diffusion of schooling. The enrolment rate for both sexes in the whole of Europe increased from a very low 16.2 per cent in 1820 to a still paltry 44 per cent in 1870 (Barro and Lee 2015). It exceeded 80 per cent only in a handful of countries, including France but not Germany or the United Kingdom.

The increase in schooling expanded the human capital of Europeans, supplementing the traditional on-the-job training via apprenticeship. This latter gave workers task- or sector-specific skills; primary schooling gave them literacy and numeracy. The numeracy is defined as the capability of counting and is measured by age-heaping – i.e. the difference between the number of people who declared their age to be a round number (20, 25, etc.) and the proportion of people who were of that age, given the normal distribution of births. Around 1820, age-heaping had already disappeared in western Europe, with few exceptions (Southern Italy, Greece) but was still widespread in eastern Europe (Hippe and Baten 2012). Trends in literacy are likely to be similar, with some lag, but data are scarce and hardly comparable. The rates were very high in Scandinavia and other Protestant countries, but quite low in the southern and eastern periphery. It was 27 per cent in Italy in 1861, but only 10–15 per cent in the South (Vecchi 2017: 379) and 22.9 per cent in the European part of the Russian empire as late as 1897 (Rushin 1956). The endowment of more advanced human capital was extremely limited: the Europe-wide enrolment rates in secondary and tertiary education did not exceed 1.5 per cent in 1870 (Barro and Lee 2015).

Modern Economic Growth: When and Where

In 1700, Europeans were quite poor: the available data on GDP per capita (Table i.1) are comparable to present-day levels in sub-Saharan Africa, and it is a small consolation that other continents were even poorer. GDP per capita stagnated, albeit with large fluctuations, throughout continental Europe in the eighteenth century, while in the nineteenth century it started to grow in the core and continued to stagnate in the periphery. Rates of growth were modest by twentieth-century standards (0.6 per cent for Belgium 1820–70), but a low rate can deliver substantial increases if sustained in the long run. GDP per capita in 1870 was almost double its 1700 level in Belgium and Germany, 70–75 per cent higher in France and the Netherlands. In contrast, only two countries in the periphery, Spain and 'Poland', achieved any significant growth in the same period, and the latter only because it was recovering from a very deep crisis. There are no data for other countries in eastern Europe, but the low (and highly tentative) 1870 estimates by Maddison imply very little or no growth at all, unless GDP per capita in 1700 was at subsistence level.

In the short run, GDP per capita can grow with additional capital and land, but ultimately modern economic growth can be achieved only if factors are used more efficiently. The relevant metric is thus total factor productivity (TFP) – i.e. the difference between rates of change in GDP and suitably weighted factors (see Introduction). Even without hard estimates for the nineteenth century, it is possible to speculate on the direction of change. The anecdotal evidence on public works, railways, roads etc. suggests that physical capital per capita may have increased. Likewise, the discussion in the previous section implies that, at least in some areas, the number of hours worked per capita increased in the eighteenth century and that total human capital grew, as well. In contrast, total cropland remained broadly constant in western Europe and increased only in some peripheral areas – most notably in eastern Europe, Scandinavia and the Balkans (Federico 2005). On balance, the most likely case seems a modest rise in inputs per capita, with substantial differences across countries. If so, the rate of growth of GDP per capita would be an upper bound for the increase in TFP.

In the long run, economic growth is bound to bring about a massive shift in the composition of GDP and employment, from agriculture to manufacturing and, in a later stage of development, to advanced services. This process predated the Industrial Revolution in England, where agriculture accounted for about a quarter of GDP already at the beginning of the eighteenth century (Broadberry et al. 2015: tab. 5.01). Continental European countries, with the notable exception of Belgium, had not reached that level by 1870 (Table 2.1). Peripheral countries were still mostly agricultural, but even in France and Germany the manufacturing sector was comparatively small, while there were huge differences between the most advanced regions, such as the Ruhr, and the rest of the country. There are no good data on occupational structure in eastern Europe, but the share of agriculture in GDP was even higher than in the periphery of western Europe – 48.7 per cent in Romania (Axenciuc 2012: tables A2 and A11), 58 per cent in Russia (Gregory 1983), 68.5 per cent in Bulgaria (Ivanov 2012).

The historical GDP estimates for the pre-statistical age are tentative and thus it is useful to seek independent confirmation about living standards from other evidence. Real wages cannot be considered independent evidence because they are very often used to estimate GDP according to the so-called demand-side approach (Fouquet and Broadberry 2015). Thus, scholars often resort to proxies, such as heights and / or urbanization rates. Heights are positively related to the intake of food, and especially of milk and meat, and

Table 2.1 The structural transformation: Europe around 1870

	% GDP		% Workforce	
	Agriculture	Industry	Agriculture	Manufacturing
Austria-Hungary	34.4	22.0	67.0	15.5
Belgium	14.0	49.0	40.0	39.0
Denmark	49.0	20.0	61.7	28.0
Finland	57.9	17.4	71.3	11.6
France	38.2	35.0	59.4	22.3
Germany	40.5	29.5	49.0	29.0
Italy	47.7	22.6	64.9	15.1
Netherlands	30.0	24.0	39.0	31.0
Norway	33.5	21.8	26.8	15.9
Spain	38.3	20.9	63.9	15.4
Sweden	40.6	19.6	67.4	17.4
United Kingdom	14.2	42.0	15.4	47.7

Sources: GDP and workforce – Belgium and Netherlands: van Zanden and van Riel (2004: tables 6.2 and 6.3); Spain: Prados de la Escosura (2016: tables 13 and 17); Sweden: Schön and Krantz (2015: tables III and VII); United Kingdom: Mitchell (1988: 104, 822); France: Toutain (1987: tables 19 and series V6, V37, and V41).
Workforce – Germany: histat.gesis.org/histat/; Italy: Giordano and Zollino (2015); other countries: Mitchell (1998).
GDP – Austria-Hungary: Schulze (2000: tables A1 and A2); Finland: Hjerppe (1996: table 5); Italy: Baffigi et al. (2013); Norway: Grytten (2015: table I); other countries: Mitchell (1998: J2).

negatively to the intensity of work and to the spread of diseases (Baten and Blum 2014). Heights did not rise in western Europe from 1810 to 1870, while they may have increased somewhat in eastern Europe and in the Russian Empire in the first half of the nineteenth century (Baten and Blum 2012). Urbanization is assumed to be positively related to the size of manufacturing and services, and thus ultimately to the level of development and GDP per capita. In the eighteenth century, the European urbanization rate, defined as the proportion of the population living in cities of more than 10,000 inhabitants, increased marginally from 9 per cent to 9.7 per cent and only as a result of the jump in the British rate from 10 per cent to 17.3 per cent (Malanima 2010). In contrast, from 1800 to 1870 the rate more than doubled in the core countries of continental Europe (from 7.1 per cent to 15.1 per cent), while it increased only by a tenth in the rest of the continent. The rise of urbanization can explain the stagnation or decline in heights even in periods of economic growth in the first decades of the nineteenth century. In fact, cities were unhealthy places, whose population could grow only thanks to immigration from the countryside. The relative prices of milk, meat, and vegetables were higher and their quality was much worse in the cities than in the countryside and the health environment was very poor.

Who did benefit from economic growth? Kuznets (1955) had argued that early industrialization caused inequality to rise, because it increased the employment share of more productive and thus better paid industrial workers and widened the gap in salaries between skilled and unskilled workers (increasing the skill premium). The evidence for this hypothesis in the period before 1870 is not strong. The number of industrial workers was still small, and the skill premium for construction workers (possibly a non-representative category) seems to have remained constant in industrializing western Europe, while increasing in the periphery (van Zanden 2009). Overall inequality depended on other sources of income, most notably profits and rent from land. In some areas, they accrued also to working-class households (e.g. peasants owning land), reducing inequality, while institutions like demesne serfdom in Poland greatly increased it (Malinowski and van Zanden 2017). Ideally, one should measure inequality in total income with household-level data. Using imaginatively all scraps of available evidence, van Zanden et al. (2014) conclude that from 1820 to 1870 the average within-country Gini coefficients (the standard measure, ranging from 0 to 1) remained broadly constant in both western and eastern Europe around 0.45. In the eighteenth century, inequality may have been higher (Alfani 2017) and its social impact was surely greater. This latter effect can be measured by the extraction ratio, the ratio of the actual Gini coefficient to the maximum feasible inequality, which could be reached when all population is at subsistence level and all the residual income accrues to the élite (Milanovic et al. 2011). The ratios in advanced countries are now around 30–40 per cent, while in pre-industrial ages they ranged from a minimum of 55 per cent in the United Kingdom in 1801 up to 100 per cent in some Third World countries – i.e. elites succeeded in squeezing all surplus above subsistence. The combination of increasing per capita income and constant Gini coefficients suggests that also in other European countries the decline in the maximum extraction rate could have started in the early nineteenth century, but the evidence is really thin.

The Causes of Growth: Technical Change

In the eighteenth and nineteenth centuries, the European technological advantage over the rest of the world became overwhelming, and differences within the continent widened a lot. By 1700, the most advanced area in the continent was Holland (de Vries and van der Woude 1997), and other areas of western Europe were arguably not far behind England. In the next century, all over the continent, 'natural philosophers' increased substantially the stock of scientific knowledge, which was disseminated by official institutions such as the French Academy of Science or the Saint Petersburg Academy of Sciences and by private undertakings – most notably the French *Encyclopédie* (Mokyr 2005). Yet technical progress in manufacturing and related sectors was almost exclusively a British affair. To be sure, there were some European innovations in the early nineteenth century, such as photography and chemical bleaching, but technical progress on the continent was essentially a story of imitation of the United Kingdom (von Tunzelman 1995). By 1870, modern industry was growing in many areas, but none could yet match Great Britain in terms of industrial technology and organization. Labour productivity in manufacturing in Germany was still about 10 per cent lower than in Britain (Broadberry 1997: table 3.1).

Imitating Britain was at the same time more necessary and easier for north-western European countries than for peripheral nations. They were geographically close, and thus were more subject to British competition, and their factor endowment and thus prices were more similar to those of Britain. They had abundant coal and fairly high wages, while capital requirements for most modern technologies were still modest. Since the mid-nineteenth century, the development of investment banks in France and Germany provided long-term funding for the few large industrial enterprises. Thus, the British factory system spread gradually in a core industrial area along a strip encompassing Belgium, northern France and western Germany, extending southwards to Switzerland and northern Italy, eastwards to the present-day Czech Republic and Austria, both then parts of the Habsburg Empire (Klein et al. 2017) and northwards to Scandinavia. Belgium was the first country to imitate England, Sweden the last in this group. It started to mechanize cotton spinning in the 1830s and industrial growth accelerated in the 1850s with the development of sawmills and the modernization of iron production (Schön 2012).

The transfer of technologies was slow because learning and adaptation to local conditions needed time. Furthermore, even small differences in factor prices could make British technology not profitable. Allen (2009) argues that French firms did not adopt Hargreaves' jenny, the first (female-powered) spinning machine, in the late eighteenth century because returns to investment were too low, although this claim is controversial (Gragnolati et al. 2011; Allen 2011b). Coke smelting, which had been invented in the 1710s and accounted for all British production of pig iron in the 1780s, started to be used in Belgium in the 1810s and in France and Germany in the following decade, but its market share reached 100 per cent only in the 1840s in Belgium and in the 1870s in France and Germany, after the spurt from rail demand (Broadberry et al. 2010). One can find a similar pattern in the adoption of the Watt steam engine, the key invention of the Industrial Revolution and the first general-purpose technology. The first machine was installed in continental Europe in 1778 (in a French mine), and by 1825 firms in France, Belgium, Germany, and Russia were able to build steam engines, with the help of British engineers (Tann and Breckin 1978). Yet by 1870 the number of steam horse power per capita was just 40 per cent of the British level in Belgium and 20 per cent of the British level in France and Prussia (Kander et al. 2013: table 6.3).

The rest of the continent trailed further behind, traditional technologies and methods still prevailing in the 1870s. In southern Europe, labour was abundant and (imported) coal expensive, so unsurprisingly the development of modern industry was patchy at best until the late nineteenth or early twentieth century. There were few, although relevant, exceptions. The Italian silk reeling industry was the world technological leader from the 1830s–1840s (Federico 1997) and Catalonia developed a huge cotton industry, which, unlike the French industry, quickly adopted the spinning jenny in the 1780s (Martínez-Galarraga and Prat 2016). Eastern Europe had coal but wages were low and anyway it was shielded from British competition by distance and by high protective duties. Thus, modernization of industry had barely begun by 1870. The Russian empire imported some cotton spinning machinery from Britain from the 1840s onwards, but other industries, including other textile sectors and metallurgy in the Urals, still operated with backward production technologies and forced labour (Markevich and Nafziger 2017). In the Balkans, there was no modern industry until the late nineteenth century (Kopsidis and Ivanov 2017).

This outline of technical progress applies to manufacturing and to some branches of the service sector, most notably transportation. From the 1780s onwards copper sheathing had increased the speed and the lifespan of sailing ships (Solar and Hens 2016), but the real game changer was the introduction of steam engines, especially on land. The gap in costs between cart and horses and railways was huge from the beginning, while steamships became competitive for long-distance commerce only after the invention of the compound engine in the 1850s. The rest of the service sector remained largely unaffected by technical progress until the twentieth century.

In agriculture there were no massive changes in organization nor major technical breakthroughs before Liebig's theory of fertilization in 1840 (a rare case of the direct contribution of science to technical progress in that period), which paved the way for the development and massive use of chemical fertilizers from the 1850s onwards. However, there is strong indirect evidence of technical progress (Federico 2005). European agriculture succeeded in feeding the growing population without a meaningful contribution from other continents and without a massive increase in land endowments, except in the periphery. Thus, most innovations were land-saving and labour-intensive. Farmers introduced new varieties of known plants (and a totally new plant, the sugar beet) and changed their agricultural practices, substituting the period of rest (fallow) with fertility-restoring plants. Fallow had long disappeared on irrigated land (e.g. in the Po Valley or in the Netherlands). The key innovation was the introduction of continuous rotation to dry land from the late seventeenth century onwards. Scholars have paid a great deal of attention to the English version of this innovation, the 'new husbandry', which substituted fallow with clover and other grasses, which could feed cattle. However, its adoption depended on factor prices and, as with all agricultural innovations, on the environment. Thus elsewhere fallow was substituted by other plants, such as potatoes where labour was abundant (most notably in Ireland and in many areas of northern Europe) and maize in the dry Mediterranean areas. Anyway, in the 1780s the gap between England and other advanced areas was not as large as in manufacturing, at least for cereal yields (Allen and Ó Gráda 1988).

The Causes of Growth: Trade and Market Integration

In the words of Persson and Sharp (2015: 4) 'Europe trades, therefore it is'. The sentence refers to the history of the continent in general, but it is surely more correct for the late eighteenth and above all for the early nineteenth century than for any other period since the fall of the Roman Empire. Trade statistics are available only for Great Britain (Mitchell 1988). They show a steady increase from 1700 to the eve of the French Revolution of about 1 per cent yearly, with a declining share of imports from Europe, from 70 per cent to 45 per cent of the total. According to O'Rourke and Williamson (2002a) European intercontinental trade increased slightly faster, at 1.26 per cent per year, but only thanks to shifts in demand and supply. Trade costs, as measured by price gaps between Asia and Europe, remained constant because the Western trading companies, such as the Dutch East India Company (VOC) and the English East India Company (EIC), exploited the monopoly on trade with their Asian possessions (Indonesia and India) to keep price differentials large, for the benefit of their shareholders and of well-connected shipowners (O'Rourke and Williamson 2002b). More recent research has shown that price gaps varied over time and in different places as the monopoly power of these companies waxed and waned with competition from other European companies and from independent merchants (de Zwart 2016). Likewise, the trade in wheat and the price gaps between the United States and Great Britain varied according to British trade policy (Sharp and Weisdorf 2013). In contrast, there is not much evidence of convergence of wheat prices before 1789 within Europe (Federico et al. 2018).

The situation changed totally after Waterloo. Total exports from continental Europe, which had remained constant during the Napoleonic Wars, increased by a third until 1830 and then by five times in the next forty years, roughly as much as world trade (Federico and Tena-Junguito 2019). Exports grew faster from the core (an increase by 6.9 times from 1830 to 1870, slightly more than from Britain) than from the periphery (4 times only, without substantial differences between countries). Thus, trade grew much more than GDP: in the same years, the ratio of total exports to GDP doubled in the United Kingdom and tripled, from 4.5 per cent to almost 15 per cent, in seven other European countries (Federico and Tena-Junguito 2017). By 1870, it reached 15.7 per cent in five core countries (and 18.7 per cent in Great Britain) and 8 per cent in eight peripheral countries.

This increase in openness implies that trade costs fell substantially in the nineteenth century. Indeed price differentials shrank both within Europe (Federico 2011; Federico et al. forthcoming), and between Europe and Asia (Chilosi and Federico 2015). The contribution of technical progress in transportation to the decline was rather small, at least until the 1850s. Maritime freights were fairly low in competitive markets, and they did not decline much (Harley 1988; 1989). Land transports were much more expensive in the eighteenth century and remained so in the early nineteenth century. Some roads were improved from the late eighteenth century onwards, but the construction of railways progressed slowly. The whole network in continental Europe totalled a mere 12,000 km in 1850, almost all in the core countries, and 73,000 km twenty years later. The rise was impressive, but the length corresponded to only a quarter of the 1913 network (a fifth in the whole periphery, a sixth in Russia). Furthermore, the rail owners, be they state or private monopolies, might have been tempted to exploit their monopolistic power to keep the gains from productivity growth rather than to transfer them to customers as lower fares. In France, the real cost of rail transport fell by 60 per cent from 1845 to 1870 but it remained three times higher than the cost of inland navigation (Toutain 1967).

Thus, arguably, trade costs changed mostly as a consequence of political decisions. The abolition of trading monopolies and their mark-up on freights accounted for most of the price convergence between Asia and Europe before 1870 (Chilosi and Federico 2015). The story of trade policy is more complex. The traditional mercantilist policies had been slowly dismantled in the second half of the eighteenth century, and in 1786 England and France signed a free trade agreement. This early liberalization did not survive the outbreak of the Napoleonic Wars: British ships blockaded the French ports and Napoleon forbade trade with Britain. After Waterloo, continental states continued to protect manufactures against British competition and for the first time in history imposed high duties on wheat, up to prohibitive levels in France and the United Kingdom to stave off Russian competition (Federico 2012). By the late 1820s, barriers to trade were arguably as high as, if not higher than, in the eighteenth century. They were slowly dismantled in the next thirty years (Lampe 2009; Tena-Junguito et al. 2012). All importing countries cut duties on wheat, in a series of autonomous decisions, while trade in manufactures was liberalized via bilateral agreements including the most-favoured nation clause – the most important being the Cobden-Chevalier treaty between the United Kingdom and France in 1861. By 1870, trade was free in all core countries, but for a few fiscal duties on specific products. Protection remained fairly high in peripheral countries, with the notable exception of the newly unified Italy.

Economic theory suggests that trade and market integration increase welfare and foster economic growth. Competition from British industry was a potent incentive to modernization of manufacturing on the continent, while growing British demand boosted the production of primary products and, in some cases, of high-quality manufactures, such as French silk cloths. Estimating these dynamic effects is impossible, but it is possible to compute a lower bound of static gains (Federico and Tena-Junguito 2017). In 1830 they amounted to 3.2 per cent of GDP in the United Kingdom, 2.5 per cent in seven European countries. In the next forty years, they doubled in the United Kingdom (to 7.5 per cent of GDP) and tripled in continental Europe (to 7.3 per cent). In 1870, the gains were substantially higher for five core countries (9.3 per cent, with a peak of 25 per cent in the Netherlands) than for seven peripheral nations (4.7 per cent on average, but less than 2 per cent in Spain and Portugal).

This period featured also the dawn of a pan-European market for capital. Modern financial techniques had been developed in Amsterdam since the late seventeenth century and in the eighteenth century the market was highly integrated with London (Neal 1990). However, the official markets were the remit of few professionals. The great innovation of the nineteenth century was the issuing of bonds by government and later private companies (e.g. railways) targeting retail investors. These sales started in the 1820s in Paris and London (Flandreau and Flores 2009), but the sums remained quite low until the late 1860s (Reinhart et al. 2016). Monetary regimes changed, as well, albeit slowly. Formally, all continental European countries adopted the traditional bimetallic system, while the United Kingdom had been de facto on a gold standard since 1717 and, after the turmoil of the Napoleonic Wars, it formally adopted the regime in the Banking Act of 1844. British economic and political power pushed most continental countries towards the gold standard. France tried to resist the tide by setting up, with Italy, Belgium, and Switzerland in 1865, a Latin Monetary Union, which issued silver coins for circulation in the partner countries. France yielded in 1873 after a collapse in the price of silver.

The Causes of Growth: Institutional Change and the Modern State

Ancien Régime institutions do not enjoy a good reputation among economic historians (Ogilvie and Carus 2014). In Western Europe they were a maze of local and social privileges, which prevented market integration, stifled innovation, and distorted incentives (Epstein 2000). East of the Elbe the overwhelming majority of the workforce was trapped by serfdom, unable to move out of the agricultural estates and exploit their talents. However, the extent of damage caused to potential development by each specific institution is still controversial. Greif (2006) has argued that merchant guilds were efficient responses to imperfect property rights, a claim strongly disputed by Ogilvie (2014). Dennison has shown how on eastern European estates landlords and serfs' communes could credibly commit to construct private-order institutions that secured incentives for serfs and adjusted the rules when necessary (Dennison and Ogilvie 2007; Dennison 2011). Cerman (2012) points out how serfdom did not prevent the development of powerful states in Austria-Hungary, Prussia, or Russia. On the other hand, Markevich and Zhuravskaya (2018) find that serfdom had negative effects on agricultural productivity, industrial output and peasant nutrition. Similarly, Jensen et al. (2018) show how the reimposition of serfdom in Denmark in 1733 reduced the wages of agricultural workers and strongly reduced the prevalence of urban apprenticeships.

It seems uncontroversial that European institutions were more conducive to economic growth in 1870 than in 1700. Domestic and foreign trade was free, restrictions on personal freedom and access to professions and trades had been abolished and, last but not least, states were able to impose and collect uniform taxes from all their citizens. The Ottoman and Russian empires were the only two major states in Europe with absolute governments and without a constitution. The nature of this change depended on the initial conditions. In some areas, such as the Netherlands, England, and, to some extent centre-north Italy, the institutions were already quite modern by 1700. In the rest of western Europe, modernization started during the Enlightenment and the process was dramatically accelerated by the French Revolution (Bogart et al. 2010). It abolished feudal privileges and traditional institutions and unified legislation and administration, and then French armies forced a similar modernization in all the Napoleonic Empire. The ripples of this shock also extended outside the empire, triggering political reforms and a shift away from absolutism to gradual democratization, which was accelerated by the revolutionary wave in 1848. Acemoglu et al. (2011) argue that differential exposure to French reforms explains differences in the level of development in Germany (as proxied by urbanization) in the nineteenth century. The accuracy of their historical reconstruction, and thus ultimately their results, has been strongly challenged by Kopsidis and Bromley (2016).

In most countries, therefore, institutional change preceded modern economic growth and is likely to have contributed substantially to it. Unfortunately, it is extremely difficult to measure this contribution and even a plain description of changes, in all their dimensions and countless local varieties, is well beyond the scope of this chapter. We will focus on three main issues, the protection of intellectual property, the abolition of serfdom, and the growth of the modern state.

Under the Ancien Régime, patents were granted as a personal concession to inventors or entrepreneurs willing to import technology. Only in England could anyone apply for a patent, providing they were willing to pay a (high) fee. Similar patent laws were approved by France in 1791 (modified in 1844), and by some other countries, such as Spain in 1811 and Russia in 1812 (Khan nd). The need for protection to foster inventions is still controversial among economists and economic historians (Moser 2013). Moser (2005) shows that only a (small) number of the exhibits at the Crystal Palace Exhibition in 1851 were patented and that the lack of a patent law in Switzerland did not hamper innovative activities. The impact of the Russian law was minimal: from 1812 to 1870 only 1,380 patents were registered in the whole empire and foreigners got more than half of all these patents (Revinskij 2002).

Serfdom was abolished in continental southern Italy in 1806 (after Napoleonic conquest), in Prussia in 1806 and in Sicily in 1812 (as a reaction to the French challenge), in Hungary in 1848, in Russia in 1861, and in Romania in 1864. Former serfs were freed from personal obligations, the land was distributed between them and the former lord, with the peasants required to pay compensation to the lord. The clauses differed across countries, being harsher in Prussia than in Hungary. In Russia, they were relatively mild, but peasants were given collective, rather than individual, rights to land. Gerschenkron (1966) argued that communal ownership hampered investments and the growth of agricultural production. Indeed the abolition of serfdom boosted economic development in the Russian Empire but the institutionalization of peasant communal land tenure as a result of the emancipation diminished growth potential (Markevich and Zhuravskaya 2018). The effects of land reforms in western Europe were less clear. The 1832 land reform in Saxony redistributed agricultural income from rents to labour without improving output or productivity growth (Pfister and Kospidis 2015). In contrast, Finley et al. (2017) find a positive correlation between the amount of land redistributed during the French Revolution and agricultural productivity in the middle of the nineteenth century.

The birth of the modern state was essentially a political process but it had far-reaching economic consequences. National governments gradually eliminated alternative political forces, abolished discrimination by status in taxation and access to economic activities, and developed centralized administrative structures that became single sources of public coercion and legislation (Dincecco 2011). Thus, modern states were able to control a rising share of national income, which they used to fund the increasingly expensive wars of the eighteenth century. England and Holland were particularly successful in increasing total revenues per capita, but they were also the richest countries in Europe (Karaman and Pamuk 2010). Other states, most notably Prussia, succeeded in increasing taxation relative to income, while the level of taxation in eastern Europe remained low (Karaman and Pamuk 2013). Government relied more on direct taxation and employed coercion and non-market instruments to enforce their collection.

These institutional changes were relevant for long-term economic growth to the extent that they removed obstacles to private initiative and created a potential for growth-fostering policies. But this potential was hardly exploited before 1870. The modern states remained minimal. In the eighteenth century, state expenditures barely exceeded 10 per cent of GDP even in Holland and Great Britain (de Vries and van der Woude 1997; White 2001). Expenditures soared during the Napoleonic Wars, but in the nineteenth century revenues remained around 10–15 per cent of GDP in all Western countries (Cardoso and Lains 2010). Furthermore, most of this money was still spent in funding the military or paying back debts from previous wars. Comparatively very little money remained for financing public goods. Indeed, states invested very little in roads in the eighteenth century and comparatively little in railways (Bogart et al. 2010). In most countries, the state limited itself to subsidizing with loans or minimum guaranteed income the private companies that built and managed the railway lines. Also, public investments in education were modest. In early modern Europe, primary education had been provided mostly by church or private institutions. The principle of public funding for compulsory primary education for all children was discussed in France in the 1790s, but was implemented only forty years later, in 1833, and only partially. Laws for public mandatory primary education were approved in Sweden in 1842 and Piedmont in 1859 (extended to the whole of Italy in 1861). However, throughout Europe, schools were funded by local authorities, while the state preferred to invest in secondary and tertiary education for the élite, rather than primary schooling. Thus, the funding was often insufficient, causing substantial regional differences within each state. The limited financial means of local authorities explains the poor school enrolment and the low literacy rates in south Italy (Cappelli 2015).

Last but not least, European states did not use their capabilities to support industrialization. Authoritative scholars such as Gerschenkron (1962) and Allen (2011a) deem state intervention indispensable in peripheral countries, whose gap with technological leaders was too large to be filled with the resources of entrepreneurs or banks. European states did adopt proactive industrialization policies towards the end of the century, but before 1870 the prevailing trend was the opposite – most countries were cutting duties and liberalizing trade.

Conclusion

Europe in 1870 was very different from Europe in 1700. The north-western regions had unambiguously started their modern economic growth, successfully reacting to the British challenge. Modern technology and the factory system were spreading from the north-western core throughout the continent. Trade was largely free and markets were more integrated than they had ever been in European history. Admittedly, many regions in the north, the east, and the Mediterranean were still mostly agricultural and backward, but almost everywhere institutions had changed in depth and were modern enough to support modern economic growth. Thus, the foundations for future growth were laid down in this period, even if actual growth was modest throughout Europe.

References

Acemoglu, D., Cantoni, D., David, S. and Robinson, J. A. (2011). 'The Consequences of Radical Reform: The French Revolution', *American Economic Review*, 101, 3286–3307.

Alfani, G. (2017). 'The Rich in Historical Perspective: Evidence for Pre-industrial Europe (ca. 1300–1800)', *Cliometrica*, 11, 321–348.

Allen, R. (2009). 'The Industrial Revolution in Miniature: The Spinning Jenny in Britain, France, and India', *Journal of Economic History*, 69, 901–927.

(2011a). *Global Economic History: A Very Short Introduction*, Oxford University Press.

(2011b). 'The Spinning Jenny: A Fresh Look', *Journal of Economic History*, 71, 461–464.

Allen, R. and Ó Gráda, C. (1988). 'On the Road Again with Arthur Young: English, Irish and French Agriculture during the Industrial Revolution', *Journal of Economic History*, 48, 93–116.

Alter, G. and Clark, G. (2010). 'The Demographic Transition and Human Capital', in Broadberry, S. and O'Rourke, K. H. (eds.), *The Cambridge Economic History of Modern Europe, vol. 1: 1700–1870*, Cambridge University Press, 44–69.

Axenciuc, V. (2012). *Produsul intern brut al României 1862–2000, vol. 1*, Bucarest: Editura economica.

Baffigi, A., Broadberry, S., Giordano, C. and Zollino, F. (2013). 'Data Appendix – Italy's National Accounts (1861–2010)', in Toniolo, G. (ed.), *The Oxford Handbook of the Italian Economy since the Unification*, Oxford University Press, 631–712.

Barro, R. J. and Lee, J-W. (2015). *Education Matters*, Oxford University Press.

Baten, J. and Blum, M. (2012). 'Growing Tall by Unequal: New Findings and New Background Evidence on Anthropometric Welfare in 156 Countries, 1810–1989', *Economic History of Developing Countries*, 27, 566–585.

(2014) 'Why Are You Tall While Others Are Short? Agricultural Production and Other Proximate Determinants of Global Heights', *European Review of Economic History*, 18, 144–165.

Bogart, D., Drelichman, M. , Gelderblom, O. and Rosenthal, J-L. (2010). 'State and Private Institutions', in Broadberry, S. and O'Rourke, K. H. (eds.), *The Cambridge Economic History of Modern Europe, vol. 1: 1700–1870*, Cambridge University Press, 71–95.

Broadberry, S. (1997). *The Productivity Race*, Cambridge University Press.

Broadberry, S., Fremdling, R. and Solar, P. (2010). 'Industry', in Broadberry, S. and O'Rourke, K. H. (eds.), *The Cambridge Economic History of Modern Europe, vol. 1: 1700–1870*, Cambridge University Press, 164–186.

Broadberry, S., Campbell, B., Klein, A., Overton, M. and van Leeuwen, B. (2015). *British Economic Growth, 1270–1870*, Cambridge University Press.

Cappelli, G. (2015). 'Escaping from a Human Capital Trap? Italy's Regions and the Move to Centralized Primary Schooling, 1861–1936', *European Review of Economic History*, 20, 46–65.

Cardoso, J. L. and Lains, P. (2010). 'Introduction: Paying for the Liberal State', in Cardoso, J. L. and Lains, P. (eds.), *Paying for the Liberal State*, Cambridge University Press, 1–26.

Cerman, M. (2012). *Villagers and Lords in Eastern Europe, 1300–1800*, Basingstoke: Palgrave Macmillan.

Chesnais, J-C. (1992). *The Demographic Transition*, Oxford: Clarendon Press.

Chilosi, D. and Federico, G. (2015). 'Early Globalizations: The Integration of Asia in the World Economy, 1800–1938', *Explorations in Economic History*, 57, 1–18.

Dennison, T. (2011). *The Institutional Framework of Russian Serfdom*, Cambridge University Press.

Dennison, T. and Ogilvie, S. (2007). 'Serfdom and Social Capital in Bohemia and Russia', *Economic History Review*, 60, 513–544.

(2014). 'Does the European Marriage Pattern Explain Economic Growth?' *Journal of Economic History*, 74, 651–693.

de Vries, J. (2008). *The Industrious Revolution: Consumer Behaviour and the Household Economy, 1650 to Present*, Cambridge University Press.

de Vries, J. and van der Woude, A. (1997). *The First Modern Economy: Success, Failure and Perseverance of the Dutch Economy, 1500–1815*, Cambridge University Press.

de Zwart, P. (2016). 'Globalization in the Early Modern Era: New Evidence from the Dutch-Asian Trade, c.1600–1800', *Journal of Economic History*, 76, 520–558.

Dincecco, M. (2011). *Political Transformations and Public Finances: Europe, 1650–1913*, Cambridge University Press.

Epstein, S. R. (2000). *Freedom and Growth: The Rise of States and Markets in Europe, 1300–1750*, London: Routledge.

Federico, G. (1997). *An Economic History of the Silk Industry 1830–1930*, Cambridge University Press.

(2005). *Feeding the World: An Economic History of World Agriculture, 1800–2000*, Princeton University Press.

(2011). 'When Did the European Market Integrate?' *European Review of Economic History*, 15, 93–126.

(2012). 'The Corn Laws in Continental Perspective', *European Review of Economic History*, 16, 166–187.

Federico, G. and Tena-Junguito, A. (2017). 'A Tale of Two Globalizations: Gains from Trade and Openness 1800–2010', *Review of World Economics*, 153, 601–626.

(2019). 'World Trade, 1800–1938: A New Synthesis', *Revista de Historia Economica*, 37, 1–33.

Federico, G., Schulze, M-S. and Volckart, O. (forthcoming). 'European Goods Market Integration in the Very Long Run: From the Black Death to the First World War', *Journal of Economic History*.

Finley, T., Franck, R. and Johnson, N. D. (2017). 'The Effects of Land Redistribution: Evidence from the French Revolution', George Mason University Working Paper in Economics, 17–29.

Flandreau, M. and Flores, J. H. (2009). 'Bonds and Brands: Foundation of Sovereign Debt Markets, 1820–1830', *Journal of Economic History*, 69, 646–684.

Fouquet, R. and Broadberry, S. (2015). 'Seven Centuries of European Economic Growth and Decline', *Journal of Economic Perspectives*, 29, 227–244.

Gerschenkron, A. (1962). *Economic Backwardness in Historical Perspective*, Cambridge, MA: Belknap Press.

(1966). 'Agrarian Policies and Industrialization in Russia', in Habakkuk, H. J. and Postan, M. (eds.), *The Cambridge Economic History of Europe, vol. 6 The Industrial Revolution and After – Incomes, Population and Technological Change*, Cambridge University Press, 707–800.

Giordano, C. and Zollino, F. (2015). 'A Historical Reconstruction of Capital and Labour in Italy, 1861–2013', *Rivista di storia economica*, 31, 155–224.

Gragnolati, U., Moschella, D. and Pugliese, E. (2011). 'The Spinning Jenny and the Industrial Revolution: A Reappraisal', *Journal of Economic History*, 71, 455–459.

Gregory, P. (1983). *Russian National Income, 1885–1913*, Cambridge University Press.

Greif, A. (2006). *Institutions and the Pattern to the Modern Economy*, Cambridge University Press.

Grytten, O. (2015). 'Norwegian Gross Domestic Product by Industry 1830–1930', Norges Bank Bicentenary Project Working Paper, 19/2015.

Harley, C. K. (1988). 'Ocean Freight Rates and Productivity, 1740–1913: The Primacy of Mechanical Invention Reaffirmed', *Journal of Economic History*, 48, 851–876.

(1989). 'Coal Exports and British Shipping, 1850–1913', *Explorations in Economic History*, 26, 311–338.

Hatton, T. and Williamson, J. G. (1998). *The Age of Mass Migration*, Oxford University Press.

Hippe, R. and Baten, J. (2012). 'Regional Inequality in Human Capital Formation in Europe', *Scandinavian Economic History Review*, 60, 254–289.

Hjerrpe, R. (1996). *Finland's Historical National Accounts 1860–1994*, Jyvaskylan: Jyvaskylan Ylopisto Historian Laitos.

Huberman, M. and Lewchuk, W. (2003). 'European Economic Integration and the Labour Compact, 1850–1913', *European Review of Economic History*, 7, 3–41.

Ivanov, M. (2012). *The Gross Domestic Product of Bulgaria 1870–1945*, Sofia: Ciela.

Jensen, P. S., Radu, C. V., Severgnini, B. and Sharp, P. (2018). 'The Introduction of Serfdom and Labor Markets', CEPR Discussion Paper 13303, cepr.org/active/publications/discussion_papers/dp.php?dpno=13303 (accessed 5 October 2020).

Kander, A., Malanima, P. and Warde, P. (2013). *Power to the People: Energy in Europe over the Last Five Centuries*, Princeton University Press.

Karaman, K. and Pamuk, S. (2010). 'Ottoman State Finances in European Perspective', *Journal of Economic History*, 70, 593–629.

(2013). 'Different Paths to Modern State in Europe: The Interaction Between Warfare, Economic Structure and Political Regime', *American Political Science Review*, 107, 603–626.

Khan, Z. (nd). 'Economic History of Patents and Patent Institutions', in Whaples, R. (ed.), EH.Net Encyclopedia, eh.net/encyclopedia/an-economic-history-of-patent-institutions/ (accessed 5 October 2020).

Klein, A., Schulze, M-S. and Vonyo, T. (2017). 'How Peripheral Was the Periphery? Industrialization in East Central Europe since 1870', in O'Rourke, K. H. and Williamson, J. G. (eds.), *The Spread of Modern Industry to the Periphery since 1871*, Oxford University Press, 63–90.

Kopsidis, M. and Bromley, D. W. (2016). 'The French Revolution and German Industrialization: Dubious Models and Doubtful Causality', *Journal of Institutional Economics*, 12, 161–190.

Kopsidis, M. and Ivanov, M. (2017). 'Industrialization and De-industrialization in Southeast Europe', in O'Rourke, K. H. and Williamson, J. G. (eds.), *The Spread of Modern Industry to the Periphery since 1871*, Oxford University Press, 91–114.

Kuznets, S. (1955). 'Economic Growth and Inequality', *American Economic Review*, 54, 1–28.

Lampe, M. (2009). 'Effects of Bilateralism and the MFN Clause on International Trade. Evidence for the Cobden-Chevalier Network (1860–1875)', *Journal of Economic History*, 69, 1012–1040.

Maddison, A. (2001). *The World Economy: A Millennial Perspective*, Paris: Organisation for Economic Co-operation and Development.

(2010). 'Statistics on World Population, GDP and Per Capita GDP, 1–2008 AD', Groningen Growth and Development Centre, www.ggdc.net/MADDISON/oriindex.htm (accessed 5 October 2020).

Malanima, P. (2009). *Pre-modern European Economy*, Leiden: Brill.

(2010). 'Urbanization', in Broadberry, S. and O'Rourke, K. H. (eds.), *The Cambridge Economic History of Modern Europe, vol 1: 1700–1870*, Cambridge University Press, 235–263.

Malinowski, M. and van Zanden, J. L. (2017). 'Income and its Distribution in Preindustrial Poland', *Cliometrica*, 11(3), 375–404.

Markevich, A. and Nafziger, S. (2017). 'State and Market in Russian Industrialization since 1870', in O'Rourke, K. H. and Williamson, J. G. (eds.), *The Spread of Modern Industry to the Periphery Since 1871*, Oxford University Press, 33–62.

Markevich, A. and Zhuravskaya, E. (2018). 'Economic Effects of the Abolition of Serfdom: Evidence from the Russian Empire', *American Economic Review*, 108, 1074–1117.

Martinez-Galarraga, J. and Prat, M. (2016). 'Wages, Prices, and Technology in Early Catalan Industrialization', *Economic History Review*, 69, 548–574.

Milanovic, B., Lindert, P. and Williamson, J. (2011). 'Pre-industrial Inequality', *Economic Journal*, 121, 255–272.

Mitchell, B. (1988). *British Historical Statistics*. Cambridge University Press.

(1998). *International Historical Statistics: Europe 1750–1993*, 4th ed., Basingstoke: Macmillan.

Mokyr, J. (2005). 'The Intellectual Origins of Modern Economic Growth', *Journal of Economic History*, 65, 285–351.

Moser, P. (2005). 'How Do Patent Laws Influence Innovation: Evidence from Historical Patent Citations', *American Economic Review*, 95, 1214–1236.

(2013). 'Patents and Innovation: Evidence from Economic History', *Journal of Economic Perspectives*, 27, 23–44.

Neal, L. (1990). *The Rise of Financial Capitalism*, Cambridge University Press.

Ogilvie, S. (2014). 'The Economics of Guilds', *Journal of Economic Perspectives*, 28, 169–192.

Ogilvie, S. and Carus, A. W. (2014). 'Institutions and Economic Growth in Historical Perspective', in Aghion, P. and Durlauf, S. (eds.), *Handbook of Economic Growth, vol 2A*, Amsterdam: Elsevier, 403–513.

Ó Gráda, C. (2009). *Famine. A Short History*. Princeton University Press.

O'Rourke, K. H. and Williamson, J. G. (2002a). 'After Columbus: Explaining Europe's Overseas Trade Boom, 1500–1800', *Journal of Economic History*, 62, 417–456.

(2002b). 'When Did Globalization Begin?', *European Review of Economic History*, 6, 23–50.

Persson, K. G. and Sharp, P. (2015). *An Economic History of Europe*, Cambridge University Press.

Pfister, U. and Kospidis, M. (2015). 'Institutions versus Demand: Determinants of Agricultural Development in Saxony, 1660–1850', *European Review of Economic History*, 19, 275–293.

Prados de la Escosura, L. (2016). 'Spain's Historical National Accounts: Expenditure and Output, 1850–2015', European Historical Economics Society Working Paper, 103.

Reinhart, C., Reinhart, V. and Trebesch, C. (2016). 'Global Cycles: Capital Flows, Commodities and Sovereign Defaults 1815–2015', *American Economic Review Papers and Proceedings*, 106, 574–580.

Revinskij, D. O. (2002). 'Patentovanie izobretenij v Rossii, 1812–1870 [Patterns in Russia, 1812–1870]', in *Ekonomicheskaya istoriya. Ezhegodnik 2001. [Economic History. 2001 Annual Volume]*, Moscow: Rosspen, 339–376.

Riley, J. (2001). *Rising Life Expectancy: A Global History*, Cambridge University Press.

Rushin, A. G. (1956). *Naselenie Rossii za sto let*. Moscow: Gosizdat.

Schön, L. (2012). *An Economic History of Modern Sweden*, London and New York: Routledge.

Schön, L. and Krantz, O. (2015). 'Swedish Historical National Accounts 1560–2010', Lund University, Department of Economic History, www.ekh.lu.se/en/research/economic-history-data/shna (accessed 29 September 2020).

Schulze, M-S. (2000). 'Patterns of Growth and Stagnation in the Late Nineteenth-Century Habsburg Economy', *European Review of Economic History*, 4, 311–340.

Sharp, P. and Weisdorf, J. (2013). 'Globalization Revisited: Market Integration and the Wheat Trade Between North America and Britain from the Eighteenth Century', *Explorations in Economic History*, 50, 88–98.

Solar, P. and Hens, L. (2016). 'Ship Speeds During the Industrial Revolution: East India Company Ships, 1770–1828', *European Review of Economic History*, 20, 66–78.

Tann, J. and Breckin, M. J. (1978). 'The International Diffusion of the Watt Engine, 1775–1825', *Economic History Review*, 31, 541–564.

Tena-Junguito, A., Lampe, M. and Tamega-Fernandes, F. (2012). 'How Much Trade Liberalization Was There in the World Before and After Cobden-Chevalier?' *Journal of Economic History*, 72, 708–740.

Toutain, J. C. (1967). 'Les transports en France de 1815 a 1965', Cahiers de l'INSEA, 1(8), 1–306.

(1987). 'Le PIB de la France de 1789 à 1982', Paris Institute de science mathematiques et economiques appliquees.

van Zanden, J. L. (2009). 'The Skill Premium and the "Great Divergence"', *European Review of Economic History*, 13, 121–153.

van Zanden, J. L., and van Riel, A. (2004). *The Strictures of Inheritance*, Princeton University Press.

van Zanden, J. L., Baten, J., Foldvari, P. and van Leeuwen, B. (2014). 'The Changing Shape of Global Inequality, 1800–2000: Exploring a New Data-set', *Review of Income and Wealth*, 60, 279–297.

Vecchi, G. (2017). *Measuring Wellbeing*, Oxford University Press.

von Tunzelman, G. N. (1995). *Technology and Industrial Progress*, Cheltenham: Edward Elgar.

White, E. N. (2001). 'France and the Failure to Modernize Macroeconomic Institutions', in Bordo, M. and Cortés-Conde, R. (eds.), *Transferring Wealth and Power from the Old to the New World: Monetary and Fiscal Institutions in the 17th Through the 19th Centuries*, Cambridge University Press.

3

Tokugawa Japan and the Foundations of Modern Economic Growth in Asia

MASAKI NAKABAYASHI

Introduction

After centuries of stagnation, Japan's output and population started to grow in the sixteenth and seventeenth centuries, and growth in output per head accelerated from the eighteenth century onwards as population numbers stabilized. In the seventeenth century, the Edo (Tokugawa) Shogunate (*bakufu*) (1600[1603]–1868) implemented institutional reforms in two directions. On the one hand, it barred foreigners from entering and Japanese from leaving the country and restricted international trade, which became negligible. On the other hand, the shogunate established property rights for land, which allowed for any use and disposition pursuant to the law, contracts, and customs, and in a 'residual claims' sense, which refers to any financial claims after all financial obligations pursuant to the law, contracts, and customs have been performed,[1] and established a judicial system to govern markets. Restrictions on the flow of people and goods are likely to have hindered growth, while the protection of property rights by the judicial system is likely to have raised growth. The aim of this chapter is twofold. First, it seeks to describe the institutional foundations of economic growth, such as the establishment of property rights and a judicial system, during the Edo shogunate. Second, it then describes the productivity growth and population dynamics which these institutional foundations supported, as well as the state capacity of the Edo shogunate.

The early modern smallholding system established in the seventeenth century protected the property rights of individual smallholders. Therefore, the transition from the medieval system to the early modern system was affected by the weather and market risks borne by cultivators, by cultivators' risk tolerance, and by risk attitudes. In medieval times, when productivity was low and farmers as a result were vulnerable to volatility in crop output due to the vagaries of the

1 For details on these concepts, see Hart (1988).

weather, an efficient second best was for multiple stakeholders to share risks under the manorial system. This institutional arrangement, however, dampened incentives for cultivators to improve productivity. Towards and beyond the seventeenth century, the shogunate and lords (*daimyo*) denied intermediate stakeholders above farmers and exclusively protected farmers' property rights. The policy enhanced farmers' incentives for productivity improvement by adopting intensive farming techniques. Improved productivity made farmers more resilient against weather risk, which in turn made property rights that exclusively impose risk on property holders more attractive.

From the late sixteenth century to late seventeenth century, Japan reunified itself into a federation. The shogunate assumed the supreme command for national defence and jurisdiction over inter-domain lawsuits, and directly ruled its own domain. Lords retained sovereignty over domestic affairs, including exclusive taxation in their own domains, and were not taxed by the shogunate. With lords given exclusive taxation rights and a stable national regime in place, the shogunate and lords invested heavily in the reclamation of alluvial plains and in urban infrastructure during the seventeenth century, resulting in rapid output and population growth. By the late seventeenth century, the shogunate and lords had vested peasants with exclusive property rights over the parcels of farmland that they cultivated and provided the judicial services to implement the rule of law, helping markets to spread. In return for the protection of their property, the owner-farmers paid a high land tax.

The physical and institutional changes of the seventeenth century paved the way for three major developments.[2] First, they brought about a modest take-off of Japan's economy in the eighteenth century, if pale compared to the acceleration after the Meiji Restoration of 1868. Japan's per capita gross domestic product (GDP), which had been 50–60 per cent of China's until the fourteenth century, surpassed China's in the eighteenth century and had caught up with the per capita GDP of peripheral European countries such as Portugal and Poland by the mid-nineteenth century (Figure 3.1).

Second, the protection of peasants' property rights and the stabilization of the peasant economy provided early modern and modern Japan with a broad and deep tax base. As of the mid-nineteenth century, land taxes amounted to 14–16 per cent of GDP. Note that the shogunate and lords delegated tax collection to villages, which meant that the cost of taxation was small. The taxation rate of 14–16 per cent was roughly twice that of other major emerging economies such as China, Turkey, and Spain at the time. The tax base financed

2 See Nagahara and Yamamura (1988) and Nakabayashi and Moriguchi (2017).

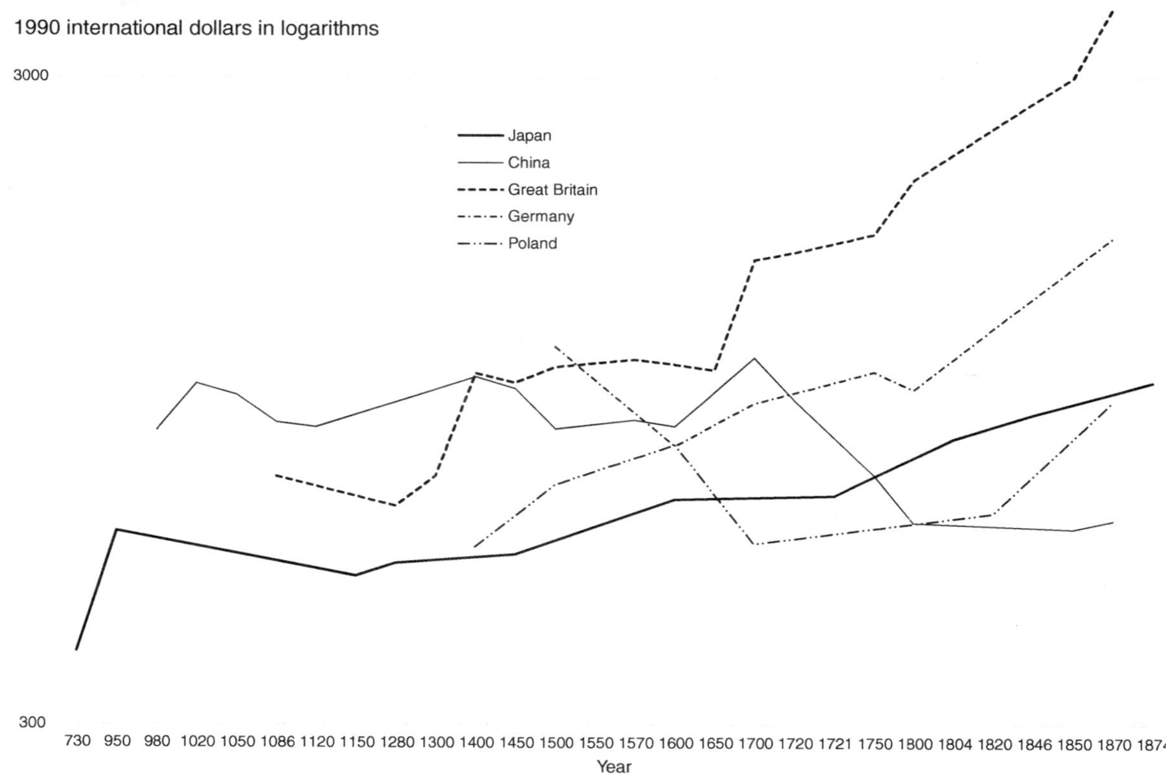

Figure 3.1 International comparison of output per person, 730–1870 (1990 international (Geary-Khamis) dollars log scale)
Sources: For Japan 730–1600: Nakabayashi et al. (forthcoming); 1721–1874: Fukao et al. (2017a; 2017b) and Bassino et al. (2019). For Great Britain and China: Bassino et al. (2019). For Germany: Malinowski and van Zanden (2017) and Palma and Reis (2019). For Poland: Malinowski and van Zanden (2017).

the building of the modern navy and the introduction of modern technology from the West in the last phase of the shogunate and the early stages of the Meiji government in the late nineteenth century. There is a growing consensus among scholars that state capacity during the early modern period helped nations accelerate modernization through investment in infrastructure.[3] In particular, it is regarded to have been a key factor in creating the 'little divergence' between Japan and China in East Asia in the nineteenth century (Grabowski 2011; Sng and Moriguchi 2014; and Koyama et al. 2018).

Third, some of the institutional changes enacted by the Tokugawa regime deprived Japan of opportunities. In particular, the isolationist policies prevented specialization in areas in which Japan had a comparative advantage and imports of goods where Japan was at a disadvantage. This meant that Japan probably had to devote more resources to food production than otherwise might have been the case, thus slowing the development of the secondary and tertiary sectors and the reallocation of labour from the farm sector to non-farm sectors. In addition, the isolationist policies also blocked the transfer of knowledge from the West. Along with Japan's class system under which *samurai* (*bushi*) exclusively occupied government jobs, these factors likely lowered Japan's growth rate.

The remainder of the chapter is organized as follows. The next section describes institutional changes towards the seventeenth century to provide the micro-foundations for Japan's economic performance from the early seventeenth to the mid-nineteenth century. This is followed by a discussion of Japan's economic performance during this period, focusing on aggregate output and output per person. The following section discusses the state capacity developed by the Tokugawa regime and its implications for Japan's economic performance. The concluding part briefly considers some legacies of the Tokugawa regime for Japan's transition to modern economic growth after the Meiji Restoration.

Institutional Framework

Creation of a Mass of Property Owners and Land Reclamation

The Taiho Imperial Legal Code of 701 stipulated that Japan's soil belongs to the emperor/empress. In practice, the Act for the Privatization of Reclaimed

3 Studies highlighting the role of early modern state capacity include: O'Brien and Hunt (1993); Dincecco (2009; 2011); Yun-Casalilla (2012); O'Brien (2012); Karaman and Pamuk (2013); Dincecco and Katz (2014); Dincecco and Onorato (2017); 't Hart et al. (2018); Messina (2019); and Cox and Dincecco (forthcoming).

Lands in Perpetuity of 743 permitted private ownership of newly reclaimed parcels of farmland. When a local ruler reclaimed a parcel of farmland, he first 'donated' the parcel to a temple or a noble. The recipient then obtained a privy seal for private ownership from the imperial court. The parcel was then recognized as a manor, and the temple or the noble who obtained the seal ruled the parcel as the manorial lord. The imperial court delegated the administration of the manor to the manorial lord. To compensate the lord for the cost of administration, the parcel was exempted from land tax.

The manorial lord typically appointed a noble or a temple as the branch office manager and a local ruler, who was often the original developer, as the local officer to maintain peace and order in the local community. The manorial lord appointed a wealthy farmer as the landlord, and the landlord made contracts with cultivators. All of the agents from the manorial lord to the landlord farmer had a claim to a fixed income from the parcel. The cultivator was the residual claimant (Nagahara 1973, 3–53; Nagahara 1975; Nishitani et al. 2017; Piggott 2018; Sakurai 2018).

Law enforcement was delegated to local officers, who were typically armed and called *samurai* (Friday 2010). Holding a monopoly in enforcing the law, the *samurai* gradually grew into a social class with increasing political powers and established the first shogunate in Kamakura in 1185 and the second shogunate at Muromachi in Kyoto in 1336. The establishment of the shogunate did not mean the immediate demise of the manorial system. *Samurai* were in charge of maintaining peace and order at the manor to which they were appointed. A new development was that their appointment was under the jurisdiction of the shogunate rather than the manorial lord. The first and second shogunates were thus a department specialized in security enforcement and national defence while manorial lords claimed about one-third of output from manors. However, after the Onin war among different *samurai* factions, which lasted from 1467 to 1477, the manorial system collapsed. Leading *samurai* emerged as feudal lords (*sengoku daimyo*) who assumed exclusive sovereign power within their domains (Ferejohn and Rosenbluth 2010).

The fourteenth and fifteenth centuries were also a period of change in agricultural techniques from extensive farming to intensive farming that improved land and labour productivity. The new techniques required dedicated cultivators, so landlord farmers encouraged cultivators to settle in the same place. Landlord farmers and cultivators together formed a village community. Landlord farmers were armed, and the village community jointly negotiated with the feudal lord about the land tax and made a contract with the feudal lord, which typically recognized the autonomy of the village as long as the stipulated land tax was paid (Inaba 2010; Nishitani 2017). This village contractor system warranted the residual claims of a village as a whole, while the lord did not identify and protect the claims of individual farm households within the village.

Hideyoshi Toyotomi, who reunified Japan, in 1588 promulgated the Ordinance of Disarmament, which banned the use of swords and other arms for negotiation over land tax with *samurai* and over water rights with neighbouring villages (Fujiki 2005). Moreover, the Toyotomi administration announced that discretionary taxation would be replaced by a land tax proportionate to the yield of a given plot of land or a fixed amount, which depended on the existing customs of each region. It also initiated cadastral surveys to identify individual farm households and their ownership of farmland. The Edo shogunate, which assumed power in 1600, inherited this policy. The shogunate registered the name of the household head and the parcel of farmland the household cultivated and vested the household with property rights to the parcel in return for payment of the land tax. The shogunate completed the cadastral surveys by the 1670s, which created a mass of small owner-peasant families in its domain. The shogunate and domain lords (*daimyo*) provided legal protection of the property rights against possible infringement by a third party, including fellow villagers. Medieval feudal lords had not identified individual households' property and the assignment of plots of farmland to individual households had been delegated to the village. Thus, legal protection of individual households' smallholdings as property rights by the state was a substantial institutional change.[4]

Tokugawa Japan was a federation (Ravina 1995; 1999). The shogunate did not assume taxation authority in the domains of lords and domain lords did not have to adopt the property law implemented in the shogunate's domain. While most lords in the more advanced regions adopted the shogunate law to protect the property rights of individual peasant families, lords in more backward regions did not necessarily do so (Brown 1993: 89–112; 2011: 58–100).

Peace under the Edo shogunate and the exclusive taxation authority enabled the shogunate and lords to massively reclaim alluvial plains in the lower reaches of large rivers, which had been left uncultivated. The shogunate and the lords also built the capital city, Edo, and domain capital cities in the seventeenth century (Nakabayashi and Moriguchi 2017).

4 For more details, see Nakabayashi and Moriguchi (2017) and Mandai and Nakabayashi (2017; 2018).

Free Market Entry, the State Court, and the Monetary Regime

Reckoning that liberalization of market entry would prompt an expansion of the market, feudal lords in the sixteenth century promulgated the Ordinance for Freedom of Market Entry and Freedom from Guilds (*Raku Ichi Raku Za Rei*). This ordinance abolished the local monopolist guilds chartered by medieval manorial lords and provided judicial functions to replace the governance that had been delegated to the chartered guilds. The Edo shogunate inherited this doctrine of free market entry (Nagahara and Yamamura 1988).

To promote expansion of the free market, the shogunate built its own judicial system. In Edo, Kyoto, Osaka, and other shogunate cities, governors (*machi bugyo*) were in charge of civil cases. For rural regions, the mayor of the village (*nanushi* / *shoya*), who was selected from among farmers of the village, served as the judge in the first instance. The magistrate (*daikan*) of the county acted as the appeal judge. Governors and most magistrates were not hereditary and were selected from among the shogunate vassal *samurai*. The supreme court was the Conference Chamber (*hyojosho*) of the shogunate, consisting of the governor of temples and shrines, the secretary of the treasury, and the governor of Edo. The shogunate judiciary operated under the case law system. If a case was difficult for a governor or a magistrate to adjudicate on the basis of previous cases, it was sent to the conference chamber.

From the thirteenth century through the early seventeenth century, hard currency in Japan was Chinese copper coins, with domestically minted coins circulating as auxiliary currency. In 1636, the Edo shogunate promulgated a three-coin system under which gold, silver, and copper coins issued by the shogunate were the fiat currency. After issuing large quantities of shogunate copper coins over the following three decades, the shogunate banned the use of Chinese copper coins in 1670 and stipulated that only the shogunate coins would be valid (Sakurai 2002: 55; 2008).

While the shogunate debased precious metal coins several times, it never issued paper notes. Although the latter policy sustained the confidence of the market in the shogunate currency, it exerted deflationary pressure on a growing economy. Therefore, the shogunate allowed lords to issue paper notes that were to circulate in their own domains and were convertible into the shogunate coins. The exchange rates between the lords' paper notes and the shogunate coins were determined in the market and depended on the fiscal position of the lord (Shimbo and Saito 1999: 351–356).

Conflicting Aims of Growth and Stability

Medieval Japan, from the eleventh century to the mid-sixteenth century, was characterized by free markets in finance, farmland, and coerced labour. Tenant cultivators actively sought loans secured by their residual claims. This agricultural finance brought about wealth inequalities. There were frequent riots by heavily indebted cultivators, who demanded that the Muromachi shogunate force the writing-off of outstanding loans (Nishitani and Nakabayashi 2017).

The Edo shogunate attempted to strike a balance between market expansion and social stability. As part of this, the shogunate in 1643 promulgated the Ban on the Perpetual Purchase and Sale of Farmland, which aimed to prevent a concentration of land ownership. However, a conundrum in implementing this ban was how to deal with loans using farmland as collateral. Agricultural finance was critical for the stability of farm households' finances, as loans using farmland as collateral enabled farmers to borrow more cheaply than using other means. In a typical loan contract, the farmer would pledge a parcel of farmland as collateral and cultivate the pledged parcel as a tenant. On maturity of the loan, the loan was repaid and the tenancy contract expired. If the farmer defaulted, the question of whether to enforce foreclosure was left to the shogunate. A key issue was how to set procedural requirements for enforcement. Tighter requirements meant higher transaction costs for lenders. The lower the transaction costs, the more likely lenders were to request enforcement of foreclosure, which would result in the concentration of ownership that the ban on sales and purchases was intended to prevent. The higher the transaction costs, the better the defaulting borrowers' interests were protected.

In 1687, the shogunate suspended the enforcement of foreclosures in cases where farmers who had borrowed by pledging a parcel of farmland and cultivated the parcel failed to repay their loan. However, this policy led to a tightening of the availability of agricultural financing, so that in 1695 the shogunate resumed the enforcement of foreclosures.

The resumption of the enforcement of foreclosures led to a renewed concentration of land ownership. Therefore, in 1722 the shogunate again banned such foreclosures. As before, this disrupted agricultural finance, so that in 1723 the shogunate repealed the ban and legalized foreclosures again. Instead, from 1723 to 1740, the shogunate introduced laws to define financial claims and procedures in the enforcement of loan contracts using farmland as collateral more clearly.

The aim of this legislation was to strike a balance between the protection of financial claims and social stability. Specifically, the new legislation stipulated the following. First, the lender was supposed to pay the land tax during the duration of the loan and the tenancy contract. Only if the lender paid the land tax was the case to be handled as a main lawsuit (*honkuji*, which in effect protected 'real right') and could the magistrate enforce foreclosure. Otherwise, a lawsuit related to either the loan contract or the tenancy contract was to be handled as a money lawsuit (*kanekuji*, which was on various financial claims) and the shogunate court did not enforce foreclosure. The land tax was collected by the mayor of the village, so that the restriction implied that the shogunate court did not protect the claims of lenders that resided outside the village in which the debtor resided. That is, the restriction in effect limited the enforcement of foreclosures to loans made between farmers who dwelt within the same village and prevented the regional expansion of a loan market using farmland as collateral. For instance, if a lender was a financier who lived in a city, his claim was not protected by the shogunate court. Second, when the lender filed a complaint that the borrower had defaulted, the magistrate was to set a new time limit for repayment. Only if the debtor failed to repay the debt within the extended period did the magistrate enforce a foreclosure. Third, the magistrate was to allow redemption of a foreclosed parcel if the debtor repaid the loan after the foreclosure within ten years from the beginning of the loan contract or the maturity of the loan contract, depending on the specifications in the contract.

In sum, the shogunate clarified the rights of debtors and added procedural requirements for foreclosure. The legislation had an asymmetric effect on loan contract interest rates. If loans were repaid punctually and foreclosure was unnecessary, interest rates tended to be lower than would have been the case otherwise. Overall, the legislation had the effect of reducing indebtedness among smallholders and lowered loan interest rates for prudent smallholders (Mandai and Nakabayashi 2018).

Thus the legislation largely achieved the conflicting aims of balancing the protection of financial claims and social stability. This can be seen, for example, in the fact that the average incomes of the different classes in the Choshu domain in the mid-nineteenth century did not differ greatly and were given by a ratio of 1.2 to 1.1 to 1.0 for *samurai*, merchants and farmers, respectively, which indicates that early modern Japan's income distribution was less skewed than that in early modern England or India (Saito 2015). Neither was inequality within classes very high. Income inequality in Japan as of the mid-1880s was greater than in Japan and Germany today, but at a similar level to the United States and the United Kingdom today, and much lower than early modern Britain (Moriguchi and Saez 2008; Milanovic, Lindert, and Williamson 2010).

Growth in Output and Population

Overview of the Growth in Output

Growth in output picked up along with the emergence of feudal lords in the fifteenth century as their rule expanded the market and their taxation power funded investment in infrastructure. Growth accelerated after the establishment of the Edo shogunate in 1600. The seventeenth century was a phase of growth driven by reclamation and population growth, that is, the increase in inputs of land and labour. The shogunate federal regime allowed for the taxation autonomy of the shogunate and lords (Ravina 1995; 1999: 16–45; Mitani 2020). The regime provided the shogunate itself and lords with strong incentives for investment in infrastructure, as reclamation directly implied an increase in tax revenue from their own domains. The reclamation of alluvial plains through investment in river control and irrigation by the shogunate and lords throughout Japan meant that land inputs in agriculture surged (Table 3.1). Reclamation of alluvial plains was largely completed by the early eighteenth century. Growth in agricultural output thus moved on to increases in the intensive margin through a rise in land and labour productivity, delivering a rise in per capita gross domestic product (Figure 3.1 and Table 3.1).

Intensive farming required long-term investment by cultivators in soil improvements. Under Japanese rice-farming techniques, land productivity was usually lowest immediately after reclamation. The shogunate and lords therefore often partially exempted newly reclaimed paddy fields from the land tax for a certain period. Farmers spent decades or even generations improving the soil to realize its full potential. Strict protection of the property right of peasants' stem families provided the incentive for such very long-term investment. However, full reclamation of alluvial plains also meant the disappearance of self-supporting sources of fertilization within a community's local ecosystem, such as burned weeds. Farmers therefore sought fertilizers provided from outside their local ecosystem, such as dried sardines and dried herrings. Loans using farmland as collateral were used to finance purchases of such fertilizers.

The shift to more intensive farming raised national average land productivity from 1.49 *koku* per *tan* in the early seventeenth century to 1.94 *koku* per

Table 3.1 Gross domestic product and population, 730–1874

	Population			Output by sector			Total output	
	Total	Urban population	Urbanization rate	Primary	Secondary	Tertiary		
	Thousands	Thousands	(%)	Thousand *koku*	Thousand *koku*	Thousand *koku*	Thousand *koku*	Million 1990 international $
730	6,100	124	2.0%	7,502	478	713	8,693	2,367
950	5,000	135	2.7%	9,471	579	885	10,924	2,975
1150	3,900	120	3.1%	6,281	399	588	7,262	1,977
1280	5,950	208	3.5%	9,836	673	1,090	11,600	3,159
1450	10,050	259	2.6%	16,615	1,374	2,223	20,212	5,504
1600	17,000	1,088	6.4%	30,677	3,663	7,284	41,624	11,334
1721	31,290	3,960	12.7%	48,810	8,430	20,360	77,600	21,131
1804	30,690	3,940	12.8%	58,800	10,090	24,400	93,290	25,404
1846	32,210	3,960	12.3%	67,060	11,700	28,140	106,900	29,110
1874	34,840	3,588	10.3%	77,103	15,888	36,551	129,542	35,276

Note: The 1990 international dollar is calculated by 1 *koku* = 272.31 dollars.
Sources: 730–1600: Nakabayashi et al. (2020); 1721–1874: Fukao et al. (2017).

Table 3.2 Output of rice and acreage of paddy fields

	Output 1000 *koku*	Acreage 1000 *tan*	Land productivity *koku* per *tan*
1600	30,678	20,650	1.486
1721	48,808	29,270	1.668
1804	58,803	30,320	1.939
1846	67,062	31,700	2.116
1874	77,103	32,340	2,384

Notes: 1 *koku* = 180.39 litres. 1 *tan* = 991 square metres. 1 acre = 0.4 hectare
Sources: Output: Fukao et al. (2017). Acreage (1600, 1729, 1800, 1850, 1872): Hayami and Miyamoto (1988: 44).

Table 3.3 Output of rice per person

	National average	East Japan	Central Japan	West Japan
1600	1.80			
1721	1.56	1.49	1.62	1.59
1804	1.92	2.04	1.65	1.92
1846	2.08	2.22	1.77	2.09
1874	2.21	2.27	2.09	2.21

Note: 1 *koku* = 180.39 litres.
Source: Fukao et al. (2017).

tan in the early nineteenth century and 2.12 *koku* per *tan* in the mid-nineteenth century (Table 3.2). The national average of rice output per person dropped from 1.8 *koku* per person from 1600 to 1.56 *koku* per person in the early eighteenth century, which indicates that this was a period of extensive growth driven by input increases rather than productivity improvement. Output per person then rose to 1.92 *koku* per person in the early nineteenth-century and 2.1 *koku* per person in the mid-nineteenth century. This was driven by catching up in eastern and central parts of Japan, which had been relatively backward in the eighteenth century, compared to western Japan, the most advanced region since medieval times (Table 3.3).

To illustrate this catching up, Figure 3.2 shows the land productivity of four farming households in different parts of Japan: the Yoshino family in the Kanto region in the eastern part of Japan, and three families in the Kinai

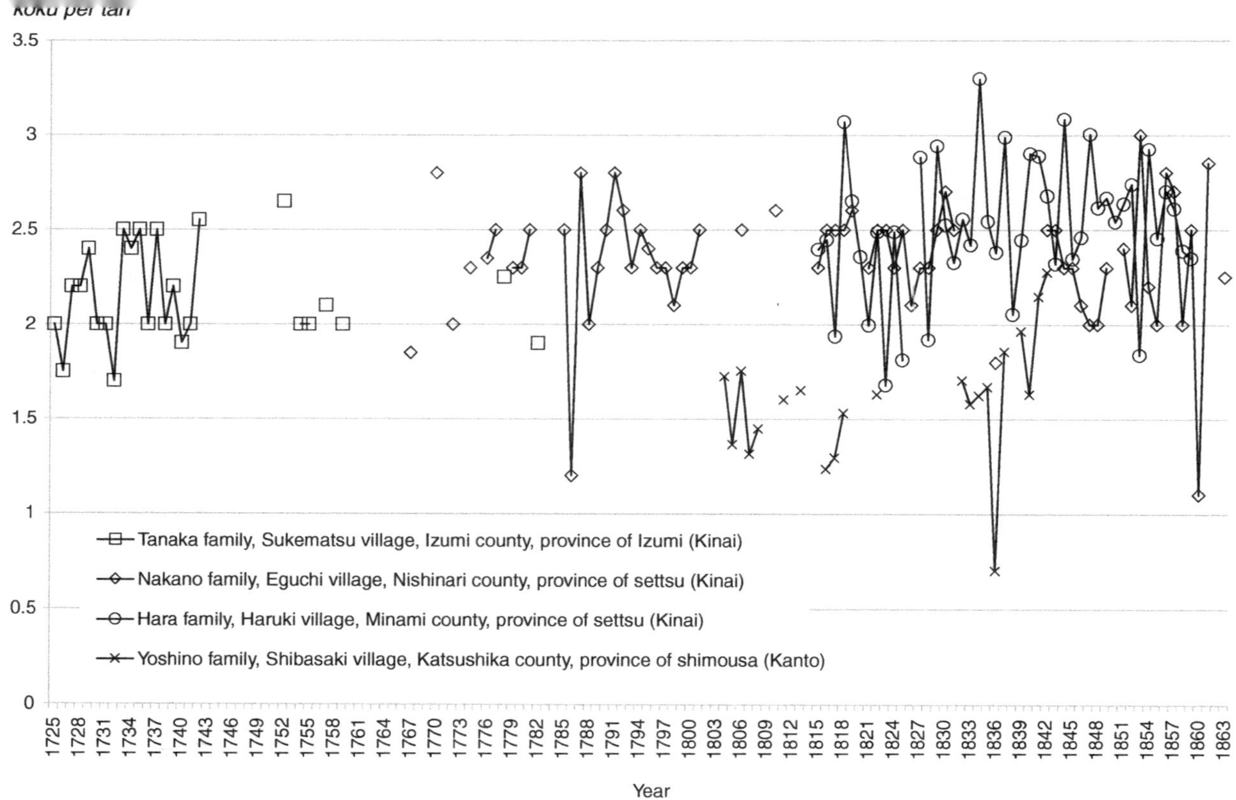

Figure 3.2 Examples of land productivity in Kinai and Kanto regions
Sources: Kinai: Mandai and Nakabayashi (2017). Kanto: Okunishi (2004: 57).
Note: 1 *koku* = 180.39 litres. 1 *tan* = 991 square metres.

region in the western part of Japan. As can be seen, the Yoshino family in eastern Japan in the nineteenth century raised productivity substantially over the course of a few decades to catch up with families in the western part of Japan.

Population Dynamics

Throughout the seventeenth century, when reclamation of alluvial plains was occurring, the children of peasant families formed new families to settle in the newly reclaimed paddy fields. The population grew from 17 million in 1600 to more than 30 million by the early eighteenth century (Table 3.1). While land and labour productivity stagnated through the seventeenth century (Tables 3.2 and 3.3), the increase in arable land fed new families.

With the scope for land reclamation vanishing, farming households ceased forming new families and pursued more intensive farming, which resulted in a rise in output per acre and per person (Tables 3.2 and 3.3). The improved productivity also implied a reduction in famines and improved nutrition, which raised the fertility potential of women. This increase in fertility potential enabled farming households to defer marriage and first birth to retain the same workforce. As a result, the age of marriage tended to increase in the eighteenth and nineteenth centuries (Saito 2002; Saito and Takashima 2017).

These patterns – the deferral of marriage combined with a stable population and a rise in output per person – were similar to those observed in Western countries in early modern times. In Japan, the switch to these patterns came about largely with the end of the period of reclamation and the subsequent improvement in land and labour productivity in the farming sector.

The Peasant Economy and Proto-industrialization

With the marriage age increasing, farming households often sent young unmarried adult members to seek by-employment in the secondary and tertiary sectors in local towns nearby while maintaining the family tie (Saito and Settsu 2007). A typical example would be for such household members to work as the servant of a merchant in a nearby town for a few years. Hand-weaving by female household members at home during the slack seasons was also common. Meanwhile, sake and soy sauce breweries hired men in winter, the slack season for agriculture (Saito 2009; Saito and Takashima 2017).

The market for coerced labour, except in the sex industry, had vanished due to the ban on coerced labour by the shogunate. Household heads were not allowed to sell their dependents legally, which meant a lower opportunity cost incurred by household heads to feed and retain dependents. Meanwhile, the household registration system under the shogunate required dependents to obtain written permission from their household head to leave home and join the urban service sector legally (Saito and Sato 2012). This raised dependents' costs of leaving agriculture. These regulations complemented those on agricultural loans to stabilize the peasant economy.

These institutional arrangements helped to create a greater division of labour in the peasant economy. Along with the shogunate's isolationist policies, this division of labour brought about specific wage dynamics. Figure 3.3 shows the real wages of carpenters and day labourers as well as the relative wage of carpenters to that of day labourers in the Kinai region. Carpenters can be regarded as representative of skilled workers in early modern Japan, while day labourers are unskilled. The real wages of carpenters and day labourers rose modestly from the seventeenth century to the nineteenth century, while they dropped as a result of inflation following the devaluation of the shogunate currency in the mid-nineteenth century. The figure also indicates that from the eighteenth century to the early nineteenth century, the relative wage of carpenters to that of day labourers declined, although it picked up from the mid-nineteenth century. Thus, arbitrage between labour markets for skilled and unskilled workers in the primary, secondary, and tertiary sectors through labour allocation within the peasant economy delivered only a modest rise in the wages of skilled workers in the secondary and primary sectors. This pattern of demand that was parallel in the primary, secondary, and tertiary sectors was reinforced by the shogunate's isolationist policies, since the growth in the non-farm population had to be accompanied by growth in the domestic food supply (Saito and Takashima 2017).

The switch in the driving force of growth from increases in land through reclamation to increases in productivity and deepening division of labour in rural regions from the seventeenth century to the eighteenth century also affected urbanization. In the seventeenth century, when the shogunate and lords built capital cities, the urbanization rate rose sharply (Table 3.1). Meanwhile, cottage industries such as silk reeling and weaving, cotton throwing and weaving, and sake and soy sauce brewing drove growth in the secondary sector, while commerce and transportation did in the tertiary sector. A substantial share of labour in non-farm sectors was supplied by

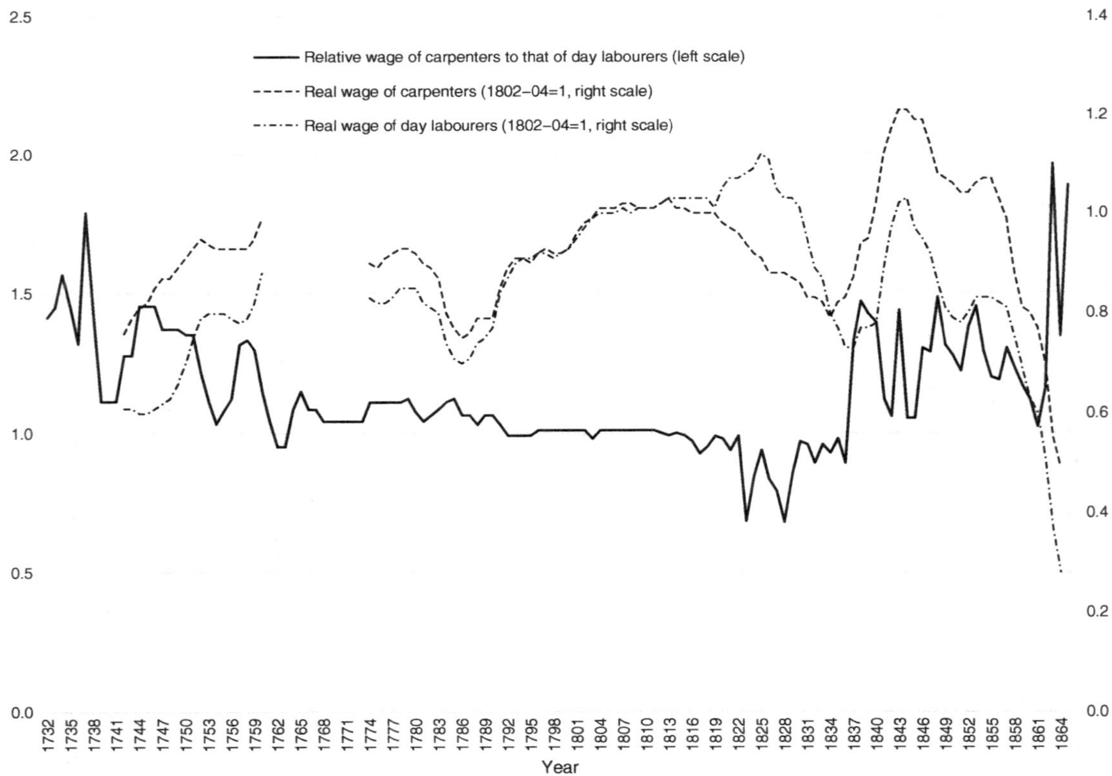

Figure 3.3 Real and relative wages of carpenters and day labourers in the Kinai region, 1732–1865
Source: Fukao et al. (2017).
Note: Carpenters: Figures up to 1818 are for the western part of Settsu province, while those from 1819 are for Kyoto and Osaka. Day labourers: Figures up to 1818 are for agricultural day labourers in the western part of Settsu province, while those from 1819 are for day labourers in Kyoto city.

farming households in the form of by-employment (Saito and Settsu 2007). As a result, the expansion of the service sector was centred on local towns that are not counted as 'urban' in Table 3.1. Furthermore, the rise in labour demand from rural towns resulted in a decrease in the population of major cities such as Edo and Osaka in the eighteenth century. These developments led to stagnation in the urbanization rate from the eighteenth century (Table 3.1).

State Capacity

Estimates of Output and Tax of the Shogunate Domain

To examine the capacity of the state during the Tokugawa period, we focus on output and land tax revenue of the shogunate domain, for which data series are available of the official predicted output on which that land tax was based and of land tax revenue.[5] The land tax was levied as a certain percentage of the official predicted output (***kokudaka***) until the early 1710s and as a fixed amount from the late 1710s due to a land tax reform to increase farmers' incentives.

When determining the land tax rate or amount, the shogunate or the lord surveyed the region under their jurisdiction to measure the area of each parcel of farmland and to estimate the agricultural output (***kokudaka***) of the parcel given the past years' crops. In practice, in the cadastral surveys on average, 15 per cent of the measured area was deducted as an allowance to provide a safety margin to stabilize owner-farmers.[6] Thus, real output per parcel was at least 1.18 (1/0.85) times the official estimated output.

Point estimates of agricultural productivity in 1600, 1721, 1804, and 1846 provided by Takashima, Fukao, and Imamura (2017) and Nakabayashi et al. (2020) show that productivity grew in the late eighteenth and the nineteenth centuries. Meanwhile, as shown in Figure 3.4, the land tax revenue of the shogunate grew until the 1710s and then stagnated. From the late 1710s the shogunate switched from setting the tax as a percentage of output to a fixed amount. The land tax trajectory therefore suggests that tax revenues did not benefit from the increase in productivity. This is not surprising, given that the shogunate and lords depended entirely on village

5 See Ono (1996: 441–448). Original sources for 1651–1715: 'Okouchike kiroku (Records of Okouchi)', Ono (2008b: 106–130); for 1716–1841: Seisai Mukoyama, ed. 'Mukoyama Seisai zakki oyobi zattetsu (Miscellaneous Records and Bound Documents of Seisai Mukoyama)', Ono (2008a): 62–80.

6 See Oishi (1969 [1794]: 73). The author, Takahisa Oishi, was a county governor of the lord of Takasaki.

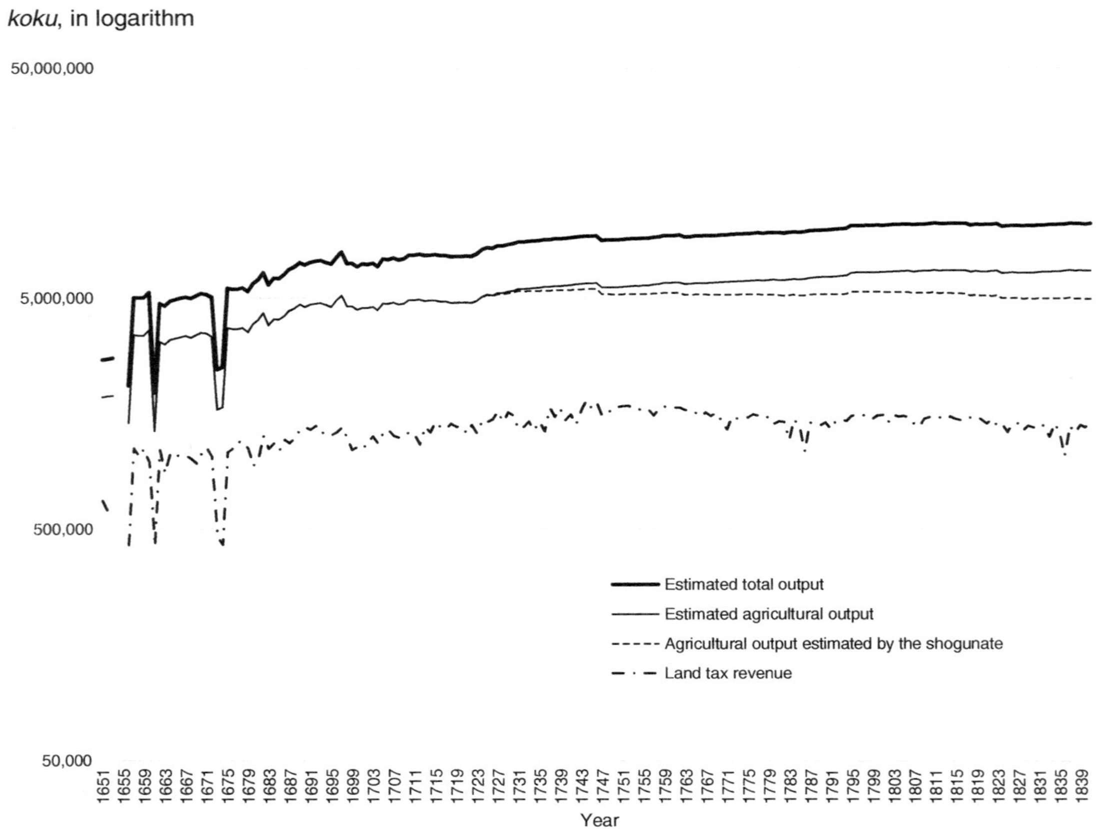

Figure 3.4 Output and land tax from the shogunate domain, 1651–1841
Sources: Output and land tax: Ono (1996: 441–448).
Note: Data are available in the online appendix of Nakabayashi et al. (forthcoming).

mayors to collect the land tax. Provided that villages served as the tax collection system, negotiation with mayors to raise tax was very difficult, and often politically almost impossible. Tax collection by coercion without accordance from mayors and other farmers was also impossible. In the case of the shogunate domain, one *samurai* official was responsible for collecting 40,000 *koku* in revenue and in charge of all administrative and judicial services. This meant that one official was in charge of 13,000 to 20,000 people. Thus, in practice, without cooperation from the villages, the shogunate and lords were not able to collect land tax. Although switching from a percentage to a fixed amount provided the shogunate and lords with stable land tax revenue, they failed to increase the amount once the land tax amount was fixed (Nakabayashi and Imamura 2017; Nakabayashi et al., 2020).

The only available information about output is the official predicted output based on cadastral surveys, which provided the basis of the land tax. As a conservative assumption, we suppose that there was no hidden farmland. Further, interpolating linearly between the estimates of agricultural productivity for years for which such estimates are available, we obtain the productivity growth trend from 1716, after which the shogunate taxation changed from the fixed rate of output to the fixed amount. We then multiply the official predicted output by 1.18 and the estimated productivity growth trend to obtain a lower bound estimate of the agricultural output in the shogunate domain, assuming no hidden farmland. If there existed hidden farmland, real output would have been higher than our estimate.

To estimate output in the secondary and tertiary sectors, point estimates for 1600, 1721, 1804, and 1846 are provided by Takashima et al. (2017). We obtain rough estimates for intervening years through linear interpolation. Further, using estimates of the relative sizes of the primary, secondary, and tertiary sectors, we multiply the estimated agricultural output by the sectoral ratio to estimate the output of the secondary and the tertiary sectors as well as the economy overall. The result is depicted by the solid thick line in Figure 3.4. The 'agricultural output estimated by the shogunate' in Figure 3.4 is the officially predicted output multiplied by 1.18.

Next, we recover the total tax revenue from the land tax record. On the official predicted output, the primary land tax (*hon nengu*) and the miscellaneous contributions (*sho yaku*) were levied in the ratio of roughly 0.8 to 0.2. There were almost no taxes on secondary and tertiary sector activities. Thus, 1.25 (=1.0/0.8) times the primary land tax was the total tax revenue. Dividing the total output and the agricultural output by the total tax, we obtain the estimated effective taxation rate in the total output and the agricultural output, which is a widely used measure of state capacity. Developments in these taxation rates over time are shown in Figure 3.5.

Under the fixed amount taxation, the land tax was temporarily reduced by switching to a fixed rate when crop output dropped more than 30 per cent, to share the risk between the shogunate and farmers (Oishi 1969 [1794]: 188–191). The fluctuations in tax revenue in Figure 3.5 are partly due to the volatility induced by this rule. Therefore, what matters in Figure 3.5 is not annual changes but the long-term trends.

The estimated effective taxation rate reached a historical high of 40 per cent of agricultural output, which was 30 per cent of total output, in the late seventeenth century, when the shogunate conducted a domain-wide cadastral survey and granted farmers property rights to their land. In return for these property rights, farmers accepted such a high taxation rate that reached 40 per cent of agricultural output. Subsequently as productivity increased, the taxation rate gradually declined to 14–16 per cent in the early nineteenth century.

Stagnant but Still Considerable State Capacity

The mass reclamation of new paddy fields provided the shogunate with a steady increase in land tax revenue in the seventeenth century. The reclamation of alluvial plains and the building of cities, roads, running water supply, and sewage in the seventeenth century meant that expenditure on the maintenance of social infrastructure rose. However, the stagnant tax revenue in Figure 3.4 indicates that from the early eighteenth century onwards increases in output due to productivity growth were not taxed.

Meanwhile, when the shogunate and lords built capital cities in the seventeenth century, they did not regularly levy taxes on merchants and craftsmen, to foster urban growth. While the shogunate introduced indirect taxes levied on guilds in the late eighteenth century, such taxes were almost negligible.

Instead of raising the land tax as agricultural output increased due to productivity growth, or imposing indirect taxes on non-farm sectors, the shogunate switched to a fixed amount of land tax in the late 1710s, and most lords in advanced regions followed suit. Facing rising costs for maintenance of physical and institutional infrastructures as the economy grew, they delegated the governance of commercial affairs to merchants' cartels and the maintenance of infrastructure to local public organizations. Specifically, while the shogunate without exception dealt with lawsuits over land ownership, tenancy contracts, and loans using land as collateral as main lawsuits (*honkuji*) and enforced contracts, it in principle encouraged merchant cartels to settle disputes about financial

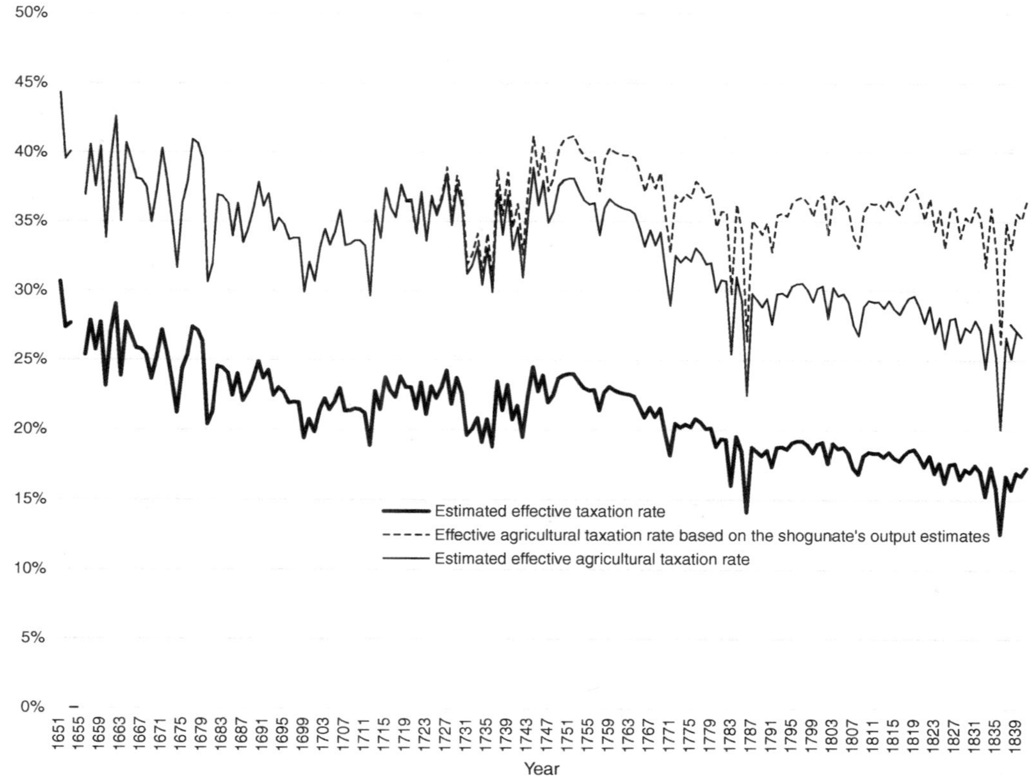

Figure 3.5 Taxation rate in the shogunate domain, 1651–1841
Sources: See notes for Figure 3.4.

claims without resorting to the courts by classifying such lawsuits as money lawsuits (*kanekuji*), whose enforcement by the shogunate court was subordinate to *honkuji* (Okazaki 2005; Mandai and Nakabayashi 2018).

Regarding the maintenance of physical infrastructure, the bodies to which such tasks were delegated were in most cases county-level organizations that consisted of all villages in the county and were run by farmers, not by *samurai*. These organizations imposed additional local taxes on member villages or collected temporary contributions. The local taxes were inherited by municipal governments after the Meiji Restoration (Kurushima 2002; Imamura and Nakabayashi 2017).

The Edo shogunate was a period of significant divergence in state capacity in countries around the world. In Japan, assuming that the shogunate domain was representative, the taxation rate fell from around 30 per cent in the mid-seventeenth century to 14–16 per cent in the mid-nineteenth century (Figure 3.5). Thus, state capacity in Japan appears to have declined considerably during this period. On the other hand, in Britain, the taxation rate climbed from less than 7 per cent to 9 per cent in the late seventeenth century, to 12 per cent in the early eighteenth century, and above 20 per cent during the Napoleonic Wars (O'Brien and Hunt 1993; Daunton 2012: 112). The taxation rate in Spain was 10 per cent in the seventeenth century (Comín Comín and Yun-Casalilla 2012: 244), that of China was 8 per cent in the mid-nineteenth century (Deng 2012: 342), and that of Turkey was less than 4 per cent until the mid-eighteenth century and 8 per cent in the mid-nineteenth century (Pamuk 2012: 321).

In summary, the state capacity of shogunate Japan was considerably higher than that of other emerging powers such as China, Spain, and Turkey from the eighteenth to the mid-nineteenth centuries. This difference in state capacity led to a 'little divergence' between Japan and China in the East (Sng and Moriguchi 2014; Koyama et al. 2018).

Tax Base Bestowed on the Meiji Government

Following the conclusion of the Treaty of Kanagawa with the United States in 1854, the shogunate increasingly consulted with the leading lords over major decisions. As part of these consultations, a growing consensus emerged among political leaders that it was necessary to consolidate state capacity. The questions were who would lead such a consolidation and how it should be implemented (Mitani 2020).

The imperial court, the Choshu domain, and the Satsuma domain declared the restoration of the imperial government and defeated the shogunate and the north-eastern allied domains in 1868. Furthermore, the imperial government abandoned the federal regime in 1871 and assumed direct rule over all of Japan by depriving lords of their sovereign powers, including taxation. The Land Tax Reform Act of 1873 reconfirmed the property rights of farmers, which had been established under the shogunate regime in advanced regions, and levied the same level of the land tax.

The abolition of the federal regime consolidated the tax base. However, the tax base itself was bequeathed from the shogunate and the lords. Because Japan waived its tariff autonomy through the treaties with Western powers in 1858, it could not raise tariffs unilaterally as a new tax base, so that the imperial government continued to rely on the land tax. The share of the land tax in total tax revenue was more than 70 per cent in the 1870s and more than 50 per cent until the early 1890s. The land tax thus to a substantial extent helped to finance modernization efforts such as the transfer of technology from the West (Nakabayashi 2012).

Conclusion

The protection of property rights, one critical condition for modern economic growth, was in place by the end of the seventeenth century under the shogunate regime. The productivity improvements from the eighteenth century are testament to the positive impacts that this protection of property rights made. At the same time, further reforms were necessary to make Japan an advanced economy. The economic gains Japan achieved after the Meiji Restoration, which opened the country to international trade and removed a range of restrictions on society and economic activity, can be regarded as indicators of the economic costs caused by the restrictions imposed by the Tokugawa regime.

Starting with trade, Bernhofen and Brown (2005) estimate that the gains from free trade after the United States forced Japan to open up in 1859 amounted to about 8–9 per cent of GDP. This estimate shows that the gains from trade – and hence the economic costs of the policy of isolation during the Tokugawa period – were quite substantial.

Next, turning to gains in productivity after the Meiji Restoration, Fukao and Settsu (2017) and Fukao et al. (2020) estimate that labour productivity in the economy overall grew at an annual average rate of 1.75 per cent between 1885 and 1899. Of the 1.75 per cent, 1.47 percentage points were due to growth in total factor productivity (TFP), since increases in the capital stock per worker contributed only 0.29 percentage points to the growth in labour productivity. These estimates show that at the beginning of Japan's industrialization process from the late 1880s onwards, growth was not driven by a jump in capital input but by growth in TFP. Meanwhile, of the 1.47 per cent growth in TFP, 0.27 percentage points were due to the reallocation of labour from the farm sector to the non-farm sector. This estimate provides a sense of the cost of social immobility before the Meiji Restoration. Other factors contributing to the increase in TFP were technology transfers from the West and improvements in human capital due to the expansion of public education. The potential of such increases in TFP can be regarded as another victim of the Tokugawa regime's isolationist policy and the policy to largely restrict public education to the *samurai* class.

Another legacy of the Tokugawa regime was the family system. As a result of the strict protection of peasant families' property, the stem family played the central role in risk-sharing and resource allocation (Saito 1998; 2000). Meanwhile, a contrasting characteristic of family law under the civil law system and the common law system is that the former commands the family to take greater responsibility. Reflecting this, the civil law system placed great emphasis on the role of filial support, obliging adult children to support their parents financially although the common law system did not contain such stipulations (Twigg and Grand 1998). When Japan's leaders modernized the family system, it was a logical choice to adopt the civil law system. In effect, the enactment of the Civil Code of 1898 formalized and augmented the role of the stem family (Nakabayashi 2019b). Also, for corporate law Japan adopted German law (Nakabayashi 2019a).

In general, the legacy of traditional law has affected the modernization of nations (Gutmann and Voigt 2020). In the case of Japan, similarities between the legal system of the shogunate and the continental civil law system prompted Japan to follow the continental European legal model after the Meiji Restoration. Furthermore, adopting the civil law system – rather than a common law system – had important implications for the path of nations that both the private and public sectors would take. For instance, countries with a civil law tradition have tended to place greater emphasis on the 'duty of support' of the family, and in such countries, the welfare state since the mid-twentieth century has increasingly taken on a greater role, replacing the supporting role originally played by the family (Haberkern and Szydlik 2010; Nakabayashi 2019b). In the private sector, corporate governance in major civil law countries such as Japan, Germany, and France tends to put greater emphasis on stakeholders beyond shareholders (Shleifer and Vishny 1997; La Porta et al. 2000; Graff 2008). Thus, directly or indirectly, the policies of the shogunate regime have had long-lasting hysteresis effects.

References

Bassino, J-P., Broadberry, S., Fukao, K., Gupta, B. and Takashima, M. (2019). 'Japan and the Great Divergence, 730–1874', *Explorations in Economic History*, Apr, 72, 1–22.

Bernhofen, D. M. and Brown, J. C. (2005). 'An Empirical Assessment of the Comparative Advantage Gains from Trade: Evidence from Japan', *American Economic Review*, Mar, 95(1), 208–225.

Brown, P. C. (1993). *Central Authority and Local Autonomy in the Formation of Early Modern Japan*, Stanford University Press.

(2011).*Cultivating Commons: Joint Ownership of Arable Land in Early Modern Japan*, Honolulu: University of Hawai'i Press.

Comín Comín, F. and Yun-Casalilla, B. (2012). 'Spain: From Composite Monarchy to Nation-State, 1492–1914. An Exceptional Case?', in Yun-Casalilla, B. and O'Brien, P. K., with Comín Comín, F. (eds.), *The Rise of Fiscal States: A Global History, 1500–1914*, Cambridge University Press, 39–66.

Cox, G. W. and Dincecco, M. (forthcoming). 'The Budgetary Origins of Fiscal-Military Prowess', *Journal of Politics*, available at doi.org/10.1086/711130 (accessed 8 January 2021).

Daunton, M. (2012). 'The Politics of British Taxation, from the Glorious Revolution to the Great War', in Yun-Casalilla, B. and O'Brien, P. K., with Comín Comín, F. (eds.),*The Rise of Fiscal States: A Global History, 1500–1914*, Cambridge University Press, 111–142.

Deng, K. G. (2012). 'The Continuation and Efficiency of the Chinese Fiscal State, 700 BC–AD 1911', in Yun-Casalilla, B. and O'Brien, P. K., with Comín Comín, F. (eds.), *The Rise of Fiscal States: A Global History, 1500–1914*, Cambridge University Press, 335–352.

Dincecco, M. (2009). 'Fiscal Centralization, Limited Government, and Public Revenues in Europe, 1650–1913', *Journal of Economic History*, Mar, 69(1), 48–103.

(2011). *Political Transformations and Public Finances: Europe, 1650–1913*, Cambridge University Press.

Dincecco, M. and Gaetano Onorato, M. (2017). *From Warfare to Wealth: The Military Origins of Urban Prosperity in Europe*, Cambridge University Press.

Dincecco, M. and Katz, G. (2014). 'State Capacity and Long-run Economic Performance', *The Economic Journal*, Feb, 126, 189–218.

Ferejohn, J. A. and McCall Rosenbluth, F. (2010). 'War and State Building in Medieval Japan', in Ferejohn, J. A. and McCall Rosenbluth, F. (eds.), *War and State Building in Medieval Japan*, Stanford University Press, 1–20.

Friday, K. (2010). 'They Were Soldiers Once: The Early Samurai and the Imperial Court', in Ferejohn, J. A. and McCall Rosenbluth, F. (eds.), *War and State Building in Medieval Japan*, Stanford University Press, 21–52.

Fujiki, H. (2005). *Katana Gari: Buki wo Fuin Shita Minshu (Sword Hunt: Arms Sealed Up by Common People)*, Tokyo: Iwanami Shoten.

Fukao, K. and Settsu, T. (2017). 'Seicho to makuro keizai (Growth and the Macro Economy)', in Fukao, K., Nakamura, N. and Nakabayashi, M. (eds.), *Iwanami Koza Nihon Keizai no Rekishi Dai-3-kan Kindai 1: 19 Seiki Kohan kara Dai Ichiji Sekai Taisen Mae (1913) (Iwanami Series on the Economic History of Japan, Volume 3, Modern Times 1: From the Late Nineteenth Century until the First World War (1913)*, Tokyo: Iwanami Shoten, 1–22.

Fukao, K., Makino, T., and Settsu, T. (2020). 'Structural Change, Capital Deepening, and TFP Growth in Japan: 1885–1970', *Social Science Japan Journal*, Summer, 23(2), 185–204.

Fukao, K., Saito, O., Takashima, M. and Imamura, N. (2017b). 'Seisan, bukka, shotoku no suitei (Estimates of Output, Prices, and Income)', in Fukao, K., Nakamura, N. and Nakabayashi, M. (eds.), *Iwanami Koza Nihon Keizai no Rekishi Dai 2 kan Kinsei: 16 Seiki Matsu kara 19 Seiki Zenhan (Iwanami Series on the Economic History of Japan, Volume 2, Early Modern Times: From the End of the Sixteenth Century to the First Half of the Nineteenth Century)*, Tokyo: Iwanami Shoten, 283–300.

Grabowski, R. (2011). 'China's Economic Takeoff', *The Chinese Economy*, 44(2), 5–24.

Graff, M. (2008). 'Law and Finance: Common Law and Civil Law Countries Compared – An Empirical Critique', *Economica*, Feb, 75, 60–83.

Gutmann, J. and Voigt, S. (2020). 'Traditional Law in Times of the Nation State: Why Is it so Prevalent?' *Journal of Institutional Economics*, 16(4), 445–461.

Haberkern, K. and Szydlik, M. (2010). 'State Care Provision, Societal Opinion and Children's Care of Older Parents in European Countries', *Ageing & Society*, 30(2), Feb, 299–323.

Hart, O. D., (1988).'Incomplete Contracts and the Theory of the Firm', *Journal of Law, Economics, & Organization*, 4(1), 119–140.

Hayami, A. and Miyamoto, M. (1988). 'Gaisetsu 17–18 seiki (Introduction: Seventeenth and Eighteenth Centuries)', in Hayami, A. and Miyamoto, M. (eds.), *Nihon Keizaishi 1 Keizai Shakai no Seiritsu (Economic History of Japan 1, Formation of the Economic Society)*, Tokyo: Iwanami Shoten, 1–84.

Imamura, N. and Nakabayashi, M. (2017). 'Josho dai-3-setsu shotoku no bunpai (Introduction: Section 3. Distribution of Income)', in Fukao, K., Nakamura, N. and Nakabayashi, M. (eds.), *Iwanami Koza Nihon Keizai no Rekishi, Dai 2 kan, Kinsei: 16 Seiki-matsu kara 19 Seiki Zenhan (Iwanami Series on the History of the Japanese Economy, Volume 2, Early Modern Times: From the End of the Sixteenth Century to the Early Nineteenth Century)*, Tokyo: Iwanami Shoten, 33–60.

Karaman, K. K. and Pamuk, Ş. (2013). 'Different Paths to the Modern State in Europe: The Interaction between Warfare, Economic Structure, and Political Regime', *American Political Science Review*, 107(3), 603–626.

Koyama, M., Moriguchi, C. and Sng, T-H. (2018). 'Geopolitics and Asia's Little Divergence: State Building in China and Japan after 1850', *Journal of Economic Behavior & Organization*, 155, 178–204.

Kurushima, H. (2002). *Kinsei Bakuryo no Gyosei to Kumiai Mura (Administration and the Associated Villages in the Early Modern Shogunate Domain)*, University of Tokyo Press.

La Porta, R., Lopez-de-Silanes, F., Shleifer, A. and Vishny, R. (2000). 'Investor Protection and Corporate Governance', *Journal of Financial Economics*, 58(1–2), 3–27.

Malinowski, M. J. and van Zanden, J. L. (2017). 'Income and its Distribution in Preindustrial Poland', *Cliometrica*, Sep, 11(3), 375–404.

Mandai, Y. and Nakabayashi, M. (2017). 'Dai-3-sho Dai-1-setsu: Kinsei no tochi hosei to jinushi keiei (Chapter 3: Section 1. The Land Law and Landlordism in Early Modern Times)', in Fukao, K., Nakamura, N. and Nakabayashi, M. (eds.), *Iwanami Koza Nihon Keizai no Rekishi, Dai-2-kan, Kinsei: 16 Seiki-matsu kara 19 Seiki Zenhan (Iwanami Series on the History of the Japanese Economy, Volume 2, Early Modern Times: From the End of the Sixteenth Century to the Early Nineteenth Century)*, Tokyo: Iwanami Shoten, 150–176.

(2018). 'Stabilize the Peasant Economy: Governance of Foreclosure by the Shogunate', *Journal of Policy Modeling*, Mar–Apr, 40(2), 305–327, doi.org/10.1016/j.jpolmod.2018.01.007 (accessed 5 October 2020).

Messina, S. A. (2019). *A History of States and Economic Policies in Early Modern Europe*, London: Routledge.

Milanovic, B., Lindert, P. H. and Williamson, J. G. (2010). 'Pre-industrial Inequality', *The Economic Journal*, Mar, 121, 255–272.

Mitani, H. (2020). 'Japan's Meiji Revolution in Global History: Searching for Some Generalizations Out of History', *Asian Review of World Histories*, 8(1), 41–57.

Moriguchi, C. and Saez, E. (2008). 'The Evolution of Concentration in Japan: Evidence from Income Tax Statistics', *The Review of Economics and Statistics*, Nov, 90(4), 713–734.

Nagahara, K. (1973). Nihon Chusei Shakai Kozo no Kenkyu (*Research on the Social Structure of Medieval Japan*), Tokyo: Iwanami Shoten.

Nagahara, K. (1975). 'Landownership under the Shöen-Kokugaryö System', *Journal of Japanese Studies*, 1(2), 269–296.

Nagahara, K. and Yamamura, K. (1988). 'Shaping the Process of Unification: Technological Progress in Sixteenth- and Seventeenth-century Japan', *The Journal of Japanese Studies*, Winter, 14(1), 77–109.

Nakabayashi, M. (2012). 'The Rise of a Japanese Fiscal State', in Yun-Casalilla, B. and O'Brien, P. K., with Comín Comín, F. (eds.), *The Rise of Fiscal States: A Global History, 1500–1914*, Cambridge University Press, 327–409.

(2019a). 'Ownership Structure and Market Efficiency: Stockholder/Manager Conflicts at the Dawn of Japanese Capitalism', *Journal of International Financial Markets, Institutions and Money*, Jul, 61, 189–212.

(2019b). 'From Family Security to the Welfare State: Path Dependency of Social Security on the Difference in Legal Origins', *Economic Modelling*, Nov, 82, 280–293.

Nakabayashi, M. and Imamura, N. (2017). 'Josho Dai-3-setsu: Shotoku to shisan no bunpai (Introduction: Section 3. The Distribution of Income and Assets)', in Fukao, K., Nakamura, N. and Nakabayashi, M. (eds.), *Iwanami Koza Nihon Keizai no Rekishi, Dai-2-kan, Kinsei: 16 Seiki-matsu kara 19 Seiki Zenhan (Iwanami Series on the History of the Japanese Economy, Volume 2, Early Modern Times: From the End of the Sixteenth Century to the Early Nineteenth Century)*, Tokyo: Iwanami Shoten, 33–49.

Nakabayashi, M. and Moriguchi, C. (2017). 'Josho Dai-2-setsu: Seifu no yakuwari (Introduction: Section 2. Role of the Government)', in Fukao, K., Nakamura, N. and Nakabayashi, M. (eds.), *Iwanami Koza Nihon Keizai no Rekishi, Dai-2-kan, Kinsei: 16 Seiki-matsu kara 19 Seiki Zenhan (Iwanami Series on the History of the Japanese Economy, Volume 2, Early Modern Times: From the End of the Sixteenth Century to the Early Nineteenth Century*), Tokyo: Iwanami Shoten, 22–33.

Nakabayashi, M., Fukao, K., Takashima, M. and Nakamura, N. (2020). 'Property Systems and Economic Growth in Japan' *Social Science Japan Journal*, Summer, 23(2), 147–184.

Nishitani, M. and Nakabayashi, M. (2017). 'Josho Dai-3-setsu Shotoku bunpai (Introduction: Section 3. The Distribution of Income)', in Fukao, K., Nakamura, N. and Nakabayashi, M. (eds.), *Iwanami Koza Nihon Keizai no Rekishi, Dai 1 Kan: 11 Seiki kara 16 Seiki Kohan (Iwanami Series of the Economic History of Japan, Volume 1: From the Eleventh Century to the Late Sixteenth Century)*, Tokyo: Iwanami Shoten, 33–49.

Nishitani, M., Hayashima, D. and Nakabayashi, M. (2017). 'Josho Dai-2-setsu Seifu no yakuwari (Introduction: Section 2. Role of the Government)', in Fukao, K., Nakamura, N. and Nakabayashi, M. (eds.), *Iwanami Koza Nihon Keizai no Rekishi, Dai-1-kan: 11 Seiki kara 16 Seiki Kohan (Iwanami Series on the History of the Japanese Economy, Volume 1: From the Eleventh Century to the Late Sixteenth Century)*, Tokyo: Iwanami Shoten, 23–33.

O'Brien, P. K. (2012). 'Afterword: Reflections on Fiscal Foundations and Contexts for the Formation of Economically Effective Eurasian States from the Rise of Venice to the Opium War', in Yun-Casalilla, B. and O'Brien, P. K., with Comín Comín, F. (eds.), *The Rise of Fiscal States: A Global History, 1500–1914*, Cambridge University Press, 442–453.

O'Brien, P. K. and Hunt, P. A. (1993). 'The Rise of a Fiscal State in England, 1485–1815', *Historical Research*, Jun, 66(160), 129–176.

Oishi, H. (1969 [1794]). *Jikata Hanreiroku Jokan (Records of Local Practices, Volume 1)*, Tokyo: Kondo Shuppansha, written and submitted to the Lord of Takasaki in 1794.

Okazaki, T. (2005). 'The Role of the Merchant Coalition in Pre-modern Japanese Economic Development: An Historical Institutional Analysis', *Explorations in Economic History*, Apr, 42(2), 184–201.

Okunishi, G. (2004). 'Kinsei koki no Shimousa chiho Sakagawa ryuiki ni okeru inasaku gijustu no tenkai (The Development of Rice Planting Technology in the Sakagawa Valley of the Shimousa District during the Late Edo Period)', *Nogyoshi Kenkyu (The Journal of Agricultural History)*, 38, 49–60.

Ono, M. (1996). *Edo Bakufu Zaisei Shiron (Fiscal History of the Edo Shogunate)*, Tokyo: Yoshikawa Kobunkan.

Ono, M. (ed.) (2008b). *Edo Bakufu Zaisei Shiryo Shusei Gekan (Collected Documents on the Fiscal Policies of the Edo Shogunate, Volume 2)*, Tokyo: Yoshikawa Kobunkan.

(2008a). *Edo Bakufu Zaisei Shiryo Shusei Jokan (Collected Documents on the Fiscal Policies of the Edo Shogunate, Volume 1)*, Tokyo: Yoshikawa Kobunkan.

Palma, N. and Reis, J. (2019). 'From Convergence to Divergence: Portuguese Economic Growth, 1527–1850', *Journal of Economic History*, Jun, 79(2), 477–506.

Pamuk, Ş. (2012). 'The Evolution of Fiscal Institutions in the Ottoman Empire, 1500–1914', in Yun-Casalilla, B. and O'Brien, P. K., with Comín Comín, F. (eds.), *The Rise of Fiscal States: A Global History, 1500–1914*, Cambridge University Press, 304–331.

Piggott, J. R. (2018). 'Estates: Their History and Historiography', in Goodwin, J. R. and Piggott, J. R. (eds.), *Land, Power, and the Sacred: The Estate System in Medieval Japan*, Honolulu: University of Hawai'i Press, 3–36.

Ravina, M. (1995). 'State-building and Political Economy in Early-modern Japan', *Journal of Asian Studies*, 54(4), 997–1022.

(1999). *Land and Lordship in Early Modern Japan*, Stanford University Press.

Saito, O. (1998). 'Two Kinds of Stem-family System? Traditional Japan and Europe Compared', *Continuity and Change*, 13(1), 167–186.

(2000). 'Marriage, Family Labour and the Stem Family Household: Traditional Japan in a Comparative Perspective', *Continuity and Change*, May, 15(1), 17–45.

(2002). 'The Frequency of Famines as Demographic Correctives in the Japanese Past', in Dyson, T. and Ó Gráda, C. (eds.), *Famine Demography: Perspectives from the Past and Present*, Oxford University Press, 218–239.

(2009). 'Land, Labour and Market Forces in Tokugawa Japan', *Continuity and Change*, May, 24(1), 169–196.

(2015). 'Climate, Famine, and Population in Japanese History: A Long-term Perspective', in Batten, B. L. and Brown, P. C. (eds.), *Environment and Society in the Japanese Islands: From Prehistory to the Present*, Corvallis: Oregon State University Press, 213–329.

Saito, O. and Sato, M. (2012). 'Japan's Civil Registration Systems Before and After the Meiji Restoration', in Breckenridge, K. and Szreter, S. (eds.), *Registration and Recognition: Documenting the Person in World History*, Oxford University Press, 113–135.

Saito, O. and Settsu, T. (2007). 'Unveiling Rural By-employment Patterns and its Implications for National Income Estimates in Early Phases of Japan's Industrialisation', Sep., paper prepared for the Hi-Stat Workshop on Historical Occupational Structures: Asian and European Perspectives Sano Shoin, Hitotsubashi University, Sep., www.campop.geog.cam.ac.uk/research/projects/internationaloccupations/inchos/saito.pdf (accessed 29 September 2020).

Saito, O. and Takashima, M. (2017). 'Jinko to toshika, ido to shugyo (Population and Urbanization, Movement and Employment)', in Fukao, K., Nakamura, N. and Nakabayashi, M. (eds.), *Iwanami Koza Nihon Keizai no Rekishi Dai-2-kan, Kinsei, 16 Seiki Matsu kara 19 Seiki Zenhan (Iwanami Series on the Economic History of Japan, Volume 2, Early Modern Times: From the End of the Sixteenth Century to the Early Nineteenth Century)*, Tokyo: Iwanami Shoten, 62–104.

Sakurai, E. (2002). 'Chusei no kahei, shinyo (Money and Credit in Medieval Times)', in Sakurai, E. and Nakahishi, S. (eds.), *Shin Taikei Nihonshi 12 Ryutsu Keizaishi (Japanese History, New Series, Volume 12, Economic History of Commerce)*, Tokyo: Yamakawa Shuppansha, 42–77.

(2008). 'Currency and Credit in Medieval Japan', *International Journal of Asian Studies*, Jan, 5(1), 53–70.

(2018). 'Medieval Japan's Commercial Economy and the Estate System', in Goodwin, J. R. and Piggott, J. R. (eds.), *Land, Power, and the Sacred: The Estate System in Medieval Japan*, Honolulu: University of Hawai'i Press, 37–58.

Shimbo, H. and Saito, O. (1999). 'The Economy on the Eve of Industrialization', in Hayami, A., Saito, O. and Toby, R. P. (eds.), *The Economic History of Japan: 1600–1990, Volume 1: Emergence of Economic Society in Japan, 1600–1859*, Oxford University Press, 337–368.

Shleifer, A. and Vishny, R. W. (1997). 'A Survey of Corporate Governance', *The Journal of Finance*, Jun, 52(2), 737–783.

Sng, T.-H. and Moriguchi, C. (2014). 'Asia's Little Divergence: State Capacity in China and Japan before 1850', *Journal of Economic Growth*, 19, 439–470.

't Hart, M., Brandon, P. and Sánchez, R. T. (2018). 'Introduction: Maximising Revenues, Minimising Political Costs – Challenges in the History of Public Finance of the Early Modern Period', *Financial History Review*, Apr, 25(1), 1–18.

Takashima, M., Fukao, K. and Imamura, N. (2017). 'Josho Dai-1-setsu Edojidai ni okeru makuro keizai (Introduction: Section 1. The Macro Economy in the Edo era)', in Nakabayashi, M. (ed.), *Iwanami Koza Nihon Keizai no Rekishi Dai-2-kan Kinsei (Iwanami*

Series on the History of the Japanese Economy, Volume 2, Early Modern Times), Tokyo: Iwanashomi Shoten, 281–300.

Twigg, J. and Grand, A. (1998). 'Contrasting Legal Conceptions of Family Obligation and Financial Reciprocity in the Support of Older People: France and England', *Ageing & Society*, 18(2), 131–146.

Yun-Casalilla, B. (2012). 'Introduction: The Rise of the Fiscal State in Eurasia from a Global, Comparative and Transnational Perspective', in Yun-Casalilla, B. and O'Brien, P. K., with Comín Comín, F. (eds.), *The Rise of Fiscal States: A Global History, 1500–1914*, Cambridge University Press, 1–35.

4

China: The Start of the Great Divergence

CHRISTOPHER ISETT

Introduction

Until the late 1990s scholars generally agreed that China, having achieved world economic leadership by 1300, was then surpassed by the much smaller upstart states of pre-industrial north-west Europe. Using national accounting estimates, Angus Maddison (2007) mapped both moments, showing how China's early advantages in statecraft and labour-intensive farming lost ground to the labour-saving commercial farming systems and merchant-led states of early modern Holland and England. His work seemed to confirm at least two historiographic traditions at the centre of post-war debates over the origins of the Great Divergence/capitalism and the formation of the modern world that followed, one concerning England and the other concerning China.

Maddison's global account was consistent with the thesis that two centuries of an agricultural and commercial revolution generated a dynamic home market for manufactures, which paved the way, in turn, for the movement of an ever-greater proportion of the labour force out of agriculture and into manufacturing and, eventually, the Industrial Revolution in England. It was also consistent with the contention that several centuries of demographically propelled expansion in late imperial China issued in stagnating and then declining labour productivity in agriculture, which made for falling real wages, a shrinking domestic market for manufactures, and environmental degradation.

Maddison's conclusions were subsequently challenged by sociologists and historians working comparatively, who placed China at the centre of their studies. Collectively, they argued that modernity's preconditions were no more advanced in early modern Europe than in Asia (Wong 1997; Frank 1998). Most famously, Kenneth Pomeranz (2000; 2002) concluded that the economies of East Asia and specifically China's most advanced region of

Jiangnan (see Figure 4.1 for a map of China) outperformed Europe's most developed zones in critical areas as late as 1820. Consequently, Pomeranz argued, England's Industrial Revolution constituted a qualitative departure from that economy's hitherto mediocre path of growth during the late medieval and early modern eras. Only good luck and fortune, he maintained, could explain the radical turn in England's trajectory after the turn of the nineteenth century.

Responding critically to this challenge, a number of economic historians improved upon and confirmed the broad trends shown in Maddison's GDP estimates, undermining Pomeranz's revision. Taken together, these new data show that England's economic performance measured in per capita GDP pulled ahead of both continental Europe and Asia in the early modern period before the onset of the Industrial Revolution. By the same token, the data show China's pre-modern economy stalling and then declining after 1730 in per capita terms. This chapter draws on published per capita GDP data for late imperial China and elsewhere as a general proxy for changes in labour productivity, as well as regional studies, to develop a general interpretation of the Qing economy between its founding in 1644 and the beginning of the Self-Strengthening Movement in 1861.

The sine qua non of modern economic growth is the systematic and ongoing rise of output per labourer because this alone generates increased GDP per capita, making possible higher real wages and/or business profits. By 1850, divergence in levels of labour productivity that had opened up between the UK and China, as reflected in the divergence in their respective levels of GDP per capita, was too great to have been the result of recent developments. English silver wages in the period 1550–1649 were already more than twice those of the Yangzi Delta, in the heart of China's most economically advanced region. In the next century, they grew to nearly seven times greater. Measured in grain purchasing power, Yangzi Delta wages fell from 87 per cent to 38 per cent of English wages in that interval (Broadberry and Gupta 2006). The cause of the divergence is complex, but it originates in the very different economic paths traced by China (including its advanced regions) and England/Great Britain during the pre-industrial period.

Between 1644 and 1850 the Qing population tripled from 150 million to 436 million, whereas farm acreage only doubled. Yields rose but labour productivity did not, as each incremental increase in food production required a greater increment of labour to produce it. Whereas labour productivity in China failed to grow, in England it nearly doubled between 1600 and 1800, with epoch-making consequences for the English economy (Overton 1996).

Figure 4.1 Map of China *c.*1912 Map credits: Redrawn based on a map from U-Spatial, University of Minnesota (uspatial.umn.edu) Data source: China Historical GIS, Natural Earth.

In England, the growth of labour productivity in agriculture brought about declining food prices, making for rising real wages. English families could thus make growing discretionary expenditures, opening the way to the rise of a dynamic home market in manufactures. In China by contrast, the economy followed what amounted to the opposite path. The decline of labour productivity in agriculture brought rising food prices, making for declining real wages. The peasant population had to devote an ever-greater proportion of its income to necessities and could make ever-fewer discretionary expenditures. Agricultural involution thus compressed the home market in manufactures, preventing the expansion of the industrial sector in China until far into the nineteenth century (Huang 1990; Ma and de Jong 2017). The remainder of this chapter will explain the Chinese path as the outcome of rational economic choices given the prevailing social conditions (Brenner and Isett 2002; Bryant 2006).

The Qing Agrarian Order

Upon the establishment of the Qing capital in Beijing in 1644, the leadership of the invading Manchu armies sought rapprochement with China's historical ruling elite in its effort to build state capacity. For centuries, Chinese emperors recruited men to the bureaucracy by testing their mastery of classical texts. Those who passed acquired legal and political status and those who earned higher degrees might be appointed to an official post. Given the arduous preparation required to sit the imperial examination, these men were predominantly scions of the wealthiest landholding families and their clans, which together constituted a self-perpetuating professional class known in English as the 'gentry' (Chang 1955; Huang 1985; Elman 1992). Faced by the fact that two-thirds of those holding the highest imperial degrees came from elite gentry families, China's new rulers had little choice but to gain their allegiance if they wished to rule and administer (Elman 2000). One of their earliest acts was, therefore, to reinstate the examination pathway to government office and salary. Equally important, however, the throne backed the collection of land rent and debt that provided the gentry the income necessary to support the preparation of its sons for high office and recognized in law important status privileges that protected degree holders and enhanced their authority over local communities and their resources. In return for these benefits, the gentry submitted in principle to the land tax, which was demanded of all landowners, though they were not subjected to the labour services required of ordinary subjects.

The Qing rulers sat atop a tax-office state that depended upon the administrative skills of degree-holding elites to collect the revenue that funded the costs of administration (including their salaries), the standing armies, territorial conquest, public works, famine relief, and some of the throne's ritual and sumptuary demands. The gentry were willing partners because office-holding, along with the degree-holding status required to become an official, afforded enormous opportunities for income. In office, the gentry took in surcharges, fines, gifts, and peculation an income eighteen times their official salaries. Out of office, they leveraged their degree-holding status to avoid the land tax, take income from tax farming, sidestep lawsuits, and secure favour from local administrators who shared their social class. The total extralegal take on the local community by office holders alone approached one and a half times annual government tax receipts (Chang 1955; 1962). The Qing state was thus an immense vehicle for facilitating private accumulation through office holding that encouraged landed and merchant elites to invest heavily in the education of their male children and, when that failed, to purchase the status and other remunerative benefits of an honorary degree.

The gentry as a class were historically local leaders who maintained authority over communities through landholdings, lineage organizations, and their control of resources. While an imperial degree provided legal protections and privileges that enhanced that authority, Qing rulers did not formally cede legal power, even if they were forced to recognize and negotiate with local gentry leaders. Taking advantage of the social unrest of the first half of the seventeenth century, the Qing sought to rebalance key social relations at the root of the economy in order to weaken the gentry's hold on peasant households and local communities. It took advantage of the gentry's retreat before widespread tenant, bondservant, and tax rebellions in the mid-seventeenth century to abolish agricultural servitude, which landholders had used successfully to hold their tenants and labourers in place and in their station. Simultaneously, the Qing strengthened the freeholding peasantry by recognizing peasant rights to land on the basis of their payment of the land tax. It added millions of households to the tax rolls by extending petty property ownership to peasants who restored abandoned estates, often at the expense of large landowners, or simply brought new land under cultivation (Oyama 1986; Guo 1991). The restoration of state fiscal solvency primarily on the backs of an independent freeholding peasantry, in charge of its own labour and land on the basis of its payment of the land tax, established the basic form of the Qing tax-office state before internal and foreign wars compelled it in the mid-nineteenth century to increase measurably the share of its revenue earned from the taxation of commerce. Until then, the land tax accounted for more than 70 per cent of revenue (Wang 1973).

On the basis of their now-strengthened communities, peasants found still more ways to enhance their independence and improve their chances of reproducing themselves. Under late imperial custom all sales of land were entailed with ongoing claims against it. In the most common practice, the seller retained the right to redeem his land no matter how much time had passed. If the right of redemption was explicitly denied, however, the seller was still entitled to supplementary payments that, in practice, recognized the seller's community-sanctioned claims against any future increase in the land's value. Imperial laws designed to cap the right to redeem at thirty years from the time of sale or to limit the number of supplementary sales were all but ineffective. Communities and local officials alike accepted these practices, despite the disputes they generated, as well as their effects on capital accumulation, because they offered a defence against the far greater threat to social order posed by landlessness and dispossession. The complete separation of peasants from the land was consequently infrequent, affecting perhaps one in ten rural inhabitants (Schurmann 1956; Huang 1996; Kishimoto 1997).

As customs establishing multiple simultaneous claims on the value of land registered to one taxpayer were recognized by communities and in legal practice, there was a parallel strengthening of the rights of tenants at the expense of landlords (Rawski 1972; Yang 1988; Shih 1992; Huang 1996; Gao 2005). By 1700, leased land was divided between surface and subsoil rights that gave landlords freedom to buy and sell claims to rent, but not to raise rent, replace tenants, supervise work, or block the transfer of surface rights between farming households. As the balance of power shifted away from landlords, tenants successfully reduced rents. In real terms, they fell by 20–40 per cent across the eighteenth century, even as population grew. Landlords succeeded in pushing them up at the end of the century, but by 1820 real rents were falling once again. Notably, sharecroppers who took up double cropping defended their second harvest against landlord claims of rent, further demonstrating the political character of rent-taking (Chang 1962; Zhou and Xie 1986; Yang 1988; Shih 1992; Jiang et al. 2000; Gao 2005). The Qing property regime that had taken shape by the 1690s had singular effects on the economy.

Most peasants had direct access to land through purchase or inheritance, especially in northern China, where tenancy was less common. In the south, where tenancy was more common, landlords were unable to tie either rent or entry fees to changes in demand for land with any regularity or predictability (Rawski 1972; Shih 1992; Mazumdar 1998; Wakefield 1998; Gao 2005). These conditions of security allowed peasants in both the north and south to focus on pursuing self-provisioning strategies with the intention of meeting most of their day-to-day needs directly through their own labour (Huang 1985; 1990; Mazumdar 1998; Myers and Wang 2002). They diversified production to the fullest extent possible while growing mostly food grains and starchy roots for household consumption. Typically, only after meeting as much of their subsistence as possible did they sell surpluses or put land in cash crops, which they did to round out their needs and pay taxes and fees (Huang 1985; 1990; Mazumdar 1998; Xu 1998; Myers and Wang 2002).

These preferences were reinforced by strategies of family formation intended to maintain the patriline while securing all important assistance in old age. Parents leaned on their control over land to support their children's early marriage as a counter against high infant mortality. Into the twentieth century, nine in ten women were married by age 24 and the average age of women at marriage was eighteen. To ensure sons had the wherewithal to maintain their wives and children, fathers divided their estates equally by partible inheritance, procuring for each son an equivalent share of land, tools, animals, etc. Early female marriage and universal partible inheritance were possible because of extraordinary parental control (Wolf and Engelen 2008). While these strategies improved chances of survival, they multiplied the number of family and farming units. But this expansion, unless countered, reduced the ratio of both land and farming capital to farmworkers as estates were broken up and fragmented (Myers 1970; Huang 1985; Wakefield 1998). For many households, security in land was paradoxically undermined, however gradually, by the very strategies of family formation it enabled.

As we shall see, those whose plots became too small to produce enough food and fibre for the family had little choice but to take up cash cropping and household manufacturing and buy their subsistence. They could do so because of the simultaneous extension of agriculture on the frontiers, where grain surpluses were initially sufficient to keep prices at levels that supported cash croppers and household manufacturers elsewhere. Nevertheless, the practices associated with the Qing property regime just described worked against those who deepened their exposure to the market under demographic pressure. Stated simply, the multiple claims on output recognized by communities and upheld in the courts hampered efforts by smallholders and tenants who might seek to accumulate through exchange. They could not easily therefore build up their farm operations to afford capital investments that would drive gains in labour productivity (Bray 1984; Huang 1985; Bray 1986; Wakefield 1998; Myers and Wang 2002). Moreover, landlords had little interest in improving their estates because, as we have seen, they could not tie rent and entry fees to changes in demand, let alone output, with any regularity (Rawski 1972; Shih 1992; Mazumdar 1998; Wakefield 1998; Gao 2005). Rents in Wuxi county in the heart of the Yangzi Delta, for example, fell so far that returns on investment in land rent declined from 10 to 2 per cent across the nineteenth century (Chang 1962). Unable to affect their tenants, landlords relocated to towns where they settled on trading in claims on rent, invested in moneylending and petty trade, purchased income-generating liturgical posts and the status that came with imperial degrees, and prepared their sons to sit the imperial exam (Chang 1955; Huang 1985).

The Decline in Farm Size and Labour Intensification

The long run effect of declining farm size and capital was the relative cheapening of labour and the corresponding adoption of what Esther Boserup (1981) identified as 'land-saving' farming, or the basis of an involutionary pattern of growth. In other words, peasants individually found that they best closed the gap between their basic needs and what their land could produce by working more hours to raise the volume of farm output even though returns per day were stagnant and falling. They could do so because their families provided excess and otherwise underemployed labour on account of their small farms (Huang 1985, 1990; Mazumdar 1998; Myers and Wang 2002; Elvin 2004).

The growth of underemployed labour was in the first instance the product of demographic growth. Although there is disagreement on the specific drivers of Qing demographic expansion, it is agreed that the population grew steadily between 1700 and 1850.[1] From 1700 to 1786 it grew from 150 to 290 million. By 1820 China's population breached 350 million and by 1850 it was as high as 436 million. Mid-century rebellions removed 30–60 million people, but by 1930 the population had surpassed its mid-century watermark, reaching 500 million.[2] Additions of land at two-thirds the pace of population

1 Wolf and Engelen (2008) give the most convincing account of the majority Han Chinese population dynamic. It is universally acknowledged that marriage for women was very early and near universal, which made for high total fertility in comparison to England.

2 Cao Shuji (2001) estimates that population grew from 150 to 311 million between 1664 and 1776 and that it reached 383 million in 1820 and 436 million by 1851. His figures are

growth caused per capita farmland to decline from 5 to 3 mu, which in turn drove up the demand for food, fibre, and fuel.[3] The looming pressures vexed eighteenth-century government officials, who considered schemes to settle the swelling numbers on the empire's frontiers (Ho 1959; Cao 1997; Marks 1998; Rowe 2001; Myers and Wang 2002).

The pressure on resources was felt first in the historical cores of the empire. Already densely populated at the end of the Ming dynasty, these regions had little untended land after 1700. Thus, the population of the north China plain (Shandong and Hebei) grew from 38 to 56.5 million between 1757 and 1850, yet farm acreage topped out at 171.1 million mu (Huang 1985). Jiangnan's population was 20 million in 1700; it reached 31 million in 1776 and 43 million in 1851. There was no expansion of acreage after 1750 (Wu 2005). Of the core regions, Guangdong's population grew perhaps the most. It more than doubled from 1690 to 1813, when it reached 19.3 million, before growing another 40 per cent by century's end. Yet farmland was added at half that pace before 1813 and half again thereafter (Marks 1998).

Inevitably, farms shrank across the eighteenth and nineteenth centuries. They contracted on average from 50 to 15 mu in Shandong-Hebei (Huang 1985; Xu 1998). Jiangnan farms, which averaged a mere 10 mu in 1750, fell to 7 mu by 1800 (Fan 1998; Hong 2005; Wu 2005). In Guangdong farms declined from perhaps 20 to 12 mu, and smaller still in the Pearl River Delta (Marks 1998). These were averages. The majority poor and middling peasants farmed as little as 4 mu in Guangdong by the late eighteenth century. In the Yangzi Delta, perhaps three-quarters of households worked less than 5 mu at a time when a household required 20 mu to achieve complete food security (Shih 1992; Ellis and Wang 1997; Wu 2005). Under these adverse conditions, families had little choice but to experiment with land-saving methods. Where they could, they added a second annual planting. They weeded more frequently, introduced high-yielding New World crops, and prepared more fertilizer. The form and timing of these extra efforts were regionally uneven, yet the pattern of intensification spread throughout the cores and then to the peripheries as peasants laboured to make up for shrinking acreage.

The most conspicuous form of intensification was the addition of a second annual crop. In north China varieties of legume were sown and harvested after spring wheat and immediately followed by sorghum or millet, to

very close to Ho (1959), who provides a population of 179 million by 1750, 353 million in 1820, and 429 million in 1850. Myers and Wang (2002) suggest 150 million in 1750, 353 million in 1820 and 380 million in 1850.

3 One mu is 0.6 acres or 0.243 hectares.

generate three harvests over two years (Huang 1985; Xu 1998). The peasants of the southern provinces, who benefited from a warmer and wetter climate, where able to harvest twice a year. By 1800 two annual rice harvests were the norm on paddies in Guangdong's most densely populated districts, while households in Jiangnan added spring wheat before paddy rice. Without the necessary farm capital improvements, however, there were limits to the spread of double cropping. Poor irrigation and drainage and a shortage of fertilizer limited the adoption of the three-in-two regime to two-fifths of cultivated area on the north China plain. In good years, this raised total grain output by only one-quarter (Huang 1985; Xu 1998). Despite the regions' permanent grain deficits, the wheat-rice regime covered no more than three-fifths of Jiangnan farmed land while in Guangdong double-rice cropping covered no more than half of the farmed area (Perkins 1969; Huang 1990; Shih 1992; Marks 1998).

Families in the cores found that the labour needed to plant and harvest more frequently was amply available at home since the time required to complete farming tasks fell with farm size. After a point, underemployment was endemic, especially in the core regions. Rural surveys conducted by John Lossing Buck in the 1920s, when demographic conditions were quite similar to the 1850s, suggest that 35 per cent of rural males farmed full time, 58 per cent did so part time, and 6 per cent went unemployed (Buck 1937). The long ascending demographic arc that extended back to the late seventeenth century, and before, not only generated underemployment among rural households but must have driven up the relative cost of capital. Peasants on smaller farms abandoned costlier tools such as seeders, carts, heavy ploughs, and mills (Buck 1937; Bray 1984; Marks 1998). They also saw a reduction in the number of heavy draft animals. By the 1800s the majority of Jiangnan farms could not support an ox and most north China farms were below the 20–50 mu needed to support a donkey (Huang 1985; 2002). In the heart of Jiangnan, around Lake Tai, hoe-ploughing was the norm in the eighteenth century, even though a ploughman with an ox performed the task nine times as fast (Shih 1992).

These more intensive farming systems required greater amounts of fertilizer. Across Guangdong, Jiangnan, and north China immense additional effort therefore went to gathering every conceivable compostable material, from grasses to canal sludge (Li 1984; Wen and Pimentel 1986a; 1986b; Ellis and Wang 1997; Huang 2002; Xue 2007). But neither crop yields nor total output responded in proportion to the overall increase in effort (Min 1984;

Huang 2005; Wu 2005; Shi 2017). In Jiangnan, where average rice yields stopped rising after 1800, the addition of wheat added only half as much output. In Guangdong and the middle Yangzi region a typical second rice planting yielded less than the first (Bray 1986; Marks 1998; Zhang 2014). The additions of labour, including those devoted to the preparation and spreading of fertilizer, did not raise yields significantly, or at all, but rather prevented them from falling as the land was planted more intensively and soil nutrients removed more quickly. Yet labour requirements certainly doubled or more in each of these examples, with the obvious implication of a decline in hourly output.

Households may have possessed means in farm equipment sufficient to survival, but this does not gainsay the improvements to labour output that would have accompanied the acquisition of more draft animals and heavier tools to speed up ploughing, planting, weeding, hoeing, and irrigating, or to power more carts, threshers, and mills (Bray 1984; 1986). But accumulation for investment in labour-saving capital required conditions that the demographic patterns did not provide. Capital and by implication fixed capital (farms, plant, and equipment) grew costly. Even in China's advanced zones the interest rate typically paid by peasants was very high, at 20–30 per cent per annum (Zhang 1996; Mazumdar 1998; Liu 2000; Peng 2008). Absent offsetting reductions in labour requirements by way of the introduction of labour-saving tools, it follows that rising farm output could only come at the price of static or falling labour productivity. Indeed, China experienced a fall of per capita output in agriculture across the eighteenth and nineteenth centuries, a decline in per capita output of calories, and a decline in well-being as measured by stature (Baten et al. 2010; Deng and O'Brien 2015; Shi 2017).

Peasant Colonization, Arbitrage Trade, and the Limits to Merchant Capital

The Qing empire's interior offered cheap land and the state promoted its settlement as a means to relieve mounting population pressure in the long-settled cores. Just as household formation strategies and their attending demographic pattern drove an involutionary dynamic of greater additions of labour for falling hourly returns, it spurred outmigration by the land-hungry to the frontiers, where the relative abundance of land sustained grain surpluses that returned to feed the otherwise overpopulated cores. By 1700, the importance of the inland grain surpluses to the populations of north

China, Jiangnan, and Guangdong was sufficiently evident that the state encouraged established merchants to profit on arbitrage opportunities, even lifting a trade ban put in place to pacify the coastal regions (Will 1990; Marks 1998; Isett 2007). The state continued to maintain granaries for the purposes of famine relief. But it relied entirely on merchants to make up for regular shortfalls, thereby fully incorporating them within its vision of proper statecraft. Given their politically necessary function, it is not surprising that merchant status improved. Anti-merchant prejudices continued, to be sure, but the state could not allow that to interfere with politically sensitive food supply. For their part, merchants sought gentry status by purchasing civil and military degrees and preparing their sons to sit the imperial exam. They also sought gentry investors in their trade, brokerage, and moneylending schemes (Chang 1962; Mann 1987; Qiao 2017). The blurring of social distinctions between merchants and gentry was partly a recognition of the role of merchants in the empire's maintenance and partly recognition by gentry of new opportunities to profit (Chang 1962). The fact that merchants and gentry secured much of their income politically made for an easy alliance between the two.

As noted, trade expansion was driven by demographic developments – but it was driven, more importantly, by the fact that demographic growth unfolded unevenly across regions. By 1790 the proportion of the total population that lived in the cores had fallen to 47 per cent, but it farmed only 28 per cent of the empire's arable land. The periphery's shares of population and arable land grew correspondingly to 53 and 72 per cent (Wang and Huang 1989). This immense imbalance fed trade as 136 million people living in districts with permanent grain deficits sought to import the grain they could not themselves grow (Myers and Wang 2002). By 1750, Jiangnan received one-fifth to one-quarter of its annual food needs from outside the region, while Guangdong imported half of the grain that it consumed (Chuan and Kraus 1975; Fan 1998; Marks 1998; Mazumdar 1998). The north China plain's poor ecology left that region especially susceptible to hunger and famine (Will 1990; Li 2007). Already engaged in the market in order to meet taxes and round out subsistence, peasants in these cores turned ever more intensively to cash crops and handicrafts in order to buy the grain they once produced (Huang 1985; 1990; Fang 1996; Mazumdar 1998).

Because merchants profited by buying cheap and selling dear they had to organize to control entry, otherwise excess competition would drive the price of their goods down to their costs. As trade grew they extended their associations, which they organized around commodities, services, and place to keep out competitors, fix prices, and capture and hoard surpluses (Mann 1987; Zhang 1996; Mazumdar 1998; Qiao 2017). Local government, which had long relied on merchant associations to maintain order in the marketplace, supported their efforts by limiting the number of brokers at major markets and recognizing their private association. In return, merchants were expected not only to maintain price stability but also to collect fees and taxes and to cover extraordinary expenses, including military campaigns, famine relief, and public works (Mann 1987; Will 1990; Mazumdar 1998). While the state saw merchant profits as the necessary cost of political stability, government officials privately collaborated with merchant brokers to pocket fees and irregular taxes (Chang 1962; Mann 1987). The Salt Gabelle and the Canton Hong were emblematic merchants in this regard. Granted state monopolies, they controlled key nodes in their respective trades in return for regular and irregular payments to the state and its functionaries. Though extraordinary in their social proximity to officialdom, they were not especially unusual in their reliance upon state power and political connections in garnering income.

The most successful merchant venturers of the Qing were arguably the Shanxi merchants. They rose on their ability to develop close political relationships with regional government and the state's recognition and protection of their trade. Excluded from established markets at the centre of the Qing empire by the power of incumbent merchant groups, petty traders and tradesmen from ecologically fragile Shanxi province travelled to Inner Asia where they acquired monopolies from a government desperate for supplies and services to support the backwater outpost of Hohot. From there the Shanxi merchants followed the Qing conquest of the steppes and, with the state's support, soon dominated the Mongol trade. As the Qing's inner Asian presence grew, the Shanxi merchants expanded into tax-farming, thereby profiting both from the collection of state revenue and that portion that came back to them in state purchases of their commodities. When the shortage of specie inhibited the Mongolian trade, they provided loans and then turned to their official connections to enforce repayment. They traded promissory notes, having received government permission to engage in quasi-banking activities. Finally, Shanxi merchants set themselves up at the centre of the empire, leveraging accumulated political connections and means to take charge of banking, lending, and commodity trade as far away as Jiangnan. Having relied upon the state for their rise, Shanxi merchants collapsed when the foundations of state power unravelled in the late nineteenth century (Qiao 2017).

With few exceptions, merchants preferred to profit on the circulation of commodities over investing and managing production (Fan 1998; Zurndorfer 2011). When merchant capital made its way into the hands of producers, it came at a cost that inhibited or even prevented ongoing accumulation. So long as the growth of trade rested, therefore, on the ability of peasants to eke out more with ever-greater inputs of labour, rather than equipping labourers with ever more capital tools, there were clear demographic limits to the system's overall expansion. By the early nineteenth century, these limits found their expression in the size of the surplus above subsistence in the two most important commodities. As late as the 1820s, only 12 per cent of all grain was traded and only half of all cotton cloth (Wu 1985; Xu and Wu 1990; Guo 1994). The countryside could support less than 7 per cent of the population in towns while no more than one in ten found full-time off-farm work. Even in advanced Jiangnan the off-farm workforce never exceeded one-sixth of the population (Rozman 1974; Skinner 1977; Xu 1992; Cao 2001; Wu 2005).

In the final analysis, the limits to the division of labour between town and country were established by the limits to the growth of the productivity of labour in agriculture. The towns of the Yangzi and the Pearl river deltas did not develop as centres of manufacturing production in response to rising demand for industrial products made possible in turn by rising agricultural productivity and lower grain prices. They emerged, on the contrary, as trans-shipment centres to house merchants who profited by growing grain imports from the periphery that were required to meet the subsistence needs of the population in the core in the face of the shortfalls of grain output there.

Alongside the growing number of merchants, a rising number of pawn shops offering high-interest loans to land-hungry peasants was established (Liu 2000). But in the absence of rising labour productivity that could make possible rising peasant incomes, the multiplication of pawnshops and the correspondingly increased supply of loans did little to reduce interest rates (Peng 2008). Peasants suffering from the declining availability of land had no choice but to step up their demand for land, pay the correspondingly higher price to acquire it, and endure whatever interest rate was necessary to afford it. They had to hold on to their plots to survive since they had nowhere else to go, so could not avoid paying whatever land price or interest rates the market demanded, and therefore had no alternative but to further intensify their labour and reduce their consumption.

In Jiangnan, the rate of interest perhaps fell from 30 to 20 per cent per annum (Hiyama 1996). Yet, because even at the new lower rate no manner of improvement in the means of production could afford repayment, peasants continued to take on debt simply to remain afloat (Pan 1996). As a consequence, those who might have been able to organize farming in a less costly manner by increasing their investments in more and better means of production and on a larger scale, found themselves continually outbid for land by the large pool of peasant families willing to compensate for lower efficiency and low rates of return on investment by intensifying labour and consuming less so as to pay higher land prices/high rents and take on higher debt if they wished to hold on to their subsistence plots in the absence of any alternative way of securing their survival (Huang 1990).

It was with a view to such limits on growth that the eighteenth-century state promoted colonization to relieve pressures on grain and other resources (Guo 1991). But, because peasants on the frontiers drew upon the market to reproduce existing patterns rather than embark on labour-saving improvements that would drive sustained growth in labour productivity, they found themselves having to bring ever-more marginal land under the plough, even clearing the hills (Ho 1959). Subject to abusive landlords and fragile ecologies, the hillside dwellers fuelled environmental degradation and filled bandit and rebel ranks. Meanwhile, grain surpluses shrank and grew less predictable as the physical limits of growth by colonization approached (Jiang 1992). Predictably, five decades or more of market integration stalled and then unravelled. First interregional markets disaggregated and after 1750 regional markets, as well, both gathering pace in the nineteenth century (Li 2007; Bernhofen et al. 2016). Driven by shortages in the grain market, relative prices turned against cash crops and household manufactures. By 1800, the limits of merchant domestic arbitrage trade were in sight, even if the main actors were not yet fully aware of its implications.

Domestic Manufacturing, Cash Cropping, and the Ongoing Extension of the Working Day

For those whose farms shrank below what was needed to provision the household with enough grain, there was some relief in putting underemployed household members freed up from farming grains to work planting cash crops and, more importantly, working up handicrafts (Myers 1972; Huang 1985; 1990). So long as grain prices were low relative to the commodities peasants could deliver, market exchange in conjunction with labour intensification proved sufficient to maintain standards of living. Had grain prices cheapened, all other things equal, households that planted cash crops or manufactured commodities would have enjoyed rising standards of living.

But, as we have seen, the terms of trade worsened for them as grain surpluses empire-wide grew less predictable and then shrank until, finally, those who took up cash cropping and domestic manufacturing to round out their subsistence found themselves having to work longer hours to grow and manufacture more just to compensate for falling hourly returns.

In Guangdong and Fujian, peasants who converted rice paddies to sugar cane in the eighteenth century, for example, found that even after growing sweet potatoes the returns from sugar were enough only to sustain households at a minimum. There was never sufficient savings to improve farming, upgrade sugar processing, and generally expand operations (Mazumdar 1998). Tools and methods remained entirely unchanged into the late nineteenth century (Daniels 1996). Peasants who grew tea did somewhat better in the eighteenth century, when rising global demand and a natural Chinese monopoly sustained prices. The appearance of Indian tea in the nineteenth century, however, undercut prices and harmed China's growers and processors. They responded to price punishment by lengthening the workday and accelerating the pace of work (Liu 2018). Annual production continued to grow until it reached 300 million lb, but this only weighed global prices down further. Low incomes and its corollary, cheap labour, again greatly hindered the introduction of cost-cutting technologies (Gardella 1994; Daniels 1996; Liu 2018). Those who planted mulberry trees and raised silk worms in order to stave off the deleterious effects of declining farm size fared poorly too (Wen and Pimentel 1986a; 1986b; Huang 1990; Shih 1992; Mazumdar 1998; Pomeranz 2000). Unable to purchase the specialized looms needed to weave silk, peasants were limited to low wage spinning. Hourly wages were far lower than if they had devoted this time to growing grains, meaning that it required many days of work to purchase a single day's consumption of food. Silk spinners were hit especially hard in the nineteenth century by a fall in domestic demand that exports failed to offset (Sun 1972).

The low set-up cost and the easy acquisition of skills needed to weave cotton cloth allowed millions of rural households to combine cotton spinning and weaving under one roof in the late imperial period. The domestic manufacture of cotton cloth spread to most of the empire, to pay taxes, clothe the household, and earn cash. The most optimistic studies show, however, that the daily earning of spinners was a considerable step down from farming. The returns on weaving were higher, but these fell in real terms as the price of grain rose. Between 1750 and 1800 the price of cloth measured against rice fell 20 per cent or more and by 1850 it had fallen by perhaps half (Xu 1992; Pomeranz 2000). It follows that households had to work twice as hard in 1850 just to acquire the same quantity of rice purchasable in 1750.

It is the character of modern economic growth that when prices fall producers lower their costs by investing in tools and equipment that increase hourly output. It is this process that leads to ever-greater production of value per worker. But Chinese rural households in the eighteenth and nineteenth century did not counter falling prices in this way because the cost of capital was high relative to the cheapness of their labour. Thus, cotton spinners did not take up the available and more efficient treadle-powered three-spindle wheel, with the exception *perhaps* of those in the eastern half of Jiangnan's Songjiang prefecture. More importantly, they never availed themselves of the five-spindle wheel (Dietrich 1972; Xu 1992). Similarly, weavers never replaced their low-technique back-strap looms with more productive though costlier draw looms (Hommel 1969; Dietrich 1972; Chao 1977). But most tellingly, households did not mechanize any part of the production process, despite vast and perhaps superior knowledge of harnessing water power: water wheels and gearing existed, but were not introduced to automate spinning or weaving by the peasants who continued to dominate production (Kuhn 1988).

The contrast with England, which experienced a much greater fall in both yarn and cloth prices over roughly the same period, is clear. English workers in the cotton industry were equipped with ever more capital, driving a fourteenfold increase in the hourly output of those manning the most advanced machines between 1780 and the 1820s. The same general pattern held in weaving, where average hourly worker output rose ninefold between 1820 and 1860 (Chapman 1972; Pollard 1981). As a result, the fall in both yarn and cloth prices was more than offset in England by rising labour productivity and falling per unit labour cost so that the contribution of cotton manufacturing to England's national income grew between 1750 and 1850. Much of this was achieved on the basis of simple water power, which remained the main motive force until 1830 (Farnie 1979).

Needless to say, the divergent patterns in Chinese and English cotton manufacturing after 1750 are apparent in the levels of productivity. By 1800 a typical Jiangnan hand-spinner needed 2,206 to 3,040 hours to produce what workers equipped with the English water-powered mules of the 1790s spun in 300 hours and the automatic mules of 1825 spun in 135 hours. If she were one of the rare few who worked a three-spindle wheel, then she still needed 1,612 hours to match (Chapman 1972; Chao 1977; Brown and Satterthwaite-Phillips 2018). England's productivity advantages in spinning were quickly replicated in weaving until the 242,000 workers employed in the English cotton industry *c.*1800 manufactured at least three times more cloth than the millions employed in Jiangnan (Chapman 1972; Farnie 1979; Xu 1992; Fan 1998; Pomeranz 2000).

China, including its advanced Yangzi Delta region, lost its technological lead to England in cotton manufacturing by the 1770s (Chao 1977). What accounts for this divergence was the very different dynamics that drove prices.[4] After 1770, China's cotton manufacturing regions felt the full effect of a demographic expansion set in motion in the 1680s. The coming exhaustion of the frontiers, in conjunction with the absence of rising labour productivity in agriculture generally, particularly among grain producers, conspired to push up basic food costs faster than the price of cotton yarn and cloth, until the relative hourly incomes of spinners and weavers fell. By contrast, the English home market grew in real terms between 1600 and 1800 as grain prices stabilized and fell relative to manufactures. This was possible because agricultural output per worker rose 60 per cent between 1600 and 1750 and 90 per cent between 1600 and 1800 (Overton 1996). Manufacturing correspondingly benefited from rising buying power in the lead-up to the Industrial Revolution, after which the technologically driven fall in the prices of manufactures were offset by continuous reductions in labour time (amount of labour required per unit of output) and England's improving terms of trade with continental grain growers (Thirsk 1984).

In the face of deteriorating prices, Jiangnan spinners and weavers would have been better off, needless to say, returning to full-time farming. But the same demographic dynamic that propelled them down what Pomeranz has called the proto-industrial dead end, of declining terms of trade and falling wages, prevented an easy *volte-face*. The return to farming required, after all, outlays of capital to build up farms and equipment that rural households did not possess. This was the flipside to cheapening wages in manufacturing. The remorseless destruction of farming capital, the exhaustion of the frontier, and mounting pressure on income conspired to make the cost of capital prohibitive. Absent the savings, and with plenty of unemployed family labour on hand, the best that most households could manage was to work more hours at the spinning wheel and loom to make up for worsening terms of trade (Dietrich 1972; Chao 1977; Fang 1996; Fan 1998).

4 On England's distinct path to industrialization, see Brenner and Isett (2002).

Divergent Endings

Comparative measurements of global performance place the beginnings of the great divergence in the sixteenth century, at which time England was one and a quarter times more productive per capita than China (Table 4.1A, 4.1B and Table 4.2). If we draw on Pomeranz's comparison of England to Jiangnan, we find that England in 1600 was more productive on a GDP per capita basis than Jiangnan's Huating district circa 1820 (Pomeranz 2000; Li and van Zanden 2012;

Table 4.1 Per capita GDP for China, Japan, and England 1500–1850

A. Indices (China in 1800=100)

	1500	1570	1600	1650	1700	1720	1750	1800	1820	1850
China	130	133	131		167	141	115	100	95	92
Huating county									165	
Japan			102			103		127		138
England	163	168	165	161	239		261	318	326	458

B. In 1990 international dollars

	1500	1570	1600	1650	1700	1720	1750	1800	1820	1850
England	1,068	1,096	1,077	1,055	1,563	1,605	1,710	2,080	2,133	2,997
Japan			667			675		828		903
China	852	873	859		1,089	925	749	654	623	600
Huating county									1,079	

Sources: China and England: Broadberry et al. (2018); Japan: Bassino et al. (2019); Huating county: Li and van Zanden (2012).

Table 4.2 Indices of output per worker in Chinese agriculture, 1600–1911 (1812=100)

	1600	1661	1685	1724	1766	1812	1850	1887	1911
Value of all agricultural goods	130	144	146	148	109	100	94	101	99
Value of grain	119	133	135	137	106	100	95	102	99

Source: Shi (2017).

Table 4.3 Comparing estimates of Chinese per capita GDP, 1600–1911 (1990 international dollars)

	1600	1661	1685	1700	1724	1766	1800	1812	1850	1887	1911
Broadberry et al.	859			1,089		749	654		600		
Xu		852	820		752	622		656	538	572	568

Sources: Broadberry et al. (2018); Xu et al. (2017).

Broadberry et al. 2018). Further comparisons show that per capita GDP in Japan surpassed China by 1800, well before the onset of the former's Meiji industrialization. Examined in isolation, Qing per capita GDP as well as agricultural output per capita stalled and then declined after 1700/1720 (Tables 4.2 and 4.3). It follows from this, that incomes in China including its advanced regions should also fall behind England. By the early nineteenth century, China's real GDP per capita was around one-third of the English level, and even in the relatively rich Huating county in the Yangzi delta it was only half the English level.

Why had such a vast gap opened by 1800? Because Chinese peasants could gain land without subjecting their families to the full discipline of the market, they could also avoid relying upon the unpredictable capacity of others to furnish their basic needs through exchange. In doing so, however, they necessarily grew higher cost low-margin crops. Initially, this was of no consequence insofar as these were intended for household consumption. Peasants sold surpluses in order to pay taxes and purchase items they could not procure directly, to be sure. But for households that came to depend more than minimally on the market because their holdings had shrunk below what was minimally needed, the path taken raised significant obstacles to expansionary developments. The customary practices in land and inheritance that pushed households more deeply into the market in order to make up for shortfalls in grain simultaneously fragmented and dissipated assets. The higher cost of capital (the cheapening of labour) propelled labour substitution that could only raise the carrying capacity of land at the cost of falling output per day insofar as investment in new equipment and tools was not possible.

The rise of population and the decline of farm assets in Jiangnan, Guangdong, and elsewhere would have pushed peasants to the wall but for the availability of land on the frontiers. The cheapness of that land relative to labour supported earlier migrants to build larger farms that produced grain surpluses. Though small on a per capita basis, these surpluses in the aggregate sustained those in the cores whose labour was cheap relative to their land. But continued demographic rebalancing in the eighteenth century ate away that surplus until the frontiers repaid the cores with higher grain prices and worsened trade terms for their manufactures. International outlets offered some respite, but as advances in production in other countries reduced costs in silk, tea, and sugar, earnings fell to subsistence levels and below in those sectors (Sun 1972; Gardella 1994; Mazumdar 1998).

The limitations of the Qing home market are apparent in the structure of economic output that showed no dynamic change in the nineteenth century (Ma and de Jong 2017). The pattern of combined and uneven growth by extension on the frontier and intensification in the cores supported the political order to 1800. Thereafter, that order faltered. Environmental degradation including hillside runoff increased the frequency and intensity of floods as well as crop failures (Marks 1998; Zhang 2014). Long-distance and regional grain markets unraveled at a quicker pace as the growth of grain exports from the middle and upper Yangzi River regions slowed (Jiang 1992; Bernhofen et al. 2016). Under economic duress, political control weakened in the face of dissident ideologies, a more distressed population willing to take up arms in revolt in larger and more destructive numbers, from the White Lotus Rebellion (1794–1804) to the Taiping Rebellion (1850–64), and foreign power incursions (Elvin 2004).

The contrast with neighbouring Japan could not be more stark. The uptick in rural prosperity that followed from rising labour productivity in the Japanese countryside after 1750, and the parallel appearance of a new social class (the *gono*), whose economic success was tied to the expansion of the home market, supported a constitutional revolution, the eventual consolidation of bourgeois rule, and the swift turning of the state to the task of supporting native industrialization (Smith 1959; Notehelfer 1990; Kwon 2002; Cohen 2015). China made no such transition. A depressed home market of poor rural households hamstrung late nineteenth-century efforts at industrialization. As it became evident that the throne no longer secured the interests of the gentry, in the face of internal rebellion and foreign incursions, sections of that elite deserted. But, with no nationally coherent equivalent to the *gono*, capable of seizing or pressuring the state towards a Meiji-style transformation, China was left in the early twentieth century politically fragmented, indebted, and easy prey.

References

Bassino, J.-P., Broadberry, S., Fukao, K., Gupta, B. and Takashima, M. (2019). 'Japan and the Great Divergence, 730–1874', *Explorations in Economic History*, 72, 1–22.

Baten, J., Ma, D., Morgan, S. and Wang, Q. (2010). 'Evolution of Living Standards and Human Capital in China in the 18th–20th Centuries: Evidences from Real Wages, Age-Heaping, and Anthropometrics', *Explorations in Economic History*, 47(3), 347–359.

Bernhofen, D., Eberhardt, M., Li, J. and Morgan, S. L. (2016). 'Assessing Market (Dis)Integration in Early Modern China and Europe', Centre for Economic Policy Research, Discussion Paper 11288.

Boserup, E. (1981). *Population and Technological Change: A Study of Long Term Trends*, Chicago: University of Chicago Press.

Bray, F. (1984). *Science and Civilisation in China: Agriculture*, Cambridge University Press.

(1986). *The Rice Economies: Technology and Development in Asian Societies*, Oxford: Blackwell.

Brenner, R. and Isett, C. (2002). 'England's Divergence from China's Yangzi Delta: Property Relations, Microeconomics, and Patterns of Economic Development', *Journal of Asian Studies*, 61, 609–662.

Broadberry, S. and Gupta, B. (2006). 'The Early Modern Great Divergence: Wages, Prices and Economic Development in Europe and Asia, 1500–1800', *Economic History Review*, 59, 2–31.

Broadberry, S., Guan, H. and Li, D. D. (2018). 'China, Europe, and the Great Divergence: A Study in Historical National Accounting', *Journal of Economic History*, 78, 955–1000.

Brown, M. J. and Satterthwaite-Phillips, D. (2018). 'Economic Correlates of Footbinding: Implications for the Importance of Chinese Daughters' Labor', PLOS ONE, doi.org/10.1371/journal.pone.0201337 (accessed September 29, 2020).

Bryant, J. (2006). 'The West and the Rest Revisited: Debating Capitalist Origins, European Colonialism, and the Advent of Modernity', *Canadian Journal of Sociology*, 4(31), 403–444.

Buck, J. L. (1937). *Land Utilization in China: Statistics*, Shanghai: University of Nanking Press.

Cao, S. (1997). *Zhongguo yimin shi: Qing-min shidai*, Fuzhou: Fujian renmin chuban she.

(2001). *Zhongguo renkoushi: Ming-Qing shiqi*, Shanghai, Fudan daxue chubanshe.

Chang, C. (1955). *The Chinese Gentry: Studies on their Role in Nineteenth-Century Chinese Society*, Seattle: Washington University Press.

(1962). *Income of the Chinese Gentry*, Seattle: Washington University Press.

Chao, K. (1977). *The Development of Cotton Textile Production in China*, Cambridge, MA: Harvard University Press.

Chapman, S. D. (1972). *The Cotton Industry in the Industrial Revolution*, London: Palgrave Macmillan.

Chuan, H-S. and Kraus, R. (1975). *Mid-Ch'ing Rice Markets and Trade: An Essay in Price History*, Cambridge, MA: Harvard University Press.

Cohen, M. (2015). 'Historical Sociology's Puzzle of the Missing Transitions: A Case Study of Early Modern Japan', *American Sociology Review*, 80(3), 603–625.

Daniels, C. (1996). *Science and Civilisation in China: Agro-Industries and Forestry*, Cambridge University Press.

Deng, K. and O'Brien, P. (2015). 'Nutritional Standards of Living in England and the Yangtze Delta (Jiangnan), circa 1644–circa 1840: Clarifying Data for Reciprocal Comparisons', *Journal of World History*, 26(2), 233–267.

Dietrich, C. (1972). 'Cotton Culture and Manufacture in Early Ch'ing China', in Willmott, W. E. (ed.), *Economic Organization in Chinese Society*, Stanford University Press.

Ellis, E. C. and Wang, S. M. (1997). 'Sustainable Traditional Agriculture in the Tai Lake Region of China', *Agriculture, Ecosystems and Environment*, 60, 177–193.

Elman, B. (1992). 'Political, Social, and Cultural Reproduction via Civil Service Examination in Late Imperial China', *Journal of Asian Studies*, 50(1), 7–28.

(2000). *A Cultural History of Civil Examinations in Late Imperial China*, Berkeley: University of California Press.

Elvin, M. (2004). *The Retreat of the Elephants: An Environmental History of China*, New Haven: Yale University Press.

Fan, J. (1998). *Ming-Qing Jiangnan shangye de fazha*, Nanjing daxue chubanshe.

Fang, X. (1996). 'Qingdai jiangnan nongmin de xiaofei', *Zhongguo jingji shi yanjiu*, 3, 91–98.

Farnie, D. A. (1979). *English Cotton Industry and the World Market: 1815–1896*, Oxford University Press.

Frank, A. G. (1998). *ReOrient: Global Economy in the Asian Age*, Berkeley: University of California Press.

Gao, W. (2005). *Zudian guanxi xinlun: dizhu, nongmin, han dizu*, Shanghai shudian chuban she.

Gardella, R. (1994). *Harvesting Mountains: Fujian and the China Tea Trade, 1757–1937*, Berkeley: University of California Press.

Guo, S. (1991). 'Qing chu shehui jingji yu Qing zhengfu de tunken zhengce', in Yuquan, W. (ed.), *Zhongguo tunken shi*, Beijing: Nongye chubanshe.

(1994). 'Qingdai liangshi shichang he shangpin liang shuliang de guce', *Zhongguo shi yanjiu*, 4, 40–49.

Hiyama, M. (1996). 'Shindai tentō-gyō no rishi-ritsu ni kansuru ichikōsatsu – Kōki ~ kenryū-ki no Kōnan o chūshin to shite', *Tōhō-Gaku*, 91, 76–89.

Ho, P. (1959). *Studies on the Population of China, 1368–1953*, Cambridge, MA: Harvard University Press.

Hommel, R. (1969). *China at Work: An Illustrated Record of the Primitive Industries of China's Masses, Whose Life is Toil, and Thus an Account of Chinese Civilization*, Cambridge, MA: MIT Press.

Hong, P. (2005). *Mingdai yilai Taihu nan'an xiangcun shehui de jingji yu shehui bianqian: Yi Wujiang xian wei zhongxin*, Beijing: Zhonghua shuju.

Huang, P. C. (1985). *The Peasant Economy and Social Change in North China*, Stanford University Press.

(1990). *The Peasant Family and Rural Development in the Yangzi Delta, 1350–1988*, Stanford University Press.

(1996). *Civil Justice in China: Representation and Practice in the Qing*, Stanford University Press.

(2002). 'Development or Involution in Eighteenth Century Britain and China? A Review of Kenneth Pomeranz's The Great Divergence: China, Europe, and the Making of the Modern World Economy', *Journal of Asian Studies*, 61(2), 501–538.

Isett, C. (2007). *State, Peasant, and Merchant on the Manchurian Frontier*, Stanford University Press.

Jiang, J. (1992). *Qingdai qianqi migu maoyi yanjiu*, Beijing University Press.

Jiang, T., Jinyu, W. and Xing, F. (2000). *Zhongguo jingji tongshi: Qingdai jingji juan* 3, edited by Xin, F., Junjian, J. and Jinyu, W., Beijing: Jingji ribao chubanshe.

Kishimoto, M. (1997). 'Min-Shin jittai no okeru 'zhaojia huishu' mondai', *Chûgoku shakai to bunka*, 12, 263–293.

Kuhn, D. (1988). *Science and Civilisation in China Volume 5. Chemistry and Chemical Technology, Part 9. Textile Technology: Spinning and Reeling*, edited by Needham, J., Cambridge University Press.

Kwon, G. (2002). *State Formation, Property Relations, and the Development of the Tokugawa Economy, 1600–1868*, London: Routledge.

Li, B. (1984). 'Ming Qing shiqi jiangnan shuidao shengchan jiyue chengdu de tigao', *Zhongguo nongshi*, 15(1), 1–14.

Li, B. and van Zanden, J. L. (2012). 'Before the Great Divergence? Comparing the Yangzi Delta and the Netherlands at the Beginning of the Nineteenth Century', *Journal of Economic History*, 72(4), 956–989.

Li, L. (2007). *Fighting Famine in North China: State, Market, and Environmental Decline, 1690s–1990s*, Stanford University Press.

Liu, A. (2018). *Tea War: A History of Capitalism in China and India*, 1834–1939. Unpublished manuscript.

Liu, Q. (2000). *Ming-Qing gaoli dai ziben*, Bejing: Shehui kexue wenxian chuban she.

Ma, Y. and de Jong, H. D. (2017). 'Unfolding the Turbulent Century: A Reconstruction of China's Historical National Accounts, 1840–1912', *Review of Income and Wealth*, 65(1), 75–98.

Maddison, A. (2007). *Contours of the World Economy 1–2030 AD: Essays in Macro-Economic History*, Oxford University Press.

Mann, S. (1987). *Local Merchants and the Chinese Bureaucracy*, Stanford University Press.

Marks, R. (1998). *Tigers, Rice, Silk, and Silt: Environment and Economy in Late Imperial South China*, Cambridge University Press.

Mazumdar, S. (1998). *Sugar and Society in China: Peasants, Technology, and the World Market*, Cambridge, MA: Harvard University Press.

Min, Z. (1984). 'Song, Ming, Qing shiqi Taihu diqu shuidao muchan liang de tantao', *Zhongguo nongshi*, 3, 37–52.

Myers, R (1970). *The Chinese Peasant Economy: Agricultural Development in Hopei and Shantung, 1890–1940*, Cambridge, MA: Harvard University Press.

(1972). 'The Commercialization of Agriculture in Modern China', in Willmott, W. E. (ed.), *Economic Organization in Chinese Society*, Stanford University Press, 173–191.

Myers, R. and Wang, Y. (2002). 'Economic Developments, 1644–1800', in Peterson, W. (ed.), *The Cambridge History of China: The Ch'ing Empire to 1800*, vol. 9, part 1, Cambridge University Press, 563–645.

Notehelfer, F. D. (1990). 'Meiji in the Rear-View Mirror: Top Down and Bottom Up History', *Monumenta Nipponica*, 45(2), 207–228.

Overton, M. (1996). *Agricultural Revolution in England: The Transformation of the Agrarian Economy 1500–1850*, Cambridge University Press.

Oyama, M. (1986). 'Large Landownership in the Jiangnan Delta Region During the Late Ming-Early Qing Period', in Grove, L. and Daniels, C. (eds.), *State and Society in China: Japanese Perspectives on Ming-Qing Social and Economic History*, Tokyo University Press, 101–163.

Pan, M. (1996). 'Rural Credit and the Concept of "Peasant Petty Commodity Production" in Ming-Qing Jiangnan', *Journal of Asian Studies*, 55 (1), 94–117.

Peng, K., Zhiwu, C. and Weipeng, Y. (2008). 'Jindai zhongguo nongcun jiedai shichang de jizhi', *Jingji yanjiu*, 5, 147–159.

Perkins, D. (1969). *Agricultural Development in China, 1368–1968*, Chicago: Aldine Publishing Company.

Pollard, S. (1981). *Peaceful Conquest: The Industrialization of Europe, 1760–1970*, Oxford University Press.

Pomeranz, K. (2000). *The Great Divergence: Europe, China, and the Making of the Modern World Economy*, Princeton University Press.

(2002). 'Beyond the East-West Binary: Resituating Development Paths in the Eighteenth-century World', *Journal of Asian Studies*, 61(2), 539–590.

Qiao, Z. (2017). 'The Rise of Shanxi Merchants: Empire, Institutions, and Social Change in Qing China', unpublished Ph.D. thesis, Stanford University.

Rawski, E. S. (1972). *Agricultural Change and the Peasant Economy of South China*, Cambridge, MA: Harvard University Press.

Rowe, W. (2001). *Saving the World: Chen Hongmou and Elite Consciousness in Eighteenth-century China*, Stanford University Press.

Rozman, G. (1974). *Urban Networks in Ch'ing China and Tokugawa Japan*, Princeton University Press.

Schurmann, F. H. (1956). 'Traditional Property Concepts in China', *Far Eastern Quarterly*, 15 (4), 507–516.

Shi, Z. (2017). *Agricultural Development in Qing China: A Quantitative Study, 1661–1911*, Leiden: Brill.

Shih, J. C. (1992). *Chinese Rural Society in Transition: A Case Study of the Lake Tai Area, 1368–1800*, Berkeley: University of California Press.

Skinner, W. (1977). 'Introduction: Urban Development in Imperial China', in Skinner, W. (ed.), *The City in Late Imperial China*, Stanford University Press.

Smith, T. (1959). *The Agrarian Origins of Modern Japan*, Stanford University Press.

Sun, E. Z. (1972). 'Sericulture and Silk Textile Production in Ch'ing China', in Willmott, W. E. (ed.), *Economic Organization in Chinese Society*, Stanford University Press, 79–108.

Thirsk, J. (1984). *The Rural Economy of England*, London: Hambledon Press.

Wakefield, D. (1998). *Fenjia: Household Division and Inheritance in Qing and Republican China*, Honolulu: University of Hawai'i Press.

Wang, Y. (1973). *Land Taxation in Imperial China, 1750–1911*, Cambridge, MA: Harvard University Press.

Wang, Y. and Guoshu, H. (1989). 'Shiba shiqi zhong zhongguo liangshi gongxu de kaochao', in *Jindai zhongguo nongcun jingji shi lunwenji*, Taipei: Academia Sinica.

Wen, D. and Pimentel, D. (1986a). 'Seventeenth Century Organic Agriculture in China: I. Cropping Systems in Jiaxing Region', *Human Ecology*, 14(1), 1–14.

(1986b). 'Seventeenth Century Organic Agriculture in China: II. Energy Flows through an Agroecosystem in Jiaxing Region', *Human Ecology*, 14(1), 15–28.

Will, P-E. (1990). *Bureaucracy and Famine in Eighteenth-Century China*, Stanford University Press.

Wolf, A. P. and Engelen, T. (2008). 'Fertility and Fertility Control in Pre-Revolutionary China', *Journal of Interdisciplinary History*, 38(3), 345–375.

Wong, R. B. (1997). *China Transformed: Historical Change and the Limits of European Experience*, Ithaca: Cornell University Press.

Wu, C. (1985). 'Lun Qingdai qianqi woguo guonei shichang', *Lishi yanjiu*, 1, 96–106.

Wu, J. (2005). *Ming Qing Jiangnan renkou shehui shi yanji*, Beijing: Qunyan chuban she.

Xu, T. (1998). *Qingdai qianzhong qi de yan hai maoyi yu Shandong bandao jingji de fazhan*, Beijing: Zhongguo shehui jingji shi yanjiu.

Xu, X. (1992). *Jiangnan tubu shi*, Shanghai shehui kexue chuban she.

Xu, X. and Wu, C. (1990). *Jiu minzhu zhuyi geming shiqi de zhongguo zibenzhuyi*, Beijing: Renmin chubanshe.

Xu, Y., Shi, Z., van Leeuwen, B., Yuping, N., Zhang, Z. and Ma, Y. (2017). 'Chinese National Income, ca. 1661–1933', *Australian Economic History Review*. 57(3), 368–393.

Xue, Y. (2007). 'A Fertilizer Revolution?: A Critical Response to Pomeranz's Theory of Geographic Luck', *Modern China*, 33(2), 195–229.

Yang, G. (1988). *Ming-Qing tudi qiyue wenshu yanjiu*, Beijing: Renmin chuban she.

Zhang, J. (2014). *Coping with Calamity: Environmental Change and Peasant Response in Central China, 1736–1949*, Vancouver: University of British Columbia Press.

Zhang, Z. (1996). *Qian jindai zhongguo shehui de shangren ziben yu shehui zaishengchan*, Shanghai: sheke xueyuan chuban she.

Zhou, Y. and Zhaohua, X. (1986). *Qingdai zudian zhi yanjiu*, Shenyang: Liaoning renmin chuban she.

Zurndorfer, H. T. (2011). 'Cotton Textile Manufacturing and Marketing in Late Imperial China and the "Great Divergence"', *Journal of the Economic and Social History of the Orient*, 54, 701–738.

5

From the Mughals to the Raj: India 1700–1858[1]

ANAND V. SWAMY

Introduction

In the year 1700 the Mughals controlled much of the Indian subcontinent. By 1858 the British Crown did. In the intervening period a range of political regimes came and went, from relatively well-governed and compact 'successor' (to the Mughals) states to states whose viability depended on warfare and extraction of tribute. And in this mix there was a peculiar hybrid entity that was part British and part Indian, part trader and part state, part 'private' and part British-Crown-controlled: The English East India Company (henceforth EIC or just Company). So an essay on the economic history of the period 1700–1858 has to foreground politics. It follows that a natural way to write it is to focus on the role of the state in promoting or undermining economic development. I will discuss four dimensions of state activity. Do they provide minimal public goods, such as law and order, so that economic activity can occur? Do they go further and provide public goods such as roads and irrigation? Do they tax so heavily as to suppress economic activity? Do they support or undermine trade and manufacturing?

Discussion of these issues will, hopefully, also shed light on the big questions that have dominated the historiography. Was the eighteenth century in India really a 'dark age' or was it a period of continued economic growth? Was the EIC's rule 'extractive'? Did colonial rule 'deindustrialize' India? Where does India fit in the Great Divergence?

I divide our period into three parts. In the first part, 1700–1765, the Mughals declined and regional powers gained strength. By 1765 the EIC was one such regional power. In the second, 1765–1818, the EIC went from being an

1 I thank Sudiksha Joshi and Rehaan Vij for research assistance. Other contributors to Volume I, especially its editors and Tirthankar Roy, provided helpful comments. Any errors are my responsibility.

important regional power to being the dominant political entity on the subcontinent. From 1818 to 1858 the Company completed its transition from being a trader to being an arm of the Crown, and consolidated British rule in India. The remainder of this chapter follows this chronology. I begin the next section by describing what the Mughal Empire looked like in its heyday. This description is essential to understanding why it declined, and what the consequences were.

The Mughals, Their Decline, and the Emergence Of Regional States: 1700–1765[2]

The Mughal State

The high point of the Mughal Empire is often identified with the rule of Akbar (1556–1605), who is credited with systematizing and rationalizing land taxation, the key source of governmental income. A small group of elite officials (*mansabdars*) was responsible for tax collection. They were paid salaries or remunerated by being given the tax revenues for a fixed area. The privilege of being a *mansabdar* came with the obligation to provide a specified number of troops. These elite noblemen were a small group, a maximum of 8,000 in one account (Pearson 1976: 221). They had to operate through a class of people closer to the ground, with local political authority, known as *zamindars*. The word *zamindar* is perhaps one of the most confusing in Indian economic history because it covers a very wide variety of types. *Zamindars* had the right to collect taxes and might also have had military obligations. Some were practically independent rulers, simply paying tribute to the Mughal emperor. At the other extreme a *zamindar* may have been what we today call a landlord. There may have been other intermediaries between the *zamindar* and the actual cultivator.

Most scholars of the Mughal Empire would probably agree with the above description. But there are two fiercely competing views on how decentralized and 'commercialized' the Mughal Empire was, and following from this, differing understandings of why it declined and the impact of this on the economy of eighteenth-century India.

2 There has been a great deal of research on the politics of the eighteenth century. Several edited collections with useful introductions can guide the reader through the literature. These include Alam and Subrahmanyam (1998), Alavi (2002), Marshall (2003) and Bhargava (2014). Roy (2013b) provides an insightful overview of the eighteenth century from the perspective of the economic historian. Subramanian (2010) is a concise history of India over the period 1707–1857, in textbook format.

The Aligarh School

In the work of Irfan Habib and others of the 'Aligarh School', the central tension in the Mughal Empire came from its desire to extract high levels of land taxes. Raychaudhuri (1982: 172) writes: '[T]he uncomplicated desire of a small ruling class for more and more material resources – an almost primitive urge to consume and acquire – was beyond doubt the primary condition on which the empire established itself.' He adds (173): 'The Mughal state was an insatiable Leviathan.' This meant, first, that the Mughals were always looking to expand the empire and seek revenues from new sources. It also meant that *zamindars* and peasants would be pressured to pay more, which sometimes provoked peasant and *zamindar* revolts. For the Aligarh School, this was the ultimate undoing of the empire.

In Habib's description, the state's revenue extraction was so successful that it permitted the noblemen to live in great luxury in substantial cities, alongside merchant communities as well as 'professionals'. Though the economy was largely agricultural, other sectors were also significant, such as iron mining, sericulture (in Bengal), and, of course, textiles. Habib estimates (1997: 90) that as much as 15 per cent of the population was urban. Much of trade was overland, and transportation was costly. The risks associated with trade, as reflected in insurance rates, were low. Money could be transferred across regions via *hundis*, bills of exchange, drawn on prominent bankers. The potential for innovation or technological change was limited, and 'the distance between India and Europe in this realm was much greater in, say, 1700, than it was in 1500' (Habib 1997: 97).

The Aligarh School views the eighteenth century as a period in which the Mughal model fell apart. Revenue extraction became difficult because of resistance from peasants and *zamindars*, especially as the empire became militarily overextended. The empire was also challenged by new regional powers, especially the Sikhs and the Marathas (see below). The collapse of the Mughals lead to anarchy and the EIC, a new and radically different political and economic entity, took advantage of the chaos and established its power.

The Revisionists

The Aligarh School has been challenged by various scholars whom Ali (1993) describes collectively as 'revisionists'. This perspective is exposited elegantly in the introduction to Alam and Subrahmanyam (1998). The revisionists view the Mughal Empire as much less centralized. They also argue that the Mughal fiscal and administrative system was not nearly as uniform as a reader of the *Ain-i-Akbari*, the famous survey commissioned by Akbar, might imagine. As the Mughals expanded the area under their control, they took their land tax terminology with them, but the actual methods of revenue collection and the position of agrarian elites changed very little, and the position of the cultivator even less. The Mughal emperor might have been all-powerful close to the capital city, but in the outer regions *zamindars* might have retained considerable autonomy.[3] The revisionists also assign greater social and political power to the merchant/creditor community, and emphasize the importance of trade, both domestic and international, as sources of government revenue (Leonard 1979: 429).

Given their view of the Mughal Empire as a looser, less centralized entity, it follows that the revisionists also take a different view of its decline. They see, within the Mughal Empire, an unfolding process of commercialization and decentralization of the economy as well as of politics. For instance, there was an increase in revenue-farming, which took a state function, tax collection, and turned it into a purchasable right. Of the early eighteenth century Bayly (1992: 459) writes 'it is better to think of decentralization or commercialization of power within the Mughal polity than of anarchy'.[4] Successor states like Bengal and Awadh were the logical end of this process; they were Mughal provinces that slowly broke away. They were (according to the revisionists) administered effectively and created environments in which agriculture could expand and trade and financial markets flourished. Indeed it has been argued that one of the causes of the Mughal decline was that the great banking firms abandoned them for their regional rivals.[5] Finally, the revisionists see the EIC as an especially successful participant in the flourishing trade and credit networks of the eighteenth century commercial world; in that sense colonial rule represented continuity rather than rupture.

The Mughal Decline: Anarchy or Prosperity?

How could India in the eighteenth century seem a picture of anarchy to some, but continuity and even prosperity to others? Partly, it depends on when and where one looks. The decline of Mughal power was fairly quick; it was greatly undermined by the 1750s. However, its moral and symbolic authority was such that even as different sections of the empire broke away, they continued to pay nominal allegiance to it, and send at least

3 Guha (2015) has described the gap between Mughal land revenue systems on paper and in practice.

4 He is referring to North India, but the point has been made more generally.

5 See Leonard (1979).

some revenues to the emperor. Bengal is a good example of this. In the early eighteenth century the amount of revenue sent to Delhi declined, and decision-making became more independent. But even in (say) 1750, when the nawab (governor) of Bengal was effectively an independent ruler, he still acknowledged the authority of the Mughal emperor. Similarly, when the EIC conquered Bengal, technically it just became the diwan (finance minister) of the Mughal emperor. The slow disentangling meant that the extent of violence and warfare was low. So economic activity was not seriously disrupted.

This picture was considerably complicated by the rise of groups like the Sikhs (in Punjab) and Marathas (in western India) who directly confronted the Mughals militarily and ideologically, drawing on different notions of religious community (Alam and Subrahmanyam 1998). The early and charismatic Maratha leader Shivaji (1630–80) began as a military commander and landholder in Bijapur, a non-Mughal sultanate in the western Deccan. The Marathas' forte was guerilla warfare. Their cavalry was very effective against the ponderous Mughal armies, whose leaders needed luxury even when marching to battle.[6] The Marathas expanded quickly and by the 1730s they were centred on their capital city, Pune, in western India in present-day Maharashtra. The de facto ruler was the minister (peshwa) to the king. The Marathas' own domains appear to have been administered along the lines of the Mughal model, with systematic procedures, record-keeping, etc. Pune could boast of wealthy banker-financiers who operated on a large scale. This was not anarchy by any measure. But the Marathas were a 'confederacy' with the peshwa at the centre. Other Maratha leaders operating in northern and central India continued the tradition of guerilla warfare. The Marathas 'raided' across northern, central and eastern India, and went as far as western Bengal. They extorted substantial payments.[7] According to Dutch sources the Marathas may have killed as many as 400,000 people in western Bengal (Marshall 1987: 73). We can understand the use of the word 'anarchy' in this context.

What was the economic impact of the Maratha raids? It is difficult to find quantitative evidence, but there is a hint in the figures for the EIC's textile

6 According to Stewart Gordon (1998: 37), 'In the seventeenth century, a main-force army . . . was a moving city.'

7 Notionally, the Marathas demanded a fourth of the land taxes (*chauth*) and another 10% called *sardeshmukhi*. In 1751 the nawab of Bengal promised the Marathas an annual sum of 1,200,000 rupees and 'the virtual cession of Orissa' as the price of peace (Marshall 1987: 80).

Table 5.1 Taxes assigned and collected, Bihar 1685–1750

Year	Tax collected in rupees	Tax collected as percentage of tax assigned
1685	8,517,683	86.39
1687–95	9,325,551	91.61
1709	9,305,431	91.41
1750	10,079,141	75.93

Source: Alam (1991: 187).

exports from Bengal. The number of pieces exported annually was 0.6 million in 1730–34 and 1740–45, but fell to 0.39 million in 1750–55.[8] This decline was at least partly due to the disruption caused by the Maratha raids into western Bengal. Even Chaudhury (1995: 190), who underplays the disruption caused by the Marathas, notes that 'the procurement of ordinary calicoes . . . which were produced mainly in Birbhum, Burdwan, and Kasimbazar areas became extremely difficult from around the mid-1740s because of the Maratha invasions'. The evidence from the important Gujarati port city of Surat is clearer. Conflict between the Mughals and the Marathas, among others, reduced trade volumes in 1750 to one-third of what they had been in 1700.[9]

It would be useful to find regional evidence on agricultural output or acreage in the eighteenth century, but there is very little to go by. The widely cited works by Muzaffar Alam (1986; 1991) suggest a contrast between Punjab, where political change was highly disruptive and Bihar, in eastern India. However, his quantitative evidence is merely the land tax collected by the Mughals, for periods that are not defined precisely. For Punjab, he reports (1986: 183) a substantial decline in the annual land tax collected from 20 million rupees in the seventeenth century to 12.5 million in Muhammad Shah's reign (1719–48). In Bihar, on the other hand, the tax collected went up slightly between the seventeenth century and 1750 (Table 5.1). For the period 1700–1722, Prakash (2002: 140) reports that the revenue collected in Bengal increased from 11.7 million rupees to 14.1 million rupees. There are two difficulties in interpreting these numbers. One is that they are nominal, and we don't know what correcting for inflation would do.[10] The other problem

8 The first figure is from Chaudhury (1995: 180), and the next from page 188.

9 This estimate is by Dasgupta (1970: 383), who cautions that 'all figures should be viewed with skepticism'.

10 The authors usually argue that prices did not change much, so the qualitative implication is valid. See Prakash (1998: 140).

Table 5.2 Population, GDP, and per capita GDP, India 1600–1871 (1871 = 100)

Year	GDP	Population	PCY
1600	71.9	55.5	129.7
1650	67.3	55.5	121.2
1700	75.7	64.1	118.2
1750	81.3	74.2	109.6
1801	87.5	80.9	108.2
1811	82.9	84	98.8
1821	79.2	80.1	98.9
1831	81.8	84.4	97
1841	87.3	82.8	105.5
1851	95.9	90.6	105.8
1861	95.6	95.3	100.3
1871	100	100	100

Source: Broadberry et al. (2015: 69).

is that if the unrest of the period was driven by conflict between the state and *zamindar* and peasant, a decline in tax collection does not necessarily reflect worsening economic conditions – it could just be that the peasants and *zamindars* kept more of the output. Conversely, an increase in tax collection might just reflect a more effective tax administration, rather than higher income or productivity.

In aggregate figures provided by Broadberry et al. (2015), the population of what came to be British India plus the princely states (modern India, Pakistan, and Bangladesh) grew roughly 15 per cent between 1650 and 1700 (see Table 5.2).[11] For the next 50 years, when the Mughal Empire unravelled, the population again increased 15 per cent. Broadberry et al. (2015) estimate that GDP grew a bit slower than population over the period 1700–50, so that an index number for per capita GDP (with base 1871 = 100) fell slightly, from 118.2 to 109.6 (Table 5.2). This performance is not consistent with the view that the decline of the Mughals was an economic calamity. Nor does it suggest economic prosperity. It is consistent with a story in which warfare and insecurity substantially undermined economic activity in some regions, whereas most other regions were only slightly affected, if at all. Thus far we have discussed trends within India in the eighteenth century. But what about

11 $(64.1 - 55.5)/55.5 = 0.15$.

levels? How does India in (say) 1750 look compared to the wealthy countries at the time?

Real Wages and Per Capita Income in India, c.1750, in Comparative Perspective

Much of the work to date suggests that real wages and per capita income in the eighteenth century were much lower in India, as compared to Britain. Roy (2010: 187) shows that per capita income in Bengal (measured in pounds or in silver) in 1763 was one-fifteenth of that in England and Wales. Per capita income expressed in grain equivalents was approximately one-fifth of that in England. Allen (2007) collected a large sample of wages and found that an adult man's wage in India would just about purchase one minimum subsistence bundle for an Indian family, whereas it would buy more than two (in Oxford) or even four (in London). Broadberry and Gupta (2006) argue that it is essential to compare worker productivity in the advanced (traded) sector, textiles. Trade should have equalized silver price of cloth between Britain and India. The silver wage in each country would have reflected worker productivity in textiles. The fact that the silver wage was much lower in India reflects the lower productivity of the Indian textile worker, a key marker that the Great Divergence had already occurred by the eighteenth century (see Table 5.3A).

Parthasarathi (1998) takes a different approach, and focuses on the 'grain wage'. He finds that, in south India, the grain wage was as high as in the rich parts of Europe, meaning Indian workers had similar access to food. Allen (2007) has compared Parthasarathi's wage data to his larger sample and finds they are unusually high.[12] Broadberry and Gupta (Table 5.3B) also find lower grain wages in India as compared to England, going as far back as the sixteenth century. The debate is by no means over, though. As Studer (2015) has shown, product markets in eighteenth century India were fragmented. It may well be that there were high-wage regions which all these scholars missed. I briefly discuss one such possibility, identified by Sivramkrishna (2009) for a slightly later period, below.

The most important long consequence of warfare and political unrest was not the destruction of assets. It was the emergence of the EIC as a regional state, with its conquest of Bengal in the Battle of Plassey (1757) and Battle of Baksar (1764). How did this come to be?

12 Measured in silver, they were approximately twice as high as the wages in the rest of Allen's sample. See his regression analysis, and discussion, pp. 16–17.

Table 5.3 Silver and grain wages of unskilled labourers in England and India 1550–1849

A. Silver wages (grams of silver per day)

Date	Southern England	India	Indian wage as % of English wage
1550–99	3.4	0.7	21
1600–49	4.1	1.1	27
1650–99	5.6	1.4	25
1700–49	7.0	1.5	21
1750–99	8.3	1.2	14
1800–49	14.6	1.8	12

B. Grain wages (kilograms of grain per day)

Date	England (wheat)	India (wheat)	(rice, on wheat equivalent basis)	Indian wage as % of English wage
1550–99	6.3	5.2		83
1600–49	4.0	3.8		95
1650–99	5.4	4.3		80
1700–49	8.0		3.2	40
1750–99	7.0		2.3	33
1800–49	8.6	2.5		29

Source: Broadberry and Gupta (2006: 17).

The EIC Becomes a Regional Power

The nawab (Mughal governor) of Bengal had to raise substantial resources to buy peace with the Marathas when they raided western Bengal in the 1740s. He had to get this money from the merchants, financiers, and *zamindars* of Bengal, and even the EIC. This weakened the nawab's political support. The nawab had also long been at odds with the Company regarding exactly what trading privileges the Mughal emperor had given it in a decree in 1717; the Company's interpretation was, of course, more expansive than the nawab's. After the death of Alivardi Khan, when a new and capricious nawab, Siraj-ud-Daulah, went to war with the Company in 1757, there was little support for him. The most important merchant-financiers of Bengal sided with the Company. Much of the nawab's army was bought off. After installing puppet regimes, the Company finally went to war again in 1764. This time the nawab of Bengal was joined by the nawab of Awadh, but the Company prevailed again. As mentioned earlier, nominally it became diwan (finance minister) of Bengal, but in fact it was now the ruling political power in Bengal.

Over the next fifty or so years the Company encountered more formidable military opponents, the Marathas, and the south Indian state of Mysore. Armies needed to be financed. This provided an incentive for all states, including the EIC in Bengal, to become more efficient at collecting taxes. It also gave them a reason to promote economic growth. The next section will look at how this played out in the period 1765–1818.

The Regional States, 1765–1818

The Company-State's Early Years: Corruption and Extraction

Bengal was one of the largest and richest provinces of Mughal India. After 1765, the Company had to administer it. Its first task in governance was the same as for any other regional state: taxation. The task was challenging because there were layers of intermediaries between the state and the actual cultivator. But there was also an internal challenge: the Company's administration in India was not structured like a state. It had governed three important port cities (Bombay, Calcutta, Madras), but ruling Bengal, with its population of 30 million, was a much greater challenge (see Figure 5.1).

One problem was lack of knowledge of local conditions. Land tenures in Bengal were complex and varied across even small distances. The Company tried as its first step to leave tax collection to the administrative structure it had inherited from the nawab. This was not a viable option in the changed political circumstances, and after 1772, the Company had to take over tax collection as well as other administrative functions.

Another issue was that the Company's officers were also freelance entrepreneurs. They were permitted to trade on their own account. This created conflicts of interest; an officer might have been more interested in acquiring goods for his private trade rather than for the Company. There was also the issue of 'corruption'. The Company's senior-most officials, including Clive, the hero of the Battle of Plassey, took enormous gifts from competing political factions in Bengal in the period leading up to 1765.

The Company also faced pressure from its shareholders. Bengal was considered a great prize; surely, they would get some returns from this. The most straightforward way for this to happen was for the Company to change how it procured the textiles it sold in Europe. Henceforth, they would

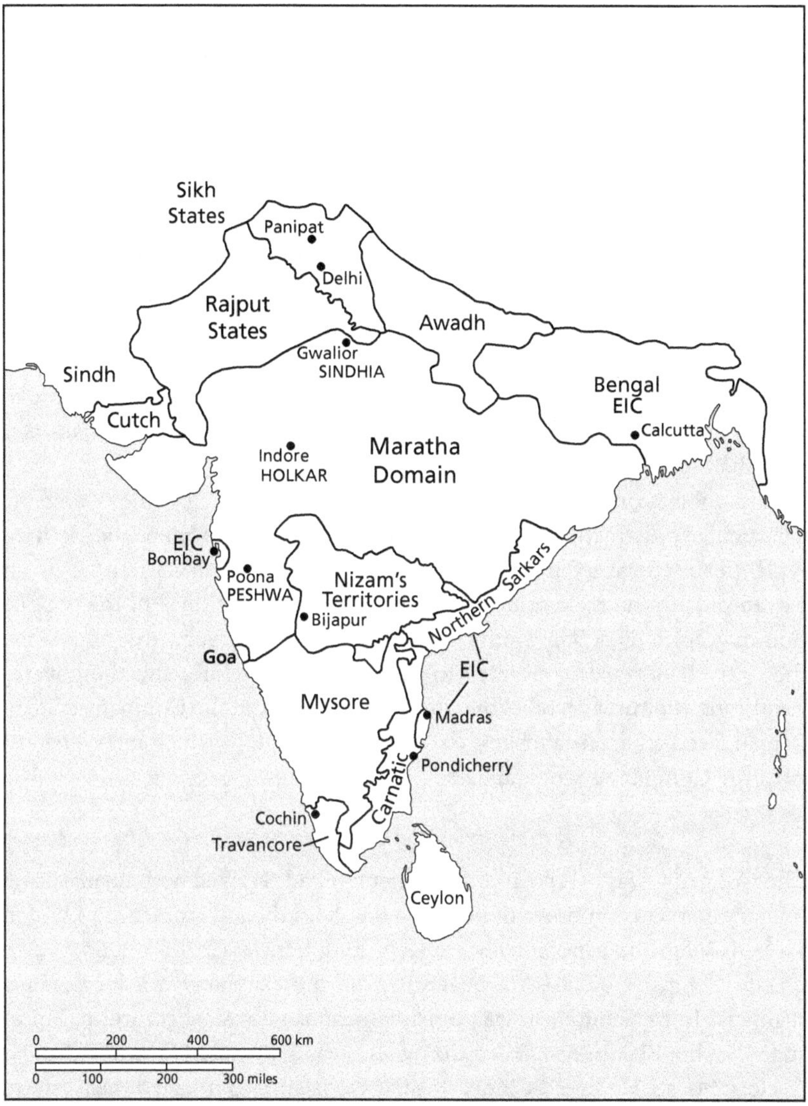

Figure 5.1 India, 1785: approximate political boundaries
Data sources: Adapted from http://etc.usf.edu/maps/pages/400/410/410.htm, Historical Atlas of India page 19 by Charles Joppen 1907 and ArcGIS Online.
Redrawn based on a map by S. J. Macklin, Williams College 2011, created using ArcGIS® software by Esri.

not be paid for in bullion. They would be purchased using the taxes extracted from Bengal.[13] Of course, this meant that land taxes had to be extracted rigidly – the Company could not, say, forgive taxes in a bad year, as was sometimes done by other Indian states.

The Company succeeded in acquiring more textiles to sell in Europe, but the methods it used were controversial. It used coercive methods both to force weavers to produce for it, as well as to exclude its rivals, such as the Dutch East India Company. Authors like Hameeda Hossain (1988) have argued that the coercive methods undermined textile production in Bengal. This is difficult to confirm, one way or the other, for Bengal as a whole. The Company's own procurement of textiles in Bengal steadily increased. The volume of sales in London, mostly by the Company, went from approximately 551,000 pieces per year in 1777–86 to 777,000 per year in 1792–1801 (Marshall 1987: 106).

A combination of factors had the potential to make the Company a particularly 'extractive' state, and this does seem to have happened, perhaps with greatest severity in the early years. In 1770 Bengal was struck by an extraordinarily severe famine, in which as much as one-third of the population may have died. The Company administration did very little to address the crisis. Land taxes continued to be collected as before, and the government's expenditures on relief measures were small. But the Company-state in Bengal faced an external check: Parliament in London, which intervened to curb the Company's worst abuses.

Rationalizing the Company-State

The Company was beholden to Parliament: it had received both financial and military assistance in times of need. By the 1760s the government in London viewed Bengal as a potentially valuable long-term asset for Britain, which greedy Company officials might destroy. So the Company was increasingly regulated from London. In 1784 a (parliamentary) board of control began to supervise the EIC. In 1786, Lord Cornwallis was appointed Governor-General to clean house. He raised Company officials' salaries, eliminated their private trade, and started the process of creating what was to become a staid and reliable governmental bureaucracy. Over the next few decades the Company's trading role shrank and by 1833 its role in India was largely administrative. The British Raj's famous 'steel frame' bureaucracy was being built.

13 See Prakash (1976).

In terms of economic policy perhaps the most (in)famous measure the Company introduced was the 'Permanent Settlement', in 1793. A varied group of *zamindars* (described above) was given ownership rights in the areas where (often) they had previously collected taxes. They were required to pay a tax on their property and would lose the land if they defaulted. The tax was set at a high level, because the Company needed cash urgently. Marshall (1987: 144) suggests that taxes increased 20 per cent in real terms compared to 1757. But the most striking feature of this arrangement was that the tax was fixed in nominal terms *in perpetuity*. This was administratively convenient. In effect the Company was giving away future revenues to satisfy present needs. The Company, and later the Crown, kept the promise not to raise the land tax, even in the face of inflation, until 1947, the year of Indian independence. By this point, the real value of the tax was negligible. The low land tax stimulated an expansion of cultivated area but starved the government of resources it could have used to create public goods.[14]

Another effort to raise revenues, the Opium Monopoly, paid off hugely in the long run for the Company. In the late eighteenth century the Company took over and systematized what appears to have been an existing monopoly. Now only the Company was permitted by law to procure opium. The Company would, via an employee-intermediary, advance capital to the peasant who would grow poppies. After the peasant delivered the poppy it would be processed in a 'factory'. Chests of opium would then be auctioned in Calcutta to private traders, who sold the opium in China. The Opium Monopoly has been highly controversial because of its adverse impact on China. There are also many reported instances, especially in the early years, of peasants being coerced to produce opium. But J. F. Richards (1981) has shown that peasants eventually benefited. The revenues from the Opium Monopoly were not private profits for the EIC; they went into the coffers of the EIC in its capacity as government. The number of chests of opium sold went from roughly 4,000 per annum in 1789–99 to 63,000 chests in 1849–59 (Table 5.4). As a percentage of the revenues of the government of India, opium profits went from 3 per cent to an astonishing 17 per cent.[15] By 1850, opium was 30 per cent of Indian exports (Table 5.5). This was partly because

14 On cultivated area, see Chaudhuri (1984: 301–304). By 1855–56 land taxes in Bengal were 35.6 per cent of governmental revenues, compared to 55.5 per cent for British India as whole (Roy 2011: 256).

15 The figures cited in this paragraph reflect the opium sold in Calcutta as well as that exported from Bombay. 'Malwa' opium was grown in princely states but taxed by the British government as it went through Bombay.

Table 5.4 Opium exports and revenues, 1789–1859 (decennial averages)

Years	Total number of chests of opium	Percentage of opium revenues to total governmental revenues
1789–99	4,083	3
1799–1809	3,908	4
1809–19	4,276	5
1819–29	4,924	8
1829–39	21,000	8
1839–49	37,167	11
1849–59	63,178	17

Source: Richards (2002: 159–160).

Table 5.5 Indian exports: commodity composition, percentage share of selected items in total value, 1811–12 to 1850–51

Year	Indigo	Piece-goods	Raw silk	Raw cotton	Opium	Sugar	Total
1811–12	18.5	33.0	8.3	4.9	23.8	1.5	90.0
1814–15	20.0	14.3	13.3	8.0		3.0	58.6
1828–29	27.0	11.0	10.0	15.0	17.0	4.0	84.0
1834–35	15.0	7.0	8.0	21.0	25.0	2.0	78.0
1839–40	26.0	5.0	7.0	20.0	10.0	7.0	75.0
1850–51	10.9	3.7	3.8	19.1	30.1	10.0	77.6

Source: Chaudhuri (1984: 842).

of expansion in cultivated area, but also because the Company's profit margins were enormous. I will return to this issue of cultivation of 'commercial crops' in the next section.

It is time to turn to a regional state with indigenous roots. Like the EIC, Indian states faced military threats. They, too, could have rationalized tax collection, and tried to promote economic growth. Roy (2013a: 1127) has argued that this is not what happened; internal warfare in India merely drove the regional states into 'fiscal crises' and 'states or quasi-states they had formed shrank in size'. Given this, it was inevitable that they neglected public goods. A possible exception to this generalization is Mysore, the Company's most formidable military opponent. The Company fought Mysore many times and finally prevailed in 1799, in collaboration with the Marathas and the nizam of Hyderabad. Mysore's ruler, Tipu Sultan, was defeated and killed.

Mysore: A 'Modernizing' State?

Like the EIC, Tipu Sultan tried to cut out intermediaries between the peasant and the state. According to a set of regulations he issued, revenue farming would no longer be practised. Preferential tax rates would be given for the cultivation of new crops and for creating new irrigation works. State officials would inspect and repair old irrigation works. There were also plans for the state to be extensively involved in trade of sandalwood, silk, spices, and other commodities.[16] Tipu also embraced European military technology, and some of the weaponry produced within Mysore was of very high quality. He also attempted to learn about manufacturing methods in France and Britain (Parthasarathi 2011: 207–208).

How high were living standards? Sashi Sivramkrishna (2009) has provided evidence that the population of Mysore was well nourished, relying on a survey commissioned by the EIC, carried out by Francis Buchanan Hamilton, who spent fourteen months touring Mysore (April 1800 to July 1801). He finds that the wages of a man and woman, taken together, if spent on ragi (a 'coarse' grain that covered most of Mysore's cultivated area) would afford the family subsistence and then some. This is a useful finding, but Sivramkrishna's wage estimates are difficult to compare with others' (see above), where the basic consumption bundle included more 'refined' (and expensive) crops and the authors focused on the purchasing power of a single wage, rather than two.

For some scholars Mysore represents a late eighteenth-century region with economic promise. The question of what would have happened had Tipu Sultan defeated the British is, as Washbrook (2004: 508) has put it 'one of the teasing counterfactuals of Southern [Indian] history'. A detailed discussion of this question is beyond the scope of this chapter, but the reader might look at the impressive range of evidence in Yazdani (2017).

After the defeat of Tipu Sultan in 1799, conflict between the EIC and the Marathas was inevitable. The Company, helped considerably by infighting among the Marathas, finally prevailed in 1818. It now dominated the subcontinent. It was time to consolidate its style of administration and governance. It would also need to shape its policies in India to respond to British economic interests.

16 This paragraph is based on Stein (1985: 402–403). Roy (2013a) questions the extent to which these measures were actually implemented.

'British India', 1818–58

Structural Change

The first half of the eighteenth century saw a change in the composition of Indian exports, with a decline in the export of piece-goods (cloth) and an increase in the importance of sugar, raw cotton, and opium (Table 5.5). The example of the Madras Presidency illustrates this process. In 1800 the Madras Presidency imported raw cotton. By 1857–58 it exported 55 million pounds of raw cotton, abroad as well as to other parts of India. Of the 12 million acres (5 million hectares) under cultivation 1 million acres (400,000 hectares) were under cotton (Kumar 1984: 366). Kumar gives much of the credit for this to the Company, which imported seeds from Malta, Mauritius, America, Egypt, and Brazil. Experimental farms were set up, to help increase productivity. All this was driven by the demand from British textile manufacturers. In contrast, there was a tax on professions and trades, called *motarfa*, which was an 'additional and heavy burden' on the Madras weaver who was facing competition from imports (Kumar 1984: 369). The government acknowledged that this was 'indefensible in principle', but did not want to give it up because it brought in substantial revenues.

Traditional manufacturing, especially textiles, took a big hit. Not only did exports of textiles fall dramatically, there was a huge increase in imports because British machine-made cloth was very cheap. Especially in the first half of the nineteenth century, India experienced 'deindustrialization'. Deindustrialization has been defined in different ways, as a decline in employment or output in industry or as a decline in the share of industry in employment or GDP. The early literature, focusing on eastern India, argued for an absolute decline in manufacturing employment over the nineteenth century (Bagchi 1976).[17] Subsequent research has suggested that this was overstated for several reasons. First, eastern India was not representative of the whole of India. Second, population growth and decrease in prices increased demand for textiles in India. Third, sectors other than textiles picked up. Fourth, even within textiles, weavers were able to recover by using cheaper imported yarn. Not surprisingly, the picture varies across time and space. Still, overall, Broadberry et al. (2015) find that the share of manufacturing in GDP fell between 1800 and 1861, with an absolute decline in industrial output in the first few decades of the nineteenth century.

17 For a critique of Bagchi see Vicziany (1979).

Clingingsmith and Williamson (2008) have provided a new explanation for deindustrialization, arguing that droughts caused by El Niño raised the price of food and hence costs for Indian manufacturing, especially in the period 1760–1810. Roy (2013b: 130) believes the authors have not fully argued their case, because the relationship between temporary and usually local climate shocks and long-term land productivity remains to be established. Still, this is a promising area for further research on the relationship between climate and economic development.

The two trends I have discussed – rise in agricultural exports and decline in domestic manufacturing – taken together suggest, for many nationalist and Marxist scholars of Indian economic history, a destructive change in the structure of the economy. India had been converted into a supplier of raw materials to British industry and a market for its products. What is the appropriate counterfactual? Parthasarathi (2011) has argued that the early nineteenth century was a missed opportunity for modern industry in India. This could have been developed with appropriate state support, such as tariff protection, government efforts to improve the technological capacity, or policies where government purchases favoured goods manufactured in India. He argues that neither capital nor entrepreneurial talent were scarce.

State-led industrialization, even if possible as a growth strategy, was politically a non-starter. Industrial interests in Britain were not about to allow the Company-state to develop its competition in India. A possible alternative was export-led agricultural growth. If agricultural production expanded rapidly, to the extent the state could tax growing incomes, it could invest in public goods like irrigation, or at a later date, in agricultural research. To what extent did this scenario play out? We have seen above that the Permanent Settlement prevented this from happening in Bengal. What about the other regions? To tell this story we need another short detour into the history of land tenure and taxation.

Agricultural Growth, Taxation, and Public Goods

By 1818 the Company was persuaded, correctly or not, that the *Zamindari* system, wherein (often) a tax intermediary was given title to land, was a mistake.[18] *Zamindars*, they believed, had merely enjoyed their rents, and not invested in their land. The Company resolved to, in principle, give ownership of land to the actual cultivator, an arrangement known as *raiyat-wari* (from *raiyat*, or farmer). As in the case of the Permanent Settlement, the

18 The discussion of law and property below relies heavily on Roy and Swamy (2016).

owner would forfeit the land tax if he defaulted. Under *Raiyatwari*, the land tax was not fixed in perpetuity; it would be revised every few decades. So, in principle, growing agriculture could have been a source of governmental revenue and investment in public goods. Initially, taxes were high in *raiyatwari* regions. But this was not to last, for reasons I discuss below.

The Company had made it easier to transfer land, by giving the owner a clean individualized title.[19] Moreover, the Company introduced its own legal system. Whereas disputes had previously typically been adjudicated within village communities, they could now be taken to more formal district courts. This was, in principle, a positive development, because a peasant could borrow from someone he did not know, with no connection to his community. The credit market expanded and became more competitive, and this facilitated growth.

It was inevitable that there would be some default, and land would change hands from peasants to their creditors. Though this was a calamity for the defaulting peasant, this did not create tension if the lender was another peasant, from the same village (say). But in relatively poor and dry regions lenders were often immigrants from other parts of India. When land passed into their hands this could lead to social tensions, including peasant riots. This made the Company uneasy. In Punjab, the huge north-western region that the Company annexed in 1849, it introduced measures from the very beginning to prevent land from passing out of the hands of a member of the village community. The preservation of the existing rural quo was becoming a priority (Washbrook 1981).

With these worries (for the Company) already in place the Mutiny in 1857 was, in present-day parlance, a game changer. It forced a re-examination of British notions of India, Indians, and how they should be governed. The *zamindars* of Awadh, dispossessed by recently introduced land tenure innovations, were important participants in the Mutiny. This hugely reinforced the notion that preservation of British rule required the appeasement of rural landowning classes. The desire to appease rural elites meant that agricultural taxes became a smaller and smaller fraction of agricultural output. Eventually, from being a state that was 'extractive', the British Raj taxed too little, and created too few public goods.[20]

19 This was true for much of the Bombay and Madras presidencies. Things were notionally a bit more complicated in parts of north India where the Company found 'brotherhoods' and some element of joint taxation was introduced.

20 The land tax was less than 5 per cent of net agricultural output by the 1930s (Roy 2011: 256).

Much of the work on Indian economic history has focused on agriculture and industry. However, in the last few decades we have seen the emergence of a rich literature on environmental history. I will now briefly touch on one of its major themes, which is of considerable contemporary relevance, before concluding this chapter.

Erosion of Customary Rights and Environmental Damage

In India, as in other parts of the world, the rural population was (and is) to varying degrees dependent on the right to use land, forests, and water bodies to which they do not have documented rights. The residents of villages may depend on the nearby woodlands or forest for firewood, hunting, medicinal plants, food, the grazing of cattle, etc. When population is thin, and industrial needs are limited, it is relatively easy to use these resources in a sustainable fashion. In India this was (and is) sometimes ensured by community-level norms, such as the designation of a forest as sacred. Citing such examples, the early literature on Indian environmental history was perhaps somewhat romantic in its view of precolonial communities living in harmony with nature. Still, it seems clear that the demands for commercial use of forest products increased dramatically under colonial rule. For instance, in the early nineteenth century the forests of the Malabar came to be valued because teak was required for the Royal Navy's ships. As was typical for the Raj, the officials engaged in a debate as to who actually owned the forests (the individual, the community, or the state) and the nature of use rights guaranteed to local users, who might protest their withdrawal. The Raj's officials were aware of the need to use the forests in a sustainable manner, so that they continued to be available for commercial use (Pathak 2002: 73). By the mid-nineteenth century officials were also pointing out that deforestation could reduce the moisture content of the air and rainfall and lead to siltation of rivers and creeks (Pathak 2002: 79).

The 'crucial watershed' in colonial policy was, however, the construction of the railways, beginning in 1853 and expanding rapidly thereafter.[21] There was a huge demand for wood to build sleepers and forests in some areas were 'felled in even to desolation'. By 1862, the Governor-General declared that forest administration until the Mutiny had been a 'melancholy failure'. This led to the Indian Forest Act of 1865, updated in 1878, as well as the formation of the Imperial Forest Department in 1864. Many historians have argued that

21 This phrase is used by Guha (1983: 1883). The remaining quotations in this paragraph are comments by British officials reported by Guha.

these and subsequent laws and institutions undermined the customary rights of populations dependent on the forests.[22] The subsequent history of their protest is beyond the scope of this short chapter. Suffice to say that the appropriate balance of various considerations – economic development, sustainable resource use, damage to the environment, and the resource needs of the poor – remains highly contentious to the present day.

Conclusion

If a Mughal observer, well acquainted with the economic history of the empire in the seventeenth century, were to travel across time and tour India in 1858, what changes would he notice? The most obvious alterations would, of course, be political and military. Mughal authority had been extinguished; the last emperor was imprisoned and languishing in Burma. Most of the subcontinent was ruled in the name of Queen Victoria. Large parts of central and northern India were still in shock from the devastation of the warfare during the Mutiny and subsequent retribution by the British; but in substantial parts of the subcontinent the British seemed firmly in control and *Pax Britannica* had made economic activity safer.

There were more people and a larger cultivated area. But that was not a surprise, because this kind of growth was also a feature of seventeenth-century history. The economy was still overwhelmingly agricultural, and, with some exceptions, highly dependent on the weather and vulnerable to famine. Agricultural techniques had barely changed.

Our traveller might notice that some new types of manufacturing had emerged. He was familiar with the factory as an organizational form. After all, in Mughal cities workers were assembled under one roof to produce luxury products for the nobility, in *karkhanas*. But now a product that seemed to be used for mundane purposes like packing material (jute) was being made in factories.[23] And the technology was now much more sophisticated, potentially allowing one man to produce a lot more. This was still a very small part of the economy, though. A new and rapid form of transport had also been introduced, the railway, but this was as yet on a small scale. Our observer might have guessed that if this were to expand, economic life might change dramatically.

22 Sivaramakrishnan (1995: 13) argues that the 'bedrock' of the 1878 Act 'was the assertion that all uncultivated land was the state's property'.

23 See Volume II Chapter 6.

One section of the population seemed to have suffered: the spinners (especially) and the weavers. They were less numerous, certainly as a fraction of the labour force. Peasants were more connected with people outside the village, more likely to sell crops that might leave the province or even the country, more likely to borrow money from an 'outsider', and more likely to migrate. Living standards had not changed dramatically. People seemed better-clothed, because cloth was cheaper, but not better-fed. The quality of life had, if anything, deteriorated slightly since 1700.

References

Alam, M. (1986). *The Crisis of Empire in Mughal North India: Awadh and Punjab, 1707–48*, Delhi: Oxford University Press.

(1991). 'Eastern India in the Early Eighteenth Century "Crisis": Some Evidence from Bihar', in Marshall, P. J. (ed.) (2003). *The Eighteenth Century: Evolution or Revolution?*, New Delhi: Oxford University Press, 43–71. First published in 1991 in *Indian Economic and Social History Review*, 27.

Alam, M. and Subrahmanyam, S. (eds.) 1998. *The Mughal State: 1526–1750*, New Delhi: Oxford University Press.

Alavi, S. (ed.) (2002). *The Eighteenth Century in India*, New Delhi: Oxford University Press.

Ali, A. M. (1993). 'The Mughal Polity: A Critique of Revisionist Approaches', *Modern Asian Studies* 27(4), 699–710.

Allen, R. C. (2007). 'India in the Great Divergence', in Williamson, J. G., Hatton, T. J., O'Rourke, K. H. and Taylor, A. M. (eds.), *The New Comparative Economic History: Essays in Honor of Jeffrey G. Williamson*, Cambridge, MA: MIT Press, 9–32.

Bagchi, A. (1976). 'Deindustrialization in Gangetic Bihar 1809–1901', in Das Gupta, A., De, B., Ray, N. R., Sarkar, J. and Chakrabarty, P. (eds.), *Essays in Honour of Prof. S. C. Sarkar*. New Delhi: People's Publishing House.

Bayly, C. (1992). *Rulers, Townsmen and Bazaars: North India Society in the Age of British Expansion 1770–1870*, Delhi: Oxford University Press.

Bhargava, M. (ed.) (2014). *The Decline of the Mughal Empire*, New Delhi: Oxford University Press.

Broadberry, S. and Gupta, B. (2006). 'The Early Modern Great Divergence: Wages, Prices and Economic Development in Europe and Asia, 1500–1800', *Economic History Review*, 59(1), 2–31.

Broadberry, S., Custodis, J. and Gupta, B. (2015). 'India and the Great Divergence: An Anglo-Indian Comparison of GDP Per Capita, 1600–1871', *Explorations in Economic History*, 55, 58–75.

Chaudhuri, B. B. (1984). 'Eastern India', in Kumar, D. (ed.), *The Cambridge Economic History of India, vol. 2: c.1757–c.1970*, Delhi: Orient Longman, 86–176.

Chaudhury, S. (1995). *From Prosperity to Decline: Eighteenth Century Bengal*. Delhi: Manohar.

Clingingsmith, D. and Williamson, J. G. (2008). 'Deindustrialization in Eighteenth and Nineteenth Century India: Mughal Decline, Climate Shocks, and British Industrial Ascent', *Explorations in Economic History*, 45(3), 209–34.

Dasgupta, A. (1970). 'Trade and Politics in Eighteenth Century India', in Alam, M. and Subrahmanyam, S. (eds.), (1998). *The Mughal State: 1526–1750*, New Delhi: Oxford University Press, 361–397. First published in Richards, D. S. (ed.), (1970). *Islam and the Trade of Asia*, Philadelphia: University of Philadelphia Press.

Gordon, S. (1998). *The New Cambridge History of India: The Marathas, 1600–1818*, New Delhi: Cambridge University Press.

Guha, R. (1983). 'Forestry in British and Post-British India: A Historical Analysis', *Economic and Political Weekly*, 44(June), 1882–1896.

Guha, S. (2015). 'Rethinking the Economy of Mughal India: Lateral Perspectives', *Journal of the Economic and Social History of the Orient*, 58, 532–575.

Habib, I. (1997). 'India during the Mughal Period', in Sridhar, S. N. and Mattoo, N. K. (eds.), *Ananya: A Portrait of India*, New York: The Association of Indians in America, 87–102.

Hossain, H. (1988). *The Company Weavers of Bengal: The East India Company and the Organization of Textile Production in Bengal, 1750–1813*, Oxford University Press.

Kumar, D. (1984). 'South India', in Kumar, D. (ed.), *The Cambridge Economic History of India, vol. 2: c.1757–c.1970*, Delhi: Orient Longman, 352–375.

Leonard, K. (1979). 'The "Great Firm" Theory of the Decline of the Mughal Empire', in Alam, M. and Subrahmanyam, S. (eds.), (1998), *The Mughal State: 1526–1750*, New Delhi: Oxford University Press, 398–418. First published in 1979 in *Comparative Studies in Society and History*, 21(2).

Marshall, P. J. (1987). *Bengal: The British Bridgehead*, Cambridge University Press.

Marshall, P. J. (ed.) (2003). *The Eighteenth Century: Evolution or Revolution?* New Delhi: Oxford University Press.

Parthasarathi, P. (1998). 'Rethinking Wages and Competitiveness in the Eighteenth Century: Britain and South India', *Past and Present*, 158, 79–109.

(2011). *Why Europe Grew Rich and Asia Did Not: Global Economic Divergence, 1600–1850*, Cambridge University Press.

Pathak, A. (2002). *Law, Strategies, Ideologies: Legislating Forests in Colonial India*, New Delhi: Oxford University Press.

Pearson, M. N. (1976). 'Shivaji and the Decline of the Mughal Empire', *Journal of Asian Studies*, 35(2), 221–335.

Prakash, O. (1976). 'Bullion for Goods International Trade and the Economy of Early Eighteenth Century Bengal', *Indian Economic and Social History Review*, 13, 159–187.

(2002). 'Trade and Politics in Eighteenth Century Bengal', in Alavi, S. (ed.), *The Eighteenth Century in India*, New Delhi, Oxford University Press, 136–164.

Raychaudhuri, T. (1982). 'The State and the Economy: The Mughal Empire', in Raychaudhuri, T. and Habib, I. (eds), *The Cambridge Economic History of India, vol. I: c.1200–c.1750*, Cambridge University Press, 172–193.

Richards, J. F. (1981). 'The Indian Empire and Peasant Production of Opium in the Nineteenth Century', *Modern Asian Studies*, 15, 59–82.

(2002). 'The Opium Industry in British India', *Indian Economic and Social History Review*, 39, 149–179.

Roy, T. (2010). 'Economic Conditions in Early Modern Bengal: A Contribution to the Divergence Debate'. *Journal of Economic History*, 70 (1), 179–194.

(2011). *The Economic History of India 1857–1947*, New Delhi: Oxford University Press.

(2013a). 'Rethinking the Origins of British India: State Formation and Military-Fiscal Undertakings in an Eighteenth Century World Region', *Modern Asian Studies*, 47(4), 1125–1146.

(2013b). *An Economic History of Early Modern India*, New York: Routledge.

Roy, T. and Swamy, A. (2016). *Law and the Economy in Colonial India*, University of Chicago Press.

Sivaramkrishnan, K. (1995). 'Colonialism and Forestry in India: Imagining the Past in Present Politics', *Comparative Studies in History and Society*, 37(1), 3–40.

Sivramkrishna, S. (2009). 'Ascertaining Living Standards in Erstwhile Mysore, Southern India, from Francis Buchanan's Journey of 1800–01: An Empirical Contribution to the Great Divergence Debate', *Journal of the Economic and Social History of the Orient*, 52(4–5), 695–733.

Stein, B. (1985). 'State Formation and Economy Reconsidered: Part One', *Modern Asian Studies*, 19(3), 387–413.

Studer, R. (2015). *The Great Divergence Reconsidered: Europe, India, and the Rise to Global Economic Power*, Cambridge University Press.

Subramanian, L. (2010). *History of India, 1707–1857*, New Delhi: Orient BlackSwan Private Limited.

Vicziany, M. (1979). 'The Deindustrialization of India in the Nineteenth Century: A Methodological Critique of Amiya Kumar Bagchi', *Indian Economic and Social History Review*, 16(2), 105–146.

Washbrook, D. (1981). 'Law, State and Agrarian Society in Colonial India', *Modern Asian Studies*, 15, 649–721.

(2004). 'South India, 1770–1840: The Transition', *Modern Asian Studies*, 38(3), 479–516.

Yazdani, K. (2017). *India, Modernity, and the Great Divergence: Mysore and Gujarat (17th to 19th C.)*, Leiden: Brill.

6

Sustainable Development in South East Asia

JEAN-PASCAL BASSINO

> Owing to high wages, and probably to this alone, the laboring classes are, upon the whole, well fed, clad, and housed. . . . The Burmese peasantry are in more comfortable and easy circumstances than the masses of laboring poor in any of our Indian provinces; and making allowance for climate, manners, and habits, might bear a comparison with the peasantry of most European countries.
>
> (*John Crawfurd, 1829, Journal of an Embassy of the Governor-General of British India to the Court of Ava, 469*).

Introduction

Early modern South East Asia can be characterized as a region of low population density, abundant natural resources, and high labour productivity in agriculture, where coastal areas were deeply involved in international trade, in particular with China and India. Reid (1993) argues that South East Asia enjoyed a remarkable prosperity during what he describes as the 'age of commerce', lasting from the fifteenth to the seventeenth century, and that the mid-seventeenth century marks the beginning of a period of relative economic decline, implying that the international trade was the main cause of prosperity. There is, however, no quantitative evidence that intra-Asian trade declined drastically after the mid-seventeenth century.

Available information on urban real wages indicates that the description of early nineteenth-century Burma, by the Governor-General of British India, applies to most parts of South East Asia until at least the mid-nineteenth century. Living standards were well above Chinese and Indian levels.[1] The population growth observed throughout the region in the eighteenth and

1 The use of real wages as a measure of living standards in early modern South East Asia is discussed by de Zwart and van Zanden (2015: 217–218) for the case of Java, which can be considered as relevant for the region as a whole.

Table 6.1 Total population and population density by kingdoms or regions

	Population (in 1000s)		Population density (sq. km)	
	1600	1800	1600	1800
Mainland South East Asia				
Burma	3,100	4,600	5	7
Laos (incl. northern Thailand)	1,200	1,200	3	3
Siam (excl. northern Thailand)	1,800	2,800	5	8
Cambodia and Champa	1,230	1,500	5	5
Vietnam (northern and central)	4,700	7,000	18	27
Malaya (incl. Patani)	500	500	3	3
South East Asian archipelago				
Sabah and Sarawak (north-west of Borneo)	200	200	1	1
Luzon and Visayas	800	1,800	4	9
Mindanao and Sulu	150	230	2	2
Sumatra	2,400	3,500	6	8
Java	4,000	5,000	30	38
Kalimantan (south and east of Borneo)	670	1,000	1	1
Sulawesi (eastern Indonesia)	1,200	1,800	6	9
Bali	600	700	80	93
Other Indonesian islands	600	900	9	14
Maluku	275	400	4	5
Total for South East Asia	23000	33000	6	8

Source: Reid (1988: 14).

nineteenth centuries suggests also a strong resilience to climate shocks and wars. The main political rulers on the mainland reinforced their authority, legitimacy, and capacity, at least until the 1850s. A number of smaller independent indigenous polities of the archipelago managed to resist Dutch and Spanish attempts to control their international trade or impose a political protectorate. The expansion of intra-Asian international trade was associated with a process of monetization and the reinforcement of the fiscal capacity of the various large and small polities. The polities considered in this chapter are listed in Table 6.1 and the territory covered by the region is shown in Figure 6.1.

To what extent was the economic transformation sustainable? To answer this question, we can use the conceptual framework proposed by Dasgupta (2009). Sustainable development at the country level is identified

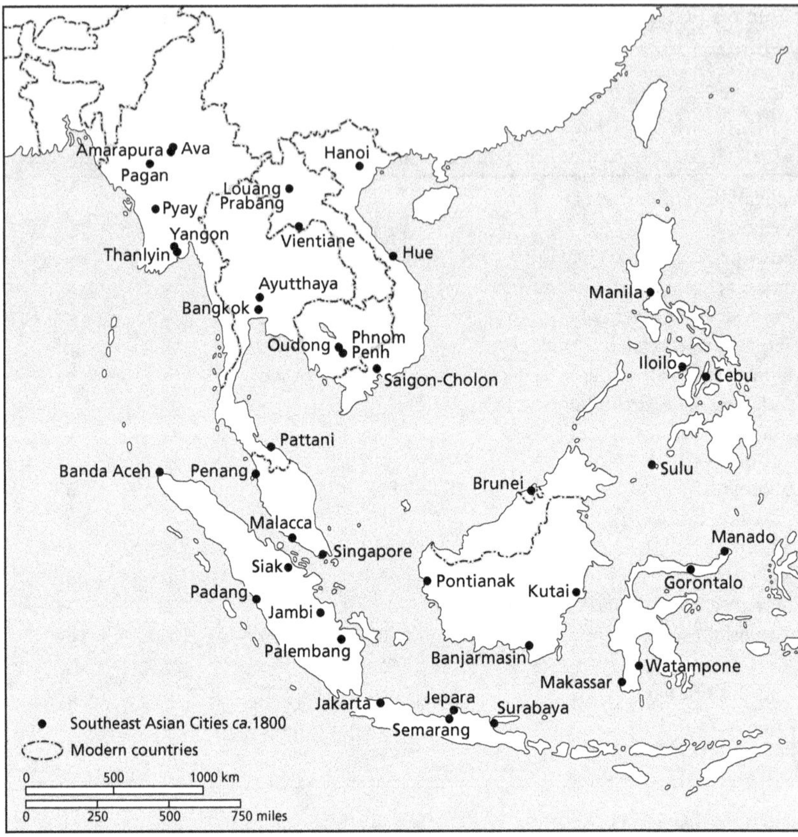

Figure 6.1 Main South East Asian cities between 1700 and 1870
Data source: IAO GIS, Natural Earth.
Map credits: Redrawn based on a map by IAO GIS, CNRS and ENS Lyon, France (iao.cnrs.fr/).
Notes: Most of the cities of the archipelago indicated on the map became colonial possessions in the sixteenth century (Cebu, 1565; Oloilo, 1566; Manila, 1571), seventeenth century (Jakarta, 1611; Manado, 1658; Padang, 1663; Makassar, 1667; Semarang and Gorontalo, 1667), eighteenth century (Surabaya, 1743; Banjarmasin, 1747; Pontianak, 1778) or early nineteenth century (Palembang, 1825; Kutai, 1844). Banda Aceh, Brunei, Jambi, Siak, Sulu, and Watampone remained the capital cities of local sultanates until the second half of the nineteenth century.

as an increase in per capita terms of comprehensive wealth, which is the total value of natural, physical (i.e. produced), and human capital stocks. Although information for early modern South East Asia is too fragmentary for a proper accounting exercise, general trends can be assessed for these three types of assets.

Urban and Rural Living Standards

In order to assess living standards in early modern South East Asia, the most abundant information is related to urban and rural wages and their purchasing power. For the sixteenth and seventeenth centuries, daily rice wages calculated by Reid (1993) for various cities, although with a small number of observations, were in the high range of European grain wages estimated by van Zanden (1999). For the later period, Java is the only area of the region for which almost continuous series are currently available. Unskilled real wages series for Batavia in 1680–1914 (de Zwart and van Zanden 2015) indicate a steady upward trend in the first half of the eighteenth century, followed by a mild downward trend until the 1880s. Welfare ratios in Batavia were always well above 1, close to or above 2 (i.e. twice the subsistence level) from the 1770s to the 1870s, higher than the estimates for Beijing, Bengal, or Leipzig. However, per capita GDP estimates by van Zanden (2003) for nineteenth-century Java constructed as annual series indicate a downward trend during the 1830s and 1840s, which corresponds to the phase of introduction of the 'cultivation system' (in place from 1830 to 1870).

High wages are also reported for mainland South East Asia, suggesting that Java can be regarded as representative for the region as a whole. For Burma in the 1820s, Crawfurd (1829: 467) indicates that nominal monthly wages of native carpenters were higher in Rangoon than in Calcutta, equivalent to 7.1 and 4.7 Mexican dollars in terms of silver content, corresponding to 1,120 and 800 lb of rice, respectively. Assuming twenty-four days worked, this implies daily rice wages of 21.2 kg in Rangoon against 15.1 kg per day in Calcutta. The same source adds that common field labourers in Rangoon received the equivalent of 9.9 kg rice per day (assuming again twenty-four days worked). For unskilled workers, this is around four times Indian wheat wages, and five times the Chinese rice wages in lower Yangzi calculated by Broadberry and Gupta (2006: 14 and 17).[2] Unskilled nominal wages were at the same level in Ava and Bassein (in upper and lower Burma, respectively), although the price of rice was lower. In Bangkok, unskilled workers received around 1863 nominal daily wages of around 10.7 g of silver (0.7 tical of 15.244 g of silver), equivalent to around 14kg of rice.[3]

South East Asian nominal silver wages were higher than in China and India, while foodstuffs, including superior goods such as sugar and fish, were locally produced and cheap, which resulted in a larger difference in terms of

2 Slightly higher than wheat wages in England, at around 8.6 kg in 1800–49.

3 Rice export price in Ingram (1964: 115).

purchasing power.[4] Some manufactured consumer goods were imported, such as white cotton fabric from India, and therefore presumably more expensive in South East Asia. But local production of cotton fabric using imported British cotton yarn increased after the 1820s (Kobayashi 2020). The most valuable garments were produced in comparatively high-population-density areas such as Java, Bali, the Sulawesi (for sarong used in Malay regions), Iloilo island for the Philippines, and around Hué for Vietnam. Other manufactured items originated from China, such as Chinaware and cast-iron cooking pots, but local substitutes produced by ethnic Chinese or native craftsmen existed (Crawfurd 1829: 81).

Information on wages in Penang[5] (a British colony since 1784) indicates sizeable difference across ethnic groups. In comparison with Burma, nominal unskilled wages in Penang were low for Malay workers, but somehow higher for Chinese workers, 2.5 and 6 Mexican dollars per month respectively, while Chinese, Indian, or Persian carpenters received 15 Mexican dollars per month, and Malay carpenters only 6 (Crawfurd 1829: 31).[6] This is only partly explained by the difference in the number of working days of Malay and Chinese workers, 26 and 30, respectively (Crawfurd 1829: 31). However, the comparatively low reward of native workers may also reflect differences in the number of working hours per day and in labour productivity rather than an ethnic premium.

A major explanation for high wages in urban areas was that labour productivity was high in agriculture. Information for the early twentieth century indicates that rice yields were not much lower than in the East Asian regions of high population density, which explains why labour productivity in rice cultivation was remarkably high in South East Asian agriculture (van der Eng 2004). Since agricultural techniques barely changed between the eighteenth and the mid-twentieth century, there is no reason to believe that

4 Information on average height is very limited before the second half of the nineteenth century. Sizeable regional differences existed. Available surveys suggest that Malay and Vietnamese were among the shortest and Burmese and Karen among the tallest, in a range between around 155 cm and 165 cm for average adult males (Bassino and Coclanis 2008: table A1). The low stature could be due to the low protein content of the diet (based on rice, vegetables, fruits, coconuts, roots, tubers, sago, beans, fish, eggs, sugar, areca nuts, and palm wine, with only small quantities of meat and no milk) and recurrent exposures to tropical diseases.

5 Singapore was founded in 1819; Malacca, the first Portuguese colony in South East Asia, established in 1511, seized by the Dutch East India Company (VOC) in 1641, and ceded to Britain in 1824. The location of the main cities is presented in Figure 6.1.

6 The price of rice is not mentioned, but it was certainly higher than in Rangoon; most of the rice consumed in Penang was imported from peninsular Malaysia, Bengal, and Burma.

the situation was different in the eighteenth and nineteenth centuries. In most areas, the land frontier remained wide open until the mid-twentieth century. Therefore, agricultural producers had a strong incentive to use techniques that were labour-saving and land-intensive. In a context of low population density, reasonably high natural land fertility, and low reclamation cost, unskilled labour in an urban area was not an attractive proposition for rural commoners.

In a predominantly agrarian society, high labour productivity in agriculture implies a low level of inequality if the tax pressure is low, which was the case in early modern South East Asia (as discussed below). The Gini coefficient for Java *c.*1880 estimated by van Zanden (2003) was 0.29 for the entire population (0.23 for the Javanese, 0.47 and 0.44 for the Chinese and European residents who had on average a higher income per head). The high urban and rural wages suggest that Java was further away from the inequality possibility frontier than *c.*1880 when the Gini coefficient was 0.39 (Milanovic et al. 2011).

Low Population Density, Demographic Growth, and Urbanization

Considering the abundance of natural resources, the region remained underpopulated until the late nineteenth century. According to data assembled by Reid (1988: 14), the entire region had around 23 million inhabitants *c.*1600 and 33 million *c.*1800, which is less than 10 inhabitants per square km (Table 6.1). A few pockets of comparatively high density (above 30 per square km) had existed in Java, Bali, and the Red River Delta for at least a millennium. In a context of relative labour scarcity, slavery, *corvée* and other types of bonded labour relations remained widespread until the nineteenth century. However, due to the availability of uncultivated land and the ability of some rural communities to remain outside the effective realm of the rulers, slaves and bonded labourers always had an exit option. This tended to mitigate the duress of their condition.

Among the various explanations for the low population density, we should distinguish natural factors from cultural or political ones. South East Asia experienced several episodes of local and region-wide collapse of population density as consequences of recurrent crop failures triggered by decadal ENSO (El Niño–Southern Oscillation) climate anomalies (Cook et al. 2000; Lieberman and Buckley 2012). But similar ENSO-related climate anomalies in India, southern China, and Japan did not result in low population densities. The same remark applies to recurrent epidemics, which are documented as having a strong impact, particularly in the case of smallpox. Although the major parts of Java and Bali have fertile volcanic soils, natural land fertility was not higher in the Red River Delta than in the deltas of the Mekong, Chao Phraya, and Irrawaddy that had comparatively much lower population density until the early twentieth century. Rice-cultivating techniques, expertise in water management, and local institutions akin to those of coastal southern China are the major explanations for the higher population density of the Red River Delta and the narrow coastal plains of central Vietnam. These lowlands certainly had a similar disease environment, but higher density had gradually reduced the prevalence of some endemic tropical diseases. However, the populations of the low-population-density highlands had some acquired adaptation to dengue and malaria.

Climate anomalies or soil fertility appear therefore less important than cultural and institutional explanations affecting both birth and death rates. *Corvée* was imposed almost exclusively on males, but it had an effect on birth rates as it frequently implied an absence for several months. It also led to a high social status for women who acted as main breadwinners. Consistent with this high status, average female age of marriage was usually above 20 (and not much higher for males), which tended to reduced fertility rates in comparison with China and India where it was usually below 20. In most areas of South East Asia, voluntary fertility restriction was practised using traditional medicine or abortion. In countries practising Theravada Buddhism (Burma, Cambodia, Laos, and Thailand) the large number of adult males living in monasteries could have reduced nuptiality rates, but this was to some extent compensated by the polygamy of the elite. Large-scale warfare and endemic violence related to blood feuds or slave hunting resulted in excess mortality of adult men, and therefore affected fertility in societies that were mostly monogamous.

Reid argues that the total population of South East Asia increased by around 50 per cent between 1600 and 1800. The main exceptions were Laos, peninsular Malaya, and north-west Borneo, which also had very low levels of density. Temporary setbacks occurred, due to large-scale warfare between the main kingdoms[7] and to climate anomalies, in particular severe droughts in 1756–68 and 1790–96 (Cook et al. 2000). Other external shocks such as the Tambora eruption of 1815 (the year without summer) had a devastating impact on agricultural output in Bali, Java, Lombok, and the Sulawesi. It is generally accepted that demographic growth accelerated

7 In particular in Burma, Siam, and Vietnam in the mid-eighteenth century.

between 1815 and 1870. Available population estimates suggest that demographic growth rates could have been above 1 per cent in Java (Boomgaard 1987) and in Luzon (Owen 1987).

This took place in the context of South East Asian countries' growing involvement in international trade and improvement in the net barter term of trade (Williamson 2008). In mainland South East Asia, population growth could have been largely due to the decline of warfare. In the Philippines and the outer islands of Indonesia, changes in military technology used by European powers drastically reduced the pressure from slave raiders based in Sulu (Warren 2007) and Eastern Sulawesi (Velthoen 1997). The gradual shift from slavery and *corvée* to wage labour also contributed to higher population growth.

Changes in urbanization patterns can be used to gauge the size of the output surplus in the primary sector and the structural transformation of the economy. The general trend between the late seventeenth and the mid-nineteenth century is characterized by an increase in the size of most capital cities, and possibly also of country-level urbanization ratios (Table 6.2). Burma and Siam had urbanization ratios *c.*1800 around 10 per cent, comparable to the average for Europe (de Vries 1984), and well above the level of the most advanced provinces of China such as Fujian, Guangdong, and Jiangsu, where it was slightly above 5 per cent (Broadberry and Gupta 2006: 9).

Java and Vietnam are major exceptions to the rising trend of urbanization. The decline of Batavia is largely compensated by the rise of Surabaya, which became the major commercial hub of Java. It is likely that the loss of political autonomy and territory controlled by the Javanese principalities of Mataram and Banten following the 'Chinese War' (1741–45) and the British invasion of Java (1811), respectively, resulted in a decline of the population of the former capitals of these political entities. In Vietnam, the population of both Hanoi and Hue declined after the reunification of the country in 1802. But the network of mid-size cities, market towns, and military outposts expanded (de la Bissachère (1812: 73–74).

Expansion of International Trade, Chinese Immigration, and Monetization

The eighteenth century witnessed an expansion of intra-Asian trade, particularly with China, and has been described as the Chinese century in South East Asian history (Reid 1997). Thai rice exports to China in particular became a major trade flow (Baker and Phongpaichit 2017: 214–216). This also applies to a large extent to

Table 6.2 Estimates of urban population from the late seventeenth to the mid-nineteenth centuries

Country/region	City	Population	Year
Indonesia (Java)	Banten	100,000	1672
	Batavia (Jakarta)	130,000	1670
	Batavia (Jakarta)	90,000	c.1870
	Jepara	100,000	1654
	Semarang	100,000	1654
	Surabaya	60,000	1625
	Surabaya	100,000	c.1870
Malaysia and Singapore	Pattani	15,000	1690
	Singapore	95,000	c.1870
Myanmar (Burma)	Ava	30,000	1688
	Pagan (Bagan)	30,000	1688
	Prome (Pyay)	25,000	1688
	Syriam (Tanlyin)	30,000	1688
	Ava	120,000	c.1820
	Amapura	120,000	c.1820
	Sagaing	120,000	c.1820
	Rangoon (Yangon)	12,000	c.1820
	Rangoon (Yangon)	100,000	c.1870
Philippines	Manila	40,000	1630
	Manila	130,000	c.1870
Siam	Ayutthaya	200,000	1686
	Bangkok	300,000	c.1830
	Bangkok	400,000	c.1850
Vietnam	Thang-Long (Hanoi)	130,000	1688
	Bac-Kinh (Hanoi)	40,000	c.1810
	Kim-Long (Hue)	150,000	1674
	Phu-Xuan (Hue)	60,000	1749
	Hué	30,000	c.1810
	Saigon-Cholon	35,000	c.1810
	Saigon-Cholon	45,000	c.1870

Notes: Present-day city names in parenthesis (Ho Chi Minh City, which includes the area of the former twin cities of Saigon-Cholon, covers also rural areas and is the administrative equivalent of a province); Syriam (Tanlyin) is located a short distance from Rangoon (Yangon), which became the capital of lower Burma after the Second Anglo-Burmese War (1852). Sagaing is located at short distance from Amapura; Siam's capital was moved to Bangkok in 1767 after the destruction of Ayutthaya by a Burmese army. Hue, the capital of the Nguyen lords ruling the central part of Vietnam (1558–1777), became capital of reunified Vietnam in 1802.
Sources: based on Reid (1993: 71–73) excluding extrapolations based on number of houses or fighters; de la Bissachère (1812) for Vietnamese cities *c.*1810; Crawfurd (1829) for Burmese cities *c.*1820; Crawfurd (1828) for Faifo *c.*1830; Roberts (1837) for Bangkok *c.*1830; Mitchell (1982) for estimates *c.*1870.

the first half of the nineteenth century, during which the United States' merchant fleet, a new foreign power, appeared in the region. North American traders played a major role in the development of pepper export from Aceh, an independent polity,[8] and of sugar and Manila hemp (abaca) export from the Philippines, which was under Spanish colonial rule but where there was a strong presence of British and Chinese traders.

Foreign trade data for the early and mid-nineteenth century suggest that the increase of export of cash crops (including rice in Burma, Thailand, and Vietnam) was more rapid than population growth. This does not imply that rural incomes increased drastically. A large part of the value added generated was related to the transportation, processing, and export, corresponding mainly to revenues of urban residents. The same remark applies to economic changes resulting from the imposition of British colonial rule (from 1824 in Arakan, Malacca, and Singapore, and 1852 in lower Burma) or French rule (from 1858 in southern Vietnam) or of what could be described as the informal British protectorate in Siam (following the Bowring Treaty of 1855).

In parallel with the growing importance of foreign trade with China, a rapid increase of migration flows from Canton and Fujian provinces took place from the eighteenth century onwards. This resulted in the establishment of sizeable Chinese communities throughout South East Asia, both in urban and rural areas (Trocki 1997). This process was reinforced by intermarriage with local women, often traders or members of the local elites. Chinese business networks rapidly became dominant in various activities related to trade and maritime transportation, in particular the export of rice to the coastal cities of southern China, as well as tin and gold mining, and sugar and pepper plantations. A contemporary British report conjectured that 1 million ethnic Chinese were residents in South East Asia *c.*1830,[9] implying that they accounted for around 3 per cent of the population, a higher share than at the turn of the twentieth century. They were mostly concentrated in Malaysia, Borneo, and Sumatra. In comparison, Indian migrants were far less numerous and played a more limited role in international trade.

Estimates of total export value for South East Asian pepper, coffee, and sugar, which were the three major commodities exported (Table 6.3), indicate a rapid expansion from the turn of the nineteenth century following the liberalization of foreign trade in the Philippines in 1789 (de Jesus 1980: 24–25)

8 Aceh accounted for around half of the world production in 1824 (Lieberman 1997: 39).

9 Newbold (1839: vol. I, p. 9); quoted in Reid (1997: 12).

Table 6.3 Annual average value by decade of three main South East Asian exports (in 1,000 silver Mexican $)

Decade	Pepper	Coffee	Sugar	Total	Growth p.a.
1750–59	408	294	319	1,021	
1760–69	467	344	602	1,413	3.4
1770–79	508	345	312	1,165	−2.0
1780–89	508	362	336	1,206	0.3
1790–99	600	395	550	1,545	2.5
1800–09	1,150	350	810	2,310	4.1
1810–19	1,008	780	532	2,320	0.04
1820–29	1,386	4,374	910	6,670	11.1
1830–39	1,760	5,782	2,646	10,188	4.3
1840–49	2,088	7,009	13,070	22,167	8.1
1850–59	2,616	12,635	17,361	32,612	3.9
1860–69	1,825	18,539	25,989	46,353	3.6
1870–79	3,527	26,020	35,991	65,538	3.5

Source: Reid (1997: 74).

and the dissolution of the Dutch East India Company (VOC) in 1799, which resulted in the establishment of Dutch colonial rule in the territories it had controlled. Coffee was essentially exported from Java to Europe, where it supplied most of demand. China was by far the biggest market for pepper and sugar. The initial phase of expansion of exports took place before the decline in shipping costs of the 1850s and 1860s (Chilosi and Federico 2015: 19). Yearly series of the export of coffee and sugar from Indonesia, which can be calculated from 1823 in volume per capita (Figure 6.2), confirm a rapid expansion before the 1850s, indicating that it was driven by the rising European and Chinese demand, respectively.

Annual series available from 1831 for exports from Singapore, which were almost exclusively re-exports, provide a more comprehensive view of the commodities traded (Kobayashi 2017: 114). In the 1830s and 1840s, non-food manufactured Asian products (mostly silk and opium, from China and India, respectively) and processed South East Asian foodstuffs accounted, respectively, for around 30 per cent and 20 per cent of total exports from Singapore, while local primary products (mostly rice, forest products, and tin) and British cotton goods accounted for less than 10 per cent each; the remainder consisted of unclassified items. The share of British cotton was on the rise in the 1860s, reaching 20 per cent *c.*1870, but overall regional trade retained its primacy in a context of the rapid expansion of foreign trade.

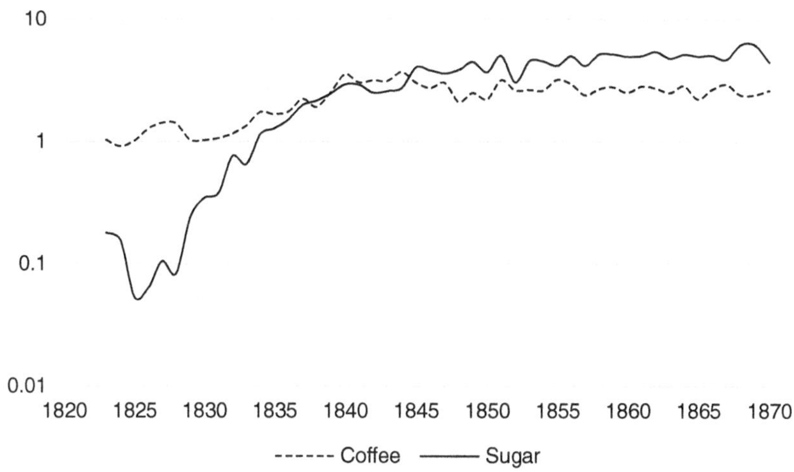

Figure 6.2 Export of coffee and sugar from Indonesia in kg per capita (log scale)
Sources: Mitchell (1982) for export volumes; Maddison (2010) for population.

The combination of a structural trade surplus and of rising foreign trade of cash crops generated an inflow of Mexican pesos in the main cities involved in international trade and also gradually in rural areas. It enabled local polities to collect additional public revenue. Export and import duties were much easier to introduce than a rise in the land tax or personal tax. South East Asian countries had until the eighteenth century used a combination of weighted silver and other metals, such as copper, tin, and lead, and barter trade for local transactions (Saito 1997; Feenstra 2014). But *corvée* and slavery were the major forms of mobilization of labour *c.*1700. The monetization of the economy enabled local authorities and political elites to reduce their reliance on *corvée* for public works and warfare, and on slavery for generating private revenues. The governments of the countries most open to international trade, such as Thailand, had therefore the ability to collect export duties and had an obvious advantage. In 1822 the volume of Bangkok's trade was already four to five times that of Rangoon; between 1740 and 1820, the portion of the revenues of the Siamese Crown derived from maritime trade rose from one-quarter or one-third to well over half (Lieberman 1997: 34–35).

The inflow of silver pesos facilitated the shift to cash for the payment of personal and land taxes. In the meantime, the perspective of reducing the actual tax burden by paying in cash rather than in kind (mostly labour, staples, and local textile products) created incentives for agricultural producers to diversify their activities, with at least one cash crop. This could explain the relatively high level of social acceptance of the 'cultivation system' in Java; although the producers were not free to decide which cash crop to cultivate, they did receive a payment in cash. A somewhat similar interpretation could be considered for the expansion of sugar cultivation in the Visayas (central part of the Philippines) and in central Luzon, where it became a major cash crop for export in the late eighteenth and early nineteenth century (Larkin 1972). The same process was observed during the nineteenth century in the Bicol peninsula (southern Luzon) in response to the payment in cash of part of the personal tax. Although the rural population was until then mostly self-sufficient and barely involved in monetary transactions, it started to cultivate abaca and process it for export. Abaca had the advantage of requiring labour input mostly during the slack season of rice cultivation; it became one of the main cash crops of the Philippines in the mid-nineteenth century (Owen 1988).

Rising State Capacity and Resistance to Colonization

The major South East Asian kingdoms on the mainland, and a few other smaller ones in the archipelago, were already powerful political entities before the eighteenth century, somewhat comparable to contemporary Japan or second-tier European kingdoms (Lieberman 2003; 2009). On the mainland, in the Burmese, Thai, Khmer, and Viet linguistic areas, relatively stable polities ruled their respective realms along the four main river transportation systems of the Irrawaddy, Chao Phraya, Mekong, and Red rivers, with large capital cities located at some distance from the coast exercising close control over the lowland people and a more indirect control over the populations of the hills and highlands belonging mostly to various smaller ethnic groups.

Indigenous polities of the Malay peninsula and archipelago, generally centred on a major port city, were of comparatively smaller size. But even in areas characterized by high population density thanks to rich volcanic soils, as in Bali and Java, and that were homogenous in both linguistic and religious terms, the polities were relatively small. This was especially the case in Bali, where seven principalities were competing for the control of taxable revenues and the labour force (total population was less than 1 million until the nineteenth century).

According to contemporary reports written by Westerners, the native polities on the mainland and the archipelago had a permanent administration managed by civil servants that the Western sources usually designated as mandarin (from the Portuguese transliteration of a Malay term derived from Sanskrit), a judicial system based on written laws, and a rather homogenous tax system. The kings, rajas, and sultans entertained diplomatic relations among themselves, and the major powers also sent tribute missions to China combining trade and diplomacy, and on occasion embassies to Japan, Mughal India, Persia, and European powers.

The revenues generated by international trade, either royal monopolies or taxations, enabled the kingdoms of the mainland to hire mercenaries from various parts of South East Asia or from Europe, India, Japan, and Persia from the sixteenth century onwards (Baker and Phongpaichit 2017: 91–94, 123) and to import modern European weaponry from the seventeenth century, in particular flintlock rifles and cannon (Lieberman 1997: 35). They were also able to attract Western military experts, either dispatched by their government or employed as foreign mandarins, for modernizing their army and navy, and upgrading their artillery. Saltpetre for the production of gunpowder was imported from India through British, Danish, Dutch, or French private traders.

The eighteenth and early nineteenth centuries witnessed a rapid reinforcement of the authority and legitimacy of the main polities and their effective control of the population living in their respective realms. It occurred in parallel in the three major kingdoms of the mainland, Burma, Siam, and Vietnam, although with temporary setbacks.[10] Understandably, the rulers of the smaller peripheral tributary polities were reluctant to accept a shift to direct rule. Political consolidation and centralization had to be imposed and was made possible by the increase of the fiscal capacity, itself permitted by the monetization of the economy.

A similar process took place in the smaller independent polities of the Malay Archipelago, in particular in Aceh, Sulu, Bali, and Lombok, and in the territories under Dutch (VOC until 1800) influence in Java or in the Philippines. In all these areas, the political institutions were based on a collaboration of the central government with the traditional local elites that benefited from the enhanced political stability and the resulting expansion of mining activities, or rice and cash crop cultivation for export. From that

10 All three kingdoms collapsed in succession between 1752 and 1786, but re-emerged immediately as strong as before.

viewpoint, the Dutch and Spanish colonial policies of the eighteenth and early nineteenth centuries did not essentially differ from those of the native polities.

The policies implemented by South East Asian states in order to raise net public revenues combined a better assessment of the tax base resulting from the improvement of land censuses and property rights,[11] a diversification of the sources of public revenue, in particular by the introduction of monopolies in opium and tobacco and a reduction of the cost of tax collection by relying on tax farming (usually undertaken by Chinese merchants). This increase of the tax pressure was made acceptable by a gradual shift to cash payment that reduced transaction costs and therefore the actual burden imposed on the taxpayers. In Burma, the ratio between cash and in-kind taxes increase steadily, from 58/42 in 1760 to 70/30 in 1804 (Lieberman 1997: 35). Overall, the tax pressure remained rather light. In Siam *c.*1830, total tax revenues (land taxes, gambling and alcohol farms, and duties) accounted for around 2.3 million tical (Roberts 1837: 426–427), equivalent to 2.7 kg rice per capita per year.

The process of monetization occurred also on the expenditure side of public finances. South East Asian rulers had traditionally relied on *corvée* labour with little more than rice distribution in terms of daily allowance. From the early nineteenth century, the compensation included at least in part a cash component. In Siam, it became common in the mid-nineteenth century to hire Chinese wages labour for digging canals or building roads, rather than relying on *corvée* labour (Ingram 1971). In a similar pattern, the compensation of civil servants gradually evolved from the traditional system of allocation of revenues from land, with *corvée* labour services attached, to monetary payments. The most elaborate case was the straightforward salary system introduced in the Chinese-style mandarin administration of Vietnam in 1839 (Vu 1997).

Clear evidence of the growing state capacity can be seen in the military might of the main polities in the mainland. The size of the major South East Asian armies and navies was already comparable to that of contemporary midsize European powers in the eighteenth century. It remained sufficient, until the early nineteenth century, for imposing their conditions by land and sea on all Westerners. The major change was their ability to sustain a long

11 Extensive land censuses were conducted in Vietnam in 1805 and 1836 (Lieberman 1997: 36). Property rights of land planted in orchards or sugar cane in areas surrounding Bangkok became also well established during the same period (Chankrajang and Vechbanyongratana 2017).

warfare mobilizing a large share of the labour force, since the army was essentially composed of peasant militias. The most impressive case was the war of more than 20 years waged successfully from 1778 by the Nguyen rulers of Cochinchina (southern Vietnam) against the Tay Son millenarian insurgency, and then the rulers of the northern part of Vietnam.

According to de la Bissachère (1812: 302–303), a Catholic missionary who was also mandarin at the court of the Vietnamese king for almost twenty years, one-third of all men aged 18–50 had been conscripted in the southern part of the country, and one-seventh in the northern part during the final phase of the war. It ended with the victory of the south, in spite of its much smaller population (compensated by a much higher involvement in foreign trade), and the reunification of the country in 1802. The same source indicates that military expenditures also included the construction of fortresses *à la Vauban* and the building of the strategic north-south 1200 km-long Mandarin road (de la Bissachère 1812: 36). The expenditures required for these public works exceeded the total amount of tax paid in cash and required therefore additional labour obtained through *corvée* and building materials requisitioned as tax in kind (de la Bissachère 1812: 298–299).

The peacetime Vietnamese army had a total of 150,000 men in 1806 (de la Bissachère 1812: 298–299), but Vietnam was by far the most militarized South East Asian polity, even accounting for the fact that it was also the most populous. The wartime army of the Burmese kingdom never exceeded 40,000 men in the late eighteenth century, for a population of 2 million, excluding peripheral tributary polities (Mantegazza 1784). Siam had an army of about the same size during the military operations in the northern, eastern, and southern peripheries, or during confrontations with Vietnam. These armies were strong enough to repel the Chinese invasions, of Burma in 1765 and of northern Vietnam in 1788. The military might of South East Asian polities was also sufficient to make British or French attempts at colonization or the territorial expansion of Dutch and Spanish colonial realms expensive and risky ventures until the modernization of their navies in the early nineteenth century gave them a superior firepower.

But this applied only to naval or coastal operations, as shown by the heavy losses suffered by the Dutch army during the Java War (1825–30). Even later in the nineteenth century, the French encountered unexpected difficulties in 1883–85 during their invasion of central and northern Vietnam, a weakened and impoverished state, although they operated from their rice-exporting colony of *Cochinchine* (southern Vietnam), which was entirely under French control from 1867 onwards. This explains how the imposition of European colonial rule in the period 1819–70[12] was a gradual process that either implied a status of protectorate or relied largely on local economic and political elites in the case of direct rule. Although Thailand had a relatively small army, it was the South East Asian country that achieved the highest fiscal capacity in the early nineteenth century. This represented a credible deterrent in front of the colonial ambitions of foreign powers, including Britain and France, that rather targeted Burma and Vietnam and acknowledged Thailand's independence.

Capital Accumulation and Sustainable Development

The paucity of quantitative information does not allow the construction of series of capital formation and capital stocks. It is, however, possible to review the available evidence in order to identify long-term trends in terms of physical, natural, and human capital, and therefore comprehensive wealth per capita, and to assess the sustainability of the transformation of South East Asian economies between the early eighteenth century and the second half of the nineteenth century.

Trends in the physical (produced) component of the stock of assets are comparatively easy to gauge. Very little machinery was imported from Western Europe, except weapons that were also produced locally. The technologies for the production of carts, vessels, and houses remained essentially unchanged. Available evidence indicates that the value of these assets was small: 5–20 dollars for a house and no more than 6 dollars for a dwelling boat in the region of the straits of Malacca in the 1820s (Crawfurd 1829: 83), where food consumption expenditures for one adult are given at 1.5 dollars per month when sago is used as the staple, and around 2.5 using rice as the staple (Crawfurd 1829: 84).

Livestock was limited to one or two cattle or buffalo per rural household, plus some poultry and pigs. Orchards of coconuts, areca, and various other fruit trees and other perennial plantations (pepper, sugar cane, betel) had a high value per hectare, the cost of land reclamation and plantation was for instance 120 Mexican dollars per acre (0.4 hectare) on Penang in the 1820s (Crawfurd 1829: 28), but total acreage was small and rather stable relative to

12 British colonial rule from 1819 in Singapore, 1826 in Arakan and Tenasserim (northern and southern coast of Burma), and 1861–62 in Lower Burma; Dutch rule from 1830 in western Java and 1830–38 in Minangkabau (Sumatra); French rule from 1861–62 in the Mekong Delta and 1864 in Cambodia.

total population. Some improvement of transportation infrastructure also took place, but mostly towards the very end of the period. Overall, the stock of physical produced capital remained stable and rather small in per capita terms.

The trend was probably different for natural capital due to population growth resulting in a dilution of the stock (decline in per capita terms). In addition, a depletion of renewable and non-renewable environmental assets occurred, with different degrees of magnitude. The most obvious aspect concerns non-renewable mining products, mostly tin in peninsular Malaya and Siam, and petrol in Burma. Thousands of workers were involved, almost exclusively ethnic Chinese in the case of tin mining, but the volumes extracted were still negligible in comparison with the late nineteenth century. Changes in the composition of export items and tax revenues provide some additional evidence of the process of depletion of renewable resources. Various products of hunting and gathering such as ivory, rhinoceroses' horn, deer skins, and bird's nests, were still reported, for instance in the public revenues of Siam in the 1830s (Roberts 1837: 426–427), but in smaller quantities or proportions than in the eighteenth century. Their share had become negligible by around 1870.

This remark does not apply, however, to the entire primary sector. In most countries, export volume was increasing steadily for forestry and fisheries products such as teak wood, rose wood, wood oil, rattan, bamboo, dried shrimps or fish, and there is no evidence that the exploitation of these resources exceeded sustainable levels. Although the scale of land reclamation was still limited in comparison with what happened in the twentieth century, the volume of rice and cash crops exported was rising fast as a consequence of a development of agricultural production that was more rapid than population growth. But the environmental impact of the consumption of natural capital was still imperceptible at the country level. Almost unspoiled forests still covered well over half of the landmass in all countries.

The declining availability in per capita terms of products from the wild (emergency foods and products from hunting) in kg per capita due to the rise in population density was largely offset by the higher carrying capacity of anthropized ecosystems. In particular, we should account for the effects of the diffusion of American crops such as cassava and maize, which reduced the need for forest products such as sago flour that were largely used as a staple in the regions close to the Straits of Malacca. Another important feature, equally difficult to document, was the gradual shift in the peripheral regions of very low population density from slash-and-burn cultivation to a specialization in irrigated rice cultivation, associated with intensive horticulture and orchards, and some cash crops. Although this resulted in an increase in land productivity, most likely in parallel with population growth, it is unlikely that labour productivity improved in terms of calories obtained from grains and roots.

The third component of comprehensive wealth, human capital, results from the transmission of existing knowledge and the accumulation of new skills. Available information suggests that South East Asia was on a trajectory of human capital accumulation. With the exception of Vietnam, where Chinese characters used for official records were studied in local schools (in principle one in each village), all South East Asian countries had used local variants of alphabets derived from Sanskrit since the end of the first millennium of the Common Era. From the seventeenth century onwards, a shift to the Latin alphabet took place in the Philippines, and to Arabic script in the Malay peninsula.

Descriptions by Western visitors mention widespread literacy and common use of written documents among males. The Philippines are the only South East Asian country for which detailed information is available: 13 per cent of males and 12 per cent of females aged 12 or above were able to read and write in *c.*1870 (in their native language; only a small percentage were able to read Spanish), and an additional 26 per cent and 12 per cent were able to read (calculation based on information reported in Cavada Mendez de Vigo 1876). This is much lower than the levels estimated for Europe *c.*1880 by Tabellini (2010: Figure 6.4). However, a number of provinces of Luzon, as well as the island of Cebu, had literacy levels comparable to the Spanish average.

Literacy levels in South East Asia, although not particularly impressive by European standards, and lower than in early nineteenth-century Japan, were probably at least as high as in India or China, and higher than in tropical regions of Africa and South America characterized by low population density and an abundance of natural resources. Estimates of numeracy derived from age-heaping measurement (Crayen and Baten 2010: 87) indicate levels for South East Asia *c.*1840 much lower than in Japan, Korea, and China (where numeracy was comparable to European and North American levels), but higher than in India. Since women had a dominant role in local trade, they were certainly at least as numerate as males.

The evolution of the numeracy estimates indicates a clear upward trend, which implies a process of human capital accumulation. The migration of ethnic Chinese in the region brought useful skills and can be regarded as a form of importation of human capital, with a gradual diffusion to the native population, particularly through intermarriage. The pattern that emerges is therefore a dual process in which the limited destruction of natural capital was offset by an increase of the stock of human capital. Comprehensive wealth per capita did not decline, and most likely increased steadily. South East Asia therefore experienced an economic transformation that can be described as sustainable development.

Conclusion

South East Asia between 1700 and 1870 can be characterized as a region of low population density, abundant natural resources, and high labour productivity in agriculture. Its coastal areas were deeply involved in international trade, particularly with China and India. Available information on urban real wages indicates that in most parts of the region, living standards were well above Chinese and Indian levels until at least the mid-nineteenth century. The population growth observed throughout the region in the eighteenth and nineteenth centuries suggests also a strong resilience to climate shocks and wars.

The main independent indigenous polities on the mainland and a few smaller ones on the archipelago reinforced their authority, legitimacy, and capacity. Trends in the main variables that form the constituent parts of comprehensive wealth, including natural, human, and physical capital, suggest that comprehensive wealth was stable or increasing in South East Asia during this period.

References

Baker, C. and Phongpaichit, P. (2017). 'Early Modern Siam as a Mainly Urban Society', *Modern Asian Studies*, 51(2), 235–267.

Bassino, J.-P. and Coclanis, P. A. (2008). 'Economic Transformation and Biological Welfare in Colonial Burma: Regional Differentiation in the Evolution of Average Height', *Economics and Human Biology*, 6(2), 212–227.

Boomgaard, P. (1987). 'Morbidity and Mortality in Java, 1820–1880: Changing Patterns of Disease and Death', in Owen, N. G. (ed.), *Death and Disease in South East Asia: Explorations in Social, Medical and Demographic History*, Singapore: Oxford University Press, 48–69.

Broadberry, S. and Gupta, B. (2006). 'The Early Modern Great Divergence: Wages, Prices and Economic Development in Europe and Asia, 1500–1800', *Economic History Review*, 59(1), 2–31.

Cavada Mendez de Vigo, A. (1876). *Historia geografica, geologica y estadistica de Filipinas*, Manila: Ramirez y Giraudier.

Chankrajang, T. and Vechbanyongratana, J. (2017). *A Brief Economic History of Land Rights in Thailand: From the Sukhothai Period to the End of King Chulalongkorn's Reign*, Bangkok: Chulalongkorn University.

Chilosi, D. and Federico, G. (2015). 'Early Globalizations: The Integration of Asia in the World Economy, 1800–1938', *Explorations in Economic History*, 57, 1–18.

Cook, E. R., Anchukaitis, K. J., Buckley, B. M., D'Arrigo, G. C., Jacoby, R. D. and Wright, W. E. (2000). 'Asian Monsoon Failure and Megadrought During the Last Millennium', *Science*, 328(5977), 486–489.

Crawfurd, J. (1828). *Journal of an Embassy from the Governor-General of India to the Courts of Siam and Cochin China: Exhibiting a View of the Actual State of Those Kingdoms*, London: H. Colburn.

(1829). *Journal of an Embassy from the Governor-General of India to the Court of Ava in the Year 1827*. London: H. Colburn; reprint Cambridge University Press, 2012.

Crayen, D. and Baten, J. (2010). 'Global Trends in Numeracy 1820–1949 and its Implications for Long-term Growth', *Explorations in Economic History*, 47(1), 82–99.

Dasgupta, P. (2009). 'The Welfare Economic Theory of Green National Accounts', *Environmental and Resources Economics*, 42, 3–38.

de Jesus, E. C. (1980). *The Tobacco Monopoly in the Philippines: Bureaucratic Enterprise and Social Change, 1766–1880*. Manila: Ateneo de Manila University Press.

de la Bissachère, P-J. L. (1812). *Etat actuel du Tunkin et de la Cochinchine, et des royaumes de Cambodge, Laos et Lac-Tho*, Paris: Belin.

de Vries, J. (1984). *European Urbanization 1500–1800*, London: Methuen.

de Zwart, P. and van Zanden, J. L. (2015). 'Labor, Wages, and Living Standards in Java, 1680–1914', *European Review of Economic History*, 19(3), 215–234.

Feenstra, A. (2014). 'Dutch Coins for Asian Growth: VOC-duiten to Assess Java's Deep Monetisation and Economic Growth, 1724–1800', *Tijdschrift Voor Sociale en Economische Geschiedenis*, 11(3), 153.

Ingram, J. C. (1964). 'Thailand's Rice Trade and the Allocation of Resources', in Cowan, C. D. (ed.), *The Economic Development of Southeast Asia*, London: Allen & Unwin, 102–106.

(1971). *Economic Change in Thailand, 1850–1970*, Stanford University Press.

Kobayashi, A. (2017). 'Price Fluctuations and Growth Patterns in Singapore's Trade, 1831–1913', *Australian Economic History Review*, 57(1), 108–129.

(2020). 'The Origin of Singapore's Economic Prosperity (c.1800–74)', in Webster, A. and White, N. (eds.), *Singapore – Two Hundred Years History of the Lion City*. London: Routledge.

Larkin, J. (1972). *The Pampangans: Colonial Society in a Philippine Province*, Berkeley: University of California Press.

Lieberman, V. B. (1997). 'Mainland-Archipelagic Parallels and Contrasts, c.1750–1850', in Reid, A. (ed.), *The Last Stand of Asian Autonomies: Responses to Modernity in the Diverse States of Southeast Asia and Korea, 1750–1900*, London: Macmillan, 27–53.

(2003). *Strange Parallels: Southeast Asia in Global Context, c.800–1830. Volume I: Integration on the Mainland*, Cambridge University Press.

(2009). *Strange Parallels: Southeast Asia in Global Context, c.800–1830. Volume II: Mainland Mirrors: Europe, Japan, China, South Asia, and the Islands*, Cambridge University Press.

Lieberman, V. and Buckley, B. (2012). 'The Impact of Climate on Southeast Asia, circa 950–1820: New Findings', *Modern Asian Studies*, 46(5), 1049.

Maddison, A. (2010). 'Statistics on World Population, GDP and Per Capita GDP, 1–2008 AD', Groningen Growth and Development Centre, www.ggdc.net/MADDISON/oriindex.htm (accessed 30 September 2020).

Mantegazza, G. (1784). 'Relation d'un voyage aux royaumes de Pegu et Ava', *Archivio Storico della Propaganda Fide, SC Indie Orientali e Cina, Misc. 10* (printed edition: R. Carmignani (ed.), (1950). *La Birmania: relazione inedita del 1784 del missionario barnabita G.M. Mantegazza*, Rome: AS).

Milanovic, B., Lindert, P. H. and Williamson, J. G. (2011). 'Pre-industrial Inequality', *The Economic Journal*, 121(551), 255–272.

Mitchell, B. R. (1982). *International Historical Statistics: Africa and Asia*, London: Macmillan.

Newbold, T. J. (1839). *British Settlements in the Straits of Malacca* (reprint Kuala Lumpur, Oxford University Press, 1965).

Owen, N. G. (1987). 'The Paradox of Nineteenth-Century Population Growth in Southeast Asia: Evidence from Java and the Philippines', *Journal of Southeast Asian Studies*, 18(1), 45–57.

(1988). *Prosperity without Progress: Manila Hemp and Material Life in Colonial Philippines*, Cambridge University Press.

Reid, A. (1988). *Southeast Asia in the Age of Commerce, 1450–1680. Volume I: The Lands below the Winds*, New Haven: Yale University Press.

(1993). *Southeast Asia in the Age of Commerce, 1450–1680. Volume II: Expansion and Crisis*, New Haven: Yale University Press.

(1997). 'A New Phase in Commercial Expansion in Southeast Asia, 1760–1850', in Reid, A. (ed.), *The Last Stand of Asian Autonomies: Responses to Modernity in the Diverse States of Southeast Asia and Korea, 1750–1900*, London: Macmillan, 57–81.

Roberts, E. (1837). *Embassy to the Eastern Courts of Cochin-China, Siam, and Muscat*, New York: Harper.

Saito, T. (1997). 'Rural Monetization and Land-Mortgage: *Thet-kayits* in Kon-Baung Burma', in Reid, A. (ed.), *The Last Stand of Asian Autonomies: Responses to Modernity in the Diverse States of Southeast Asia and Korea, 1750–1900*, London: Macmillan, 153–184.

Tabellini, G. (2010). 'Culture and Institutions: Economic Development in the Regions of Europe', *Journal of the European Economic Association*, 8(4), 677–716.

Trocki, C. A. (1997). 'Chinese Pioneering in Eighteenth-Century Southeast Asia', in Reid, A. (ed.), *The Last Stand of Asian Autonomies: Responses to Modernity in the Diverse States of Southeast Asia and Korea, 1750–1900*, London: Macmillan, 83–101.

van der Eng, P. (2004). 'Productivity and Comparative Advantage in Rice Agriculture in South-East Asia Since 1870', *Asian Economic Journal*, 18(4), 345–370.

van Zanden, J. L. (1999). 'Wages and the Standard of Living in Europe, 1500–1800', *European Review of Economic History*, 3(2), 175–197.

(2003). Rich and Poor Before the Industrial Revolution: A Comparison Between Java and the Netherlands at the Beginning of the 19th century', *Explorations in Economic History*, 40(1), 1–23.

Velthoen, E. J. (1997). '"Wanderers, Robbers and Bad Folk": The Politics of Violence, Protection and Trade in Eastern Sulawesi 1750–1850', in Reid, A. (ed.), *The Last Stand of Asian Autonomies: Responses to Modernity in the Diverse States of Southeast Asia and Korea, 1750–1900*, London: Macmillan, 367–388.

Vu, M. G. (1997). 'Reform Tendencies in Nineteenth-Century Vietnam', in Reid, A. (ed.), *The Last Stand of Asian Autonomies: Responses to Modernity in the Diverse States of Southeast Asia and Korea, 1750–1900*, London: Macmillan, 411–424.

Warren, J. F. (2007). *The Sulu Zone, 1768–1898*, 2nd ed., Singapore: NUS Press.

Williamson, J. G. (2008). 'Globalization and the Great Divergence: Terms of Trade Booms, Volatility and the Poor Periphery, 1782–1913', *European Review of Economic History*, 12(3), 355–391.

7
The Ottoman Empire, 1700–1870

ŞEVKET PAMUK

The Ottoman Empire stood at the crossroads of intercontinental trade, stretching from south-eastern Europe and the Black Sea region through Anatolia, Syria, Mesopotamia, and the Gulf to Egypt and most of the North African coast for six centuries until World War I. As a large literature has already examined in detail, the nineteenth century was an era of major changes for the Ottoman Empire. In contrast, much less was known until recently about the eighteenth century. Fortunately, while there are still many gaps in our knowledge, we have a better idea today about what happened to the Ottoman economy during the eighteenth century.

Making use of the evidence that has been gathered by economic historians in recent decades, I will argue that two very different periods or conjunctures can be identified for the Ottoman economy during the eighteenth century. The decades until the end of the 1760s were a period of relative peace and economic expansion. There is evidence that incomes tended to rise and commercial and monetary linkages inside the empire grew stronger during this period. In contrast, from the end of the 1760s until the 1820s was a period of wars and domestic political struggles when long-distance trade as well as agricultural and manufacturing output was frequently disrupted, state finances were under pressure and the frequent debasements by governments at Istanbul and Cairo in response to the financial difficulties led to inflation. Even though trade and more generally economic interaction between the Ottoman Empire and Western Europe increased during the eighteenth century, its volume remained small by the standards of the nineteenth century. As a result, both urban and rural crafts and manufacturing activities in the Ottoman Empire remained mostly intact and specialization in agriculture for export was not yet strong at the end of the eighteenth century. The low levels of trade with other regions of the world provided a good deal of room for local actors, merchants, and manufacturers, as well as local institutions and organizations, to survive and respond to changing circumstances.

The nineteenth century was a period quite different from the earlier era. In the face of the growing European challenge and territorial losses of the empire in the Balkans and North Africa including Egypt, it was characterized, on the one hand, by major efforts of Western style reform in administration, education, law, and justice, as well as economic, fiscal, and monetary affairs. It was also a period of integration into world markets and rapid expansion in trade with industrial Europe that transformed the Ottoman economy into an exporter of primary products and importer of manufactures. Direct investments by European companies in railways, trade, ports, and other areas after mid-century supported this process.

The last part of the chapter will review the evidence presented by the recent studies on real wages and estimates of GDP per capita before and after the Industrial Revolution. This evidence will allow us to evaluate better the case of the Ottoman Empire with respect to the debate on the Great Divergence. These studies show that the purchasing power of the wages of skilled and unskilled construction workers in the leading cities in north-western Europe (Britain and the Low Countries), were more than 50 per cent higher than those in Istanbul during the eighteenth century. The gap in GDP per capita between north-western Europe and the different regions of the Ottoman Empire was somewhat higher. These differences increased further during the nineteenth century and until World War I. The gap in real wages and GDP per capita between southern Europe (Italy and Spain) and the Ottoman Empire was more limited during the eighteenth century, but this gap also increased during the nineteenth century, especially after 1870.

I begin with a note on population trends. The evidence on the population of the Ottoman Empire during the early modern era is not very detailed, but some basic trends can be established. The population of the Ottoman Empire covering territories in south-eastern Europe, western Asia and northern Africa increased from about 26 to 28 million between 1700 and 1820. In contrast, the population of Europe as a whole increased from 120 million in 1700 to 200 million in 1820 and 315 million in 1870. The population of South Asia is estimated to have increased from 165 million in 1700 to 200 million in 1820 and 240 million in 1870 (McEvedy and Jones 1978). The slow increase in the population of the Ottoman Empire before the nineteenth century was in part due to the losses of territory in Europe, but population increases in the remaining areas of the empire was also limited. One important reason for the latter was the frequent recurrence of the plague around the eastern Mediterranean and the Middle East from the fourteenth century until the 1830s. Even though the population of the territories that remained part of the Ottoman Empire increased more rapidly after 1820, the rise of independent states in south-eastern Europe and the de facto independence of Egypt led to the decline of the total population of the empire. In 1870, the population of the European provinces of the empire stood around 7 million and the Asian territories of Turkey, Syria, Iraq, and Arabia at around 17 million. The population of Egypt is estimated at 6.5 million for the same year. The trend towards urbanization in the Ottoman Empire was also modest. The share of the population living in urban areas is estimated to have increased from around 12–13 per cent in 1700 to about 17–18 per cent in 1870.

Land Regime and State Finances

The agricultural sector provided the economic livelihood for close to 80 per cent of the population as well as key fiscal support for the Ottoman state during the early modern era. The durability of the empire, its achievements, and its limitations were closely related to its agrarian institutions. In the core regions of the empire in the Balkans and Anatolia, state ownership of agricultural lands was established as the basic form. Hereditary usufruct of these lands was given to peasant households, which typically cultivated with a pair of oxen and family labour. The peasant family farm that typically cultivated land with a pair of oxen and family labour thus emerged as the basic economic and fiscal unit in the countryside (İnalcik 1994: 103–179). However, locally powerful families always exerted control over land in different parts of the empire. In addition, large amounts of land were controlled by Islamic *waqfs* or pious foundations. Peasant families cultivated the land as sharecropping tenants in these large holdings.

Despite the decline in the power of the central government and the rise of urban notables (*ayan*) in the provinces during the seventeenth and especially the eighteenth centuries, the central administration refused to recognize private ownership in most agricultural lands with the exception of orchards and vineyards. Records from these Islamic courts provide details of land sales before the nineteenth century, but these were small in number. Usufruct in most state lands remained in the hands of peasant households. In contrast, urban real estate did change hands quite easily (Keyder and Tabak 1991: 1–16).

Nonetheless, increasing control of taxation gave locally powerful groups greater control of agricultural land during the eighteenth century. The

Ottoman central administration relied on the tax-farming system to collect taxes in both rural and urban areas. Only the local powerful and well-connected individuals could participate in the auctions where the tax-farms were sold to the highest bidder. Frequent wars and deterioration of state finances increased the pressures on the central government to rely on the tax-farming system for the purposes of domestic borrowing, as well. With the introduction of the *malikane* system at the end of the seventeenth century, some of the revenue sources of the central administration began to be farmed out on a lifetime basis in return for large initial payments to be followed by annual payments (Özvar 2003: 29–92). For both the well-connected individuals in the capital city and those in the provinces, getting a piece of government tax revenues thus became an activity more lucrative than investing in agriculture, trade, or manufacturing (Salzman 1993: 393–423). The option of borrowing in the European financial markets was not available to the Ottoman government until the middle of the nineteenth century.

Urban Economy

In the urban economy, manufacturing and trade remained under the control of the guilds. The guilds sought and obtained the support of the government whenever merchants tried to organize production outside the guilds. In return, the government expected the guilds to contribute to the urban economy and to the army during periods of war. At the same time, there existed considerable tension between the government and guild membership, both Muslim and non-Muslim. While the guilds tried to preserve their independence, they were viewed with suspicion for the heterodox religious beliefs of their membership (Faroqhi 2009a). The Ottoman state encouraged the activities of merchants, domestic manufacturers, and moneychangers. These groups could accumulate wealth and capital, but the properties of government bureaucrats were often confiscated after their death. Despite the rise of locally powerful groups in the provincial urban centres during the seventeenth and eighteenth centuries, merchants and domestic producers did not become powerful enough to influence the central government to change or modify its policies. Only in the provinces, locally powerful groups were able to exert increasing degrees of influence over the provincial administrators (İnalcık 1969: 97–140).

It has often been assumed that the prohibition of interest in Islam prevented the development of credit, or at best, imposed rigid obstacles in its way. Similarly, the apparent absence of deposit banking and lending by banks has led many observers to conclude that financial institutions and instruments were, by and large, absent in Islamic societies. However, Islamic law had provided several means by which the anti-usury prohibition could be circumvented, just as the same prohibitions were circumvented in Europe in the late medieval period. There did not exist an insurmountable barrier against the use of interest-bearing loans for commercial credit. Instead, numerous other commercial techniques were used, including a variety of business partnership forms such as *mudaraba* and other credit arrangements sanctioned by religious theory. Ottoman institutions of private credit and finance thus retained their Islamic lineage and remained mostly uninfluenced by the developments in Europe until the nineteenth century. Dense networks of credit developed in and around Ottoman urban centres despite the Islamic prohibitions against interest (Çizakça 1996).

The State and Provincial Elites

The Ottoman state was relatively strong during the sixteenth century and was able to provide security, law, and order, build some infrastructure such as roads and irrigation, and protect the domestic trade routes. However, its capacity in these areas diminished considerably during the seventeenth and eighteenth centuries with the rise of the *ayan* in the provinces. The new power-holders in the provinces came from two different groups: prominent notables whose families had been among the local elites and centrally appointed officials who subsequently put down local roots. The *ayan* played important roles maintaining security and urban life in their districts and ensuring the safety of the trade routes (Hourani 1966: 83–110; Inalcik 1980: 283–337; Yaycioglu 2016: 65–116). Despite the rise of the power of the *ayan*, however, the central administration did not lose control of the law and the judiciary and continued to oppose private ownership on agricultural land, for example.

Nonetheless, even in the eighteenth century when the power and influence of the provincial notables were at their peak, they could not establish new formal political institutions that reflected the existing balances between the centre and the provinces. The central administration often tried to prevent the provincial elites from joining forces, resorting to the 'divide and rule' method whenever necessary. Cooperation and coordination amongst the provincial elites was also made more difficult by the fact that the empire covered a large geographical area and different ethnic groups. In turn, the local elites needed the sultan in Istanbul as a source of legitimation

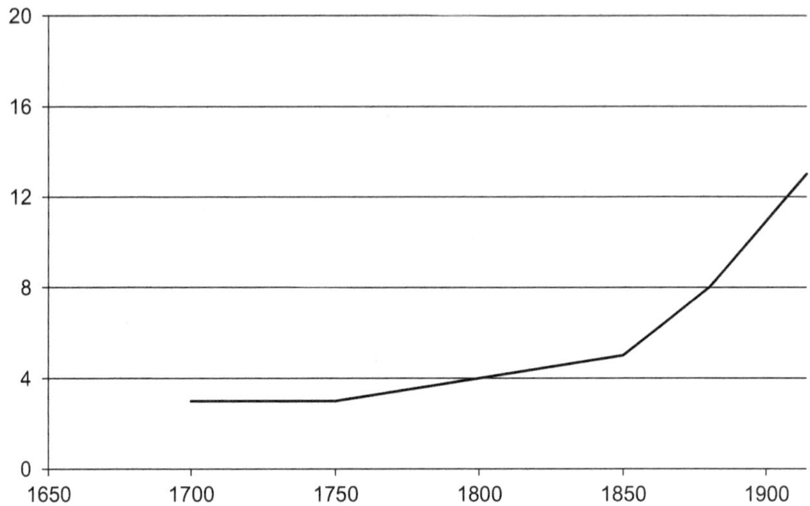

Figure 7.1 Revenues of the Ottoman central government as percentage of GDP, 1700–1914 (estimated)
Source: Pamuk (2012: 317–329).

in order to be able to continue to collect taxes in his name (Barkey 1994: 229–242; Yaycioglu 2016: 203–238).

As the central administration's power in the provinces declined, so did its ability to collect taxes and bring the revenues to the centre. The local notables, together with various other groups at the centre, began to control the tax collection process and retained a large part of the revenues. Tax revenues that reached the central treasury remained low in both absolute and relative terms. Annual tax revenues reaching the central treasury are estimated at 3 per cent of the GDP of the empire during the eighteenth century (Figure 7.1). Another recent estimate indicates that the annual per capita tax revenues that reached the central treasury in Istanbul did not exceed three days of wages of an unskilled labourer in the capital city until the end of the eighteenth century. The Ottoman central government was able to achieve virtually no increase in per capita tax collections until late in the eighteenth century. In contrast, the pressures of warfare helped most states across Europe to increase the revenues they collected at the centre during the seventeenth and especially the eighteenth centuries. Towards the end of the eighteenth century, taxes collected by central governments exceeded 10 per cent of GDP in the Dutch Republic and Great Britain and was approaching those levels in a number of other countries in western and central Europe. Available evidence suggests that taxes collected by central administrations across Asia also remained low, often below 5 per cent of GDP during the eighteenth century (Dincecco 2009; Karaman and Pamuk 2010; 2013).

Trade with South Asia and Western Europe during the Eighteenth Century

One important economic priority for the Ottoman central administration was the provisioning of the urban areas, which was seen as necessary for political stability. The central government wanted to assure a steady supply of goods, especially for the capital city and the army. The Ottoman government did not hesitate to intervene in local and long-distance trade to regulate the markets and ensure the availability of goods (İnalcık 1994: 179–217). The emphasis on provisioning also necessitated an important distinction between imports and exports. Imports were encouraged as they added to the availability of goods. As a result, the Ottomans never used protectionism as economic policy. Promoting long-distance trade and gaining control over trade routes, both overland and maritime, remained an important part of the Ottoman strategy across the eastern Mediterranean. The Ottomans supported the flourishing trade across the Black Sea and across Anatolia to and from Persia. Ottoman merchants, especially those from the Arab provinces including Egypt, also developed trading networks in South Asia and North Africa (İnalcık 1970: 207–218; Hanna 1998: 43–99).

Exports from India consisted of: Indian fabrics, especially cotton and mixed textiles; spices; drugs; dyestuffs, especially indigo; and at times porcelains from China. Exports from the Ottoman Empire included animals, raw materials, and dyestuffs. Imports into the Ottoman Empire far exceeded exports to India, however, giving rise to large outflows of specie, often in the form of Dutch and Spanish silver coinage. The growing volume of textile imports from India raised concerns for both local production and the outflows of specie towards the east. Because Ottoman government policy favoured the consumer over the producer and aimed at keeping the urban markets well supplied rather than protecting the domestic producers, it did not attempt to prohibit the importation of the textile products from India.

The popularity of most of the textile imports from India was due primarily to their better colour, design, and overall quality. Nonetheless, cotton textile products from India faced stiff competition in the Middle East from local producers. Both Ottoman and Persian manufacturers began to produce successful imitations of Indian textiles, especially the cotton and mixed varieties including muslins, hand-painted chintzes and, to a lesser extent, lower-priced calicoes at the lower end of the market. Over time the peasant women also began to produce imitations of the Indian fabrics in their homes. Nonetheless, the quality fabrics imported from India remained important symbols of luxury and prestige in urban areas across the Ottoman Empire until the early decades of the nineteenth century (İnalcık 1992; Veinstein 1999; Faroqhi 2009b). Imports of cotton manufactures from India to Egypt through the Red Sea continued during the eighteenth century (Raymond 1973–1974).

Most of the Ottoman trade with Europe was controlled by European merchants and trading companies. While the governments of European countries often encouraged, backed, and supported merchants who were their subjects or citizens, Ottoman governments did not view the protection of their own merchants as a priority. Moreover, from the twelfth century onwards, most European countries promulgated laws forbidding foreign nationals, including Muslims, to make a lengthy sojourn, settle permanently, or engage in commerce. As a result, Muslim merchants began to lag behind non-Muslim Ottoman merchants who were able to take advantage of their growing international networks and connections with European merchants (Gilbar 2003: 1–36).

In addition, the Ottoman government, like others in the Middle East since the medieval era, was willing and ready to offer commercial and legal privileges to European merchants. Among the privileges granted to European merchants living in Ottoman port cities, the most important were the right to trade and travel within the empire, to transfer products from one region to another, and to use vessels carrying the flag of their own countries. Through these privileges, the rulers sought to increase the circulation of goods, especially luxury goods in their local markets, and increase state revenues from trade. Another motive was to use the privileges as an instrument of foreign policy and gain influence and friendship in Europe. The privileges gradually expanded and ceased to be unilateral grants during the eighteenth century. Some of the new privileges began to conflict with the sovereignty of the empire, such as the right for European traders to set up their own tribunals in the Ottoman Empire, and to take trade disagreements to these courts. In addition, customs duties paid by European merchants were kept at the lowest levels, and in many cases, foreign traders paid less customs taxes than local traders (İnalcik 1971; Boogert 2005; Artunç 2015).

Ottoman trade with western Europe expanded and probably more than doubled during the eighteenth century. Ottoman imports consisted mostly of high-income goods, woollen textiles for high-income groups, and, to a lesser extent, the so-called colonial goods, including sugar, coffee, and some dyestuffs. Ottoman exports consisted of mostly agricultural goods and some textiles early in the century. Trade with Great Britain conducted by the Levant Company was small and stagnated for most of the eighteenth century. In contrast, Ottoman trade with France showed considerable dynamism. Woollen textiles purchased by higher-income groups also made up the largest share in imports from France. Amongst the woollen textiles, *londrins seconds* purchased by high- but not the highest-income groups had the largest share. In addition, colonial goods such as sugar and coffee were also significant in imports from France, but their value was smaller than woollen textiles. Even in the latter part of the century, however, one cannot talk of the destruction of the guilds or the domination of the markets as a result of the imports from Europe (Eldem 1999).

During the eighteenth century, Egypt's long-distance trade also began to shift from the Red Sea towards the Mediterranean and Europe. One reason was the decline in the imports of coffee from the Red Sea along with the rise of coffee imports from the Americas through Europe. Another reason was the rise in the imports of higher-priced woollen textiles, especially from France. The shift of the alliances of the ruling mamluk beys of Egypt from the Red Sea merchants to European merchants also helped bring Egypt's economy closer to the European economy during the eighteenth century (Hanna 2011).

The ratio of exports and imports to GDP for the empire as a whole increased slowly during the eighteenth century. It was probably not higher than 2 or 3 per cent for each at the end of the century, but it is difficult to provide precise estimates. The share of external trade was higher along the coastal areas of the Balkans, western Turkey, along the Syrian coast, the Nile Delta and parts of the Gulf and lower in the interior areas (Pamuk 1987: 1–17). As a result, not only did the exports of agricultural commodities remain limited but also Ottoman crafts and manufacturing, including those in Egypt, remained mostly intact and continued to produce for the large domestic market across the empire (Braudel 1979: 467–484; İnalcık 1992: 254–306). In fact, Ottoman textile manufacturers continued to export some of their products to Europe during the first half of the eighteenth century and to the north of the Black Sea until the end of the century. Similarly, exports of cotton yarn and cloth from Ambelakia in central Greece to the Habsburg Empire continued until early in the nineteenth century.

Reforms and Centralization After 1820

From the beginning of the nineteenth century, the Ottoman government was confronted with important developments at home and abroad. The Ottomans could not yet foresee the implications of the economic changes in western Europe, but Napoleon's invasion of Egypt in 1798 illustrated clearly the consequences of European military advances. Inside the empire, provincial notables and local lords were acting independently of the central government and effectively controlled large territories, retaining a major share of tax revenues. The expansion of external trade strengthened the position of non-Muslim merchants in the Balkans. Inspired by the currents of thought unleashed by the French Revolution, they began to take the lead in nationalist movements aiming to secede from the Ottoman Empire. Serbia became the first country to gain its independence, followed by Greece and Romania. In Egypt, Muhammad Ali Pasha and his descendants were able to establish their autonomy, if not formal independence, and pursue a course different from the rest of the empire.

The reformist sultan Selim III and his successor sultan Mahmud II tried to create a new army and sought to increase the power of the central government against both external and domestic challenges. They believed that, in order to achieve these objectives, the government needed to increase its tax revenues at the expense of the local groups in the provinces. The reforms pursued by Muhammad Ali in Egypt provided Mahmud II with a powerful model. Ottoman reform efforts entered a new stage with the proclamation of the *Tanzimat* (literally reorganization) in 1839. The government promised to grant all Ottoman subjects the same basic rights and equality before the law, irrespective of their religion. The government also promised to strengthen the property rights of all subjects and formally ended the centuries-old custom of confiscating the wealth of government officials who had lost their positions and, at times, even the wealth of the provincial notables. It also attempted to build a better-functioning system of taxation as well as a more modern and efficient central and provincial bureaucracy. A new commercial code and a new maritime code along European lines were introduced. Not only the institutions of the state but also those of the Christian *millets* began to be secularized, most importantly those of the Armenian and Greek communities. Education was an important component of the reforms. A three-tier education system was established early, but the spread of the new schools to the provinces could gain momentum only towards the end of the century (Hourani 1966; Zürcher 2004: 36–70).

The reform programme was the result of genuine belief on the part of the high-level officials that the only way to save the empire was through European-style institutional change. However, many of the reforms were quite expensive and required effective enforcement. In contrast, the fiscal, administrative, and legal capacities of the state were limited and the state could not effectively enforce the new laws and policies. While laws could be changed and new policies could be announced overnight, the fiscal, administrative, and legal capacities of the state improved slowly. The state's capacity to penetrate the rural areas where the great majority of the population lived and implement the reforms as well as deliver infrastructure, health services, and education remained low. The effectiveness of the reforms also differed from province to province and from period to period, depending on the abilities of the government officials in charge (Zürcher 2004: 60–61).

The 1838 Treaty and the Expansion of Foreign Trade

The reform efforts of the Ottoman government had important implications for the economy. For political support against external and internal threats, as well as support for the reform process itself, the government often turned to western European states, most importantly Great Britain and France. The recurring financial needs of the central government only added to the search for external support. The British as well as the other European governments saw the reforms and the reinforcement of the Ottoman state as an important aspect of their policy in the eastern Mediterranean. In exchange for the military, political, and financial support, European states demanded the creation of a market economy specializing in agriculture and trade, which was open to the outside world and provided privileges to European companies and citizens. As the economy opened up to European trade and investment, the power of European states and businesses within the empire kept growing. In contrast, the influence of various domestic groups, landowners, guilds, merchants, and financiers remained limited (Owen 1981: 57–153; Issawi 1982: 1–43).

The most important change in Ottoman economic institutions during the reform era was the signing of the Baltalimanı free trade treaty with Great Britain in 1838 just before the proclamation of the reform programme *Tanzimat*. It was followed by other free trade treaties containing similar provisions, signed with France and other European states. Trade with western Europe had been growing rapidly since the end of the Napoleonic Wars, but the Treaty changed the Ottoman customs regime for the rest of the century. Before 1838, the Ottoman state collected customs duties of 3 per cent on both imports and exports. In addition, local and foreign merchants had to pay an 8 per cent internal customs tax when transferring products from one region of the empire to another. The treaty increased the tax on exports to 12 per cent while fixing the duty on imports at 5 per cent. In addition, while local merchants continued to pay internal customs, foreign merchants were exempted from this practice. While European merchants secured an important advantage, the Ottoman state thus lost an important source of revenue to which it had turned especially during periods of financial crises. Equally importantly, the Ottoman government agreed not to create local monopolies in foreign trade (Pamuk 1987: 18–21).

For the Ottoman government, the main motivation in signing the free trade treaty was political. Muhammad Ali Pasha, an officer of the Ottoman army in Egypt, had seized the governorship after Napoleon and the French armies were driven out, declared independence from Istanbul, and launched a reform programme aimed at establishing a powerful state. Thanks to measures designed to improve the efficiency of tax collection and the creation of state monopolies in foreign trade, he had bolstered the state finances. With the financial resources he raised, Muhammad Ali established a number of state industrial enterprises and, above all, a strong army and navy (Panza and Williamson 2015: 79–100). After the defeats it suffered against Muhammad Ali in the 1830s, the Ottoman government faced the risk of losing not only Egypt and Syria but also large parts of Anatolia. There was even the possibility that he might replace the Ottoman dynasty in Istanbul. The Ottoman government needed the support of the British government to keep the empire together. In many ways, the free trade treaty was the price to be paid for that support. For its part, the British government also wanted to abolish Muhammad Ali's state monopolies on foreign trade and state industries, as they were hurting British interests in Egypt. The treaty brought about the end of Muhammad Ali's project of state-led industrialization in Egypt (Owen 1981: 57–76; Zürcher 2004: 46–49; Panza and Williamson 2015: 79–100).

At the end of the eighteenth century and in the early nineteenth century, trade within the empire was far more important than foreign trade. Furthermore, trade with India and parts of eastern Europe had a significant share in the external trade of the empire. During the century from the end of the Napoleonic Wars to World War I, this picture changed significantly. The volume of trade with the industrializing countries of

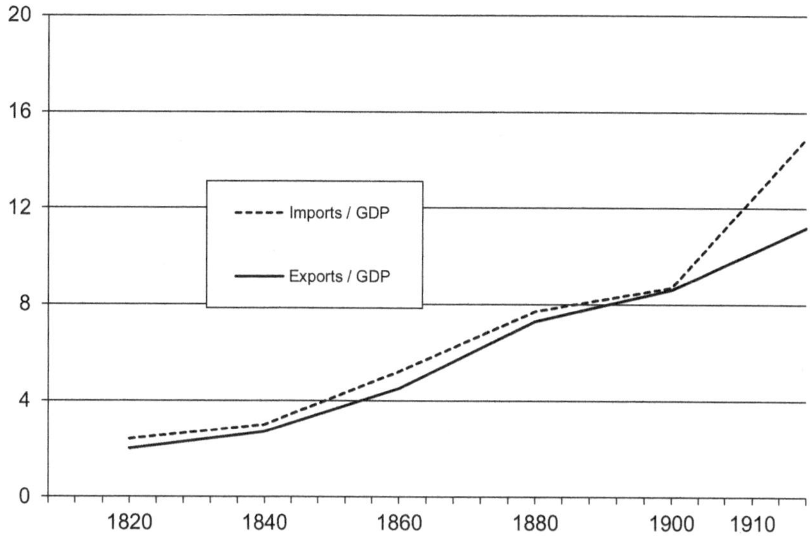

Figure 7.2 Growth of external trade of the Ottoman Empire: ratio of exports and imports to GDP, 1820–1914 (estimated and in per cent)
Source: Pamuk (1987: 18–40).

western and later central Europe expanded rapidly. The Ottoman economy was increasingly transformed into an exporter of agricultural commodities and raw materials and an importer of manufactures and some food items (Pamuk 1987: 18–54, 148–171).

Annual exports of the Ottoman Empire increased from less than 4 million British pounds in the early 1820s to about 20 million pounds in the early 1870s at annual rates above 5 per cent. Imports increased at about the same pace. The ratio of exports or imports to GDP increased from 2–3 per cent in the early 1820s to about 7 per cent in the early 1870s and to 11 per cent on the eve of World War I (Figure 7.2). An important characteristic of the exports was their diversity. Agricultural commodities such as tobacco, wheat, barley, raisins, figs, raw silk, mohair, hazelnuts, opium, cotton, and olive oil were the leading exports from the Balkans, Anatolia, and Syria. In contrast, only one commodity, cotton, accounted for more than 90 per cent of the exports from Egypt.

From the 1850s, the opening of the economy took on an additional dimension. European companies and individual investors began to establish enterprises within the borders of the Ottoman Empire. The largest share, approximately two thirds, of foreign direct investment went into railway companies. In addition, significant amounts of European capital began to be invested in trade companies, banking, insurance, ports, and municipal services such as water and utilities (Pamuk 1987: 62–81).

Fiscal Centralization and External Borrowing

As part of the centralizing reforms, the Ottoman government sought to increase its tax revenues not by negotiating with the notables but by undermining their power and their hold on the tax collection process as well as raising the tax burden of the population. Political centralization thus went hand in hand with fiscal centralization for the rest of the century (Figure 7.1 and Karaman and Pamuk 2010: 619–625). Tax revenues reaching the treasury increased from an estimated 4 per cent of the GDP of the empire around 1800 to 7 per cent in 1870 and to more than 11 per cent of GDP of the empire on the eve of World War I. Rising fiscal demands on the agricultural producers contributed to the growing challenges to Ottoman rule, especially in southeastern Europe. Moreover, even though the central government's revenues began to rise, its expenditures also rose during the nineteenth century. Financial difficulties as well as the efforts to reduce and finance the budget deficits continued until World War I. In response to the frequent wars late in the eighteenth century and during the first half of the nineteenth century, the central government tried to finance the deficits by domestic borrowing and by resorting frequently to debasements or reductions in the silver content of the currency. This strategy provided additional revenue during the wars but also led to monetary instability and high rates of inflation.

With the monetary reform of 1844, the Ottoman government abandoned debasements and adopted the bimetallic system. European financiers and state representatives then began to urge the Ottoman government to turn to long-term foreign borrowing as a solution to its financial problems. After the outbreak of the Crimean War sharply increased the need for revenue, the Ottoman government started selling long-term bonds in European financial markets in 1854. It borrowed large amounts at interest rates significantly higher than those paid by most other countries at the time. An important part of the borrowed funds was used to cover current expenditures, including military expenditures. Only a small fraction was directed to infrastructure investments that might increase future tax revenues. By the second half of the 1860s, the Ottoman government had to secure new debt in order to continue its interest and principal payments. As the impact of the financial crisis of 1873 began to be felt in the European financial markets, securing new funds became much more difficult. The Ottoman state's long-term and mostly externally held debt had reached close to £200 million. Annual principal and interest payments began to exceed half of the revenues of the Ottoman treasury. The government announced in the autumn of 1875 that it would halve all its debt payments and stopped all debt repayments the following year (Owen 1981: 100–121; Pamuk 1987: 56–62).

The external borrowing experience of Egypt during the nineteenth century showed many similarities to that of the Ottomans. The government of Egypt led by the descendants of Muhammad Ali began borrowing from European banks also around mid-century. The sharp increase in the price of cotton during the American Civil War encouraged the government to increase its external borrowing and invest more heavily in irrigation projects and other infrastructure designed to expand cotton production. However, the decline in cotton prices after the end of the American Civil War created major difficulties for Egyptian state finances and eventually led not only to default in the mid-1870s but also to the British occupation of Egypt in 1882 (Owen 1981: 122–135).

Commercialization of Agriculture

The expansion of commodity exports as well as the reform efforts of the government had far-reaching consequences for agriculture, which was the principal source of income for close to 80 per cent of the population of the empire. While precise estimates are not available, existing evidence points to slowly rising total and per capita production in agriculture. Moreover, a rising share of the agricultural output was directed to urban and export markets and the rural population was drawn into market relations more strongly than in earlier periods. In comparison, changes in technology, in land ownership patterns, and tenancy relations proceeded more slowly during the nineteenth century.

One basic cause of the increases in agricultural production was the improvements in security after a very difficult and long period of wars. Rural population began to leave remote settlements away from roads and cities and to move to the valleys, where they started producing on more fertile land. Secondly, the population of the empire began to increase, albeit slowly. Part of the increase in agricultural production was directed to urban markets. In addition, along with the expansion in foreign trade, agricultural exports to European markets increased steadily. Thirdly, the terms of trade between agriculture and industry began to shift in the aftermath of the Industrial Revolution and remained in favour of agriculture. In addition, railways and steamships began to reduce the costs of transportation for the bulkier agricultural commodities and improved the prices obtained by the agricultural producers. Supported by these trends, the rural population increased its specialization in agriculture. A large share of the rural population started buying in local markets some of the imported textile products such as yarn and cloth that they previously produced for their own consumption and started devoting a greater share of their time to agriculture (Pamuk 1987: 18–26, 150–153).

Along with the growing power of the provincial notables during the eighteenth century, there was an increase in large holdings and to a lesser extent in large farms producing for the market across the empire. Large landholdings continued to produce for both the domestic urban and export markets during the nineteenth century. However, a large part of the agricultural production for markets came from family farms, which cultivated around 4–6 hectares every year using family labour and a pair of oxen. The migration of millions of Muslim families from the Crimea, the Caucasus and later from the Balkans to the empire also supported the family farms in Anatolia and Syria. The government settled most of these families in rural areas and gave them land where uncultivated land was available (Karpat 1985: 60–77; Keyder and Tabak 1991: 1–16).

Egypt presents one of the strongest cases of monoculture anywhere in the world during the nineteenth century. Most of Egypt's population and agricultural land was located along the Nile Valley and especially in the Nile Delta. Linking this fertile and homogeneous region to export ports and world markets was relatively easy. In addition to geography, the state also supported growing specialization in agriculture and in cotton. The distribution of land was very unequal, especially around the Delta. The family of Muhammad Ali Pasha and the elites around them had a great deal of economic and political power. After the signing of the free trade treaties with European powers in 1838, the government in Egypt strongly supported the development and growing export orientation of agriculture. State policies in support of agricultural development such as irrigation, distribution of seeds, and investment in transportation that began with Muhammad Ali Pasha in the early part of the century were continued. These investments were made with funds borrowed in European financial markets at the height of the cotton boom during the 1860s (Owen 1969; 1981: 122–152).

Decline of Manufacturing

The volume of cotton textiles and other manufactures imported from Britain and other European countries expanded rapidly after 1820. Faced with competition from the products of the Industrial Revolution, some branches of craft-based production activities were able to resist, but many others declined. The most important craft-based branch of production was textiles, both in rural and urban areas. With the increase in productivity achieved in Europe after the Industrial Revolution, prices of cotton textile products declined by as much as 80 per cent in the first half of the century. While these price decreases increased the consumption of cotton textiles, they also made it very difficult for local production to survive, initially in the coastal regions followed by both the urban and rural areas in the interior.

By the middle of the nineteenth century, many local and European observers were pointing out that in the face of competition from the rapidly growing volume of imported products, yarn-spinning and weaving were declining in Salonica, Istanbul, Bursa, Diyarbakir, Aleppo, Damascus, and elsewhere. The complaints issued by owners of small workshops and guild workers about the competition of imported products lasted throughout the century. The share of imports in domestic consumption of cotton textiles varied considerably between the coastal regions and the interior. For the empire as a whole, it is estimated that this share increased from less than 10 per cent in 1820 to more than 50 per cent in 1870 and more than 70 per cent by 1914. The local producers did not fold without resistance, however. Local weavers, using imported yarn that was cheaper and more durable, struggled to maintain their existence by producing varieties of textiles that were popular in local markets (Issawi 1980: 298–305; Pamuk 1987: 108–129; Quataert 1993: 49–104; Pamuk and Williamson 2011: 159–184).

Low tariffs and the competition from imported manufactures also made it difficult for private manufacturing establishments to adopt the steam engine. In fact, during the period until 1870, the most important attempts to adopt the new technology came from the two governments in Cairo and Istanbul. Beginning as early as 1814, Muhammad Ali Pasha in Egypt embarked on an industrialization drive mostly to support his military. The economic and military successes of Muhammad Ali impressed the Istanbul government. As part of the initial reforms in the 1830s and 1840s, the Istanbul government also imported new machines from Europe for a series of state-owned factories, cotton and wool weaving plants, a fez factory, the armoury, the shipyards, and the foundries, essentially to meet the needs of the army and the navy. Highly paid engineers, technicians, and even labourers were brought in from Europe to work in these factories. However, the free trade treaty of 1838 reduced tariffs and opened these state manufacturing enterprises in the Cairo and Istanbul regions to the competition of imports. Although their output was bought mostly by the state, many of these factories could not sustain their operations for long (Clark 1974: 65–76; Owen 1981: 57–76).

Trends in per Capita Incomes, 1700–1870

It is now possible to distinguish between two different economic conjunctures for the Ottoman Empire including Egypt during the eighteenth century. The period up to the end of the 1760s was a relatively peaceful time of expansion, slowly rising incomes, and price stability. Available evidence on production is limited, but it does point to an increasing trend for agriculture and artisanal activity, as well as an investment in manufacturing in many parts of the Balkans and Anatolia. In the Balkans, large-scale farms *(çiftlik)* specialized in grain production for Istanbul and other long-distance markets. Commercial linkages between the markets of Anatolia, Syria, and Egypt grew stronger during this period. With the growth of the European trade in the second half of the century, Istanbul began to develop into an international exchange centre, joining the multilateral payments network involving the leading European centres of commerce (Pamuk 2000: 159–170).

In contrast, from the end of the 1760s until the 1830s was a period of frequent wars with European neighbours Russia and Austria as well as political and military conflict between central government and powerful notables in the provinces, which resulted in the decline of production, long-distance trade and incomes. The state finances frequently experienced large budget deficits arising mostly from wars, and, to a lesser extent, from the costs of centralizing reform, including the creation of a new army. In response, the government in Istanbul attempted to increase its control over revenue sources, made use of various forms of internal borrowing, and when the short-term fiscal pressures mounted, resorted to debasements. The silver content of the Ottoman currency declined by more than 90 per cent and the price level increased more than twelvefold from 1770 to 1840 (Pamuk 2000: 188–204). The central government also responded to the growing political and military pressures during the wars and domestic conflict with greater economic interventionism, creating fiscally motivated regional trade monopolies and raising its demands on agriculture and especially manufacturing establishments (Genç 1995). In other words, while the Industrial Revolution was taking place in Britain and later in north-western Europe, the Ottoman central administration struggled with frequent wars and domestic conflict as well as a severe and prolonged fiscal crisis.

The economy of Egypt experienced similar trends during the eighteenth century. In his classic study on eighteenth-century Cairo, André Raymond pointed to a relatively peaceful period of expansion and slowly rising incomes from the beginning of the century until the end of the 1760s followed by a period of domestic turmoil and more frequent wars, which led to declining production and declining incomes as well as debasements and higher rates of inflation from the end of the 1760s until the end of the 1820s (Raymond 1973–1974). More recently, Nelly Hanna has also argued that Egypt's exports, and more generally trade with both Asia and Europe, expanded until the end of the 1760s. In contrast, rivalry and conflict between the *mamluk* households or local state elites intensified after the 1760s. Rising domestic political tensions and military conflict led to the decline in production and incomes until the early decades of the nineteenth century (Hanna 2011).

The Ottoman Empire began to open to foreign trade and foreign investment after 1820. While the share of manufacturing activities declined, agricultural production for long-distance markets, both domestic and foreign, expanded – especially in the coastal regions. Growing specialization in agriculture was accompanied by slow increases in per capita incomes. The available evidence from a variety of sources – real wage series and foreign trade series, as well as central government tax revenues – suggests that per capita incomes increased by about 0.5 per cent per year or by a total of about 30 per cent in the period between 1820 and 1870 (Pamuk 2006). The cultivation of new land and the shift to cash crops that brought higher revenues were the leading causes of the increase in agricultural incomes. The overall growth rate was not any higher in part because the market orientation of agriculture remained limited to the coastal regions. The decline of craft-based manufacturing and the absence of industrialization also kept the increase in average incomes limited.

Recent studies on wages in the leading cities in Europe and in the Ottoman Empire have provided additional insights into the trajectories of per capita incomes before and after the Industrial Revolution. These studies showed that the purchasing power of the wages of skilled and unskilled construction workers in the leading cities of north-western Europe (in Britain and the Low Countries) were approximately 50 per cent higher than those in Istanbul during the eighteenth century and this gap increased further during the nineteenth century. The gap between the real wages in the leading cities of southern Europe and those in Istanbul was more limited during the eighteenth century but this gap also increased during the nineteenth century, especially after 1870 (Allen 2001; Özmucur and Pamuk 2002).

Recent estimates of GDP per capita for the Ottoman Empire and for various European countries are consistent with these trends (see Introduction to Volume I). Along with some regional variation, GDP per capita in the Ottoman Empire as a whole is estimated to have increased modestly from about $640 in 1700 to about $720 in 1820, measured in 1990 international prices. GDP per capita in north-western Europe increased more strongly and the gap between this region and the Ottoman Empire widened during the eighteenth century. The per capita income gap between the Ottoman Empire and southern Europe remained more limited until 1820.

GDP per capita in the Ottoman Empire began to increase, albeit slowly, during the nineteenth century to about $850 in 1870, again measured in 1990 international prices (Pamuk 2006; 2009). Thanks to industrialization, per capita incomes in north-western Europe continued to increase more rapidly than those in the Ottoman Empire. As a result, the per capita income gap between the Ottoman Empire and the north-western European economies continued to widen until 1913. Increases in per capita incomes in southern Europe were limited until 1870. However, as industrialization picked up in the second half of the century, their per capita incomes also increased more strongly until World War I. As a result, the per capita income gap between southern European countries and the different regions of the Ottoman Empire remained limited until 1870 but increased from 1870 until 1913. Per capita incomes in large parts of Asia including India and China did not increase and even declined during the eighteenth and nineteenth centuries. The economic performance of the Ottoman Empire during the eighteenth and nineteenth centuries thus looks better in comparison to these latter regions (see Introduction to Volume I).

In the absence of detailed evidence, it is difficult to talk about changes in income distribution across the Ottoman Empire during the period 1700 to 1870. However, it would be safe to say that merchants, landowners, and the market-oriented agricultural producers in the coastal regions benefited from the growing commercialization of agriculture and the rise in the relative prices of agricultural cash crops in both the eighteenth and especially the nineteenth centuries. For both the eighteenth and nineteenth centuries, the top income groups in the rural areas remained those controlling large amounts of land, especially in the coastal regions, and producing for domestic and export markets. During most of the eighteenth century and in the early part of the nineteenth century, many of the highest income groups in the urban areas were connected to the networks of tax collection. It has been estimated that some 1,000–2,000

Istanbul-based individuals, together with some 5,000–10,000 individuals in the provinces, as well as innumerable contractors, agents, and managers controlled an important share of the state's tax revenues. Non-Muslims were often prohibited from holding tax-farming contracts, but Greeks, Armenians, and Jews were very much part of this elite as financiers, partners, brokers, and accountants. In the provinces, the wealthiest people in the urban areas belonged to the notable families that controlled tax collection and retained a large fraction of the tax revenues. Many of these notables were also engaged in long-distance trade and owned land, but their economic power was tied, above all, to tax collection (Salzman 1993: 393–423).

As a result of the increasing political and fiscal centralization after 1820, the urban notables in the provinces began to be squeezed out of tax collection and a larger fraction of the tax revenues flowed to the central treasury. While tax collection declined as the leading source of private income and wealth, agricultural exports and long-distance trade, especially with European countries, took its place. The leading Ottoman merchants during the nineteenth century were Greeks and Armenians living in port cities such as Salonica, İstanbul, İzmir, Beirut, and Alexandria who sometimes partnered with European merchants or merchant houses (Keyder et al. 1993: 519–558). In comparison to the rest of the empire, large landowners were more powerful both economically and politically in Egypt. To a greater extent than elsewhere in the region, the wealthiest families in nineteenth-century Egypt were the large landowners producing cotton for export markets.

There is evidence that life expectancy at birth began to increase slowly in the Ottoman Empire during the nineteenth century until 1870. I have estimated that life expectancy at birth in the Ottoman Empire increased from around 26–28 years in 1820 to 29–31 years in 1870. These levels of and the limited increases in life expectancy are not very different from the existing estimates of life expectancy at birth in other developing regions during the nineteenth century (Zijdeman and de Silva 2014: 101–116). There was considerable regional variation around these averages. The disappearance of the plague after the 1830s contributed to rising life expectancy. Public health measures such as the quarantine of ships played a role in the disappearance of the plague. Rising agricultural production per capita and slow improvements in nutrition also contributed to the slow decline in mortality in the more commercialized coastal regions until 1870.

References

Allen, R. C. (2001). 'The Great Divergence in Wages and Prices from the Middle Ages to the First World War', *Explorations in Economic History*, 38(4), 411–447.

Artunç, C. (2015). 'The Price of Legal Institutions, The *Beratli* Merchants in the Eighteenth-Century Ottoman Empire', *Journal of Economic History*, 75(3), 720–748.

Barkey, K. (1994). *Bandits and Bureaucrats: The Ottoman Route to State Centralization*, Ithaca: New York.

Boogert, M. H. van den. (2005). *The Capitulations and the Ottoman Legal System, Qadis, Consuls and Beratlis in the 18th Century*, Leiden: Brill.

Braudel, F. (1979). *Civilisation matérielle, économie et capitalisme, XVe–XVIIIe siècle. Vol 1. Les structures du quotidien*, Paris: Armand Colin.

Çizakça, M. (1996). *A Comparative Evolution of Business Partnerships, the Islamic World and Europe*, Leiden: Brill.

Clark, E. C. (1974). 'Ottoman Industrial Revolution', *International Journal of Middle East Studies*, 5(1), 65–76.

Dincecco, M. (2009). 'Fiscal Centralization, Limited Government, and Public Revenues in Europe, 1650–1913', *Journal of Economic History*, 69(1), 48–103.

Eldem, E. (1999). *French Trade in Istanbul in the Eighteenth Century*, Leiden: Brill.

Faroqhi, S. (2009a). *Artisans of Empire: Crafts and Craftspeople Under the Ottomans*, London and New York: I. B. Tauris.

(2009b). 'Ottoman Cotton Textiles, The Story of a Success that Did Not Last, 1500–1800', in Riello, G. and Parthasarathi, P. (eds.), *The Spinning World, A Global History of Cotton Textiles, 1250–1850*, Oxford University Press, 89–103.

Genç, M. (1995). 'L'Economie Ottomane et la guerre au XVIIIe siecle', *Turcica* 27, 177–196.

Gilbar, G. (2003). 'The Muslim Big Merchants-Entrepreneurs of the Middle East, 1860–1914', *Die Welt des Islams*, 43(1), 1–36.

Hanna, N. (1998). *Making Big Money in 1600: The Life and Times of Isma'il Abu Taqiyya, Egyptian Merchant*, American University in Cairo Press.

(2011). *Artisan Entrepreneurs in Cairo and Early-Modern Capitalism (1600–1800)*, New York: Syracuse University Press.

Hourani, A. (1966). 'Ottoman Reform and the Politics of Notables', in Hourani, A., Khoury, P. S. and Wilson, M. C. (eds.), *The Modern Middle East*, London and New York: I. B. Tauris, 83–110.

İnalcık, H. (1969). 'Capital Accumulation in the Ottoman Empire', *Journal of Economic History*, 29(1), 97–140.

(1970). 'The Ottoman Economic Mind and Aspects of the Ottoman Economy', in Cook, M. A. (ed.), *Studies in the Economic History of the Middle East*, Oxford University Press, 207–218.

(1971). 'Imtiyazat: the Ottoman Empire', in *Encyclopedia of Islam, vol. 3*, 2nd ed., Leiden: Brill, 1179–1189.

(1980). 'Military and Fiscal Transformation in the Ottoman Empire, 1600–1700', *Archivum Ottomanicum*, 6, 283–337.

(1992). 'The Ottoman Market in Cotton Fabrics, India and England: the Role of the Cost of Labor in Commercial Rivalry', in İnalcık, H., *The Middle East and the Balkans Under the Ottoman Empire, Essays on Economy and Society*, Bloomington: Indiana University Press, 254–306.

(1994). 'The Ottoman State: Economy and Society, 1300–1600', in İnalcık, H. and Quataert, D. (eds.), *An Economic and Social History of the Ottoman Empire, 1300–1914, Part I*, Cambridge University Press, 11–409.

Issawi, C. (1980). *The Economic History of Turkey, 1800–1914*, University of Chicago Press.

(1982). *An Economic History of the Middle East and North Africa*, New York: Columbia University Press.

Karaman, K. and Pamuk, Ş. (2010). 'Ottoman State Finances in Comparative European Perspective, 1500–1914', *Journal of Economic History*, 70(3), 593–627.

(2013). 'Different Paths to the Modern State in Europe: The Interaction between Warfare, Economic Structure and Political Regime', *American Political Science Review*, 107(3), 603–626.

Karpat, K. (1985). *Ottoman Population, 1830–1914, Demographic and Social Characteristics*, Madison: University of Wisconsin Press.

Keyder, Ç. and Tabak, F. (1991). *Landholding and Commercial Agriculture in the Middle East*, Albany: State University of New York Press.

Keyder, Ç., Özveren, E. and Quataert, D. (1993). 'Port Cities in the Ottoman Empire', *Review, Fernand Braudel Center*, 10, 519–558.

McEvedy, C. and Jones, R. (1978). *Atlas of World Population History*, Harmondsworth: Penguin Books.

Owen, R. (1969). *Cotton and the Egyptian Economy, 1820–1914*, Oxford University Press.

(1981). *The Middle East in the World Economy 1820–1914*, London and New York: Methuen.

Özmucur, S. and Pamuk, Ş. (2002). 'Real Wages and Standards of Living in the Ottoman Empire, 1489–1914', *Journal of Economic History*, 62(2), 292–321.

Özvar, E. (2003). *Osmanlı Maliyesinde Malikâne Uygulaması*, Istanbul: Kitabevi Yayınları.

Pamuk, Ş. (1987). *The Ottoman Empire and European Capitalism 1820–1913: Trade, Investment and Production*, Cambridge University Press.

(2000). *A Monetary History of the Ottoman Empire*, Cambridge University Press.

(2006). 'Estimating Economic Growth in the Middle East since 1820', *Journal of Economic History*, 66(3), 809–828.

(2009). 'Estimating GDP per capita for the Ottoman Empire in a European Comparative Framework, 1500–1820', paper presented at the XVth World Economic History Congress, Utrecht.

(2012). 'The Evolution of Fiscal Institutions in the Ottoman Empire, 1500–1914', in Yun-Casalilla, B., O'Brien, P. and Comin Comin, F. (eds.), *The Rise of Fiscal States. A Global History*, Cambridge University Press, 304–331.

Pamuk, Ş. and Williamson, J. G. (2011). 'Ottoman De-Industrialization 1800–1913: Assessing the Magnitude, Impact and Response', *Economic History Review*, 64(1), 159–184.

Panza, L. and Williamson, J. G. (2015). 'Did Muhammad Ali foster Industrialisation in 19th-Century Egypt?', *Economic History Review*, 68(1), 79–100.

Quataert, D. (1993). *Ottoman Manufacturing in the Age of Industrial Revolution*, Cambridge University Press.

Raymond, A. (1973–1974). *Artisans et Commerçants au Caire au XVIIIe Siècle*, 2 vols, Damascus: Institut Français de Damas.

Salzman, A. (1993). 'An Ancien Regime Revisited: Privatization and Political Economy in the Eighteenth-Century Ottoman Empire', *Politics and Society*, 21(4), 393–423.

Veinstein, G. (1999). 'Commercial Relations Between India and the Ottoman Empire (Late Fifteenth to Late Eighteenth Centuries): A Few Notes and Hypotheses', in Chaudhury, S. and Morineau, P. (eds.), *Merchants, Companies and Trade, Europe and Asia in the Early Modern Era*, Cambridge University Press, 95–115.

Yaycioglu, A. (2016). *Partners of the Empire, the Crisis of the Ottoman Order in the Age of Revolutions*, Stanford University Press.

Zijdeman, R. L. and Ribeiro de Silva, F. (2014). 'Chapter 6: Life Expectancy Since 1820', in van Zanden, J. L., Baten, J., Mira d'Ercole, M., Rijpma, A., Smith, A. and Timmer, M. (eds.), *How Was Life? Global Well-Being Since 1820*, Paris: OECD Publishing and International Institute of Social History, 101–116.

Zürcher, E. J. (2004). *Turkey, A Modern History, Third Edition*, London and New York: I. B. Tauris.

8

The Economic History of North America, 1700–1870

JOSHUA L. ROSENBLOOM

The first permanent European settlements were established in North America shortly after 1600. Between 1700 and 1870, these European colonial settlements consolidated into nation states, expanded to continental scale, began the process of industrialization, and achieved substantial improvements in the living standards of their citizens. By 1870 the foundations of modern North America had been established. This transformation was a remarkable economic success and one that commands the focus of our attention. Yet it is not the only history one might tell. From the perspective of the aboriginal peoples of North America, the expansion of European settlement was more tragedy than success. Similarly, the experience of enslaved Africans and their descendants was one of remarkable hardships that produced a legacy of racial segregation and tensions that are still palpable.

Colonial Origins

In 1607 British colonists established the first permanent European settlement in North America at Jamestown, Virginia. The following year a French colony was established in Quebec. By 1700 the population of the British and French colonies that would become the United States and Canada numbered about 250,000, most living close to the Atlantic coast, from South Carolina to present-day Maine. British colonists greatly outnumbered their French counterparts in Canada and Spanish settlers in the South-west and Florida. Nonetheless competition between European colonizers allowed the indigenous peoples to play one power off against the other. Competition also prompted European powers to encourage efforts to expand the territory under their control and thus pre-empt settlement by other powers.

The spread of diseases such as smallpox and measles from European explorers to the native population affected native peoples even before colonization. Ubelaker (1988: 292) estimated that the native population east of the Mississippi River declined from roughly 560,000 in 1500 to 500,000 by 1600. The resulting disruption of native groups greatly facilitated early European colonization by reducing native resistance to the new arrivals. After 1600 the decline of native populations accelerated. Between 1600 and 1700 native populations fell to about 250,000 (Ubelaker 1988: 292).

Meanwhile, among the colonial population high rates of natural increase and migration, both voluntary immigration from Europe and the involuntary importation of African slaves, produced rapid growth. By 1700, European and African settlers in North America approximately equalled the native population and by the time of the American Revolution the colonial population exceed 2.5 million (McCusker 2006). As the number of colonists increased, the area of settlement spread, extending southwards to below Savannah, Georgia, and inland to the foothills of the Appalachian Mountains. Rapid population growth was mainly due to the abundance of land and natural resources, which made entry into farming relatively easy, encouraging early marriage and high rates of marital fertility. American conditions also contributed to lower mortality: abundant food and forest-products meant a better-nourished, better housed, and healthier population, and low population density discouraged the transmission of diseases.

In economic terms, labour scarcity relative to land and natural resources raised the marginal value of labour. But the cost of migration amounted to nearly a year's income for a British labourer, and the expense of establishing oneself as an independent producer pushed the cost even higher. Few potential migrants could pay these costs. Innovative credit arrangements helped to overcome this barrier to migration, however. Many migrants entered into agreements with shipowners in which they committed to repay the cost of their passage by working for a period of time, in most cases three to five years, after arrival in America. These contracts, called indentures, were sold to colonists seeking to hire labour. Galenson (1981) estimated that perhaps 70 per cent of the half-million European migrants to North America before 1776 came as indentured servants.

Indentured servants settled mainly in the rich agricultural regions of Pennsylvania, New York, and New Jersey. Few were attracted to the poorer soil and less hospitable climate of New England, and the growing reliance of planters further south in Virginia, Maryland, and the Carolinas on enslaved labour to produce tobacco, rice, and other exports discouraged voluntary migration. The reluctance of free migrants to settle in the Southern colonies in turn reinforced reliance on slave labour. As a result, over the course of the eighteenth century the Black share of population increased, reaching close to 40 per cent of the population in the Southern colonies by the 1770s.

Colonial Economic Performance

Population statistics make clear that the British and French colonies in North America experienced an historically unprecedented rate of extensive economic growth. After 1700, colonial populations approximately doubled every twenty years, prompting Thomas Malthus to argue that in the absence of constraints population would increase at a geometric rate (Galenson 1996: 169). The hallmark of the post-1800 period has been sustained improvements in gross domestic product (GDP) per capita. Prior to 1800, though, per capita incomes were relatively stagnant.

With limited data, efforts to estimate pre-1800 economic growth rely on backward projection from known values *c.*1800 and have focused only on the precursors to the United States. Mancall and Weiss (1999: 26) placed the 1800 GDP per capita for the United States at $67 (in 1840 prices). Comparisons of purchasing power over long time periods are problematic, but this suggests per capita incomes in the range of $1,600 and $1,900 in 2014 prices (Measuring Worth) (Johnston and Williamson 2016). The Maddison Project Database, version 2013 estimated US per capita GDP in 1800 at $1,296 in 1990 dollars (about $2,700 in 2018), and British per capita income at $2,097. Lindert and Williamson (2016: 103–106) argued, however, that with proper adjustment for living costs, US per capita income would actually be higher than in Britain. International comparisons of this sort are quite sensitive to the bundle of consumer goods used to adjust for differences in the cost of living (Lindert and Williamson 2016: 68–69; Geloso 2019). In particular, abundant land and natural resources in the United States kept the cost of basic consumption goods much lower than in Britain, though luxury goods were more expensive in the United States.

Mancall and Weiss (1999) estimated colonial American income levels before 1800 by extrapolating backwards based on estimates of agricultural productivity, changes in population composition, and a small number of other series. They concluded that GDP per capita was largely unchanged during the eighteenth century, rising from $64 in 1700 to $67 by 1774 (in 1840 prices) and then remaining flat for the next quarter-century. Put differently, the incomes of British colonists in North America were already remarkably high in 1700. Consistent with their estimates Allen et al. (2012) found no clear trend in real wage series constructed for several North American cities in the eighteenth century. Their real wage series also implied, consistent with Lindert and Williamson, that the living standard of urban workers in Boston, Philadelphia, and Baltimore was higher than for comparable workers in London. Geloso (2019) extended this approach to French Canada, arguing that living standards in Quebec were 40–60 per cent of those in Philadelphia and Boston in the 1760s. but were above those of workers in France at the time.

Supporting the conclusion that the colonial incomes were roughly stable, there is little evidence of significant technological or institutional changes. Agriculture dominated the economy of North America in 1700 and agricultural techniques changed little over the century (Mancall et al. 2002). Increased population size and better organization contributed to improvements in transatlantic and coastal shipping (Walton and Shepherd 1979), but trade constituted a small part of the overall economy, so that even large advances in efficiency had limited effects on the economy. Given rapid population growth, the ability to sustain stable and relatively high incomes over the century represents a remarkable achievement in itself.

Probate inventories offer another perspective on colonial living standards. When data are available over time they imply an accumulation of material possessions that suggests a growing level of material comfort (Main and Main 1988). It is difficult to extrapolate from data for selected communities to a broader colony-wide level, but the data appear consistent with stable per capita incomes.

Probate data offer a clearer picture of regional variations within the colonies. Alice Hanson Jones (1980) collected probate inventories from 1774 in randomly selected counties throughout British North America. Figure 8.1 summarizes her estimates of total wealth and wealth per capita by colonial region. Looking simply at average wealth per free capita one might conclude that the Southern colonies were much more successful than those in the mid-Atlantic or New England regions. These comparisons are distorted, however, by the concentration of slaves in the South, where they are included in the total wealth figure and excluded from the population. In the South, slavery had created a much more unequal distribution of wealth than in the North, greatly benefiting free European-Americans at the expense of an enslaved African American population. Focusing on non-human wealth and including slaves among the Southern population tells a substantially different story, showing that physical wealth per person was quite similar across colonial regions.

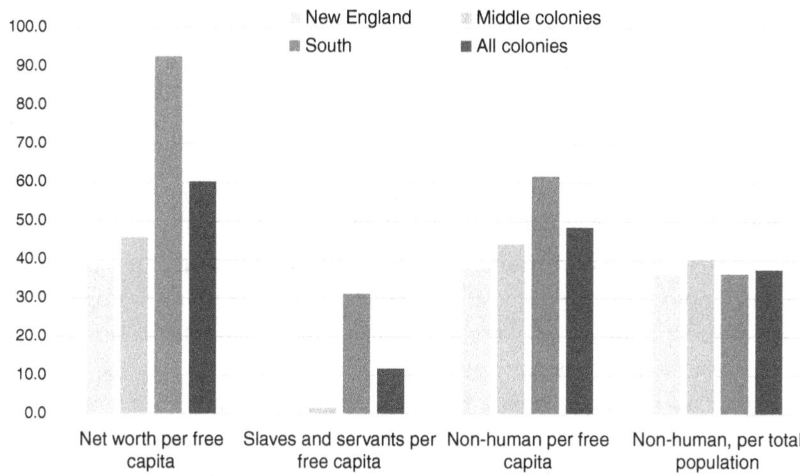

Figure 8.1 Probate wealth per capita by region, 1770 (pounds sterling)
Source: Jones (1980: 54, 58).

American Independence

In 1776 thirteen of Britain's North American colonies – from Georgia to New England – declared independence from Britain. Britain's Canadian colonies opted not to join the rebellion; a choice that can be attributed to their dependence on exports of furs and fish to Britain and the fact that recent shifts in imperial policy had affected them differently than their neighbours to the South.

The movement for independence had emerged relatively quickly after the conclusion of the Seven Years War in 1763. Until then, the North American colonies had enjoyed a relatively benign neglect. British policy, embodied in the Acts of Trade and Navigation (first introduced in 1651), sought to promote trade within the British Empire and reduce external trade. The Acts prohibited colonists from producing some manufactured goods and required that manufactures imported into the colonies come from Britain. They also required that major colonial exports – e.g. tobacco, rice, and indigo – be shipped through Britain regardless of their final destination, in effect imposing an additional tariff on long-distance trade. Economic historians have concluded, however, that the welfare effects of the Navigation Acts were small and largely offset by the benefits of membership of the British Empire – including protection of American shipping by the Royal Navy (McClelland 1969).

Rather, the causes of conflict are to be found in shifts in British policy after 1763. The end of the Seven Years War shifted the geopolitical balance in North America: France ceded most of its colonies to Britain, and Spain relinquished claims to Florida and the Gulf Coast, while acquiring New Orleans from France. No longer in competition for control of the continent, Britain placed new restrictions on colonial settlement, hoping to avoid costly conflicts with the native population. Colonists, however, viewed settling western territories as a source of economic profit and resented this constraint. Another source of tension arose from new British taxes imposed to recover some of the costs of the war. The colonists interpreted Parliament's actions as evidence they were being treated unfairly.

The shifts in British policy provoked a growing resistance movement centred among the mercantile and trading elite in New England and middle Atlantic port cities (Taylor 2016). In 1765, responding to the Stamp Act, nine colonies sent representatives to a Stamp Act Congress in New York. As the first such meeting of representatives of the colonies, this was an important step in the emergence of a sense of national identity. Tensions continued to rise in the following years, and in 1773 colonists protesting the Tea Act, which granted the East India Company a monopoly on tea imports, dumped a load of tea in Boston Harbor. Britain ordered the complete closure of the port and sent a large military force to occupy it. Responding to these actions, the colonists convened the first Continental Congress in Philadelphia in 1774, and by early 1775 the tensions had devolved into an armed conflict precipitated by the British march on Lexington and Concord.

Support for independence was far from universal: Loyalists, who favoured remaining part of the empire, were almost as numerous as Revolutionaries, and a large part of the rural population remained uncommitted to either side (Taylor 2016). The Revolution thus entailed significant internal conflicts. Moreover, the Revolutionaries confronted practical challenges in taking on the much larger and better supported British Army. In the end, failures of British leadership and the cost and difficulty of fighting a war of attrition far from home allowed the Revolution to succeed.

Economic Performance: 1783–1870

Having achieved independence, the economic prospects of the United States did not appear especially promising. No longer part of the British Empire, American merchants found themselves excluded from lucrative trading routes while local manufacturing enterprises faced a flood of cheap

British imports. The federal government emerged from the war with substantial debts and no reliable source of income. It was largely unable to protect western settlers or American shipping interests and lacked authority to negotiate more favourable tariff rates with foreign governments.

Quantitative evidence for the late 1780s and early 1790s is limited, but most accounts suggest that these conditions depressed urban growth and reduced national income. Rosenbloom and Weiss (2014), for example, estimated that international exports from the middle Atlantic region fell by almost 50 per cent between 1770 and 1791, and conjecture that regional per capita GDP may have fallen 18 per cent. Lindert and Williamson (2016) similarly argued that the post-Revolution economy suffered a significant depression. Yet one should not read too much into these estimates. Only a small fraction of the population lived in cities, and the consequences of reduced trade for the predominantly rural population may have been limited.

As in the colonial era, the newly independent United States and Britain's Canadian colonies continued to experience sustained extensive growth. From just under 4 million at the time of the first decennial census in 1790, the US population increased nearly tenfold, reaching close to 40 million at the time of the 1870 Census (Haines and Sutch 2006: series Aa7), a growth rate of approximately 3 per cent per year. Canadian population grew even more quickly, but from a much lower base, rising from about 200,000 to 3.6 million by 1870. Canadians were about 5 per cent of the North American population in 1790; by 1870 they were about 10 per cent. Much of this growth was due to high rates of fertility among North American residents, including the enslaved population of the US South. In addition, as the costs of transatlantic passage fell, the inducement of high American wages attracted a growing number of European migrants. As Figure 8.2 illustrates, international migration to the United States began to increase gradually in the 1820s and 1830s in both absolute numbers and relative to the resident population; immigration further accelerated in the mid-1840s due to the push of the Irish potato famine and political turmoil in Germany.

Meanwhile the displacement of native populations, advances in transportation and communication technologies, and the successful social organization of settlement meant that new resources continued to be brought into play. The continued expansion of land and natural resources meant that despite rapid population growth, North American economic development took place under conditions of endogenous disequilibrium that sustained the relative scarcity of labour.

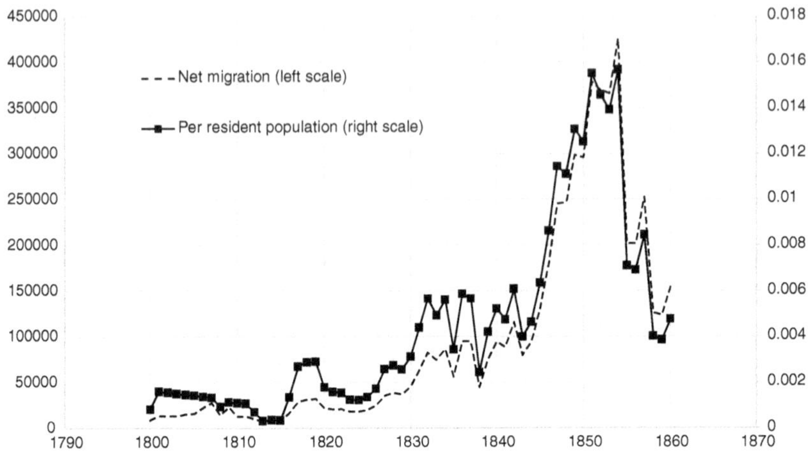

Figure 8.2 Net migration and number of migrants relative to population, 1800–60
Source: Carter et al. (2006: table Ad1–89).

After 1790 rapid population growth was coupled with increases in GDP per capita, signalling the beginnings of modern economic growth. Estimates for this period, especially those for the years before 1840, are not as sound as those for the post-1860 period, but there is little doubt about the significant rise in productivity and incomes that characterized this period (Rhode and Sutch 2006). The generally accepted path of GDP per capita growth is plotted in Figure 8.3, which shows decadal benchmark estimates and annual interpolations based on a variety of less comprehensive data. The rate of growth varied considerably, but there is an apparent acceleration over time, and by 1870 real per capita income had nearly tripled. Over the entire period the annual average rate of growth of per capita GDP was 0.9 per cent.

The growth accounting framework decomposes increases in output or output per capita into the contributions of greater use of inputs (e.g. capital and labour effort) and greater efficiency. Output per capita (y) is assumed to be produced according to a production function $y=AF(k, l)$, where k and l are measures of the quantity of capital and labour per capita employed in production and A measures changes in efficiency, also called total factor productivity (TFP). For the United States, much of the growth in per capita income in the nineteenth century reflected increased inputs per capita, rather than growth in TFP (see Table 8.1). From 1800 to 1855 labour input per capita accounted for close to half of the observed growth, while increased capital per worker and greater TFP each explained slightly less than one-quarter of

Table 8.1 The proximate sources of growth, US 1800–90

	Rates of growth (% per year)				
Period	Real GDP per capita	Man hours per capita	Capital per man hour	TFP	TFP share
1800–55	0.87	0.48	0.19	0.20	23.0%
1855–90	1.47	0.41	0.69	0.37	25.2%

Source: Abramovitz and David (2000: 8, 14, 21).

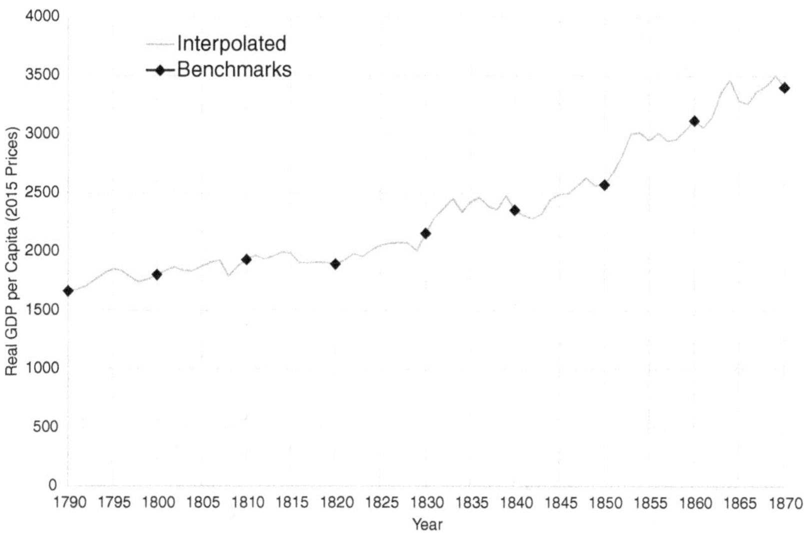

Figure 8.3 US real GDP per capita, 1790–1870
Source: Carter et al. (2006: table Ca9-19).

the growth. In the second half of the century, TFP growth accelerated but continued to account for a minority of the total per capita income growth. An important caveat, however, is the assumption that TFP growth was 'factor neutral'. There are good reasons to believe that in the nineteenth century technological progress was capital-using, meaning that conventional approaches to growth accounting will understate the impact of TFP growth and overstate that of capital accumulation.

Growth accounting is only the beginning of an explanation of the growth of the North American economy after 1790. A more complete account requires an investigation of the factors that contributed to both increased factor inputs and TFP growth. The remainder of this chapter offers a narrative account that draws out several key themes for the North American economy. First, economic progress after 1790, and especially after 1820, owed a great deal to technological innovations that began in the British Industrial Revolution. The mechanization of factory production, especially in textiles, rapid advances in the efficiency of the steam engine, and improved transportation technologies quickly diffused from Britain to the United States and were central to reshaping the American economy. The diffusion of these technologies was by no means automatic, however, a fact emphasized by the uneven uptake of these innovations across Europe in the first half of the nineteenth century. Second, a favourable institutional context and the emergence of a domestic technological community capable of adapting European innovations were both important ingredients in American success.

The Constitution

Recent work by economists and economic historians has emphasized the role of institutions in determining economic performance (North et al. 2009; Acemoglu and Robinson 2012; Engerman and Sokoloff 2012). The US Constitution, which came into effect in 1788, marked an important institutional paradigm shift that helped set the stage for subsequent economic growth. The Constitution has been remarkably successful, but its passage was by no means inevitable. Moreover, the political compromises that were necessary for its passage perpetuated sectional conflicts that would ultimately lead to an enormously costly Civil War.

The American Revolution had launched Britain's former colonies on a journey of institutional experimentation without clear precedents or obvious models. Over the preceding 170 years colonists had developed effective institutions of self-governance within their respective colonies, but there was little precedent for how a federation of independent states should be collectively governed. Shortly after declaring independence in July 1776 the members of the Continental Congress set to work to establish a federal government. The Articles of Confederation were completed in 1777, but were not formally ratified by all thirteen states until 1781.

In the wake of having rejected the authority of the British Crown, the Articles of Confederation were written to avoid creating a new power to replace it. Instead the federal government was essentially a creature of the states. Congress was empowered to direct the war against Britain, but it lacked the authority to tax directly or independently raise an army. Not surprisingly, the states failed to fully comply with congressional requisitions, and on several occasions the army nearly disbanded because of lack of troops and funds. Unable to fund its operations Congress resorted primarily to issuing paper currency, so-called 'Continentals', which depreciated rapidly in value during the war.

The situation did not improve with independence. Unable to independently and reliably raise funds, the federal government was largely powerless to address the challenges it confronted. It could neither repay loans undertaken during the war nor access capital markets to borrow for other activities. It was unable to field sufficient military forces to adequately protect the nation's territories in the trans-Appalachian west. And it could not establish a coherent international trade policy that would protect nascent manufacturers from a flood of cheap British imports, open foreign ports to American shipping or oblige Spain to allow the movement of goods on the Mississippi River (Mittal et al. 2010: 28).

Gradualist efforts to amend the Articles foundered on the fact that any changes required unanimous approval by all thirteen states. When delegates from every state except Rhode Island gathered in Philadelphia in the summer of 1787, they embarked on a different tack, drafting an entirely new document that would establish an independent but limited federal government. Much of the resulting document was concerned with defining the respective spheres of influence of the states and the federal government and creating a complex, multipart federal government capable of responding to new and unforeseen circumstances that might arise. The Constitution reserved for the federal government the power to negotiate international treaties, impose tariffs and duties, coin money, regulate interstate commerce, establish and regulate patents and copyrights, and provide a postal service.

Beard (1913) argued that provisions of the Constitution reflected the efforts of urban and commercial interests to reassert their authority at the expense of rural and agricultural debtors. More recent quantitative analyses offer a more nuanced picture of how the interests of individual delegates may have influenced their voting. In the most thorough analysis of voting at the congressional convention, Heckelman and Dougherty (2013) rejected Beard's arguments that narrow economic interest motivated voting but found evidence that slave owners tended to support a stronger national government.

In retrospect, it is apparent that the Constitution created a context in which the new nation was able to harness forces of phenomenal growth. But this growth was not so much a direct effect of the passage of the

Constitution as of the stable environment of 'market-preserving federalism' it created, in which states competed with each other to promote their own economic fortunes within limits established by the federal government (Mittal et al. 2010). At the same time, however, it is important to note the Constitution's imperfections. To balance the competing interests of slave and free states, delegates to the convention created a bicameral legislature giving each state equal weight in the Senate and apportioning seats in the House of Representatives by population, with the proviso that each slave was the equivalent of three-fifths of a free citizen. While these measures achieved a temporary success, territorial expansion led to sectional imbalances that would threaten this compromise. In 1820 and 1850, the tensions were averted, but in 1860 they sparked the American Civil War, resulting in enormous human and financial losses.

Banks, Money, and Finance

One area of the economy directly and immediately affected by the ratification of the Constitution was the nation's monetary system. The Constitution granted the federal government exclusive authority to mint coins and regulate the money supply. The federal government's power to levy duties on foreign commerce also provided a reliable source of revenues that helped establish federal debt obligations as a sound investment. On these foundations, the new nation established an increasingly sophisticated and adaptive financial system that facilitated commerce and mobilized capital to support its development.

Alexander Hamilton, the nation's first Treasury Secretary, made the dollar the new nation's monetary unit. Hoping to increase the supply of money, he opted for a bimetallic standard, in which either silver or gold could be minted, with gold valued at 15 times silver. Because of market fluctuations, however, the value of the two metals rarely corresponded to the ratio at the mint, with the result that only the undervalued metal circulated as currency.

Although states were prohibited from issuing paper currency, they had the power to charter banks and other corporations. State-chartered commercial banks began to proliferate in the 1790s; they accepted deposits and issued paper banknotes to their customers. The notes could be redeemed at the issuing bank for specie, and the requirement that the bank be able to meet the demand for redemption served to regulate note issue. Because they facilitated commerce, however, banknotes circulated from hand to hand and not all were quickly returned to the issuing bank, allowing banks to hold only fractional reserves and thus increase the supply of money. Rousseau and Sylla (2005) argued that the expansion of the financial sector helped mobilize capital and stimulated economic development.

By issuing notes, banks affected the money supply with possible consequences for macroeconomic fluctuations. In the antebellum period, there was no central authority to regulate the supply of money; economic historians have been interested in the extent to which market forces were effective in regulating note issuance by commercial banks. The evidence suggests unsound note issue was relatively rare, and mostly affected smaller banks in frontier areas. Nonetheless, the financial system remained subject to external forces that contributed to economic instability. In the 1830s, lower British interest rates led to an inflow of specie and a rapid expansion in credit for investments in rail and canal projects. When international credit conditions tightened after 1839, however, rising interest rates drained specie and led to a contraction of note issue. As a result, many borrowers were left unable to repay their loans and were forced to default, triggering a significant financial crisis (Temin 1969).

Territorial Expansion

The enormous natural resources of North America in combination with European technologies were a source of potential wealth. The greater part of North American economic development in the nineteenth century was consumed with realizing this potential by privatizing land-ownership, developing transportation technologies to make the land accessible, settling the land, and putting it into production. How the gains (and losses) from this enterprise would be distributed was one of the central issues of collective choice with which American political institutions wrestled during the century.

The Treaty of Paris, signed in 1783, ending the American Revolutionary War and recognizing the independence of the United States, granted the new country sovereignty over that part of North America east of the Mississippi River, south of the Canadian border, and north of Spanish possessions in Florida and a narrow strip of the Gulf Coast in what would become Alabama and Mississippi. Further territorial additions proceeded rapidly. In 1803, the Louisiana Purchase nearly doubled the land area of the United States. In 1819, Spain relinquished Florida to the United States. In 1845 Texas, which had gained its independence from Mexico in 1836, was annexed; in 1846 disputes with Britain over the border with Canada were resolved, opening the Oregon territory to settlement and in 1848 victory in a war with Mexico resulted in the acquisition of California, and the rest of the American South-west.

The blueprints for how this land would be settled were laid out in two land ordinances drafted by Thomas Jefferson and adopted by Congress in 1785 and 1787. Crucially, these ordinances established the principle that new territories would, when they reached a sufficient population, enter the country as states just like those already in existence. The ordinances also stipulated a uniform government survey based on a rectangular grid, established a system of townships, and set aside land in each township for the support of public schools. Once surveyed, fee-simple title to the land was to be sold at auction. Finally, and fatefully, the Northwest Ordinance of 1787, which dealt with the territory that would ultimately become the states of Ohio, Indiana, Illinois, Michigan, and Wisconsin, prohibited the introduction of slavery into territories north of the Ohio River.

How quickly land would be sold and on what terms soon emerged as a source of political conflict. Federalists, led by Alexander Hamilton, advocated higher prices and slower sales, hoping to increase federal revenues and encourage higher population density and greater commercial development. Anti-federalists, led by Thomas Jefferson, argued for lower prices and rapid sales to encourage an agrarian republic of small landholders. Initially advocates for slower land sales prevailed; a minimum lot size of 640 acres and a price of at least $1 an acre effectively excluded most small purchasers. Most land was purchased by investors who in turn sold small lots and offered more favourable credit terms. Over time, however, land sales provisions were relaxed, culminating in the 1860s with the Homestead Act, which allowed settlers to acquire land in exchange only for their commitment to develop it.

Transportation Revolutions

Access to transportation was a crucial determinant of land values. At first settlement followed navigable rivers. Early settlers in the Ohio River Valley shipped their crops to market on flatboats to New Orleans. In 1807 Robert Fulton used a steamboat to travel up the Hudson River from New York to Albany. Within a few years, steamboats were in wide use. By 1860 it is estimated there were more than 800 steamboats in service on interior rivers, and freight costs for upstream shipments had fallen by almost 90 per cent relative to their 1815 level (Cain 2006).

Developing areas further from navigable rivers required costly investment in canals or, after 1830, railways. Because of the large capital costs of construction and positive externalities that these investments generated they were often the result of public-private partnerships, with state or local governments anticipating that their investment would be repaid through increased property taxes collected as nearby land values increased.

The Erie Canal, traversing upstate New York and linking New York City to the Great Lakes, opened in 1825 and was enormously successful. Settlement along its route and on lands accessible to the Great Lakes increased, and the state's investment was quickly repaid. Hoping both to imitate this success and to prevent New York from monopolizing trade with the interior, Pennsylvania and Maryland both invested in competing routes. States in the Midwest also invested heavily in canals in the 1830s, but few of these investments proved profitable and a number were forced to suspend bond payments or default after the financial panic of the 1830s.

After the 1830s, the focus of internal improvements shifted to railways. Unlike canals, railways were mainly built by private investors, but often with investments from towns and cities seeking to ensure service to their community. Whether railway construction followed demand for their services, or if settlement, and hence demand, followed the railways remains a matter of debate among economic historians (Atack et al. 2010).

Agriculture and Manufacturing

As one might expect, in a land-abundant country, agriculture dominated the American economy in the first half of the nineteenth century. In 1800 close to 75 per cent of the US labour force was employed on farms (see Table 8.2); over the next seven decades the agricultural labour force increased by a factor of 7.5, an average annual rate of growth of 2.9 per cent. Yet agriculture's share of total employment fell to just half of total employment in 1870, while manufacturing's share of employment increased from only about 5 per cent of the labour force in 1800 to 20 per cent in 1870.

Driving these sectoral shifts and, at least in part, producing the rise in per capita incomes noted earlier were technological advances that raised the productivity of labour and capital. In the manufacturing sector, automation, the growing use of water and steam power, and organizational innovations combined to produce especially rapid increases in the value of labour and encourage the sector's relative growth. In agriculture, continued access to virgin land interacted with mechanical and biological innovations to increase output and enable a smaller share of the labour force to support a rapidly growing population.

Table 8.2 US labour force 1800–70

				Non-agricultural			
	Total	Agricultural		Total		Manufacturing	
Year	(1,000s)	(1,000s)	%	(1,000s)	%	(1,000s)	%
1800	1,713	1,274	74.4%	439	25.6%		
1810	2,337	1,690	72.3%	647	27.7%	128	5.5%
1820	3,163	2,249	71.1%	914	28.9%		
1830	4,272	2,982	69.8%	1,290	30.2%		
1840	5,778	3,882	67.2%	1,896	32.8%	454	7.9%
1850	8,193	4,889	59.7%	3,304	40.3%	1,063	13.0%
1860	11,293	6,299	55.8%	4,994	44.2%	1,461	12.9%
1870	12,785	6,378	49.9%	6,407	50.1%	2,577	20.2%

Sources: Carter et al. (2006: table Ba 814–830).

In 1790, few observers would have predicted these developments. Yet, as a result of a combination of accidents, policy choices, and market imperfections, the technologies of the Industrial Revolution were successfully transferred across the Atlantic Ocean and adapted to North American conditions, giving rise to a distinctive American system of manufacturing characterized by the substitution of machinery and standardized parts for skilled craft labour and supported by a growing community of local mechanics and engineers.

The early growth of American textile manufacturing was stimulated by protection from British imports during the embargo of 1807 and the War of 1812. The disruption of international trade between 1807 and 1815 both raised the profitability of domestic manufacturing and encouraged New England merchants to shift financial resources away from trade and into manufacturing ventures (Rosenbloom 2004). Among the leaders of this transition was the Boston Manufacturing Company, established by Francis Lowell in Waltham, Massachusetts. Lowell's innovations were both technological and organizational. He introduced a novel mechanical loom, and the vertical integration of all of the steps in cloth production under one roof. To deal with the scarcity of factory labour, Lowell recruited young women from farms in the surrounding countryside, building dormitories to provide them with housing and supervised living arrangements (Field 1978).

Despite these innovations, Lowell's venture would have failed without tariff protection after 1816. Fearing the effects of a flood of European imports at the end of the War of 1812, newly established manufacturers appealed to

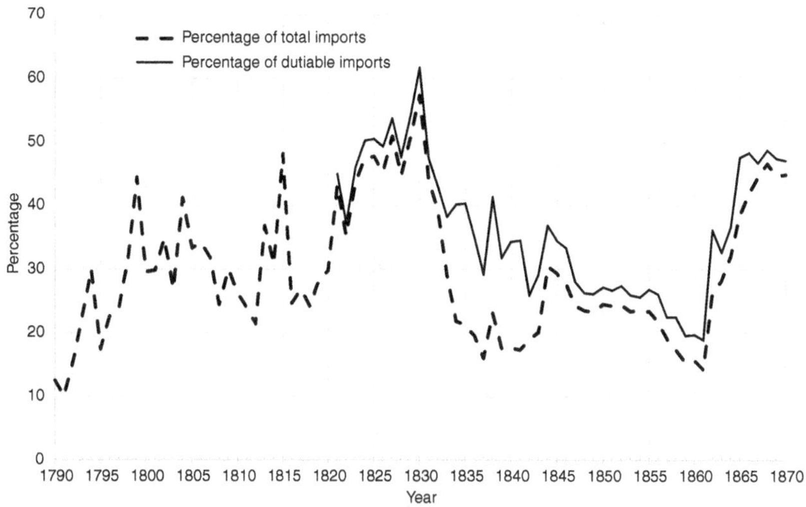

Figure 8.4 US revenue from duties as a percentage of the value of imports, 1790–1870
Source: Carter et al. (2006: table Ee424–430).

Congress for increased tariffs. But any tariff required winning support from Southern cotton exporters. Lowell's tariff proposal establishing a minimum valuation for cotton textile imports of $0.25 per yard cleverly excluded low-priced Asian cloth that competed directly with his company's product but had much less effect on higher-quality and more expensive British cloth produced from American cotton. This strategy enabled Lowell to win Southern votes and gain protection (Rosenbloom 2004). As Figure 8.4 illustrates, tariff protection increased substantially between 1816 and 1830.

With tariff protection the distinctive, large-scale, vertically integrated approach to textile production pioneered by Lowell thrived. Over the next decade, as Lowell and his chief engineer, Paul Moody, improved manufacturing methods, productivity advanced quickly, making tariff protection less important. By the middle of the nineteenth century, the United States had emerged as the world's second largest producer of textiles. As the industry grew and matured, textile machine manufacturers were spun-off as independent enterprises and diversified into a broader range of equipment manufacturing, including the production of steam locomotives.

Precision manufacturing using interchangeable parts emerged in the early nineteenth century as another distinctive American enterprise (Rosenbloom 1993). Much of the impetus for early innovations in this industry arose from military demand and key advances were made at government armouries. By mid-century, however, American technology was attracting the attention of British manufacturers. Techniques developed first in firearms production helped the machine tools industry and were important in typewriter, bicycle, and eventually automobile production in the late nineteenth and early twentieth centuries (Rosenberg 1963).

Despite the dramatic changes in manufacturing in the first half of the nineteenth century, agriculture still dominated the economy. Settling the frontier offered significant potential for capital gains as population density increased and land values rose. Land was abundant, and could be purchased at relatively low prices, but the costs of farm-making constrained the pace of settlement. Clearing land, building a house, and acquiring livestock, ploughs, and other necessary implements pushed the costs well above the purchase price of raw land. Atack and Bateman (1987) estimated that establishing an 80-acre (30-hectare) farm in the Midwest cost $1,715 in 1860, roughly ten times per capita income, while the cost of a comparable farm in the North-east was over $3,138.

Relying primarily on family labour, Northern farms produced a mix of grains, livestock, and produce. Much of this was consumed on the farm, but as the century progressed a growing surplus made its way to urban markets at home and abroad. Yields per acre showed little trend in the nineteenth century, and rising production of grain and livestock was primarily the result of increases in the number of acres farmed per person. This in turn was due mainly to the introduction of improved ploughs, seeders, mechanical reapers, and threshers. Yet as Olmstead and Rhode (2002) argued, we should not discount the importance of biological innovation. Developing new varieties was essential both to respond to pests and disease and to enable the spread of production into territories with different climatic conditions.

In the South, a climate conducive to growing cotton combined with access to slave labour produced a very different pattern of development. The falling cost of factory-produced cotton textiles created an enormous demand for cotton. Responding to this demand, Southern planters increased production from a few thousand bales in the 1790s to more than 4 million before the outbreak of the Civil War (Figure 8.5). Slavery facilitated the South's transition to cotton production by speeding the movement onto fertile soils in the interior. At the same time, new varieties of cotton substantially increased the productivity, and hence value, of slave labour (Olmstead and Rhode 2008).

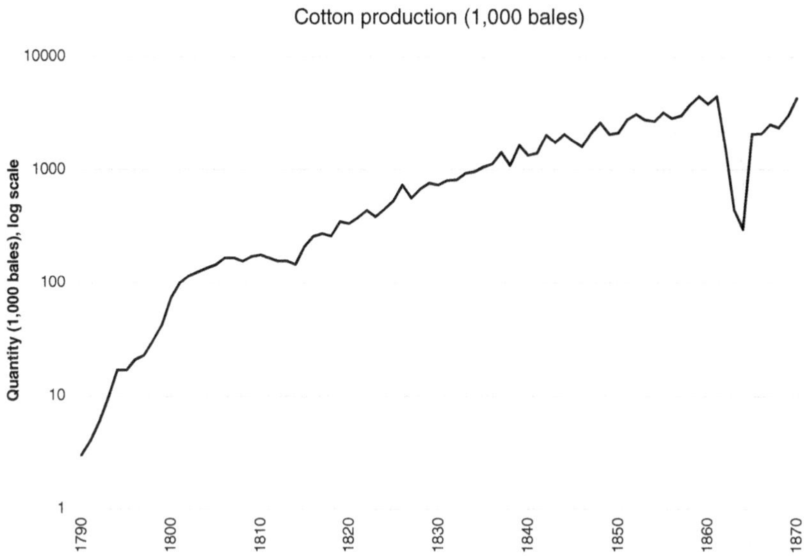

Figure 8.5 US cotton production, 1790–1870
Source: Carter et al. (2006: table Da755–765).

Slavery

Despite the common influence of abundant land, Northern and Southern development diverged sharply. The prohibition of slavery in the North and its persistence in the South set up a sort of natural experiment between competing economic systems, distinguished by this difference in property rights regimes (Wright 2006). Given the centrality of slavery to the nation's economic and political development, it is important to remember that at the time of the Revolution slavery was legal in all of the British colonies, and there were slaves and slave owners in every state.

Revolutionary rhetoric about resisting colonial enslavement, however, helped crystallize anti-slavery sentiments, at least in those states with relatively few slaves. The Vermont state constitution, adopted in 1777, provided that 'no male person, born in this country, or brought from over sea, ought to be holden by law, to serve any person as a servant, slave or apprentice, after he arrives at the age of twenty-one years, nor a female, in like manner...' (quoted in Wright 2006: 49). Pennsylvania adopted a gradual emancipation law in March 1780, and the rest of the New England states had abolished slavery within a year of the end of the Revolutionary War. New York (1799) and New Jersey (1804), the states with the greatest numbers of slaves, were the last Northern states to legislate abolition. Paralleling Northern abolition, however, Southern states were developing new rationalizations and legal protections of the institution.

The passage of the Northwest Ordinance, prohibiting slavery north of the Ohio River, ensured that the regional division between the original states would be perpetuated as the country expanded. As Wright (2006: 41–46) documents, many of the early settlers in these territories advocated for the introduction of slavery but were prevented from doing so by the Ordinance.

At the time of the Revolution, North and South had nearly equal populations and strikingly similar accumulations of non-human wealth (Wright 2006: 57). Of course, slavery had allowed free Southerners to accumulate more human wealth than their Northern counterparts, and total wealth (including slaves) per free capita in the South was vastly higher than in the North. Beginning in the 1790s, cotton displaced tobacco, rice, and indigo as the principal employer of slave labour. Fuelled by growing demand for cotton and enabled by Eli Whitney's development of a cotton gin capable of processing the variety of cotton that grew well in the American South, Southern slave owners expanded their production of the crop. Rising demand, improvements in productivity, and the prohibition on imports of new slaves to the United States imposed by the Constitution drove slave prices sharply higher in the decades before the Civil War (Figure 8.6). For slave owners, rising prices were a form of capital gains, contributing to the enormous wealth accumulation for large plantation owners. This Southern elite came to see their fortunes tied to the value of their enslaved labourers.

While investments in slaves emerged as the primary form of wealth accumulation in the South, land became the leading investment in the North. Land is immobile while labour is mobile, and this difference had profound effects on regional development. In the North, landowners encouraged the development of towns, promoting commercial services, transportation, and other place-specific improvements that would attract settlers and enhance land values. In the South, slavery facilitated the movement of crops and people into the interior and onto the most fertile soils, and discouraged investment in immobile forms of capital.

Regional differences in investment translated into regional divergence in demographics. Because slavery limited opportunities to break into farming and discouraged the emergence of markets in free labour, immigrants largely avoided the South. Rates of natural increase were high in both regions but growing numbers of European immigrants in the North meant that the Northern population grew much more rapidly. Having begun in the late 1770s with nearly equal

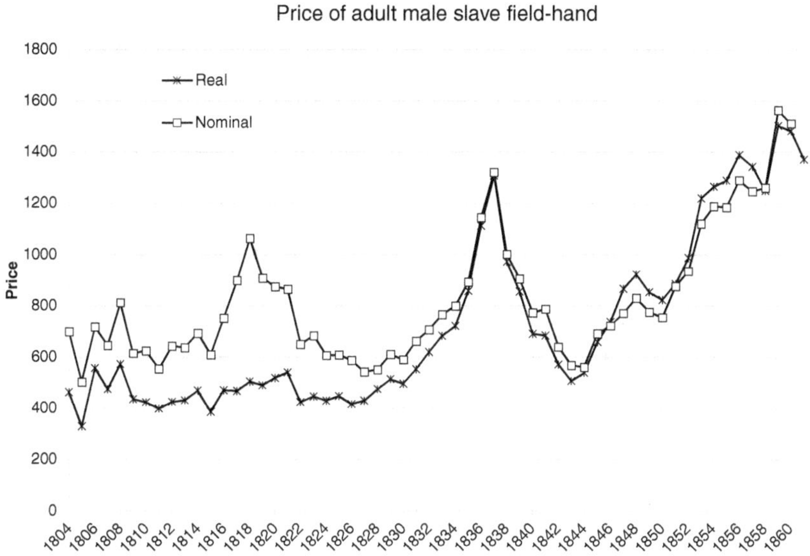

Figure 8.6 Slave prices, 1804–60
Source: Carter et al. (2006: table Bb209–214).

populations, by 1860 the population of the non-slave states exceeded that of the slave states by a ratio of almost two to one (Wright 2006: chapter 2).

The Civil War: Causes and Consequences

In April 1861, the United States was plunged into a bloody and destructive Civil War that lasted until 1865. Although the immediate events that precipitated the conflict concerned the constitutional question of whether individual states were free to leave the United States, the underlying sectional conflict concerned slavery. Politically and economically, the Southern states were thriving, incomes for free whites were high and the value of slave property was growing. Since 1848, Southern opposition to tariffs had been largely successful and tariff rates falling. Yet the tension between slave and free states embedded in the Constitution had never been far from the surface, and in the past conflict had been averted only by ensuring that territorial expansion maintained a balance of free and slave states. The addition of Minnesota, Oregon, and Kansas as free states with no balancing slave states, however, provoked Southern concern about future threats to their slave property. Southern leaders may also have misjudged the willingness of Northerners to fight to preserve the union.

The war proved enormously costly. Goldin and Lewis (1975) estimate that the total cost of the war – including wartime expenses on both sides, the loss of life, debilitating injuries, and destruction of physical capital – amounted to over $6.5 billion, roughly 1.5 times annual GDP in 1860. This was more than twice what it would have cost to compensate all Southern slave owners for the emancipation of their slaves (Goldin 1973).

Earlier generations of economic historians viewed the Civil War as a turning point in American industrialization. Quantitative measures suggest continuity in the rate of growth of industry before and after the war, however. Nonetheless, the war was important in resolving the long-simmering political dispute between slave and free regions of the country. And it had profound implications for the economic organization of the Southern states. With emancipation, slaveholders lost their investment in slaves. And former slave owners (who retained title to most of the region's land and physical capital) and formerly enslaved workers had to develop new productive arrangements. The dominant solution to these constraints was the emergence of sharecropping.

Emancipation also affected regional development. As Wright (1986) documents, by the end of the nineteenth century regional patterns of economic development converged. Urbanization, investment in transportation, and industry all accelerated in the South. Yet the region also suffered a significant economic setback. Regional incomes fell sharply relative to the North. This shock appears to reflect the combined impact of slowing world demand for cotton, which remained the region's dominant product, with reductions in labour supply by former slaves (Temin 1976).

Conclusion

Writ large, the economic history of North America from 1700 to 1870 is a story of the response to the opportunities created by land abundance. North America's land and resources, in combination with European institutions and technologies, created enormous opportunities for wealth creation. Transatlantic migration, high rates of natural increase, and investment in capital formation were the vehicles by which wealth creation was realized. In the 170 years covered by this chapter, the non-native population increased by a factor of close to 160 (while total population grew fortyfold), and the value of output produced per person more than doubled.

In detail the story becomes more complex. There was nothing inevitable about the response to economic incentives that characterized this history. The varied experiences of other European settlements in the Americas demonstrates that resource abundance alone did not guarantee sustained and stable economic growth. Choices and historical contingencies mattered in numerous ways. Imperfections in labour and financial markets, for example, slowed transatlantic migration and encouraged the use of unfree labour, both indentured servants and slaves. These and other choices had enormous implications for how the fruits of economic growth would be distributed. This is most starkly obvious in the institution of slavery, which dispossessed captives of ownership of their persons and the surplus they produced. The implications of slavery manifested themselves in the political organization of the United States and shaped patterns of regional investment and economic development throughout the pre-Civil War era. Slavery also created regional tensions that ultimately produced a destructive and costly Civil War.

Slavery was by no means the only economic issue that generated political conflicts. Land ownership and access to the resources necessary to bring land into productive economic use similarly emerged as a recurrent source of political tensions. Federalists and anti-federalists coalesced around differences in how quickly and on what terms new lands should be transferred to private ownership. On a smaller scale, individuals vied to acquire new lands on favourable terms. Meanwhile, tariff policy and numerous other political decisions created winners and losers and affected the distribution of economic returns. We can understand these conflicts in economic terms, but only by studying them historically can we gain an appreciation of the contingent nature of the choices that were made and the forces that influenced them.

References

Abramovitz, M. and David, P. A. (2000). 'American Macroeconomic Growth in the Era of Knowledge-Based Progress: The Long-Run Perspective', in Engerman, S. L. and Gallman, R. E. (eds.), *The Cambridge Economic History of the United States, vol. 3*, Cambridge University Press, 1–92.

Acemoglu, D. and Robinson, J. (2012). *Why Nations Fail: The Origins of Power, Prosperity, and Poverty*, New York: Crown.

Allen, R. C., Murphy, T. E. and Schneider, E. B. (2012). 'Colonial Origins of the Divergence in the Americas: A Labor Market Approach', *Journal of Economic History*, 72(4), 863–894.

Atack, J. and Bateman, F. (1987). *To Their Own Soil: Agriculture in the Antebellum North*, Ames: Iowa State University Press.

Atack, J., Bateman, F., Haines M. and Margo R. A. (2010). 'Did Railroads Induce or Follow Economic Growth? Urbanization and Population Growth in the American Midwest, 1850–1860', *Social Science History*, 32(2), 171–197.

Beard, C. A. (1913). *An Economic Interpretation of the Constitution of the United States*, New York: Dover, reprinted 2004.

Cain, L. (2006). 'Transportation', in Carter, S. B., Gartner, S. S., Haines, M. R., Omstead, A. L., Sutch, R. and Wright, G. (eds.), *Historical Statistics of the United States, Earliest Times to the Present: Millennial Edition*, Cambridge University Press.

Carter, S. B., Gartner, S. S., Haines, M. R., Omstead, A. L., Sutch, R. and Wright, G. (eds.) (2006). *Historical Statistics of the United States, Earliest Times to the Present: Millennial Edition*, Cambridge University Press.

Engerman, S. L. and Sokoloff, K. L. (2012). 'Factor Endowments and Institutions', in Engerman, S. L., Sokoloff, K. L. and Haber, S. (eds.), *Economic Development in the Americas since 1500: Endowments and Institution*, National Bureau of Economic Research Series on Long Term Factors in Economic Development, Cambridge University Press, 31–56.

Field, A. J. (1978). 'Sectoral Shift in Antebellum Massachusetts: A Reconsideration', *Explorations in Economic History* 15, 146–171.

Galenson, D. (1981). *White Servitude in Colonial America*, New York: Cambridge University Press.

(1996). 'The Settlement and Growth of the Colonies: Population, Labor, and Economic Development', in Engerman, S. L. and Gallman, R. E. (eds.), *The Cambridge Economic History of the United States, vol. 1: The Colonial Era*, Cambridge University Press, 135–208.

Geloso, V. (2019). 'Distinct within North America: Living Standards in French Canada, 1688–1775', *Cliometrica*, 13, 277–321.

Goldin, C. D. (1973). 'The Economics of Emancipation', *Journal of Economic History*, 33(1), 66–85.

Goldin, C. D. and Lewis, F. D. (1975). 'The Economic Costs of the American Civil War: Estimates and Implications', *Journal of Economic History*, 35(2), 299–326.

Haines, M. R. and Sutch, R. (2006). 'Population: 1790–2000 [Annual estimates], Table Aa6–8', in Carter, S. B., Gartner, S. S., Haines, M. R., Olmstead, A. L., Sutch, R. and Wright, G. (eds.), *Historical Statistics of the United States, Earliest Times to the Present: Millennial Edition*, Cambridge University Press.

Heckelman, J. C. and Dougherty, K. L. (2013). 'A Spatial Analysis of Delegate Voting at the Constitutional Convention', *Journal of Economic History* 73(2), 407–444.

Johnston, L. and Williamson, S. H. (2016). 'What Was the U.S. GDP Then?', MeasuringWorth, measuringworth.com / usgdp / #

Jones, A. H. (1980). *Wealth of a Nation to Be: The American Colonies on the Eve of the Revolution*, New York: Columbia University Press.

Lindert, P. H. and Williamson, J. G. (2016). *Unequal Gains: American Growth and Inequality since 1700*, Princeton University Press.

Maddison Project Database, version 2013, Bolt, J. and van Zanden, J. L. (2014). 'The Maddison Project: Collaborative Research on Historical National Accounts', *Economic History Review*, 67(3): 627–651, working paper.

Main, G. L. and Main, J. T. (1988). 'Economic Growth and the Standard of Living in Southern New England, 1640–1774', *Journal of Economic History*, 48(3), 27–46.

Mancall, P. C. and Weiss, T. (1999). 'Was Economic Growth Likely in Colonial British North America?', *Journal of Economic History*, 59(1), 17–40.

Mancall, P. C., Rosenbloom, J. L. and Weiss, T. (2002). 'Agricultural Labor Productivity in the Lower South, 1720 to 1800', *Explorations in Economic History*, 39, 390–424.

(2004). 'Conjectural Estimates of Economic Growth in the Lower South, 1720 to 1800', in Guinnane, T. W., Sundstrom, W. and Whatley, W. (eds.), *History Matters: Economic Growth, Technology, and Population, Essays in Honor of Paul A. David*, Stanford University Press, 387–424.

McClelland, P. (1969). 'The Cost to America of British Imperial Policy', *American Economic Review*, 59, 370–381.

McCusker, J. J. (2006). 'Population by Race and by Colony or Locality: 1620–1780: Table Eg1-59', in Carter, S. B., Gartner, S. S., Haines, M. R., Olmstead, A. L., Sutch, R. and Wright, G. (eds.), *Historical Statistics of the United States, Earliest Times to the Present: Millennial Edition*, Cambridge University Press.

Mittal, S., Rakove, J. N. and Weingast, B. R. (2010). 'The Constitutional Choices of 1787 and their Consequences', in Irwin, D. and Sylla, R. (eds.), *Founding Choices: American Economic Policy in the 1790s*, University of Chicago Press, 25–56.

North, D. C., Wallis, J. J., Weingast, B. R. (2009). *Violence and Social Orders: A Conceptual Framework for Interpreting Recorded Human History*, Cambridge University Press.

Olmstead, A. L. and Rhode, P. W. (2002). 'The Red Queen and the Hard Reds: Productivity Growth in American Wheat, 1800–1940', *Journal of Economic History*, 62(4), 929–966.

(2008). 'Biological Innovation and Productivity Growth in the Antebellum Cotton Economy', *Journal of Economic History*, 68(4), 1123–1169.

Rhode, P. W. and Sutch, R. (2006). 'Estimates of National Product Before 1929' in Carter, S. B., Gartner, S. S., Haines, M. R., Olmstead, A. L., Sutch, R. and Wright, G. (eds.), *Historical Statistics of the United States, Earliest Times to the Present: Millennial Edition*, Cambridge University Press.

Rosenberg, N. (1963). 'Technological Change in the Machine Tool Industry, 1840–1910', *Journal of Economic History*, 23 (4), 414–443.

Rosenbloom, J. L. (1993). 'Anglo American Technological Differences in Small Arms Manufacturing', *Journal of Interdisciplinary History*, 23, 683–698.

(2004). 'Path Dependence and the Origins of Cotton Textile Manufacturing in New England', in Farnie, D. A. and Jeremy, D. J. (eds.), *The Fibre that Changed the World: The Cotton Industry in International Perspective, 1600–1990s*, Oxford University Press, 365–391.

Rosenbloom, J. L. and Weiss, T. (2014). 'Economic Growth in the Mid-Atlantic Region: Conjectural Estimates for 1720 to 1800', *Explorations in Economic History*, 51, 41–59.

Rousseau, P. L. and Sylla, R. (2005). 'Emerging Financial Markets and Early US Growth', *Explorations in Economic History*, 42, 1–25.

Taylor, A. (2016). *American Revolutions: A Continental History, 1750–1804*, New York: W. W. Norton.

Temin, P. (1969). *The Jacksonian Economy*, New York: W. W. Norton.

(1976). 'The Post-Bellum Recovery of the South and the Cost of the Civil War', *Journal of Economic History*, 36, 898–907.

Ubelaker, D. H. (1988). 'North American Indian Population Size, A.D. 1500 to 1985', *American Journal of Physical Anthropology*, 77, 289–294.

Walton, G. M. and Shepherd, J. F. (1979). *The Economic Rise of Early America*, Cambridge University Press.

Wright, G. (1986). *Old South, New South: Revolutions in the Southern Economy since the Civil War*, New York: Basic Books.

(2006). *Slavery and American Economic Development*, Baton Rouge: Louisiana State University Press.

9

Latin America: 1700–1870

REGINA GRAFE

A Latin American perspective on the economic history of the period 1700 to 1870 is an interesting challenge. The chronology fits the conventional periodization of economic processes in Brazil rather well. Though Brazil became independent in 1822, it did so as a kingdom/empire. There was no abrupt political rupture from a political economy framework shaped by the reforms imposed on the colony in the eighteenth century by the Portuguese minister, Pombal. There were repeated episodes of political instability but according to Schulz (2016) existing elites moved to adapt to independence astutely. Significant economic and demographic development continued to build on cycles of gold mining and plantations. Despite the abolition of the slave trade in the 1850s, Brazil's elites resisted the abolition of slavery until 1888, just before a republican transition. Growth was urban as well as rural. Rio de Janeiro's population, for example, expanded by a factor of more than ten during the period under consideration, driven first by the arrival of more enslaved Africans and after the 1850s by European immigration.

At the same time the chronology moves right across the sharp break during the 'age of revolutions' that dominates political and economic history periodization for Spanish-speaking America. The eighteenth-century economic history of Spanish America moved in parallel with Brazil. There were reforms to the established rules of the Spanish imperial economy that underpinned observable economic expansion, a process of market deepening within and between the various imperial viceroyalties, a forceful demographic expansion, agricultural diversification, and a decentralization of trade flows. Newer commercial centres on the Atlantic such as Buenos Aires and older ones such as Havana expanded fast, even if transatlantic integration in staple products remained limited in volume and in terms of price convergence. Overall the centre of economic gravity shifted more clearly from the Pacific to the Atlantic and relations with British American commercial circuits intensified. Silver mining experienced a notable revival. As in Brazil the process was not a transition to modern economic growth in a sense of incipient industrialization, but it brought sustained expansion for most of the century.

As the century drew to a close in Spanish America average standards of living began to fall. Distributional issues and the limitations of growth within the imperial constellation became more visible. But the growth process only went decisively into reverse with the implosion of the Spanish Empire between 1808 and 1825. The remaining Spanish colonies, Cuba and Puerto Rico, accelerated their transition into plantation economies focused on sugar and coffee, accompanied by an unprecedented number of arrivals of enslaved Africans. The mainland markets meanwhile fragmented. Initially twelve, later sixteen new republican states struggled to establish legitimate forms of government and fiscal systems, and were mired in civil and internecine war. New tariff walls, monetary fragmentation, and high war expenditure added to obstacles to market development. A continent that had seen repeated large epidemics but which had been unfamiliar with famine for more than two centuries witnessed the disruption of vital supply lines within.

Hard data are few. But it is clear that the independence crisis and the wars of the first half of the nineteenth century firstly set back economic growth significantly, and secondly were followed by several decades of stagnation in much of Spanish America. By mid-century, however, several Spanish American Republics rejoined the growth process. Those Latin American republics that had struck lucky in both of the geographical lotteries, as producers of sought-after mineral or agricultural commodities and with access to the rapidly expanding Atlantic supply lines of European early industrializers, became more deeply integrated into the global economy. The question remains, however, why so late, why so slowly, and why was the growth pattern characterized by very high levels of inequality?

Colonial Latin America in the Eighteenth Century

Over the past two decades two very different models of the governance and political economy of the Iberian empires have competed in the literature. The more traditional, still favoured by economists like Acemoglu and Robinson (2012), is a centre-periphery model of imperial control. In the words of Kalamovitz (2008):

> The original sin that the colonies of Spain and Portugal inherited was absolutism ... a monarchical system with few constitutional and legal restrictions, secured in the organisation of corporation and *castas* [ethnic/racial groups], which gave rise to iron social hierarchies and profound economic inequality. The Catholic Church ... gave faith to the divine, and therefore unquestionable, power of the king.

In Spanish America over the eighteenth century a new monarchy of French descent, the Bourbons, reinforced centralization and aggravated the lack of political representation of colonial elites, not to mention the great majority of indigenous, mestizo, African-origin, and poor European immigrants. Bértola and Ocampo (2012) argue that unpredictable decision-making by a faraway monarchy, the inefficient regulation of property rights, a heavy tax burden, low public investment, the large colonial surpluses siphoned off to the imperial centre, and the commercial monopoly of the metropolis were to blame for the gap that had opened between Latin American per capita income and that of North America and Europe by the end of the colonial period.

By contrast Cardim et al. (2012) argue that Spanish and Portuguese governance evolved in a multipolar network of political centres including Mexico City, Lima, Rio, Havana, Madrid, and Lisbon. Grafe and Irigoin (2012) and Grafe (2015) argue that in a polycentric or stakeholder empire policymaking was overwhelmingly the outcome of negotiations between elites in the various centres, and between elites and non-elite groups within each centre. According to Irigoin and Grafe (2008) and Grafe (2012) local and regional decision-making was paramount and Halperin Donghi (1992) claimed that the monarch (who had never been considered to have any divine attributes) filled the crucial but not centralizing role of legitimate arbiter in the system. Extractive practices were mostly a result of the strength of local power groups, which could put pressure on the general population, rather than absolutist extraction from a remote centre.

Both models provide clear predictions regarding political governance, the development of growth and inequality, the insertion into global trade, fiscal and financial structures, and the role of different productive sectors. These will therefore be discussed in turn.

Administration, Commercial Regulation, and the Fiscal State

The eighteenth century was one of reform and economic expansion in Latin America on the whole, though the pace and strength diverged spatially and chronologically. In the Hispanic territories, Lynch (1973) described the

Bourbon reforms as a 'second conquest' that replaced hands-off governance structures of the previous Habsburg period with improved administrative techniques and central control. Change was slow and haphazard, though, and the notion of the second conquest has been called into question.

Administrative reforms created new viceroyalties. New Granada (1717/1739), today's Colombia, parts of Ecuador and Venezuela, and Rio de la Plata (1776), today's Argentina, and parts of Uruguay and Bolivia, were carved out of the existing Viceroyalty of Peru. Together with the Viceroyalty of Mexico they brought the number of major administrative units to four (Kuethe and Andrien 2014). Reforms also formally confirmed the transfer of the centre of economic gravity from Peru to Mexico, which had been underway since the seventeenth century. Burkholder and Chandler (1977) demonstrated that reformers pushed back against the domination of the administration by American-born creoles. Many more European officials were sent to the Americas, a move that created considerable political conflict. In Brazil the discovery of gold and a shift in plantation production moved the centres of population southwards. New administrative units were created in Sao Paulo and Minas de Ouro (1709), Minas Gerais (1720), and Mato Grosso and Goias (1748). More emblematic was the move of the capital from Salvador do Bahia to Rio de Janeiro in 1763.

The second set of reforms affected the trading regime. The Spanish regulatory framework for colonial trade was known since the sixteenth century as *Carrera de Indias* in the Atlantic. The Manila galleon connected Acapulco and the Philippines across the Pacific. The *Carrera* was never a monopoly system in economic terms, notwithstanding the pervasive confusion in the literature. It combined staple ports, such as Cadiz, Veracruz, and Havana, with convoys (called *flotas y galeones*), and compulsory guild membership (*Consulados*). Individual merchants competed on their own account. There was no joint stock, and no monopoly rights to the shipment of particular goods. In the English Atlantic non-British/British American merchants and shipowners were legally excluded creating a de facto exclusive British Atlantic (Zahedieh 2010). In the Spanish case the control of participation in the trade was by contrast based on guild membership rather than control of vessels' and merchants' origin. Outsiders could de facto access the system via the payment of a commission/bribe to a guild-member. This structure created insider benefits but not a closed Spanish Atlantic.

Thus the eighteenth century reforms of transatlantic trade were not the abolition of a monopoly as often implied. Instead, they deregulated the staple and convoy features. But paradoxically they also introduced two proper monopoly joint-stock companies in regionally restricted spaces. Convoys became increasingly unimportant from the 1730s, and between 1757 and 1788 only about 15 per cent of all wares travelled in the *flotas y galeones*; everything else went in single ships or small ad hoc flotillas organized for protection (Lamikiz 2009). Regular packet boats improved the flow of information. In 1765 nine Spanish peninsular ports were allowed direct navigation with the Caribbean, and in 1778 the *decreto de comercio libre* all but abolished the staple and convoy regulations. Even after the abolition of the Cadiz staple, however, four-fifths of the now considerably expanded trade volume went through this port. As Baskes (2013) has argued, both staple and convoys had fulfilled an important economic function in reducing uncertainty (rather than risk). Merchants struggled to replace those mechanisms thereafter. The rise of maritime insurance companies in Cadiz led to a wave of bankruptcies and the American markets suffered extreme price volatility. Meanwhile joint stock companies were introduced for trade with Caracas (1728) and Havana (1740), partially monopolizing the expanding exports of several key commodities: cocoa, sugar, and tobacco (Gárate Ojanguren 1990; 1994).

Portugal's colonial trading regime was more successful in turning Lisbon and Porto into the 'mandatory emporium' in the words of Pedreira (2000). Because of its size the Brazilian plantation and gold-mining economy was in many ways the tail that wagged the peninsular dog. Nonetheless, the commercial reforms of the Pombal period (1750–77, partially continued thereafter) served to reinforce the role of the European metropolis. A set of reforms successfully aimed at increasing the re-export trade, 85 per cent of which consisted of sugar and cotton. The creation of the most important of three new monopoly trade companies, that for the regions of Pará and Maranhão (founded 1755) began to promote cotton production after 1760, causing a dramatic expansion.

In addition, colonial exchange in Asia and Africa was much more important for Portugal than for Spain. The imperial economy interlinked trades in Asian textiles and enslaved Africans with exports of initially sugar and gold, later also cotton and coffee from Brazil and the European markets, from whence European manufactures were mostly exported to Brazil. According to Pedreira (2000) by the later eighteenth century about 20 per cent of those were of peninsular Portuguese origin, a reasonable share considering the small size of the Portuguese economy. Only the slave trade was almost entirely in the hands of Brazilians and, to a lesser extent, residents of the African colonies and never passed through Portugal at all.

The Portuguese reforms sidelined the British carrying trade and its position in the metropolitan economy, previously dominant thanks to the Methuen treaty (1703). They also imposed a clear metropolitan preference, most visibly by prohibiting sugar-refining in Brazil in favour of Portuguese refineries. In many ways Portugal took more leaves out of Britain's book in commercial regulation than out of Spain's. Indicative of the difference between the Iberians are recent estimates by Costa et al. (2015) and Palma (2016) that suggest wages of workers in peninsular Portugal were raised by almost 23 per cent as a consequence of the colonial contribution in the late eighteenth century. For Britain the estimate is 18–19 per cent, but for peninsular Spain a meagre 6 per cent. There has been a long debate whether British dominance and gold inflows from Brazil led to a 'Dutch disease' problem in peninsular Portugal, but Costa et al. (2016) would suggest that in the Portuguese case the European metropolis reaped very significant benefits, not least in fiscal terms. In one way or another Brazil accounted for 40 per cent of Portuguese royal revenues at mid-century and still 20 per cent in 1762–76 (Costa et al. 2013).

Administrative reform and changes in the regulation of transatlantic trade were accompanied by changes in fiscal governance also in Spanish America as first outlined by Klein and Tepaske (1982) and Klein (1998). Fiscal organization consisted of an increasing number of Treasury districts, by the late eighteenth century more than 100 (see Figures 9.1 and 9.2 for mainland districts). A side effect of this decentralization was that the modalities of taxes differed significantly from district to district. Revenue collection was strongly influenced by local decision-making resulting in different tax rates across sectors of the economy, corporate groups of taxpayers, and products subject to taxation.

The revenue-raising capacity per capita in Spanish America was quite similar to that in peninsular Spain (Figure 9.3). That contrasts with most European imperial formations in the eighteenth century, including Portugal and particularly Britain. The relative closure of the Portuguese and British Atlantic trading systems (notwithstanding intercolonial smuggling in the Americas) went hand in hand with a strategy that derived fiscal benefits mostly in the form of taxation levied on commodities at the point of importation into the European metropolis. Re-exports were eventually favoured by systems of drawbacks and rebates reinforcing the entrepôt trade, and colonial subjects in North America and Brazil were more lightly taxed than metropolitan ones. By contrast, taxation within Spanish-America *per capita* differed notably between districts, but across larger regions it matched taxes in the peninsula by the 1780s and surpassed it by the 1790s (Figure 9.3).

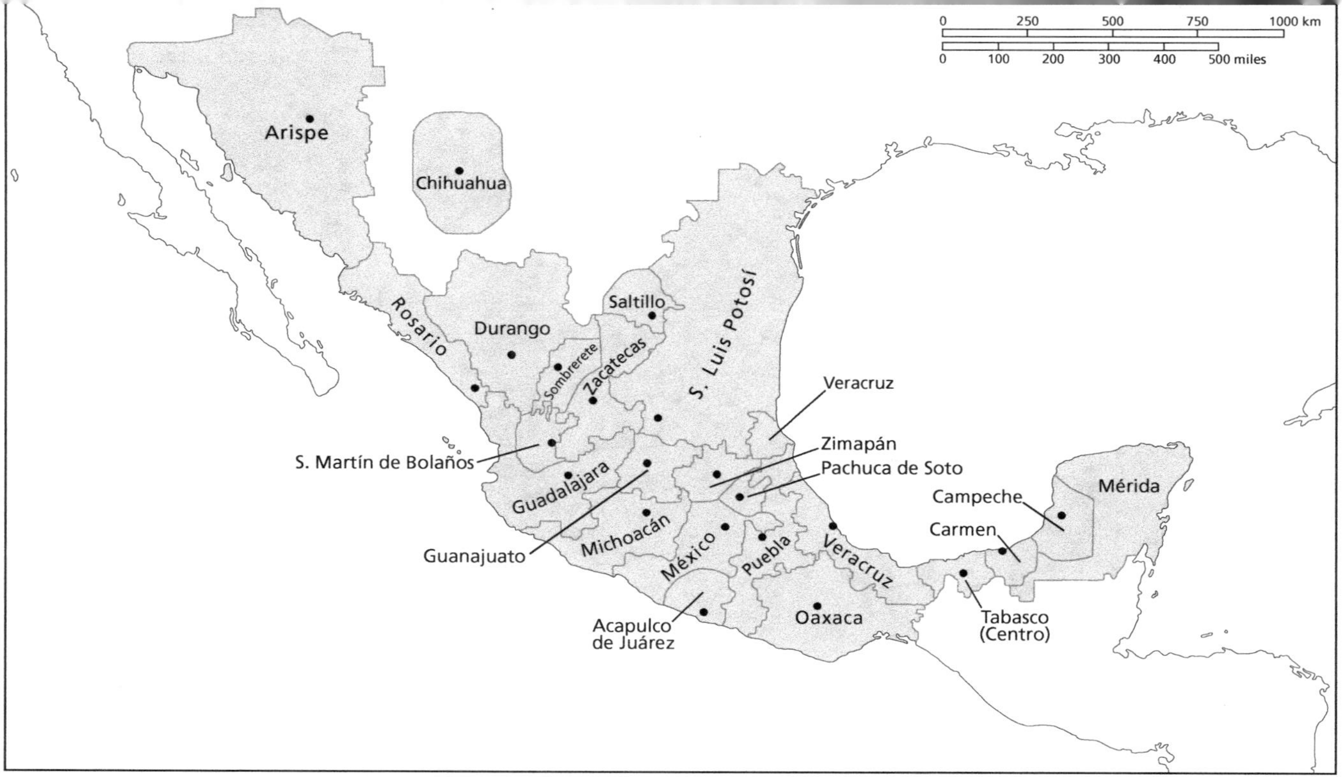

Figure 9.1 The fiscal governance structures: treasury districts (*cajas*) in New Spain (late eighteenth century)
All maps in this chapter were created with financial support from a British Academy Small Grant SG113363. Redrawn based on a map by Alejandra Castrodad with data compiled by M. A. Irigoin and the author.

Figure 9.2 Treasury districts (*cajas*) in Ecuador, Peru, Upper Peru, Rio de la Plata, and Chile (late eighteenth century)
All maps in this chapter were created with financial support from a British Academy Small Grant SG113363. Redrawn based on a map by Alejandra Castrodad with data compiled by M. A. Irigoin and the author.

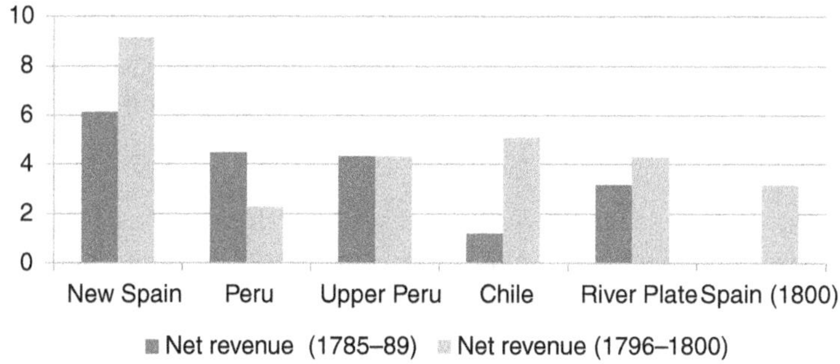

Figure 9.3 Net revenue in Spanish America and Spain 1785–1800
Source: Grafe and Irigoin (2012).

The combination of economic growth over the eighteenth century and administrative reform led to an unprecedented expansion of the fiscal state in Spanish America. Revenues and expenditure increased from about 10 million *pesos* per annum in the 1730s to 40 million in the late 1780s, and 70 million at the turn of the century. Until the very late eighteenth century revenues in the Americas grew faster than remittances to Spain, which fell from 12 per cent of total American expenditure in the 1730s to 4–5 per cent in the late 1790s (Irigoin and Grafe 2008). Arroyo Abad and van Zanden (2016) estimate the cost of direct transfers from Peru to Spain at below 1 per cent of gross domestic product (GDP) throughout the eighteenth century. On the receiving side Grafe and Irigoin (2012) show that tax income derived in one way or the other from the Americas never accounted for more than 13 per cent on average for any decade of the royal revenue in Spain over the century, considerably less than in Portugal as seen above.

Thus, for Spanish America there is little evidence that revenue was siphoned off to Europe, as claimed by the centre-periphery model cited by Bértola and Ocampo (2012). Instead, it was redistributed within Spanish America. Grafe and Irigoin (2012) also show for five-year samples in the early 1730s, the late 1780s, and the late 1790s that intracolonial transfers between treasuries, so-called *situados*, accounted for anything between one-quarter and 42 per cent of total net expenditure of these regional treasuries. The very large transfers were instrumental in guaranteeing the continued expansion of colonial rule. They subsidized certain regions and made local elites invest in the system in the most literal way, by lending to the local treasuries and by using transfers as a system of spatial redistribution of capital.

Arguably that created in Spanish America a commitment of economic elites to the imperial bond despite higher taxes than in Brazil, where the bond was felt largely as a tax on exports, which produced few gains for Brazilian elites.

Credit and Mining

Economic historians long argued that Latin American credit markets were underdeveloped during the colonial period. One aim of eighteenth-century reforms in Brazil was to sever the stranglehold that English merchants were perceived to have held on Brazilian trade as creditors. The trio of institutions articulating financial markets in the richest European regions – banks, shareholding companies, and public bonds – were also of relatively minor importance in Spanish America. However, on the Spanish side an alternative set of three core institutions articulated a sizeable credit market: religious institutions, merchant guilds (*consulados*), and local treasuries.

As in the Islamic world, religious institutions provided local, regional, and increasingly superregional credit. Convents, religious fraternities, hospitals, and the Inquisition provided access in the form of loans, often guaranteed by real property. Their deep pockets and interest in long-term, stable investments made them almost ideal lenders, rather like modern pension funds. Von Wobeser (1990) claims that by the late eighteenth century the standard interest rate they charged had come down to 5 or even 4 per cent per annum in a market of huge proportion. Debtors were almost anyone in colonial society: small property owners, powerful *hacendados,* mine-owners, shopkeepers, and parish priests. For those with only moveable property to pawn, a *Monte de Piedad* on the Italian model was created in late eighteenth-century Mexico. *Consulados* increasingly acted as merchant banks. They pooled the investments of individuals and religious institutions, syndicating large loans to the public treasury. Regional treasuries relied on such loans, provided at about 6 per cent interest per annum, instead of issuing bonds. In turn, treasuries' intracolonial transfers were effected generally by turning over funds to private individuals, who would use them as zero-interest loans in interregional trade, creating de facto a *giro* system in Spanish America.

There is very little research on this, but it stands to reason that in the silver-rich Spanish American economy, relaxed liquidity constraints helped the development of a system of public and private credit that was sui generis. Like the fiscal system, with which it was deeply intertwined, the financial system was decentralized, competitive, and provided impersonal sources of capital successfully and cheaply, if compared to contemporary banks, shareholding companies, and bond markets. But because of its institutional peculiarities, financial historians have often mistaken the absence of more familiar financial structures for an absence of a developed credit market.

Next to transatlantic trade, mining was the single largest source of capital. In Spanish America as well as in Brazil, mining was a private activity with one exception; mercury, which was an indispensable input into silver mining, was a monopoly of the monarch in the Spanish Empire. Mining (mostly silver) in the most populous regions of Spanish America, Peru/Upper Peru (today's Bolivia) and Mexico, accounted for less than 10–15 per cent of employment. Half of the economy was agricultural, the remainder consisting of a large service sector. Mining regions were more important because they turned into poles of economic integration as Assadourian (1983) was the first to show. They articulated interregional commercial exchanges that supplied manufactures, foodstuffs, and draught animals to the mining centres.

In Mexico almost all mining labour consisted of wage earners. In Peru and Upper Peru the *mita* labour draft and free labour coexisted. Often the same workers participated in both, but the reduced *mita* wages constituted an in-kind transfer from indigenous labourers to mine-owners. Only in the New Granada (Colombia) region of Choco did the relatively minor gold-mining sector (see Figure 9.4) rely on slaves. By contrast the rapid expansion of gold mining in Brazil towards the mid-century relied almost entirely on slavery as a labour system.

The Brazilian cycle of gold mining, which expanded until the 1740s then contracted, first slowly and then rapidly from the 1770s, is largely explained by the discovery and depletion of new deposits. The resurgence of silver mining in Mexico and Peru resulted from more complex factors. New discoveries were made. Still, over time the quality of deposits had a tendency to decline and overall profits were determined by the relation between labour costs, taxation, and, most importantly, the price of mercury. The lower the quality of ore, the larger the need for mercury in amalgamation. One of the most successful reforms in the Spanish case was the decision to expand dramatically the production of mercury – a royal monopoly – and to lower its price. As Dobado and Marrero (2014) have argued, the fiscally counterintuitive measure to forgo short-term revenue from the monopoly at a time of high demand was fundamental in the impressive recovery and expansion of silver mining (Figure 9.4). This had very positive long-term results for the treasuries, something also shown by Contreras (2010) for Peru.

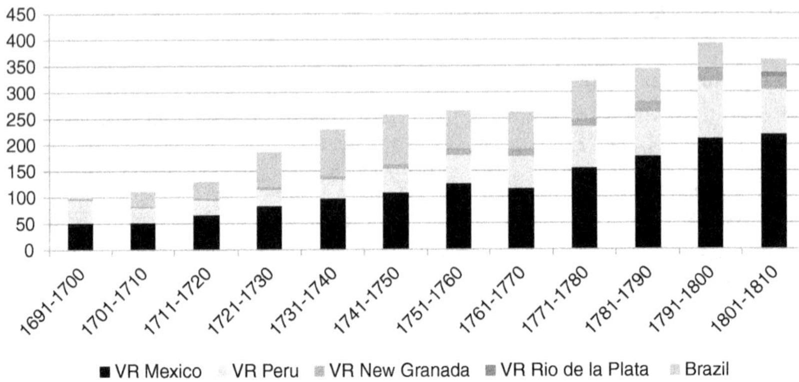

Figure 9.4 Production of precious metals in the territories of the Spanish viceroyalties and Brazil 1680–1810 (millions of silver pesos of 272 maravedis equivalent)
Sources: TePaske and Brown (2010), Palma and Silva (2016).

Growth and Living Standards

In Spanish America, growth in mining and finance was accompanied by an increasing diversification of agriculture over the eighteenth century. Cash crops such as tobacco, sugar, and cocoa became increasingly important. Mazzeo (2010) demonstrates, for example, that exports of cocoa from El Callao (Peru) increased seven times between the 1740s and the 1770s. After the short-lived English occupation in 1762, Cuba began importing significant numbers of enslaved Africans, turning within a few decades into a slave-based plantation economy. When the Haitian Revolution destroyed the sector in the French colony, the expansion of sugar in Cuba and Brazil accelerated even more. Because plantation regions were not self-sufficient in food stuffs, interregional trade expanded, too. In mainland Spanish America, slave occupations were very diverse, ranging across most urban and rural activities (Newson 2006). Venezuela and Buenos Aires, two of the regions with the largest labour scarcity, increasingly turned to slave imports in addition to free immigrants. Peru counted 90,000 enslaved Africans by the end of the eighteenth century. Only in New Spain did the transformation and expansion of the primary sector occur largely without slavery. Even as slavery's importance increased fast in Spanish America, the number of enslaved who arrived in Brazil, where all important sectors relied on slavery, was until the 1850s a multiple of that of Spanish America (Figure 9.5).

At the transatlantic end of the slave trade, Spanish involvement was minimal before the nineteenth century and most Africans were sold by

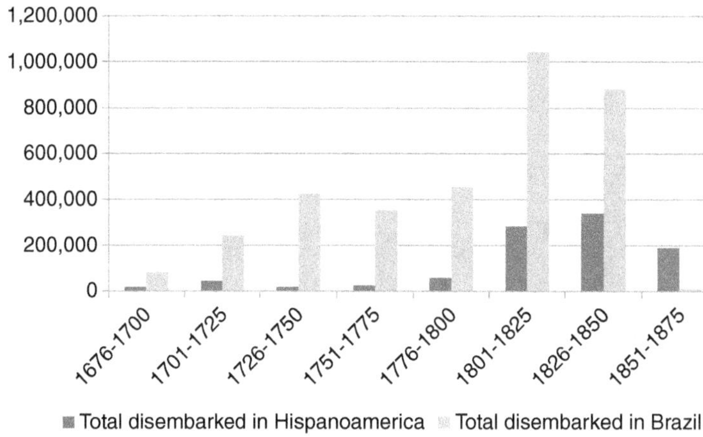

Figure 9.5 Enslaved Africans disembarked in Latin America 1675–1875
Source: Transatlantic slave database www.slavevoyages.org/voyage/database (accessed 27 October 2020).

Portuguese/Brazilian or other European traders. By the end of the eighteenth century the slave population of Brazil has been estimated as about 1.5 million, while the US and the French Caribbean (pre-revolution in Haiti) were an unwelcoming new home to about 700,000 each, with the British Caribbean accounting for another half-million. Spanish America's slave population had increased to more than 300,000 (Bergad 2007). The large increase of slavery was an integral part of the economic growth model. It reflected a vast increase in 'productive' investment in commodified people, while in Cuba, in particular, Santamaria Garcia (2011) found evidence that the labour productivity per enslaved worker increased in the second half of the eighteenth century. Forms of forced labour of indigenous people, on the other hand, prevailed by the eighteenth century only on the economically least productive frontiers of the Spanish territories – with the notable exception of the mining *mita*, which combined draft labour with wage payments. Indigenous slavery had been outlawed in Spanish America since 1542 but it persisted in regions such as the north of Mexico. In Brazil it was only formally abolished in the eighteenth century and had been sizeable. But Reséndez (2016) is right to say that it is poorly researched.

Growth was necessarily regionally diverse between core and 'frontier' regions. There are few estimates for GDP and Maddison's (2010) figures are probably wildly off the mark for eighteenth century Latin America. Arroyo Abad and van Zanden (2016) have recently provided estimates in 1990 Geary

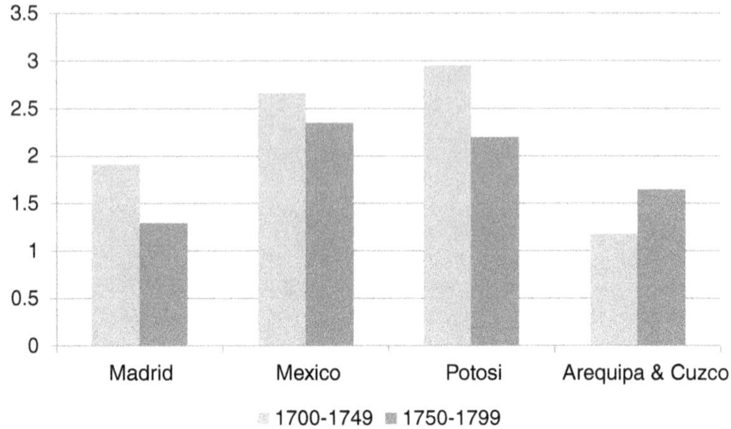

Figure 9.6 Welfare ratios in bare-bones baskets in Spain, New Spain, Alto Peru, and Peru 1700–1800
Source: Arroyo Abad and van Zanden (2016).

Khamis dollars for the two most populous regions of Spanish America, Mexico ($800–900) and Peru (rising from $700 to $800 over the eighteenth century), broadly in line with Contreras Carranza (2014) and Seminario (2016). In both cases, growth turned moderately negative in the last two decades of the eighteenth century, but these data mean that Mexico's GDP per capita exceeded that of peninsular Spain while Peru's was just a little lower. Arroyo Abad and van Zanden (2016) argue that in the period 1725 to 1775 GDP growth rates per annum, 0.36 per cent and 0.44 per cent respectively, exceeded those of Britain (0.13 per cent), and especially peninsular Spain (0.02 per cent). Growth rates in Cuba, Venezuela, and Rio de la Plata were probably much higher, even on the basis of the limited evidence available, and unlike Peru and Mexico they continued to expand until the end of the century. Tax data for the late eighteenth-century bishopric of Buenos Aires, for example, kept growing according to Fradkin and Garavaglia (2009). In short, there is a consensus that this was an economy in expansion at least until the final quarter of the eighteenth century.

The picture of expansion visible in mining, agriculture, the fiscal system, and the introduction of enslaved workers is also reflected in measures of standards of living, an area of intense debate (Arroyo Abad et al. 2012; Arroyo Abad and van Zanden 2015; Dobado González 2015; Arroyo Abad and van Zanden 2016). But by and large, measures of welfare using multiples of 'bare-bones baskets' and anthropometric studies point in the same direction. Figures 9.6 and 9.7

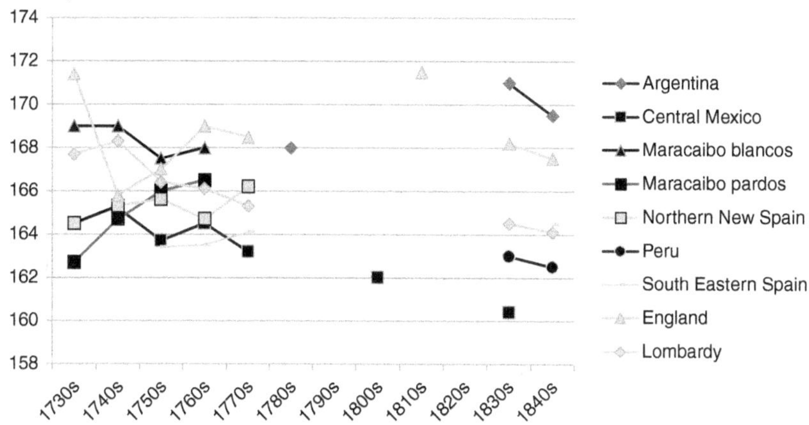

Figure 9.7 Average height of adult males, 1730s to 1840 (cm)
Source: Dobado González (2015); Floud et al. (1990).

show the diversity between Spanish American regions. Data on welfare ratios suggest that life was considerably harder in Peru than in almost any of the other regions, mirroring to a certain extent also the fiscal data. But even in Peru subsistence was generally not in danger and standards of living expressed in subsistence baskets were comparable to European peripheral regions, though clearly below those of Europe's or Latin America's richest regions.

Meanwhile anthropometric measures (Figure 9.7), too, suggest that the biological welfare of eighteenth-century Latin American birth cohorts was within the range of European variations, with Argentineans standing particularly tall (all Latin American series are black, European grey for easier comparison). But the data also suggest wide and increasing disparities across regions, and data not displayed here draw additional attention to the significant differences among the *castas* in the same regions.

Eighteenth-century Latin American societies – like European ones – were Ancien Régime societies. The social structure was based on the notion of collective rights and duties of distinctive social groups defined along the lines of race, ethnicity, gender, religious, military, or lay status, and others. A male member of the indigenous nobility, a creole nun, a slave of African descent, a poor white urban craftsman, and a poor indigenous peasant could be taxed differently if they sold the same piece of cloth. Their access to the labour market would be restricted or promoted by their status and *casta,* and their strategies of economic survival conditioned by support from a religious fraternity or access to the communal lands of the indigenous village. Some of the boundaries between corporate groups were notably weaker in Spanish and lusophone America than others. Boundary-crossing was not impossible – race was not a completely fixed category (yet), for instance – leaving room for individuals to move out of their corporate place.

The collective rights of corporate groups were, however, not only restrictions to be overcome. They were also the foremost protection mechanism, especially for the lower social strata. Owensby (2008) has argued that thanks to the skilful use of Spanish courts of law indigenous communities had, for example, maintained significant amounts of collectively held land in many regions. Indigenous institutions by the late eighteenth century were very different from their sixteenth-century antecedents. The dramatic demographic collapse during the sixteenth and early seventeenth centuries had turned economies in the Andes and Mesoamerica, which had been labour-rich and land-poor, into economies with a low labour to land ratio. Therefore, even if some land was held with collective title in indigenous villages, more often than not plots were farmed as family plots, as Duenas (2010) shows. Religious institutions enjoyed often enormous wealth and important privileges. But they were also patient lenders, providing long-term funding for agricultural improvement and short-term funds in crises. Free coloured people were more often required to serve in the militias than whites. Yet Vinson (2001) demonstrates that their military service also could serve to claim collective special rights (freedoms/*fueros*) traditionally granted to militiamen for all people of African descent.

Collective bargaining for social, economic, and political rights was the fundamental organizational practice. The monarchy was the ultimate arbiter but mostly adjudicated conflicts ex-post. Reforms in the eighteenth century brought administrative capacity, a mining expansion, more trade, a more diversified agriculture, and vastly expanded fiscal capacity. They also led to a large number of conflicts over the rights and duties of the corporate groups in society. Paradoxically, they effected in many cases an increased decentralization, such as the subdivision of administrative and fiscal units. Deeper goods and financial markets were accompanied by the foundation of more institutions, such as merchant or mining guilds, that moved large amounts of capital. The expansion of the fiscal state led in the context of regional elite control to an empowering of those elite groups. An increasing number of conflicts and rebellions did not question imperial rule as such. Yet they throw light on the need for realignments and new bargains, especially where elites rolled over the increasing tax burden on the weakest in society, as seems to have happened for example to indigenous villages in the Andes in the late eighteenth century.

By the end of the eighteenth century, strains showed in some macro regions, notably Peru and Mexico, with their large populations. The corporatist social order of Latin American societies had shown a remarkable growth potential, though, and neither Spanish nor Portuguese rule in the Americas collapsed under their own weight. Independence, when it came, was triggered by the French invasion of the Iberian Peninsula in 1808.

Independence and Post-Independence Latin America

Until 1808, only Haiti had undergone a revolutionary process of independence, in which armed slaves forced an end to slavery and that of the plantation economy. But ten years after the revolution its white population had declined from 40,000 to 10,000 through death and flight, there were about 20,000 surviving mulattos, and one-third to half of the former slave population had perished (Gelman 2011). The political influence of the independence of the thirteen British colonies and the French Revolution should not be underplayed. But outside Haiti it was the imprisonment of the Spanish king by French troops in 1808 and the removal of the Portuguese royal family from Lisbon to Brazil that set off a process that would end, seventeen years later, in the independence of most of the Spanish American republics with which we are familiar today and an independent Brazilian Empire.

Over the next three decades, Spanish America was subjected to civil wars that sometimes turned into international wars, as Gran Colombia split into three countries Venezuela, Ecuador, and Colombia (1830) and Bolivia separated from Peru (1825). The Central American Federation split in the late 1830s into Nicaragua, Honduras, Costa Rica, El Salvador, and Guatemala. Only Cuba and Puerto Rico remained Spanish colonies. The various provinces in the Rio de la Plata would not settle into Argentina on one bank of the river and Uruguay on the other until mid-century.

Debates about the transition from colony to independence pitch 'pessimists' like Coatsworth (2006), who blame the colonial legacy for at least five decades of stagnation, against (relative) 'optimists' like Prados de la Escosura (2009), who argue that independence and post-independence should not be blamed for the fact that Latin America fell behind in comparison with North America or Europe. The only point on which pessimists and optimists agree is that the extremely violent and protracted nature of the independence and post-independence wars and civil conflicts led to the large-scale destruction of human, physical, and financial resources. It set most regions back very seriously – with the possible exception of Chile. But the exact nature of that destruction is less often discussed.

Both views have merit. But both also omit important parts of the story. The pessimists have a hard time reconciling their view with the fact that the late colonial regime was one of economic expansion. If the colonies were capable of substantial growth, why should the legacy have been so devastating? Acemoglu et al. (2002) and Acemoglu and Robinson (2012) famously claimed that the centralizing and extractive nature of colonial institutions was to blame for a 'reversal of fortunes' after independence, in which exclusive institutions and extractive practices prevailed in most of Latin America, while inclusive institutions in North America paved the way to growth. However, given what we now know about the structure of colonial economic governance, extraction and centralization turned out to be straw men.

The optimists rightly argue that Latin America did not fall behind Asia, Africa, the Middle East, or even the European periphery in the period, but only against those regions in North America and mostly north-western Europe that were surging ahead thanks to the Industrial Revolution. Prados de la Escosura (2009) rejects the notion that a colonial legacy was at fault because economic performance was simply average, both measured against the majority of the contemporary 'rest of the world' and against the economic fortunes of post-independence experiences in other parts of the world in the twentieth century. But unlike Spain, which had grown only slowly already in the eighteenth century, most of Latin America had experienced fast economic development in the late imperial period, at least by the standards of pre-industrial societies. Thus the change in perspective does not alter the fact that on the whole the growth performance of Latin American economies in the first half of the nineteenth century was poor in relation to its own past performance. Clearly they had been knocked off their path of relatively steady pre-industrial growth.

Figure 9.8 uses GDP per capita data by Bértola and Ocampo (2012) but regroups countries. By 1820 almost all of the territories that would become the new Spanish American republics had suffered from the destruction of war. Chile's economy grew fast over the next five decades and turned from a relatively poor colonial backwater into one of the richest societies in Latin America. The relatively short and less violent process towards independence may have been one of the reasons. Despite the endemic violence that reigned in the Rio de la Plata for most of the rest of our period, the provinces that

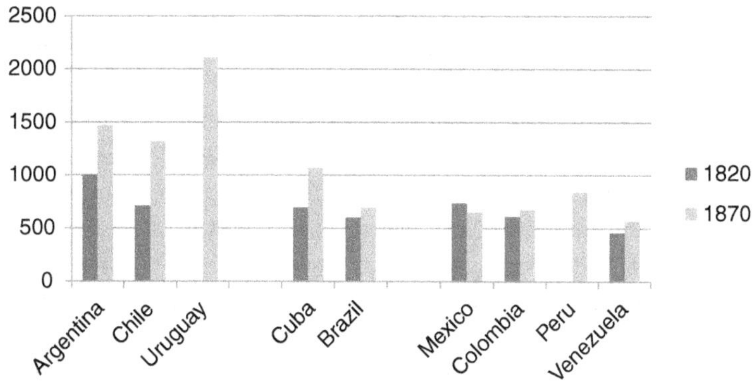

Figure 9.8 GDP per capita 1820–70 (1990 international dollars)
Source: Bértola and Ocampo (2012).

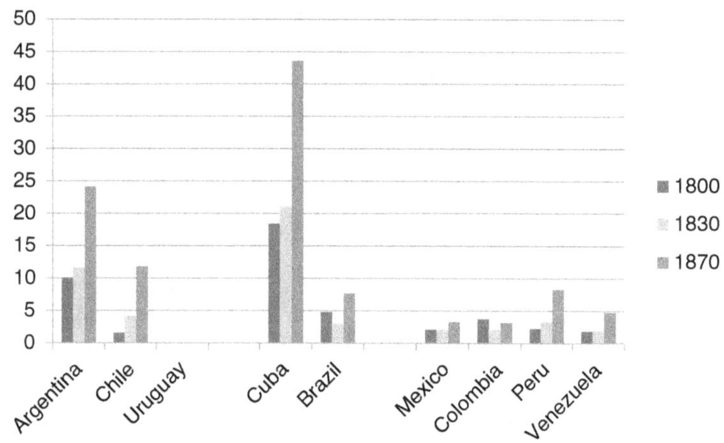

Figure 9.9 Exports per capita 1800–70 (thousands of dollars)
Source: Bértola and Ocampo (2012).

were to become Argentina and modern Uruguay experienced strong economic expansion. However, this should not be interpreted as continuing a process visible in the eighteenth century. In fact, most of the growth occurred after 1850. Before mid-century growth was elusive in the Rio de la Plata as the development of exports shown in Figure 9.9 suggests.

A second group of countries, the plantation economies of Brazil and Cuba, maintained slavery and continued to expand throughout. In both countries sugar producers were the big beneficiaries of the demise of the Haitian sugar sector. Santamaria Garcia (2011) provides data that track Cuba's evolution from a minor player compared not only to pre-revolutionary Haiti but also the British Caribbean (14,000 tons in Cuba, 130,000 in Haiti, and 103,000 in the British islands), to overtaking British production by the later 1830s, i.e. even before the abolition of slavery in the British colonies. As the trade in Africans dried up, the island turned to the introduction of 150,000 Chinese between 1840 and 1872 in similarly abusive ways (Santamaria Garcia 2011). Cuba also became the first Latin American country with a railway network. But the social savings and positive feedback between railways and exports were likely at a lower scale than those shown by Bignon et al. (2015) for Latin America's largest countries, which introduced railways after the 1870s. Growth in Cuba occurred even though it was the only commodity exporter in Spanish America whose terms of trade deteriorated. In Brazil voluntary immigration began to complement the still expanding slave-labour sector (Figure 9.5). Nevertheless, the acceleration of growth only really began after the 1870s. Leff (1997) linked this to transports costs, which in turn were owed to the late arrival of railways. This is consistent with Bignon et al. (2015), who showed very large social savings for a later period when Brazil finally developed a large network. Brazil, however, not only avoided the destruction of the Spanish American Wars of Independence. It also managed to avoid the second curse of its Spanish-speaking neighbours, public defaults on domestic and international debt.

That brings us to the third group of countries, comprising more than half of the Latin American population: Mexico (and the Central American countries), Colombia, Venezuela, and Peru (and Ecuador and Bolivia). Though there are only data for some of these, they are the clearest examples of the five lost post-independence decades. On balance there was little more than stagnation. When growth returned, it was weaker than in the late colonial period. There are a number of factors that account for this. First, they had a number of challenges in common with all other countries bar Cuba and Brazil. The creation of a large number of smaller polities presented all of them with the challenge of how to finance not only a new administration, but also the ongoing costs of war. The fiscal dire straits of the early Spanish American republics were extreme. Not surprisingly, the boundaries of the new republics often resembled those of the old Treasury districts. In the 1820s, the new republics embarked on an ill-advised foray into borrowing on the London market. Almost all of them defaulted immediately on their loans in – as Marichal (1989) discusses – the first of many recurrent debt crises.

New states with little legitimacy and rising expenditures relied primarily on two devices. Customs aggravated the effect of the disintegration of internal markets. Debasements and inflationary fiat money doubled down on the new obstacles to internal trade. The colonial Spanish silver peso had not only constituted the most important international money of exchange of the eighteenth century, but also the largest existing monetary union, as Irigoin (2000; 2008) shows. The result of the destruction of that union and that of a common trading zone was naturally worst in countries like Bolivia, which ended up without easy access to the coast and affordable transport. In addition, the old centres of population and in particular mining were among the most fought over, for obvious reasons. Seminario (2016) suggests that Peru lost about one-third of its GDP per capita between 1804 and 1824. While the disintegration of markets is difficult to document with hard data, there is plenty of information rarely used by economic historians. In the early Independence period the most important indigenous languages in the Andes – Quechua and Aymara – made a comeback at the expense of Spanish, according to Pearce (2011). This was a clear sign that markets had become more local and more dominated by indigenous actors.

Control over mining areas became an important battle. It was also a part of the destruction of capital stock from which it was particularly difficult to recover. Flooded mines could not simply be brought into operation, but needed large investments. To make matters worse, independence cut the silver-producing areas of Spanish America off from the supply of cheap mercury. The effects are visible in Figure 9.10. While the low point of production was passed earlier in Peru and Mexico than in Bolivia, production recovered nowhere in the old mining centres before the 1840s, if then.

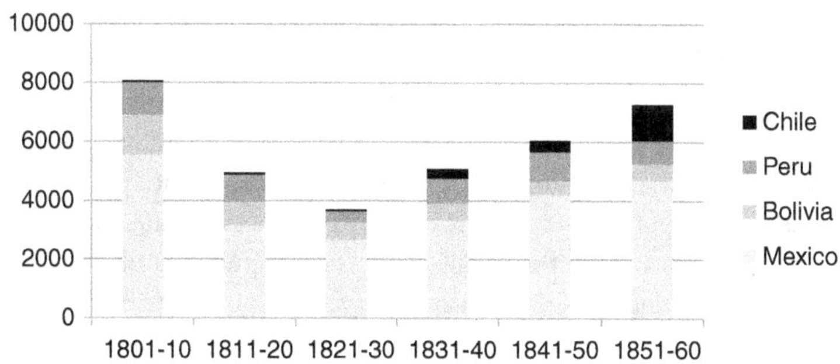

Figure 9.10 Silver production in Latin America 1800–60 (tons)
Source: Gelman (2011) and Contreras (1999).

Both the pessimist and the optimist views of post-Independence Latin America acknowledge the costs. What both views underplay is that the transition from colony to nation states in Latin America came not only with the considerable costs of war and destruction or even the cost of setting up twelve then sixteen new state apparatuses, monetary and commercial disintegration, and a brutal war. It also constituted a regime change that was costly because it further dislocated markets and especially because institutions and organizations which had co-evolved fell apart.

This is clearly visible in the credit sector. By the late eighteenth century not only Mexican *hacendados* had made liberal use of cheap credit. Then, successive waves of disentailment starting in the late colonial period but accelerating in the nineteenth century closed down the basic units of credit provision. Liberal reformers and many economic historians saw religious property primarily as dead-hand property and an obstacle to functioning land markets. But because of their credit services they had in fact underpinned agricultural and commercial investment. As liberal reformers pressed for money to finance new states and expropriated the most important credit institutions, the effects reverberated through the economy. A similar effect resulted from the dislocation of the *situado* system for interregional commerce and the interspatial transfer of capital, which isolated interior mining regions from the coast. Regions that had financed their public administration through transfers, such as Buenos Aires, struggled badly to replace those payments. Regions in the hinterland were cut off from the larger trade networks on the Atlantic and Pacific shores when trade was not lubricated any longer by large injections of public money.

The transformation of land markets and access to land was a second area where regime change caused unintended problems. From an economic standpoint, the liberalization of land markets and the conversion of land held in common property by indigenous communities should have improved productivity. Liberal reformers' convictions and elites' convenience led to the sale not only of religious institutions' landholdings (destroying the 'bank capital' used to secure their lending) but also that of many indigenous communities. Elsewhere, especially where the land frontier had not yet been closed, as in parts of Venezuela or the Rio de la Plata, the concentration of landholdings was more the result of the sale of public lands, as Ocampo (2011) argues for Venezuela. But almost everywhere land distribution became dramatically more unequal as a result, with far-reaching consequences for inequality in the longer run. Nor were larger holdings necessarily more productive. Especially after credit markets had been severely curtailed, the impact on productivity differed from region to region and product to product. Furthermore, as mentioned above, most 'common lands' had been farmed de facto as family holdings, in any case.

Regime change also transformed labour relations. Slavery was only abolished early in those parts of the former empire where its economic importance was modest. In slavery-dependent Venezuela, abolition occurred only in the 1850s. Tribute paid by indigenous communities was not eliminated in the Andean countries until mid-century. But tribute is another example of the complexities of regime change. Indigenous communities in Bolivia, for example, realized that tribute payments constituted proof of land rights. While liberal reformers saw tribute as one of the horrors of colonial exploitation, which should be abolished as soon as possible, indigenous peasants had relied on them as a way to protect their access land. They were only too aware that, no sooner had tribute been abolished, then their land would be gone, too, as Platt (1984) has shown.

The costs of regime change were not straightforward and in most cases they were very unevenly distributed across social strata. As in other transitions from corporatist social orders to proto-liberal ones at the turn of the nineteenth century, the transition more often than not left the weakest sectors of society very exposed. Indigenous people in many parts of Spanish America would be chided by nationalists and liberals in the nineteenth century for siding generally with royal forces rather than with those who tried to bring independence and for not understanding that they had to throw off their yoke. A yoke of exploitation at the hands of colonial elites they had born. Yet the end of the corporatist system of the old regime, reliant as it was on collective bargaining among social groups, removed not only collective restrictions but also protections long before a system that might protect the individual came into place.

Weak states became hostages to elite groups in ways that colonial administrations had not been, because collective bargaining offered a minimum of protection and because the empire guaranteed access to legal procedures. That is not to say that the removal of corporatist restrictions did not offer the potential for economic growth. But most Latin Americans had to wait for a very long time for that potential to become realized. In the absence of a new regulatory and legal framework that could check the abuse of power, inequality increased. Even when commodity exports began to offer improved earnings and healthier fiscal balances, growth was aligned with increased inequality. The history of the short-lived guano boom in mid-century Peru is a good example. The demand of intensifying European agriculture drove an enormous expansion of the exports of bird droppings from the south of Peru as fertilizers. At its peak in 1853 guano accounted for 74 per cent of Peruvian exports, leaving silver a distant second. But while standards of living had slowly recovered to reasonable levels by mid-century, the GDP growth guano drove was actually associated with *falling* standards of living as inflation reduced real wages. As Arroyo Abad (2014) argues, in the brave new world of republican Latin America, growth and inequality were not moving in the same direction.

References

Acemoglu, D. and Robinson, J. A. (2012). *Why Nations Fail: The Origins of Power, Prosperity, and Poverty*, New York: Crown.

Acemoglu, D., Johnson, S. and Robinson, J. (2002). 'Reversal of Fortune: Geography and Institutions in the Making of the Modern World Income Distribution', *Quarterly Journal of Economics*, 117(4), 1231–1294.

Arroyo Abad, L. (2014). 'Failure to Launch: Cost of Living and Living Standards in Peru During the 19th Century', *Revista de Historia Economica / Journal of Iberian and Latin American Economic History*, 32(1), 47–76.

Arroyo Abad, L. and van Zanden, J. L. (2015). 'Optimistic but Flawed? A Reply', *Revista de historia Economica/Journal of Iberian and Latin American Economic History*, 33(1), 77–82.

(2016). 'Growth under Extractive Institutions? Latin American Per Capita Gdp in Colonialtimes', *Journal of Economic History*, 76(4), 1182–1215.

Arroyo Abad, L., Davies, E. and van Zanden, J. L. (2012). 'Between Conquest and Independence: Real Wages and Demographic Change in Spanish America, 1530–1820', *Explorations in Economic History*, 49(2), 149–166.

Assadourian, C. S. (1983). *El Sistema De La Económia Colonial*, Mexico: El Mercado Interior, Regiones Y Espacio Económico.

Baskes, J. (2013). *Staying Afloat : Risk and Uncertainty in Spanish Atlantic World Trade, 1760–1820*, Stanford University Press.

Bergad, L. (2007). *The Comparative Histories of Slavery in Brazil, Cuba, and the United States*, Cambridge University Press.

Bértola, L. and Ocampo, J. A. (2012). *The Economic Development of Latin America since Independence*, Oxford University Press.

Bignon, V., Esteves, R. and Herranz-Loncán, A. (2015). 'Big Push or Big Grab? Railways, Government Activism, and Export Growth in Latin America, 1865–1913', *Economic History Review*, 68(4), 1277–1305.

Burkholder, M. A. and Chandler, D. S. (1977). *From Impotence to Authority. The Spanish Crown and the American Audiencias, 1687–1808*, Columbia: University of Missouri Press.

Cardim, P., Herzog, T., Ruiz Ibáñez, J. J. and Sabatini, G. (2012). *Polycentric Monarchies: How Did Early Modern Spain and Portugal Achieve and Maintain a Global Hegemony?*, Portland: Eastbourne.

Coatsworth, J. H. (2006). 'Political Economy and Economic Organization', in Bulmer-Thomas, V., Coatsworth, J. H. and Cortés-Conde, R. (eds.), *The Colonial Era and the*

Short Nineteenth Century, vol. 1 of *The Cambridge History of Latin America*, Cambridge University Press, 237–273.

Contreras Carrenza, C. (1999). 'En la mineria hispoamericana después de la independencia. Estudio comparative de Bolivia, Chile, México y Peru', in Bornemann, M. M. (ed.), *In dos décados de investigación en historia económica comparada en América Latina: Homage a Carlos Sempat Assadourian*. Mexico: El Colegio de México, Centro de Estudios Históricos, 255–283.

(2010). 'La Mineria En El Peru En La Epoca Colonial Tardia, 1700–1824', in Chocano, M., Contreras, C., Quiroz, F., Mazzeo, C. A. and Flores, R. (eds.), *Compendio De Historia Economica Del Peru, Tomo 3: Economia Del Periodo Colonial Tardio*, Lima: Banco Central de Reserva del Peru – El Instituto de Estudios Peruanos, 103–168.

(2014). 'Crecimiento Económico En El Perú Bajo Los Borbones, 1700 – 1820', working paper PUCP Depto de Economia.

Costa, L. F., Rocha, M. M. and Sousa, R. M. de. (2013). *O Ouro Do Brasil*, Lisbon, Impresa Nacional-Casa da Moeda.

Costa, L. F., Palma, N. and Reis, J. (2015). 'The Great Escape? The Contribution of the Empire to Portugal's Economic Growth, 1500–1800', *European Review of Economic History*, 19, 1–22.

Costa, L. F., Lains, P. and Miranda, S. M. (2016). *An Economic History of Portugal, 1143–2010*, Cambridge University Press.

Dobado González, R. (2015). 'Pre-Independence Spanish Americans: Poor, Short and Unequal . . . or the Opposite?', *Revista de Historia Economica / Journal of Iberian and Latin American Economic History*, 33(1), 15–59.

Dobado, R. and Marrero, G. (2014). 'El *Mining-Led* Growth En El México Borbonico, El Papel Del Estado Y El Coste De La Independencia', in Hausberger, B. and Ibarra, A. (eds.), *Oro Y Plata En Los Inicios De La Economia Global: De Las Minas a La Moneda*, Mexico: El Colegio de México, Centro de Estudios Históricos, 177–216.

Duenas, A. (2010). *Indians and Mestizos in the 'Lettered City': Reshaping Justice, Social Hierarchy, and Political Culture in Colonial Peru*, Boulder: University Press of Colorado.

Floud, R., Wachter, K. and Gregory, A. (1990). *Height, Health and History: Nutritional Status in the United Kingdom, 1750–1980*, Cambridge University Press.

Fradkin, R. and Garavaglia, J. C. (2009). *La Argentina Colonial: El Río De La Plata Entre Los Siglos Xvi Y Xix*, Buenos Aires: Siglo Veintiuno Editores.

Gárate Ojanguren, M. (1990). *La Real Compañía Guipuzcoana De Caracas*, San Sebastian: Sociedad Guipuzcoana de Ediciones y Publicaciones.

(1994). *Comercio Ultramarino E Ilustración: La Real Compañía De La Habana*, San Sebastian; Donostia.

Gelman, J. (2011). 'Senderos Que Se Bifurcan. Las Economias De América Latina Luego De Las Independencias', in Bértola, L. and Gerchunoff, S. (eds.), *Institucionalidad Y Desarrollo Economico En América Latina*, Santiago: Comisión Económica para América Latina y el Caribe (CEPAL), 19–42.

Grafe, R. (2012). *Distant Tyranny. Markets, Power and Backwardness in Spain 1650–1800*, Princeton University Press.

(2015). 'Tyrannie À Distance: La Construction De L'état Polycentrique Et Les Systèmes Fiscaux En Espagne (1650–1800)', in Beguin, K. (ed.), *Ressources Publiques Et Construction Étatique En Europe*, Paris: Open Edition Books, 167–186.

Grafe, R. and Irigoin, A. (2012). 'A Stakeholder Empire: The Political Economy of Spanish Imperial Rule in America', *Economic History Review*, 65 (2), 609–651.

Halperin Donghi, T. (1992). 'Backward Looks and Forward Glimpses from a Quincentennial Vantage Point', *Journal of Latin American Studies* Supplement, 219–234.

Irigoin, A. (2000). 'Inconvertible Paper Money, Inflation and Economic Performance in Early Nineteenth Century Argentina', *Journal of Latin American Studies*, 32(2), 333–359.

(2008). 'Gresham on Horseback: The Monetary Roots of Spanish American Political Fragmentation in the Nineteenth Century', *Economic History Review*, 62(3), 551–575.

Irigoin, A. and Grafe, R. (2008). 'Bargaining for Absolutism: A Spanish Path to Empire and Nation Building', *Hispanic American Historical Review*, 88(2), 173–210.

Kalamovitz, S. (2008). 'Las Consecuencias Economicas De La Independencia En América Latina', *Revista de Economía Institucional*, 10(19), 207–233.

Klein, H. S. (1998). *The American Finances of the Spanish Empire. Royal Income and Expenditures in Colonial Mexico, Peru, and Bolivia, 1680–1809*, Albuquerque: University of New Mexico Press.

Klein, H. S. and Tepaske, J. J. (1982). *The Royal Treasuries of the Spanish Empire in America*, Durham: Duke University Press.

Kuethe, A. J. and Andrien, K. J. (2014). *The Spanish Atlantic World in the Eighteenth Century: War and the Bourbon Reforms, 1713–1796*, Cambridge University Press.

Lamikiz, X. (2009). 'Patrones De Comercio Y Flujo De Información Comercial Entre España Y América Durante El Siglo Xviii', *Revista de Historia Economica*, 25(2), 233–260.

Leff, N. (1997). 'Economic Development in Brazil, 1822–1913', in Haber, S. (ed.), *How Latin America Fell Behind*, Stanford University Press, 34–64.

Lynch, J. (1973). *The Spanish American Revolutions, 1808–1826*, New York: W. W. Norton.

Marichal, C. (1989). *A Century of Debt Crises in Latin America: From Independence to the Great Depression, 1820–1930*, Princeton University Press.

Mazzeo, C. (2010). 'El Comercio Colonial a lo Largo del Siglo XVIII y su Transformación, Frente a las Coyunturas de Cambio', in Chocano, M., Contreras, C., Quiroz, F., Mazzeo, C. A. and Flores, R. (eds.), *Compendio De Historia Economica Del Peru. Tomo 3: Economia Del Periodo Colonial Tardio,* Lima: Banco Central de Reserva del Peru – El Instituto de Estudios Peruanos, 223–294.

Newson, L. A. (2006). 'The Demographic Impact of Colonisation', in Bulmer-Thomas, V., Coatsworth, J. H. and Cortés-Conde, R. (eds.), *The Cambridge History of Latin America*, Cambridge University Press, 143–184.

Ocampo, J. A. (2011). 'La Historia Divergente De Las Economias Grancolombianas', in Bértola, L. and Gerchunoff, S. (eds.), *Institucionalidad Y Desarrollo Economico En América Latina*, Santiago: Comisión Económica para América Latina y el Caribe (CEPAL), 191–223.

Owensby, B. P. (2008). *Empire of Law and Indian Justice in Colonial Mexico*, Stanford University Press.

Palma, N. (2016). 'Sailing Away from Malthus: Intercontinental Trade and European Economic Growth, 1500–1800', *Cliometrica*, 10, 129–149.

Palma, N. and Silva, A. C. (2016). 'Spending a Windfall: American Precious Metals and Euro-Asian Trade 1492–1815', GGDC Research Memorandum.

Pearce, A. J. (2011). 'Reindigenization and Native Languages in Peru's long Nineteenth Century (1795–1940)', in Heggarty, P. and Pearce, A. J. (eds.), *History and Language in the Andes*, London: Palgrave Macmillan, 135–163.

Pedreira, J. M. (2000). 'From Growth to Collapse: Portugal, Brazil, and the Breakdown of the Old Colonial System (1760–1830)', *Hispanic American Historical Review*, 80(4), 839–864.

Platt, T. (1984). 'Liberalism and Ethnocide in the Southern Andes', *History Workshop Journal*, 17, 3–28.

Prados de la Escosura, L. (2009). 'Lost Decades? Economic Performance in Post-Independence Latin America', *Journal of Latin American Studies*, 41(2), 279–307.

Reséndez, A. (2016). *The Other Slavery : The Uncovered Story of Indian Enslavement in America*, Boston: Houghton Mifflin Harcourt.

Santamaria Garcia, A. (2011). 'Dos Siglos De Especializacion Y Dos Decadas De Incértidumbre. La Historia Economica De Cuba 1800–2010', in Bértola, L. and Gerchunoff, S. (eds.), *Institucionalidad Y Desarrollo Economico En América Latina*, Santiago: Comisión Económica para América Latina y el Caribe (CEPAL), 135–223.

Schulz, K. (2016). 'Atlantic Transformations and Brazil's Imperial Independence', in Tutino, J. (ed.), *New Countries. Capitalism, Revolutions, and Nations in the Americas, 1750–1870*, Durham, NC: Duke University Press, 201–230.

Seminario, B. (2016). *El Desarrollo De La Economia Peruana En La Era Moderna. Precios, Demanda Y Produccion Desde 1700*, Lima: Universidad del Pacifico.

TePaske, J. J. and Brown, K. W. (2010). *'A New World of Gold and Silver'*, E-book, Leiden: Brill, www.scribd.com/document/273627347/A-New-World-of-gold-an-silver (accessed 30 September 2020).

Vinson, B. (2001). *Bearing Arms for His Majesty: The Free-Colored Militia in Colonial Mexico*, Stanford University Press.

von Wobeser, G. (1990). 'La Inquisicion Como Institucion Crediticia En El Siglo Xviii', *Historia Mexicana*, 39(4), 849–879.

Zahedieh, N. (2010). *The Capital and the Colonies : London and the Atlantic Economy, 1660–1700*, Cambridge University Press.

10

Africa: Slavery and the World Economy, 1700–1870

PATRICK MANNING

In economic history for the period from 1700 to 1870, the most prominent African issue is the institution of slavery and the long-distance slave trade – especially from Africa to the Americas but also across the Indian Ocean, across the Sahara to North Africa, and the capture and exploitation of slaves within Africa. This chapter, titled to reflect that primacy, addresses volume and direction of slave trade, theories of enslavement, and the value of sub-Saharan Africa's total exports and slave exports, 1700–1870. Following a review of the social implications of slavery in Africa and overseas, the chapter turns to interpretation of African economic life in local, regional, and global contexts, concluding with contending frameworks for assessing African economic growth.

Africa is distinctive as a world region in its populations, economies, and cultures. Yet Africa had been connected throughout time – physically and by migration of people – to other parts of the eastern hemisphere. Unquestionably, the interconnections of Africa with other areas of the world grew dramatically in the period from 1700 to 1870, though our interpretations will differ according to whether we think of these as the expansion of existing links or the forging of new ties. The size of the African continent is immense and the magnitude of African population has been a substantial portion of the human total. The physical area of Africa is more than 55 per cent that of all Eurasia.[1] Africa's population in 1700 was roughly 140 million – thus roughly equal to the populations of Europe, China, or India, and far greater than the population of the Americas, so that Africa was populated at moderate density on a world scale (Manning 2014a). Meanwhile, the fluctuations in African climate have largely paralleled those of the rest of

1 The sparsely populated Sahara is big, but so is Siberia; the difference is that the Sahara separates the dense populations on either side of it, while Siberia has a populous region only on one side.

the world. For Africa, as for other regions, the eighteenth and nineteenth centuries were a time of gradual rise in temperature and humidity after the low point of the Little Ice Age in the mid-seventeenth century.[2] The monsoons from the Atlantic expanded the grasslands of West Africa; the monsoons from the Indian Ocean expanded the grasslands of the northern and southern halves of Eastern Africa.

Because of the physical extent of Africa, the analysis will pay attention to variations among the continent's main regions – West, Central, Southern, Eastern, and North – as well as offering summary statements for the continent as a whole. Figure 10.1 shows the five great regions and the major river systems within each region.[3]

Each of these regions has a particular set of regional ecologies, major food crops, and centres of population.[4] West Africa consists mostly of savannah, with a northern band of desert and forest at the south. Yams were the principal forest crop; sorghum and millet were the principal savannah crops; rice was grown along the western coast and Upper Niger Valley. Maize had been adopted in recent centuries. Domestic animals in the savannah included cattle, with donkeys as the main beast of burden and horses for warfare; sheep, goats, pigs, chickens were everywhere. Both coast and savannah are densely populated; over half the region's population was in modern Nigeria. In Central Africa, the equatorial forest straddles the equator, with savannah to the north and south of the forest. Yams were the principal forest crop, along with bananas; millet was pre-eminent in the savannah; manioc, recently adopted, gained importance in forest and savannah. Central African population, while relatively sparse, was densest in the southern savannah. Eastern Africa, the most ecologically diverse region, includes regions of desert in north and east, temperate climate in Ethiopian and Great Lakes highlands, savannah in the middle Nile and south-eastern regions, forest in the Zambezi Valley, and the great island of Madagascar. Millet and recently adopted maize were grown in the savannah, bananas in the Great Lakes highlands, and wheat in Ethiopian highlands. Cattle were prominent in the region; camels in the deserts. Eastern Africa's population was densest in the highlands of Ethiopia and those surrounding the Great Lakes. Southern Africa

2 The Medieval Warm Period, from roughly 900 to 1300 CE, encouraged population growth throughout Africa and other regions; temperature and humidity declined regularly but unevenly until roughly 1650.

3 These regions, drawn to coincide with modern national boundaries, are virtually identical to those used in United Nations reports. The Zambezi Valley, in contrast to the others shown in Figure 10.1, includes portions of three regions: Central, Eastern, and Southern Africa.

4 For a more detailed summary of these descriptive points, see Austen (1987).

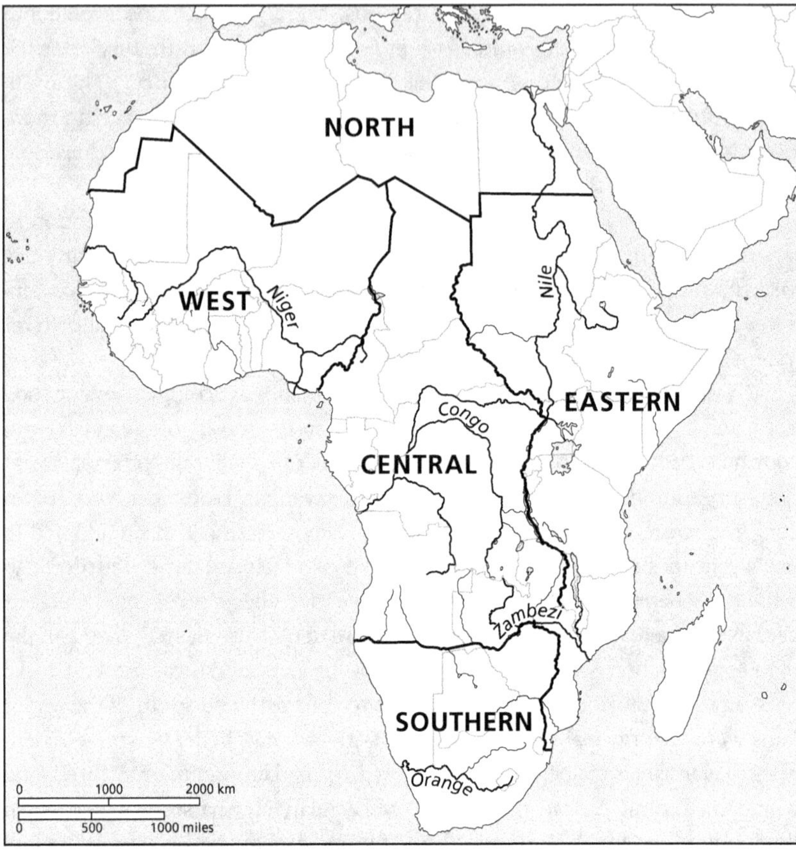

Figure 10.1 African regions and major rivers
Map credit: Redrawn based on a map by Patrick Manning.
Data source: Base map in Eckert IV projection; regions as classified by the author.

consists of savannah in south and east, desert in north and west; millet and maize were the principal crops and cattle were numerous, especially where population was densest in the well-watered regions of the eastern coast. In North Africa, wheat was the principal food crop; cattle, sheep, and goats were herded, along with camels in the extensive desert. Population was densest in the Nile Valley, along the Mediterranean shore, and in the Atlas highlands. In artisanal work, iron and steel ware, pottery, textiles, and leather goods have long been manufactured in most African regions; copper mining and manufacture was prominent in Central Africa. Construction has been in stone, wood, and thatch but mostly in adobe.

African Slavery and Slave Trade, 1700–1870

The export of captives from sub-Saharan Africa to centres of wealth can be traced far back in time, to seizure of captives from the Middle Nile Valley in the days of the Old Kingdom of Egypt. Fifteenth-century Portuguese visitors to West Africa began seizing and purchasing captives, and this new Atlantic slave trade expanded until, by 1650, it exceeded the volume of trans-Saharan slave trade (Manning 1990).

Research in progress is preparing revised estimates of African population and migration, using the best available methodology. These estimates are to provide decennial populations for Africa – by region, sex, age, and free or slave status – for the continent from 1650 to 1950. Table 10.1 provides a compact summary of current estimates for some major variables.[5] The full range of projections includes volumes of slave exports, levels of enslavement within Africa, and total size of slave populations in Africa and abroad. Of these demographic variables, the levels of capture and the size of enslaved populations are the most difficult to estimate, but the inclusion of such estimates is essential to an understanding of African economies, especially for the nineteenth century. Table 10.1 shows regional populations, the enslaved populations within African regions, and annual export of captives – for the decades of the 1700s, 1790s, and 1870s. These figures show a modest growth in African continental population throughout the two centuries, but show significant population declines for West and Central Africa. The annual number of persons captured and transported from sub-Saharan Africa doubled from 1700 to 1790 then fell back to the earlier level by 1870 – but the enslaved population within Africa grew to more than 10 per cent of the continental total by 1870.[6] Population in North Africa grew not only because of natural growth but because of the settlement of sub-Saharan captives whose descendants came to comprise at least 10 per cent of the regional population.[7]

More detailed tabulations show the moments of regional peaks in enslavement: the 1790s for West African slave exports, the 1830s for central African

5 These estimates of population and migration rely on analysis by demographic simulation, work that has met delays and is still incomplete. Programming of the simulation requires improvements in the linkage of estimates from one decade to another, especially the estimates of enslaved populations within Africa. The results reported in Table 10.1 are therefore preliminary: Manning et al. (2014–2015); Manning, African Population and Migration Dataverse.

6 Estimates of enslaved populations within Africa, necessarily speculative, are now undergoing more systematic analysis.

7 For southern Africa in the Dutch era, up to roughly 1800, captives brought to southern Africa were mostly of Asian rather than African origin.

Table 10.1 Total and slave populations, selected decades

	1700			1790			1870		
Region	Pop $\times 10^6$	Est. slave pop $\times 10^6$	Annual slave exports $\times 10^3$	Pop $\times 10^6$	Est. slave pop $\times 10^6$	Annual slave exports $\times 10^3$	Pop $\times 10^6$	Est. slave pop $\times 10^6$	Annual slave exports $\times 10^3$
West	**50**	1	32	**46**	2	45	**41**	5	5
Central	**22**	0.5	8	**17**	1	40	**19**	3	1
Eastern	**39**	0.5	8	**44**	2	10	**46**	6	35
North	**17**	1	0	**23**	2	0	**29**	4	0
Southern	**10**	0	0	**12**	0.5	0	**10**	0.5	0
Continent	**138**	**3**	**48**	**141**	**7.5**	**95**	**145**	**18.5**	**41**

Sources: Eltis et al. (2010); Manning, 'Africa: Slavery and the World Economy', doi.org/10.7910/DVN/COK6XE.

exports, the 1870s for exports from Eastern Africa, and the 1850s–70s for the size of continental slave populations (Manning 1990; Eltis et al. 2010). The directions of transportation of African captives varied considerably by region. West African captives went to the Caribbean, South America, North America, and North Africa. Central African captives went mostly to Brazil, then to the Caribbean and with some to North America. For Eastern Africa, as for West Africa, captives went in many directions: to West Asia, South Asia, North Africa, the Indian Ocean islands, Southern Africa, and to the Caribbean.

The principal demographic results for Africa arising from study of the slave trade are that enslavement limited and reallocated population within Africa, that the African diaspora (in all directions) rose in its aggregate population to some 10 per cent of the continental population by the mid-nineteenth century, and that the enslaved population within Africa grew, especially during the nineteenth century, to more than 10 per cent of the continental population. Regional variations in the impact of enslavement varied significantly: West Africa underwent the longest and most consistent losses; Central Africa experienced serious losses from 1750 to 1850; and Eastern Africa experienced serious losses in the nineteenth century.

Recurring efforts to theorize slavery and the slave trade have led to recent advances, and the increase in available data gives promise of further improvements in theory. Gareth Austin completed a 2005 analysis of slavery in the Asante Kingdom during the nineteenth century, which explored comprehensively the land/labour ratio that has been the subject of much previous analysis, notably by Nieboer (1900) and Domar (1970). H. J. Nieboer, writing in 1900 about slavery among ethnic communities in the nineteenth-century Dutch East Indies, argued that a relative shortage of labour encouraged landowners to engage in enslavement in order to gain low-priced labour for agricultural production. Evsey Domar, writing in 1970 with regard to European serfdom but at the time of an expanding literature on the enslavement of Africans, made similar arguments; A. G. Hopkins (1973: 23–27) drew more explicitly on Nieboer in his economic history of West Africa. Austin (2005: 153–170) applied these frameworks to the specifics of the Asante, using the full range of available prices to gain a sense of the relative prices and elasticities of labour and land. He went further, arguing that politics and culture needed to be added to the analysis, and concluded that slavery was a Hobson's choice within the Asante economy, so that the demand for labour was sufficient to pay for slave labour but not for wages to free labourers. Austin (2005: 170) notes that 'the Nieboer hypothesis is inadequate once the analysis is extended beyond the borders of the slave-importing economy to include the areas from which the captives came'.

Another line of theorization has sought to go beyond slavery in a domestic economy, to explain the export of slaves from Africa to other regions. This discussion, too, analysed the land/labour ratio, but in different terms. Henry Gemery and Jan S. Hogendorn (1974) proposed a version of the vent-for-surplus model for export commodities: they argued that labour was in relative surplus within Africa, and that the sale of captives to overseas markets enabled the purchase of desired import goods; Gemery and Hogendorn drew inspiration from Myint (1964). Philip Curtin (1979: 15–16) addressed the prices of those initially captured, arguing that they corresponded to 'fencing' – they were held artificially low because the captives were stolen goods that needed to be sold in a hurry. Taking a different approach, Jack Goody (1971: 25) pointed out the technological difference between 'people of the hoe' (in Africa) and 'people of the plough' (on other continents), noting that physical productivity was higher in the latter. Patrick Manning (1990: 33–34) adopted this observation to argue that European slave purchasers in Africa, offering prices based on the productivity of labour in the Americas, were able to outbid African purchasers of labour, free or slave. Stefano Fenoaltea (1999) focused instead on the cost of transportation within Africa: given high costs of head transportation, Africans could purchase imports most easily by selling a commodity that could move itself (though under duress) to the ports.

In sum, while the rise and persistence of enslavement within a given economy has been shown to be susceptible to theorization along lines running from Nieboer to Austin, theorization of the sale of captives from one domestic economy to another, along with the initial seizure of captives, has shown to be relatively intractable. The various hypotheses address quite different aspects of the overall problem of slave trade, and not much work has gone into efforts to link them. But because long-distance slave trade has been a major historical and social issue, and because documentation is growing in quantity and consistency, one may hope for new analyses.

As European powers seized African territories in the Scramble for Africa from the 1880s to the early twentieth century, the new authorities generally had the power to halt slave raiding. With the exception of a few cases, the European powers did not proclaim general emancipation of slaves either on their initial conquest or during their later administration. As a result, the number of persons enslaved in Africa reached a peak in the 1870s and gradually declined until it reached a low level in the 1930s.

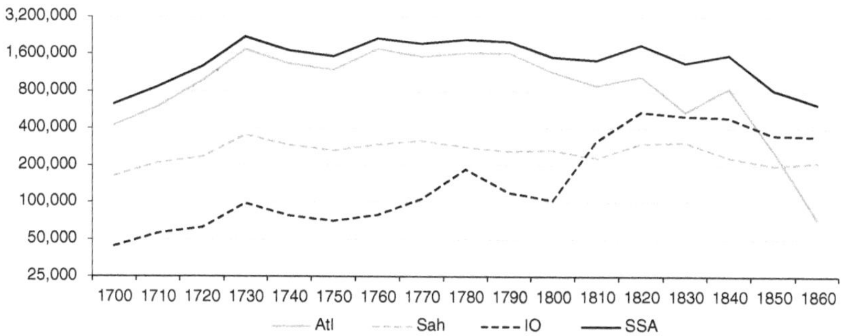

Figure 10.2 Value of sub-Saharan African slave exports in 1913 pounds, by region
Notes and sources: Average annual total value of persons embarked in sub-Saharan Africa for sale as slaves, by decade. Estimated f.o.b. value at African port of dispatch. Prices are Atlantic African f.o.b. prices, as listed in Manning (1982: 332–333). Volume figures are as listed in Manning, 'Africa: Slavery and the World Economy', doi.org/10.7910/DVN/COK6XE.

To facilitate comparisons both within Africa and globally, I offer estimates of the total value of African exports in constant 1913 prices, 1700–1870, distinguishing the value of slave exports from the value of all other commodities. Slave export values are shown in Figure 10.2, with total export values in Figure 10.3. These figures are approximate, but they indicate that the total value of exports from sub-Saharan Africa remained below £4 million sterling for the period up to 1850, and then rose rapidly because of diamond and then gold exports from South Africa.[8]

The values shown in Figure 10.2 reflect what African sellers got out of the external slave trade. The value of enslaved persons in the Atlantic economy overall was much greater, as it included the cost of commodities traded for slaves, the cost of vessels and crews, and especially the productivity of slave workers. In the nineteenth century, the value of 'legitimate trade' from Africa exceeded the value of slave trade only from the 1850s or conceivably from the 1840s.

Implications of African Slavery for Life in Africa and Overseas

The expansion of slavery in early modern and modern times brought transformation to society in all the regions where slavery flourished, and to regions beyond (Manning 1990; Lovejoy 2011). For Africa, the expansion in brutality

8 As Munro (1976: 35) notes, J. D. Fage (1969: 91–92) estimated the total trade of West Africa in the eighteenth century (imports plus exports) at £4 million, roughly the same order of magnitude as the exports of slaves for the Atlantic shown in Figure 10.2.

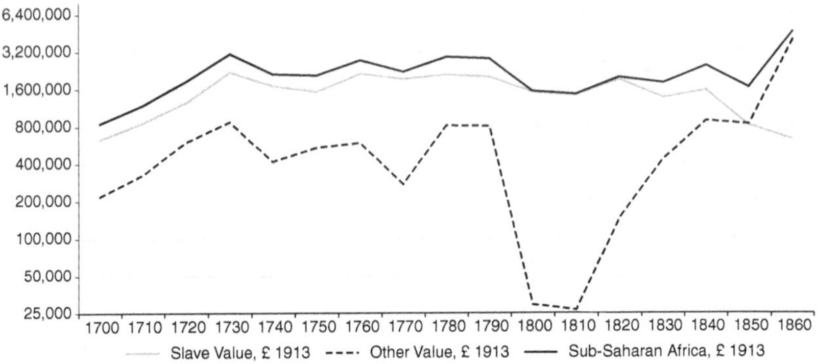

Figure 10.3 Sub-Saharan African annual export value, in £ 1913
Sources and notes: The value of slave exports is as shown in Figure 10.1. For 1700–1800, non-slave export values include English import values from Africa and French import values from Senegal; not included are African exports via Dutch, Portuguese, Indian Ocean or trans-Saharan merchants. Non-slave export values, 1800–70, include West African exports of palm products and groundnuts, East African cloves, and South African wool and diamonds. Not included for 1800–70 are exports of ivory, gum, lumber, cotton, hides, dyes, grains, textiles, and other commodities. Sources: de Kiewiet (1941); Brooks (1975: 34); Curtin (1975: 62–70, 100–101); Manning (1986: 208–209); Sheriff (1987: 62–64); and Johnson (1990). See Manning, 'Africa: Slavery and the World Economy', doi.org/10.79/DVN/COK6XE.

brought by warfare, kidnapping, and other devices for enslavement made for wide disruption. In addition to the recurring seizure and transportation of people of all ages, the gendered, age-specific, and ethnic dimensions of slavery were substantial. Captives traded across the Atlantic included twice as many males as females; the captives were dominantly young adults. As a result, slave populations in the Americas were consistently short of females, while populations in West and Central Africa were consistently short of males. Patterns of marriage and sexual division of labour on each side of the Atlantic were distorted for the whole era of the slave trade. In the Americas, African-descended women had most of their children with African-descended men, so that a distinctive African-descended community remained large. Nevertheless, European men fathered a significant minority of the children of African-descended women: while most of these offspring lived their lives as slaves, some became free and lived in an intermediate caste of colour.

In coastal West Africa and Central Africa, where most of those dispatched were male, the slave trade kept the proportion of adult females well over the normal 50 per cent for two centuries, though with great local variation. Many of these adult women were in slave status, living in isolation from their own families; they had responsibility for the care of their children, but had little say in the destiny of those same children, who belonged to the fathers. The institution of marriage was undermined as larger numbers of female partners became available to free men, who could now enjoy extended dominance without taking on family responsibilities. Conversely, the slave traders crossing the Indian Ocean and the Sahara transported nearly twice as many females as males. In these cases, slave populations in Eurasia and North Africa were consistently short of males, while populations in Eastern Africa were commonly short of females. In Eurasia and North Africa, the children of most African women were fathered by men of the master class, so there was a steady tendency towards social and biological integration of the Africans into the dominant society – distinctive African communities existed, but remained relatively small (Manning 1990). In Eastern Africa and in interior West Africa, where most of those dispatched were female, the slave trade generated a proportion of adult males over the normal 50 per cent. Many of these men were in slavery, and were liable to execution at any time. African social orders evolved as the slave trade expanded. In coastal West Africa and in Central Africa, the shortage of men meant that women took over tasks that had previously been performed by men. Inversely, in Eastern Africa and in the interior of West Africa, the shortage of women meant that men took over tasks that had previously been performed by women.

The severity and the duration of these social changes depended on the rise and fall in the volume of enslavement. For West Africa, Atlantic slave exports grew at 1 per cent per year throughout the eighteenth century to 60,000 per year, then declined at an average 2 per cent per year for the first half of the nineteenth century. For Central Africa, Atlantic slave exports grew at 1 per cent per year during the eighteenth century to 30,000 per year, remained at that level from 1800 to 1850, then ended suddenly. The export slave trade from East Africa and across the Sahara totalled roughly 15,000 per year for most of the eighteenth century, then rose at 1 per cent per year to 45,000 per year by 1840, remained at that level until 1870, then declined very rapidly.

War and enslavement commonly correlated in Africa. Prior to 1700, African states were not especially warlike – seventeenth-century exceptions were the wars in Senegambia, the Gold Coast, and Kongo. States forming or expanding thereafter relied heavily on war: Asante, Segou, and Dahomey in eighteenth-century West Africa and, in the nineteenth century, Merina in Madagascar, and Bunyoro in Eastern Africa (Thornton 1983; Campbell 2005; Médard and Doyle 2007). The kingdom best known for its wars, the Zulu state (founded 1816), conducted very little trade in slaves. Nevertheless, the response to expanding enslavement was more complex than simple growth of warfare. In several cases, states carried on campaigns to limit or abolish enslavement, but were eventually drawn back into the prevailing ethos of enslavement. Examples include the kingdoms of Waalo, Benin, and Kongo in the seventeenth century; Asante and Dahomey in the eighteenth century, and the Sokoto Caliphate in the nineteenth century (Akinjogbin 1967; Ryder 1969; Thornton 1983; Barry 1985). Along with the expansion in warfare, refugee populations grew substantially in the eighteenth and nineteenth centuries in many parts of the continent: common tactics were the dispersion of populations to mountaintops, forests, and marshes.

With time, practices of enslavement expanded to most areas of the continent. The mechanism of this expansion remains in need of further study. Was it a localized social 'infection', as enslavement in one region caused the practice to be adopted in neighbouring regions? Was it the relentless economic pressure of high and well-funded demand at the coast? Did the dynamic change in some way to bring about the expansion in continental African enslavement during the nineteenth century? The incentives to enslave were such that one knew the price on every head, by age and gender. In this sense, the African continent underwent an extreme monetarization during these two centuries. In the nineteenth century, as enslavement grew within Africa and slave exports declined, the sex ratios among the enslaved tended to even out. This facilitated the development of a new political economy of slavery – one focused on the creation of slaves as an inferior social class in place of attaching them to owners in individual servitude. In the West African savannah, hundreds of 'slave villages' were formed, in which male and female slaves formed family units but worked under the direction of overseers acting on behalf of the owners.[9]

The 'second slavery', focusing on expanding enslavement in the early and mid-nineteenth century, has gained significant attention in recent scholarship. The analysis has emphasized slavery in the United States, Cuba, and Brazil, tied closely to capitalist development, especially from the 1820s to the 1860s (Tomich and Zeuske 2008). At largely the same time, enslavement expanded in the Eastern Hemisphere tropics and semi-tropics. The expansion of slavery in nineteenth-century Africa, long acknowledged but not analysed with care, tended to be treated as simply a spillover effect from the external

9 Slave rebellions and the formation of maroon communities took place in Africa as in the diaspora: these are best-documented for the nineteenth century. On slave villages and the constitution of slave social classes, see Mason (1973) and Campbell (2005). On rebellion and emancipation, see Diouf (2003), Alpers et al. (2005), Cooper (1980) and Scully and Paton (2005).

slave trade. But as major studies appeared on the expansion of slavery in the Indonesian archipelago, in Thailand and Burma, in south India, and in the lands of West Asia, there came to be reason to study the expanding enslavement in Africa more carefully (Ewald 1990; Beemer 2013).

Local, Regional, and Global Economic Context

A. G. Hopkins (1973), in his foundational study of West African economic history, relied on the analytical categories of 'domestic economy' and 'external trade' for his analysis: these categories have dominated studies in African economic history ever since, including the present study. The distinction is logical, but the manner of its application has led to distortion in analysis: most studies focus primarily on external trade, even though the domestic economy accounted for the great majority of economic activity. There is an advantage, therefore, to assuming the interplay of several domestic sectors. These can include the sectors of self-sufficient production or foraging (a small sector in the aggregate, but commonly connected to other sectors); a local-exchange sector (including village and regional activities of agriculture, manufacturing, exchange, and consumption, commonly with local moneys); a sector of interregional and continental trade (monetary); and tertiary sectors from local to interregional levels (providing government, exchange of specialized knowledge, and cultural production) (Manning 2014a: 141–142).

For the eighteenth century, the local exchange sector can be addressed through changes in production and production system. One striking case of local transformation is that of the Weme Valley (in modern Benin) where people were driven as refugees by the expansion of Dahomey in the seventeenth century. These settlers gradually built an intensive system of agriculture, relying on the annual flood of the river, which spilled over the banks and fertilized adjoining fields. In succeeding seasons these farmers grew manioc, maize, and beans in the floodplain, as well as crops under rainfall on the plateau. Channels were dug each year to enable waters to re-enter the rivercourse; fish were held in these ditches and then harvested once a year; cattle were kept in island pens during the flood season. These peasants participated in a network of markets organized on a four-day calendar, and in the nineteenth century they added production and sale of palm oil to their activities (Manning 1982: 87).

In other transformations, artisanal production grew in the villages of Gold Coast during the seventeenth century, in association with the expanding gold trade, but late in the century an expansion of warfare and firearms exports brought growth in slave exports and a decline in artisanal production. The increase in prices of slaves at the opening of the eighteenth century was such that gold came to be imported (from Brazil) in exchange for slaves, reversing previous flows (Kea 1982). Meanwhile, commercial flows in the interior, relying on the institution of the trade diaspora, moved commodities among centres of population. In West Africa, kola nuts, consumed as a stimulant, were transported in caravans from Asante through the market centre at Salaga to the commercial metropolis of Kano. In Central Africa, trade routes focused on Malebo Pool on the lower Congo, while in East Africa commercial routes centred on Lake Victoria; Egyptian grains and Ethiopian coffee flowed to Marseille and Istanbul through Alexandria (Issawi 1947; Gray and Birmingham 1970; Martin 1972; Curtin 1975; Gran 1979; Lovejoy 1980; Issawi 1982). Textiles were produced and exchanged throughout the continent, relying on cotton in West Africa and Eastern Africa, while fibre from the raffia palm was woven throughout Central Africa. The principal African import in exchange for slaves was textiles, including some European woollens but mostly Indian cottons; English cottons began to replace Indian textiles in the nineteenth century. The interplay of domestic and imported textiles in various African regions is an issue requiring further study (Martin 1972; 1987; Kriger 2006; Kobayashi 2018).

It is useful to compare continental histories of colonialism, to see where Africa fits in. On one side were the Americas, where conquest and colonization came early – a chapter that ended by 1830 with independence for the mainland territories – although the rest of the Caribbean (except Hispaniola) remained under colonial rule until the twentieth century. The other major early colonization was that of the Ottomans and their sixteenth-century colonial occupation of the Arab Middle East, the Balkans, and most of North Africa; the Ottomans held North Africa until the nineteenth century.

For most of Asia and for Africa except for the Mediterranean littoral, local economies participated in maritime trade not through colonization but through trading posts, well into the nineteenth century. The biggest exception was India, which had fallen fully under British sway by 1818; in addition, the Dutch gained control of key territories in the East Indies. Africa and the rest of the eastern hemisphere, while long escaping direct colonization, still shared experiences of empire: the wars among imperial powers and the shifts in great-power commercial policy. Coastal trading posts changed hands among the Portuguese, Dutch, French, English, and Danish during the War of Austrian Succession, the Seven Years War, the American Revolution, and the Napoleonic Wars. Parallel global influences radiated, in the nineteenth century, from the British abolition of oceanic slave trade, British free trade policy, and the gold standard, not to mention the Opium War, the 1848 revolutions, and the great triad of mid-century social upheavals – the Indian Rebellion of 1857, the Taiping Revolt, and the American Civil War. The latter had an unmistakable impact on Africa, in that production and export of cotton rose dramatically, if briefly, in Egypt and Angola.

Only Portugal governed substantial African territory, in Angola. Other African lands interacted with European economies in different ways. As Joseph Inikori (2002) has argued, African labourers and consumers, both at home and under English rule in the diaspora, contributed substantially to the Industrial Revolution in England through the instrument of the British Empire. Inikori, working under the premise that English industrial growth arose primarily out of external trade rather than from the domestic market, argues that African labourers produced essential raw materials for industry (in Africa as well as in the Americas) and, in addition, consumed the produce of English industry.

The range of commodities exported from Africa grew in the nineteenth century, beyond the Central African beeswax, Senegambian gum, and Ethiopian coffee of the eighteenth century. This shift was signalled by the rising exports of palm oil from the Niger Delta, then followed by the spread of palm oil exports along much of the West African coast, and by the subsequent expansion of palm kernels from the same source. Soon thereafter, exports of groundnuts from Senegambia began a steady increase, while clove production expanded on the island of Zanzibar. For all these commodities, slave labour was important in production, though independent peasants also participated in exports. Cocoa, brought from Venezuela to the Spanish-controlled island of Fernando Po, was then planted in Gold Coast, where the cocoa industry grew for several decades before reaching its peak. The expanding ivory market brought great quantities of elephant tusks to the Indian Ocean coast, principally for sale in India. Woollens exported from South Africa sometimes reached the value of palm oil from West Africa (Dike 1956; Meillassoux 1971; Houghton 1975; Gutkind et al. 1978; Manning 1982; Coquery-Vidrovitch and Lovejoy 1985; Iliffe 1987; Manning 1997; Kriger 1999; Austin 2005; Campbell 2005).

Silver currency grew rapidly in importance throughout the continent. This appears to have depended in part on shifts in silver flows after the end of Spanish control of the mines, and on the growing importance of London as a financial centre. Another factor important for West Africa was that, in the era of illegal slave trade, transactions had to be made rapidly, so that oceanic merchants purchased slaves quickly with silver coin instead of the previous complex packages of imported goods. Gujarati merchants in Mozambique exchanged silver sent from Brazil, slaves from Africa, and textiles from Gujarat (Machado 2014). As of 1850, steam shippers opened regular service to the West African coast: their dependable schedules transformed the patterns of trade. German merchants imported great quantities of cowrie shells from the East African coast and exchanged them in West Africa for palm products. Maritime workers of Kru ethnicity signed on to the steamers in Sierra Leone, worked on voyages that went to the mouths of the Niger or the Congo, and collected their pay as they were dropped off on the return trip (Brooks 1972).

The political economy of the African continent underwent numerous and contradictory changes during the nineteenth century. The expansion in continental slavery brought widespread disruption and militarization of the continent, yet it concentrated wealth in the hands of elites and expanded commerce in certain commodities. While the export slave trade continued, migrants came to Africa from various directions: returnees from the African diaspora of the Americas, merchants and indentured workers from India, and European settlers in Algeria and South Africa. Where slavery declined, ex-slaves formed themselves into peasant communities, some of which prospered. Systems of money and credit changed. It is difficult to know whether the positive or negative changes predominated, within each region and especially for the continent as a whole. In any case the African continent, with this complex and contradictory heritage, was next to face an even bigger set of changes as European conquest and formal colonial rule began after 1870 (Rodney 1972; Munro 1976; Manning 1982; Hogendorn and Johnson 1986; Sheriff 1987; Inikori 2002; Manning 2006; Prestholdt 2008).

Growth and Decline, 1700–1870

The issue of economic growth, while it has been discussed less fully for Africa than for other world regions in the eighteenth and nineteenth centuries, remains an issue of relevance. The reluctance of economic policymakers to consider African historical patterns is gradually giving way to a lively interest in African economic history. This chapter concludes by summarizing available theses on economic growth in Africa, most of them advanced some time ago, in the hope that the current relaunch of African economic history will bring a more robust exploration of African economic growth.

A. G. Hopkins (1973: 123), implicitly assuming that economic growth was unlikely without significant external contact, concluded that international trade did not serve as an engine of growth for precolonial Africa. As he saw it the export sector – whether in slaves or in agricultural commodities – was small and weakly linked to the domestic economy.[10] To illustrate such weak links, he proposed a parallel of precolonial African trade to the enclave economies of the postcolonial era, in which there is substantial remittance of profits overseas.[11] Manning (1982), in contrast, assumed that domestic economies might lead in a 'mechanism of accumulation' producing growth as long as external factors did not counterbalance domestic investment, providing empirical estimates of export revenue and the links of external and domestic economies for the period 1640–1960 in the region of southern Bénin Republic.[12] Ralph Austen (1987: 268–271), in a long-term interpretation of African economic history, draws on both of these approaches as he observes a pairing of autonomy in African economic life and marginalization in African links to the world, so that periodic episodes of African economic brilliance arose, but that 'direct exposure to world oceanic trade . . . provided little incentive for intensification of productive technology and organization'. Further, in a demographic approach to growth, Manning estimated rough stasis in African population from 1700 to 1900, in contrast to estimates such as that of Maddison (2001: 175, 183), which propose steady growth in African population through the whole era of slave trade.[13]

To clarify rates of precolonial African economic growth, we need estimates of aggregate domestic income, population estimates, and detailed narratives of regional economic change. Since study of the economic history of Africa is now integrated increasingly into economic history generally, there is hope that the relevant data collection, analysis, and linkage of issues within the continent and externally may now advance substantially.

10 A notable predecessor to Hopkins was Allan McPhee, whose 1926 analysis argued, more optimistically, that British government and international trade opportunities had caused rapid growth in British West Africa. See McPhee (1971) [1926]; Hopkins (1973: 119–123).

11 On remittance of profits and its limitation of African national income in postcolonial years, see Manning and Drwenski (2016).

12 Philip Curtin (1975) made similar arguments for a shorter period for Senegambia; Donald Wright (2010) made parallel arguments for the much smaller region of Niumi, Gambia.

13 Maddison proposed an African population rising from 61 million in 1700 to 123 million in 1913, as compared with roughly 140 million estimated by Manning for 1700 to 1900. See Manning (1990); Manning (2010); Manning (2014a).

References

Akinjogbin, I. A. (1967). *Dahomey and its Neighbours, 1708–1818*, Cambridge University Press.

Alpers, E. A., Campbell, G. and Salman, M. (eds.) (2005). *Slavery and Resistance in Africa and Asia*, London: Routledge.

Austen, R. (1987). *African Economic History: Internal Development and External Dependency*, London: James Currey.

Austin, G. (2005). *Labour, Land and Capital in Ghana: From Slavery to Free Labour in Asante, 1807–1956*, University of Rochester Press.

Barry, B. (1985). *Le Royaume du Waalo: Le Sénégal avant la conquête*, rev. ed., Paris: Karthala.

Beemer, B. (2013). 'The Creole City in Mainland Southeast Asia: Slave Gathering, Warfare and Cultural Exchange in Burma, Thailand and Manipur, 18th–19th C', unpublished Ph.D. thesis, University of Hawai'i.

Brooks, G. E., Jr. (1972). *The Kru Mariner in the Nineteenth Century: An Historical Compendium* (Newark: University of Delaware Department of Anthropology).

Brooks, G. E. (1975). 'Peanuts and Colonialism: Consequences of the Commercialization of Peanuts in West Africa, 1830–70', *Journal of African History*, 16, 29–54.

Campbell, G. (2005). *An Economic History of Imperial Madagascar, 1750–1895: The Rise and Fall of an Island Empire*, Cambridge University Press.

Cooper, F. (1980). *From Slaves to Squatters: Plantation Labor and Agriculture in Zanzibar and Coastal Kenya, 1890–1925*, New Haven: Yale University Press.

Coquery-Vidrovitch, C. and Lovejoy, P. E. (eds.) (1985). *The Workers of African Trade*, Beverly Hills: Sage Publications.

Curtin, P. D. (1975). *Economic Change in Precolonial Africa: Senegambia in the Era of the Slave Trade, Supplementary Evidence*, Madison: University of Wisconsin Press.

(1979). 'The African Diaspora', in Craton, M. (ed.), *Roots and Branches: Current Directions in Slave Studies*, papers presented at a conference entitled 'Slave Studies: Directions in Current Scholarship', held in Waterloo, Ontario in March 1979.

de Kiewiet, C. W. (1941). *History of South Africa, Social and Economic*, Oxford: Clarendon Press.

Dike, K. O. (1956). *Trade and Politics in the Niger Delta, 1830–1895*, Oxford: Clarendon Press.

Diouf, S. (2003). *Fighting the Slave Trade: West African Strategies*, Athens: Ohio University Press.

Domar, E. D. (1970). 'The Causes of Slavery or Serfdom: a Hypothesis', *Journal of Economic History*, 30, 18–32.

Eltis, D. et al. (2010). 'Slave Voyages: The Transatlantic Slave Trade Database', slavevoya ges.org. (accessed 30 September 2020).

Ewald, J. J. (1990). *Soldiers, Traders, and Slaves: State Formation and Economic Transformation in the Greater Nile Valley, 1700–1885*, Madison: University of Wisconsin Press.

Fage, J. D. (1969). *A History of West Africa*, Cambridge University Press.

Fenoaltea, S. (1999). 'Europe in the African Mirror: The Slave Trade and the Rise of Feudalism', *Rivista di Storia Economica*, 15, 123–165.

Gemery, H. A. and Hogendorn, J. S. (1974). 'The Atlantic Slave Trade: A Tentative Economic Model', *Journal of African History*, 15, 233–246.

Goody, J. (1971). *Technology, Tradition, and the State in Africa*, Cambridge University Press.

Gran, P. (1979). *Islamic Roots of Capitalism: Egypt, 1760–1840*, Austin: University of Texas Press.
Gray, R. and Birmingham, D. (1970). *Pre-colonial African Trade: Essays on Trace in Central and Eastern Africa Before 1900*, Oxford University Press.
Gutkind, P. C. W., Cohen, R. and Copans, J. (eds.) (1978). *African Labor History*, Beverly Hills: Sage Publications.
Hogendorn, J. S. and Johnson, M. (1986). *Shell Money of the Slave Trade*, Cambridge University Press.
Hopkins, A. G. (1973). *An Economic History of West Africa*, London: Longman.
Houghton, D. H. (1975). *The South African Economy*, 4th ed., Oxford University Press.
Iliffe, J. (1987). *The African Poor: A History*, Cambridge University Press.
Inikori, J. E. (2002). *Africans and the Industrial Revolution in England: A Study in International Trade and Economic Development*, Cambridge University Press.
Issawi, C. (1947). *Egypt: An Economic and Social Analysis*, Oxford University Press.
(1982). *An Economic History of the Middle East and North Africa*, New York: Columbia University Press.
Johnson, M. (1990). *Anglo-African Trade in the Eighteenth Century: English Statistics on African Trade 1699–1808* (edited by Thomas Lindblad, J. and Ross, R.), Leiden: Centre for the History of European Expansion.
Kea, R. A. (1982). *Settlements, Trade and Politics in the Seventeenth-Century Gold Coast*, Baltimore: Johns Hopkins University Press.
Kobayashi, K. (2018). 'The British Atlantic Slave Trade and Indian Cotton Textiles: The Case of Thomas Lumley and Co.', in Shiroyama, T. (ed.), *Modern Global Trade and the Asian Regional Economy*, Singapore: Springer, 59–85.
Kriger, C. (1999). *Pride of Men: Ironworking in 19th-Century West Central Africa*, Portsmouth, NH: Heinemann.
(2006). *Cloth in West African History* (Lanham, MD: AltaMira Press).
LeVeen, E. P. (1977). *British Slave Trade Suppression Policies, 1821–1865*, New York: Arno Press.
Lovejoy, P. E. (1980). *Caravans of Kola: The Hausa Kola Trade, 1700–1900*, Zaria: Ahmadu Bello University Press.
(2011). *Transformations in Slavery: A History of Slavery in Africa*, 3rd ed., Cambridge University Press.
Machado, P. (2014). *Oceans of Trade: South Asian Merchants, Africa, and the Indian Ocean, c.1750–1850*, Cambridge University Press.
Maddison, A. (2001). *The World Economy: A Millennial Perspective*, Paris: Organisation for Economic Co-operation and Development.
Manning, P. (1982). *Slavery, Colonialism and Economic Growth in Dahomey, 1640–1960*, Cambridge University Press.
(1986). 'Slave Trade, "Legitimate" Trade, and Imperialism Revisited: The Control of Wealth in the Bights of Benin and Biafra', in Lovejoy, P. E. (ed.), *Africans in Bondage: Studies in Slavery and the Slave Trade*, Madison: African Studies Program, University of Wisconsin, 203–233.
(1990). *Slavery and African Life: Occidental, Oriental, and African Slave Trades*, Cambridge University Press.
(2006). 'African Connections with American Colonization, 1400–1850', in Bulmer-Thomas, V. and Coatsworth, J. (eds.), *The Cambridge Economic History of Latin America*, Cambridge University Press, 43–71.

(2014a). 'Africa's Place in Globalization: Africa, Eurasia, and their Borderlands', *Journal of Globalization Studies*, 59(1), 65–81.

(2014b). 'African Population, 1650–2000: Comparisons and Implications of New Estimates', in Akyeampong, E., Bates, R. H., Nunn, N. and Robinson, J. A. (eds.), *Africa's Development in Historical Perspective*, Cambridge University Press, 131–150.

African Population and Migration Dataverse, dataverse.harvard.edu/dataverse/WH_AfricanPopMigration.

Manning, P. and Drwenski, M. (2016). 'The Differences of Inequality in Africa', in Hudson, P. and Tribe, K. (eds.), *The Contradictions of Capital in the Twenty-First Century: The Piketty Opportunity*, Newcastle upon Tyne: Agenda Publishing, 207–222.

Manning, P., Nickleach, S., Yi, B. and McGill, B. (2014–2015). 'Demographic Models for Projecting Population and Migration: Methods for African Historical Analysis', *Journal of World-Historical Information*, 2–3(1), 23–39.

Martin, P. M. (1972). *The External Trade of the Loango Coast, 1576–1870: The Effects of Changing Commercial Relations*, Oxford: Clarendon Press.

(1987). 'Power, Cloth and Currency on the Loango Coast', *African Economic History*, 15, 1–12.

Mason, M. (1973). 'Captive and Client Labour and the Economy of the Bida Emirate, 1857–1901', *Journal of African History*, 14, 453–471.

McPhee, A. (1971) [1926]. *The Economic Revolution in British West Africa*, 2nd ed., with an introduction by Anthony G. Hopkins, London: Frank Cass.

Médard, H. and Doyle, S. (eds.) (2007). *Slavery in the Great Lakes Region of East Africa*, Oxford: James Currey.

Meillassoux, C. (ed.) (1971). *The Development of Indigenous Trade and Markets in West Africa*, Oxford University Press.

Munro, J. F. (1976). *Africa and the International Economy 1800–1960*, Totowa, NJ: Rowman and Littlefield.

Myint, H. (1964). *The Economics of the Developing Countries*, London: Hutchinson.

Nieboer, H. J. (1900). *Slavery as an Industrial System*. The Hague: M. Nijhoff.

Prestholdt, J. (2008). *Domesticating the World: African Consumerism and the Genealogies of Globalization*, Cambridge University Press.

Rodney, W. (1972). *How Europe Underdeveloped Africa*, London: Bogle–L'Ouverture Publications.

Ryder, A. F. C. (1969). *Benin and the Europeans, 1485–1897*, Harlow: Longmans.

Scully, P. and Paton, D. (eds.) (2005). *Gender and Slave Emancipation in the Atlantic World*, Durham, NC: Duke University Press.

Sheriff, A. (1987). *Slaves, Spices, and Ivory in Zanzibar: Integration of an East African Commercial Empire into the World Economy, 1770–1873*, London: James Currey.

Thornton, J. K. (1983). *The Kingdom of Kongo: Civil War and Transition, 1641–1718*, Madison: University of Wisconsin Press.

Tomich, D. and Zeuske, M. (eds.) (2008). 'Introduction, the Second Slavery: Mass Slavery, World-Economy, and Comparative Microhistories', *Review*, 31, 91–100.

Wright, D. (2010). *The World and a Very Small Place in Africa: A History of Globalization in Niumi, the Gambia*, 3rd ed., Armonk, NY: M. E. Sharpe.

11

Australia: Geography and Institutions

DAVID MEREDITH

Australia experienced enormous economic and social changes between 1700 and 1870. The long isolation of the Australian people was broken, first by the Macassans in the early eighteenth century and then – and with far greater impact – by British invasion and occupation from 1788. This chapter outlines the economy of Australia prior to 1788, the subsequent period of British expansion in the nineteenth century and the consequences for these two economies.

Geologically Australia is the quiet continent. The relative lack of seismic activity created a landscape of plains and plateaus, rather than high mountain ranges or deep rift valleys. It has some of the world's oldest surface rocks. The age of the surface, however, and the way it was relatively undisturbed meant that most of the continent was not renewed by the volcanic upheavals necessary for more fertile soils. As a result, Australia has by far the poorest soil of any continent: the soil is old, badly leached, and lacking in nutrients. Australia is one of the world's warmest continents, but also the driest with the exception of Antarctica. Similar in size to continental US, Australia has only one-quarter of the area receiving more than 40 inches rainfall per year. High temperatures reduce the effectiveness of rainfall through evaporation. Eastern Australia's climate is strongly influenced by the Pacific Ocean: the El Niño Southern Oscillation brings alternate periods of drought and flood in recurring but unpredictable cycles. All these conditions severely constrain plant growth and therefore agriculture, but there are exceptions. The main areas that combine fertile soils with adequate rainfall – and were thus suitable for agriculture using nineteenth-century technology – run in patches from the north-east Highland zone to the south-east Lowland zone, and are also found in the south-west corner of Western Australia, southern South

My thanks to Dr. Barrie Dyster for very helpful comments on an earlier draft.

Australia and in north-central and south-east Tasmania. Together these areas made up 8 per cent of the continent's land mass. The rest of Australia was difficult or unsuitable for agriculture even where rainfall was adequate because of poor soil quality. But over much of the continent the rainfall is not adequate: two-thirds of the continent is arid or semi-arid (Heathcote 1975: 8, 25–28; Flannery 1994: 77–83, 112). This, then, is how Australia's first order geography stood in 1700 (see Chapter 14).

The continent's long period of relative isolation, perhaps 50 million years, gave rise to its unique and wide range of flora and fauna. Australian flora is characterized by scleromorphy – small plants, small leaves, and small distances between leaves – caused by adaptation to poor soils. Fauna then adapted to the flora, as illustrated by koalas, wombats, kangaroos, and *O. paradoxus* – the platypus. A low reproduction rate was a common adaptive technique. In the evolving Australian environment marsupials outcompeted placental mammals and carnivorous reptiles were more successful than carnivorous mammals. As a result, and unlike other continents, there were no large mammals that could be domesticated.

In 1700 Australia was home to about 900,000 people whose economy depended on hunting and foraging (Williams 2013; Hunter 2015: 93). Population fluctuated with climate and technological changes. The largest decline was in the Last Glacial Maximum (LGM), 21,000–18,000BP when the population declined by 60 per cent over 3,000 years. The population rebuilt slowly reaching pre-LGM levels about 10,000BP. Growth was somewhat faster in recent millennia as technological changes intensified (Lourandos 1997: 76–79). The organization of production in this hunter-gatherer economy was significantly influenced by the range and seasonality of resources and with only limited storage available people had to move to where food was most available for immediate consumption. Food security was a constant issue. Movement of groups around *country* was not aimless wandering but organized and logistical (Hunter 2015: 78). Where resources were relatively plentiful, as on the tropical coast, groups were semi-sedentary; in the most difficult environments, such as the Western Desert, people were far more mobile in their search for seasonal sources of food and for water. Networks of exchange over very large areas and regular ceremonial gatherings involving people from different groups integrated Australian Aboriginal society (McBryde 1987).

Much of the technology employed in the Aboriginal economy was concerned with food production. Some equipment required teamwork – canoes, large nets, and fish traps – other tools were designed for a single user: digging stick, spear and spear thrower, axe, hatchet, hammer. The use of fire in land management also required people working together. Ian Keen categorized production technology by function: extractors such as hatchets; entrainers (hides, lures); immobilizers: weapons such as harpoons, spears, and boomerangs and facilities like nets, traps, and snares; and retrievers, for example fish-hooks. Food preparation required equipment such as spatulas, spoons, and containers, together with grindstones, mullers, graters, sieves, and so forth. Some plants were poisonous and required the application of leaching techniques. And food was cooked in ovens and in open fires (Keen 2004: 89, 94). Fish traps on coasts, rivers, and lakes were permanent facilities built of stone and wood. There were also large-scale drainage systems constructed to manage water levels in swamps and to catch eels and other fish (Lourandos 1987: 306; 1997: 220).

Fire, Aboriginal Australia's main source of energy, had multiple uses: it entered into ritual, was used for food processing and cooking, for warming humans, shaping and hardening raw materials, and making artefacts. Smoke was used as an insect repellent and to mask the smell of the hunter from the hunted. Fire was used to increase food supply by raising the absolute productivity, and therefore carrying capacity, of the land. Australians' deployment of fire was precise and deliberate. Low-intensity (or 'cool') fire was used to control wildfires by preventing the build-up of fuel. It had an immediate use in large-scale hunting but its longer-term impact was to modify the environment to increase species diversity and raise output. The Australian landscape was anthropogenic: according to Gammage, fire was used to create particular types of landscape, such as grassy paddocks and plains, open forests with a clear understorey, edges and copses where animals ate and sheltered. The unnatural (but highly pleasing) appearance of the Australian landscape was favourably commented upon by numerous Europeans in the early nineteenth century (Gammage 2011: 199). These practices added value to the land.

Australians used other techniques in replenishing their earth: in the tropical north and on the west coast the practice of replanting yam-tops was followed, as well as seed-planting in several locations; digging roots and separating them to encourage growth; planting grass trees to encourage grubs, relocating a scented bush to attract bees. The dingo (wild dog) was domesticated to aid hunting and young cassowaries were captured and tethered and fattened. These interventions, together with fire-stick farming, marine management, and land drainage systems, have highlighted the blurry border between foraging and farming. Keen suggests that the term 'hunter-gatherer-cultivators' might be more appropriate to describe Aboriginal production (Keen 2004: 96).

There was a considerable degree of gender segmentation in the indigenous Australian workforce. Women worked harder than men, more regularly, for longer periods of time and were more productive. They not only foraged but processed and cooked food. Women worked well into old age whereas men's productiveness peaked at an earlier age. It was women, not men, who were responsible for social reproduction. Specialization of labour made the best use of the human resources available to maximize food production. Child labour was common though varied in extent between poorer and richer environments. In the Western Desert children collected vegetable foods, eggs, caterpillars, small birds (using snares), nuts, and small animals and reptiles that had been burnt by fire. Boys joined in kangaroo hunts by barking like dogs to herd the animals in the direction of the adult hunters. In the richer northern tropics children did less (Keen 2004: 320).

Women made tools, wooden dishes, string, bags, apparel, children's toys, baskets, cloaks, and stone flakes for spear heads. They built huts. They foraged vegetable foods, grubs, insects, and hunted small animals and reptiles. Where available they fished, dived for mussels, gathered shellfish, and captured crabs. Women processed and prepared food by winnowing, grinding, and cooking and they collected firewood and water.

Men concentrated their work efforts on toolmaking and hunting. Their manufacturing activities involved stone-knapping and edge-grinding, hafting hatchets and adzes, making string and rope. They made weapons, nets, baskets, dishes, canoes and rafts, fish-traps and ritual objects. Spears, spear-throwers, lures, snares, nets, and brush fences were deployed in hunting large and small game. On the coast men hunted dugong and turtles from canoes (with and without outriggers), rafts, and reef platforms. Men climbed trees to catch koalas, dug for wombats, swam and dived for marine animals and used spears, nets, and traps to obtain fish. They used canoes on swamps to collect eggs. They killed crocodiles by swimming underneath and attacking with a stone knife.

Distribution and consumption were governed by kin relationships, as a result of which all adults had reciprocal obligations of some kind. Sharing was ubiquitous. With limited facilities for food storage, accumulation was limited and all provisions were distributed in accordance with well-defined social rules. Although there were many variations, a common distributive institution was for a married man to support his wife's father, who in turn made further distributions. Gender relations were unequal in varying degrees among different groups, a relatively high level of polygyny being an indication of greater inequality (Keen 2004: 269).

Australians developed a complex economy over many thousands of years that remained viable through considerable climatic challenges. Their economy provided a material base for a society that was rich in culture and spirituality and it provided time and space for the development and enjoyment of these attributes (Berndt and Berndt 1988). Europeans did not usually describe the indigenous people they met as underfed or stunted, and often admired their physique. The hunter-gatherer economy was small-scale and low-intensity, but was characterized by high levels of human and social capital accumulated over long periods. It was far more innovative and resourceful than is implied by Maddison's stylized depiction of an unchanging society living close to or at the bare subsistence necessary for human reproduction (Maddison 2006: 450; Maddison 2007: 310; Clark 2009: 1157; Introduction to Volume I).

Australia was isolated but not unvisited. From the seventeenth century fishermen from South Sulawesi (Macassa) came to northern Australia to fish in shallow coastal waters for trepang (sea slug), which they profitably re-exported to China. In the eighteenth century up to 3,000 Macassans worked the Australian coast annually from November to April. The visitors also traded with the Australians for sea-turtle shell, pearl shell, pearls, sandalwood, and some minerals, goods that the local population stockpiled in anticipation (Veth and O'Connor 2013: 40–41). In return the Macassans introduced new products and technologies: the dugout canoe with sails, metal harpoons, steel axes, pipes and tobacco, cloth, food and drink, knives, and tomahawks. These items then entered into the extensive trading networks that criss-crossed the continent. But their interaction was not all positive: Macassans introduced smallpox to Australia, to which the indigenous population had no immunity, and it spread across the country as far as the south-east coast, causing major outbreaks of mortality (Campbell 2002; Hunter 2015: 86–87).

European sailors visited infrequently, often accidentally, sometimes staying a few days on the coast. The British government organized Captain James Cook's voyage, which charted the east coast in 1770 carrying among its company Sir Joseph Banks, gentleman botanist. At the end of a four-month voyage along the east coast, south to north, involving a short stop at 'Botany Bay' and one of seven weeks for repairs in Queensland, Cook declared 'eastern Australia' for Britain and planted a flag at Cape York. While the ship was being repaired, Banks, out of scientific curiosity, measured the height of local men: they ranged from 62 to 69 inches with an average of 65 inches (Blainey 2009: 264). Banks undoubtedly proved the most influential visitor. By 1785 the British government was searching for a place to send convicts, America now being closed to them for this purpose, and Banks strongly advocated eastern Australia, nominating Botany Bay as a suitable spot. He was listened to by the parliamentary committee looking into this problem because he was a member of the British elite, and President of the Royal Society. He was also the most senior of the expedition still alive, James Cook having died in 1779 on his third voyage (Atkinson 1997: 71).

The development of the European economy in Australia comprised a number of broad phases. During the first forty years, 1788–1828, international exports were limited to whaling and sealing, the latter quickly reaching over-exploitation. Despite this low level of viable exports, international trade in the form of international imports was vigorous from the start of British settlement. As penal colonies, New South Wales and Tasmania were supported financially by the British government and imports were financed by this subsidy. The majority of the European population were convicts, predominantly males in their twenties, or ex-convicts ('emancipists'). Convict labour was coerced, backed up by severe physical punishment, its deployment determined by the colonial government. However, convicts in Australia were not slaves. The convict status itself was a temporary one, occupying in most cases seven years of an adult lifespan. Moreover, the coerced labour of convicts was limited on a daily basis: after 3pm each day (and on Sundays) convicts were free to work for wages for whoever was willing to employ them. Well-behaved convicts became eligible for a ticket-of-leave after serving half of their sentence, enabling them to work full-time in the market economy (subject to certain restrictions). Upon expiration of their sentence, or early release through obtaining a pardon, some emancipists received land grants, and the right to the assignment of convict labour. These arrangements were considered necessary to ensure sufficient labour was available to keep the European population fed and supplied with other goods and services. Government regulations stipulating minimum rations and wages also underpinned the domestic economy (Dyster 1988).

In a different league were the military officers and government officials who made up the social elite in the colony. They received land grants running into thousands of acres, and large numbers of convict workers to labour for them; they also controlled virtually all private international imports. That some of these officers and officials made substantial fortunes in the colonial economy was not very surprising and quite in keeping with contemporary norms regarding the private economic benefits associated with public and military office. What was more surprising, perhaps, was that some emancipists also amassed significant riches through trade, livestock, real estate, and money lending (Dow 1974). For the less fortunate emancipists their post-bond future depended on wage employment, possibly supplemented by small-scale production, petty trade, or becoming a publican. Farming (including livestock) and trade in domestic and imported produce were the mainstays of the early colonial economy, but construction, transport, and commercial services also developed. Sydney and Hobart were busy ports and even without a recognizable international export trade they developed commercial and financial services, including, in 1817, the first bank, the Bank of New South Wales. The establishment of these economic institutions and the nucleus of an urban economy produced an environment that would shape future economic development (Abbott and Nairn 1969).

As long as the British penal subsidy flowed into the colony it continued to grow, but threats to its continuance led some to consider the necessity of developing a viable export staple. Livestock did much better in the hinterland of Sydney than arable farming and grasslands were extensive. Several members of the elite began experimenting with wool production and embarked on the slow process of importing suitable animals and building up flocks separate from those kept for meat. Raising and cross-breeding merino flocks by trial and error with no immediate financial return required patience and considerable capital. Making contact with a potential market in Britain for fine wool from Australia that would challenge German imports involved activities only members of the elite could perform.

By 1815 graziers were beginning to move west across the Blue Mountains in search of more land, a process helped by the government building a road from Sydney over the mountain and founding a new town, Bathurst, on the western plain. Trial consignments of fine wool in the mid-1820s were successful and in 1828 the British government removed tariff barriers to colonial wool imports, opening the door to the first Australian wool boom. Australian real GDP increased tenfold between 1800 and 1828, but the European population, driven by greater convict arrivals, grew faster after the war, so real GDP per capita declined.

From the late 1820s to the mid-1840s the pastoral economy expanded rapidly north, west, and south from Bathurst and north through the midlands of Tasmania from Hobart. In 1835 graziers from Tasmania crossed to Port Phillip and expanded across the southern portion of New South Wales (Boyce

2011). There were, apparently, 800,000 sheep in the colony in 1828, by 1846 ten times as many; 340,000 cattle increased to 1.4 million over the same period (Butlin, N. et al. 1987: 107). In line with government policy, land grants and convict labour were made available to immigrants with capital, but many graziers simply moved onto lands beyond the government's borders and established sheep runs as 'squatters', taking their convict labourers with them. The incentive to do so increased after 1831 when the British government, under the influence of the ideas of Edward Gibbon Wakefield, ended the practice of free land grants and required colonial governments to sell Crown land at auction. Although squatters lacked legal property rights in the land they occupied they carried on their enterprise as if they did possess them, and the government was not willing, or able, to evict them. Most lived in Sydney and ran their grazing operations with salaried managers and convict shepherds (McMichael 1984). Their overheads were minimal, but sheep were expensive to purchase. A constant stream of newcomers deployed what capital they had brought with them from Britain, together with funds borrowed from Sydney merchants, to get started. Graziers' incomes came from sale of wool to a consignment agent in Sydney and sale of sheep to those starting out or wishing to augment their flocks, plus wethers for meat. Profits depended on both sources: without the demand for sheep from newcomers and butchers, the squatters struggled to cover their costs (Abbott 1971). Many became indebted to Sydney mercantile houses that made advances on the wool clip and supplied goods and services required by the squatter. The colonial government passed a Wool Lien Act in 1843 that facilitated using both sheep and wool as collateral (Butlin, S. 1953: 340–345). Thus merchant capital penetrated wool production. Wool exports rose rapidly and by 1835 accounted for half of domestic exports from New South Wales, rising to 75 per cent 1841–1850 (Butlin, N. et al. 1987: 109).

The continued influence of Wakefield's 'systematic colonization' ideas resulted in the establishment in 1836 of a new colony, South Australia, whose economic viability, its promotors considered, was threatened by cheap convict labour in neighbouring New South Wales. They therefore lobbied the British government to end penal transportation. To some extent they were pushing an open door as by this time many employers felt the supply of convicts was too restricted and that a much bigger pool of cheap labour existed in Britain among the poor, some of whom could be subsidized to emigrate to Australia using the revenue obtained from land sales. Potential immigrants, however, were put off by Australia's penal status. In Britain, it was suspected that penal transportation to such prosperous colonies had lost the 'dread' necessary to deter crime. Moreover, by now there was a substantial number of emancipists in the colony whose personal experience of the convict system led them to add their voice against penal transportation, but in any case the working class generally regarded the continued inflow of convicts as detrimental to their wage level. By 1837 it was clear that penal transportation to New South Wales would shortly cease and the last regular shipload of convicts arrived in 1840 (Meredith 1988).

By 1850 the real GDP of Australia was ten times its size in 1828 and had grown faster than the European population, resulting in a 47 per cent rise in real GDP per head over these two decades. In 1851 gold was discovered in both New South Wales and Victoria, a new colony carved out of the southern part of New South Wales in 1850. The 'gold rush' that followed had far-reaching consequences, not least because gold finds continued to be made over the next two decades, from Tasmania in the south to Queensland (separated from New South Wales in 1859) in the north. None were as spectacular as the Victorian gold discoveries in 1851, but they kept alive the popular view of eastern Australia as a gold-rich land (McLean 2013: 80–90). Real GDP increased fivefold between 1850 and 1870 while the European population grew by a factor of four, thus producing a further rise in real GDP per head.

The immediate impact of the 1851 gold rushes, however, was to cause widespread economic disruption as thousands left their jobs and headed to the diggings. Prices and wages increased sharply and farmers and graziers turned to indigenous Australians to provide labour to keep their operations going. By 1853 immigrants began to arrive in substantial numbers, from Britain, Europe, the United States, and China (Coghlan 1918 vol. 1: 563–587). Over the decade Australia's European population rose from 405,000 in 1850 to 1,146,000 in 1860. The colonial governments struggled to keep order on the gold fields and facilitate the movement of people, goods, and gold, but government revenues increased substantially through issuing mining licences and the imposition of a gold export tax. Government expenditure matched this increase so that the value of the gold retained by the state was recycled through the domestic economy, much of it spent on improving transport infrastructure. The eastern Australian gold rushes were highly democratic: anyone could go to the gold fields, and did, in large numbers. Gold was found at or near the surface, often in or near streams, so that fossicking involved a lot of hard manual labour with shovel and sieve but not much capital. It was not possible for a single person to monopolize gold production: Australia had no equivalent of Cecil Rhodes. The end of convict transportation together

Figure 11.1 Australia, real GDP per head, European population, 1801–90 ($A2010–11)
Source: Butlin, M. et al. (2015).

with these effects of the gold rush reduced income inequality even while average real incomes were rising (Panza and Williamson 2019). The increased wealth and rapidly rising population was a stimulus to local production, particularly to farming and livestock for meat, though also to trade, services, and manufacturing. As a result the economy grew rapidly in the 1850s, levelled off in the 1860s (but did not decline) and expanded to new heights in the 1870s and 1880s (Figure 11.1 and Volume II Chapter 11). Thus, from the 1840s, Australia achieved 'modern economic growth' (Kuznets 1966: 65).

Mining as a share of GDP declined from its early 1850s level and by 1870 there was a convergence between the main components (Figure 11.2), but the long-term rise in the share of manufacturing and construction continued into the future. Services (48 per cent) and manufacturing and construction (16 per cent) in 1870 indicated a surprisingly large urban economy.

Following the gold discoveries the European population in Australia accelerated sharply (Figure 11.3). This was an unusual population. It was heavily dependent on immigration: in 1861 only 37.2 per cent of the European population had been born in Australia; and it was more urban than might be expected of an economy dependent on extensive land resources – in 1861 39.2 per cent lived in a capital city or other town (Caldwell 1987: 41; Price 1987: 8). Perhaps the most abnormal characteristic

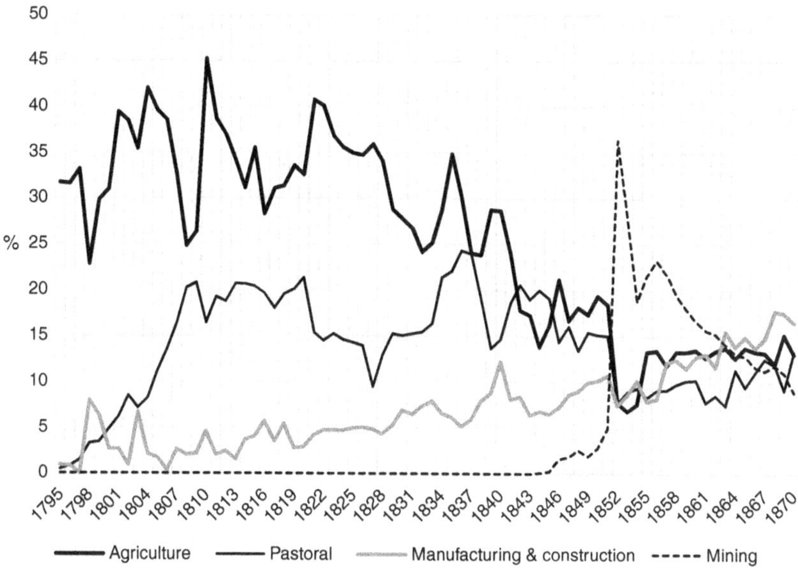

Figure 11.2 Australia, industry shares of GDP (percentage)
Source: Butlin, N. and Sinclair (1986).

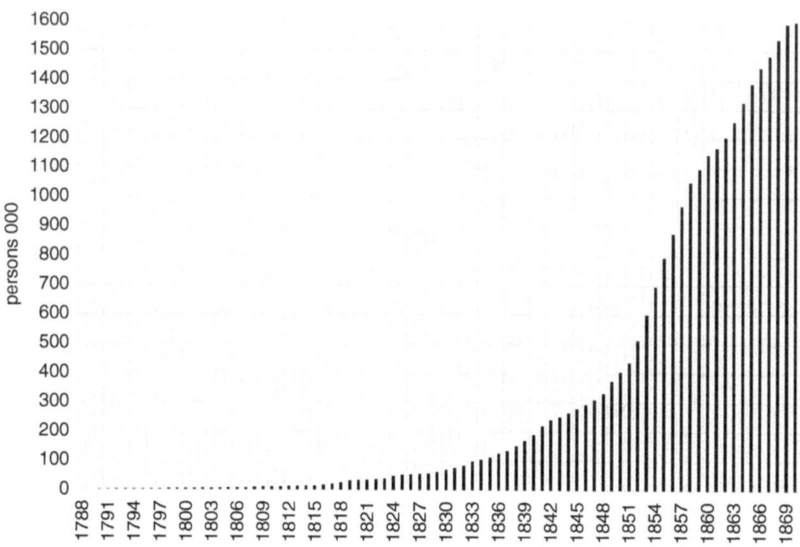

Figure 11.3 Australia, European population, 1788–1870 (thousands of persons)
Source: Butlin, M. et al. (2015).

of the settler population in the early nineteenth century was its structure, resulting from the preponderance of convict immigrants, most of whom were male. The sex ratio (males per 100 females) stood at 281.1 in 1821 and ten years later there were three males for every female. In the 1830s non-convict immigration and natural increase lowered the ratio, down to 187.5 in 1841. It continued to decline, despite the gold rush bringing far more men to the colonies than women, and in 1871 was 120.1. The sex ratio among adults (over 15 years of age) was higher: 168.9 in New South Wales in 1871 (Butlin, M. et al. 2015). An obvious effect of these ratios was that a considerable number of men never married, leading to a low dependency ratio in the first half of the century that implied an increased proportion of people of working age in the population and therefore a higher rate of GDP growth per head.

Human capital includes the knowledge and capabilities of an individual as well as their physical attributes and health (Volume I Chapter 12). Convicts were not lacking in measurable human capital, but as coerced labour they often lacked the incentive to work (Oxley 1996; Meredith and Oxley 2015). Literacy is a relevant and convenient measure of human capital in the post-convict era. Overall settler literacy was high: 84 per cent among urban adults in New South Wales in 1856, 68 per cent in rural areas (New South Wales Census 1856). Health was one measure where Australians thought they did well and mortality tables supported this opinion. As F. B. Smith (1997: 29) puts it, 'comparative life expectancies and general death rates showed Australia to be the healthiest nation on earth'.

In 1788 indigenous Australians were already under some pressure from smallpox introduced by Macassans. The rate of population decline accelerated after that, particularly from the 1820s when the wool boom brought graziers and their sheep into vast areas of Aboriginal lands. The decline continued under the impact of the gold rushes from the 1850s and the expansion of the pastoralist frontier north of Capricorn in Queensland, northern South Australia and the Kimberleys (Bottoms 2013; Curthoys 2014). Population decline at the frontier continued into the early twentieth century. Estimates made by Noel Butlin (1986: 107), put the decline in Aboriginal population between 1788 and 1860 at 66 per cent, from 1.1 million to 375,000, with the Aboriginal and European populations being just about equal in 1850. Population decline was the end result of a complex demographic process whereby Aboriginal populations lost structural viability, imploding as the normal demographic relationships collapsed.

For Europeans, Australia seemed a healthy place, there being no endemic diseases to which they were susceptible. Until the arrival of outsiders the same was perhaps true for Aboriginal Australians, but they lacked immunity to a range of diseases brought by newcomers that caused illness and death on a wide scale. The speed of population decline in areas of greatest European impact was astonishing: 60 per cent in the space of 15 years in both Tasmania and Victoria (Ryan 2014). Diseases to which Europeans had developed immunity from childhood, but which were deadly to the indigenous population, explain only part of their demographic catastrophe. The brief description of the indigenous economy at the beginning of this chapter indicated that sustaining a population of somewhere around 1 million people required access to all the land and its resources on a daily basis. Movement around *country* to hunt and forage as the seasons changed was essential to maintain production. People had lived in Australia for such a long time that there were no places they did not occupy. Settlers also required the land and its resources. Arable farmers made permanent settlements that obliterated Aboriginal access to land, but the area under arable agriculture at this time was quite limited. Similarly, mining operations were devastating, but they occupied even smaller areas of land. Pastoral farmers, however, practised transhumance – they were as 'nomadic' as the Aborigines – and their flocks and herds were enormous.

Drawing an international perspective, Adhikari has argued that commercial stock farmers employed a mode of production that was particularly damaging when coming into contact with hunter gatherer economies (Adhikari 2014: 1–31). Partly this was due to the impact of the introduced animals themselves, which consumed and contaminated water supplies, ate grasslands, and trampled plants, causing a large-scale decline in native fauna. But it was also due to the commercial nature of the invading graziers. They were producing wool for distant global markets, profits per sheep were small, but total profits high if flocks were large enough. Their capital stock – the sheep – reproduced themselves at a rate of around 60 per cent per annum, but as the flocks expanded, and the number of stock farmers increased, the area of grazing land rose exponentially. Access to water became more problematic as their flocks moved into more arid regions. There was, suggests Adhikari, a 'get-rich-quick' mentality among commercial stock farmers that made them intolerant of obstacles to expansion and thus highly aggressive towards the people they found living in the areas into which they were moving. From the Aboriginal point of view this invasion must be resisted and the invaders forced to retreat. Moreover, as the impact of the flocks and herds continued, the local inhabitants became more desperate through the contraction of their food supply. Resistance to invasion led to reprisals and an escalation of violence. Small Aboriginal groups were vulnerable to attack if they could be located; isolated shepherds and stockmen – not the persons generally who owned the sheep or the wool – were highly exposed to Aboriginal violence. At first, Europeans found the guerrilla tactics of the Aborigines difficult to defeat and were surprised at the power and accuracy of their spears and other weapons. But in time settlers' access to firearms, horses, and logistical support from the coast tipped the balance in their favour. As pastoralists organized vigilante forces, extreme exterminatory rhetoric escalated into indiscriminate exterminatory violence and 'total war on a local scale' was the result (Adhikari 2014: 18).

The wars on Australia's moving frontier and the massacres they involved have been well documented (Reynolds 1981; Milliss 1992; Boyce 2008; Foster and Nettelbeck 2012; Ryan 2012; Curthoys 2014; Ryan 2014). Of longer-term impact was the assault, abduction, rape, and forcing into sexual slavery of indigenous women by settler men (Reynolds 1990: 117; Boyce 2008: 89–102; Clements 2014). The European population at the frontier consisted overwhelmingly of adult males. Venereal disease spread rapidly and not only caused death directly but compromised fertility and childbirth (Butlin, N. 1983: 77–79; Hunter 2015: 87–92). Demographic recovery was difficult and further constrained by the widespread practice of kidnapping Aboriginal children to keep them as servants (Hetherington 2002; Boyce 2008: 86–89). An integrated mix of disease, malnutrition, and violence produced a demographic decline of massive proportion over a relatively short space of time.

In some regions – Tasmania, Victoria – the onslaught was so complete that few Aborigines survived; in others the survivors had to adjust to their new subordinate position. Despite the decline in their numbers, those who survived were highly valued workers, men in the management of livestock and women for childminding and the heavier domestic work on pastoral stations. The remuneration received by Aboriginal men and women employed as workers on cattle ranches and sheep stations did not reflect their productivity, as racial prejudice prevented settlers from paying them wages. Instead they received rations and some clothing and were allowed a limited time to pursue their traditional way of life. They were not free to leave the station and thus appear more akin to serfs than free wage labour. Yet across the 'outback' Europeans constantly attested that they could not manage to run their properties and homes without the assistance of Aboriginal workers (McGrath 1987; May 1994; McGrath 1995; McGrath et al. 1995; Goodall 1996; Curthoys 2014). The cattle industry rapidly expanded in the latter part of the nineteenth century when the new technology of refrigeration opened up an international market for Australian beef. The reliance of cattle farmers from Queensland to Western Australia on Aboriginal labour intensified. This was not assimilation: Aboriginal workers were not treated as equals and it is far from clear that they wanted to be part of white society: working for Europeans was a compromise that might allow their culture to survive and their numbers to increase but it was not a substitute for what they had lost (Reynolds 1990).

Dispossession, then, was part and parcel of the expansion of the European economy from 1788. As Hunter has pointed out, dispossession occurred in two stages: legal dispossession occurred from the start of Governor Phillip's rule: under English law 'Aboriginal people were at once trespassers on their own ancestral land' (Hunter 2015: 88). Physical dispossession took place over more than a century, though at particular places and times it was very swift. Kercher has explained that British law 'placed Aborigines in an ambiguous position'. The instructions given to Phillip were 'to open an intercourse with the natives, and to conciliate their affections, enjoining all of our subjects to live in amity and kindness with them. And if any of our subjects shall wantonly destroy them, or give them any unnecessary interruption in the exercise of their several occupations, it is our will and pleasure that you do cause such offenders to be brought to punishment according to the degree of the offence' (Kercher 1995: 6). Phillip and subsequent governors of New South Wales and Tasmania failed to follow these instructions and in particular by granting Aboriginal land to settlers they denied the indigenous population any property rights in land. As Aborigines were not allowed to appear in court because they were not Christians they effectively had no legal rights at all. The legal fiction of *terra nullius* ('empty land') was developed to provide legitimacy to this process and was not successfully challenged in Australian courts until 1992 (Chesterman and Galligan 1997). Nor did the State act effectively to prevent the murder of indigenous Australians, clearly illegal acts, but not ones for which settlers or the militia were restrained by the implementation of law (Milliss 1992). There were many Europeans in Australia and Britain, some in powerful political positions, who deplored the violence and demographic destruction taking place: after all, this was the era of anti-slavery (Reynolds 1998; Foster and Nettelbeck 2012). Committees in the British Parliament discussed the question, interrogated a range of European observers, and issued critical reports. Had they been successful in stopping the expansion of the settler economy it would have undoubtedly saved lives and Aboriginal society, but economic considerations prevailed at all times. Secure property rights for settlers could only be ensured by insecure rights, or a complete absence of rights, for indigenous Australians.

Conclusion

Let no one think much of a trifling expense
Who knows what may happen a hundred years hence!
The loss of America what can repay?
New colonies seek for at Botany Bay.
Public Advertiser, 23 November 1986
(Christopher and Maxwell-Stewart 2013: 88)

Perhaps nothing could console Britain for the loss of the American colonies, and for a while the tiny military base at Sydney, full of criminals and scheming officers and officials on the make, costing the British Treasury rather more than a 'trifling expense', was an embarrassment rather than a substitute America. But perhaps Britain also learned a lesson in imperial governance and avoided the mistakes of Lord North. By 1870 the view from Britain was rather different. British goods, capital, enterprise, and emigrants flowed to the Australian colonies, not on the scale of similar flows to the United States in the nineteenth century, but to a far greater extent than might have been expected in 1788. Australia supplied Britain with a vital raw textile material in quantities that transformed woollen manufacturing and enabled it to industrialize. From 1851 Australian gold flowed to Britain and helped to underpin the gold standard, augmenting the provision of international liquidity at a time when international trade expanded faster than output. For the first time, Australia emerged on the global stage, and its newest city, Melbourne, was viewed as a marvel of the age (Wilson 2016: 47–50). The European economy in Australia was established and expanded in a period coterminous with the British Industrial Revolution, which itself produced a shift in economic ideology from mercantilism to industrial capitalism that found a reflection in the growing Australian economy (Kociumbas 1992: chapter 4).

Moreover, the Australian settler economy appeared highly successful between 1830 and 1870, and indeed up to the crisis of 1890 (Volume II Chapter 12; Broadberry 2015: 306; Butlin, M. et al. 2015: 557). Noel Butlin's calculations appear to confirm the widely held view in Australia at the time that the settlers enjoyed high per capita incomes. It is evident from Figure 11.4 that from 1830 to 1860 real GDP per head among the European population in the Australian colonies was higher than in Great Britain, implying these

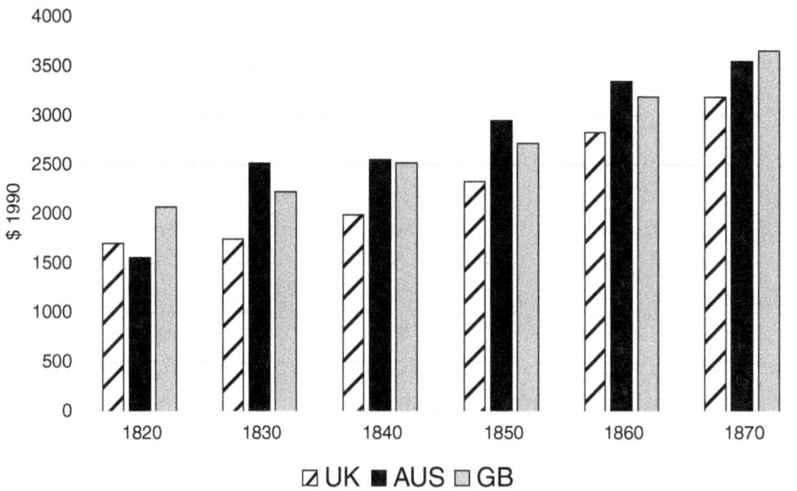

Figure 11.4 Real GDP per head, Australia (European population), UK and Great Britain, 1820–70 (1990 international dollars)
Source: UK and Australia: Maddison (2006: 437, 449); Great Britain: Broadberry et al. (2015).

settlers (1.7 million in 1871, most of whom came from the UK), were the richest people on the planet.

Australia's rapid economic growth resulted from a high land-to-population ratio, substantial immigration, and British investment. A market economy, including in labour, developed at an early stage of British settlement, together with urban manufacturing industries and services, albeit on a small scale. Immigrants from Britain noticed a subtle change in the labour market once they arrived in the colonies, from a buyer's market in Britain, to a seller's in Australia. Until the 1840s this effect was masked by the availability of convict labour but emerged more strongly thereafter. Employers turned to indentured labour, rather unsuccessfully, and to stringent labour laws, Master and Servant legislation, and fought against the market power of labour in the courts (Buckley and Wheelwright 1988: 62–63; Patmore 1991: 24–38; Quinlan 2018). And workers fought back. High wages stimulated the urban economy and consumption. Gold brought more immigrants but created more demand for labour, and real wages rose through the gold decade of the 1850s (Coghlan 1918 vol. 2: 687–829). Significantly, skilled artisans used some of their bargaining power to reduce work effort by demanding an eight-hour day, achieved in most trades by 1870 (Patmore 1991: 56–65). They also supported worker organizations, trades unions, friendly societies, and similar institutions, and increased their saving rate by use of savings banks and building societies. In 1870 Australia had the highest labour productivity in the world (Maddison 1995: 249). The French sociologist Albert Métin, visiting New Zealand and Australia at the end of the century, saw the colonies as 'a worker's paradise', an exaggeration that nevertheless reflected real differences in the labour market between western Europe and Australia (Metin 1901; Patmore 1991: chapter 3).

Institutional arrangements evolved. Commercial and financial institutions were transferred from Britain and adapted to local colonial conditions (Butlin, S. 1953; Abbott and Nairn 1969). Over the period 1788 to 1870 governance made a transition from military rule to parliamentary democracy, achieving universal male suffrage by 1860. Generally speaking, the institutional arrangements that developed from the 1820s supported settler capitalism, while avoiding democratic deficits and white-on-white conflict. Certainly, they could be counted as beneficial to economic outcomes as far as the settlers were concerned (Volume I Chapter 15). Colonial governments proved highly capable. The Commissariat was a major economic institution until the 1820s, facilitating imports, local production, and consumption (Butlin, N. 1994: 64). Governors were good at managing and disciplining coerced convict labour and directing this to ends that appeared desirable, such as building transport infrastructure and port facilities. Similarly, urban construction was a high priority for government, including the construction of many fine public buildings that impressed visitors to a penal settlement. Government was instrumental in encouraging free immigration, of both working class and capitalist. From 1832 the colonial governments used revenue from land sales to subsidize assisted immigration on a considerable scale, targeting single females, families, and workers with particular skills and continued to do this even during the gold rush. Governmental response to the gold rush enhanced economic growth. Governors were less successful, however, in controlling settlers who defied local regulations, eventually losing control over vast areas of the interior to grazier 'squatters' (Roberts 1935). And their record in protecting the rights and lives of indigenous people was abysmal.

A combination of geography and institutions was responsible for the success of the British economy in Australia by 1870, and for the destruction of the pre-existing indigenous economy and society. The Aboriginal economy developed complex institutions over a long period to ensure that production of food and other supplies from the land's natural resources was maximized and efficiently distributed among the whole population. The British settlers in Australia applied different sets of institutions, including those of the global economy, to production and distribution from the same land and natural resources, with markedly different results. The arrival of the British in 1788 was not a result of globalization, though it may have been caused by war and empire in the eighteenth century (Volume I Chapter 19). But the growth of the settler economy in the Australian colonies from the 1820s was clearly an early, perhaps outstanding, manifestation of nineteenth-century globalization (O'Rourke and Williamson 2002). The Australian colonies benefited from the liberalization of international trade and capital, while British rule effected transfers of cultural norms and institutions, as well as British and Irish immigration. In nineteenth-century Australia, globalization and British imperialism went hand in glove.

References

Abbott, G. J. (1971). *The Pastoral Age: A Re-Examination*, Melbourne: Macmillan.

Abbott, G. J. and Nairn, N. B. (eds.) (1969). *Economic Growth of Australia 1788–1821*, Melbourne University Press.

Adhikari, M. (ed.) (2014). *Genocide on Settler Frontiers: When Hunter-Gatherers and Commercial Stock Farmers Clash*, Cape Town, UCT Press.

Atkinson, A. (1997). *The Europeans in Australia, vol. 1*, Oxford University Press.

Berndt, R. M. and Berndt, C. H. (1988). *The World of the First Australians: Aboriginal Traditional Life, Past and Present*, Canberra: Aboriginal Studies Press.

Blainey, G. (2009). *Sea of Dangers: Captain Cook and His Rivals*, Camberwell: Penguin Group (Australia).

Bottoms, T. (2013). *Conspiracy of Silence: Queensland's Frontier Killing Times*, Sydney: Allen & Unwin.

Boyce, J. (2008). *Van Diemen's Land*, Melbourne: Black Inc.

(2011). *1835: The Founding of Melbourne and the Conquest of Australia*, Melbourne: Black Inc.

Broadberry, S. (2015). 'Review Essay', *Australian Economic History Review*, 55(3), 301–310.

Broadberry, S., Campbell, B., Klein, A., Overton, M. and van Leeuwen, B. (2015). *British Economic Growth, 1270–1870*, Cambridge University Press.

Buckley, K. and Wheelwright, T. (1988). *No Paradise for Workers: Capitalism and the Common People in Australia 1788–1914*, Oxford University Press.

Butlin, M., Dixon, R. and Lloyd, P. J. (2015). 'Statistical Appendix: Selected Data Series, 1800–2010', in Ville, S. and Withers, G. (eds.), *The Cambridge Economic History of Australia*, Cambridge University Press, 555–594.

Butlin, N. (1983). *Our Original Aggression: Aboriginal Populations of Southeastern Australia 1788–1850*, Sydney: Allen & Unwin.

(1986). 'Contours of the Australian Economy 1788–1860', *Australian Economic History Review*, 26, 96–125.

(1994). *Forming a Colonial Economy, Australia 1815–50*, Cambridge University Press.

Butlin, N. and Sinclair, W. (1986). 'Australian Gross Domestic Product 1788–1860: Estimates, Sources and Methods', *Australian Economic History Review*, 26, 126–147.

Butlin, N., Ginswick, J. and Statham, P. (1987). 'The Economy Before 1850', in Vamplew, W. (ed.), *Australians: Historical Statistics*, Sydney: Fairfax, Syme & Weldon.

Butlin, S. (1953). *Foundations of the Australian Monetary System 1788–1851*, Sydney University Press.

Caldwell, J. C. (1987). 'Population', in Vamplew, W. (ed.), *Australians: Historical Statistics*, Sydney: Fairfax, Syme & Weldon, 23–41.

Campbell, J. (2002). *Invisible Invaders: Smallpox and Other Diseases in Aboriginal Australia 1780–1880*, Melbourne University Press.

Chesterman, J. and Galligan, B. (1997). *Citizens Without Rights: Aborigines and Australian Citizenship*, Cambridge University Press.

Christopher, E. and Maxwell-Stewart, H. (2013). 'Convict Transportation in Global Context, *c*.1700–88' in Bashford, A. and Macintyre, S. (eds.), *The Cambridge History of Australia, vol. 1: Indigenous and Colonial Australia*, Cambridge University Press, 68–90.

Clark, G. (2009). 'Review of *Contours of the World Economy, 1–2030AD: Essays in Macro-Economic History* by Angus Maddison. Oxford University Press, 2007', *Journal of Economic History*, 69, 1156–1161.

Clements, N. (2014). *The Black War: Fear, Sex and Resistance in Tasmania*, St. Lucia: Queensland University Press.

Coghlan, T. (1918). *Labour and Industry in Australia, vols. 1, 2*, Oxford University Press.

Curthoys, A. (2014). 'Indigenous Dispossession and Pastoral Employment in Western Australia during the Nineteenth Century: Implications for Understanding Colonial Forms of Genocide', in Adhikari, M. (ed.), *Genocide on Settler Frontiers: When Hunter-Gatherers and Commercial Stock Farmers Clash*, Cape Town: UCT Press.

Dow, G. (1974). *Samuel Terry: The Botany Bay Rothschild*, Sydney University Press.

Dyster, B. (1988). 'Public Employment and Assignment to Private Masters, 1788–1821', in Nicholas, S. (ed.), *Convict Workers: Reinterpreting Australia's Past*, Cambridge University Press, 127–151.

Flannery, T. (1994). *The Future Eaters*, Kew: Reed Books.

Foster, R. and Nettelbeck, A. (2012). *Out of the Silence: The History and Memory of South Australia's Frontier Wars*, Adelaide: Wakefield Press.

Gammage, B. (2011). *The Biggest Estate on Earth: How Aborigines Made Australia*, Sydney: Allen & Unwin.

Goodall, H. (1996). *Invasion to Embassy: Land in Aboriginal Politics in New South Wales 1770–1972*, Sydney: Allen & Unwin.

Heathcote, R. (1975). *Australia*, London: Longman.

Hetherington, P. (2002). *Settlers, Servants and Slaves: Aboriginal and European Children in Nineteenth-Century Western Australia*, Perth: University of Western Australia Press.

Hunter, B. (2015). 'The Aboriginal Legacy', in Ville, S. and Withers, G. (eds.), *The Cambridge Economic History of Australia*, Cambridge University Press, 73–96.

Keen, I. (2004). *Aboriginal Economy and Society: Australia at the Threshold of Colonisation*, Oxford University Press.

Kercher, B. (1995). *An Unruly Child: A History of Law in Australia*, Sydney: Allen & Unwin.

Kociumbas, J. (1992). *The Oxford History of Australia, vol. 2, 1770–1860: Possessions*, Oxford University Press.

Kuznets, S. (1966). *Modern Economic Growth: Rate, Structure and Spread*, New Haven: Yale University Press.

Lourandos, H. (1987). 'Swamp Managers of South-Western Victoria', in Mulvaney, D. and White, J. (eds.), *Australians: To 1788*, Sydney: Fairfax, Syme & Weldon, 292–307.

(1997). *Continent of Hunter-Gatherers: New Perspectives in Australian Prehistory*, Cambridge University Press.

Maddison, A. (1995). *Monitoring the World Economy 1820–1992*, Paris: Organisation for Economic Co-operation and Development.

(2006). *The World Economy*, Paris: Organisation for Economic Co-operation and Development.

(2007). *Contours of the World Economy, 1–2030 AD: Essays in Macro-Economic History*, Oxford University Press.

May, D. (1994). *Aboriginal Labour and the Cattle Industry: Queensland from White Settlement to the Present*, Cambridge University Press.

McBryde, I. (1987). 'Goods from Another Country: Exchange Networks and the People from the Lake Eyre Basin', in Mulvaney, D. and White, J. (eds.), *Australians: To 1788*, Sydney: Fairfax, Syme & Weldon, 252–273.

McGrath, A. (1987). *Born in the Cattle: Aborigines in Cattle Country*, Sydney: Allen & Unwin.

(ed.) (1995). *Contested Ground: Australian Aborigines under the British Crown*, Sydney: Allen & Unwin.

McGrath, A., Saunders, K. and Huggins, J. (1995) (eds.), *Aboriginal Workers*, special issue of *Labour History*, 69, Sydney: Australian Society for the Study of Labour History.

McLean, I. (2013). *Why Australia Prospered: The Shifting Sources of Economic Growth*, Princeton University Press.

McMichael, P. (1984). *Settlers and the Agrarian Question: Capitalism in Colonial Australia*, Cambridge University Press.

Meredith, D. (1988). 'Full Circle? Contemporary Views on Transportation', in Nicholas, S. (ed.), *Convict Workers: Reinterpreting Australia's Past*, Cambridge University Press.

Meredith, D. and Oxley, D. (2015). 'The Convict Economy', in Ville, S. and Withers, G. (eds.), *The Cambridge Economic History of Australia*, Cambridge University Press, 97–122.

Metin, A. (1901). 'The Worker's Paradise', in Manne, R. and Feik, C. (2012) (eds.), *The Words that Made Australia*, Melbourne: Black Inc.

Milliss, R. (1992). *Waterloo Creek: The Australia Day Massacre of 1838, George Gipps and the British Conquest of New South Wales*, Sydney: University of New South Wales Press.

New South Wales Census (1856). doi:10.26193/MP6WRS (accessed 27 October 2020).

O'Rourke, K. and Williamson, J. (2002). 'When Did Globalisation Begin?', *European Review of Economic History*, 6, 23–50.

Oxley, D. (1996). *Convict Maids: The Forced Migration of Women to Australia*, Cambridge University Press.

Panza, L. and Williamson, J. (2019). 'Australian Squatters, Convicts, and Capitalists: Dividing up a Fast-Growing Frontier Pie, 1821–71', *Economic History Review*, 72(2), 569–594.

Patmore, G. (1991). *Australian Labour History*, Melbourne: Longman Cheshire.

Price, C. (1987). 'Immigration and Ethnic Origin', in Vamplew, W. (ed.), *Australians: Historical Statistics*, Sydney: Fairfax, Syme & Weldon.

Quinlan, M. (2018). *The Origins of Worker Mobilisation: Australia 1788–1850*, London: Routledge.

Reynolds, H. (1981). *The Other Side of the Frontier: Aboriginal Resistance to the European Invasion of Australia*, Ringwood: Penguin Books.

(1990). *With the White People: The Crucial Role of Aborigines in the Exploration and Development of Australia*, Ringwood: Penguin Books.

(1998). *This Whispering in our Hearts*, Sydney: Allen & Unwin.

Roberts, S. H. (1935, 1964). *The Squatting Age in Australia, 1835–1847*, 2nd ed., Melbourne University Press.

Ryan, L. (2012). *Tasmanian Aborigines: A History since 1803*, Sydney: Allen & Unwin.

(2014). '"No Right to the Land": The Role of the Wool Industry in the Destruction of Aboriginal Societies in Tasmania (1817–1832) and Victoria (1835–51) Compared', in Adhikari, M. (ed.), *Genocide on Settler Frontiers: When Hunter-Gatherers and Commercial Stock Farmers Clash*, Cape Town: UTC Press, 185–209.

Smith, F. B. (1997). 'The First Health Transition in Australia, 1880–1910', in Jones, G. W., Douglas, R. M. , Caldwell, J. C. and D'Souza, R. M. (eds.), *The Continuing Demographic Transition*, Oxford: Clarendon Press.

Veth, P. and O'Connor, S. (2013). 'The Past 50,000 Years: An Archaeological View', in Bashford, A. and Macintyre, S. (eds.), *The Cambridge History of Australia, vol. 1, Indigenous and Colonial Australia*, Cambridge University Press, 72–42.

Williams, A. (2013). 'A New Population Curve for Prehistoric Australia', *Proceedings of the Royal Society B*, 280(1761).

Wilson, B. (2016). *Heyday: Britain and the Birth of the Modern World*, London: Weidenfeld & Nicolson.

PART II

★

FACTORS GOVERNING DIFFERENTIAL OUTCOMES IN THE GLOBAL ECONOMY

12

Population and Human Development since 1700

ROMOLA DAVENPORT AND OSAMU SAITO

Introduction

'In traditional societies, fertility and mortality are high. In modern societies, fertility and mortality are low. In between there is the demographic transition' (Demeny 1972: 153). Before this transition, women bore half a dozen children or more, but between one-third and half of those born died before reaching reproductive age, while high levels of mortality made any long-term planning over one's life course difficult. According to classical theories of the demographic transition, economic and societal changes enabled mortality levels to decline. This generated an unprecedented increase in population, but married couples responded to the progressive impact of rising life expectancy and associated population growth by limiting their family size, eventually bringing the population growth to a halt. Indeed, the period before 1870 saw the level of mortality declining in many west European countries. Falls in mortality were especially marked in urban populations, where mortality levels had been most severe. These improvements in urban life expectancies were essential to the unprecedented rates of urbanization achieved by early industrializing nations in the nineteenth century. The end of our period, the 1870s, witnessed the onset of fertility transition in western Europe and the Anglophone neo-Europes (or Western offshoots), and a decline in population growth rates. Between 1870 and 1930 all countries in these areas experienced significant and historically unprecedented fertility declines, such that crude birth rates fell from a range of 25–45 births per 1,000 population to less than 20 in all cases, and total fertility rates (TFRs) from around 5 births per woman to less than 3 by the 1930s (Chesnais 1992: 117–128).

However, this classic interpretation is no longer tenable. The actual patterns of interactions with economic and social factors were far more complex than earlier generations of scholars thought. The next section sets out issues to be explored and approaches we will take, followed by an examination of the situation prior to the transition. Then we will explore the relationships between population change and economic growth before discussing the implications of demographic changes by taking a look at health status and labour productivity.

Issues and Approaches

There are several factual findings that are at odds with presumptions of the classical demographic transition model. The first is that the beginning of mortality decline started earlier than previously thought: in northern Europe the decline began well before industrialization (Flinn 1981; Wrigley et al. 1997). The second is that urbanization operated to offset improvements in health and longevity, at the individual level via increased exposure to diseases and at the population level through the redistribution of population from healthier rural to unhealthy urban environments. The other three findings are concerned with fertility. The first of the three is that there are countries whose fertility rose before the onset of fertility decline (Dyson and Murphy 1985; Wrigley et al. 1997: chapter 7), and the second is that the mortality transition did not trigger an immediate decline in fertility, as a result of which it took a long period, sometimes more than 100 years, for leaders of the demographic transition to complete the whole process (Chesnais 1992: chapters 3–4). Finally, the decline did not necessarily stop at the level at which the population replaces itself: in many countries today, fertility is below replacement levels. This has happened not only in European and North American countries but in East Asian nations as well, and has been dubbed, controversially, the second demographic transition (Lesthaeghe 2014).

According to economic theories since the time of Malthus, mortality has been linked to nutritional status and, hence, to family income. But it was the epidemiologist Thomas McKeown who argued explicitly for the first time that an increase in nutritional intake resulting from economic growth after the Industrial Revolution was the major factor accounting for the mortality decline in England and Wales (McKeown and Record 1962; McKeown 1976). McKeown's thesis was criticized by public health historians and researchers and the current consensus is that public health measures were more important than nutritional improvements in reducing mortality, although the balance may have varied from disease to disease (Szreter 1988; Woods 2000; Harris 2004). For a later period, Samuel Preston showed from nation-level data that there was a non-linear, positive relationship between longevity and national income per capita, but his conclusion was that 84 per cent of the gain in life expectancy between the 1930s and the 1960s was attributable to an exogenous upward shift of the curve and only 16 per cent to a move along the longevity-income function, i.e. an increase in income per capita (Preston 1975). This seems to confirm the findings of the McKeown debate: the income effect was small in size compared to other factors. However, it is not certain whether this would hold for a period before the mid-nineteenth century. Simon Kuznets once remarked that a decline in the level of mortality was 'an indispensable prerequisite for modern economic growth' (Kuznets 1979: 136), suggesting a reverse causality. While he did not specify in what sense it was a prerequisite, we are now in a better position to clarify how mortality decline and economic growth were related to each other.

Early fertility decline was achieved largely by control of fertility within marriage (rather than by falls in marriage rates), and by traditional means of contraception, especially withdrawal and abstinence. The causes of this transition remain hotly debated, with economic theories emphasizing the changing costs and benefits to parents of having (or averting) children or offspring quantity-quality trade-offs (Guinnane 2011; Galor 2011), and ideational theories emphasizing the spread of novel ideas, behaviours and technologies (Cleland and Wilson 1987). This lack of consensus reflects three main difficulties confronting any universal explanation (in addition to very considerable issues of data quality and measurement): (1) the wide heterogeneity of starting conditions at the onset of fertility decline with respect to levels of fertility, child survival, income per capita, labour force participation of women and children, educational enrolment, dependency levels and adult literacy; (2) the potential endogeneity of key explanatory variables (especially early life mortality); and (3) the coincidence of multiple profound economic and social changes accompanying fertility declines in all cases (Mason 1997; Guinnane 2011). The most notable factors common to nearly all fertility declines are the roles played by more affluent and more highly educated social groups, and urban populations, in leading declines. These patterns have been interpreted as supporting both economic and ideational models, but they are also consistent with a combination of economic motivations for some sub-populations and the wider diffusion of new norms or aspirations. Acceleration of the pace in fertility transition took place after the turn of the twentieth century in many European countries.

In the following sections, we will first take a brief look at pre-transition demography to see if early modern origins of the transition are found. Then we will focus on the early phase of mortality decline, exploring successive changes in cause-of-death patterns. Also explored is the mortality-income link. As causation is unlikely to have been one-way, whether or not the rise in life expectancy exerted a positive impact on long-term economic growth will be tested. Finally, we will set the issues in a broader conceptual framework. The most influential attempt to date to capture aspects of development additional to the standard measure of economic growth is the United Nations' concept of human development. Its human development index (HDI) combines indices of life expectancy at birth (e_0), educational attainment, and gross domestic product (GDP) per capita (UNDP 1990; Crafts 1997). Economic historians have extended this approach especially in the field of anthropometrics, where measures of stature have been used extensively to estimate the 'biological standard of living' in childhood. Since the 1950s these non-economic indices have been found to be correlated with income per capita (van Zanden et al. 2014: 253). Education, especially of women, has been assigned a critical role in driving life expectancy increases over the last half century (Lutz and Kebede 2018). Conversely, improvements in health and nutrition are also argued to have contributed to progressive improvements in cognitive capacities (Floud et al. 2011). As we demonstrate in this chapter, however, the relationships between GDP per capita, health, and educational attainment were positive but weaker in the past, in part because of the antagonistic effects of early urbanization on health and longevity.

Pre-Transition Demography and the Onset of Demographic Transition

Pre-transitional mortality patterns were characterized by relatively high volatility, caused by epidemic diseases and by subsistence crises usually accompanied by epidemic diseases. The onset of mortality decline was generally preceded by an attenuation of crises, with no necessary reduction in the average level of mortality. In England subsistence crises abated over the sixteenth and seventeenth centuries, but the average level of mortality rose, a phenomenon attributed to the progressive integration of the English economy, which promoted agricultural specialization and the efficient distribution of grain but also operated to speed the introduction and circulation of infectious diseases (Walter and Schofield 1989).

The frequency of famines declined markedly in western Europe as a whole after the mid-eighteenth century. There is no consensus on the roles played in this decline by market integration, climate warming, institutional changes, and the adoption of New World crops (most notably maize, which has been argued to have stabilized food supply in northern Italy as well as China, whereas potato monoculture was notoriously the proximate cause of the great Irish famine of 1845–49, and associated subsistence crises in northern and central Europe) (Flinn 1981; Alfani and Ó Gráda 2017; Deng and Sun 2019). Nonetheless the wider weakening and disappearance of mortality responses to short-term wage fluctuations was accompanied by substantial improvements in agricultural productivity in England and in Sweden (Allen 2000; Bengtsson 2004; Livi-Bacci 2012: table 4.2; Burnette 2014; Broadberry et al. 2015: table 3.2). At the other end of Eurasia, Japan's last nationwide famine took place as late as the 1830s. But the frequency of famine occasioned by drought had already begun declining from the early eighteenth century onwards, together with reduced variations in rice harvests. During the 125-year period from 1721, while population remained stationary, primary-sector output increased by one-third (Saito and Takashima 2016: table 12.2). It remains an open question whether the strong growth of the Chinese population after 1700 was driven by similar or pan-Eurasian factors (Deng and Sun 2019).

Another factor is epidemiological. As William McNeill set out in his *Plagues and Peoples*, the initial effect of increasing trade and urbanization was to raise mortality. The effects of sudden epidemiological integration are most evident in the massive die-offs associated with 'virgin soil' epidemics in the New World, but progressive integration also operated to raise infectious disease mortality in nineteenth-century India and parts of Africa (Doyle 2013; Dyson 2018). Urbanization contributed to rising mortality levels in England in the seventeenth and in the US in the early nineteenth century (Haines 2001). However, McNeill also argued that these initial rises in epidemic mortality were followed by a gradual process of accommodation between host and pathogen that involved a decline in pathogen virulence. Thus, as once-rare epidemic diseases became childhood diseases they also became less lethal (McNeill 1976; Kunitz 1983; Walter and Schofield 1989). This assumption was based on the recognition that pathogens that disable or kill their hosts are less likely to be transmitted to a new host. However, over the last thirty years this paradigm has been overturned, with the recognition of the complexity of selective forces operating on the determinants of virulence. In fact, for the most lethal diseases of the early modern period (smallpox, plague, typhus, typhoid, cholera, malaria, and yellow fever), there was no necessary selection for avirulence since they did not depend on ambulatory human victims for transmission. Crucially, though, these particularly lethal diseases are also relatively susceptible to the disruption of transmission by human interventions (quarantine, isolation, vaccination, control of insect vectors, and clean water supplies). Because these diseases were relatively lethal, crude but successful preventative measures against them produced disproportionately large gains in longevity (Davenport 2015). In other words, wherever a reduction of mortality volatility took place, it was due to the reduction in the frequency of epidemic outbreaks or the stabilization of harvests, or both.

Despite the gains in longevity made possible by the control of the most virulent diseases, reductions in mortality from less lethal but highly infectious diseases did not follow immediately. These less lethal diseases (childhood infections, respiratory and diarrhoeal pathogens) proved more difficult to control. They flourished in high-density populations and were fatal mainly to the young, the elderly, and the malnourished. Their high infectiousness and person-to-person transmission made prevention difficult, and therefore reductions in mortality required improvements in nutritional status (to increase resistance), sanitation, and personal hygiene. It is no surprise, therefore, that late nineteenth- and early twentieth-century reformers of public health focused on slum conditions as well as child and maternal health. The early stages of mortality decline thus involved a transition from a regime of relatively high adult mortality, with little distinction by wealth, to one in which mortality was increasingly concentrated at the extremes of life and amongst the poor. While it is initially surprising that socioeconomic differentials in mortality should have become more marked as subsistence crises diminished, studies of medieval and early modern crises indicate that the epidemics that often accompanied harvest failures were relatively egalitarian in effect, except when the rich had recourse to flight, as in the case of plague (Galloway 1987; Kelly and Ó Gráda 2014).

Pre-transition urban demography was migration-related and density-dependent. As mortality rates were higher in urban than in rural populations, urbanization acted to raise average mortality rates (the so-called urban graveyard effect), both through the redistribution of population to high mortality environments and, in the early stages, through increased circulation of infectious diseases via transport and trade networks. There, infant and child mortality was generally high, but recent immigrants of all ages also suffered high mortality because they encountered relatively lethal diseases against which they had acquired no immunity in childhood. Urban mortality rates therefore varied substantially depending on cultural habits (especially infant-feeding practices) and prevailing pathogens. What was at work in urban society, moreover, was in sharp contrast with the rural sector before the transition: urban mortality tended to rise when trade was brisk. As Richard

Smith has suggested, for an extremely 'open' society and economy like England in the seventeenth century, openness meant a greater exposure to pathogens imported from abroad, for their domestic circulation was intensified by urban growth (Smith 2001). Dramatic reductions in urban mortality were therefore essential to modern rates of urbanization (de Vries 1984; Dyson 2011).

Turning to the fertility side, with the striking exception of France where fertility decline was initiated in the early nineteenth century, and the US (Bailey and Hershbein 2018) it is likely that fertility generally rose in the first stage of demographic transition. In England fertility rose between 1750 and 1850 as a consequence both of higher marriage rates and of higher fertility within marriage. This rise in marital fertility coincided with falls in stillbirth and neonatal mortality rates, and probably reflected an improvement in living standards, especially in the availability of foodstuffs (Wrigley 2004; Woods 2009). Similar pre-transitional rises in fertility have been observed across the world regions – from nineteenth-century Europe and Japan to twentieth-century Asia, Latin America and Africa (Dyson and Murphy 1985; Saito 2014). These rises reflect a variety of proximate changes including improving adult survival and health, falls in breastfeeding and marriage booms, but generally suggest that 'fertility conditions in pre-modern societies more nearly approximate an excess demand situation than one of excess supply' (Easterlin 1978: 131).

While pre-transition fertility levels were well above what is now sufficient for 'replacement', they were far below theoretical biological maxima. Although most pre-modern societies were unplanned, 'natural' fertility populations, a variety of nuptial and other practices operated to modulate fertility levels. Where marriage ages were relatively high and not all women married, as was broadly the case in western and especially north-western Europe, then marriage practices could eliminate as much as half of the population's reproductive potential. However, fertility *within* marriage also varied considerably across world regions. For example, the average total marital fertility rate (TMFR), a standardized measure of the number of children born within marriage, for pre-transitional Japan, Korea, and rural China was 5.6, with a range of 5.8–5.3, while that for five European counterparts, England, France, Germany, Spain, and Sweden, stood at 8.1 with the range of 8.7–7.4 (Saito 2014: figure 12.1; note that England, the lowest in Europe, was higher than Japan, the highest in East Asia). *Total* fertility rates (taking into account married and unmarried women) were broadly similar in these societies, ranging between roughly 4 and 6 children per woman (Saito 2014). Therefore as argued by Hajnal (1965; 1982), in north-west European countries where the nuclear family system prevailed the gap between TFR and TMFR could be very wide, while in societies with more complex family systems the two measures tended to come closer. But even amongst west European countries there existed room for substantial variation in the level of 'natural' fertility before the transition.

The coincidence between a distinctive system of marriage and household formation and the areas in which modern economic growth first emerged has led a number of authors to argue that the north-west European marriage pattern (EMP) promoted economic growth. The EMP was characterized by late age at marriage, non-universal marriage, and neo-local household formation at marriage. These features, it is argued, reduced population pressure, and promoted female labour-force participation and mobility, and greater investments in human capital (Hajnal 1965: 132; de Moor and van Zanden 2010; Wrigley 2014; Carmichael et al. 2016). However, the association between marriage systems and economic performance is not straightforward. First, fertility of north-west European countries was not unusually low, despite late and non-universal marriage. Rather, evidence from a range of historical societies indicates that most populations exercised norms and behaviours that served to regulate family size and realized fertility, including abortion, infanticide, neglect, prolonged breastfeeding, adoption, sexual abstinence, and taboos against widow remarriage. Second, the level of female labour-force participation appears to have varied widely, depending on the extent to which women could combine childbearing with non-domestic work, which was constrained by the type of work available for females outside the home. In England for example, while employment of unmarried women was high, employment of married women contracted with the mechanization of spinning, and was concentrated by the mid-nineteenth century in a limited number of districts where textiles, straw-plaiting and lace-making offered jobs for female labour (You 2020). In Africa and Asia, by contrast, married women provided the bulk of agricultural labour, and therefore early and universal marriage was compatible with high female labour-force participation (e.g. Boserup 1970; Goody 1976); but there are cultures in which women's participation in productive work was discouraged, be it domestic production or paid work. In the Indian subcontinent, the south represents the former and the north the latter type (Dyson and Moore 1983). A similar contrast may be found between Japan and Korea in East Asia, but it is difficult to find an East Asian parallel to the contrast between western and eastern Europe (contra Wolf and Hanley 1985: 3–4; see Saito 2014). While female autonomy, however specified, *may* well have been conducive to economic growth, its effects did not necessarily operate through marriage patterns.

To sum up, first, the process of mortality decline tended to be much longer than previously thought. Second, there were cases in which fertility increased before the onset of modern fertility decline, suggesting that in those countries the burden of population pressure was further heightened. Third, the prolonged process of mortality decline meant that its effect on the burden of population pressure could have been a complex one. The 'pressure' is comprised of two components – one comes from the rising rate of growth and the other from the increasing dependency ratio. The issue of population pressure in the transition to modern economic growth is, therefore, more complex than has often been assumed.

Longevity and Economic Growth

The question about the link between mortality and income can be examined with reference to the Preston curve for earlier periods. Figure 12.1 plots life expectancies against GDP per capita in two time periods in the long nineteenth century. The 1850 sample consists of twelve countries, of which eight are European, two North American (Western offshoots), and two Asian, while the 1913 sample has more non-Western cases with fourteen European, four Western offshoots, two Asian and four Latin American. The statistical association was unambiguous in 1913 whereas it was not in 1850. It is not the inclusion of non-Western cases that disturbs the 1850 correlation. In fact, dispersion within Europe was considerable, suggesting that the correlation was weaker in earlier years, but the association evolved by 1913 (see also Riley 2007: table 12.3). This interpretation seems to be consistent with the two-stage hypothesis we put forward about mortality decline in the previous section: in the earlier stage of lethal epidemics income and wealth did not come to the fore as defining variables, and it was in the later stage of less lethal but more infectious diseases that the income-mortality link began to operate.

The next task is to check if the varied levels of longevity in 1850 had any influence on economic performance over the 1850–1913 period. Although none of the transition theorists framed the question in this way, there are grounds to believe that the reverse causation may have also been at work. One is that the gains in life expectancy over the same period were rather poorly correlated with the levels of GDP per capita in the initial year ($R = 0.33$, excluding India whose mortality transition had not started yet). The other is that given the

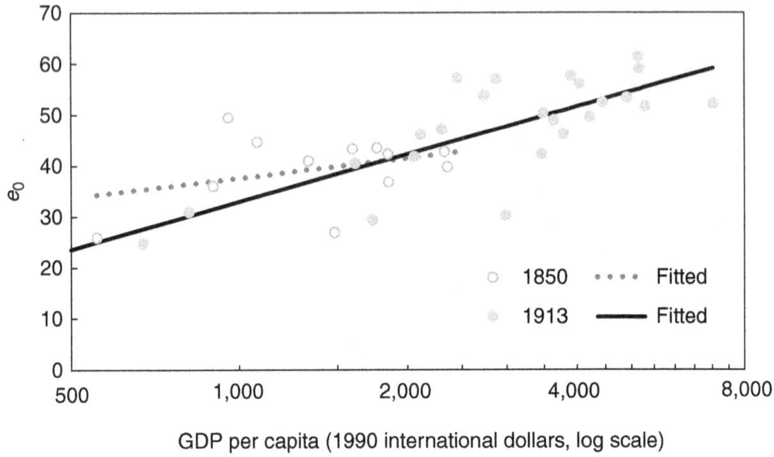

Figure 12.1 The Preston curves: real GDP per capita and life expectancy at birth (e_0) in 1850 and 1913

Sources and notes: Crafts (1997; 2002) and van Zanden et al. (2014), except for Japan's per capita GDP estimates, which are taken from Settsu et al. (2016): table A.9; and Saito and Takashima (2016): table 12.2.

Names of countries for which data are available, listed by benchmark year:

1913: Argentina, Australia, Austria, Belgium, Brazil, Canada, Chile, Denmark, Finland, France, Germany, India, Ireland, Italy, Japan, Mexico, the Netherlands, New Zealand, Norway, Spain, Sweden, Switzerland, the UK, the US (twenty-four countries).

1850: Belgium, Canada, Denmark, France, India, Italy, Japan, Netherlands, Norway, Sweden, the UK, the US (twelve countries).

When the fitted lines are drawn, per capita GDP is logarithmically transformed. *R* for 1850 is 0.345, and *R* for 1913 is 0.755.

premise that longevity is an important element for the formation of human capabilities (UNDP 1990), one can argue that in the period under review the causal link was from the initial level of life expectancy to the subsequent performance in economic growth. Figure 12.2 is a correlation diagram plotting twelve countries' average annual growth rates over the 1850–1913 period against their life expectancies in 1850. Ten plots come close to the fitted line. Of the ten, Norway and Sweden (far right) show the highest life expectancies while India and Italy (far left) are the lowest. In between there are six countries – Denmark, France, the UK, Belgium, the Netherlands, and Japan. Above the line are two Western offshoots, Canada and the US. Their life expectancies are intermediate, but because of an advantageous combination of resource abundance and better institutions, they enjoyed a 0.7-point higher growth performance. For both groups of countries, the regression line is

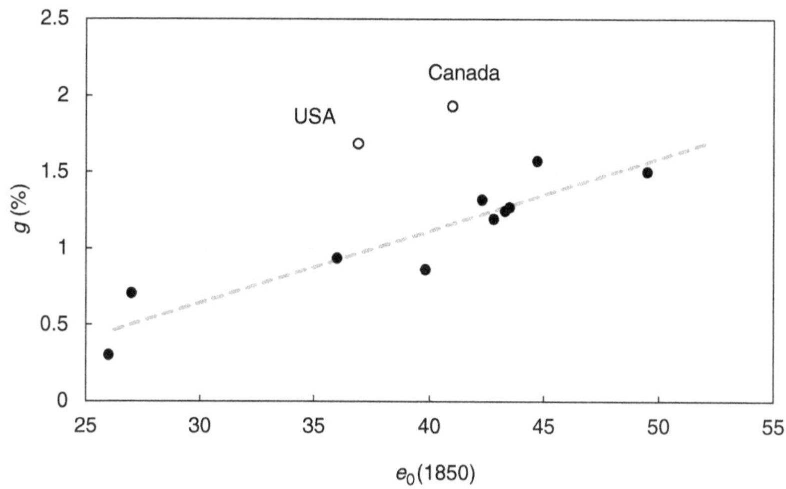

Figure 12.2 Life expectancy at birth (e_o) in 1850 and the average annual rate of growth in real GDP per capita (g) over the period 1850–1913.
Sources and notes: See Figure 12.1 above. The estimated regression equation is:
g = -0.778 + 0.047 e_o + 0.744 W-Offs; adjusted R^2 is 0.894 with N = 12.
All the coefficients are statistically significant at the 1 per cent level.

upward-rising; hence, this suggests that what happened to people's health before the mid-nineteenth century was crucial for the performance of modern economic growth in the industrialization period.

The attained level of GDP per capita must have had an effect on fertility change over time, and moreover, given the fact that the correlation between GDP per capita and the level of educational attainment (a weighted average of adult literacy and combined school enrolment) in 1870 is reasonably high (R = 0.748), the reduction in fertility must also have been influenced by the level of education in the initial period. Figure 12.3 looks at the former and Figure 12.4 at the latter relationship. In both graphs, Japan was the only nation where TFR was increasing, and India's was close to zero; Japan was in the middle of the period of pre-transition fertility increase, which was the stage yet to come for India. Among the other sixteen Western countries where fertility was on the decrease, it is evident that its decline was conditioned by the initial levels of income and educational attainment. Clearly, improved survival, despite its immediate effect being to enlarge the denominator of GDP per capita, generated further growth through its enhancement effect on people's physical and mental capabilities, which in turn exerted a promoting effect on fertility decline. While the fertility transition may not have been triggered by the

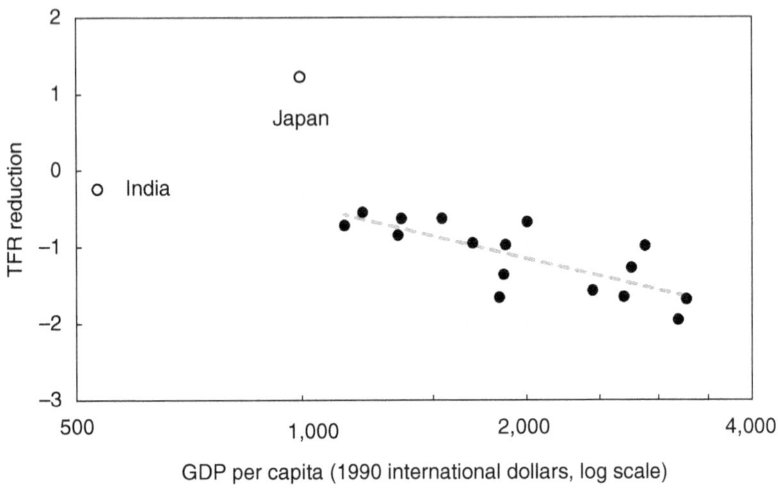

Figure 12.3 Real GDP per capita in 1870 and the reduction in total fertility rate (TFR), 1870–1913

Sources and notes: TFR estimates are taken from Gapminder.org, "Babies per woman (total fertility rate)", www.gapminder.org/data/. For GDP per capita, see Figure 12.1 above. *R* is 0.766 with *N* = 16 (as in Figure 12.4, Japan and India are excluded).

decline in mortality, changes initiated by the rise in life expectancy resulted eventually in the fertility transition, and this interpretation is consisted with what unified growth theory has postulated (Galor 2011).

Health Status and Labour Productivity

Falls in mortality are often but not always associated with improvements in population health. Where health did improve, initially through reduced exposure to disease and dearth, then such improvements could have increased productivity, through greater strength and endurance, enhanced cognitive capacities, and less time spent in ill health. Fogel and colleagues have gone so far as to argue that the process of economic development was one of 'technophysio-evolution', where gains in human physical and cognitive capacities drove gains in output that promoted further improvements in health in a virtuous spiral of increasing productivity (Floud et al. 2011). However, health need not improve in tandem with life expectancy, if the causes of mortality are acute diseases with few after-effects, or if increasing survival leaves more of the population in a state of debility.

The evidence for changes in population health derives mostly from anthropometric studies of adult male heights, data that become more

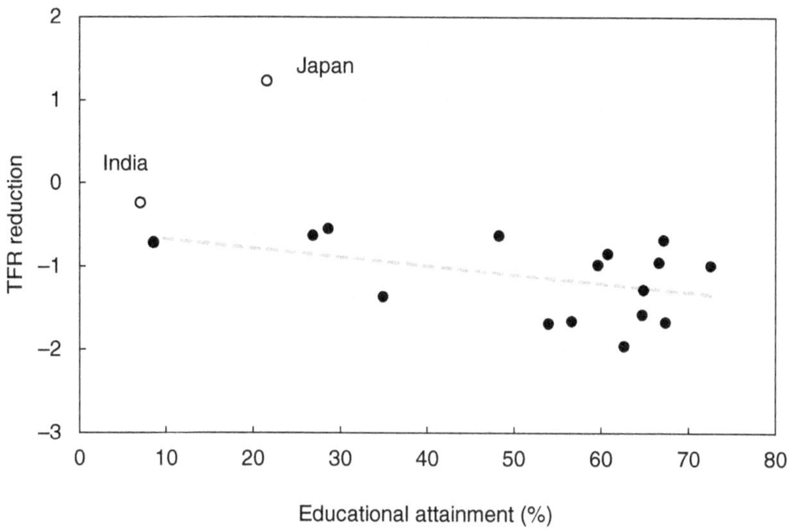

Figure 12.4 Educational attainment in 1870 and the reduction in total fertility rate (TFR), 1870–1913

Sources and notes: See Figure 12.3 above. Educational attainment is a weighted average of adult literacy (× 0.667) and combined school enrolment (× 0.333), and TFR reduction is defined as TFR in 1913 *minus* TFR in 1870. R is 0.423 with N = 16. Japan and India are excluded from computation since fertility decline in both countries had not begun by 1913.

abundant from the second half of the nineteenth century onwards. While individual heights are strongly affected by genetic factors, for large populations, inter-population variations in average adult heights are a (complex) outcome of maternal health and nutritional status in childhood. Nutritional status is determined by the quality and quantity of food intake, and energy demands arising from work and disease. In addition to sheer calorific intake, growth is sensitive to the intake of specific nutrients, especially protein and calcium, and heights may therefore differ also between populations because of ecological and economic factors affecting cattle–human ratios and access to milk, or as a result of dietary preferences (Baten and Blum 2014). The mean heights of populations may also vary according to their migrant composition, because heights of adult migrants reflect conditions in the area where they spent their childhood. Migrants may also be positively selected for tallness (Humphries and Leunig 2009; Baten et al. 2010).

In those European populations in which height data derive from conscript armies average adult male heights appear to have risen fairly steadily from at

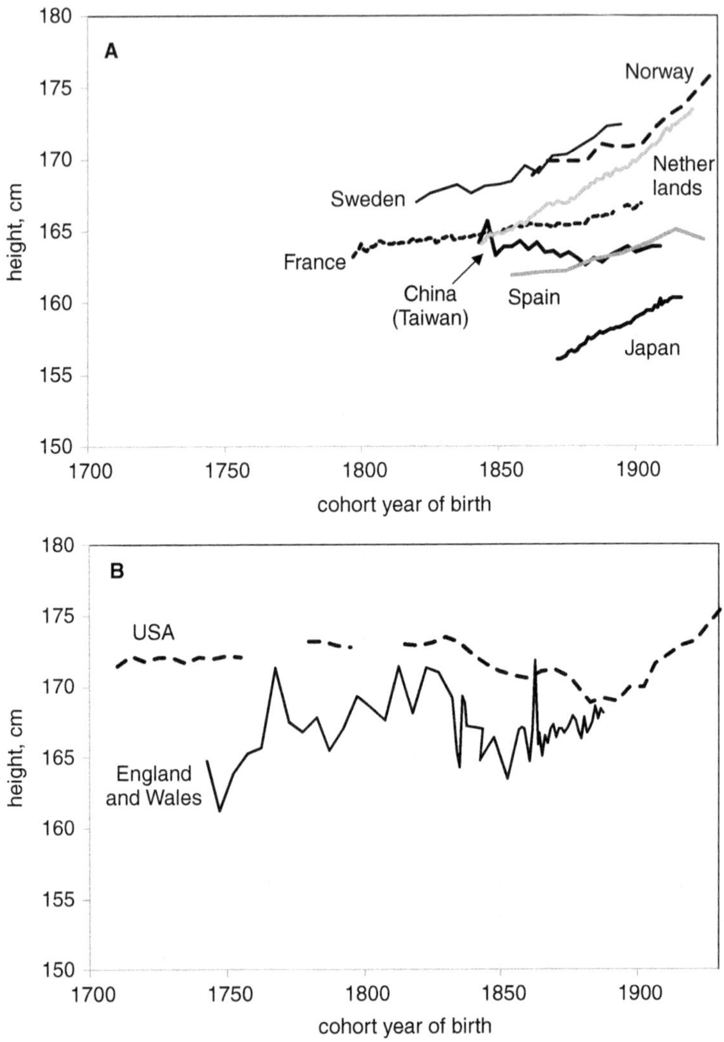

Figure 12.5 Estimated average adult male height, national populations, born 1710–1930
Sources: Steckel and Floud (1997: tables 5B.1, 9A.1, 9A.2); Floud et al. (1990: table 4.1); Fogel (1986: table 9.A.1); Hatton and Bray (2010: appendix 2); María-Dolores and Martínez-Carrión (2011: table 1); Olds (2003: table 3); Steckel and Floud (1997: table 4.1); Shay (1994).

least the mid-nineteenth century (Figure 12.5A). However, in Anglophone populations (Figure 12.5B) in which heights data derive mainly from volunteer armies, slaves (for the US), and prison populations, an initial advantage in stature in cohorts born before *c.*1830 was reversed for cohorts born between *c.*1830 and *c.*1850 (for the UK) or *c.*1830–90 (for the US). This reversal coincided with the onset of secular increases in real wages, and, it has been argued, indicates a trade-off between income and health during the Industrial Revolution, a phenomenon dubbed the 'industrialization puzzle' or the 'antebellum paradox'. In this scenario urbanization and industrialization were associated with increased exposure to infectious diseases, higher workloads, and reduced quality of diet. A compelling alternative explanation is that the composition of military volunteers fluctuated with alternative opportunities in the labour market, making military service or crime relatively unattractive when wages were buoyant (Bodenhorn et al. 2017). If this were indeed the case then the relatively tall stature of Anglophone recruits and criminals, despite their low social status, would suggest that the Anglophone populations from which military volunteers were drawn were indeed substantially taller than continental European populations throughout the nineteenth century. Such a conclusion would strengthen the observed relationship between GDP per capita and male heights in the nineteenth century, in which Anglophone samples otherwise present an anomaly (Baten 2000).

Few comparable data exist for non-European populations. Figure 12.5A includes data only for populations where the sampling process used to obtain height measurements was considered relatively unaffected by potential selection biases. Heights of the Chinese male population of Taiwan, measured under Japanese rule, showed some deterioration amongst cohorts born in the period after 1850, and no overall trend. The population consisted largely of relatively recent migrants from southern China, who may have been taller than the populations that they left. The Japanese data derive from military conscripts and indicates that the Japanese population was markedly shorter than European populations in the same period, but also experienced rapid growth during the period of rapid economic development after 1870.

Taken together, these data indicate that heights of conscripted males in a number of national populations rose in tandem with life expectancy, urbanization, and economic development in the second half of the nineteenth century, suggesting synergistic relationships between these variables (e.g. Steckel and Floud 1997). However, whether these positive relationships held before the mid-nineteenth century is unclear. Sources for the investigation of heights of cohorts born before the early to mid-nineteenth century are relatively fragmentary and liable to selection biases, which may explain some of the apparently trendless fluctuations in height in eighteenth-century populations. If we accept that the male populations of Britain and America were taller than their contemporaries by the early nineteenth century then it remains unclear when this advantage emerged. Americans enjoyed greater and more equitable access to food and land, and suffered lower exposure to infectious diseases as a consequence of isolation and low population densities. Britain, however, experienced rapid population growth and urbanization, factors expected to promote disease exposure and to dampen rises in per capita consumption. Nevertheless, as we have argued, mortality fell, especially in cities, and this together with increasing agricultural output and the safety net provided by the English poor laws may have improved population health despite apparently unpromising conditions. Two changes in particular are likely to have promoted gains in stature and health before the mid-nineteenth century.

First, although early declines in mortality benefited adults more than children, improvements in maternal health also conferred large benefits on very young infants. In England adult mortality, maternal mortality, stillbirths, and early neonatal mortality all fell in tandem across the eighteenth century, consistent with strong improvements in maternal health (Wrigley et al. 1997; Smith and Oeppen 2006; Woods 2009). This had important implications for stature and child development, because gestation is one of the most critical developmental periods, when insults *in utero* can result in premature birth or growth retardation with enduring negative consequences for height (Luo and Karleberg 2000; Cole 2003). The most important environmental effects on foetal development are maternal infection and severe nutritional deprivation, factors that changed markedly in the initial stages of the mortality transition. The recession of famines reduced the incidence of severe maternal nutritional deficits. Endemicization and the control of the more lethal diseases reduced the risk of infections in pregnancy, and also increased maternal immunity and therefore the transfer of passive acquired immunity against childhood diseases to the foetus, with protective effects in early infancy.

The second relevant effect of early mortality declines on adult heights is via their impact on survival prospects of rural-urban migrants. What slim historical evidence we have suggests that rural to urban migrants were generally positively selected for skills and probably height and robustness. However, before the dramatic reductions in urban mortality that commenced in the mid-eighteenth century in north-western Europe, migration to towns entailed a high mortality risk from diseases against which height and good nutritional status offered no protection (including plague, smallpox, typhus, and typhoid). Migration to towns therefore operated selectively to eliminate the most robust adults from the population. Conversely, declines in urban mortality reduced the trade-offs between longevity and wealth, and reduced negative selection against tallness and other positive migrant attributes, allowing the emergence of a positive association between health and longevity, with positive consequences for human capital formation.

The early gains in population health that we have outlined here were probably enough to counterbalance the malign effects of urbanization, at least in the early stages of industrialization in Britain. However, there may have been periods where the rapidity of urbanization outweighed improvements in health. A very common finding in research on stature is that urban populations were shorter than rural ones. This was the case for Britain, Sweden, the US, Australia, and Japan in the nineteenth century, although apparently not for parts of Germany and Spain (Floud et al. 1990: chapter 5; Shay 1994; Steckel and Floud 1997: chapters 4, 8, and 10; Baten 2009). At the national level the level of urbanization, it has been argued, explains much of the cross-sectional variation in height between countries (Steckel and Floud 1997: chapter 11). However, urbanization was no impediment to height gains in the late nineteenth century, and rapid rates of urbanization were associated with concomitant increases in stature, and a convergence (or crossover) between rural and urban heights. This waning of an urban height penalty is consistent with the progressive disappearance of excess urban mortality in these populations by the early twentieth century. According to our argument, the disappearance of the urban height penalty represents the final stage in a progressive reduction in rural-urban differentials in health and mortality that began for north-western European populations in the mid-eighteenth century. There may nonetheless have been periods of reversal. Life expectancy and infant mortality rates were relatively stagnant in England between 1820 and 1860, and worsened in the US, in association with rapid rates of urbanization in the early nineteenth century (Haines 2001). Woods (1985) attributed the British pattern to the extensive redistribution of the population from relatively healthy rural to unhealthy urban areas, against a backdrop of gradually improving mortality in most settlement types. In this case rapid population redistribution could have resulted in lower average stature even if rural-urban differentials in height were narrowing. This contrasts with fairly continuous improvements in life expectancy and infant mortality after 1750 in Sweden, where urbanization was negligible before the late nineteenth century (and where heights of conscripts rose monotonically for birth cohorts born after 1840).

Finally, adult heights reflect maternal health and living conditions in childhood, and may be an inadequate guide to *adult* health. Unfortunately, more direct evidence of trends in the health of adults is elusive. Sources that report sickness are difficult to interpret both because the sources are selective, and because ill health is subjective and may display what Johansson termed a 'cultural inflation of morbidity' (Johansson 1991). Drawing on evidence from working men's friendly societies (cooperative associations that provided sickness benefits and sometimes healthcare), Riley argued in his book *Sick not Dead* (1997) that mortality improvements in nineteenth-century Britain were associated with increasing levels of morbidity. Illnesses became less frequent, but the average length of sick spells increased. More recent work on similar sources, adjusted for age, has not supported Riley's (or Johansson's) conclusions (e.g. Harris et al. 2012).

Taken together, the evidence from adult male heights suggests both wide variation in nutritional status between populations, and substantial improvements in the economically most advanced countries over the course of the nineteenth century. It is likely that males in Britain and the Anglophone neo-Europes enjoyed a substantial advantage in height over other European populations by 1800. While heights should not be used as an absolute indicator of adult capacity in cross-country comparisons, the growth in adult male stature of nineteenth-century European populations suggests significant improvements in population health and therefore in human capital in this period. Improvements in urban mortality would have increased the returns to height and health, by reducing the risks of migration.

Conclusion

Not all economies that achieved economic growth during the period in question were characterized by invariably high mortality and fertility. The initial levels of the two varied considerably from culture to culture. But what was common to all those economies was the progressive impact that rising life expectancy and associated population growth exerted on the growth process, on the one hand, and on the demographic transition process from disorder to order and from waste to efficiency, on the other.

The immediate effect of the decline in mortality must have been a pressure on the standard of living since the resultant increase in total population tended to increase food prices and, hence, to decrease real wages while the worsened dependency ratio was another burden to the working population. Eventually, however, increased longevity resulted in better growth performance through its positive effects on population health and human capital accumulation. Moreover, the mortality transition was accompanied by shifts in major causes of death. When comparatively lethal infectious diseases were major killers, nutritional intake did not afford much protection. It was only when they were under control that a positive feedback between longevity and living standards started working – through increased nutrition and better public health services the state began to provide. In his seminal article Preston (1975) suggested that an increase in income accounted only for 16 per cent of the rise in life expectancy, but this positive effect is likely to have become a little clearer in later stages of the transition. Also likely is that the decline in mortality in general, and probably that in under-5 mortality in particular, led to fertility decline in later stages, although only after 1870.

We have characterized mortality declines before 1870 as a function of two overlapping processes. First, famine control and the consequent stabilization of mortality was often accompanied by increasing disease exposure (as a consequence of economic and epidemiological integration). Second, control of the most lethal diseases made towns in particular less dangerous and facilitated rapid urbanization. These two processes were sequential in England but overlapped elsewhere. Critically, these processes were a ubiquitous feature of demographic transition, occurring virtually everywhere before 1950. In parts of India, Africa, and Oceania mortality appears to have risen in the nineteenth century as a consequence of increasing trade and the impacts of colonization, and then underwent a very marked stabilization and decline in mortality after *c.*1920 as a consequence of control measures against both famine and the most lethal epidemic diseases (especially plague, smallpox, and cholera) (Doyle 2013: chapter 2; Dyson 2018). Similar measures were implemented slightly earlier in parts of Latin America. These improvements in survival were often associated with increases in fertility (and fecundity), and account for the very rapid rates of population growth evident in most developing country populations by 1950. Fertility declines were also more rapid in these populations than amongst the forerunners in the demographic transition (with some marked mainly sub-Saharan exceptions) and show similar variety with respect to levels of economic development.

References

Alfani, G. and Ó Gráda, C. (2017). *Famine in European History*, Cambridge University Press.

Allen, R. C. (2000). 'Economic Structure and Agricultural Productivity in Europe, 1300–1800', *European Review of Economic History*, 4, 1–26.

Bailey, M. and Hershbein, B. (2018). 'US Fertility Rates and Childbearing in American Economic History', in Cain, L. P., Fishback, P. V. and Rhode, P. W. (eds.), *The Oxford Handbook of American Economic History vol. 1*, Oxford University Press, 75–100.

Baten, J. (2000). 'Heights and Real Wages in the 18th and 19th Centuries: An International Overview', *Jahrbuch für Wirtschaftsgeschichte*, 41, 61–76.

(2009). 'Protein Supply and Nutritional Status in Nineteenth-Century Bavaria, Prussia and France', *Economics and Human Biology*, 7, 165–180.

Baten, J. and Blum, M. (2014). 'Why Are You So Tall While Others Are Short? Agricultural Production and Other Proximate Determinants of Global Heights', *European Review of Economic History*, 18, 144–165.

Baten, J., Ma, D., Morgan, S. and Wang, Q. (2010). 'Evolution of Living Standards and Human Capital in China in the 18th–20th Centuries: Evidence from Real Wages, Age-Heaping, and Anthropometrics', *Explorations in Economic History*, 47, 347–359.

Bengtsson, T. (2004). 'Mortality and Social Class in Four Scanian Parishes, 1766–1865', in Bengtsson, T., Campbell, C., Lee, J. Z. (eds.), *Life Under Pressure: Mortality and Living Standards in Europe and Asia, 1700–1900*, Cambridge, MA: MIT Press.

Bodenhorn, H., Guinnane, T. and Mroz, T. A. (2017). 'Sample-Selection Biases and the Industrialisation Puzzle', *Journal of Economic History*, 77, 171–207.

Boserup, E. (1970). *Woman's Role in Economic Development*, London: Allen & Unwin.

Broadberry, S., Campbell, B. M. S., Klein, A., Overton, M. and van Leeuwen, B. (2015). *British Economic Growth 1270–1870*, Cambridge University Press.

Burnette, J. (2014). 'Agriculture, 1700–1870', in Floud, R. and McCloskey, D. N. (eds.), *The Economic History of Britain since 1700, vol. 1: 1700–1870*, Cambridge University Press, 89–117.

Carmichael, S. G., de Pleijt, A., van Zanden, J. L. and De Moor, T. (2016). 'The European Marriage Pattern and its Measurement', *Journal of Economic History*, 76, 196–204.

Chesnais, J.-C. (1992). *The Demographic Transition. Stages, Patterns and Economic Implications*, Oxford: Clarendon Press.

Cleland, J. and Wilson, C. (1987). 'Demand Theories of the Fertility Transition: An Iconoclastic View', *Population Studies*, 41, 5–30.

Cole, T. J. (2003). 'The Secular Trend in Human Physical Growth: A Biological View', *Economics and Human Biology*, 1, 161–168.

Crafts, N. F. R. (1997). 'The Human Development Index and Changes in Standards of Living: Some Historical Comparisons', *European Review of Economic History*, 1, 299–322.

(2002). 'The Human Development Index, 1870–1999: Some Revised Estimates', *European Review of Economic History*, 6, 395–405.

Davenport, R. J. (2015). 'The First Stages of the Mortality Transition in England: A Perspective from Evolutionary Biology', Centre for Competitive Advantage in the Global Economy (CAGE) Working Paper, University of Warwick.

Demeny, P. (1972). 'Early Fertility Decline in Austria-Hungary: A Lesson in Demographic Transition', in Glass, D. V. and Revelle, R. (eds.), *Population and Social Change*, London: Edward Arnold, 153–172.

de Moor, T. and van Zanden, J. L. (2010). 'Girl Power: The European Marriage Pattern and Labour Markets in the North Sea Region in the Late Medieval and Early Modern Period', *Economic History Review*, 63, 1–33.

de Vries, J. (1984). *European Urbanization 1500–1800*, London: Methuen.
Deng, K. and Sun, S. (2019). 'China's Extraordinary Population Expansion and its Determinants during the Qing Period, 1644–1911', *Population Review*, 58, 20–77.
Doyle, S. (2013). *Before HIV: Sexuality, Fertility and Mortality in East Africa, 1900–1980*, Oxford University Press.
Dyson, T. (2011). 'The Role of the Demographic Transition in the Process of Urbanization', *Population and Development Review*, 37, S1, 34–54.
(2018). *A Population History of India*, Oxford University Press.
Dyson, T. and Moore, M. (1983). 'On Kinship Structure, Female Autonomy, and Demographic Behaviour in India', *Population and Development Review*, 9, 35–60.
Dyson, T. and Murphy, M. (1985). 'The Onset of Fertility Transition', *Population and Development Review*, 11, 399–440.
Easterlin, R. A. (1978). 'The Economics and Sociology of Fertility: A Synthesis', in Tilly, C. (ed.), *Historical Studies of Changing Fertility*, Princeton University Press, 57–113.
Flinn, M. W. (1981). *The European Demographic System, 1500–1820*, Baltimore: Johns Hopkins University Press.
Floud, R., Wachter, K. and Gregory, A. (1990). *Height, Health and History: Nutritional Status in the United Kingdom, 1750–1980*, Cambridge University Press.
Floud, R., Fogel, R.W., Harris, B. and Hong, S. C. (2011). *The Changing Body: Health, Nutrition, and Human Development in the Western World since 1700*, Cambridge University Press.
Fogel, R. W. (1986). 'Nutrition and the Decline in Mortality since 1700: Some Preliminary Findings', in Engerman, S. L. and Gallman. R. E. (eds.), *Long-Term Factors in American Economic Growth*, University of Chicago Press, 439–555.
Galloway, P. R. (1987). 'Differentials in Demographic Responses to Annual Price Variations in Pre-Revolutionary France', *European Journal of Population*, 2, 269–305.
Galor, O. (2011). *Unified Growth Theory*, Princeton University Press.
Goody, J. (1976). *Production and Reproduction: A Comparative Study of the Domestic Domain*, Cambridge University Press.
Guinnane, T. (2011). 'The Historical Fertility Transition: A Guide for Economists', *Journal of Economic Literature*, 49, 589–614.
Haines, M. R. (2001). 'The Urban Mortality Transition in the United States, 1800–1940', *Annales de Démographie Historique*, 101, 33–64.
Hajnal, J. (1965). 'European Marriage Patterns in Perspective', in Glass, D. V. and Eversley, D. E. C. (eds.), *Population in History*, London: Edward Arnold, 101–143.
(1982). 'Two Kinds of Pre-Industrial Household Formation System', *Population and Development Review*, 8, 449–494.
Harris, B. (2004). 'Public Health, Nutrition, and the Decline of Mortality: The McKeown Thesis Revisited', *Social History of Medicine*, 17, 379–407.
Harris, B., Gorsky, M., Guntupalli, A. M. and Hinde, A. (2012). 'Long-Term Changes in Sickness and Health: Further Evidence from the Hampshire Friendly Society', *Economic History Review*, 65, 719–745.
Hatton, T. J. and Bray, B. E. (2010). 'Long Run Trends in the Heights of European Men, 19th–20th Centuries', *Economics and Human Biology*, 8, 405–413.

Humphries, J. and Leunig., T. (2009). 'Was Dick Whittington Taller Than Those He Left Behind? Anthropometric Measures, Migration and the Quality of Life in Early Nineteenth-Century London?', *Explorations in Economic History*, 46, 120–131.

Johansson, S. R. (1991). 'The Health Transition: The Cultural Inflation of Morbidity during the Decline of Mortality', *Health Transition Review*, 1, 39–68.

Kelly, M. and Ó Gráda, C. (2014). 'Living Standards and Mortality since the Middle Ages', *Economic History Review*, 67, 358–381.

Kunitz, S. J. (1983). 'Speculations on the European Mortality Decline', *Economic History Review*, 36, 349–364.

Kuznets, S. (1979). 'Population Trends and Modern Economic Growth: Notes Towards a Historical Perspective', in *Growth, Population and Income Distribution: Selected Essays*, New York: W. W. Norton.

Lesthaegue, R. (2014). 'The Second Demographic Transition: A Concise Overview of its Development', *Proceedings of the National Academy of Sciences of the United States of America*, 111, 18112–18115.

Livi-Bacci, M. (2012). *A Concise History of World Population*, 5th ed., Chichester: Wiley-Blackwell.

Luo, Z. C. and Karleberg, J. (2000). 'Critical Growth Phases for Adult Shortness', *American Journal of Epidemiology*, 152, 125–131.

Lutz, W. and Kebede, E. (2018). 'Education and Health: Redrawing the Preston Curve', *Population and Development Review*, 44, 343–361.

McKeown, T. (1976). *The Modern Rise of Population*, London: Edward Arnold.

McKeown, T. and Record, R. G. (1962). 'Reasons for the Decline of Mortality in England and Wales during the Nineteenth Century', *Population Studies*, 16, 94–122.

McNeill, W. H. (1976). *Plagues and Peoples*, New York: Anchor.

María-Dolores, R. and Martínez-Carrion, J. M. (2011). 'The Relationship Between Height and Economic Development in Spain, 1850–1958', *Economics and Human Biology*, 9, 30–44.

Mason, K. O. (1997). 'Explaining Fertility Transition', *Demography*, 34, 443–454.

Olds, K. (2003). 'The Biological Standard of Living in Taiwan Under Japanese Occupation', *Economic and Human Biology*, 1, 187–206.

Preston, S. H. (1975). 'The Changing Relation Between Mortality and Level of Economic Development', *Population Studies*, 29, 231–248.

Riley, J. C. (1997). *Sick not Dead: The Health of British Working Men During the Mortality Decline*, Baltimore: Johns Hopkins University Press.

(2007). *Low Income, Social Growth, and Good Health: A History of Twelve Countries*, Berkeley: University of California Press.

Saito, O. (2014). 'Demographic Regimes in the Asian Past', Paper presented at the Conference to celebrate the 50th Anniversary of the Founding of the Cambridge Group for the History of Population and Social Structure, Downing College, Cambridge.

Saito, O. and Takashima, M. (2016). 'Estimating the Shares of Secondary- and Tertiary-Sector Outputs in the Age of Early Modern Growth: The Case of Japan, 1600–1874', *European Review of Economic History*, 20, 368–386.

Settsu, T., Bassino, J.-P. and Fukao, K. (2016). 'Revisiting Economic Growth in Meiji Japan: Industrial Structure, Labour Productivity and Regional Inequality [in Japanese]', *Economic Review*, 67, 193–214.

Shay, T. (1994). 'The Level of Living in Japan, 1885–1938: New Evidence', in *Stature, Living Standards, and Economic Development. Essays in Anthropometric History*, in Komlos, J. (ed.), University of Chicago Press, 173–204.

Smith, R. M. (2001). 'Plagues and Peoples. The Long Demographic Cycle, 1215–1670', in Slack, P. and Ward, R. (eds.), *The Peopling of Britain: The Shaping of a Human Landscape*, Oxford University Press, 177–210.

Smith, R. M. and Oeppen, J. (2006). 'Place and Status as Determinants of Infant Mortality in England *c.*1550–1837', in Garrett, E., Galley, C., Shelton, N. and Woods, R. (eds.), *Infant Mortality: A Continuing Social Problem*, Aldershot: Ashgate, 53–78.

Steckel, R. H. and Floud, R. (eds.) (1997). *Health and Welfare During Industrialisation*, University of Chicago Press.

Szreter, S. (1988). 'The Importance of Social Intervention in Britain's Mortality Decline, *c.*1850–1914: A Re-Interpretation of the Role of Public Health', *Social History of Medicine*, 1, 1–37.

United Nations Development Programme (UNDP) (1990). *Human Development Report*, Oxford University Press.

van Zanden, J. L., Baten, J., d'Ercole, M. M., Rijpma, A., Smith, C. and Timmer, M. (eds.). (2014). *How Was Life? Global Well-Being since 1820*, Paris: OECD Publishing and International Institute of Social History.

Walter, J. and Schofield, R. (1989). 'Famine, Disease and Crisis Mortality in Early Modern Society', in Walter, J. and Schofield, R. (eds.), *Famine, Disease and Social Order in Early Modern Society*, Cambridge University Press, 1–74.

Wolf, A. P. and Hanley, S. B. (1985). 'Introduction', in Hanley, S. B. and Wolf, A. P. (eds.), *Family and Population in East Asian History*, Stanford University Press, 3–4.

Woods, R. (1985). 'The Effect of Population Redistribution on the Level of Mortality in Nineteenth-Century England and Wales', *Journal of Economic History*, 45, 645–651.

(2000). *The Demography of Victorian England and Wales*, Cambridge University Press.

(2009). *Death Before Birth: Fetal Health and Mortality in Historical Perspective*, Oxford University Press.

Wrigley, E. A. (2004). 'Explaining the Rise in Marital Fertility in the "Long" Eighteenth Century', in Wrigley, E. A. (ed.), *Poverty, Progress and Population*, Cambridge University Press, 317–350.

(2014). 'European Marriage Patterns and Their Implications', in Briggs, C., Kitson, P. M. and Thompson, S. J. (eds.), *Population, Welfare and Economic Change in Britain 1290–1834*, Woodbridge, Suffolk: Boydell.

Wrigley, E. A., Davies, R. S., Oeppen, J. E. and Schofield, R. S. (1997). *English Population History from Family Reconstitution 1580–1837*, Cambridge University Press.

You, X. (2020). 'Women's Labour Force Participation in Nineteenth-Century England and Wales: Evidence from the 1881 Census Enumerators' Books', *Economic History Review*, 73(1), 106–133.

13

Proximate Sources of Growth: Capital and Technology, 1700–1870

ALESSANDRO NUVOLARI AND MASAYUKI TANIMOTO

Introduction

This chapter is concerned with two fundamental drivers of the process of 'modern economic growth': capital accumulation and technical change. Economists dealing with contemporary data routinely provide decompositions of rates of economic growth, sorting out the relative contributions of these two 'proximate' sources. It turns out that major data limitations prevent the systematic implementation of standard growth accounting exercises of this kind to the period before 1870. The approach of this chapter will be therefore less sanguine and more circumspect. We shall try to provide an appraisal of the role played by capital accumulation and technical change by pulling together heterogeneous sources and pieces of evidence. Whenever possible, we shall try to back up our reconstruction of historical trends of capital accumulation and technical progress with qualitative accounts.

Broadly speaking, there are two opposing interpretations of the dynamics of world economic growth before the Industrial Revolution, which, for convenience sake, can be labelled as the Malthusian and Smithian accounts (Broadberry et al. 2015: 266–278). The Malthusian account, most eloquently articulated by Clark (2007), argues that before the Industrial Revolution all societies were characterized by overall stagnation in income per capita, with no steady growth. In this context, cross-country variations in income per capita were, by and large, accounted for by demographic factors. The Smithian perspective contends that, notwithstanding the powerful limitations exerted by resource constraints and the rudimentary state of technology, it was still possible for some successful pre-industrial economies such as Holland and England after 1500 to experience substantial phases of economic

We would like to thank Steve Broadberry, Nick Crafts, Giovanni Federico, and Kyoji Fukao for useful comments, and Bob Allen for sharing data.

growth, albeit at very low rates (e.g. 0.2–0.3 per cent per year of per capita gross domestic product [GDP]).[1] Since the most sophisticated versions of the modern Malthusian model contemplate some technical change (which in the long run is progressively 'reabsorbed' by growing population), it is difficult to discriminate empirically between the two perspectives.

Be this as it may, it is interesting to remark that both the Malthusian and Smithian perspectives suggest a very similar 'stylized' characterization of the structural transformation of the production process taking place at the beginning of modern economic growth (Hansen and Prescott 2002). In a nutshell, in most of the literature (assuming for sake of simplicity a Cobb-Douglas specification), a pre-industrial economy is characterized by an aggregate production function of this kind:

$$Q = AT^{\alpha}L^{1-\alpha} \text{with } 0 < \alpha < 1 \tag{1}$$

In equation (1), Q is aggregate output, A is the level of technology, T represents land and natural resources and L is the labour input in the production process (measured, for example, using the number of workers). This representation of the production process, clearly, reflects the notion that agricultural goods and related products accounted for the predominant share of the output of pre-industrial societies. Land is a fixed factor. Hence, as population grows, diminishing returns set in. Remarkably, in this specification, the accumulation of physical capital does not even feature explicitly in the production function, while technical change is assumed to be characterized by very sluggish and sporadic advances.[2] In other words, neither capital accumulation nor technical change is regarded as a significant driver of economic growth for pre-industrial economies.

For industrial economies, the most common characterization of the production process is instead the production function of the standard Solow growth model:

1 According to the estimates of Fukao et al. (2017: 285) for the period 1721–1846 Japan also experienced a growth rate of about 0.2–0.25 per cent annually. Despite the lack of significant indigenous technological change, the assimilation of technologies originating from China and Korea raised the overall level of production throughout Japan's archipelago (Tanimoto, forthcoming).

2 For recent contributions using this type of characterization of the production process for pre-industrial economies, see Voigtlander and Voth (2009) and Ashraf and Galor (2011). Non-Malthusian and Smithian approaches tend, however, to favour a two-sector modelling approach (Persson 1988). Interestingly enough, even disaggregated sectoral models of pre-industrial growth abstract from including capital in the production function, see Sharp et al. (2012) and Kelly (1997).

$$Q = AK^{\alpha}L^{1-\alpha} \text{again with } 0 < \alpha < 1 \qquad (2)$$

In equation (2), K is the stock of physical capital. In this representation of the production process, physical capital features explicitly as a factor of production, alongside labour, whereas the role played by land and natural resources is completely overlooked.[3] Furthermore, technical change is no longer regarded as sluggish and sporadic, but rather, in most empirical growth accounting exercises, it turns out to be the key driver of growth in income per capita.

In this framework, a fundamental transformation in the mechanics of the growth process lies at the heart of the transition from a pre-industrial economy to 'modern economic growth'. This amounts to a major shift in the relative contributions of the proximate sources of economic growth, with capital accumulation and technical change playing a relative minor role before the Industrial Revolution and becoming the fundamental drivers of economic growth thereafter.

This characterization of the transition to 'modern economic growth' is a very crude summary picture, whose purpose is to stress the fundamental differences between modern economic growth and pre-industrial economic systems. A more articulated depiction, which takes into account that land and natural resources are not simply 'given' but require significant investments for being appropriated, maintained and developed was suggested by Angus Maddison (1982) and is represented in Table 13.1.

Maddison's more detailed characterization of the production process in different economic epochs highlights two important points. The first is that the emphasis on capital accumulation as a distinctive feature of modern economic growth, which emerges from the 'Malthus to Solow' meta-narrative, should not lead us to neglect the major investments in the 'augmentation' and development of land and other natural resources that were carried out in many pre-industrial societies. The second is that the emergence of modern economic growth should not be regarded as a sudden shift, but as a more gradual culmination of a number of progressive changes in the quality of the inputs of the production process and in their interaction.

3 The exclusion of land from the aggregate production function used to describe economic growth since the industrial economies is essentially motivated by the fact that farmland rents represent a very small share of income in modern economies and for this reason the contribution of variations in the input of land to economic growth is bound to be relatively insignificant (Clark 2007: 198–200).

Table 13.1 The production process in six economic epochs

Epoch	Production function
Pre-Agrarian (hunting and gathering) societies	Q=F(A,T, L)
Agrarianism	Q=F(A,T',L', K)
Ancient imperialism (Egypt, Rome, China)	Q=F(A',T',L'',K') + p
Reversion to agrarianism (Middle Ages)	Q=F(A',T',L',K)
Advancing agrarianism (1500–1650)	Q=F(A',T',L',K')
Merchant capitalism (1650–1750)	Q=F(A',T',L'',K'') +p'
Modern economic growth (1700–1870)	Q=(A'',T'',L''',K''')+p''

Sources and notes: Q=output
A= technical progress (residual), essentially serendipitous; A'= technical change driven by scale effects and learning by doing; A''= technical change driven by systematic search for innovations
T=land and natural resources; T'= land and natural resources appropriated and maintained, T''=land and natural resources developed and augmented
K= moderate stock of working capital; K'= K + investment in infrastructure (roads, aqueducts and urban facilities); K''=K' but capital deepening more significant; K'''= working capital+fixed capital. Investment (replacement, widening, deepening) in all types of capital (connection between investment and embodied technical change)
L=raw labour; L'= labour force with a modicum of skills; L''= labour force with a modicum of skills and specialization; L'''= labour force comprising some formal education and on-the-job training
p= plunder (unrequited levies on products and manpower in colonized areas); p'= plunder augmented by monopolistic trade; p''=residual or negative plunder.
Adapted from Maddison (1982: 5).

The Changing Nature of Capital Accumulation

The role played by fixed capital goods in the production processes of pre-industrial economies was fairly limited. Most production processes were extremely rudimentary in technological terms, using relatively simple tools and equipment. Furthermore, these tools and equipment were not particularly expensive. Thus, according to Hicks, in pre-industrial economies, working or circulating capital, in the form of raw materials, intermediate goods, and finished goods, played such an overwhelming, dominant role, that one can indeed define industrialization as a process in which 'the range of fixed capital goods that were used in production . . . began noticeably to increase. It was not simply an increase in capital accumulation, but an increase in the *range and variety* of the fixed capital goods in which investment was embodied' (Hicks 1969: 142–143, italics in the text).

Table 13.2 Number and power of European waterwheels, 1200–1800

Year	Number of waterwheels	Average power (HP)	HP per capita
1200	300,000	2	0.008
1800	750,000	3	0.012

Source: Makkai (1981: 178).

Cipolla (1976: 80–91) argued, that in general terms, Hicks' notion of the Industrial Revolution as a shift from circulating to fixed capital, was broadly correct and it probably touched upon a particularly significant dimension of the industrialization process. However, Cipolla also noticed that, since the Middle Ages, the European economy had been already characterized by an expansionary drive in certain forms of fixed capital. This preliminary phase of accumulation represented an important base from which the subsequent industrialization spurt was launched in the eighteenth century.[4] First, there was a significant expansion in construction of water- and windmills. Cipolla estimated that, by the end of the eighteenth century in Europe, there were more than half a million watermills (Cipolla 1976: 81). More recent estimates of the expansion in the number and power of waterwheels provided by Makkai (1981) reported in Table 13.2 confirm the expansion in waterwheels highlighted by Cipolla. Other quantification exercises seem even to suggest a more rapid increase (Reynolds 1983: 123–125; Kander et al. 2013: 69 suggests that it is not far-fetched to estimate that in the eighteenth century the number of waterwheels had reached 1 million). Makkai's estimate of the power output of watermills around 1800 is probably also too low: according to Reynolds, the average power of eighteenth-century waterwheels was between 5 and 7 HP (Reynolds 1983: 174). Concerning windmills, Kander et al. (2013: 69) suggest that in the eighteenth century their number was likely to range from 30,000 to 100,000 (their estimate for the total number of windmills in France, England, Germany, the Netherlands, Belgium, and Finland is 50,000–60,000). Notably, alongside this expansion of prime movers, Kander et al. (2013: 79) suggest that pre-industrial Europe was plausibly characterized by significantly higher energy consumption than other contemporary agrarian civilizations. They put forward three possible factors for the emergence of a peculiar European

4 These trends in capital accumulation were coupled with significant streams of technological improvements, see MacLeod and Nuvolari (2012).

energy consumption pattern: 1) the colder climate, which resulted in a higher fuel consumption; 2) the more intensive use of higher-yield cereals and tubers outside Europe, which allowed a lower per capita surface for ensuring the reproduction of population; 3) the relative scarcity of pastures outside Europe. According to Kander et al. (2013: 79), pre-industrial Europe was probably characterized by a per capita consumption of energy of about 63–84 MJ (15–20,000 kcal), whereas non-European civilizations were probably characterized by per capita consumption of around 21–42 MJ (5–10,000 kcal).

The second distinctive trend in 'fixed' capital accumulation in Europe pointed out by Cipolla is the growth of farm livestock. Broadberry et al. (2015: 388–389) recently revived this theme by highlighting that the substantial endowment of livestock could have played an important role in the economic success of the North Sea regions of Europe in the early modern period. The growth of livestock (especially horses) meant a more capital-intensive agriculture, also characterized by an intensive use of non-human energy, focused on the production of relatively high value products that required more processing. In contrast, major irrigation infrastructures played a central role as agrarian fixed capital in enhancing land productivity in rice-cropping areas such as Japan. In fact, the number of dike facilities increased by 4.38 times between the 1740s and 1830s in the *Bōchō* region in the western part of Japan's archipelago, whereas the number of livestock increased only by 1.25 times (Akimoto 1987: 186).

A third important trend in pre-industrial fixed capital accumulation was the expansion of the European merchant fleet. Table 13.3 sets out some tentative estimates by van Zanden, suggesting a growth from 200,000 tons in 1500 to more than 3,000,000 tons in 1780, which amounts to almost a tenfold increase in per capita terms. This trend was also coupled with a significant expansion of military navies, spurred by the endemic conflict between European states.

Table 13.3 The west European merchant fleet

Year	Total fleet (thousand tons)	Tonnage per inhabitant
1500	200–250	3.2–4
1600	600–700	7.7–9
1670	1,000–1,100	12.8–14.1
1780	3,372	30.7

Source: van Zanden (2001: 82).

John Brewer (1988: 34–35) has aptly noticed that ships of the line were possibly the most expensive 'capital goods' of the eighteenth century. In terms of outlays they costed between £30,000 and £60,000, vastly exceeding that of the largest industrial plants of the time. By comparison, a coke blast furnace at the end of the eighteenth century cost about £4,000 (Davies and Pollard 1988: 96), while a fully equipped Arkwright-type mill for cotton spinning cost about £3,000 (Chapman and Butt 1988: 106).

These figures also suggest that the fixed capital requirements of the new technologies of the First Industrial Revolution were not particularly expensive. These modest capital requirements account for the relative ease with which English businessmen and entrepreneurs were able to fund their innovative investments. Hence, even if one can notice important limitations in English banking, financing, and company legislation that could have potentially exerted an inhibiting effect on savings and investment, there is abundant evidence that local ('country') banks, partnerships combining innovators with businessmen with credit connections, in combination with internal sources ('ploughed-back profits') were in most cases sufficient to provide the capital resources necessary to start and expand firms and other ventures using new technologies (Crouzet 1972).[5]

In comparative perspective, the English approach to financing investment during the Industrial Revolution remained somewhat idiosyncratic, providing support for Gerschenkron's notion that latecomer countries had to resort to a number of institutional innovations such as 'mixed banks' or 'investment banks' for recruiting funds and channelling them into manufacturing investment. By and large, this outcome was due to an increasing trend in capital requirements and in capital intensities and in the scale of operations that emerged as an important feature of the technological trajectories of the First Industrial Revolution (Allen 2012).

Tables 13.4 and 13.5 provide a synthetic perspective on the transformation of the structure of the capital stock in England from 1760 to 1860 using the statistical reconstruction of Feinstein (1988).[6] Concerning Table 13.4, the point that merits attention is the shift in the structure of the capital stock from agriculture to manufacturing and services (railways, transport, and gas/electricity). In Table 13.5, the key-point is obviously the growth of the share of

5 Brunt (2006) shows that, in many instances, English 'country banks' operated as *ante-litteram* venture capitalists.

6 Broadberry and de Pleijt are currently working at new estimates of capital stock for Britain for the period 1270–1870. For some preliminary results see Broadberry and de Pleijt (2018).

Table 13.4 Structure of capital stock (percentage share) in Great Britain by sector, 1760–1870

Year	Agriculture	Mining and quarrying	Manufacturing	Gas, water, and electricity	Distribution and other services	Railways	Other transport	Public services	Dwellings	Total (millions of current £)
1760	36.82	0.42	7.11	0.00	9.21	0.00	8.37	9.62	28.45	239
1800	31.86	0.51	9.20	0.00	10.39	0.00	12.78	8.35	26.92	587
1830	22.75	0.98	12.06	0.49	11.76	0.20	12.55	7.55	31.67	1,020
1850	18.31	1.21	14.55	1.34	9.99	10.26	10.60	6.44	27.30	1,491
1870	15.92	1.57	17.28	2.83	8.01	14.31	10.16	5.97	23.94	2,795

Source: Feinstein (1988: 433).

Table 13.5 Structure of capital stock (percentage share) in Great Britain by type of asset, 1760–1870

	Buildings (dwellings and industrial and commercial buildings)	Plant, machinery, and equipment	Rolling stock and vehicles	Ships	Total (millions of current £)
1760	85.36	10.88	1.26	2.51	239
1800	82.11	12.78	1.36	3.75	587
1830	84.66	10.82	1.18	3.34	1,020
1850	82.90	12.61	1.88	2.62	1,491
1870	77.10	16.71	2.90	3.29	2,795

Source: Feinstein (1988: 435).

capital invested in plant and machinery. However, as Field (1985) has remarked, it is also worth noting that even in the second half of the nineteenth century the lion's share of the structure of the capital stock was represented by buildings.

It is instructive to compare Tables 13.4 and 13.5 with the estimates of the capital structure in Japan in 1878 by Ohkawa et al. (1966: 148, 152). In this case, the breakdown of gross capital stock into industrial sectors in 1878 shows that the primary sector accounted for 73.9 per cent and non-primary industries 26.1 per cent. Machinery and equipment represented only 3.8 per cent of the entire capital stock of non-primary industries. Thus, the structure of the capital stock in mid-nineteenth century Japan was concentrated largely in the agrarian sector, not in industry, so that the overall pattern of capital accumulation was still characterized by relatively limited investments in machinery.

Table 13.6, taken from Feinstein (2003), reports estimates of investment as a share of gross national product in a group of selected countries. Overall, Table 13.6 shows a common pattern of growth in the share of investment from the relatively low pre-industrial levels (which Rostow and Lewis hypothesized to be around 5 per cent of income) up to levels around 15–20 per cent, which is the range that most countries had reached by 1913.

The Maddison project has provided a fundamental contribution to the reconstruction of comprehensive historical series of GDP per capita at the national level, paying particular attention to the issue of the comparability over time and across countries (Bolt and van Zanden 2014). In this respect, for the period 1700–1870, statistical comparative reconstructions of long run patterns of capital accumulation have not witnessed the same progress.

Table 13.6 Investment as share (percentage) of gross national product in selected countries, 1770–1913

Years	United Kingdom	United States	France	Germany	Italy	Sweden	Denmark	Spain	Japan	Russia	Australia	Canada
1770–1800	4	8										
1800–09	7	8										
1810–19	13	8										
1820–29	13	8	11									
1830–39	8	8	11									
1840–49	10	16	13									
1850–59	10	20	16	14				5				
1860–69	12		17	18	7	9		8			7	
1870–79	13	18	12	20	8	11	10	8			11	9
1880–89	13	18	15	18	10	8	7	9	14	13	10	10
1890–99	12	20	16	22	10	11	9	9	14	14	9	8
1900–09	13	19	18	23	18	11	11	12	12	15	16	16
1910–13	15	17	17	24	17	14	11	14	15	18	16	17

Source: Feinstein (2003: 45). Ratios are at current market prices and averages of percentages of individual years.

Table 13.7 Capital per worker in selected countries ($1985)

	1820	1850	1880
Belgium		4,426	8,874
Denmark			1,906
France	1,883	4,109	5,731
Germany	2,332	3,500	5,336
India		357	550
Italy		1,890	2,047
Japan			634
Netherlands	3,521	3,266	3,773
Norway			6,196
Spain		441	1,156
Switzerland			6,821
UK	1,841	2,388	3,599
US	1,804	2,400	4,325

Source: Allen (2012).

Overall, in this field, the data are still fragmentary and limited to a handful of countries. A preliminary attempt to convert the scattered national estimates into a common currency (1985$) is in Allen (2012). Table 13.7 reports Allen's data on capital intensity (capital per worker) for the period 1820–80. Interestingly enough, Table 13.7 shows that some European 'followers' such as Belgium, France, and Germany were characterized by rates of capital intensity higher than those of the US and the UK, whereas, on the other hand, non-Western countries such as India and Japan by 1880 were still characterized by very low levels of capital intensity.

The 'Technology Profile' of the First Industrial Revolution

Historians of technology have remarked aptly that the breadth and depth of technical innovations of the Industrial Revolution are difficult to summarize under a single rubric (Landes 1969). Still, for interpretative purposes, it is possible to consider the most significant advances as related to the development of two major technological trajectories (Dosi 1982), namely: 1) mechanization, that is the substitution in a growing number of production processes of machines for human skills; and 2) the use of new power sources, in particular steam power (von Tunzelmann 1995).

These two technological trajectories proceeded at rather different paces, both considering the invention and the diffusion phases. More precisely, 'mechanization' actually *preceded* the deployment of steam power on a large scale. For this reason, we would maintain – as suggested originally by Cipolla (1962) and later on, in a more articulated way, by Wrigley (2004) – that rather than regarding the Industrial Revolution as a unitary process, it is more appropriate to consider it as the combination of two distinct technological trajectories, with different origins and rates of improvement, but progressively interacting and reinforcing each other.

The first phase of the Industrial Revolution, covering approximately the years 1700–1820, was characterized by the early mechanization of production processes in some key industries – first and foremost, cotton spinning and other textiles, but also brewing, papermaking, printing, and many others. Indeed, several historians (see, among others, Paulinyi 1986; von Tunzelmann 1995: 104–122) consider 'mechanization' and the related rise of a technological system capable of producing 'machines to make machines' as the *key technological element of the early phases of industrialization*. This view of the Industrial Revolution also links up with the 'high-wage economy' interpretation of the British Industrial Revolution put forward recently by Allen (2009). According to Allen, the Industrial Revolution took place in Britain because inventors and entrepreneurs were prompted to search for more capital-intensive technologies by the high level of real wages prevailing in Britain throughout the eighteenth century.[7] The fundamental feature of Allen's account is that technological opportunities were richer on the capital-intensive side of the spectrum of available techniques. More precisely, in Allen's model, capital-intensive techniques are characterized by faster rates of improvement than labour-intensive techniques (see Figure 13.1).[8]

In this historical phase, the search for capital-intensive technology consisted, by and large, in the design and refinements of machines, so that historians of technology have been frequently inclined to epitomize this historical phase as the 'age of machinery' (Cookson 2018). Table 13.8

7 Allen's 'high-wage economy' interpretation of the Industrial Revolution is, currently, at the centre of a very lively debate. Criticisms concern the estimates of real wages constructed by Allen and the estimates of the cost effectiveness of machine-technology in different countries. For a complete list of references and a compact rejoinder, see Allen (2018).

8 This pattern of technical change, in which technological opportunities are not evenly distributed along the spectrum of the available techniques but are clustered in the capital-intensive region, was originally proposed by David (1975) to interpret the differences between American and British technological practices during the nineteenth century highlighted by Habakkuk (1962).

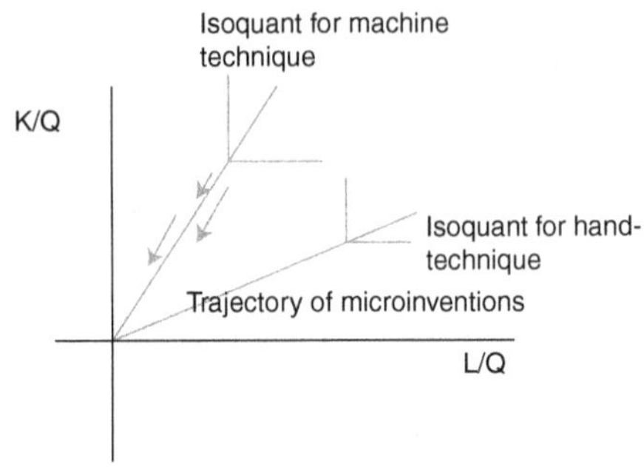

Figure 13.1 Choice of technique and differential rates of technical progress
Sources and notes: Allen (2009). The key assumption of Allen's interpretation is that technical progress originating from the capital-intensive technique is faster than from the labour-intensive technique.

Table 13.8 Labour productivity in cotton spinning

Technology	OHP (Operating hours to process 100lb of cotton)
Indian hand spinners (18th century)	50,000
Crompton's mule (1780)	2,000
100-spindle mule (1790)	1,000
Power-assisted mules (1795)	300
Roberts' automatic mules (1825)	135
Most efficient contemporary machines (1972)	40

Source: Chapman (1972).

shows the major impact of mechanization on labour productivity in cotton spinning.

The view of the central role of mechanization in fostering technical progress during the British Industrial Revolution owes much to the discussion contained in Chapter XV of the first volume of Marx's *Capital* (see Rosenberg 1974; 1976a for an insightful interpretation). In that chapter, Marx emphasized that the distinctive technological feature of modern industry was precisely the 'mechanization' of production. When production is performed by means of 'systems of machinery', Marx noted, production processes become susceptible to self-sustained and continuous improvement. This is because the adoption of 'systems of machinery' and the ensuing reconfiguration of production processes that are increasingly independent of human intervention open the door to the systematic application of the principles of science and engineering to the sphere of production (Marx 1990: 501–502).

Marx remarks that the expansion of mechanization determined the emergence of an independent machine-making industry. Initially, in this sector, machines were produced by means of traditional handicraft methods. However, in the course of time machines were applied to the construction of machine themselves. When this stage is reached, the realization of the full productive possibilities of modern industry finally becomes possible, and a process of self-sustained economic growth is irreversibly triggered. In Marx's view, the beginnings of this historical phase can be dated to the early 1850s.

Rosenberg (1963a; 1963b), in two very influential papers, has carried out a penetrating historical reconstruction of the emergence of an independent machine-making industry in the United States. The stages of the historical process described by Rosenberg are similar to those identified by Marx. Initially, machines were developed and produced by their users. Following the expansion of production in the user industries, a number of firms began to specialize in the production of machines themselves. Typically, these firms began as 'specialist' producers of well-defined classes of machines. However, as the skills and the techniques used in the production of individual machines could be relatively easily 'stretched' and employed in the production of other types of machinery, quite soon these firms extended their range of products. In a second phase, following an analogous process, machine-tool producers split off from the machine-making industries. Interestingly enough, machine-tool producers were normally highly specialized, limiting their operations to a narrow range of products. However, each of these individual machine tools could, with minor modifications, be adapted to cater to the needs of a wide range of possible users. Rosenberg labels this phenomenon 'technological convergence'. The process is represented in Figure 13.2.

To sum up, Rosenberg regards the evolution of the mechanical engineering industry during the nineteenth century as characterized by a process of progressive 'vertical disintegration'. This process of vertical disintegration was driven by two distinct sets of forces. The first was the expansion of output in user industries, which determined a sustained demand for machines and machine tools. The second was the process of technological convergence mentioned above. According to Rosenberg, the high degree of specialization characteristic of the US machine tool industry would have not been economically sustainable without the trend towards technological convergence. In this

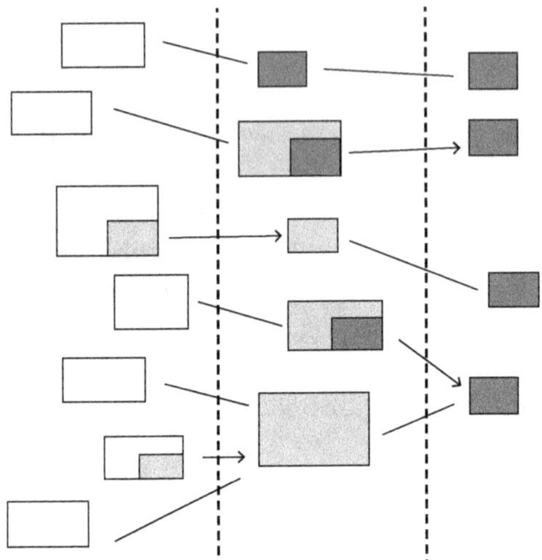

Figure 13.2 The expansion of mechanical engineering (vertical disintegration, specialization, and technological convergence)

case, it is likely that the restricted size of the market would have prevented the emergence of 'specialist' producers of machine tools (Rosenberg 1963b: 17). This pattern of specialization also affected the dynamics of innovative activities. Technically sophisticated industries imposed stringent requirements on the performance attributes of the various machines, stimulating innovations in design and favouring the consolidation among machine-tool producers of bodies of (technological) knowledge and skills.[9] This knowledge base could then be used for improving and refining the design of machine tools performing similar functions in less sophisticated industries. In this perspective, the emergence of an independent machine-tool industry played a key role in assuring a rapid dissemination of new technologies across industries. In addition, Rosenberg noted the existence of other processes of technological learning on the users' side that fed back on the accumulation of technological knowledge in machine-tool producers. Overall, the emergence of a specialized machine-making industry may be regarded as one of the most important

9 Examples are knowledge of the properties of metals in different conditions of use, properties of various lubricants, properties of feedback mechanisms and other control devices in various conditions of use. Most of this knowledge could not be fully articulated and codified and for this reason, it was very often embodied in workers' skills. See Rosenberg (1963b: 16).

factors accounting for the acceleration in the rate of technical progress during the nineteenth century (Rosenberg 1963a). Rosenberg's studies provide important support for Allen's account of technical change during the Industrial Revolution, since they provide a compelling account of the factors accounting for a more rapid technological change on the capital-intensive side of the spectrum of available techniques.

Rosenberg's contributions on the development of the mechanical engineering industry have been influential, but they are essentially based on the American experience. Some explorative reconstructions of the emergence of the machine-making industry in Britain suggest that Rosenberg's model can probably also be applied to interpret the British case (MacLeod and Nuvolari 2009; Cookson 2018). An important area of future research for historians of technology and economic historians would be to check whether the patterns of development highlighted by Rosenberg were characteristic also of other countries.

A particularly interesting feature of this first spurt of industrialization driven by the mechanization of production is that the energy base of the economy, in a qualitative sense, remained unchanged. In a quantitative sense, the adoption of water power grew remarkably. The efficiency of waterwheels was also raised considerably by a number of technical innovations. At all events, in the first phase of the Industrial Revolution the traditional mixture of human, animal, wind, and water power (although in changing proportions) continued to provide the bulk of power to the economy.

Traditional accounts of the British Industrial Revolution have instead, more or less explicitly, assumed that a wide range of industrial sectors rapidly benefited from the development of steam-power technology. Rostow's work can be considered representative of this view. Rostow dated the British 'take-off' to the years 1783–1802, linking it explicitly with the commercialization of the Boulton and Watt steam engine (Rostow 1975: 164–167; Landes, 1969: 99–103). More recent research has suggested that such a direct link between steam power and early industrialization is actually spurious. The available shreds of evidence suggest that during the late eighteenth and early nineteenth centuries, the British economy was still dominated by the extensive use of animal, wind, and water power (Kanefsky 1979: 188–233).

Estimates of the extent of steam usage are set out in Table 13.9. Kanefsky's (1979) data consider total steam HP employed in manufacturing and mining. It is important to note that these data are intended to cover power capacity installed rather than actual power use. Although the picture of the diffusion of steam power emerging from Table 13.9 is probably roughly correct, in our

Table 13.9 Sources of power in use in Britain (mainly mining and manufacturing)

	Steam		Water		Wind	
Year	HP	(%)	HP	(%)	HP	(%)
1760	5,000	5.88	70,000	82.35	10,000	11.76
1800	35,000	20.59	120,000	70.59	15,000	8.82
1830	160,000	47.06	160,000	47.06	20,000	5.88
1870	2,060,000	89.57	230,000	10	10,000	0.43
1907	9,659,000	98.14	178,000	1.81	5,000	0.05

Source: Kanefsky (1979: 338).

judgement, these figures still contain some overestimation of the extension of the use of steam vis-à-vis the two other sources of power, especially for the years 1760, 1800, and 1830. This is mainly because very small productive units (which typically employed wind and water) are likely to have gone unnoticed. Notwithstanding this consideration, the slow growth of steam power until the first quarter of the nineteenth century is still apparent.

Furthermore, the economy-wide repercussions of the progressive adoption of steam technology remained circumscribed until at least the 1840s. Therefore, it seems that traditional accounts have improperly conflated the early development of the steam engine (and in particular the invention of the Watt engine) with its economic significance. In contrast, von Tunzelmann (1978) and Crafts (2004) point out that the widespread adoption of the steam engine had to await a number of improvements that progressively reduced its power costs relative to other energy sources. Crafts' recent growth accounting calculations of the contributions of steam power to labour productivity growth are set out in Table 13.10. Table 13.10 shows that steam power began to contribute significantly to overall productivity growth only from the 1830s and that it exerted its major impact only in the second half of the nineteenth century, when it accounted for a yearly growth rate of about 0.1–0.15 per cent per year of aggregate labour productivity (Total contribution A+B).

Recently, growth economists have put forward the notion of 'general purpose technologies' (GPTs). These are technologies that: 1) display rapid rates of technological progress; 2) can be employed in a wide range of application sectors; and 3), when adopted, stimulate innovations also in the application sectors (Lipsey et al. 2005). Steam power, electricity, and ICT are the prime examples of GPTs highlighted in the literature. An interesting feature of GPTs is that they are supposed to generate important

Table 13.10 Contributions of steam power to labour productivity growth by stationary steam engines, 1760–1910 (percentage)

Years	1760–1800	1800–30	1830–50	1850–70	1870–1910
Rates of growth:					
Steam HP per worker	4.3	3.9	4.2	5.2	3.9
TFP in steam technology	2.8	0.06	1.2	3.5	1.7
Contributions:					
Capital deepening (A)	0.004	0.02	0.02	0.06	0.09
TFP (B)	0.005	0	0.02	0.06	0.05
Total contribution (A+B):	0.01	0.02	0.04	0.12	0.14
Steam income share (%)	0.1	0.4	0.5	1.2	2.2
Social Savings (as % of GDP)	0.2	0	0.3	1.2	1.8

Source: Crafts (2004: 344).

macroeconomic effects. The general idea is that prolonged phases of rapid economic growth alternating with others of relative stagnation can be accounted for by the diffusion of specific GPTs.

GPT growth models are intuitively appealing because they hold the promise of providing a simple, albeit insightful account in which the long-term dynamic of productivity growth is driven by the diffusion of radical innovations (following the well-known S-shaped path).[10] However, when moving from the models to their application to economic history, the matter becomes immediately thorny (see Field 2011: 206–228 for an insightful critical discussion).

Table 13.11, which gives estimates of the share of steam capital in the total capital stock, provides further evidence on the process of diffusion of steam power technology in Britain. In particular, we have computed two figures: one for the share of steam in the total capital stock in mining and manufacturing; and one by type of asset, which considers the share of steam in the 'plant, machinery and equipment' stock of the total economy. This can be taken as a rough indication of the relative 'weight' of steam technology in the stock of capital. Rather consistently with what we have noticed so far, the share of steam seems to attain a sizeable share in the stock of capital of the overall economy only in the very late nineteenth century.

In this respect, a hypothetical GPT account of industrialization depicting an economy powered exclusively by steam would be clearly wide of the mark (Crafts and Mills 2004: 170). In fact, the progress of steam-powered

10 For an example of this approach see Jovanovic and Rousseau (2005).

Table 13.11 Share of 'steam' capital in the total capital stock (Britain, 1760–1907)

Year	Steam capital (in millions of current £)	% of steam in the gross stock of capital (mining and manufacturing)	% of steam in the gross stock of capital (plant, machinery, and equipment)
1760	0.21	1.17	0.81
1800	1.96	3.44	2.61
1830	9.6	7.22	7.87
1870	51.5	9.77	11.03
1907	144.885	12.26	12.81

Sources and notes: Calculated using data on steam capital cost per HP (replacement costs) from Crafts (2004), data on total HP installed from Kanefsky (1979: 338) and data on the gross capital stock from Feinstein (1988: 437–440).

mechanization was far from being uniform both across and within industries. Even in sectors that employed steam intensively, a number of critical phases of the production process continued to be carried out using hand tools well up to the late nineteenth century (Samuel 1977).

The message emerging from these considerations is that the focus on the diffusion of a single key technology such as steam power is much too narrow a perspective for the study of the connection between technology and economic growth during the nineteenth century. Rather, following Kander et al. (2013), it is probably more insightful to focus on the emergence and progressive consolidation of a broad constellation of technologies ('development block') constituted by machinery – machine tools – steam engines – coal – iron-production techniques. This perspective has the advantage of acknowledging explicitly the interdependencies among technological trends at technology and sector level in a much more explicit way than the successive GPT literature, which insisted on the life cycle of a single generic technology (Nuvolari 2019).

Figure 13.3 shows the comparative diffusion of steam-power technology in some major Western countries. Figure 13.3 provides further corroboration that the genuine 'age of steam' of the world economy was the second half of the nineteenth century. Remarkably, the relative pace of adoption of steam power across countries is consistent with the relative degree of backwardness of nineteenth-century Europe posited by Gerschenkron (1962).

After having discussed the general 'technology profile' of the First Industrial Revolution, it is useful to discuss the major 'drivers' of technical change in this historical phase.

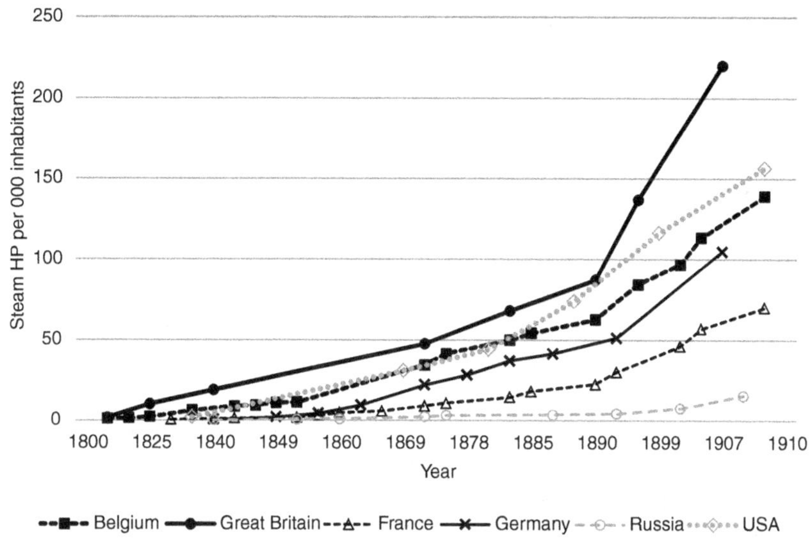

Figure 13.3 The international diffusion of steam power technology
Source: van Neck (1979); Fenichel (1966).

Institutions (patent systems)

Following a cue from Douglass North (1981), many historians have claimed that the creation of modern patent systems provided a fundamental stimulus to inventive activities in this period, prompting the acceleration of technical change of the British Industrial Revolution. Khan and Sokoloff (2001), arguing along similar lines, have suggested that the effectiveness of the nineteenth-century US patent system was the crucial factor accounting for the ascendancy of the US among the world technology leaders. These claims are controversial. Petra Moser (2005), using evidence from the catalogue of the Crystal Palace exhibition, has demonstrated that in the mid-nineteenth century the large bulk of inventive activities was undertaken outside the coverage of the patent system. Furthermore, case studies show that many critical technologies such as high-pressure steam, steamboats, and iron-production techniques were developed outside patent protection, and often with inventors sharing knowledge, adopting models of behaviour similar to open-source software (Bessen and Nuvolari 2016). The main conclusion from this line of research is that patents represented one among several possible 'appropriability tools' that inventors could use in this period. In many contexts, inventors could resort to alternative appropriability strategies that did not contemplate the use of patents (such as lead times, reputation, secrecy, complementary assets), which were feasible and effective.

Hence considering the emergence of modern patent systems as the fundamental institutional prerequisite prompting the acceleration of technical change of the Industrial Revolution is probably misleading (MacLeod and Nuvolari 2016).

Science and Useful Knowledge

Mokyr (2002) has argued that another important driver of technical change in this period was the progressive coalescence of science and technology. Mokyr introduces the concept of 'industrial enlightenment' to describe this more direct interaction between science and inventive activities. Since Mokyr recognizes that the *direct* contribution of science to technology in the early phases of industrialization was probably rather limited, he suggests the notion of 'useful knowledge' to define the knowledge base underlying all the techniques mastered by a society. 'Useful knowledge' is a much broader set than scientific knowledge, containing not only systematic knowledge about natural phenomena but also other types of practical knowledge about the properties of the natural world that may potentially have a bearing on the design of artefacts. The main achievement of the 'industrial enlightenment' was to establish the conditions for a self-sustaining process of accumulation of 'useful knowledge' by reducing its production, storage, and dissemination costs. Accordingly, Mokyr emphasizes the adoption of a scientific method and an experimental attitude as the key to improvements in technology (Mokyr 2002: 36–39, 80–85).

Learning-By-Doing and Learning-By-Using

Other authors (von Tunzelmann 1995; Allen 2009) have, in contrast to Mokyr, emphasized the role of learning-by-doing and learning-by-using. These forms of learning resulted in a search for innovations driven by and large by tweaking, adaptation, and the slow accumulation of empirical rules of thumb. They typically resulted in incremental improvements, but in many sectors their cumulative effect was without doubt highly significant (Rosenberg 1976b). Furthermore, in several instances these forms of learning were reinforced by knowledge-sharing taking place within inventors' communities (Bessen and Nuvolari 2016).

Drawing a comprehensive balance between the relative weight of a more scientific approach to the search for innovations and the role of more empirical forms of learning is probably impossible. Rather than searching for a predominant driver of technological learning, it is perhaps more important to stress the historical significance of the emergence and consolidation of a 'pluralistic' innovation system characterized by multiple drivers of technical advance, increasingly interacting and reinforcing each other.

Concluding Remarks

The Industrial Revolution represented a fundamental turning point in human history. Before it, economic growth was sluggish and, with few exceptions, stagnation in living standards and material prosperity appeared to be one of the defining characteristics of economic life. The Industrial Revolution, which began in Britain between 1700 and 1850, marked the beginning of a new historical phase characterized by sustained economic growth: the origins of the contemporary world economy are found in the changes it introduced. Notwithstanding the enormous literature on the subject, historians are still debating the causes of the Industrial Revolution without sign of imminent closure. The debate is not short of conjectures often built around one or few fundamental determinants such as institutions, geography, culture, etc. Clearly, we do not have the space here to provide a comprehensive reassessment of these contributions. Rather, a more suitable way to conclude our chapter is to provide a compact summary of the salient features that characterized the patterns of technical change and capital accumulation in this historical phase.

Concerning technical change, the most important conclusion is that, even if it is possible to identify some macro-trends such as 'mechanization' and the use of inanimate energy sources, inventive activities displayed a remarkable degree of differentiation concerning the characteristics of the inventors, the knowledge base they exploited, and the organizational set-ups informing innovation processes.

In this perspective, perhaps the period 1700–1870 should be interpreted as an historical phase in which in the leading countries such as the UK and US, there was the emergence and consolidation of an effective 'pluralistic' innovation system. The key idea underlying the notion of innovation systems is that innovation processes are inherently social processes in which many different interacting actors are involved (Soete et al. 2010). In this historical phase, one can point to increasing interactions between inventors, entrepreneurs and financial backers, scientists (i.e. natural philosophers), engineers, artisans, skilled workmen, and users. Furthermore, inventive activities were organized using different organizational set-ups and they also differed in terms of the procedures adopted for exploiting diverse knowledge bases. Rather than trying to articulate accounts of technical advance in terms of simple and general causal factors, a more fruitful approach could be to consider explicitly the wide variety of organizational set-ups and institutional arrangements that were informing innovation processes in this historical phase and their complementarities.

Concerning capital accumulation, growth accounting exercises aimed at assessing the relative contributions of capital accumulation vis-à-vis technical change for the period 1700–1870 are presented in other chapters of the book (see also Crafts 2009). Overall the picture emerging from these decompositions suggests that, for the limited number of countries for which data are available, the period 1700–1870 is an historical phase in which the capital-deepening contribution seems to dominate the TFP contribution to economic growth. In other words, the available evidence indicates that TFP growth dominates capital deepening only when the industrialization process has been launched on a relatively large scale; before that, capital deepening represents the main driver of economic growth (Crafts 2009). This interpretation is plausible, but, following Abramovitz and David (1973; 2001), it is also possible to put forward an alternative explanation. If technical change was capital-using, it is possible that part of the estimated capital-deepening contribution will reflect also the contribution of technical change (Abramovitz 1993).

Abramovitz and David's (2001) interpretation of the growth accounts for the nineteenth-century US is that the small contribution of TFP before 1890 and the much larger contribution thereafter reflects a fundamental change in the nature of technical progress, which was basically capital-using in the nineteenth century and 'neutral' thereafter (Abramovitz 1993).

As a final consideration, it is interesting to note that the large role of capital deepening is also consistent with the view of Allen (2012) who regards nineteenth-century technical change as essentially 'embodied' in capital goods. Allen examines the 'spread' of the Industrial Revolution in the nineteenth and twentieth centuries using aggregate data on capital stocks and productivity growth. As we already mentioned, Allen regards the Industrial Revolution as resulting from the adoption of capital-intensive techniques ('mechanization'), which are much more 'dynamic' from an innovation point of view than labour-intensive technologies. This view of technical change can explain the large emphasis on capital deepening by latecomer industrializers.

References

Abramovitz, M. (1993). 'The Search for the Sources of Growth: Areas of Ignorance Old and New', *Journal of Economic History*, 53, 217–243.

Abramovitz, M. and David, P. (1973). 'Reinterpreting Economic Growth: Parables and Realities', *American Economic Review*, 63, 428–439.

(2001). 'Two Centuries of American Macroeconomic Growth: From Exploitation of Resource Abundance to Knowledge-Driven Development', Stanford Institute for Economic Policy Research working paper.

Akimoto, H. (1987). *Zenkōgyōkajidai no Keizai (Economy in the Pre-industrial Period)*, Kyoto: Mineruvashobō.

Allen, R. C. (2009). *The British Industrial Revolution in Global Perspective*, Cambridge University Press.

(2012). 'Technology and the Great Divergence: Global Economic Development Since 1820', *Explorations in Economic History*, 49, 1–16.

(2018). 'Spinning Their Wheels: A Reply to Jane Humphries and Benjamin Schneider', Oxford Discussion Papers in Economic and Social History, 166, www.economics.ox.ac.uk/materials/working_papers/4650/166julyallen.pdf (accessed 9 November 2020).

Ashraf, Q. and Galor, O. (2011). 'Dynamics and Stagnation in the Malthusian Epoch', *American Economic Review*, 101, 2003–2041.

Bessen, J. and Nuvolari, A. (2016). 'Knowledge Sharing Among Inventors: Some Historical Perspectives', in Harhoff, D. and Lakhani, K. (eds.), *Revolutionizing Innovation: Users, Communities and Open Innovation*, Cambridge, MA: MIT Press, 135–155.

Bolt, J. and van Zanden, J. L. (2014). 'The Maddison Project: Collaborative Research on Historical National Accounts', *Economic History Review*, 67, 627–651.

Brewer, J. (1988). *The Sinews of Power. War, Money and the English State, 1688–1783*, Cambridge, MA: Harvard University Press.

Broadberry, S. and de Pleijt, A. (2018). 'Capital and Economic Growth in Britain, 1270–1870', paper presented at World Economic History Congress, Boston.

Broadberry, S., Campbell, B., Klein, A., Overton, M. and van Leeuwen, B. (2015). *British Economic Growth 1270–1870*, Cambridge University Press.

Brunt, L. (2006). 'Rediscovering Risk: Country Banks as Venture Capital Firms in the First Industrial Revolution', *Journal of Economic History*, 66, 74–102.

Chapman, S. (1972). *The Cotton Industry in the Industrial Revolution*, London: Macmillan.

Chapman, S. and Butt, J. (1988). 'The Cotton Industry, 1775–1856', in Feinstein, C. and Pollard, S. (eds.), *Studies in Capital Formation in the United Kingdom, 1750–1920*, Oxford: Clarendon Press, 105–125.

Cipolla, C. M. (1962). *The Economic History of the World Population*, Harmondsworth: Penguin.

(1976). *Before the Industrial Revolution. European Society and Economy, 1000–1700*, London: Routledge.

Clark, G. (2007). *A Farewell to Alms. A Brief Economic History of the World*, Princeton University Press.

Cookson, G. (2018). *The Age of Machinery. Engineering the Industrial Revolution, 1770–1850*, Woodbridge: Boydell.

Crafts, N. F. R. (2004). 'Steam as a General-Purpose Technology: A Growth Accounting Perspective', *Economic Journal*, 114, 338–351.

(2009). 'Solow and Growth Accounting: a Perspective from Quantitative Economic History', *History of Political Economy*, 41, 200–220.

Crafts, N. F. R. and Mills, T. (2004). 'Was the 19th century British growth steam powered? The climacteric revisited', *Explorations in Economic History*, 41, 156–171.

Crouzet, F. (1972). 'Editor's Introduction', in Crouzet, F. (ed.), *Capital Formation in the Industrial Revolution*, London: Methuen.

David, P. (1975). *Technical Choice, Innovation and Economic Growth*, Cambridge University Press.

Davies, R. and Pollard, S. (1988). 'The Iron Industry, 1775–1850', in Feinstein, C. and Pollard, S. (eds.), *Studies in Capital Formation in the United Kingdom, 1750–1920*, Oxford: Clarendon Press, 73–104.

Dosi, G. (1982). 'Technological Paradigms and Technological Trajectories: A Suggested Interpretation of the Determinants and Directions of Technical Change', *Research Policy*, 11, 147–162.

Feinstein, C. (1988). 'National Statistics, 1760–1920' in Feinstein, C. H. and Pollard, S. (eds.), *Studies in Capital Formation in the United Kingdom, 1750–1920*, Oxford: Clarendon Press, 257–471.

(2003). 'National Income Accounts: Investment and Savings', in Mokyr, J. (ed.), *The Oxford Encyclopedia of Economic History*, Oxford University Press.

Fenichel, A. H. (1966). 'Growth and Diffusion of Power in Manufacturing 1838–1919', in Brady, D. (ed.), *Output, Employment and Productivity in the United States after* 1980, Chicago: National Bureau of Economic Research, 473–479.

Field, A. (1985). 'On the Unimportance of Machinery', *Explorations in Economic History*, 22, 378–401.

(2011). *A Great Leap Forward. 1930s Depression and US Economic Growth*, New Haven: Yale University Press.

Fukao, K., Nakamura, N. and Nakabayashi, M. (eds.) (2017). *Nihonkeizai no Rekishi (History of Japanese Economy), vol. 2*, Tokyo: Iwanamishoten.

Gerschenkron, A. (1962). *Economic Backwardness in Historical Perspective*, Cambridge, MA: Harvard University Press.

Habakkuk, H. J. (1962). *American and British Technology in the Nineteenth Century*, Cambridge University Press.

Hansen, G. and Prescott, E. (2002). 'Malthus to Solow', *American Economic Review*, 92, 1205–1217.

Hicks, J. (1969). *A Theory of Economic History*, Oxford University Press.

Jovanovic, B. and Rousseau, P. (2005). 'General Purpose Technologies' in Aghion, P. and Durlauf, S. (eds.), *Handbook of Economic Growth, vol. IB*, Amsterdam: Elsevier, 1181–1224.

Kander, A., Malanima, P. and Warde, P. (2013). *Power to the People. Energy in Europe over the Last Five Centuries*, Princeton University Press.

Kanefsky, J. W. (1979). *The Diffusion of Power Technology in British Industry, 1760–1870*, unpublished Ph.D. thesis, University of Exeter.

Kelly, M. (1997). 'The Dynamics of Smithian Growth', *Quarterly Journal of Economics*, 112, 939–964.

Khan, B. Z. and Sokoloff, K. L. (2001). 'The Early Development of Intellectual Property Institutions in the United States', *Journal of Economic Perspectives*, 15, 233–246.

Landes, D. S. (1969). *The Unbound Prometheus. Technological Change and Industrial Development in Western Europe from 1750 to the Present*, Cambridge University Press.

Lipsey, R. G., Carlaw, K. I. and Bekar, C. (2005). *Economic Transformations: General Purpose Technologies and Long-Term Economic Growth*, Oxford University Press.

MacLeod, C. and Nuvolari, A. (2009). '"Glorious Times": the Emergence of Mechanical Engineering in Early Industrial Britain, *c.*1700–1850', *Brussels Economic Review*, 52, 215–237.

(2012). 'Technological Change' in Doyle, W. (ed.), *The Oxford Handbook of the Ancien Regime*, Oxford University Press, 448–466.

(2016). 'Inventive Activities, Patents and Early Industrialization: A Synthesis of Research Issues', *Rivista di Storia Economica*, 32, 77–107.

Maddison, A. (1982). *Phases of Capitalist Development*, Oxford University Press.

Makkai, L. (1981). 'Productivité et exploitation des sources d'energie (XII–XVII siècle') in Mariotti, S. (ed.), *Produttivita' e Tecnologie nei Secoli XII–XVIII*, Florence: Le Monnier.

Marx, K. (1990). *Capital*, vol. 1, Harmondsworth: Penguin.

Mokyr, J. (2002). *The Gifts of Athena: Historical Origins of the Knowledge Economy*, Princeton University Press.

Moser, P. (2005). 'How Do Patent Laws Influence Innovation? Evidence from Nineteenth Century World Fairs', *American Economic Review*, 95, 1213–1236.

North, D. C. (1981). *Structure and Change in Economic History*, New York: W. W. Norton.

Nuvolari, A. (2019). 'Understanding Successive Industrial Revolutions: a "Development Block" Approach', *Environmental Innovation and Societal Transitions*, 32, 33–44.

Ohkawa, K. et al. (1966). *Chōkikeizaitōkei vol. 3 Shihon Sutokku (Estimates of Long Term Economic Statistics of Japan since 1868, vol. 3, Capital Stock)*, Tokyo: Tōyōkeizaishinpōsha.

Paulinyi, A. (1986). 'Revolution and Technology', in Porter, R. and Teich, M. (eds.), *Revolution in History*, Cambridge University Press, 261–289.

Persson, K. G. (1988). *Pre-Industrial Economic Growth. Social Organization and Technical Progress in Europe*, Blackwell: Oxford.

Reynolds, T. S. (1983). *Stronger than a Hundred Men: A History of the Vertical Water Wheel*, Baltimore: Johns Hopkins University Press.

Rosenberg, N. (1963a). 'Capital Goods, Technology and Economic Growth', *Oxford Economic Papers*, 15, 217–227; reprinted in Rosenberg, N. (1976). *Perspectives on Technology*, Cambridge University Press.

(1963b). 'Technological Change in the Machine Tool Industry, 1840–1910', *Journal of Economic History*, 23, 414–446; reprinted in Rosenberg, N. (1976). *Perspectives on Technology*, Cambridge University Press.

(1974). 'Karl Marx on the Economic Role of Science', *Journal of Political Economy*, 82, 713–728.

(1976a). 'Marx as a Student of Technology', *Monthly Review*, 28, 56–77.

(1976b). *Perspectives on Technology*, Cambridge University Press.

Rostow, W. W. (1975). *How It All Began: Origins of the Modern Economy*, London: Methuen.

Samuel, R. (1977). 'Workshop of the World: Steam Power and Hand Technology in mid-Victorian Britain', *History Workshop*, 3, 5–72.

Sharp, P., Strulik, H. and Weisdorf, J. (2012). 'The Determinants of Income in a Malthusian Equilibrium', *Journal of Development Economics*, 97, 112–117.

Soete, L., Verspagen, B. and ter Weel, B. (2010). 'Systems of Innovation' in Hall, B. and Rosenberg, N. (eds.), *Handbook of the Economics of Innovation*, vol. 2, Dordrecht: Elsevier, 1160–1180.

Tanimoto, M. (forthcoming). 'Introduction and Diffusion: How Did Useful and Reliable Knowledge Feature in the Industrial Development in Early Modern Japan?', *Technology and Culture*, 62.

van Neck, A. (1979). *Les Debuts de la Machine a Vapeur dans l'Industrie Belge, 1800–1850*, Bruxelles: Palais des Academies.

van Zanden, J. L. (2001). 'Early Modern Economic Growth: A Survey of the European Economy, 1500–1800', in Prak, M. (ed.), *Early Modern Capitalism. Economic and Social Change in Europe, 1400–1800*, London: Routledge, 69–87.

von Tunzelmann, G. N. (1978). *Steam Power and British Industrialization to 1860*, Oxford: Clarendon Press.

(1995). *Technology and Industrial Progress. The Foundations of Economic Growth*, Aldershot: Edward Elgar.

Voigtlander, N. and Voth, J. (2009). 'Malthusian Dynamism and the Rise of Europe: Make War, not Love', *American Economic Review*, 99, 248–254.

Wrigley, E. A. (2004). *Poverty, Progress and Population*, Cambridge University Press.

14

Underlying Sources of Growth: First and Second Nature Geography

PAUL CARUANA-GALIZIA, TOMOKO HASHINO, AND MAX-STEPHAN SCHULZE

Introduction

Economic growth over the period from the mid-seventeenth to the late-nineteenth century was associated with profound changes in the spatial distribution of economic activity across the world. The *Great Divergence* (Pomeranz 2000; 2011) between Europe and Asia had been under way before the Industrial Revolution. In terms of per capita output, the early leader China had likely already fallen behind Italy by the start of the fourteenth century. About a century or so later, England and Holland had caught up, too, and moved well ahead (Broadberry et al. 2018). The income and productivity gap between the global West and East widened dramatically over the next two hundred years, just as within Europe income differentials between the North/North-west and South/South-east increased. In the mid-eighteenth century, China and India still accounted for well over half the world's manufacturing output (Bairoch 1982). About 125 years later, this share had declined to about one-sixth, while that of Europe and North America had risen to 75 per cent. A similar, if somewhat less stark, pattern of relative rise and decline is also evident in total economy output.

This chapter asks to what extent 'geography' helps explain the changes in the global distribution of economic activity since 1700 and up to the onset of the Second Industrial Revolution. First nature, or physical geography, characteristics – climate, coasts, rivers, mountain ranges, prevailing wind directions, natural endowments with land and mineral resources etc. – confer different geographic advantages or disadvantages for economic activity across different regions or countries of the world. For example, being landlocked or faced with very rugged terrain raises transport costs, while an adverse disease environment or poor soil quality lower (agricultural) productivity. Second nature geography, by contrast, is concerned with the spatial aspects of human activity – the 'geography of interactions between economic agents' (Venables 2006). Road building, railway and canal construction or the formation of cities, for instance, alter the costs of economic interaction across space.

However, geography is just one among the fundamental sources of economic growth and cross-country income differences typically identified in the literature.[1] Rodrik et al. (2004) maintain that much of standard growth theory, with its focus on physical and human capital accumulation and technological change, addresses 'at best the proximate causes of growth' but not its deeper determinants. Hence the question remains what ultimately makes some economies accumulate and innovate – and so grow – more quickly than others. They distinguish three main lines of thought in the literature that is explicitly concerned with the *fundamental* causes of growth and cross-country income differentials. The first strand attaches particular significance to physical geography and its influence on agricultural productivity and human resources (e.g. Diamond 1997; Sachs 2001). A second line of argument centres on the productivity gains to be had from international trade and market integration as main drivers of growth (e.g. Sachs and Warner 1995; Frankel and Romer 1999; Dollar and Kray 2004). Much in the wake of North's (1990) seminal study, a third set of causal analyses concentrates on the quality of institutions – broadly conceived as referring to both formal and informal rules and subsuming 'culture' – and their central importance for growth and development. Examples of work in this vein are the cross-section studies by Acemoglu et al. (2001; 2002), Easterly and Levine (2003), and Hall and Jones (1999). Whilst it is reasonable to take physical geography as an exogenous determinant of income (up to a point, as we shall see below), this does not hold for institutions or trade where feedback effects are bound to be significant. A key issue in the literature then has been not just finding serviceable measures of institutional quality and openness, but appropriate instruments with which to address endogeneity problems econometrically. In an effort to assess the independent contribution of geography, institutions, and integration to cross-country differences in income levels, Rodrik et al. (2004) incorporate the three main hypotheses on the fundamental factors of growth into a common cross-sectional analytical framework, drawing on Acemoglu et al. (2001) and Frankel and Romer's (1999)

1 Rodrik et al. (2004) question whether trade ought to be treated as one of the ultimate determinants of growth but include it in their analysis in light of an extensive literature that assigns a central causal role to trade. In contrast, Acemoglu (2009) identifies geography, institutions and culture as well as luck as fundamental causes.

instruments for institutions (settler mortality) and integration (predicted trade/gross domestic product [GDP] ratios derived from gravity equations for bilateral trade flows), respectively. They conclude that 'institutions rule' – in contrast to institutional quality, physical geography exerts only weak direct effects on income whilst trade has no direct effects.[2]

The 'institutions rule' argument and the conceptual approach upon which it is based have been challenged from a range of different angles. Glaeser et al. (2004) argue that the indicators of institutional quality and the instrumenting techniques commonly used in the literature to show that institutions cause growth are conceptually unsuitable. Instead, they maintain, human capital is a more fundamental source of growth than institutions. In their assessment, it is good policies that matter, not institutions *per se*. Institutional quality, in turn, improves with rising incomes. Carstensen and Gundlach (2006), too, caution against the 'primacy of institutions' in accounting for cross-country differences in economic development. If appropriately measured via malaria incidence, they argue, geography turns out to be as important as institutional quality. Krugman (1991), Redding and Venables (2004), Head and Mayer (2011) and other writings in the 'new economic geography' literature stress a different aspect: the physical geography of a region determines not just its own physical characteristics but also its location *relative* to other regions. This, in turn, can have a strong effect on a given region's access to market, the location of activity and income.[3]

The focus here is on exploring to what extent 'geography', broadly conceived, mattered for economic development across the globe. The rest of the chapter is organized as follows. The next section sets out the pattern of comparative aggregate growth for a sample of major economies between 1700 and 1870 and documents the shift from East to West in the global economic centre of gravity. In a sense, this maps out the issues to be accounted for by looking at the role of geography. The next section surveys the comparative evidence on key first nature geographical characteristics that have been identified in the literature as potentially critical for long run economic development. This is followed by an exercise that seeks to assess quantitatively whether and to what comparative extent first

2 Further and with regards to the links between determinants, geography is found to have a significant influence on institutional quality and thus *indirectly* on incomes while institutional quality affects integration positively.

3 Bosker and Garretson (2009) adds to that perspective by arguing that institutional quality itself is correlated with neighbouring economies' institutional set up, i.e. distance to 'good' or 'bad' institutions matters.

nature characteristics, second nature geography forces, and institutional quality can account for the observed income trajectories across a sample of thirteen major economies in America, Asia, and Europe. The analysis draws on a simple panel regression framework. Finally, a case study on shifting comparative advantage in the textile industry over the course of the nineteenth century illustrates the outcomes of technical change within a changing global economic geography. The conclusion summarizes the main argument of this chapter: changes in trade costs, agglomeration economies and differential access to markets with associated productivity gains likely played a major role in moving the economic centre of gravity towards the West. The West became absolutely and relatively richer not just because of better institutions, but also, and significantly so, because of more favourable geographies. In that sense, institutions did *not* rule supreme.

A Moving Economic Centre of Gravity: Long Run Divergence between East and West

Recent country-specific estimates of GDP and population allow for a more reliable assessment of output levels and growth across the major economies of the world than earlier approximations. This holds, in particular, for the centuries before 1800. Table 14.1 reports on the course of GDP per capita between 1700 and 1870. It shows the extent to which the Western economies, especially Belgium, Britain, and the Netherlands, moved ahead – compared to the once-leading economy of China – from what was already a distinctly advantageous income position in 1700 to a huge lead by the mid-nineteenth century.

However, the data show not only a 'racing ahead' of the richest European economies, and later the United States, but more broadly a significant widening in income dispersion over the eighteenth and nineteenth centuries. Individual countries' growth experiences were different for a range of reasons, including *inter alia* the timing and pace of initial industrialization and structural change. As a result, income differentials increased significantly. The change in the world's leading economies' relative income (GDP per capita) position reflects developments in world manufacturing. According to Bairoch (1982), the 'rise of the West' was associated with a dramatic decline in China's and India's share in world manufacturing between 1750 and 1880 (Table 14.2). This shift in the location of activity is even more pronounced if one looks at Bairoch's (1982) per capita levels of industrialization (Table 14.3).

Table 14.1 GDP per capita (1990 Intl. $)

	1700	1750	1800	1850	1870	Δ1870/1700	Δ1870/1800
Belgium	1,375	1,361	1,479	1,847	2,692	0.40	0.86
China	1,089	749	654	600	530	−0.42	−0.30
Finland	839	936	764	957	1,140	0.18	0.57
France	1,063	1,052	1,126	1,597	1,876	0.33	0.73
Great Britain	1,513	1,695	2,097	2,718	3,657	0.52	0.80
Germany	939	1,051	987	1,428	1,839	0.40	0.89
Habsburg Empire			936	1,090	1,223		0.38
India	622	576	569	556	526	−0.10	−0.11
Italy	1,513	1,571	1,397	1,516	1,635	0.05	0.23
Japan	675	675	828	903	1,011	0.24	0.29
Mexico	919	806	812	656	651	−0.20	−0.32
Netherlands	1,620	1,811	2,007	2,371	2,774	0.32	0.46
Ottoman Empire	700		740		825	0.10	0.16
Peru	726	693	664	593	694	−0.03	0.06
Portugal	880	1,188	754	923	975	0.06	0.37
South Africa/Cape	1,703	1,692	959	654	807	−0.44	−0.25
Spain	913	902	974	1,155	1,365	0.24	0.48
Sweden	1,298	1,008	885	1,112	1,392	0.04	0.65
United States	1,238	1,277	1,296	1,849	2,445	0.40	0.91

Sources and notes: Derived from Maddison Project Database (versions 2013 and 2018) and the following: Belgium: Buyst (2011); China: Broadberry et al. (2018); France: Ridolfi (2016); Germany: Pfister (2011); Great Britain: Broadberry et al. (2015a); Habsburg Empire: new estimates 1800–60 based on Schulze (2000), Kausel (1979), Komlos (1983); India: Broadberry et al. (2015b); Italy: Malanima (2011); Japan: Bassino et al. (2019); Mexico, Peru: Arroyo Abad and van Zanden (2016); Netherlands: van Zanden and van Leeuwen (2012) and personal communication, Bas van Leeuwen; Portugal: Palma and Reis (2018) and personal communication, Nuno Palma; South Africa: Fourie and van Zanden (2013); Spain: Álvarez-Nogal and Prados de la Escosura (2013) and personal communication, Leandro Prados de la Escosura; Sweden: Schoen and Krantz (2015); United States (non-native population): Sutch (2006), Mancall and Weiss (1999). Belgium 1800=1812; Japan 1700=1721; Ottoman Empire 1800=1820; Spain: 11-year moving average.

According to this measure, the West's industrialization found its counterpart in the East's de-industrialization.

Figure 14.1 below summarizes and illustrates graphically the East to West shift in the economic centre of gravity between 1700 and 1870 on the basis of sample GDPs. It is the task of the following sections to consider the extent to which this shift was an outcome of broadly perceived 'geography'. The next part will first review the evidence on physical geography and how this shaped the patterns of economic activity across the globe.

Table 14.2 Shares in world manufacturing output (percentage)

	1750	1800	1830	1860	1880
Europe	24.4	28.6	34.2	53.3	61.3
UK	3.3	5.0	8.4	19.9	22.9
USA	0.1	0.7	2.5	7.2	14.7
China	32.3	32.9	29.8	24.4	12.5
India	24.1	19.6	17.6	8.6	2.7

Sources: Bairoch (1982), amended for 1750 and 1800 to account for Crafts and Harley's (1992) revisions of UK industrial production index; cf. Broadberry et al. (2010).

Table 14.3 Per capita levels of industrialization (UK in 1860 = 100)

	1750	1800	1830	1860	1880
World	11	9	11	11	14
Europe	13	13	17	27	38
UK	28	30	39	100	136
USA	6	14	22	33	59
China	13	9	9	6	6
India	11	9	9	5	3

Sources: See Table 14.2.

First Nature Characteristics – Physical Geography and Economic Activity

Environmental characteristics such as natural resource endowments, climatic conditions, landscape shapes and access to rivers, lakes, and the sea have long featured in the historical and economics literature on long run development, the diffusion of modern economic growth, and industrialization (e.g. Pollard 1981). This section's focus is on documenting some of the large differences in such characteristics across the globe and their economic implications. To illustrate one aspect of the issue: *ceteris paribus*, poor soils in an adverse disease environment yield lower outputs than agriculture in temperate, largely disease-free regions benefiting from high inherent soil quality. Such differences in geography, then, can have far-reaching consequences for economic change and well-being over the very

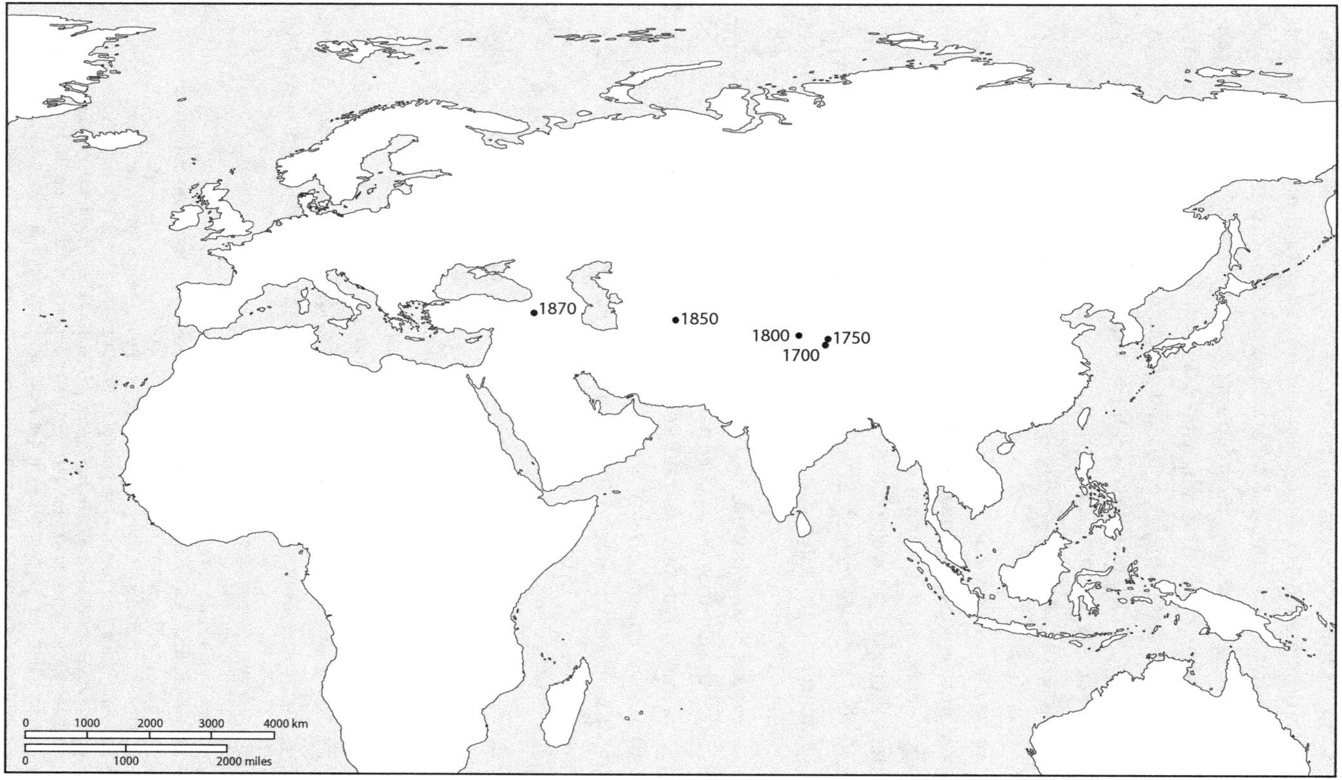

Figure 14.1 The shift in the economic centre of gravity
Source: Map redrawn based on sources that can be found in the text.

long term.[4] However, once attention shifts to less readily accessible natural resources such as mineral deposits, the analytical problem becomes more complicated than the soil quality example seems to suggest. It makes little sense to perceive, say, coal deposits as economically strictly exogenous and time-invariant. After all, it takes initiative, incentives, and significant financial means to prospect for and gain knowledge about them in the first place – and substantial investment to exploit them subsequently. We know that access to coal (and water power) played a major role in underpinning the industrialization of Europe (Pollard 1981; Fernihough and O'Rourke 2014).

Most of the world's coal deposits (including those known of and once exploited but no longer mined as, for example, in Britain and Belgium) are spatially concentrated in certain regions.[5] In terms of its share in global coal resources, Europe was well placed.[6] What mattered economically, though, was societies' ability to identify, access, and exploit such resources and not just their existence, i.e. the interaction of 'first nature' characteristics and human intervention. To the extent that output data can serve as a rough guide, Europe, and especially Britain, had a significant lead in the late eighteenth and nineteenth centuries over other parts of the world (Mitchell 2013).

Next we look at natural constraints on food production. In this context, the concept of inherent soil quality is of particular relevance. This refers to 'the quality of land before human interference or natural processes affected it' (Beinroth et al. 2001). In that sense, we can take this as a genuinely exogenous variable.

Figure 14.2 shows that land quality is extremely uneven across the world. The top quality 'class I, II and III' land occupies only a small fraction of the global land surface (16.5 million km^2 [6.4 million square miles], 12.7 per cent). These lands are generally free of constraints for most agricultural uses' (Beinroth et al. 2001: 569). On this score, parts of North America, Europe, and the Black Sea region as well parts of India, areas in Southern and Eastern Africa and South America were comparatively well endowed with

4 For a broad, general treatment see Diamond (1997).

5 *Encyclopedia Britannica*, (n.d.) 'World Distribution of Coal'; Open University (n.d.).

6 On the basis of sedimentary rock strata, almost half of the world's total coal *resources* (i.e. total amount of coal available) are estimated to be in Europe (including Russia), with North America accounting for 29 per cent and Asia for about 14 per cent (Australia – 6 per cent; Africa and South America – 1 per cent). The distribution changes only marginally if the far narrower (and time-variant) concept of economically and technically recoverable *reserves* is employed. See *Encyclopedia Britannica* (n.d.), 'Coal mining'. For Europe, see Fernihough and O'Rourke (2014).

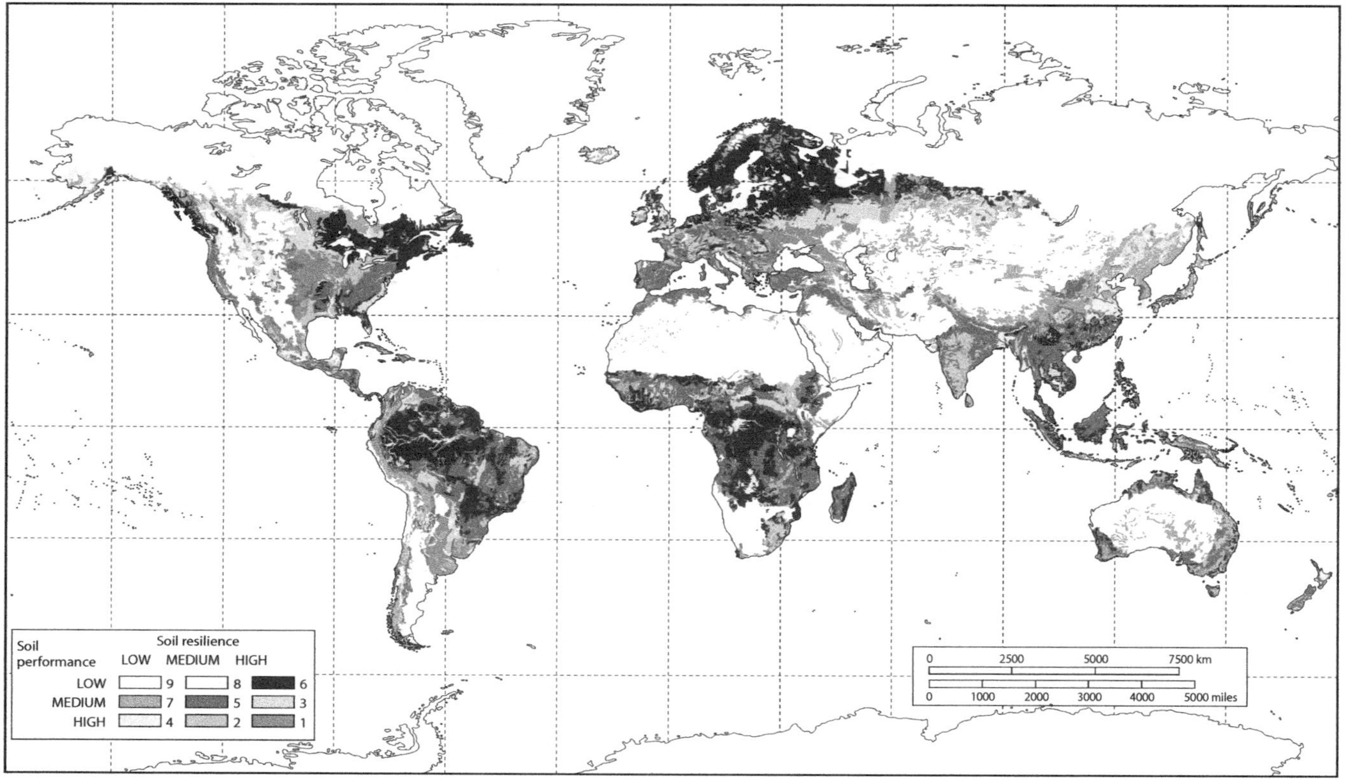

Figure 14.2 Inherent land quality
Source: Redrawn based on a map by Beinroth et al. (2001).

high-quality land. The issue is whether such advantages translated into comparative developmental gains. Looking into this and fully adjusting for nineteenth-century borders, we draw on a sample of seventeen economies with GDP per capita data available back to 1700 and corresponding soil fertility measures from Nunn and Puga (2012) that build on the same FAO-UNESCO Soil Map of the World and linked global climatic database as Beinroth et al. (2001).[7] Our sample data suggest that there is a positive, fairly strong, and significant correlation between soil quality and population density. This holds for both 1700 (.531) and 1870 (.579). But did areas with better soil quality display a tendency towards extensive growth, driven by population growth that was positively responding to the domestic food supply? The corresponding association with GDP per capita is initially weak (1700: .095) but turns stronger and significant for 1870 (.446). Over the longer term, and in the given sample, higher levels of inherent soil quality do not appear to have worked against intensive (or productivity) growth and improvements in living standards.

Malaria prevalence is regarded as a key risk in the disease environment that affects economic development (cf. Carstensen and Gundlach 2006). Some authors (e.g. Sachs 2001; Sachs and Malaney 2002; Sachs 2003) have argued that the disease ecology may have direct effects on income and development, while others maintained that it is through their impact on institutions, i.e. indirectly, that first nature characteristics such as malaria prevalence affect economic growth (e.g. Acemoglu et al. 2001; Rodrik et al. 2004). The jury is still out on this issue. Though imprecise as to the historical dating, Figure 14.3 shows that North American, East Asian, and European regions that are now largely unaffected by malaria were once areas of considerable environmental risk. Some parts of America and Eurasia were never affected but much of Africa, South America, and South East Asia still is today.

The location of countries, the ruggedness of their terrain, and their access to waterways shape the ease or difficulty of communication over distance. A favourable geography providing good 'natural' transportation networks conferred economic advantage. In the eighteenth and early nineteenth centuries, the costs per ton mile of transport across and along rivers, lakes, and the sea were far lower than over land by pack animals or wagon (Cain 2006; Grafe et al. 2010). Coastal areas and regions endowed with navigable waters were thus in a more favourable position in terms of access to domestic and

7 With exception of the Ottoman Empire, all economies listed in Table 14.1 are included in the sample.

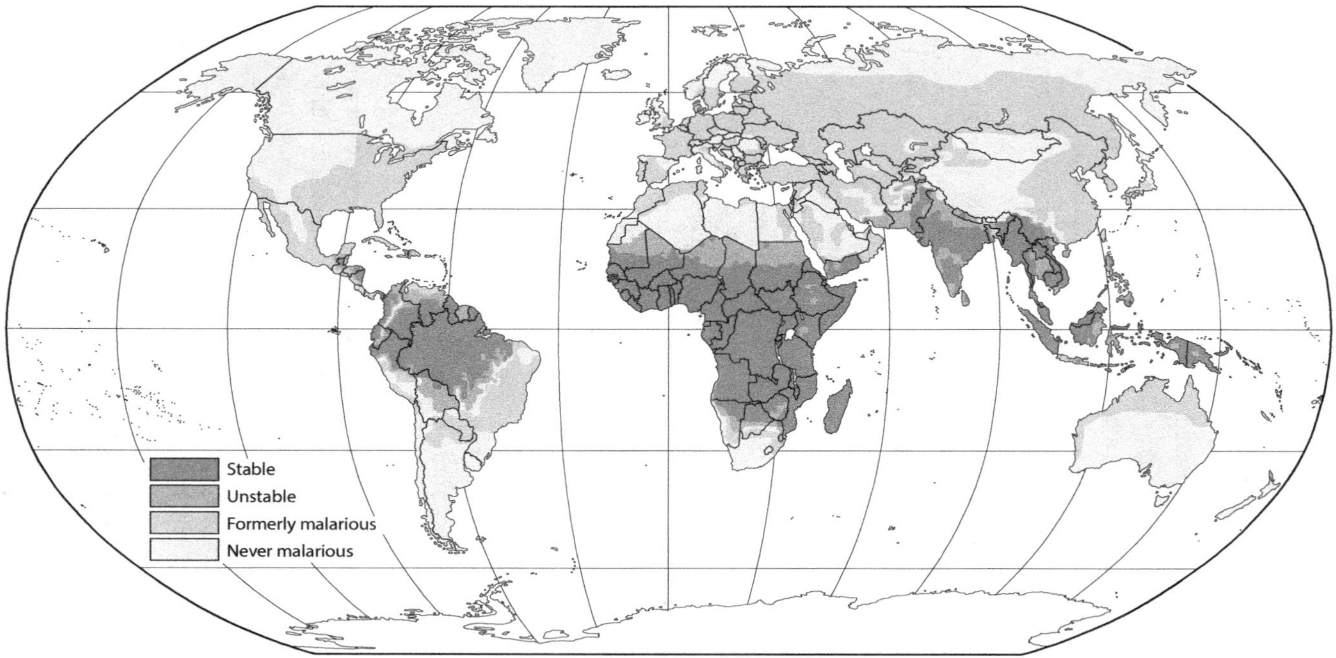

Figure 14.3 Past and current malaria prevalence
Source: Redrawn based on a map by the World Bank (2009). Creative commons licence CC BY 4.0 (link: ccsearch.creativecommons.org/photos/17ffffde-a6af-4b46-a9bd-8777fe578840).

foreign markets, trade, and the gains to be had from increasing interregional division of labour than landlocked regions and those with poor inland waterways. One way to illustrate the effects of access to water on human activity is to consider the location of cities as centres of population. It is not by chance that almost all of the world's largest cities in the eighteenth and nineteenth centuries were either port cities or located on large rivers, offering ready communications across distance (Table 14.4). This is, of course, not to say that the locus of cities was determined solely by 'first nature' geography. Bosker and Buringh's (2017) long run study on the origins of the European city system suggests, though, that proximity to water was particularly important for the formation of cities and their growth. All this matters since it is cities where, historically and up to today, much of societies' productivity advances and the related institutional, commercial, and technological changes originate (Glaeser 2011).

Table 14.4 illustrates another important issue. There was a pronounced shift in the global hierarchy of cities. In the seventeenth and eighteenth centuries, Asian cities were still dominating. Led by London, this changed rapidly and by 1875 the five largest cities were either in Europe or America. This shift cannot be accounted for by 'first nature' geography. Rather, it is a reflection of the gradual movement of the economic centre of gravity from East to West and tallies with de Vries' (1984) observation that the extent of urbanization was positively associated with the level of economic development.

Second Nature Geography – Human Action, Market Access and Change in the Location of Economic Activity

'New economic geography' reasoning holds that exogenous first nature geography advantages or disadvantages become amplified rather than reduced by economic forces as maintained in standard theory: regions or countries characterized by 'good' geography will attract people and firms, which – given the 'proximity-productivity' nexus – will lead to further advances in productivity. By the same token, regions with 'bad' geography will display lower levels of activity and attract fewer people, further lowering productivity. In other words, if workers and firms move to where productivity is high, this will further raise productivity and so generate a changing and uneven spatial distribution of activity. The implication is that reductions in the costs of interaction, e.g. the costs of internal and external trade, may have

Table 14.4 World's largest cities (population, thousands)

	1700		1750		1800		1850		1875
Istanbul	700	Beijing	900	Beijing	1,100	London	2,320	London	4,241
Tokyo	688	Tokyo	694	London	861	Beijing	1,648	Paris	2,250
Beijing	650	London	676	Guangzhou	800	Paris	1,314	New York	1,900
London	550	Istanbul	625	Tokyo	685	Guangzhou	875	Berlin	1,045
Paris	530	Paris	556	Istanbul	570	Istanbul	785	Vienna	1,020
Ahmedabad	385	Osaka	413	Paris	547	Tokyo	780	Beijing	900
Osaka	380	Guangzhou	400	Naples	430	New York	646	Istanbul	873
Esfahan	350	Kyoto	362	Hangzhou	387	Mumbai	580	Philadelphia	791
Kyoto	350	Hangzhou	340	Osaka	383	St. Petersburg	502	Tokyo	781
Hangzhou	303	Naples	310	Kyoto	377	Berlin	446	St. Petersburg	764
Amsterdam	210	Amsterdam	219	Moscow	248	Hangzhou	434	Mumbai	718
Naples	207	Lisbon	213	Suzhou	243	Vienna	426	Calcutta	680
Guangzhou	200	Mashhad	200	Lucknow	240	Philadelphia	426	Guangzhou	670
Aurangabad	200	Xian	195	Lisbon	237	Liverpool	425	Liverpool	650
Lisbon	188	Seoul	187	Vienna	231	Calcutta	413	Glasgow	635
top 10									
% Asia	0.64		0.59		0.61		0.39		0.12
% Europe	0.36		0.41		0.39		0.54		0.70
top 15									
% Asia	0.60		0.59		0.57		0.39		0.21
% Europe	0.40		0.41		0.43		0.52		0.64

Source: Reba et al. (2016).

asymmetric and clustering rather than dispersion effects. Regions close to large and growing markets confer advantages to increasing returns to scale industries, which will be attracted to such regions. Further, depending on the strength of amplification effects, these can even generate disparities between locations that are identical in their (exogenously given) underlying characteristics. Trade, then, does not necessarily lead to a diminution in regional income differentials (Krugman 1991). A key insight here is that even with perfect institutions across the globe, regional or international market integration can lead to divergence in incomes as economic activity becomes more concentrated.

The period from the early eighteenth century up to the 1870s witnessed profound technical and organizational changes that affected the cost of interaction between spatially distant economic agents over short as well as very long distances: these included the construction of new canals, the pavement of roads and extension of road networks just as much as improvements in port facilities and sailing technology. These changes led to declining transport costs even before the gradual transition to steam propulsion (shipping, railways) beginning in the early nineteenth century.[8] Thereafter, growing adoption of the new technology on land and at sea 'contributed to the re-orientation of trading patterns within and beyond Europe' (Grafe et al. 2010).

Trade costs 'include all costs incurred in getting a good to a final user other than the marginal cost of producing the good itself: transportation costs (both freight costs and time costs), policy barriers (tariffs and non-tariff barriers), information costs, contract enforcement costs, costs associated with the use of different currencies, legal and regulatory costs, and local distribution costs (wholesale and retail)' (Anderson and van Wincoop 2004: 691–692). While transport costs, especially across the seas, are fairly well documented for the early nineteenth century (e.g. Harley 1988; Findlay and O'Rourke 2007), the same cannot be said for the other components of trade costs. Trade cost approximations derived from the estimation of gravity models employing bilateral trade and output data are available for the late nineteenth and twentieth century (e.g. Jacks et al. 2010), but not for the historical period of interest here. However, given their large component weight, transport costs can still offer a meaningful, approximate take on the development of trade costs. Figures 14.4 and 14.5 illustrate the trend decline in the costs of economic interaction over land and sea from the mid-eighteenth century. This decline fostered not only the rapid expansion in international trade during the

8 Cf. Bogart (2014) on Britain or Grafe et al. (2010) on Europe.

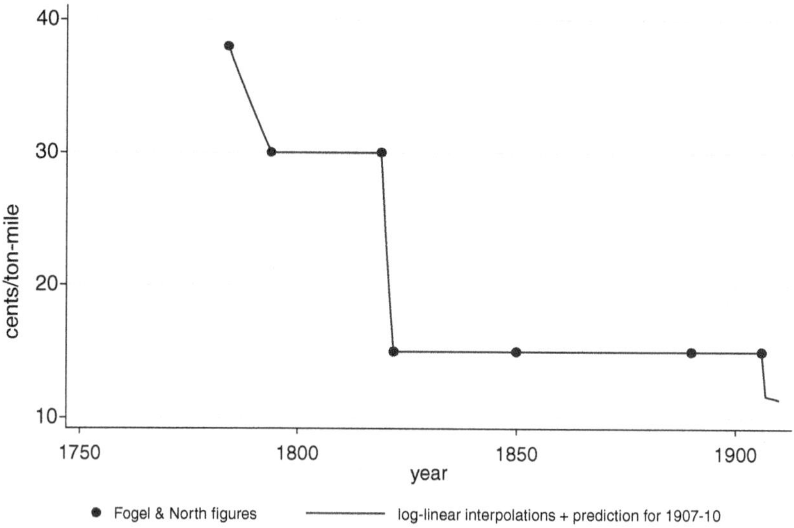

Figure 14.4 Wagon freight cost
Sources: Fogel (1964), Cain (2006, citing North (1965)).

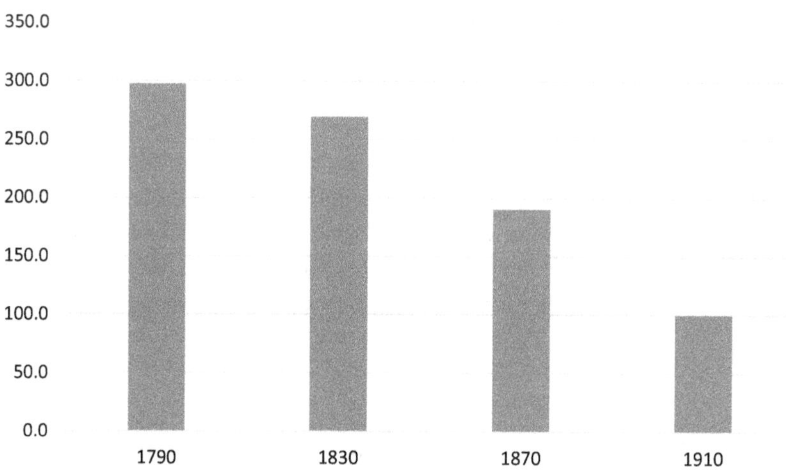

Figure 14.5 Index of ocean shipping costs (1910=100)
Source: Harley (1988).

nineteenth century (Findlay and O'Rourke 2007; O'Rourke et al. 2010), but also major shifts in the location of economic activity across space.

Urbanization

Before exploring inter-economy differences in access to markets and their effects on comparative income development, let us consider changes in the geographical distribution of activity from a different angle – urbanization. The extent of urbanization can be viewed as an outcome of the balance between '*centripetal* forces that tend to pull population and production into agglomerations and *centrifugal* forces that tend to break such agglomerations up' (Krugman 1996: 7). Typically, the former include natural factors providing favourable conditions such as ready access to water or geographically central locations, external economies related to market size (backward and forward linkages; thick labour markets), and 'pure' externalities like knowledge spillovers.[9] The historical evidence would suggest that these forces came to prevail over the long term, and especially so in Europe and North America. Global population growth (about 0.5 per cent during 1700–1870)[10] was associated with an increase in the spatial concentration of population – across the world, the share of people living in cities rose from about 5 per cent in 1700 to *c*.16 per cent in 1900. However, in Europe and North America urbanization proceeded at such rates that by 1880 the proportion of the population living in urban areas (29 per cent) was about three times as large as in Asia (Table 14.5). By that time, Europe and the United States had replaced Asia as the locus of the world's largest cities (Table 14.4).

In the eighteenth and nineteenth centuries, urbanization, i.e. spatial concentration of population in cities (observed at continental, national, or regional levels) and the location of production were closely associated. In 1750, Europe and the US accounted for 20 per cent of the world's population, but produced *c*.25 per cent of global manufacturing output (Table 14.2). By 1880, the output share of these two – by then most urbanized – regions of the world had increased dramatically to 75 per cent whilst having less than 30 per cent of the world's population. The evidence is consistent with the view that urbanization, the 'pull into agglomerations', was positively related

9 In contrast, market-mediated forces such as commuting cost, urban land rents and the pull of dispersed resources (e.g. farmland) as well as non-market factors like congestion and pollution tend to work against agglomeration (Krugman 1996).

10 Note that population growth in Europe and, especially, its 'western off-shoots' was markedly faster than in Africa and Asia. See ourworldindata.org/world-population-growth.

Table 14.5 Share of the population living in urban areas (percentage)

	1600	1700	1750	1800	1850	1880	1900
Africa				4.0	4.0	4.0	5.0
Asia				10.0	10.0	10.0	10.0
Europe	7.6	9.2	9.5	10.0	16.7	29.0	
North America (US)	0.7	2.0		6.1	15.4	28.6	40.0
Latin America & Carib.				14.0	13.0	17.0	20.0
World	5.2	5.1		7.3			16.4
China	7.0	5.9		6.0			6.6
India	4.6	4.9		6.4			10.0
Japan	4.4	5.0		5.0			11.9
European regions							
Central	5.0	7.1	7.5	7.1	12.5		26.8
Eastern	1.4	2.6	3.5	4.2	7.5		18.0
Mediterranean	13.7	11.7	11.8	12.9	18.6		22.2
North & West	8.2	13.1	13.6	14.9	26.1		43.4
Middle East	1.7	2.1		5.7			15.8

Sources and notes: Our World in Data – ourworldindata.org/urbanization. For European regions, the 1900 values refer to 1890.

to economic development and productivity growth (e.g. de Vries 1984). Physical proximity to other people (producers, consumers, workers) saved on trade costs and allowed for economies of scale which arise from locating in areas of intense economic activity.

Market Access and Economic Growth

Access to markets as a 'second nature' geography measure has been identified in the literature as one of the key determinants of cross-country income differences (Redding and Venables 2004; Mayer 2009; Head and Mayer 2011; Jacks and Novy 2018). In this literature, the derivation of market access is explicitly grounded in theory and typically based on twentieth-century data explored in either cross-section or panel settings. For reasons of data constraints, such an approach is as yet not feasible in the early nineteenth-century context. Instead, we draw on an older yet pioneering informal 'model' in which the notion of market potential was first introduced (Harris 1954). Here, a region's market potential (or access to markets) is measured as the sum of transport (or trade) cost weighted GDP in that region and in other adjacent or distant regions (or countries). Estimating market potential requires data on domestic and foreign GDP as well as transport costs. With these data in place, we estimated market potential for a balanced sample of thirteen economies and at decadal intervals over 1800 to 1860.[11] Changes in market potential (or access) are the outcome of changes in income (countries' own as well as that of other countries) and/or changes in the distance-related costs of accessing this income or purchasing power. A reduction (or rise) in transport costs will, therefore, affect countries' access to markets.

The new market potential estimates are based on land-mass-bounded geodesic overland distances, sailing distances for sea routes, river routes as well as ocean shipping freight rates and estimated overland freight rates (wagon freight), allowing for multiple nodes within each economy. In the absence of more precise data, freight rates for river routes are assumed to be equal to sea freight rates. These data were digitized and put together in a Geographical Information System (GIS), enabling us to calculate the lowest-cost route from any one regional node to another. Steam shipping and railways gained significance only towards the very end of the period under review. While railway construction in Europe and North America began before 1870, the mid-nineteenth century railway networks were of limited extension wherever in the world (cf. Mitchell 2013) and failed to connect a number of important nodes. Most regions in our sample did not have railways at all until the late nineteenth century (all of China, for example). Sailing was the main mode of sea transport – in terms of tonnage – throughout the early to mid-nineteenth century. Here, routing builds on the world's main sailing lines, taking into account whether lines were eastbound or westbound (Rodrigue 2013), augmented by connecting routes from the main regional ports to the nearest major shipping line. They ensure that every regional port has a connection to the global ocean lines. Freight rates for overland transport are derived from Fogel (1964) and North (1965), while those for sea-based transport have been estimated on the basis of Findlay and O'Rourke (2007) and Kaukianinen (2006).

11 Note that for each of the thirteen economies, the country-level estimates of market potential are derived from underlying regional market potentials. The latter, in turn, are based, first, upon the distribution of a country's GDP across its regions and, second, the costs of transport from any region in a given country to all other domestic and foreign regional nodes (economic centres) in the sample, which serve as GDP access weights. The sample includes *c.*300 regions across the thirteen economies. In the given Harris-type setting of calculating market potential, the main advantage of a procedure that builds on regional rather than country-level data is the avoidance of serious distortions in estimated costs of access to both domestic and foreign purchasing power that would result from using single country nodes. This would be particularly problematic for geographically very large countries such as, say, Canada, China or the US.

Table 14.6 Market potential (GB = 100)

	1800	1830	1860
Australia*	77	81	74
Canada	84	87	82
China	101	100	87
France	82	81	79
GB	100	100	100
Germany	89	92	88
Habsburg Empire	44	42	40
India	90	90	81
Italy	88	90	84
Japan	90	91	81
Spain	88	90	83
Sweden	83	85	78
US	85	88	84

*Including New Zealand.
Sources and notes: See text.

Table 14.6 above documents the development of market potential in the first half of the nineteenth century. Note that at the beginning of the century, China's market potential was slightly larger than Britain's; by 1860 it had declined by 14 percentage points relative to Britain. Although all economies in the sample appear to have lost out in relative terms vis-à-vis Britain to some varying but overall modest degree up to 1860, the key observation here is the far stronger adverse development for the Asian economies of China, India, and Japan – i.e. those economies that were falling behind more rapidly advancing Europe and America.

The task now is to assess quantitatively whether and to what comparative extent first nature characteristics, second nature geography forces – 'the changing costs of economic interactions across distance' (Crafts and Venables 2003) – and institutional quality account for changes in the global distribution of economic activity and income. The discussion builds on a simple panel regression framework and our balanced sample of thirteen major economies across America, Asia, and Europe. The explanatory variables include 'exogenous' first nature characteristics (such as terrain ruggedness, soil quality, and malaria stability) and second nature variables such as our measure of market potential; as a control, we include a measure of railway density and finally we use an institutional quality variable that is constructed from data in Polity IV. Note that all sample economies had access to the sea. Further, all of them produced coal (anthracite and / or lignite) from some time during or throughout the nineteenth century (Mitchell 2013), i.e. each country in the sample had more or less significant coal deposits.[12] However, evidence on proven, recoverable coal reserves is available only for the later twentieth and early twenty-first century. All explanatory variables have been constructed or adjusted so as to match with countries' nineteenth-century boundaries – an issue of particular relevance in the cases of the Habsburg Empire and India.[13]

By construction, the market potential measure includes economies' own GDP and that of other economies. With GDP per capita as the dependent variable, this raises potential reverse-causation and endogeneity problems. We address these issues by relying on two-stage-least-squares estimation and instrumenting market potential with the sum of the inverted distances to London, Luxembourg, New York, and Tokyo.

The results are reported in Table 14.7. All coefficients have the expected signs and are highly significant, apart from that on ln(Railway Density) whose insignificance is not surprising given the then low rates of railway diffusion and the associated lack of network density effects across the sample economies. The coefficient on ln(MP) is fully within the range observed in other recent studies concerned with market potential. On balance, these results add up to considerable support for arguments that stress the importance of geography in economic development. Both first nature characteristics and second nature forces mattered for inter-economy income differentials between 1800 and 1860. Controlling for key characteristics of the physical environment, economies enjoying better access to markets fared far better in terms of per capita income. Particularly rugged terrain imposed a penalty just as much as high soil quality conferred income advantages. Most striking, though, is the powerful effect on income of an adverse disease (malaria) environment. This tallies with Carstensen and Gundlach's (2006) point that, if appropriately measured, geography as captured in (exogenous) malaria risk does indeed matter at least as much as institutional quality. According to our results, institutions are clearly part of the explanation of the observed income differentials among the sample economies. However, the West became

12 Given the lack of internationally comparative historical evidence on proven, recoverable coal reserves in the first half of the nineteenth century, we do not include a measure of the extent of such deposits among the explanatory variables.

13 The measures of terrain ruggedness and soil quality are derived on the basis of data from Nunn and Puga (2012); for malaria ecology we rely on Kiszewski et al. (2004) index measuring the stability of malaria transmission based on geographically-specific vector mosquitoes. This measure, too, is time-invariant and highly region-specific.

Table 14.7 GDP per capita and market potential

dep. var.	(1) ln (GDPpc)		(2) ln (GDPpc)		(3) ln (GDPpc)		(4) ln (GDPpc)	
ln (MP)	0.5076	***	0.4228	***	0.4456	***	0.3027	***
	0.1722		*0.1589*		*0.1372*		*0.0053*	
Institutional quality	0.0203	***	0.0231	***	0.0230	***	0.0316	**
	0.0039		*0.0029*		*0.0028*		*0.0130*	
Ruggedness	−0.2477	***	−0.2127	***	−0.2163	***		
	0.0414		*0.0387*		*0.0379*			
Soil quality	0.0117	***	0.0100	***	0.0104	***		
	0.0024		*0.0018*		0.0015			
Malaria ecology	−0.8513	***	−0.7917	***	−0.8007	***		
	0.0911		*0.0742*		*0.0637*			
ln (railway density)	−0.0296		0.0063					
	0.0390		*0.0201*					
Constant	−4.6737		−2.4940		−3.0354		−0.2807	***
	4.0901		*3.6409*		*3.1226*		0.0212	
R-squared	0.573		0.683		0.680		0.878	
Obs.	91		91		91		91	
Year FE	N		Y		Y		Y	
Country FE	N		N		N		Y	

Robust standard errors in *italics*; ***p<0.01, **<0.05, *≤0.10
2nd stage results, 2-stage-least-squares; instrument: ln of sum of inverted distances to London, Luxembourg, New York, Tokyo.

absolutely and relatively richer not just because of better institutions, but also, and significantly so, because of more favourable geographies.

Case Study: Changes in Competitive Advantage and the Location of Production in Cotton Textiles – India and Britain

It is well known that the cotton industry originated where raw materials were easily available, in other words, where the climate was hot or mild enough for the cultivation of cotton. In this sense, India was the original home of cotton cultivation and cotton spinning – activities well suited to the local climate (Farnie 2004: 395). However, over the long term technological change induced a shift in competitive advantage in cotton textile production away from India and in Britain's favour. This shift was associated with a major change in the location of the industry, which from the late eighteenth century became spatially highly concentrated in Britain and, specifically so, in Lancashire.[14] In other words, favourable first nature characteristics did not *per se* confer a permanent advantage in terms of industrial location.

India was the largest producer and exporter of cotton goods in the world during the early modern period, exporting to Britain on a large scale from the seventeenth century. 'By the early nineteenth century, however, Britain had become the world's most important cotton textile producer, dominating world export markets and even exporting to India' (Broadberry and Gupta 2009: 279). In the fifty or so years around the turn of the eighteenth to the nineteenth century, cotton textile production in Britain rose about thirtyfold (Riello 2016: 144). This shift from Indian to British predominance in cotton textiles can, up to a point, be accounted for in terms of technological change in response to factor-price differentials. Growing imports of cotton cloth from India through the East India Company during the seventeenth century triggered moves towards import substitution in Britain (cf. Inikori 1989). British producers, including makers of fine woollen and linen fabrics, became increasingly concerned about their products being substituted with cheaper and fashionable Indian printed cottons. High wages in Britain meant that cotton textiles produced domestically employing traditional labour-intensive methods could not compete with Indian goods. The outcome was a search for new, capital-intensive methods of production that ultimately led to a shift of competitive advantage in Lancashire's favour. Broadberry and Gupta (2009) identify four stages in the evolution of this shift.[15]

During the first stage, from about 1700 to the 1770s, domestic producers pressured the government successfully for protective legislation. While this helped to advance a domestic industry in Lancashire, whose output eventually replaced imports from India, British producers could still not compete with India in third markets. Whereas cheap skilled labour was readily available in India, the wage rate of unskilled labour was about four to five times higher in Britain as early as the seventeenth century. It was in the second stage (*c.*1770s–90s) that competitive advantage began to shift in Britain's favour, driven by rapid technological progress in more

14 See Crafts and Wolf (2014) for a detailed quantitative examination of first and second nature factors shaping the location of the cotton industry within early nineteenth-century Britain.

15 Unless noted otherwise, the following discussion relies on Broadberry and Gupta (2009). See also Inikori (1989).

machine-intensive manufacturing that was responding elastically to high wage rates. The outcome was a dramatic rise in productivity. Yet the British FOB (free on board) price remained far above the CIF (cost, insurance, and freight) price of Indian goods in Britain as wage and raw cotton costs moved in favour of Indian producers, offsetting the gains from productivity growth. In the third stage, between the 1790s and the 1820s, swift technological change was associated with sustained productivity growth in Britain while the Anglo-Indian differential in raw cotton prices narrowed substantially. Raw cotton cost after the end of the Napoleonic Wars declined enough to realize the benefits of rapidly increasing productivity, The British FOB price now fell below the CIF price of Indian goods in Britain. Indian cloth was increasingly displaced by British cloth in the British market, while Lancashire producers found it easier to compete with India in third markets such as Africa, where transport costs were similar for both countries. Finally, and from about 1830, technology-driven productivity gains in Britain reduced British FOB prices to such an extent that the British selling price in the Indian market, inclusive of transport costs, fell below the Indian FOB price in at least some products. Britain's share of the Indian market grew from 3 per cent in the 1830s to 61 per cent in the 1880s.[16]

However, the shift in the global centre of gravity in cotton textiles production over the eighteenth and nineteenth centuries was not just an outcome of technological advance in Britain. It was also, and critically so, shaped by a changing geography of trade and the reinforcing effects of the interaction of productivity growth and access to markets. Changes in the pattern of international trade removed the constraints imposed on British producers by the distinct lack of nearby supplies of raw cotton. Crucially, they also opened up export opportunities, dramatically increasing the size of the market and thus the scope for the scale economies that British cotton textile manufacturers were able to exploit. The removal of input constraints and the expansion of output markets were intricately linked in the slave-based economy of the Atlantic system and its triangular trade with Britain as a central actor.[17]

Up to the end of the seventeenth century and in the absence of significant local cultivation, Europe, including Britain, had relied mainly on imports of raw cotton from the Levant to produce small quantities of fustians, i.e. mixed

16 Broadberry and Gupta (2009) also identify comparatively low interest rates and rental prices of capital as well as a functioning patent system as advantageous to Britain.

17 For a detailed discussion of the significance of the slave-based Atlantic economy in British industrial development see Inikori (1989; 2002).

linen-cotton fabrics. With growing demand and, in particular, a shift in consumer tastes towards finer cotton fabrics, these sources proved inadequate. The potential alternative of importing large quantities of raw cotton from distant Asia was ruled out by high transport costs (Riello 2016). Instead, the focus turned to developing cotton (and other) plantations in the Americas, exploiting the labour of African slaves bought on the coasts of West Africa and their enslaved descendants. Their production of colonial cash crops such as raw cotton was destined for export as inputs in British manufacturing. In turn, British-made cotton textiles were sold on the domestic market and exported in rapidly growing quantities to Africa, British North America, and eventually India and markets across the world. With British commercial interests backed up by the Royal Navy's command of the seas, it was in the Atlantic economy that a considerable part of the success of the British cotton textile industry in the eighteenth and nineteenth century originated.

Productivity growth in British cotton manufacturing had cumulative effects through its interaction with second nature geography forces. It was at once a source and an outcome of growing access to markets and purchasing power. Variations in relative wage and raw material costs notwithstanding, over the longer term technology-based productivity advances were instrumental in the rise of British firms' competitiveness vis-à-vis Indian cotton producers, underpinning their growing share in expanding domestic and international markets. The demand offered by a larger market encouraged firms to enter the industry and exposed those engaged in the production for exports to 'stiff competition with cheap and high-quality Indian cotton goods ... and induced them to adopt innovations that reduced costs and raised quality. These developments ... enabled the industry to successfully invade major European markets and those of the Americas from the late eighteenth century onward' (Inikori 1989: 345). The long run outcome was an industry that, in the global context, became heavily concentrated in Britain and, more specifically, Lancashire. Following Marshall (1920), theory tells us that gains from industry agglomeration – or geographical concentration of economic activity – arise when and where proximity reduces the costs of moving goods, people, and ideas (Ellison et al. 2010). Market-size related external economies making for the agglomeration of people and activity typically derive from access to output and input markets as well as thick labour markets as distinct from 'pure' external economies such as knowledge spillovers (Krugman 1996). There is, then, a nexus between market size, agglomeration, and productivity. The historical evidence would suggest that these forces can indeed account to a significant extent for Lancashire's rise as the world's centre of cotton textiles production. According to a broad consensus in the literature, the nineteenth-century Lancashire cotton industry gained substantially from external economies of scale that resulted *inter alia* from productivity-enhancing networks of large numbers of co-locating small but highly specialized and interconnected firms, the ready transmission of tacit knowledge and deep pools of labour (cf. Broadberry and Marrison 2002; Leunig 2003; Crafts and Wolf 2014).[18]

In short, our case study shows how over the course of the eighteenth and early nineteenth centuries the production base of the cotton textiles industry shifted from a part of the world with natural advantages (or favourable first nature characteristics) to a new area that developed technological advantages and was able to gain from a changing geography of trade.

Conclusion

This chapter has considered the historical evidence on whether and to what extent 'geography', as one among the fundamental sources of economic growth and cross-country income differences typically identified in the literature, can account for the changes in the global distribution of economic activity since 1700 and up to the onset of the Second Industrial Revolution. Notwithstanding the impact of institutions, our findings suggest that geography in both its first and second nature incarnations did indeed matter for the East to West shift in the world's economic centre of gravity over the period observed.

References

Acemoglu, D. (2009). *Introduction to Modern Economic Growth*, Princeton University Press.

Acemoglu, D., Johnson, S. and Robinson, J. (2001). 'The Colonial Origins of Comparative Development', *American Economic Review*, 91, 1369–1401.

(2002). 'Reversal of Fortune: Geography and Institutions in the Making of the Modern World Income Distribution', *Quarterly Journal of Economics*, 117(4), 1231–1294.

Álvarez-Nogal, C. and Prados de la Escosura, L. (2013). 'The Rise and Fall of Spain (1270–1850)', *Economic History Review*, 66(1), 1–37.

Anderson, J. E. and van Wincoop, E. (2004). 'Trade Costs', *Journal of Economic Literature*, 42 (3), 691–751.

18 This is not to imply that first nature geography characteristics played no role in the location of the industry. Cf. Crafts and Wolf (2014).

Arroyo Abad, L. and van Zanden, J. L. (2016). 'Growth Under Extractive Institutions? Latin American Per Capita GDP in Colonial Times', *Journal of Economic History*, 76, 1182–1215.

Bairoch, P. (1982). 'International Industrialization Levels from 1750 to 1980', *Journal of European Economic History*, 11, 269–331.

Bassino, J.-P., Broadberry, S., Fukao, K., Gupta, B. and Takashima, M. (2019). 'Japan and the Great Divergence, 730–1870', *Explorations in Economic History* (forthcoming).

Beinroth, F. H., Eswaran, H. and Reich, P. F. (2001). 'Global Assessment and Land Quality', in Stott, D. E., Mohtar, R. H. and Steinhardt, G. C. (eds.), *Sustaining the Global Farm*, published by the International Soil Conservation Organization in cooperation with United States Department of Agriculture, Agricultural Research Service, and National Soil Erosion Research Laboratory and Purdue University, 569–574.

Bogart, D. (2014). 'The Transport Revolution in Industrializing Britain', in Floud, R., Humphries, J. and Johnson, P. (eds), *The Cambridge Economic History of Modern Britain, vol. 1: 1700–1870*, 4th ed., Cambridge University Press, 53–88.

Bosker, M. and Buringh, E. (2017). 'City Seeds: Geography and the Origins of the European City System', *Journal of Urban Economics*, 98, 139–157.

Bosker, M. and Garretsen, H. (2009). 'Economic Development and the Geography of Institutions', *Journal of Economic Geography*, 9, 295–328.

Broadberry, S. and Gupta, B. (2009). 'Lancashire, India, and Shifting Competitive Advantage in Cotton Textiles, 1700–1850: The Neglected Role of Factor Prices', *Economic History Review*, 62(2), 279–305.

Broadberry, S. and Marrison, A. (2002). 'External Economies of Scale in the Lancashire Cotton Industry, 1900–1950', *Economic History Review*, 55(1), 51–77.

Broadberry, S., Fremdling, R. and Solar, P. (2010). 'Industry, 1700–1870', in Broadberry, S. and O'Rourke, K. H. (eds.), *The Cambridge Economic History of Modern Europe, vol. 1: 1700–1870*, Cambridge University Press, 164–186.

Broadberry, S., Campbell, B., Klein, A., Overton, M. and van Leeuwen, B. (2015a). *British Economic Growth, 1270–1870*, Cambridge University Press.

Broadberry, S., Custodis, J. and Gupta, B. (2015b). 'India and the Great Divergence: An Anglo-Indian Comparison of GDP Per Capita, 1600–1871', *Explorations in Economic History*, 55, 58–75.

Broadberry, S., Guan, H. and Li, D. (2018). 'China, Europe and the Great Divergence: A Study in Historical National Accounting', *Journal of Economic History*, 78, 955–1000.

Buyst, E. (2011). 'Towards Estimates of Long Term Growth in the Southern Low Countries, ca.1500–1846', paper for the 'Quantifying Long Run Economic Development' conference at the University of Warwick in Venice, March 22–24.

Cain, L. P. (2006). 'Transportation – Inland Freight Rates, by Type of Transportation: 1784–1900 (Series Df17-21)', *Historical Statistics of the United States Millennial Edition Online*, Cambridge University Press, hsus.cambridge.org/HSUSWeb/HSUSEntryServlet (accessed 8 October 2020).

Carstensen, K. and Gundlach, E. (2006). 'The Primacy of Institutions Reconsidered: Direct Income Effects of Malaria Prevalence', *The World Bank Economic Review*, 20(3), 309–339.

Crafts, N. and Harley, C. K. (1992), 'Output Growth and the Industrial Revolution: A Restatement of the Crafts-Harley View', *Economic History Review*, 45, 703–730.

Crafts, N. and Venables, A. J. (2003). 'Globalization in History: A Geographical Perspective', in Bordo, M., Taylor, A. and Williamson, J. G. (eds.), *Globalization in Historical Perspective*, University of Chicago Press, 323–364.

Crafts, N. and Wolf, N. (2014). 'The Location of the UK Cotton Textiles Industry in 1838: A Quantitative Analysis', *Journal of Economic History*, 74(4), 1103–1139.

Diamond, J. (1997). *Guns, Germs and Steel: A Short History of Everybody for the Last 13,000 Years*, reprint 2005, London: Vintage Books.

Dollar, D. and Kray, A. (2004). 'Trade, Growth and Poverty', *Economic Journal*, 114, 22–49.

Easterly, W. and Levine, R. (2003). 'Tropics, Germs, and Crops: How Endowments Influence Economic Development', *Journal of Monetary Economics*, 50, 3–39.

Ellison, G., Glaeser, E. L. and Kerr, W. R. (2010). 'What Causes Industry Agglomeration? Evidence from Coagglomeration Patterns', *American Economic Review*, 100, 1195–1213.

Encyclopedia Britannica (n.d.). 'Coal-mining', www.britannica.com/technology/coal-mining (accessed 7 October 2020).

Encyclopedia Britannica (n.d.). 'World Distribution of Coal', www.britannica.com/science/coal-fossil-fuel/World-distribution-of-coal (accessed 7 October 2020).

Farnie, D. A. (2004). *The English Cotton Industry and the World Market 1815–1896*, Oxford University Press.

Fernihough, A. and O'Rourke, K. H. (2014). 'Coal and the European Industrial Revolution', University of Oxford, Discussion Papers in Economic and Social History, no. 124.

Findlay, R. and O'Rourke, K. H. (2007). *Power and Plenty: Trade, War, and the World Economy in the Second Millennium*, Princeton University Press.

Fogel, R. W. (1964). *Railroads and American Economic Growth: Essays in Econometric History*, Baltimore: Johns Hopkins University Press.

Fourie, J. and van Zanden, J. L. (2013). 'GDP in the Dutch Cape Colony: The National Accounts of a Slave-Based Society', *South African Journal of Economics*, 81, 467–490.

Frankel, J. and Romer, D. (1999). 'Does Trade Cause Growth?', *American Economic Review*, 89(3), 379–399.

Glaeser, E. L. (2011). *Triumph of the City: How Our Greatest Invention Makes Us Richer, Smarter, Greener, Healthier, and Happier*, New York: Penguin.

Glaeser, E. L., La Porta, R., Lopez-de-Silanes, F. and Shleifer, A. (2004). 'Do Institutions Cause Growth?', *Journal of Economic Growth*, 9, 271–303.

Grafe, R., Neal, L. and Unger, R. W. (2010). 'The Services Sector', in Broadberry, S. and O'Rourke, K. H. (eds.), *The Cambridge Economic History of Modern Europe, vol. 1: 1700–1870*, Cambridge University Press, 187–213.

Hall, R. and Jones, C. L. (1999). 'Why Do Some Countries Produce So Much More Output Per Worker than Others?', *Quarterly Journal of Economics*, 114(1), 83–116.

Harley, C. K. (1988). 'Ocean Freight Rates and Productivity, 1740–1913: The Primacy of Mechanical Invention Reaffirmed', *Journal of Economic History*, 48(4), 851–876.

Harris, C. (1954). 'The Market as a Factor in the Localization of Industry in the United States', *Annals of the American Geographers*, 64, 315–348.

Head, K. and Mayer, T. (2011). 'Gravity, Market Potential and Economic Development', *Journal of Economic Geography*, 11, 281–294.

Inikori, J. E. (1989). 'Slavery and the Revolution in Cotton Textile Production in England', *Social Science History*, 13(4), 343–379.

(2002). *Africans and the Industrial Revolution in England: A Study in International Trade and Economic Development*, Cambridge University Press.

Jacks, D. S. and Novy, D. (2018). 'Market Potential and Global Growth over the Long Twentieth Century', *Journal of International Economics*, 114, 21–237.

Jacks, D., Meissner, C. and Novy, D. (2010). 'Trade Costs in the First Wave of Globalization', *Explorations in Economic History*, 47, 127–141.

Kaukianinen, Y. (2006). 'Journey Costs, Terminal Costs, and Ocean Freight Rates: How the Price of Distance Declined from the 1870s to 2000', *International Journal of Maritime History*, 18(2), 17–64.

Kausel, A. (1979). 'Österreichs Volkseinkommen 1830–1913', in Österreichisches Statistisches Zentralamt (ed.), *Geschichte und Ergebnisse der zentralen amtlichen Statistik in Österreich 1829–1979*, Vienna: Österreichisches Statistisches Zentralamt.

Kiszewski, A., Mellinger, A., Spielman, A., Malaney, P., Ehrlich Sachs, S. and Sachs, J. (2004). 'A Global Index Representing the Stability of Malaria Transmission', *American Journal of Tropical Medicine and Hygiene*, 70(5), 486–498.

Komlos, J. (1983). *The Habsburg Monarchy as a Customs Union: Economic Development in Austria-Hungary in the Nineteenth Century*, Princeton University Press.

Krugman, P. (1991). *Geography and Trade*. Cambridge, MA: MIT Press.

(1996). 'Urban Concentration: The Role of Increasing Returns and Transport Costs', *International Regional Science Review*, 19 (1 & 2), 5–30.

Leunig, T. (2003). 'A British Industrial Success: Productivity in the Lancashire and New England Cotton Spinning Industries a Century Ago', *Economic History Review* 56(1), 90–117.

Maddison Project Database, version 2013. Bolt, J. and van Zanden, J. L. (2014). 'The Maddison Project: Collaborative Research on Historical National Accounts', *Economic History Review*, 67(3), 627–651.

Maddison Project Database, version 2018. Bolt, J., Inklaar, R., de Jong, H. and van Zanden, J. L. (2018), 'Rebasing "Maddison": New Income Comparisons and the Shape of Long-Run Economic Development', University of Groningen, Groningen Growth and Development Centre Research Memorandum GD-174.

Malanima, P. (2011). 'The Long Decline of a Leading Economy: GDP in Central and Northern Italy, 1300–1913', *European Review of Economic History*, 15, 169–219.

Mancall, P. C. and Weiss, T. (1999). 'Was Economic Growth Likely in Colonial British North America?', *Journal of Economic History*, 59(1), 17–40.

Marshall, A. (1920). *Principles of Economics*, London: Macmillan.

Mayer, T. (2009). 'Market Potential and Development', Centre d'Études Prospective et d'Information Internationales, Document de Travail No. 24.

Mitchell, B. R. (2013). *International Historical Statistics: 1750–2010*, Basingstoke: Palgrave Macmillan, www.worldcat.org/title/international-historical-statistics-1750-2010/oclc/838564900 (accessed 9 November 2020).

North, D. (1965). 'The Role of Transportation in the Economic Development of North America', in *Les Grandes Voies Maritimes dans le Monde XV–XIX Siécles*, École des Hautes Études en Sciences Sociales, 244–245.

(1990). *Institutions, Institutional Change, and Economic Performance*. New York: Cambridge University Press.

Nunn, N. and Puga, D. (2012). 'Ruggedness: The Blessing of Bad Geography in Africa', *The Review of Economics and Statistics*, 94(1): 20–36, online data, diegopuga.org/data/rugged/ (accessed 8 October 2020).

Open University (n.d.). 'Global Distribution of Coal', www.open.edu/openlearn/nature-environment/environmental-studies/energy-resources-coal/content-section–4.5, (accessed 8 October 2020).

O'Rourke, K. H., Prados de la Escosura, L. and Daudin, G. (2010). 'Trade and Empire', in Broadberry, S. and O'Rourke, K. H. (eds.), *The Cambridge Economic History of Modern Europe, vol. 1: 1700–1870*, Cambridge University Press, 96–121.

Our World in Data (n.d.). 'Urbanization', ourworldindata.org/urbanization (accessed 9 October 2020).

Palma, N. and Reis, J. (2018). 'From Convergence to Divergence: Portuguese Economic Growth, 1527–1850', Maddison Project Working Paper WP-11.

Pfister, U. (2011). 'Economic Growth in Germany, 1500–1850', paper for the 'Quantifying Long Run Economic Development' conference at the University of Warwick in Venice, March 22–24.

Pollard, S. (1981). *Peaceful Conquest: The Industrialization of Europe 1760–1970*, reprint 1986, Oxford University Press.

Pomerantz, K. (2000). *The Great Divergence: China, Europe, and the Making of the Modern World Economy*, Princeton University Press.

Reba, M., Femke, R. and Seto, K. C. (2016). 'Spatializing 6,000 Years of Global Urbanization from 3700 BC to AD 2000', Scientific Data 3: 160034, https://pubmed.ncbi.nlm.nih.gov/27271481/, dataset 'ChandlerV2': https://urbanization.yale.edu/data (accessed 9 November 2020).

Redding, S. and Venables, A. J. (2004). 'Economic Geography and International Inequality', *Journal of International Economics*, 62, 53–82.

Ridolfi, L. (2016). 'The French Economy in the Longue Durée: A Study on Real Wages, Working Days and Economic Performance from Louis IX to the Revolution (1250–1789)', unpublished Ph.D. thesis, IMT School for Advanced Studies, Lucca, e-theses.imtlucca.it/211/1/Ridolfi_phdthesis.pdf (accessed 9 October 2020).

Riello, G. (2016). 'Cotton: The Making of a Modern Commodity', *East Asian Journal of British History*, 5(1), 35–149.

Rodrigue, J. P. (2013). *The Geography of Transport Systems*, New York: Routledge.

Rodrik, D., Subramanian, A. and Trebbi, F. (2004). 'Institutions Rule: The Primacy of Institutions over Geography and Integration in Economic Development', *Journal of Economic Growth*, 9, 131–165.

Sachs, J. D. (2001). 'Tropical Underdevelopment', National Bureau of Economic Research Working Paper 8119.

(2003). 'Institutions Don't Rule: Direct Effects of Geography on Per Capita Income', NBER Working Paper 9490.

Sachs, J. D. and Malaney, P. (2002). 'The Economic and Social Burden of Malaria', *Nature*, 415, 680–685.

Sachs, J. D. and Warner, A. (1995). 'Economic Reform and the Process of Global Integration', *Brookings Papers on Economic Activity*, 26(1), 1–118.

Schoen, L. and Krantz, O. (2015). 'New Swedish Historical National Accounts since the 16th Century in Constant and Current Prices', Lund Papers in Economic History no. 140.

Schulze, M. S. (2000). 'Patterns of Growth and Stagnation in the Late Nineteenth Century Habsburg Economy', *European Review of Economic History*, 4(3), 311–340.

Sutch, R. (2006). 'National Income and Product', in Historical Statistics of the United States Online Edition, hsus.cambridge.org/HSUSWeb/HSUSEntryServlet (accessed 9 October 2020).

van Zanden, J. L. and van Leeuwen, B. (2012). 'Persistent but not Consistent: The Growth of National Income in Holland 1347–1807', *Explorations in Economic History*, 49, 119–130.

Venables, A. J. (2006). 'Shifts in Economic Geography and their Causes', Centre for Economic Performance Discussion Paper no. 767.

World Bank (2009). *World Development Report, Part I: Reshaping Economic Geography*, Washington, DC: World Bank.

15

Institutions

JOHN JOSEPH WALLIS

The world of 1870 was very different from the world of 1700. In 1700, most of the New World, North and South America, was divided into colonies of European powers: Spain, Portugal, Britain, France, and the Netherlands. By 1870, after two large waves of revolutionary independence movements and several smaller ones, integrated nation states had appeared throughout the hemisphere and, with a few small remnants primarily in Canada and the Caribbean, the European powers had withdrawn. By 1870, Japan was in the middle of a thoroughgoing revolutionary reorganization of military, political, and economic power: the Meiji Restoration. Europe itself underwent a similar and profound change in structure, with the consolidation of modern fiscal nation states in Britain, France, the Netherlands, and Switzerland and the gradual agglomeration of pieces and the beginning of consolidated nation states in Italy, Germany, Spain, and the Scandinavian countries.

The revolutionary changes in the structure of the political and economic systems of these countries, many of them becoming 'countries' for the first time, clearly resulted in part from the dislocations and changes occurring in the world because of the economic and technological changes that we refer to as the 'Industrial Revolution', which make up a central narrative theme of the economic history of the modern world. Equally, however, it seems that the nature of the revolutionary changes in their political and economic institutions was a key determinant of whether these countries industrialized. Some have suggested, for example, that the institutions that developed in British North America were key to their ability to take advantage of the new industrial technologies, while the institutions that developed in Spanish Latin America crippled their ability to industrialize.[1] One of the central questions in economic history is

1 Acemoglu, Johnson, and Robinson, 'Colonial Origins' and 'Reversal of Fortune'.

how much of modern economic development is the result (or cause) of changes in political and economic institutions.

The economic historian Douglass North defined institutions as 'the rules of the game and the means of enforcement' or alternatively as 'humanly devised constraints on human behaviour'. In common use the word institution means many things. The Catholic Church is an institution, democracy is an institution, speed limits are institutions, and marriage is an institution, but clearly the church, democracy, speed limits, and marriage are not all the same type of social phenomenon. Economic historians who think about institutions tend to divide them into two types: norms and rules. Norms are patterns of behaviour that constrain individual choices. In this chapter I focus on institutions as agreed-upon rules, not institutions as norms. The institutional structure of a society is made up of the agreed-upon rules that govern the internal relationships between members of organizations as well as the relationships between organizations. We can think of societies as organizations of organizations, and some of the organizations in a society are governments. A central part of the history of institutions between 1700 and 1870 is the rise of bigger and more organized governments.

Economic historians have long understood that institutions as agreed-upon rules have a direct effect on economic performance. Most societies before the modern period were agrarian. Rules governing the use, ownership, and ability to transfer land between individuals (by buying or selling, inheritance, or violence) play a fundamental role in the productivity of agriculture. These rules are 'primary rules', rules that directly affect the decisions that people make. For example, under feudalism, many peasant landowners had secure use of their property, they could use it year after year, but they could not sell their land to someone else.

Property laws regarding land are agreed-upon rules, and agreed-upon rules require an agreement. How do societies structure the process by which groups decide upon what rules they will recognize? In other words, what are the rules for forming (or changing) rules? The legal theorist H. L. A. Hart called these rules for creating or changing rules 'secondary rules'.

This chapter lays out a simple framework for how we might think about how political and economic institutions interact by focusing on primary and secondary rules. In the most general and abstract way, secondary rules structure the political system and primary rules the economic system. The interaction of primary and secondary rules throughout a society is central to understanding the institutional structure and how it changes over time.

Why the emphasis on primary *and* secondary rules? Most economic historians agree that institutions governing the use of land, labour, capital, and other resources, as well as rules governing the ability of people to contract and exchange have an effect on economic performance. Yet, despite a wide understanding that secure and alienable property rights in land could improve agricultural productivity, many societies are unable to create and enforce primary rules that enable secure property rights in land or in other economic activities. In fact, in most societies the agreed-upon rules tend to favour some groups over others, and are often not enforced in an unbiased way that enables people to believe that the rules will be credibly enforced. That makes secure property rights in land or other possessions problematic. Why is that?

The answer lies in the interaction of primary and secondary rules. Secondary rules determine *who* gets to determine the rules and under what conditions and processes. If the individuals endowed with the ability to make and change the rules do not find it in their interest to create secure property rights in land and to enforce the rules that make property secure, then property rights will not be secure. The secondary rules go a long way to explaining why primary rules promote growth or do not. As we will see, credible secondary rules are a problem in many societies. If the secondary rules are insecure, then so, too, are the primary rules that depend on the secondary rules.

This chapter develops these institutional concepts and uses them to examine three historical cases between 1700 and 1870: Spain and her colonies; Britain and her colonies; and Japan during the Tokugawa Shogunate and, very briefly, after the Meiji Restoration. What we will see is that in Spain and in Japan, the societies at the time of significant institutional change had trouble adopting clear secondary rules, while the British institutions in the United States were transformed into much clearer and credible secondary rules.

Since the secondary rules determine who gets to set the rules under what conditions, primary rules must always be consistent with the interests of those with the power to make and enforce the rules. The primary rules can promote or retard economic performance. It may be in the interests of the decision-makers to impoverish the general population to enrich themselves, for example. The primary rules, and the economic outcomes they produce, create the circumstances under which the secondary rules might change, that is the conditions under which the decision-makers find it in their interests to change the secondary rules. Since secondary rules are the rules for changing rules, there are also secondary rules for changing the existing secondary rules.

One of the conditions for modern development to occur is the presence of clear and stable secondary rules. In most societies, secondary rules are vague and unpredictable. If the actual secondary rule in place is that whichever group is in power gets to make the rules, and who is in power changes unpredictably from time to time, then the secondary rules will be uncertain. Those conditions describe Japan in both the Tokugawa and Meiji periods. In both Spain and Britain, and in the Spanish and British Empires, the secondary rules were clear and stable, but resulted in very different patterns of primary rules. In the late eighteenth and early nineteenth centuries, the Spanish institutions proved incapable of dealing with the rapid changes occurring throughout the Latin American world, and countries in South and Central America have trouble with credible secondary rules to this day. In parts of the British Empire, notably the United States and Canada, the British domestic and colonial institutions were transformed into clear and credible secondary rules.

This chapter gives you an idea of what institutions are in a way that enables you to see how institutions varied in each of the three cases. The framework enables you to see why certain aspects of the primary rules promoted economic growth in some of the societies, how secondary rules supported those primary rules, and how primary and secondary rules interact.

The Colonial Heritage in the New World

The Heritage

Although both Spain in 1500 and England in 1600 were kingdoms when they began to expand their reach into colonies around the world, their internal institutions were quite different. Spain had recently integrated under a common monarch. Government in Spain was relatively decentralized while the monarchy was relatively strong. Much of the actual business of government was spread widely across subordinate kingdoms and, particularly, towns and cities, who negotiated with the king for things like taxes and defence. Because Spain had been reconquered from the Moors over several centuries, towns and local nobility gained significant privileges as the reconquest proceeded. Local privileges were necessary to ensure local stability, and because they were created at different times and in different circumstance, local privileges varied from town to town. The Crown, or more accurately crowns, negotiated these privileges on a piecemeal basis and continued to do so even after the monarchy consolidated under Ferdinand and Isabella.

The secondary rule in Spain was whatever rules the king negotiated with the towns and local notables were legitimate recognized rules. This meant that the rules varied from region to region and town to town within Spain. The King was 'absolute', but only in the sense that he and his agents were the only entity that negotiated with everyone. In practice, as Irigoin and Grafe (2008) have shown, the king was not able to coerce the towns through threats of violent retribution.

Government in England had similar origins in conquest, the Norman Conquest in 1066. To secure England the Normans and the Norman king, William, seized land and divided it up between military leaders who owed allegiance to William. Royal towns were recognized or created by William and kings that followed. The Royal towns enjoyed privileges like the towns in Spain: some measure of self-governance, tax preferences, recognition as organizations, and the ability to structure organizations like guilds within the town. Not all towns were royal towns, some towns owed their existence to powerful feudal lords, but those towns did not possess the same privileges as the Royal towns.

The English king, while the most powerful individual in the country, had to negotiate constantly with bodies of nobles and towns, just as in Spain. Civil wars were infrequent but not uncommon events. Rather than dealing with the nobles and towns piecemeal, as in Spain, however, organized groups developed to coordinate the collective actions of aristocrats and towns with respect to the king in the form of the House of Lords and the House of Commons. Royal towns were represented in Parliament. The impetus for representing towns in the House of Commons appears to have been the coordination of tax policy and revenue generation. The results were taxes, obligations, and privileges granted to towns and notables that applied more or less equally throughout the kingdom.

The historian J. A. Elliot has termed the European system of governance 'composite monarchy', meaning that most emerging states in Europe around this time were made up of pieces ruled by independent or quasi-independent leaders who were brought into a coalition of powerful organizations under a monarch (Elliot 1992). The relationship of the pieces to the Crown constituted a central part of the institutional structure of each society, particularly in terms of primary and secondary rules. In Spain, the king negotiated agreements with towns and aristocrats individually. The secondary rule was that these agreements between the king and the towns would constitute legitimate primary rules. As a result, the rules, the taxes, and the rights and privileges varied between towns (Irigoin and Grafe 2008; Grafe 2012).

In contrast, in England the king negotiated rules, taxes, and privileges with the nobility and towns through representative bodies and, as a result, the rules created by the king were more or less the same throughout the kingdom. A series of conflicts between the king and the barons, and between groups of barons, led to compromises that created mutual obligations on the part of the king and the barons. Magna Carta was an early example that set the constitutional relationship between the king and the nobles. The relationship in Magna Carta created several secondary rules. It would not be until the late 1600s that Parliament would attain constitutional equality with the king in rule-making. Local lords also maintained their own courts whose rules differed from lord to lord. Nonetheless, from early on, the king's rules applied across the kingdom; they were 'common laws'.[2]

In neither Spain nor England in 1500 were political and economic institutions democratic, representative, or inclusive. It isn't clear that one or the other set of institutions were 'better' in an economic sense of increasing (or decreasing) the standard of living in the two countries. In both countries the institutions were the result of bargains between elites. The king got the best deal, but more powerful elites got better treatment in terms of rules and enforcement of rules than less powerful elites, and elites in general got a much better deal than the mass of the population. It is equally true to say that individuals who received better treatment under the rules became more powerful. The institutions in the two countries displayed patterns of relationships within the elites that shaped how rules were made and enforced – and would carry over into their establishment of colonies in the New World.

Spanish Latin America

Spanish settlement in the New World began with Columbus' landing on Hispaniola in 1492, his return in 1493, and the establishment of a permanent colony. A second colony was established on Cuba in 1511. A series of missions, the third headed by Cortes, led to the conquest of Mexico between 1518 and 1521. The Spanish spread settlements throughout the Caribbean and on its shores. Peru became a colony in 1533.

Four features of Spanish colonization contributed to the unique institutional development of Latin America. First, as in Spain, the king maintained relationships with the colonies on an individual basis. The formal Spanish hierarchy in the New World was weak in the sense that the colonial

2 Spain had representative bodies, indeed the first parliament appears to have been called in Leon in Spain by King Alfonso IX in 1188 (van Zanden et al. 2012: 838).

government structure did not vest power in a central authority, such as a viceroy, who controlled the other colonial offices and officers. In fact, the Crown subverted the hierarchy as much as it sustained it. For example, Cortes acted against the direct orders of the Governor of Cuba when he set off to conquer Mexico, yet the king confirmed Cortes' position in New Spain. Pizarro acted without the permission of the Governor of Panama when he conquered Peru, and the king confirmed his position in Peru. While Cortes and Pizarro's claims and conquests were recognized by the king, they remained the subject of contention. In this, the relationship between New World elites and the monarchy mirrored the relationship between elites and the monarchy in Spain itself. As in the Old World, the king and his agents negotiated directly with local elites to determine what rules would be created and enforced. Rather than ruling through a hierarchy, the king ruled through direct contact with towns, courts, and other government organizations.

Second, the existence of two large, thriving civilizations in the New World enabled the Spanish *conquistadors* to insert themselves into the ruling positions of the Inca and Aztec societies, taking over patterns of tribute and labour control already in existence. The relatively small Spanish population was, in part, able to govern a large native population through the native governance institutions already in place. Third, the Spanish colonists initially established a method for confirming Spanish claims to land and labour together in the *encomienda*. Control over land and native labour was parcelled out among the initial *conquistadors* and those who soon followed. Reallocations periodically occurred in some places, the *repartmiento*. Eventually the *encomienda* system was reformed by the New Law in 1552. How control of land and labour evolved from 1500 on varied widely in the different regions of the Spanish Empire. Property rights in land and labour were negotiated and renegotiated in Latin America. No one owned land free and clear, control of land was always subject to renegotiation and depended on political relationships. As a result, the primary rules were idiosyncratic, varying from colony to colony, town to town, group to group, and even on occasion individual to individual.

Finally, the presence of gold and large silver deposits meant that the Spanish colonies could be a paying proposition for the Spanish Crown. Silver mines in New Spain (Mexico) and Peru formed the financial backbone of the empire. Governance units were created under control of viceroys or captain-generals, appointed by the king; treasuries to monitor the flow of silver from the mines to the king's accounts in Spain, the *cajas*; and courts, the *audiencias*, to resolve disputes about mines, lands, labour, and other conflicts that arose in the colonies. In principle, all these offices were filled by the king and occupied at his pleasure. The *cajas* and *audiencias* were not under the direct control of the viceroy or captain-general. It was in this sense that hierarchy in the Spanish Empire was weak.

As in Spain, these local government organizations dealt with and negotiated with the king and his agents directly. The king did not levy a tax on the *cajas* that applied equally everywhere in the empire. The king negotiated individually with the *cajas* in ways that enabled him to coordinate across the different areas of the empire. There were significant fiscal flows within the empire, some *cajas* were taxed to provide revenues used to subsidize other colonies, as Irigoin and Grafe (2008) demonstrate.

There were royal officials in each region, the two viceroyalties, the captain-generalities, and other minor divisions, the treasuries, and the courts. The king created privileges for corporate groups, the *fueros*, that applied to the church, the towns, guilds, and militias. Power was not hierarchical, power was distributed horizontally and disputes over power and arrangements were mediated by the king and his agents. This was a composite monarchy in which negotiation between the king and the elite groups was critical to the stability and survival of the system. The monarchy, the king and his agents, was the single most powerful player, but the king was embedded in a set of institutional arrangements, primary and secondary rules, in which his absolute power was moderated by the need to negotiate coordination. As Irigoin and Grafe (2008) stress, the arrangements were the result of negotiations, not of coercion. Although the Spanish King was an absolute monarch, he did not possess absolute coercive power.

British North America

The settlement of colonies in British North America (including colonies in the Caribbean) was similar in many ways to the Spanish settlement in Latin America, but with a few key differences that turned out to matter over time. The first permanent British colony was Virginia, established at Jamestown in 1607 by the Virginia Company. The Virginia Company was a corporation chartered by the king in 1606. The charter gave a group of shareholders rights to establish a colony under certain conditions and, in return, to claim the protection of the king and the rights of British citizens under the king. The corporate charter was significant. Rather than granting privileges directly to a person, such as Cortes or Pizarro, who held those privileges at the pleasure of the king, the Virginia Company was granted privileges that belonged to the corporation, which was, in a legal sense, perpetually lived – that is, the corporation's existence was independent of the lives of its members. When a member died or withdrew, the corporation lived on. Not that the Virginia Company lasted long. Two new charters were issued, in 1609 and 1612, and in 1619 the company granted the colonists the right to hold an assembly. But beset by many difficulties, the company was eventually dissolved in 1624. Administration of the colony was taken over by the king, and so could have developed relationships similar to the Spanish colonial relationships with the monarchy.

The Virginia Company charters required that land be held in the land tenure of free and common socage, one of the many kinds of land tenure in Britain. Land held in free and common socage could be sold, was 'alienable', could be divided, and was inheritable. Landowners had certain 'fixed and certain incidents' that they had to pay to the landlord in order to maintain control of the land. But if they paid those incidents (like today's property taxes) the owner had secure title and freedom to use his land, or to sell it to someone else who owned the land as long as he paid the incidents. It was the clearest, simplest, and most predictable way of owning land in Britain, and it would eventually apply to all the British colonies (with a few exceptions). It was a clear primary rule.

The charters of the Massachusetts Bay Company, 1629, and Maryland, 1632, also required free and common socage. In Virginia, Massachusetts, and Maryland, secondary rules were established in the colonial charters and the acts of the colonies themselves. While the king retained authority in the colonies, what made a rule legitimate was the process of enactment by the colonial assembly in agreement with the governor, subject to the approval of the king and his representatives.

Land was central to the economy of the British colonies, as most people were farmers. The colonial legislatures began structuring rules for establishing who owned which pieces of land through publicly available land registries at the level of counties (or townships). Clear and secure property rights in land became part of both the primary and secondary rules in the colonies. Property rights in land were more secure in both Britain and her colonies than they were in the Spanish colonies, but property rights in land in the British colonies also became much more clearly delineated (see Priest, 2021).

Two more colonies, Connecticut and Rhode Island, were created out of the land granted to Massachusetts, but then the formation of new colonies stopped as events in Britain overtook the colonization process. A series of conflicts between the king and Parliament led to a civil war, the beheading of a king, a period of parliamentary rule, the restoration of the monarchy, and the deposition of another king in 1688. The long-running conflict between the king and Parliament was not a conflict over primary rules, it was a conflict over secondary rules. Although nominally over taxation, the central conflict was over how rules about taxation could be changed. How would British elites collectively decide what the rules would be? Was it in the hands of the king, determined through individual negotiations with colonies, towns, and powerful elites (as in Spain)? Or was it an ongoing process in which the king and Parliament, like the governor or proprietor and the assemblies in the colonies, should both have a role?

The British colonies also differed from the Spanish colonies in a lack of readily exploited gold and silver. The British colonies could not pay for themselves through the extraction of precious metals. To minimize their fiscal drain on the Crown, the colonies were required to finance themselves and were, accordingly, allowed to govern themselves with a minimum of supervision, what the historian James Henretta calls 'salutary neglect'. For the most part, colonies operated on funds raised by the colonial legislatures through taxes on themselves. In practice, in combination with the presence of assemblies in all of the British colonies, this meant that the colonies enjoyed considerable latitude in establishing the rules that controlled the internal affairs of each colony, and developed well-established secondary institutions governing the rules for making rules. The colonial institutions mirrored the institutions in England.

The Seven Years War and its Consequences in British and Spanish America

As late as 1750 there was no general call for independence in either British or Spanish America. But events set in motion by the Seven Years War of 1756–63 (called the French and Indian War in the North American colonies), would lead to independence for some of the British North American colonies in 1776. Further consequences of the war would eventually lead to independence in Spanish Latin America, as well, beginning in 1808 and culminating in the 1820s. In both cases, the war left the finances of the imperial powers in a parlous state and both empires moved to increase revenues from their colonies. Although Britain was victorious in the war, its territorial gains, particularly in Canada and India where the French were expelled from both, required a larger peacetime military presence in the now enlarged British Empire. The Spanish had suffered serious military losses in the colonies for the first time. The British seized Havana and Manila, and while Spain regained control of Cuba and the Philippines in the peace settlement, Spain now faced the daunting challenge of defending its New World Empire in the face of determined British expansion. Both Spain and Britain turned to their colonies for more revenues.

Demand for higher revenues from the colonies set in motion the forces that led to independence in the British colonies, but not so in Spain. British attempts to raise revenues produced a constitutional crisis in the colonies. Specifically, they produced conflict over the nature of the secondary rules within the institutional structure of the empire. Attempts to raise revenue in Spanish Latin America were sometimes successful, sometimes not, but never were constitutional/institutional issues brought into conflict.

When the war ended in 1763, the British announced their intention to raise taxes and in 1765 introduced the Stamp Act, which required that certain documents be accompanied with a revenue stamp. The taxes imposed by the Stamp Act were the same in every colony. The Act was resisted by the colonists who argued, with some reason, that the institutional arrangements for levying taxes internal to the colonies required an act of the colonial assemblies, the appropriate secondary rule for creating new rules.

The colonists argued that the secondary rules governing their laws duplicated the same secondary rules agreed between the Crown and Parliament in the Glorious Revolution of 1688. The debate was about who, and by what process, rules would be made or changed. As the American historian Gordon Wood (2002) argues that the American Revolution 'was a revolution to save the British Constitution, not to change it'. The American colonists believed that the British constitution was being corrupted by the influence of the king in Parliament. They were trying to save the existing set of constitutional arrangements, essentially the secondary rules that governed the formation of primary rules. These were rules drawn up through a process of deliberation according to agreed-upon procedures. They believed they had created the essence of that system in the colonies through a political administration with royal governors, councils, and colonial assemblies. Independence inevitably involved a change in those institutions, both primary and secondary rules, to which we will return after considering independence in the Spanish New World.

The Spanish Empire's need to raise revenues to pay for improved defences led to a series of policies called the 'Bourbon Reforms'. Attempts to raise tax revenue, in the Spanish manner, were more successful in some places than others. Negotiations with sugar planters in Cuba, in the 1770s the richest per capita income colony, led to an increase in tax revenues in exchange for privileges and arrangements that benefited the growers. In New Spain attempts were made to shore up the existing revenue arrangements and ensure a steady flow of silver from the mines.

The attempts to raise revenues were not 'resisted' as they were in the British colonies, but were, as Irigoin and Grafe (2008) argue, 'negotiated'. Legitimate changes in the rules about taxation could occur in negotiation between the king and his representatives and the local elites affected by the changes. That the new taxes did not everywhere produce the same results should not be surprising.

Latin American scholars like John Lynch (1986) consider the Bourbon reforms to be a turning point in the relationship between the colonies and the empire. Perhaps these changes would have reached a new equilibrium, but a series of conflicts involving Britain, France, the Dutch, and the Spanish culminated in the Napoleonic Wars and, in 1808, Napoleon forced Charles VI of Spain and his son, Ferdinand VII, to abdicate and placed his brother, Joseph Bonaparte, on the throne as King Joseph I.

The response to King Joseph I was identical in Spain and her colonies. Joseph was denounced as an illegitimate king and independence and revolutionary movements began organizing in Spain and in the New World. The end of the Napoleonic Wars led to the restoration of the monarchy in Spain. Ferdinand VII was reinstated as king in 1813, but independence had attained sufficient momentum in many colonies to sustain movements that the Spanish could not suppress. By 1828, most of Spanish Latin America was independent.

Tokugawa Institutions and the Meiji Restoration

In 1868, the existing political and economic institutions of Japan were dramatically changed by the 'Meiji Restoration'. For several centuries before 1868 the Japanese political economy was structured around the emperor and his court, located in Kyoto; the *daimyo*, the military leaders, landowners, and governors who controlled local domains (the *han*) and were served by administrators and warriors, the *samurai*; and an alliance or coalition of the *daimyo*, headed by the shogun, located in Edo (now Toyko). The Tokogawans had seized power during a period of civil war, under the leadership of Tokugawa Ieyasu, who was shogun from 1603 to 1605, followed by his son Tokugawa Hidetada. The Tokugawa Shogunate lasted from 1603 to 1867 under the leadership of 15 shoguns. Ieyasu built a coalition of *daimyo* capable of ruling Japan, but not capable of displacing the most powerful *daimyo* who had opposed the Tokugawans. Ieyasu's power rested with and within the coalition of *daimyo*:

> The *shogun* and the *daimyo* of the Tokugawa period collectively monopolized a previously dispersed authority over land and its resources, military force, law and judicature, cities and commerce. The new and extraordinary prerogatives of rule, all concerned with social control, were the effective instruments of the elite's very transformation. Appropriation of the right to disarm civilians, to divest *samurai* of land, to deny changes of station or residence, and to superintend the church and the imperial court served, at once, to identify, to contract the membership of, and to protect from assault the political masters of the realm. The coercive and intrusive powers of early modern regimes, singularly dramatic in range, were also the instruments of unprecedented public peace (Berry 1986: 237–238).

The accomplishment of the Tokugawans was peace. It was a peace sustained within a highly stratified society, with clear status markers, where the privileges of powerful elites kept them from going back to civil war. Peace was maintained because the privileges the secure elites actually enjoyed were more valuable than the uncertain gains they might have enjoyed if the existing order was overthrown. Shoguns had existed in Japan since the twelfth century but were not always able to provide peace. Elites were sometimes convinced that their best interests lay in overthrowing the existing arrangements. The Tokugawa Shogunate ultimately fell when a coalition of elites displaced them. That coup resulted in the Meiji Restoration.

What can we say about primary and secondary rules under the shogunate? When Ieyasu began building his coalition of *daimyo* after his military victory, he dispossessed opponents and replaced them with his sons and close associates. Assembling a network of military and landholding elites had been the pattern of earlier shoguns, and the shogun's government and bureaucracy, the *bakufu*, was designed to incorporate elites into privileges that bound them to the coalition.

Control of land was central to the Tokugawan coalition. A *koku* was a unit of weight, roughly the amount of rice needed to sustain a person for one year. Landholdings were rated by *koku*, representing not their acreage but how much rice they could produce. After the Tokugawa took power 'eighty-seven warrior houses were extinguished and three reduced in size, as a total of 6,222,690 *koku* of assessed land changed hands' (Jansen 2000: 34). There were roughly 26,000,000 *koku* of assessed land at the end of the formative period of the Tokugawa ascendancy around 1700 (Jansen 2000:

42). Roughly one-third of the land was redistributed within the *daimyo* coalition between 1603 and 1700. Much of this redistribution was not expropriation, as the early confiscations had been, but transfers of land within the coalition recognizing that some members had become more powerful and some less.

The *bakufu* network was part a government and part a patronage network. It was the manifestation of how 'The shogun and the *daimyo* of the Tokugawa period collectively monopolized a previously dispersed authority over land and its resources, military force, law and judicature, cities and commerce' (Berry 1986: 237). The whole system of governance is more aptly called the *bakufuhan* system by Japanese scholars. Much of the actual governance of Japan was done by the *daimyo* at the domain (*han*) level. There was no central tax system or fiscal administration. There was no central legal code or central court system. Members of the *bakufu* network controlled local governance, but there was no centralized set of rules or organizations that operated at the national and local level.

Power and authority were determined by the status of elites in the network. Just as in Latin America after independence, the Japanese system required that privileges be created for elites that would bind their interests to supporting the coalition. The privileges were reflected in a very detailed status system. *Daimyo* that were Tokugawan vassals were termed *fudai*, those *daimyo* and houses with close connections to the Tokugawans. Those *daimyo* and houses who had opposed the Tokugawans or were outside the Tokugawan network were termed *tozama* or outside lords. Tokugawa house vassals were part of the *bakufu* network and were allowed to serve in the *bakufu* organizations within the Tokugawan government. *Tozama daimyo* were outside the *bakufu* network. Privileges available to *fudai daimyo* were not available to *tozama daimyo*. *Tozama daimyo* and their *samurai* would form the backbone of the coup leading to the Meiji Restoration, particularly from the provinces of Satsuma, Chosu, Tosa, and Saga.

Daimyo were further ranked by their *koku* ratings: those with domains with more *koku* ranked higher in the hierarchy of elites than those with less. An elaborate and very precise method of ranking an individual elite's status allowed each to be placed in the shogun's 'galaxy'. Those outside that galaxy were outside the key circles of power, and those within knew their place. By manipulating and reordering the *daimyo*, the *bakufu* coalition was able to maintain power, order, and peace. This was not a static status system, but one in which active manipulation of privileges was used to maintain the integrity of the coalition.

What does this tell us about primary and secondary rules? The most basic secondary rule was that whatever the shogun said was a rule, was a rule: 'Once a shogun was invested by the court he was an absolute ruler. During his minority there might be a regent, and after he reached maturity he issued orders through bureaucratic institutions that developed, but in theory there was nothing that could constrain him' (Jansen 2000: 44). The shogun and his close associates needed the flexibility to change the rules. Just as we saw with Spain, a theoretically absolute ruler does not necessarily rule absolutely. Like Spain, government at the centre was intimately involved with government at the local level, what Japanese scholars call the *bakufu-han* system. Unlike Spain, however, there was no central tax system. The shogunate did not collect taxes, although it did require contributions of men and resources for projects. Neither were there *bakufu* courts. Codes of conduct for the *daimyo* and *han* were created in the 1660s, but there was no centralized enforcement of the codes. Shoguns and the *bakufu* backed the power of the *daimyo*, not the rules of the *daimyo*.

The laws and customs that structured much of life in Japan were created and enforced at the local level. The *daimyo* were doubly privileged in this system, for they were able to make and enforce rules within their domain and be supported in that role by the larger shogunate coalition, at the same time as they had privileged access to official positions within the *bakufu* network of organizations. It might be most appropriate to say that the secondary rules within the *bakufu* network were personal rather than legal. Institutional arrangements gave specific individuals the opportunity to hold offices and make decisions, rather than detailing rules that governed how rules would be made that applied across the society. The arrangement was durable because the truly dangerous people – the political, social, and military elites – all had well-defined position in the network and stakes in maintaining the institutional arrangements. It was, however, an institutional system with weak and vague secondary rules, weaker than in either the British or Spanish empires.

The Meiji Restoration was a coup carried out by a minority coalition of regional powers in Japan. The central players were the *tozama daimyo* and their *samurai* from the provinces of Satsuma, Chosu, Tosa, and Saga. Unlike the new Latin American republics that lost their king and had to devise some arrangement to replace him, the Japanese lost their shogun but recovered their emperor in the process. The reasons for the Meiji revolution were complicated, but one element was the growing pressure placed on Japan by European powers. The restoration of the emperor, who had never lost symbolic importance in Japanese society, gave the new coalition a legitimate ideological and symbolic head. But that did not solve the problem of secondary rules.

Independence and Development

The events that led to independence in Latin and North America, as well as the restoration of the Meiji emperor in Japan, were tremendously rich and complicated events with different patterns of change. In the United States, the king was expelled, in Latin America the king disappeared, in Japan the emperor was restored to power. One might naturally ask whether it was the institutions in place before independence, the events that led up to and occurred during independence, or changes that occurred after independence that mattered most to the subsequent economic performance of these societies. The best explanations involve elements of all three.

Focusing on the secondary rules in place at the time of independence enables us to get at these questions about independence and what follows. In what became the United States, there were well-established secondary rules within the colonies themselves. The dispute between the colonists and the king in Parliament centred on the secondary rules within the empire, and when relationships broke down and fighting broke out, the colonists were able to quickly transform the secondary rules that already existed within their colonies into secondary rules for now independent states. This did not mean that the process was easy; it was not. But the states were able to take their colonial institutions as a basis for new institutions, primary and secondary. All of the original states had written their own constitutions by 1780. The states began to negotiate with each other over the primary and secondary rules that might govern a confederation (1781) or union (1788) of states. The first national constitution, written in 1777 and ratified in 1781 was 'The Articles of Confederation'. The Articles were replaced by the second national Constitution written in 1787, ratified in 1788, and operationalized in 1789.

Latin America's institutional legacy put the region in a much more difficult situation when the king disappeared. The characteristic secondary rule for forming primary rules was that the monarchy would negotiate with local elites, in the case of towns and cities, and other powerful elite organizations, the *fueros*, over primary rules. When the king disappeared, there was no obvious way to structure agreements about rules: the existing secondary rules were wiped out at independence. Even when the king was restored after the defeat of Napoleon, the situation in many areas of Latin America had progressed to the point where the king was no longer able to reach credible agreements with local elite groups, not only because new groups of elites were rising, but because old elites found themselves in new configurations after the king was removed. In Buenos Aires, for example, trade was a central economic activity and it was difficult to maintain relationships between commercial elites in the light of new alliances between peninsulares merchants (born in Spain) and creole merchants (born in the Americas of mixed-race parentage). Eventually, a new configuration and coalition of elite groups emerged, centred around Juan Manuel de Rojas. De Rojas was a *caudillo,* a military leader from the Pampas, the pastoral agricultural area outside Buenos Aires (Lynch 1981).

Similar scenarios played out across Latin America from 1808 to the 1820s. In the absence of the monarchy to negotiate agreements with elites, the elites found themselves without an institutional mechanism to coordinate agreements: the old secondary rules did not work and new secondary rules were not immediately forthcoming. Competition between elite groups, old and new, was difficult to contain when powerful actors could not see clear ways to reach credible agreements.

This institutional legacy of colonialism in Spanish Latin America proved to be very costly. In many places, units of government disintegrated rather than integrated. Credible secondary rules proved very difficult to establish. Disintegration cannot continue forever, however. The forces that stopped disintegration were not rooted in the pre-existing Spanish or Latin American institutions, but in the logic of creating social order in the midst of violence. Powerful leaders and organizations, both military and social, needed to come to some agreement to cease using violence and to begin to construct rules that enabled relationships between groups to be restored. Commitments between powerful groups are much less likely to be credible when violence occurs regularly, as it did after 1808. One way to attempt to ensure that promises are honoured is to endow the powerful individuals and groups with economic rents through privileged control of resources and, importantly, rules and rule enforcement biased in their favour. If their privileges are adversely affected by outbreaks of violence, then it may be possible for a coalition of powerful groups to maintain a fragile peace that can be built upon. North et al. (2009) call this the 'logic of the natural state'.

This is what appeared to happen in many Latin American societies between 1808 and the establishment of more stable governments and social arrangements. Inequality increased with independence. Elites redistributed resources among themselves in ways that might lead to more stable intraelite arrangements. Primary rules, such as who controlled land, were manipulated to make secondary rules more credible.

Institutional arrangements in Tokugawa Japan were structured to allow the shogun and the *bakufu* to manipulate economic and social privileges to maintain peace and social order. The secondary rules were weak in order to preserve the power of the coalition to change the rules. Tokugawa Japan was more successful at establishing peace than the nineteenth-century Latin American governments and elites were. During and after the Meiji Restoration, the *daimyo* and *samurai* that led the revolt needed to use their consolidated power. Power remained highly personal, despite the acknowledged absolute power of the emperor to make and change the rules. In theory, the absolute power of the shogun over the rules was restored to the emperor. In practice, this meant that those who controlled access to the emperor, like the *bakufu* before them, controlled the rules. The leaders of the revolt who became powerful in the Meiji period were known as 'oligarchs'. The oligarchs wrote a constitution that the emperor decreed in 1887. Even though the constitution created an elected legislature, the Diet, the constitution never gave power over the rules completely to the Diet. The ability to make and change the rules still lay with the group that controlled access to the emperor, and the rules for determining who was in that group were contested. When the Army and Navy exerted control over access to the emperor in the 1910s and 1920s, there was no constitutional block to their accession. Secondary rules remained weak in the Meiji period as they had in the Tokugawa period.

Agreements reached between powerful groups in a fragile equilibrium always have a fragile and contingent character themselves. Those who are currently more powerful, which really means the leaders and groups capable of putting together the largest and best-organized coalitions, have an advantage in reaching agreements, whether those agreements correspond to a written constitution or not. In Latin America after 1808, leaders often emerged who were themselves military leaders or leaders of strong organizations that included military resources. These leaders were known as *caudillos*.

Into the Future

Tempting as it is to assume that the institutions that mattered for growth and development, or their absence, were set in 1790 in the United States, in 1830 in Latin America, and in 1868 in Japan, this would be a serious mistake. One important aspect of good institutions that North stressed was 'adaptive efficiency', the ability to adapt to changing circumstances. Here, too, the difference between primary and secondary institutions plays a key role.

In Latin America, most of the new nations found it difficult to settle on a credible set of secondary rules. It was not that Latin America lacked the intellectual capacity to form secondary rules; in fact, Latin American countries engaged in a very creative attempt to write constitutions that would structure social order. As Dye (2006) reports, the average Latin American country wrote thirteen new constitutions between 1810 and 2000 (including Brazil) and an average of six constitutions between 1830 and 1914. Nonetheless, rule-based constitutions proved to be aspirational rather than institutional. The repeated attempts to write new secondary rules into constitutions was regularly frustrated by regime changes outside the constitutional process. Rule changes often accompanied regime changes.

Simply being a British colony was not enough to ensure that modern development followed. British colonial policy changed after the American Revolution. The British abolished the slave trade in 1807 and slavery itself in 1833. This was an intervention in the internal affairs of the colonies far more dramatic than the Stamp Act. The benign neglect that had characterized British colonial policy in the eighteenth century, which resulted in the building of both secondary and primary rules in the colonies, including the Caribbean colonies, was gradually changed. Britain administered its colonies, and the new colonial policy did not build the kind of institutions in its colonies in India or Africa that it had developed, unintentionally, in the North American colonies. European colonial policy in the latter half of the nineteenth century, in Africa and Asia, followed different paths than the North American experience as well.

Institutions in what became the United States were not fixed in 1790, either. Despite the apparent stability of the national constitution, state governments in the United States continued to experiment with their constitutions. The typical state wrote two constitutions between the founding date of statehood and 1860. All of the original states had constitutions by 1780, and the national constitution was more a mirror of provisions in the state constitutions than a model for states. The initial secondary rules for forming laws constrained the executive and legislative branches of government, and those constraints were tightened considerably in the 1840s, when half of the existing states wrote new constitutions (Wallis 2005). In a series of constitutional changes, both by amendment and by writing entirely new constitutions, states gradually constrained their legislatures to pass 'general' laws for a wide variety of purposes. General laws applied equally to everyone, in contrast to special or local laws, which applied differently to different individuals or groups. General laws for forming corporations, for forming local governments, and for a number of government functions were widespread in the United States by the 1880s (Hennessey and Wallis 2017). These were secondary rules constraining the form that primary rules could take.

Conclusions

Can we bring together all the strands of the argument to understand how institutions form a foundation for the underlying sources of growth? With the important caveat that institutions are never set in stone, we can draw some tentative conclusions.

First, the idea that specialization and division of labour, supported by the size of the market, is an important source of growth suggests that institutions that enable larger social entities to form and can integrate political and economic arrangements among larger groups of people will be more productive. The experience of the United States and Japan, where revolutionary events led to greater social integration and higher rates of growth, appears to be consistent with this idea. The Latin American experience, where revolutionary events produced disintegration, is also consistent. In all three societies, the process of revolution and independence was costly in the short run, but integration appears to have been better for growth in the long run.

Second, integration depends on credible secondary rules. Spain, England, and Japan were endowed by their histories with different sets of secondary rules and institutions. Those differences carried over into the organization of the Spanish and British empires. Whether one set of institutions was better than the other before 1770 is problematic. There were areas of the Spanish Empire doing just as well as areas of the British Empire in the late 1700s. One clear lesson seems to be that the effect of independence was magnified, for better or worse, by their institutional endowments. When the monarchy was withdrawn from its coordinating role in the secondary rules of Spain and the Spanish Empire, the costs were significant and disruptive. When the monarchy was expelled from what became the United States, coordination through secondary rules was able to continue with largely the same initial institutions that developed in the colonial period, albeit with the need for substantial adjustments over the next seventy years.

In Japan, both the Tokugawan shoguns and the Meiji emperor were able to provide relatively peaceful social orders. When they shifted the locus of power from the shogun back to the emperor there was violence for a time, but order was restored. Japan continued to integrate its economy and society, but under secondary rules that left it open to control by more narrow factions of elites, as happened with the Army and Navy in the early twentieth century.

Third, primary rules mattered, as well. Property rights in land, fundamental primary rules, were more clearly defined in British North America than in Spanish Latin America. Although this resulted in part from conditions in the colonies, it was also an accident of the requirement that land be held in free and common socage from the Virginia Company charter onwards. Nonetheless, property rights in land mattered enormously. Control of land in the Spanish Empire continued to be associated with political and social power, and security of landholdings depended on the landowner's place in the social order. Control of land was essential to sustaining social order in Tokugawa Japan, as well. Land ownership on the United States largely became impersonal and secure.

Are institutions underlying sources of growth and development? The answer seems irrefutably to be yes. Do we understand how institutions change over time, and what institutions are best for producing growth and development? There we are still wrestling with complicated and fascinating problems, both in conceptualizing what institutions are and how they work historically.

References

Acemoglu, D., Johnson, S. and Robinson, J. A. (2001). 'The Colonial Origins of Comparative Development: An Empirical Investigation', *American Economic Review*, 2001(91), 1369–1401.

(2002). 'Reversal of Fortune: Geography and Institutions in the Making of the Modern World Income Distribution', *Quarterly Journal of Economics*, 2002(117), 1231–1294.

Berry, M. E. (1986). 'Public Peace and Private Attachment: The Goals and Conduct of Power in Early Modern Japan', *The Journal of Japanese Studies*, 12(2), 237–271.

Dye, A. (2006). 'The Institutional Framework', in Bulmer-Thomas, V., Coatsworth, J. and Cortés-Conde, R. (eds.), *The Cambridge Economic History of Latin America. vol. 2: The Long Twentieth Century*, Cambridge University Press, 169–208.

Elliot, J. H. (1992). 'A Europe of Composite Monarchies', *Past & Present*, 137, 48–71.

Grafe, R. (2012). *'Distant Tyranny': Markets, Power, and Backwardness in Spain (1650–1800)*, Princeton University Press.

Hennessey, J. and Wallis, J. J. (2017). 'Corporations and Organizations in the United States after 1840', in Lamoreaux, N. R. and Novak, W. J. (eds.), *Corporations and American Democracy*, Cambridge University Press, 74–105.

Irigoin, A. and Grafe, R. (2008). 'Bargaining for Absolutism: A Spanish Path to Nation-State and Empire Building', *Hispanic American Historical Review*, 88(2), 173–209.

Jansen, M. B. (2000). *The Making of Modern Japan*, Cambridge, MA: Harvard University Press.

Lynch, J. (1981). *Argentine Dictator: Juan Manuel de Rosas, 1829–1852*, Lanham: SR Books.

(1986). *The Spanish American Revolutions, 1808–1826*, 2nd ed., New York: W. W. Norton.

North, D. C., Wallis, J. J. and Weingast, B. R. (2009). *Violence and Social Orders: A Conceptual Framework for Interpreting Recorded Human History*, Cambridge University Press.

Priest, C. (2021). *Credit Nation: A History of Property Laws and Institutions in Early America*, Princeton University Press.

van Zanden, J. L., Buringh, E. and Bosker, M. (2012). 'The Rise and Decline of European Parliaments, 1188–1789', *Economic History Review*, 65(3), 835–861.

Wallis, J. J. (2005). 'Constitutions, Corporations, and Corruption: American States and Constitutional Change, 1842 to 1852', *Journal of Economic History*, 65(Mar), 211–256.

Wood, G. S. (2002). *The American Revolution: A History*, London: Weidenfeld and Nicolson.

16

Consequences of Growth: Living Standards and Inequality

JAN LUITEN VAN ZANDEN, BAS VAN LEEUWEN, AND YI XU

Introduction

Well-being is the ultimate goal of economic activity. Whereas for millennia people had lived close to the subsistence level, with substantial levels of inequality, major changes have taken place over the past centuries (e.g. Koepke and Baten 2005) resulting in a much higher level of well-being. This is well documented for the late nineteenth and twentieth centuries (e.g. Prados de la Escosura 2015). However, for the eighteenth and nineteenth centuries more controversy exists. This controversy covers four major debates.

The initial, classic debate concerns the consequences of the Industrial Revolution for living standards – in particular in England, although similar discussions have been going on for other countries, as well. The three subsequent debates have broadened the initial debate by including comparisons with other parts of the world. The second of the four debates relates to the Little Divergence: why is it that north-western and southern Europe grew apart? The third adds a further international dimension: in the 'Great Divergence' debate the issue is at what time did the standard of living of the population of western Europe start to diverge significantly from that of the rest of the world, in particular from China? Kenneth Pomeranz (2000) maintains that this did not happen until the final decades of the eighteenth century. Specifically, up until about 1780 the standard of living of the Chinese was the same, or nearly the same, as that of the inhabitants of Great Britain. The fourth, related, debate adds yet another region by focusing on the comparison of well-being between Great Britain and the United States (or

The research leading to these results received funding from the European Research Council under the European Union's Horizon 2020 Programme/ERC-StG 63769 – HinDI, as part of the project 'The Historical Dynamics of Industrialization in North-Western Europe and China c.1800–2010: A Regional Interpretation'.

before 1776, the North American colonies). New research by, amongst others, Allen et al. (2012) and Lindert and Williamson (2015) concludes that the standard of living of North American settlers was at least on a par with, and probably even higher than, that of British workers.

These debates link up with the literature, which suggests that there was an 'early growth paradox': that the growth of GDP that can be estimated for industrializing countries did not result in matching increases in the standard of living of the labouring class (Komlos 1998). The link with inequality is obvious: part of the explanation for the paradox appears to be the rise in income and wealth inequality during early industrialization.

These debates about historical trends and comparisons have taken place against the background of a more general discussion about how to measure well-being. Thanks to work by Kuznets, Maddison and others, gross domestic product (GDP) has come to be used as the key measure of the economic performance of countries. It is, however, becoming increasingly clear that well-being is a multidimensional phenomenon, including health, education, political justice, personal security etc., none of which can be ignored when studying historical changes in the standard of living (van Zanden et al. 2014). However, data on these other dimensions are often scarce, and it is not clear prima facie how to weigh these different indicators. The contribution of this chapter is to present historical estimates for the three dimensions of the Inequality-Adjusted Human Development Index (IHDI) – real income, life expectancy, and education – to discuss trends and international disparities for the period 1700–1900, and, finally, to present for the first time for the countries concerned a set of estimates of that IHDI, which is arguably the best guide to the evolution of well-being that we can construct.

Real Income

Starting with the first dimension, real income, the estimates as presented by Maddison and the Maddison Project that followed in his footsteps are at the moment arguably the best estimates of the purchasing power of a population. The recent revision of the Maddison data set has tried to address as well as possible the problems of comparing real incomes in time and space (Bolt and van Zanden 2018). Various updates for north-western Europe have been made by, for example, van Zanden and van Leeuwen (2012) for Holland and Broadberry et al. (2015a) for Great Britain. Largely confirming the start of the Industrial Revolution in the late-eighteenth (England) or late-nineteenth (Netherlands) century, the main contribution of these new studies has been

Table 16.1 GDP per capita in 1990 international dollars

A. Selected European countries

	GB	Netherlands	Germany	Italy	France	Spain	Poland	Russia
1700	1,517	2,123**	942	1,404*	1,065	865	619	540
1800	2,103	2,632**	989	1,419*	1,119	944	567	639
1850	2,725	2,376	1,431	1,613*	1,601	1,073	620	757
1900	4,776	3,337	2,992	2,050	2,918	1,683	1,698	1,149

B. Selected non-European countries

	Argentina	Brazil	Mexico	US	Australia	India	China	Zimbabwe
1700			928	1,112		731	1,089	
1750			815			672	749	
1800	933	545	821	1,601	519	650	654	
1850	1,254	545	663	2,284	1,980	596	540	300
1900	2,882	550	1,146	5,055	4,023	631	611	400

Sources and notes: Part A: Great Britain from Broadberry et al. (2015a); Netherlands from van Zanden and van Leeuwen (2012);* Northern Italy,** Holland.
Part B: Zimbabwe from Prados de la Escosura (2012); India from Broadberry et al. (2015b); China from Broadberry et al. (2018).
Maddison Project Database, version 2019, Bolt et al. (2018).

the conclusion that per capita income in north-western Europe had already been above subsistence levels prior to 1700 (Table 16.1A).

International comparisons have also increased in number. For the Great Divergence debate these recent updates have produced highly relevant results: whereas both Pomeranz and Maddison thought that GDP per capita (or more generally, the standard of living) in China was more or less stable between 1500 and 1800, the new research suggests that this conclusion may have been too optimistic, and that real incomes were declining already in the eighteenth century (Table 16.1B). At the onset of our period of interest, in 1700, there is a substantial gap between the most advanced economies of Europe – England and the Netherlands – and China, but GDP per capita in the latter compares well with that in the rest of western Europe (and seems to be higher than for India). Yet, at the end of the nineteenth century, it is argued that real wages in China were comparable to those of India or even Africa (Frankema and Waijenburg 2012).

The gap between the North Sea region and the rest of the world increased due to the growth of real income in the West and its decline in Asia. Not all European countries did well, however. As for example Cvrcek (2013) points out, the further east and south one goes the more real wages stagnated, with Poland and Italy being examples of countries suffering such stagnation until the mid-nineteenth century.

For the Americas, a debate remains about their relative position in the global economy. Whereas Acemoglu et al. (2002) ranked North America substantially behind Latin America up to 1800, and Coatsworth (2008) argues for a smaller gap, Allen et al. (2012), using so-called subsistence ratios, showed income per worker in the British colonies in the eighteenth century to be already higher than in Latin America, and even on a par with north-western Europe. The new estimates in Table 16.1B also confirm the positive assessment of real income growth in North America.[1]

Population and Life Expectancy

The traditional story about life expectancy is that it was very low until the Industrial Revolution, that it rose very slowly (or barely at all) during the first stage of industrialization, and only started to increase rapidly after the demographic transition of the final decades of the nineteenth century. Moreover, Pomeranz (2000) maintains that life expectancy in the most advanced parts of China during the eighteenth century was probably higher than in western Europe, while even in the settler colonies of the West (such as the US) mortality was arguably lower than in many other parts of the world (Acemoglu et al. 2001; Table 16.2).

As regards this traditional story, it is fair to say that there is increasing evidence that already before 1750 life expectancy in parts of Europe began to improve – slowly, but more or less steadily. The new research that supports this is sometimes based on rather problematic samples. In a detailed reconstruction of the life histories of more than 300,000 famous people, de la Croix and Licandro (2015) show that human longevity began to increase from the 1640s onwards – clearly preceding the Industrial Revolution.

1 The same is true for the subsistence ratio literature. Allen (2001) and Allen et al. (2011) developed this method to estimate the number of 'bare bones' baskets that could be acquired with that income; Allen put together a very basic consumption basket that only contained the bare necessities for a family of four (the 'bare bones' basket) and estimated how many such baskets a wage earner could afford to buy with his income.

Table 16.2 Mean age at death for the population over five years of age

A. Selected European countries

	England	Netherlands	Germany	Italy	France	Spain	Poland	Russia
1700	57.9	56.0	46.6	46.7	59.4	36.6		
1750	55.6	63.5	51.7	50.8	45.2	45.6	49.6	
1800	51.6	60.0	53.3	52.5	46.3	51.8	45.5	49.6
1850	50.3	48.6	51.6	47.6	62.7	51.9	43.6	48.6
1900	55.3	56.2	55.2	56.9	59.1	56.8	46.1	42.6
1930	60.8	60.7	62.3	60.4	53.9	61.8	49.8	42.3
1930 e_5	61.7	63.3	62.6	60.7	58.4	56.9	57.2	56.8*

B. Selected non-European countries

	Argentina	Brazil	Mexico	USA	Canada	Australia	India	China	Zimbabwe
1700	44.4		41.3	51.8	48.6			62.9	
1750	36.0	40.9	34.0	50.8	57.5			55.8	
1800	41.5	43.4	39.0	52.9	55.1	35.7		60.7	
1850	44.3	41.1	39.9	46.7	48.9	39.6	38.2	56.5	
1900	47.6	41.2	45.0	52.9	54.1	52.4		54.2	31.1
1930	55.2	44.6	50.9	58.4	60.2	63.3	37.8*	58.9	31.8
1930 e_5	55.7	47.9	47.9	59.4	62.7	64.1	37.8	52.0*	48**

Sources and notes: Family History Library (familysearch.org/search/). We excluded non-representative sources, such as Germans in Russia and Europeans in Africa. For countries with few observations we took ten years around the benchmark, for example 1690–1710 for 1700. 1930 data were taken from the United Nations *Demographic Yearbook 1948*, table 34. 1930 e5 is estimated life expectancy at age 5 in 1930.
Part A: * European part of the USSR
Part B: China taken from Chen (1959); 1930 data for Argentina and Zimbabwe from the United Nations *Demographic Yearbook 1957*, table 24; Zimbabwe 1930 from the United Nations *Demographic Yearbook 1960*, table 23. 1930 e5 is estimated life expectancy at age five in 1930.
* Taiwan
** Rhodesia: life expectancy at birth, 1954

Cummins (2017) analysed a different segment of the European population – members of the nobility – and arrived at even more 'optimistic' conclusions: their life expectancy had already increased during the late-medieval period (roughly the fourteenth century, spanning the period of the Black Death), but noted that this 'growth spurt' ended in the sixteenth century. Life expectancy began to increase again around 1650, confirming de la Croix and Licandro's analysis of the famous people. 'Everywhere in Europe, the modern sustained increase in longevity originates around 1650 for European nobility' (Cummins 2017: 431). Since de la Croix and Licandro focused on educated people, the fact that there was apparently a rise in their life expectancy, whereas this was less clear in the population as a whole (according to de la Croix and Licandro 2015), points to the importance of human capital as an explanation of this fundamental shift. This also seems to be confirmed by the positive correlation between the education and age-at-death inequality that we note later. Yet, as a similar increase occurred in China without education increasing markedly, it has been argued that climate and disease-related factors also played a role (Lee et al. 1994). Indeed, part of the decline in age-specific death rates is related to the lesser impact that warfare – direct violence – had on the nobility, who, from being medieval monopolists of violence were gradually 'pacified' (Pinker 2011). This suggests that an increase in life expectancy also occurred for commoners in the second half of the seventeenth and much of the eighteenth centuries. Then followed what has been coined an 'Engels pause' (Allen 2009) or a 'Malthusian intermezzo', i.e. a period in which wages stagnated but labour productivity rose, resulting – in the late-eighteenth century and the first half of the nineteenth century – in a stagnation of life expectancy.

On the basis of similar sources – family trees available online – we have estimated the evolution of the mean age at death (as a proxy for life expectancy) of the population over the age of five years. To this we have added estimates of the mean age at death of Chinese citizens who left a gravestone (collected and published by Chen 1959). Keeping possible biases in mind,[2] it is clear that in the eighteenth century life expectancy was probably the highest in England, the Netherlands, and arguably China, followed by the US (or rather the North American colonies). In the first half of the nineteenth century various European countries appear to have suffered from Engels' pause, but much progress in this respect was made after 1850. Other countries outside north-western Europe, such as Italy, seem to have been less prone to Engels' pause. They often show remarkable stability in life expectancy until the late nineteenth century, before

2 Both sets of data are slightly biased: people with many children and grandchildren have a greater chance of being included in family trees, which have usually been put together by their (distant) offspring. The bias in the Chinese sources is even more pronounced, as not many families could afford to pay for a gravestone (moreover, the quality of the stone had to be good enough to survive through the ages and be included in Chen's [1959] survey). To get an idea of this bias, we compare, for 1930, with actual life expectancy for that year (at age five years); clearly, the difference for Western Europe and Argentina is very small, and larger for China.

starting their demographic transitions (Lo Cascio and Malanima 2005), which, however, lasted a much shorter time than in north-western Europe. Hence, in the nineteenth century the gap between the various countries disappeared.

So far, we have mostly focused on mortality after the age of five years, hence ignoring child mortality. This choice is mostly determined by difficulties with the data rather than by the unimportance of child mortality (Kannisto 2001). Indeed, a common problem is that, frequently, children below the age of five years were not recorded in mortality data. Obviously the pre-1850 European increase in longevity that we show in Table 16.2 may be enhanced by declining child mortality (Schofield et al. 1991). That this is not a uniquely European phenomenon can be seen in the case of China (Lee et al. 1994: 401). Since China was economically stagnating at the same time as child mortality was declining, this suggests that factors other than just economic ones played a major role.

These early falls in child mortality, however, were restricted to certain world regions and continued after 1800. Even though on a global scale the mortality of children below five years of age declined from, on average, 43 per cent in 1800 to 39 per cent in 1900 (Gapminder.org), the differences were mostly to be found in Western countries: England, for example, declined from 33 per cent to 23 per cent and the US from 46 per cent to 23 per cent; China, India, Latin America, and Africa stagnated. Only after 1900 did the share of surviving children outside Europe and the Western offshoots increase significantly.

Education

Another important aspect of well-being concerns education. Education gives access to reading (e.g. books), the economy (reading contracts), and social status. Yet for the eighteenth century relatively little information about education is available. For the years around 1800, Reis (2005: 202) presents male literacy rates for various parts of Europe that indicate a literate core in Britain, the Netherlands, Belgium, and northern France of approximately 70 per cent versus 20–40 per cent for various other regions in Europe. That these low male literacy rates are characteristic for many places is also shown by literacy rates of approximately 40 per cent and 50 per cent, respectively, in late-nineteenth century China and Japan (Ohkawa and Rosovsky 1973: 8; Rawski 1979).

Even though these literacy rates around 1800 seem to suggest significant eighteenth-century development in north-western Europe (Reis 2005), evidence for the pre-1800 period is scarce. Yet, looking at book titles per million inhabitants, we note, with the exception of England, a growth between 1700 and 1800 for north-western Europe and stagnation for other regions (van Zanden and

Baten 2008; Fink-Jensen 2015). The same can be observed by looking at the ABCC index, i.e. the share of people that were numerate (able to state their age correctly). In 1700 this was, at a percentage point in the low 80s, relatively similar in most parts of the world. Yet by around 1800 north-western Europe had forged ahead (A'Hearn et al. 2009; Baten 2013; Prayon and Baten 2013).

Whereas before 1800 only a modest change could be witnessed, mostly in north-western Europe, developments in the nineteenth century were more spectacular with a nearly universal increase in mass education. Even though numeracy data do also exist for this period, average years of education may be a more efficient indicator for the period after 1800, since it also picks up education above bare literacy; see the data in Table 16.3. From these data it seems that developed, north-western European countries and 'Western offshoots' were able to build on their eighteenth century gains to expand mass education rapidly. Even though other countries improved, they remained far behind the UK, US, and the Netherlands.

As regards the drivers of this diversity in educational patterns, it has been argued that in the first phase before 1940, among other things, economy, culture, and religion played major roles (Benavot and Riddle 1988: 201–203). This view has been criticized by Meyer et al. (1992), based on the observation that the expansion of mass education occurred in many cases before the Industrial Revolution and, hence, cannot be directly related to economic growth. Likewise, mass education, albeit in rudimentary form, started in many places irrespective of culture and religion. Meyer et al. offer as an alternative explanation that mass education started as an inherent part of nation-state formation and, hence, followed a global diffusion pattern (Meyer et al. 1977). But no matter who is right, only after 1940 did this 'world development of education' start to lead to convergence.

Levels of Inequality in the Inequality-Adjusted Human Development Index (IHDI)

As pointed out in the introduction to this chapter, we follow the method of calculation of the United Nations (2018) with the dimension indices[3] of GDP, age at death, and education, which together make up the so-called Human Development Index (HDI):

3 The dimension indices are calculated as (actual value – minimum value)/(maximum value – minimum value). Based on tables 16.1–16.3, for GDP per capita we set the maximum value at US$7,000 and the minimum value at US$400; for years of education we set the maximum at ten years and the minimum at zero; and for age at death the maximum is set at seventy years and the minimum at thirty years. The GDP dimension index is logarithmic.

Table 16.3 Average years of education

A. Selected European countries

	UK	Netherlands	Germany	Italy	France	Spain	Poland	Russia
1800	1.7	2.1						
1850*	2.6	3.0	5.4	0.8	4.2	1.5		0.5
1900	5.3	5.6	6.5	2.4	6.3	3.1	2.4	0.7
1930	6.7	6.4	7.7	3.9	7.7	3.8	2.5	2.1

B. Selected non-European countries

	Argentina	Brazil	Mexico	US	Canada	Australia	India	China	Zimbabwe
1800								0.3	
1850*	1.5	0.5	0.6	5.6	5.7	3.1	0.1	0.8	0.01
1900	2.1	0.7	1.1	7.1	7.1	6.3	0.3	1.2	0.03
1930	3.7	1.3	1.5	8.5	8.5	8.4	0.7	3.9	0.56

Sources and notes: van Zanden and van Leeuwen (2012); van Leeuwen and Li (2014); de Pleijt (2018). * 1870

$$HDI = \left(I_{GDP} \cdot I_{age\ at\ death} \cdot I_{education}\right)^{1/3} \tag{1}$$

Yet well-being is also influenced by inequality: higher inequality is considered to lower overall well-being. This occurs in a great many ways, ranging from reduced access to crucial services like education and healthcare to fewer opportunities for one's children. Measuring national averages only may therefore give a biased picture of well-being, and a correction for inequality is required. This can be captured by the Atkinson index, which takes a value between 0 and 1 that indicates the share in a dimension a person is willing to forgo to arrive at perfect equality. Hence, each of the three dimensions is multiplied by its 1-inequality, implying that if inequality is equal to zero the Inequality-adjusted Human Development Index (IHDI) is equal to the HDI, or proportionally lower otherwise,[4] i.e.

4 In line with the literature, inequality is calculated using the Atkinson index, in which, via the chosen weight ε, the level of aversion to inequality is set. This value can run from 0 (no inequality aversion, i.e. higher mean income, education or age at death implies

$$I_x^* = (1 - A_x) \cdot I_x \tag{2}$$

Combining equation (1) and (2), we arrive at the IHDI as follows:

$$IHDI = (I_{GDP}^* \cdot I_{age\ at\ death}^* \cdot I_{education}^*)^{1/3} \tag{3}$$

Given that the Atkinson index can be interpreted as the percentage of well-being a person is willing to give up in order to achieve equality, the percentage difference between the IHDI (Equation 3) and HDI (Equation 1) can be interpreted as welfare loss due to inequality. We find that welfare loss does differ among countries but only to a limited extent (for estimates and sources see the following section; footnote 5). For example, around 1700 welfare loss was lowest in north-western Europe at 13.4 per cent, as against 18.7 per cent in eastern Europe and 16.5 per cent in Latin America. Yet, whereas the percentage welfare loss stagnated in north-western Europe, in all other regions it was declining up to 1900. This decline in welfare loss was, however, reversed in 1930, when all regions – with the exception of north-western Europe, southern Europe and the Western offshoots – would start on a path of increasing welfare loss.

In order to tentatively explain these trends, we have to look at the underlying inequalities (income, age at death, and education), and their effect on the IHDI. The first factor, income inequality, was rather stable between 1700 and 1900. These patterns are often related to the Kuznets curve, which states that initially income inequality increases with rising income until a certain threshold is reached, after which it then declines. Such a curve was first argued for the nineteenth-century Industrial Revolution (see, for example, Williamson 1985). Yet, given recent studies pointing to pre-modern (i.e. pre-eighteenth century) growth, it has also been argued that rising inequality as expressed in a Kuznets curve already existed for the pre-modern period (van Zanden 1995; Hoffman et al. 2002).

Whereas the pre-modern rise in inequality for western and southern Europe is relatively uncontroversial, its rise during the nineteenth-century Industrial Revolution is more in doubt (see, for example, Feinstein 1988). In part, this may be due to more equal growth than hypothesized during the period of the

a comparable higher welfare level, irrespective of the changes in inequality) to infinity (higher inequality aversion will mean that increases of lower income groups, lower educational levels and/or groups with lower life expectancy will weigh more heavily in increasing the welfare of the entire population) (Bellu and Liberati 2006). Since this choice is subjective, in our case we set it at 1 implying moderate inequality aversion.

Industrial Revolution. However, this doubt may also be caused in part by the situation that the Kuznets curve is conditional on factors such as the ability of the elite to extract income, factor endowments, population density, and colonialism, all of which vary widely across regions and over time.

Indeed, the most remarkable pattern is the decline of income inequality in Latin America after the eighteenth century, which runs counter to that of western Europe. Before 1800, inequality was slightly higher than that of western Europe, mostly driven by a declining land–labour ratio in combination with rising GDP per capita, which allowed for rising extraction of income by the colonial elite. The inequality started to decline on the eve of Latin American independence – caused by decolonization – and continued to decline for the following five decades (1820–70) due to turmoil, lack of urbanization, and poor economic growth (Williamson 2010). However, we need to stress that differences in income inequality around the world in the period 1700–1900 were small. Indeed, as also pointed out by Williamson (2010), western European countries in similar phases of industrialization had levels of income inequality comparable with those in Latin America, an argument made on a global scale by Milanovic et al. (2011).

The second factor, inequality of age at death, again shows more or less stable patterns, with only occasional peaks and troughs. There are two theories that are usually named when explaining this pattern. On the one hand, there is the constancy hypothesis, which argues that differences in life expectancy among social classes are, by and large, constant over time given similar disease environments and socio-economic characteristics (Bengtsson and van Poppel 2011: 345). Short-term deviations due to changes in both factors, such as during the Industrial Revolution, are, however, possible. The second hypothesis, based on the work of Antonovsky (1967), is the divergence-convergence theory. It argues that, before *c.*1650, the disease environment was highly virulent and targeted both upper and lower socio-economic classes alike. With the increases in income and levels of sanitation achieved between 1650 and 1850, nutritional causes of death became more prevalent, thus increasing the gap in life expectancy between the elite and common labourers. After 1850, this trend reversed (Bengtsson and van Poppel 2011: 346).

In general, therefore, recent findings on inequality of age at death seem to support the divergence-convergence theory (see, for example, Woods and Williams 1995). Yet, rather than awarding the Industrial Revolution a key role as the main driver of inequality in life expectancy, the main conclusion is that increasing inequality had mostly occurred before that time, due to rising population densities and urbanization (Bengtsson and van Poppel 2011: 354).

The third factor, educational inequality, showed larger differences than for income inequality. Nevertheless, patterns here also show stability in western Europe versus declining inequality in most other regions up to 1800 and stability afterwards. This was mostly the result of the high levels of literacy already attained in western Europe in the eighteenth century that resulted in lower initial levels of inequality.

Global Change in Well-Being

The IHDI results are reported in Table 16.4 and Figures 16.1–16.2.[5] Clearly, north-western Europe and the Western offshoots were leading the world, with a marginally higher score for north-western Europe both in 1700 and 1800. However, during the nineteenth century the American offshoots advanced more than England and the Netherlands. England, being the first industrializer, experienced the fastest growth in IHDI in north-western Europe during the eighteenth century, even though this was accompanied by increasing income inequality and falling age at death. In comparison, income growth in the Netherlands started only in the nineteenth century, but was also accompanied in that period by declining age at death. This suggests the importance of Engels' pause in early industrialization, and it has been debated whether that 'pause' was exacerbated by urbanization taking place in this period (Williamson 1981).

The Little Divergence between north-western and southern Europe is something that appears in the data, as well. Yet, whereas in terms of GDP there was divergence, the IHDI shows an eighteenth-century convergence by southern Europe, which was mainly the result of increases in age at death. This Little Divergence in GDP between north-western and southern Europe has been widely discussed. Some have argued that this divergence in income can be explained by institutional changes (van Zanden et al. 2012; Carmichael

5 The data have been derived from Tables 16.1–16.3. Data lacking for the early nineteenth, and eighteenth, centuries, mostly for education, were obtained by linking years in primary school with the numeracy estimates of Baten (2013). Inequality for education and age at death were directly calculated from the underlying data. In cases where data were lacking, again mostly for education, we extrapolated backwards to 1700 using 1-ABCC index as a proxy of educational inequality. Income inequality was obtained from van Zanden et al. (2014) and Moatsos et al. (2014) and, where applicable, extended using the Williamson index of income inequality. The index we used is GDP÷real wage. The higher this index, the less income goes to the bottom of society, i.e. income inequality is higher. Various sources were used including Allen (2001), Studer (2008), Allen et al. (2011), Frankema and Waijenburg (2012), Arroyo Abad et al. (2012), and Challú and Gómez-Galvarriato (2015).

Table 16.4 Inequality-adjusted human development index

A. Selected European countries

	England	Netherlands	Germany	Italy	France	Spain	Poland	Russia
1700	0.383	0.357	0.273	0.206	0.296	0.154	0.180	
1800	0.400	0.412	0.352	0.231	0.277	0.238	0.165	0.121
1850	0.426	0.382	0.384	0.229	0.470	0.268	0.183	0.147
1900	0.579	0.561	0.452	0.396	0.584	0.413	0.320	0.171
1930	0.685	0.675	0.530	0.525	0.609	0.509	0.360	0.260

B. Selected non-European countries

	Argentina	Brazil	Mexico	USA	Canada	Australia	India	China	Zimbabwe
1700			0.139	0.351	0.346*			0.181	
1800	0.176	0.097	0.126	0.389	0.373		0.058	0.142	
1850	0.237	0.094	0.120	0.444	0.426	0.293	0.055	0.159	
1900	0.336	0.111	0.211	0.603	0.577	0.564	0.085	0.195	0.022
1930	0.485	0.191	0.276	0.719	0.719	0.549	0.120	0.316	0.089

Sources and notes: Calculated based on Tables 16.1–16.3. * 1750

et al. 2016),[6] while others have argued for the effect of human capital (de Pleijt and van Zanden 2016) and international trade (Allen 2001). Nevertheless, given its importance in explaining overall well-being in southern Europe, the focus should be on rising age at death. As mentioned earlier, this may be related to rising levels of education. Indeed, a simple correlation of our data shows that health and educational inequalities are positively correlated. Likewise, better climate and a more favourable disease environment may have played a beneficial role. Engels' pause in north-western Europe may, however, have obstructed this positive development for that region.

The rise in IHDI of North America showed a very different pattern with growth mostly being driven by income in the eighteenth century and education being added in the nineteenth century. This was enough to stay abreast, or ahead, of north-western Europe. An explanation for this was in part stability in age at death, arguably the result of an unchanging

6 But for a critique of this point of view, see Dennison and Ogilvie (2014).

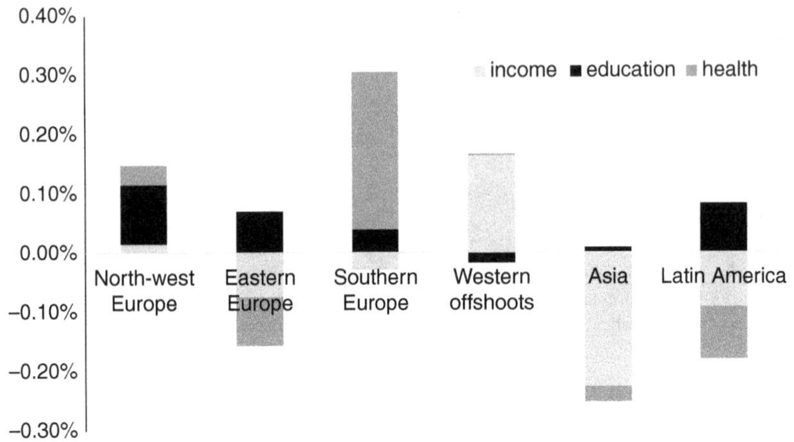

Figure 16.1 Compound annual per capita growth rate of IHDI, c.1700–1800
Sources and notes: See Tables 16.4A and 16.4B. North-western Europe = Netherlands and UK; eastern and middle Europe = Germany, Poland, and Russia; southern Europe = France, Spain, and Italy; Western offshoots = Australia, Canada, and US; Asia = China and India; Latin America = Argentina, Brazil, and Mexico.

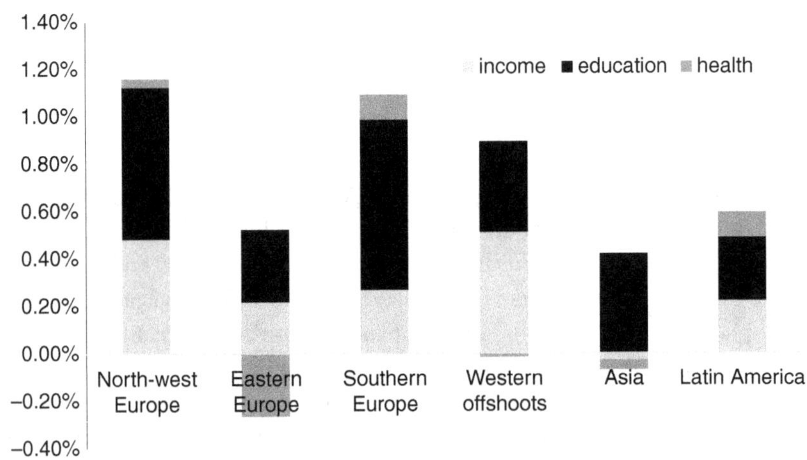

Figure 16.2 Compound annual per capita growth rate of IHDI, c.1700–1900
Sources and notes: See Figure 16.1. North-western Europe = Netherlands and UK; eastern and middle Europe = Germany, Poland, and Russia; southern Europe = France, Spain, and Italy; Western offshoots = Australia, Canada, and US; Asia = China and India; Latin America = Argentina, Brazil, and Mexico.

disease environment. Another, but related, explanation is the omission of child mortality from our data: by excluding the rapid fall in child mortality in the US (Gapminder.org) we ignore most of the increase in life expectancy at birth.

For income growth, again both institutional and factor endowment explanations exist. In terms of institutions, this links up well with the Little Divergence: the institutions transplanted from England to North America, such as secure property rights and small government, were more efficient in enhancing market exchange than those transferred from southern Europe to Latin America (North et al. 2000; see also Field 1985). For factor endowments, it has been argued that those countries with plantations based on slave labour generated economic and social inequalities (Engerman and Sokoloff 1997; Sokoloff and Engerman 2000). Another reason for creating extractive institutions, as brought forward by Acemoglu et al. (2001), was high settler mortality in Latin America, which resulted in extractive institutions being created by the colonizers.[7]

Of course, in almost all cases societal well-being was the product of a combination of the colonizer being willing to extract wealth – via force and/or trade – and the available factor endowments. Low labour costs and a high concentration of land in the hands of a few resulted in systems like *encomienda* in Latin America, where rich men were granted land and forced labour (after abolishing forced Indian labour, African slaves were increasingly imported). This concentration of wealth in a few hands resulted in high levels of inequality (de Ferranti et al. 2004; Milanovic et al. 2011).[8] This was also true for education (Allen et al. 2012: 865): Juif and Baten (2012), for example, show that numeracy among the Inca was about half that of the Spanish conquistadores. In North America, the scarcity of labour generated high wages, which, combined with less profitable crops, created fewer opportunities to generate excessive inequality of wealth (Allen et al. 2012).

The discrepancy between the West and Asia, specified in the Great Divergence debate, can in many ways be considered an extreme variant of what happened in Latin America, with the same pattern of negative growth in income and health in the eighteenth century and minor improvements in the nineteenth century. The explanation of the effect of this strongly negative growth in well-being for Asia consists, for the eighteenth century, of per capita income decline, which, for the nineteenth century, is compounded with a rise in education. Our results thus do not confirm the view developed

7 For a critique see Albouy (2012). 8 For a critique see Williamson (2010).

by the 'California School' that up to the eighteenth century China and India were on a par with north-western Europe (Pomeranz 2000; Parthasarathi 2011). In reality, the gap with England and the Netherlands (Holland) was in 1700 already large for both China and India, which is confirmed by most recent research (e.g. Allen 2007; Allen et al. 2011; Xu et al. 2017; Broadberry et al. 2018). However, in 1700 the gap between East Asia and parts of southern and eastern Europe was very limited.

The dating of this gap is of importance for its explanation. For example, the argument that India and China were unable to develop their own industrial revolution due to Western (colonial) policy loses its point because divergence had, in fact, started earlier (Parthasarathi 2011 for India; von Glahn 1996: 1–2, for the Sprouts of Capitalism debate in China). This clears the way for explanations that reinforce the importance of factors of production. Clark (1987), for example, argues for higher labour productivity in England, with corresponding higher wages, thus clearing a path for increases in technology. Pomeranz (2000) in explaining nineteenth-century Chinese stagnation, argued that, compared to China, England was blessed with coal reserves and overseas consumer markets. A similar 'stroke of luck' for Europe can be distilled from Rosenthal and Wong (2011), who claim that the continent's violent past resulted in higher demand for capital-intensive technologies and rising urbanization, both of which led to growth.

Conclusion

The period 1700–1900 witnessed a most dramatic break with previous global economic history: the transition from a more or less stagnant, or at best – in western Europe – very slow-growing, economy to the 'modern economic growth' of the nineteenth and, ultimately, twentieth centuries. This radical break, also known as the Industrial Revolution, began in the region of the world that already before 1800 attained the highest levels of real income, a region in which other dimensions of well-being – life expectancy and education – had also attained relatively high levels. In Great Britain this was indeed closely linked to the process of industrialization, but in other parts of the North Sea area comparable changes in services and agriculture produced comparable advances in well-being. Similarly, in the Western offshoots the standard of living was often as high as in the most advanced parts of Europe, even though the industrialization processes often started much later than in Great Britain. To explain why the offshoots were able to achieve such high levels of well-being already before their Industrial

Revolution – for which a wide variety of institutional and factor-endowment theories have been suggested – is beyond the scope of this chapter.

The 'Great Divergence', the nineteenth-century combination of rapid economic growth in the core regions of the world economy and stagnation in the rest, was in many ways a continuation of trends already at play in the eighteenth century. In the West occasional signs of a 'growth paradox' can be found, in the sense that GDP growth did not always lead to comparable advances in other dimensions of the standard of living. Yet the overall tendency is one of a long-term improvement in well-being. In the non-Western world, however, the picture is more mixed, with some countries such as Argentina registering increased prosperity, but giants (in terms of population) such as China and India showing hardly any development. Disparities in the world economy sharply increased as a result. The world in 1900 was much more unequal than in 1700.

References

Acemoglu, D., Johnson, S. and Robinson, J. A. (2001). 'The Colonial Origins of Comparative Development: An Empirical Investigation', *American Economic Review*, 91(5), 1369–1401.

(2002). 'The Reversal of Fortune: Geography and Institutions in the Making of the Modern World Income Distribution', *Quarterly Journal of Economics*, 117(4), 1231–1294.

A'Hearn, B., Baten, J. and Crayen, D. (2009). 'Quantifying Quantitative Literacy: Age Heaping and the History of Human Capital', *Journal of Economic History*, 69(3), 783–808.

Albouy, D. Y. (2012). 'The Colonial Origins of Comparative Development: An Empirical Investigation: Comment', *American Economic Review*, 102(6), 3059–3076.

Allen, R. C. (2001). 'The Great Divergence in European Wages and Prices from the Middle Ages to the First World War', *Explorations in Economic History*, 38(4), 411–447.

(2007). 'India in the Great Divergence', in Williamson, J. G., Hatton, T. J., O'Rourke, K. H. and Taylor, A. M. (eds.), *The New Comparative Economic History: Essays in Honor of Jeffrey G. Williamson*, Cambridge, MA: MIT Press, 9–32.

(2009). 'Engels' Pause: Technical Change, Capital Accumulation, and Inequality in the British Industrial Revolution', *Explorations in Economic History*, 46(4), 418–435.

Allen, R. C., Bassino, J.-P., Ma, D., Moll-Murata, C. and van Zanden, J. L. (2011). 'Wages, Prices, and Living Standards in China, 1738–1925: In Comparison with Europe, Japan, and India', *Economic History Review*, 64(1), 8–38.

Allen, R. C., Murphy, T. E. and Schneider, E. B. (2012). 'The Colonial Origins of Divergence in the Americas: A Labor Market Approach', *Journal of Economic History*, 72(4), 863–894.

Antonovsky, A. (1967). 'Social Class, Life Expectancy and Overall Mortality', *The Milbank Memorial Fund Quarterly*, 45, 31–76.

Arroyo Abad, L., Davies, E. and van Zanden, J. L. (2012). 'Between Conquest and Independence: Real Wages and Demographic Change in Spanish America, 1530–1820', *Explorations in Economic History*, 49(2), 149–166.

Baten, J. (2013). 'Numeracy Estimates (ABCC) by Birth Decade and Country, Both Before and After 1800', Clio-infra, clio-infra.eu/Indicators/NumeracyTotal.html (accessed 9 November 2020).

Bellu, L. and Liberati, P. (2006). 'Policy Impacts on Inequality: Welfare-Based Measures of Inequality – The Atkinson Index', EASYPol Series, 50, Rome: Food and Agriculture Organization of the United Nations.

Benavot, A. and Riddle, P. (1988). 'The Expansion of Primary Education, 1870–1940: Trends and Issues', *Sociology of Education*, 61(3), 191–210.

Bengtsson, T. and van Poppel, F. (2011). 'Socioeconomic Inequalities in Death from Past to Present: An Introduction', *Explorations in Economic History*, 48, 343–356.

Bolt, J., Inklaar, R., de Jong, H. and van Zanden, J. L. (2018), 'Rebasing "Maddison": New Income Comparisons and the Shape of Long-Run Economic Development', University of Groningen, Groningen Growth and Development Centre Research Memorandum GD-174.

Broadberry, S. N., Campbell, B. M. S., Klein, A., Overton, M. and van Leeuwen, B. (2015a). *British Economic Growth 1270–1870*, Cambridge University Press.

Broadberry, S. N., Custodis, J. and Gupta, B. (2015b). 'India and the Great Divergence: An Anglo-Indian Comparison of GDP Per Capita, 1600–1871', *Explorations in Economic History*, 55, 58–75.

Broadberry, S. N., Guan, H. and Daokui Li, D. (2018). 'China, Europe, and the Great Divergence: A Study in Historical National Accounting, 980–1850', *Journal of Economic History*, 78(4), 955–1000.

Carmichael, S., de Pleijt, A., van Zanden, J. L. and de Moor, T. (2016). 'The European Marriage Pattern and its Measurement', *Journal of Economic History*, 76(1), 196–204.

Challú, A. E. and Gómez-Galvarriato, A. (2015). 'Mexico's Real Wages in the Age of the Great Divergence, 1730–1930', *Revista de Historia Económica*, 33(1), 83–122.

Chen, N. (1959). *A Collection of Gravestone Inscriptions in the Qing Dynasty*, Beijing: Zhonghua Book Company (陈乃乾, 清代碑传文通检, 中华书局 1959年2月).

Clark, G. (1987). 'Why Isn't the Whole World Developed? Lessons from the Cotton Mills', *Journal of Economic History*, 47(1), 141–173.

Coatsworth, J. H. (2008). 'Inequality, Institutions and Economic Growth in Latin America', *Journal of Latin American Studies*, 40(3), 545–569.

Cummins, N. (2017). 'Lifespans of the European Elite, 800–1800', *Journal of Economic History*, 77(2), 406–439.

Cvrcek, T. (2013). 'Wages, Prices, and Living Standards in the Habsburg Empire, 1827–1910', *Journal of Economic History*, 73(1), 1–37.

de Ferranti, D., Perry, G. E., Ferreira, F. H. G. and Walton, M. (2004). *Inequality in Latin America: Breaking with History?* World Bank Latin American and Caribbean Studies. Washington, DC: World Bank.

de la Croix, D. and Licandro, O. (2015). 'The Longevity of Famous People from Hammurabi to Einstein', *Journal of Economic Growth*, 20(3), 263–303.

Dennison, T. and Ogilvie, S. (2014). 'Does the European Marriage Pattern Explain Economic Growth?', *Journal of Economic History*, 74(3), 651–693.

de Pleijt, A. M. (2018). 'Human Capital Formation in the Long Run: Evidence from Average Years of Schooling in England, 1300–1900', *Cliometrica*, 12(1), 99–126.

de Pleijt, A. M. and van Zanden, J. L. (2016). 'Accounting for the "Little Divergence": What Drove Economic Growth in Pre-Industrial Europe, 1300–1800?', *European Review of Economic History*, 20(4), 387–409.

Engerman, S. L. and Sokoloff, K. L. (1997). 'Factor Endowments, Institutions, and Differential Paths of Growth Among New World Economies: A View from Economic Historians of the United States', in Harber, S. (ed.), *How Latin America Fell Behind: Essays on the Economic History of Brazil and Mexico, 1800–1914*, Stanford University Press, 260–304.

Family History Library (https://familysearch.org/search/).

Feinstein, C. H. (1988). 'The Rise and Fall of the Williamson Curve', *Journal of Economic History*, 48(3), 699–729.

Field, B. C. (1985). 'The Evolution of Individual Property Rights in Massachusetts Agriculture, 17th–19th Centuries', *Northeastern Journal of Agricultural and Resource Economics*, 14(2), 97–109.

Fink-Jensen, J. (2015). 'Book Titles per Capita', Clio-infra,handle.net/10622/AOQMAZ (accessed 10 October 2020).

Frankema, E. and Waijenburg, M. (2012). 'Structural Impediments to African Growth? New Evidence from Real Wages in British Africa, 1880–1965', *Journal of Economic History*, 72(4), 895–926.

Gapminder.org, 'Child Mortality (0–5 year-olds dying per 1,000 born)', www.gapminder.org/data/ (accessed 9 November 2020).

Hoffman, P. T., Jacks, D. S., Levin, P. A. and Lindert, P. H. (2002). 'Real Inequality in Europe since 1500', *Journal of Economic History*, 62(2), 322–355.

Juif, D.-T., and Baten, J. (2012). 'On the Human Capital of Inca Indios Before and After the Spanish Conquest: Was There a "Pre-Colonial Legacy"?' University of Tuebingen Working Papers in Economics and Finance 27, University of Tuebingen, Faculty of Economics and Social Sciences.

Kannisto, V. (2001). 'Mode and Dispersion of the Length of Life', *Population: An English Selection*, 13(1), 159–171.

Koepke, M. and Baten, J. (2005). 'The Biological Standard of Living in Europe during the Last Two Millennia', *European Review of Economic History*, 9(1), 61–95.

Komlos, J. (1998). 'Shrinking in a Growing Economy? The Mystery of Physical Stature during the Industrial Revolution', *Journal of Economic History*, 58(3), 779–802.

Lee, J., Feng, W. and Campbell, C. (1994). 'Infant and Child Mortality Among the Qing Nobility: Implications for Two Types of Positive Check', *Population Studies*, 48(3), 395–411.

Lindert, P. H. and Williamson, J. G. (2015). 'American Colonial Incomes, 1650–1774', *Economic History Review*, 69(1), 54–77.

Lo Cascio, E. and Malanima, P. (2005). 'Cycles and Stability: Italian Population Before the Demographic Transition (225 B.C.–A.D. 1900)', *Rivista di Storia Economica*, 21(3), 5–40.

Maddison Project Database, version 2018. Bolt, J., Inklaar, R., de Jong, H. and van Zanden, J. L. (2018), 'Rebasing "Maddison": New Income Comparisons and the Shape of Long-Run Economic Development', University of Groningen, Groningen Growth and Development Centre Research Memorandum GD-174.

Meyer, J. W., Ramirez, F. O., Rubinson, R. and Boli, J. (1977). 'The World Educational Revolution, 1950–1970', *Sociology of Education*, 50, 242–258.

Meyer, J. W., Ramirez, F. O. and Nuhoglu Soysal, Y. (1992). 'World Expansion of Mass Education, 1870–1980', *Sociology of Education*, 65(2), 128–149.

Milanovic, B., Lindert, P. and Williamson, J. (2011). 'Pre-Industrial Inequality', *The Economic Journal*, 121(551), 255–272.

Moatsos, M., Baten, J., Foldvari, P., van Leeuwen, B. and van Zanden, J. L. (2014). 'Income Inequality Since 1820', in van Zanden, J. L., Baten, J., Mira d'Ercole, M., Rijpma, A., Smith, A. and Timmer, M. (eds.), *How Was Life? Global Well-Being Since 1820*, Paris: OECD Publishing and International Institute of Social History, 199–215.

North, D. C., Summerhill, W. and Weingast, B. R. (2000). 'Order, Disorder, and Economic Change: Latin America vs. North America', in Bueno de Mesquita, B. and Root, H. (eds.), *Governing for Prosperity*, New Haven: Yale University Press, 17–58.

Ohkawa, K. and Rosovsky, H. (1973). *Japanese Economic Growth: Trend Acceleration in the Twentieth Century*, Stanford University Press.

Parthasarathi, P. (2011). *Why Europe Grew Rich and Asia Did Not: Global Economic Divergence, 1600–1850*, Cambridge University Press.

Pinker, S. (2011). *The Better Angels of our Nature: Why Violence Has Declined*, Harmondsworth: Penguin.

Pomeranz, K. (2000). *The Great Divergence. China, Europe, and the Making of the Modern World Economy*, Princeton University Press.

Prados de la Escosura, L. (2012). 'Output per Head in Pre-Independence Africa: Quantitative Conjectures', *Economic History of Developing Regions*, 27(2), 1–36.

(2015). 'World Human Development, 1870–2007', *Review of Income and Wealth* 61(2), 220–247.

Prayon, V. and Baten, J. (2013). 'Human Capital, Institutions, Settler Mortality, and Economic Growth in Africa, Asia and the Americas', Working Paper, University of Tuebingen.

Rawski, E. (1979). *Education and Popular Literacy in Ch'ing China*, University of Michigan Press.

Reis, J. (2005). 'Economic Growth, Human Capital Formation, and Consumption in Western Europe Before 1800', in Allen, R. C., Bengtsson, T. and Dribe, M. (eds.), *Living Standards in the Past*, Oxford University Press, 195–225.

Rosenthal, J.-L. and Bin Wong, R. (2011). *Before and Beyond Divergence: The Politics of Economic Change in China and Europe*, Cambridge, MA: Harvard University Press.

Schofield, R., Reher, D. and Bideau, A. (eds.) (1991). *The Decline of Mortality in Europe*, Oxford University Press.

Sokoloff, K. L. and Engerman, S. L. (2000). 'Institutions, Factor Endowments, and Paths of Development in the New World', *Journal of Economic Perspectives*, 14(3), 217–232.

Studer, R. (2008). 'India and the Great Divergence: Assessing the Efficiency of Grain Markets in Eighteenth and Nineteenth Century India', *Journal of Economic History*, 68 (2), 393–437.

United Nations (1948). *Demographic Yearbook 1948*, New York: United Nations.

United Nations (1957). *Demographic Yearbook 1957*, New York: United Nations.

United Nations (1960). *Demographic Yearbook 1960*. New York: United Nations.

United Nations (2018). *Human Development Indices and Indicators: 2018 Statistical Update*, New York: United Nations Development Programme.

van Leeuwen, B. and Li, J. (2014). 'Education Since 1820', in van Zanden, J. L., Baten, J., Mira d'Ercole, M., Rijpma, A., Smith, A. and Timmer, M. (eds.), *How Was Life? Global Well-Being Since 1820*, Paris: OECD Publishing and International Institute of Social History, 87–100.

van Zanden, J. L and Baten, J. (2008). 'Book Production and the Onset of Modern Economic Growth', *Journal of Economic Growth*, 13(3), 217–235.

van Zanden, J. L., Baten, J., Foldvari, P. and van Leeuwen, B. (2014). 'The Changing Shape of Global Inequality 1820–2000: Exploring a New Dataset', *Review of Income and Wealth*, 60(2), 279–297.

van Zanden, J. L., Buringh, E. and Bosker, M. (2012). 'The Rise and Decline of European Parliaments, 1188–1789', *Economic History Review*, 65(3), 835–861.

van Zanden, J. L. and van Leeuwen, B. (2012). 'Persistent but not Consistent: The Growth of National Income in Holland 1347–1807', *Explorations in Economic History*, 49(2), 119–130.

van Zanden, J. L. (1995). 'Tracing the Beginning of the Kuznets Curve: Western Europe During the Early Modern Period', *Economic History Review*, 48(4), 643–664.

von Glahn, R. (1996), *Fountain of Fortune: Money and Monetary Policy in China, 1000–1700*, Berkeley: University of California Press.

Williamson, J. G. (1981). 'Urban Disamenities, Dark Satanic Mills, and the British Standard of Living Debate', *Journal of Economic History*, 41(1), 75–83.

(1985). *Did British Capitalism Breed Inequality?* Boston: Allen & Unwin.

(2010). 'Five Centuries of Latin American Income Inequality', *Revista De Historia Económica / Journal of Iberian and Latin American Economic History*, 28(2), 227–252.

Woods, R. and Williams, N. (1995). 'Must the Gap Widen Before It Can Be Narrowed? Long-Term Trends in Social Class Mortality Differentials', *Continuity and Change*, 10, 105–137.

Xu, Y., Shi, Z., van Leeuwen, B., Ni, Y., Zhang, Z. and Ma, Y. (2017). 'Chinese National Income, *c*.1661–1933', *Australian Economic History Review*, 57(3), 368–393.

17

International Transactions: Real Trade and Factor Flows

WOLFGANG KELLER, MARKUS LAMPE, AND CAROL H. SHIUE

Introduction

The link between trade and global economic development defines one of the most enduring debates in all of economic history. The question goes to the heart of whether the origins of the Industrial Revolution of the late eighteenth century can be traced to one economy or one region in Europe, or whether industrialization was the result of global connections. By the mid-eighteenth century, the world saw an overall increase in openness and the movement of goods across national borders, with considerable growth in trade between European countries and their North American colonies. Concurrently, industrialization started in a small set of countries in western Europe and on the North American east coast, initiating a global divergence in national incomes. This chapter discusses the main drivers of trade in this period and reviews the factors that contributed to increasing trade.

We begin with a survey of the broad regional and temporal trends in trade, as well as the key factors driving differences in trade costs. We then lay out the theoretical reasons why trade can be mutually beneficial to trading partners before examining historical arguments and evidence, along with available quantitative estimates of gains from trade. The chapter then moves on to suggest additional mechanisms that could dynamically result in multiplier effects of trade on growth, concluding that trade contributed to global divergence. We conclude that basic resource gains from trade are likely to have a limited impact on growth. Instead, the most important impacts of trade and factor flows are likely to emerge in terms of interactions with other factors such as institutions and technology transfer.

Historical Background 1700–1870

The Evolution of Domestic and International Trade

Table 17.1 shows low volumes of international trade before 1800. Data on trade volumes and openness are scarce for the period before 1800, and the existing data might somewhat underestimate actual trade flows, given the limited state capacity to record economic activity. Nevertheless, this and further evidence shows that international goods were only available to a minority of households at this time.

Though the timing and intensity of trade varied by region, on average trade increased much faster after 1800 than before, both in absolute terms and with respect to total production. The rapid acceleration of trade in the nineteenth century should be seen in the light of its very low initial levels. Global trade grew three times as fast as global output from 1500 to 1820: 1.0 per cent per annum versus 0.3 per cent per annum (Maddison 2005: 22). Between 1820 and 1870, global trade volumes (not including the slave trade) and world production increased faster than ever before, at 4.8 per cent per annum (Federico and Tena 2017) and 0.9 per cent per annum, respectively – shares of exports in domestic production also rose almost everywhere.

Commodity price analysis provides another, complementary, assessment of trade. For example, markets may be highly efficient if information about prices is transmitted rapidly; in this case, we may observe little or no trade, but prices are highly correlated, conditional on inter-market distance and local shocks. Market integration measures typically use prices of traded goods, from everyday staple grains like wheat and rice to (initially) scarcer and more luxury goods like spices, tea, sugar, coffee, or fine textiles of silk and cotton. Since the possibility of trade implies that price differences of similar goods in different locations will be arbitraged away (up to the level of the trade costs between locations) – price behaviour across different markets reveals valuable evidence about the degree of market integration between different locations, relative efficiency, and changes in trade costs. The advantage of this approach is that it can provide insights into the degree of 'national', regional, and intercontinental market integration even in the absence of trade volume data.

Studies on integration have typically shown declining price gaps over time in Europe (Federico 2012; Chilosi et al. 2013). Although market integration within domestic markets and across international markets did not always move together (since there were differences in domestic and international costs of trade), this finding, like the volume estimates, produces an overall

Table 17.1 Openness and the growth of trade

Region (example)	Openness 1700	Openness 1760	Openness 1820	Openness 1870	Trade growth 1700–60	Trade growth 1760–1820	Trade growth 1820–70	Share of world exports in 1870
United Kingdom	8	15	8	19	1.6%	1.8%	4.9%	19.5%
Continental Europe (France)			5	12	2.3% (1716–80)	-2.1% (1787–1821)	4.6%	44.4% (France: 11.2%)
Japan				3			14.3% (1860–70)	0.3%
India				7	(0.2%) (EIC) (-2.2%) (Surat)	(2%) (EIC)	3.8%	5.5%
China			0 (1840)	1			1.8% (1830–70)	2.1%
South East Asia (Dutch East Indies)			(1)	(5)	?	(2.6%) (VOC exports)	4.8% (1822–70)	2.1% (Dutch East Indies: 0.9%)
Ottoman Empire	<2	<2	2	6			4.3%	1.7%

Latin America (Mexico)			(8)	(12)		(0.6%)	2.2%	Latin America and Caribbean: 9.0% (Mexico: 0.6%, Brazil: 1.9%)
Latin America (Brazil)			27	23		0.1% (1800–30)	4.9%	
Africa (Nigeria)				(Africa: 16)			3.2%	3.1% (Nigeria: 0.1%)
Africa (Slave trade)	0.3	0.7 (1790)	0.3	0	0.8%	?	-100%	n/a
Australia			7 (1826)	21			10.7%	1.6%
United States	(9 Mid-Atlantic/24 Lower South, 1720s)	(9 Mid-Atlantic/22 Lower South, 1770)	6	5	3.7% Mid-Atlantic / 4.3% Lower South 1720–70	2.0% (US, 1790–1820)	4.3%	8.4%

Sources and notes: Openness=exports/gross domestic product in current prices (if in parenthesis, data refer to estimates in constant prices). Trade growth per year is measured in constant prices. Share of world exports is measured current prices and refers to 1913 borders. Data for 1820 and 1870 based on Federico and Tena-Junguito (2016; 2017; 2018); for periods before 1870 refer to chapters 1, 5, 6 and 10 of this volume and the sources given in Keller et al. (2020), and Appendix 17.1.

picture of nineteenth-century markets being, on average, much more interconnected than seventeenth-century markets. In Asia, the absence of an industrial revolution did not mean there was little intra-regional trade. On the contrary, markets in western Japan and the Yangzi Delta were highly integrated before 1800, and general domestic integration in Japan and China was not sharply different in comparison to regional market integration in western Europe (Shiue and Keller 2007; Dobado-González et al. 2015). The extent of grain-market integration between Asian and European markets, however, was relatively very weak in the seventeenth century (Dobado-González et al. 2015). Comprehensive intercontinental market integration in competing goods was generally not observed in the eighteenth century. Early globalization was generally limited to high value-to-weight goods: spices, sugar, tea, porcelain, Asian textiles. Moreover, global trade between Europe and Asia, Africa, and the Caribbean was possible only through the advantages conferred by European privileged companies (O'Rourke 2006; de Zwart and van Zanden 2018).

Understanding the Basis and the Costs of Trade

Although the historical and the economics literature employ different terms to describe the basis of trade, both literatures share the key idea that differences between trading partners form the sources of, or basis for trade. The first and most fundamental economic definition of these differences is comparative advantage. Differences in opportunity costs[1] lead to gains from specialization between, for example, individuals, households, clans, regions, or countries. Adam Smith's *Inquiry into the Nature and Causes of the Wealth of Nations* (1776) gave specialization and the division of labour a central role in understanding why some places are rich and others poor. Two key insights of Smith's work are that specialization creates improvements in the production of different goods and that the degree of such specialization is determined by the 'extent of the market'.

Second, technology differences between trading partners can also be a reason to trade. The first rigorous formulation of the determinants of the pattern of trade – which economy exports which good – is due to David Ricardo. Inspired by the Methuen Treaty of 1703 between England and Portugal, Ricardo realized that there were benefits in Portugal making port

1 Opportunity costs are the costs of an alternative use of resources not chosen, e.g., in a cost-benefit analysis of making all goods yourself instead of specializing in the production of one and exchanging its surplus for the production of others.

wine while England produces textiles, even if Portugal in principle could produce both cheaper. Developing the concept of comparative advantage, he showed that an economy that is relatively inefficient (has higher opportunity costs) in producing certain goods should import these in exchange for goods that the country produces relatively efficiently (low opportunity costs).

Third, resource differences are potentially an important source of trade. Swedish economists Eli Heckscher and Bertil Ohlin developed the theory of comparative advantage further by noting that differences in the availability of production factors, or 'factor abundance', is an important determinant of relative production costs across countries. For example, an economy with large amounts of arable land would, in the absence of trade, have a relatively low price of land, and thus would be able to produce goods that use land intensively with relatively low cost. In contrast, manufactured (or artisanal) goods would tend to be cheaper in countries that have an abundance of labour, and therefore relatively low-cost workers.

While Ricardo saw differences in production technologies as the primitive basis determining the pattern of trade since it directly affected relative autarky prices, Heckscher and Ohlin saw relative autarky prices determined by differences in the relative factor abundance across economies. These lead to opportunity cost differences and thus trade even if the production technologies that Ricardo emphasized are the same across countries. Both theories, however, are theories of comparative advantage in that trade is driven by opportunity cost differences across economies (Lampe and Sharp 2019). Empirically, it has been challenging to separate the roles of production technology versus factor abundance differences (Trefler 1995).

Finally, another potential difference between countries may be institutional quality. Depending on the context, institutional differences may be less important than the other three, but following a similar logic, economies with good institutions would tend to export institutions-intensive goods. For example, countries with better contract enforcement will, all else equal, be able to produce goods that are relatively contract-intensive (in analogy to Heckscher-Ohlin's labour- or land-intensiveness) at lower autarky prices compared to an economy with weak enforcement of contracts and therefore export those products abroad (Nunn 2007).

Even if the basis for trade may exist, the extent to which countries can realize trade gains will depend on the costs of trade. If, for example, England were to export textiles to Portugal in exchange for wine, the price of English textiles in Lisbon would not be the same as that in Liverpool, as long as there are non-negligible trade costs. Trade costs will drive a wedge between the prices in the two countries.[2] In particular, trade costs that are too high, relative to differences in comparative advantage, will result in several economies all producing the same type of good at home because trade is not feasible. Thus, falling trade costs will lead to more trade of the same goods ('intensive margin'), but also increase the range of goods that can be traded ('extensive margin').[3] The expansion of trade along both margins can be seen over the period 1700 to 1870, when not only did the spice trade increase between South and South East Asia and Europe, but trade in grain and goods with relatively low value-to-weight ratios increased, too.

The central result of trade theory is that given certain conditions, the trade equilibrium has weakly higher welfare than seen in autarky equilibrium, that is, all else equal, people in a world with trade are better off than without it.[4] While such gains from trade have been proven at various levels of generality (Dixit and Norman 1980), the theoretical result that trade cannot lead to lower welfare follows from the fact that when the economy can engage in trade with other economies, the no-trade situation continues to be an option, and an increase in the set of choices – from one (autarky) to two (autarky or trade) – cannot lower welfare.

Despite the positive implication of overall gains, it is important to emphasize that it rests on key assumptions about the relevant conditions. In the absence of these conditions, free trade may or may not be the optimal policy as a matter of theory. For example, free trade generally remains the best policy in the presence of increasing returns to scale and monopolistic competition (Helpman and Krugman 1985). At the same time, if an economy has monopoly power in trade, this country can do better than a free trade policy by implementing an import tariff of a certain size because this improves the country's terms of trade.[5] The size of this 'optimal' tariff would be chosen to maximize the country's welfare, not global welfare. At least theoretically, in that case, mercantilist and protectionist policies can maximize a country's welfare. In practice, however, such goals are hard to achieve because often

2 Trade practitioners speak of the fob versus the cif price, for 'free on board' and 'cost, insurance, freight' inclusive price, respectively, with the latter being higher.

3 With increasing returns to scale, falling trade costs can also lead to the agglomeration of economic activity, as highlighted in the 'new economic geography' literature (Krugman 1991).

4 Among the conditions that ensure gains from trade are (1) convex technologies (no increasing returns to scale), (2) perfect competition (no market power), and (3) the equality of social and private net costs (no externalities).

5 The terms of trade is the ratio of export to import prices. By influencing the prices for imported goods on world markets through tariffs, a large country can shift income from foreign producers to the domestic government.

there will be retaliation with tariffs by other countries, lowering welfare in all countries (a so-called *trade war*).

Furthermore, it is important to note that the distributional implications are such that the presence of overall gains from trade to a country is consistent with trade lowering the welfare of certain individuals. Thus, trade does not unambiguously increase the welfare of everyone even when the relevant conditions are fulfilled. One of the most important results in the Heckscher and Ohlin world is that when there are multiple factors of production, opening up trade will lower the welfare of factors used intensively in the import-competing production, while raising the welfare of factors intensively used in the export sector (Stolper and Samuelson 1941). That is, the impact of trade on welfare is heterogeneous across factors of production. Such distributional effects have been extensively analyzed in work on the period 1700–1870 (O'Rourke and Williamson 1999), and they may also matter because they affect the incentives of certain factor-using versus factor-saving technological changes that some argue played a role in why Europe industrialized first (Allen 2011).

Drivers of Increasing Market Integration and Trade

Several major drivers were responsible for increasing market integration and trade over the eighteenth and nineteenth centuries. One of the most basic of these factors was reduction in the costs of transport (shipping), which rise with distance because greater distance increases fuel, crew, equipment, and the opportunity (time) cost of shipping. Road improvements, canals, railways, and steamships naturally reduced transport costs. While trade costs fell substantially over the period 1700 to 1870, the fact that trade declines with geographic distance even today (commonly referred to as the *gravity equation of trade*) gives powerful evidence for the importance of trade costs in shaping trade patterns at any given point in time.

The quality of roads and the transport infrastructure had a direct impact on costs of transportation. In the Netherlands and the UK, considerable investments in internal road construction and canal building contributed to improving the infrastructure in both regions from 1700 to 1870. This helped to deepen the integration of domestic markets and thus also improved the connection of ports to their hinterland (Bogart 2014). By contrast, for example, Indian markets were relatively fragmented in the eighteenth and early nineteenth century, but became more integrated as railway building (for British military purposes) advanced (Studer 2008; Donaldson 2018).

Technological improvements in transport are important for reducing trade costs. In shipping, for example, copper sheeting (Solar and Hens 2016), better navigation instruments, and improved understanding of wind patterns (Kelly and Ó Gráda 2019) not only improved transport but also increased the reliability and speed of information transmission carried via the post. The largest advances in shipping and land transport technology were concentrated in the nineteenth century (de Zwart and van Zanden 2018: 32–37). Such advances were reinforced in the early nineteenth century with the invention of steamships, which apart from their early use as gunboats became important for trade from around 1865 (Pascali 2017). From the 1850s, the international telegraph network also spread, but it took until the 1870s to effectively facilitate worldwide access to the technology as a means of communication, allowing information to travel faster than people and commodities (Steinwender 2018).

A second factor driving market integration includes the taxes on domestic and international trade (tariffs), as well as non-tariff barriers such as quantitative restrictions on the volume that can be traded. In Europe, the eighteenth century represented the final stage of European colonial expansion following the age of discoveries, and the intellectual and practical means by which that expansion was achieved: namely, mercantilist policies and the domination of trade by the state-backed monopoly trading companies. The degree of market integration thus depended importantly on the policy stance towards free markets and associated tariff reductions. Under classical mercantilism, western European powers attempted to capture value-added and employment by monopolizing trade routes for the benefit of their shipping and trading companies, while granting national industries exclusive access to colonial raw materials. A famous example of such a measure was the English Navigation Acts, first stipulated under Cromwell in 1651, and finally revoked in 1854. They were aimed at excluding (more efficient) Dutch shippers and traders from transporting goods from and to England and its colonies, and keeping manufacturing concentrated in Britain.

The back and forth on protectionism imply not only that 'free trade' was not the norm but also that there was no uniform 'progress' towards integration and free trade. The British government was financed by tariff revenues and the average ratio of import duties relative to the value of imports was between 30 per cent and 50 per cent from 1790 to 1840, on goods such as sugar, wine, tea, coffee, tobacco, and other high value-to-weight products, rather than timber, useful as it was for building British warships. The Corn Laws protected landed interests and kept the price of grain high – tariffs had to be raised as high as 40 per cent to keep cheap foreign grain from entering Britain during years when the harvest was good.

Between 1840 and 1870, mercantilist and other trade barriers were slowly dismantled in Europe (Tena-Junguito et al. 2012). The trend proved to be short-lived, however, and in the post-1870s political backlash resulted in a reversal in the free trade stance for Germany, France, and other countries. Increasing protectionism also occurred beyond Europe, in the United States and much of Latin America after independence, and again from the mid-1800s (see chapters 8 and 9 of Volume I). Nevertheless, the decades of reduced protectionism in the nineteenth century had coincided with ongoing national integration. The first and most important customs union of the German states, the *Zollverein*, was officially established in 1834. It resulted in the abolition of tariff barriers among member states, contributing to lower internal trade barriers and increased market integration (Keller and Shiue 2014), but it also established higher trade barriers for some of its neighbours. Recent work by Chilosi and Federico (2015) attributes most of the improvements in the extent of market integration in the transatlantic trade to these types of institutional change and declines in tariffs, as well as to the dismantling of the monopolies of European trading companies. Western powers also used military technology to force markets like China and Japan into the world economy by means of 'gunboat diplomacy'.

Third, there are other costs that are less straightforward to quantify, such as the costs related to the institutional environment in which trade takes place. For example, a relatively high risk of expropriation will increase trade costs because forward-looking traders will want to be compensated through higher prices for the additional risk. Expropriation may be due to the manner of governance (which results in an unwillingness or an inability to protect property rights), the actions of private agents' (such as unfettered piracy), or a combination of the two. We may see both trade increasing, and, price gaps going down when institutions change.

The historical examples of the development of market access in the US, India, and Europe suggest institutional changes are closely linked to the development of the domestic infrastructure that ultimately improved market integration (Fogel 1964; Donaldson 2018). Developments in domestic markets may in turn be closely tied to international trade as increased domestic market integration and urbanization tends to concentrate economic activity, making specialization and international openness and trade much more feasible (Keller et al. 2017).

One way to study the link between trade and institutions is to consider periods of institutional change or reform. Wars were sometimes fought because of trade conflicts and political hostilities. For example, in the late seventeenth century, England and the Netherlands fought a series of trade wars, followed by trade-related conflicts between Britain and Spain in the early eighteenth century. The increasingly global wars between Britain and France left their mark on the 1760–1820 period. Mercantilist trade rivalries accompanied the deepening of European colonization of the world and paradoxically increased trade costs through the militarization of trade (Thomas and McCloskey 1981: 93–97; Findlay and O'Rourke 2009: chapter 5; O'Rourke et al. 2010: 97–101).

Wars and revolutions were also important flashpoints that, either temporarily or permanently, changed the trajectory of trade by changing the underlying laws and institutions. A clear example of how war changed international trading regimes is the Opium Wars, in which the British went to war to force open Chinese markets to European traders (Keller et al. 2011). Other examples include how the French armies occupied and reformed many of the institutions of the European countries they occupied; or how the American Revolutionary War changed the relationship between the colonizer and the colonists. Among the colonies that did benefit, both trade and institutional transfer appear to be part of the story (Acemoglu et al. 2001; 2005).

Empire-building and colonial ties affected not only the amount of trade but also the kind of goods traded and the rules of engagement – and not always positively. The gains from trade before 1870 were unevenly distributed, due to colonialism, disease, and exploitation, in particular with respect to Africa and the native populations of North and South America and Oceania (Zahedieh 2014: 395; de Zwart and van Zanden 2018: 5–8; Volume I, chapters 8–11). Some, but not all, colonies of the industrializing nations could reap gains from specialization in raw material provision.

Fourth, there is a set of trade costs that are typically found to be highly significant in empirical analysis, but which can also be hard to capture. These are exemplified by 'border' effects. It makes sense, for example, that common language tends to increase trade, and border effects exist even after we control for distance, size, and border taxes (Shiue 2005; Jacks 2009). While differences in institutional regulation and 'doing business' across the border might play important roles, they do not explain everything (Head and Mayer 2014).

Trade and Industrialization from 1700 to 1820

Quantitative Estimates of the Gains from International Trade

Theoretically, specialization and trade according to comparative advantage have led to an increase in efficiency that has increased world production, for given resources and technology levels. Trade also distributes the increased production to consumers, raising overall welfare. The magnitude of these potential gains and the importance of trade in explaining the divergence in incomes have been the subject of numerous studies.

In contrast to explanations of industrialization that locate the sources of growth in capital accumulation, the Enlightenment, or political revolutions within the British or European region, Immanuel Wallerstein's (1974) influential world systems theory argues that divergence is the result of a process of western European colonialism from the sixteenth century onwards and the concurrent rise of a new capitalist world system. In his view, trade between the capitalist centre (characterized by free labour and productive cities) and the peripheries (which were subject to serfdom, feudal land tenure regimes, or slavery) magnified the differences in living standards and development between the two regions. The peripheries increasingly specialized in cash-crop production with coerced labour, while the centre absorbed a large share of the profits from high productivity goods – the newly established order thus deprived the peripheries of their own development potential (Wallerstein 1974: 86–102; 349–350).

Although Wallerstein emphasized regional disparities in society and institutions, the idea that trade can result in specialization in certain activities with different development potential is familiar to economic theory, as well, although the assumptions behind such models warrant as much attention as those for the free trade case. It is well known that comparative advantage in agricultural production will naturally lead to specialization in agricultural production. In Matsuyama (1992), for example, a small, open economy with high agricultural productivity that opens to world trade will specialize in agriculture and see industrial stagnation because innovation occurs more rapidly in manufacturing activities. In Grossman and Helpman (1991: chapter 6), opening up to trade leads to specialization in low-tech, low-learning industries, which results in permanently lower rates of growth compared to the no-trade equilibrium.

Like Wallerstein, Kenneth Pomeranz also argued for the central importance of trade between the Old and the New World in the century from 1760 to 1860, but he shifted the emphasis to differences in the ability of different continents, Europe and Asia, to address their shared problem of resource scarcity. Here, Europe's ecological constraints were significantly lessened both by imports of agricultural products such as sugar, timber, and cotton, and other factors that provided a new flush of resources and price adjustments that were critical to industrialization. According to Pomeranz, without this world trade, eighteenth-century living standards would have been 'unlikely to lead to a thoroughgoing industrialization, and might even have impeded it' (Pomeranz 2002: 445).

How much of the divergence in per-capita income from 1700 to 1870 can be attributed to gains from trade? In light of these extensive qualitative arguments that attribute European success to trade in consequence of the age of discoveries, it is notable that quantitative estimates of gains from trade have, more often than not, failed to find empirical support for trade as a substantial engine of European growth. Studies based on comparative static methods have found the importance of trade and the periphery for the development of the centre to have been overstated (O'Brien 1982), and the extent to which European colonization before 1800 penetrated the world to have been relatively limited. This literature argues that trade was of little importance even for the cotton industry, where industrialization was fastest and most pronounced: first, it accounted for only a small share of economic activity, and furthermore, there would have been domestic substitutes for both inputs and markets at relatively little opportunity cost (Thomas and McCloskey 1981; O'Rourke et al. 2010: 110; Zahedieh 2014).

The disagreement is not about whether 'ghost acreage' derived from the land and labour of the New World expanded the economy of western Europe, as there is agreement that it did even among the critics. Rather, the objection is that the magnitude of the actual contribution was not that big relative to what is needed to explain income divergence. McCloskey reckoned that at most 13 per cent of any change in income in England can be explained by foreign trade (McCloskey 1994). Furthermore, export markets in cotton could not have been an engine of growth if they only acquired prominence at a point well into the industrialization process (Thomas and McCloskey 1981).

The relevant question seems to be not whether Britain would have survived a more limited comparative advantage in food production, but whether Britain was dependent on trade to such an extent that without it, industrialization would have failed. Harley estimates that self-sufficiency in 1860 would have cost Britain 6 per cent of national income, a minor fraction of the total rise in output that needs to be explained.[6] From 1855 to 1913, output per worker in Britain rose by roughly 80 per cent, and thus trade, as Harley (1994) notes, would seem to account for 'only one-thirteenth of the story'.

If imports were not that high, could it be that a significant part of the Industrial Revolution was financed by repatriated profits from slave trading and slave plantations to Britain, as the so-called 'Williams' hypothesis' argues? Like the above calculation on imports, one critic of this hypothesis concluded that the argument would 'founder on the numbers' (O'Brien 1982: 16): total profits, as such, did not make up a large share of British investments. A counterargument is that such calculations rely on the strong assumption of full employment of resources (i.e. there is an almost equally valid alternative with little opportunity cost), and that most individual magnitudes are small in comparison to national income (Findlay 1990; Zahedieh 2014).

As rough and simplistic as they are, the calculations of Thomas, McCloskey, Harley, and other authors dovetail with the recent theoretical and empirical literature by trade economists that have quantified the gains of trade for more recent periods with fully specified general equilibrium models. Based on theory and employing a variety of counterfactuals, Costinot and Rodriguez-Clare (2014) compute the welfare of forty countries (twenty-seven in Europe and thirteen other major countries) based on the observed levels of international trade in the year 2008. They then recompute incomes for the counterfactual case where trade costs are infinite, implying there is no international trade. The difference in incomes can be thought of as the welfare gains of going from autarky to the observed levels of trade in 2008. On average, across all countries, this is about 15 per cent of annual GDP (Costinot and Rodriguez-Clare 2014: table 4.1).[7] Specifically, for the Netherlands, gains are around 24 per cent; for Great Britain, about 12 per cent; and for the larger countries China and the US, about 4 per cent. Alternatively, they calculated hypothetical welfare losses of applying 40 per cent tariffs on all trade partners – only 1.5 per cent of income in 2008, suggesting that even a fairly large decline in trade barriers generates limited gains.

Although these estimates are for contemporary periods, the fact that trade as a fraction of national income was much smaller in the past suggests that in

6 Assuming a prohibition of trade would have reduced the price of exportables to importables by 50%, and the share of imports in income is assumed to be half of what it actually was (25%) = 50% x 12.5%, or 6%.

7 We focus here on the most plausible model assumptions for the period 1700 to 1870, shown in columns 2 and 3, with multiple sectors but no intermediate goods trade.

the eighteenth or nineteenth century trade gains would have been below the estimated 15 per cent of annual income. The result shows that at least as far as the static effects of trade are concerned, the potential gains from international trade are unlikely to have generated the large divergence in growth rates in global developments of the nineteenth century, even if it did contribute to them.

Of course, the extent to which actual trade flows and specialization patterns follow Ricardian differences in efficiency, differences in endowments, or other factors is difficult to ascertain empirically given the multitude of factors that affect trade historically. But one rare example where specialization patterns and shifts in relative prices have been assessed in a specific historical context is the forced opening of the Japanese market after 1853. Employing a factor abundance trade model with detailed data before and after Japan's opening, the estimated comparative advantage-based gains from autarky to trade is between 5 per cent and 9 per cent of GDP (Bernhofen and Brown 2005: table 17.4). While non-negligible, these estimates are consistent with comparative advantage-based, specialization-based gains from trade being fairly small relative to the differences in income between countries that need to be explained (in Japan's case, the income change of before versus after the Meiji Restoration).

Trade and Domestic Market Efficiency

An important part of the European story of growth is not only the Atlantic trade between the Old World and the New World, or trade between the developed and lagging parts of Europe, but also the very rapid growth in trade and integration of markets within western Europe from the eighteenth to the nineteenth centuries. As discussed earlier, a standard method of evaluating the efficacy of trade for different time periods and regions comes from price studies, since the behaviour of prices in different markets is affected by all types of trade costs, even those related to institutions or property rights. Unlike the estimates that focus on the value of imports or the profits from trade, which tend to capture specific aspects of the value or quantity of trade in the aggregate, or of goods categories, price studies tend to focus on questions of the efficiency of markets.

Price data confirm the key elements of the qualitative history about when and where markets developed first, showing that a critical juncture can be dated to between the late eighteenth century and the early nineteenth century. To compare market performance visually, we plot bilateral correlations between grain markets – since grain is a commonly traded commodity, grain markets will reflect aspects of market conditions more generally. Price correlations tend to decline the further apart markets are, consistent with the idea that as distance increases, trade becomes more costly, and so the higher the correlation, the more integrated the markets.

European markets in the nineteenth century were very different from how they had been in the preceding centuries. Figure 17.1, based on Shiue and Keller (2007), plots bilateral price correlations for wheat between ten centrally to moderately important markets in Europe, conditional on distance for two twenty-five-year periods: 1770–94 and 1825–49. The two samples are slightly different due to data availability, but both samples are based on central locations in France, the German-speaking regions, and the Low Countries. Significant improvement in market performance from the late eighteenth to the nineteenth century is apparent: the correlation at all distances increases strongly and the slope of the correlation declines much more slowly with distance in the nineteenth century compared to the eighteenth.

To understand what this improvement means in global terms, Figure 17.2 plots the late eighteenth-century European sample against a Chinese sample consisting of all prefectural markets in the ten central and southern provinces. The Chinese sample is more comprehensive than the European sample (a total of 14,520 points are plotted for China) and includes not only key trading hubs, but also peripheral regions. Nevertheless, there is a great deal of overlap and little evidence that Europe was exceptionally more integrated than China before the nineteenth century.

The economies of England and western Europe became notably more integrated simultaneously with their industrialization, or even after industrialization had begun. Market integration in England in the late eighteenth century was somewhat higher than in the Yangzi Delta for distances under 400 km (250 miles) – but English markets were also performing better than France, Germany, and other European markets (Shiue and Keller 2007). With respect to England, since industrialization in England is commonly believed to have already started by 1770, the high levels of integration seen in the late eighteenth century do not predate industrialization. It is also instructive to consider France, a country that would industrialize soon after Britain. Up until the late eighteenth century, integration among markets in France was comparable to that of the Yangzi Delta; see Figure 17.3.

Of course, inefficient markets – and the numerous and varied reasons behind why markets might perform poorly – will reduce the likelihood of

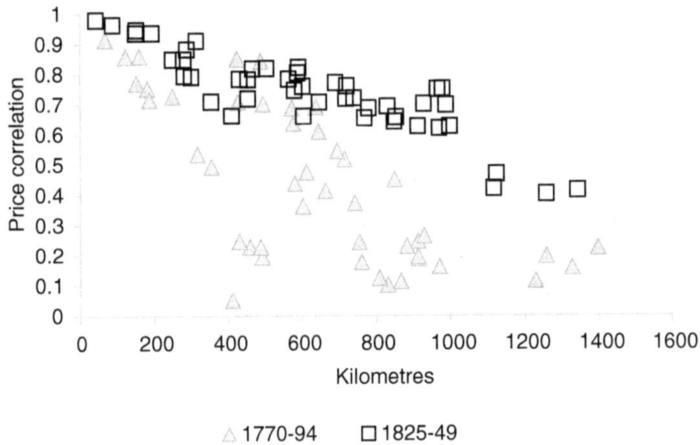

Figure 17.1 European markets 1770–94 and 1825–49

growth occurring. However, if we ask whether market efficiency can consistently *predict* growth, or in this case, give rise to the Great Divergence, the results are in line with the estimates of the gains of trade. Efficiency may have contributed to welfare increases, but the advantage enjoyed by the earlier industrializers, if there was any, was unlikely to have been a necessary and sufficient condition for generating industrialization.

Growth Effects of Trade

The low static gains from trade reported above are not the end of the link between trade and growth. Econometric estimates in the framework of growth regressions typically suggest larger gains than those based on static general equilibrium models (Frankel and Romer 1999). This requires an explanation of how trade affects growth besides static efficiency gains. For example, trade might be a proxy of underlying changes in institutions that promote growth more effectively than trade itself. The institutions that make trade possible are also likely to make property rights more secure. Trade also contributes to knowledge about new products, markets, practices, preferences, organizations, opportunities, religions, and legal systems. The question seems to be whether we can separate observable qualities about institutions that benefit the economy anyway, from those institutions that exclusively impact on trade (Shiue and Keller 2007; Nunn and Trefler 2014). Keller and Shiue (2020) investigate the impact of institutional change on

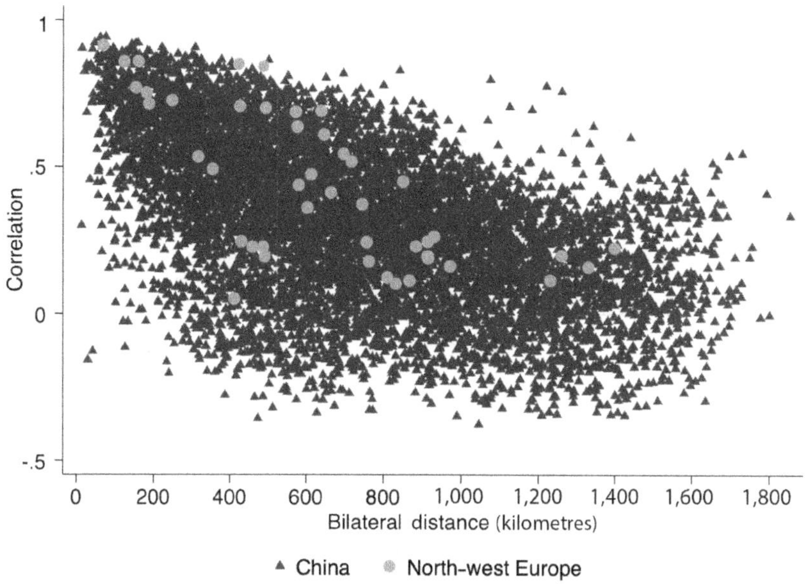

Figure 17.2 China and north-west Europe, 1770–94

market integration, showing not only that institutional reforms can lead to changes in a given economy, but also that the impact is multiplied through openness and the integration of markets.

One influential argument at the intersection of trade and institutional changes is that by Acemoglu et al. (2005) who show that trade is positively related to urbanization. Here, contrary to the static considerations above, international trade does not matter in itself so much as through the effect of trade on improving institutional quality. They argue that in the non-absolutist countries of western Europe, relatively open access to trading aided the economic, and later political, rise of new capitalist merchant elites that changed the institutional environment towards more secure property rights, which later also benefited industrial innovators and entrepreneurs, and thus contributed to industrialization. On the other hand, societies that failed to achieve such an institutional framework – as a consequence of European intervention (Acemoglu et al. 2001) or because of control of trade through the Crown (as in Spain and Portugal) – also failed to reap the institutional and long run economic benefits (Pascali 2017).

Furthermore, trade and general openness to ideas can be a vehicle for the transfer of ideas and a stimulus for technological development. In a simple

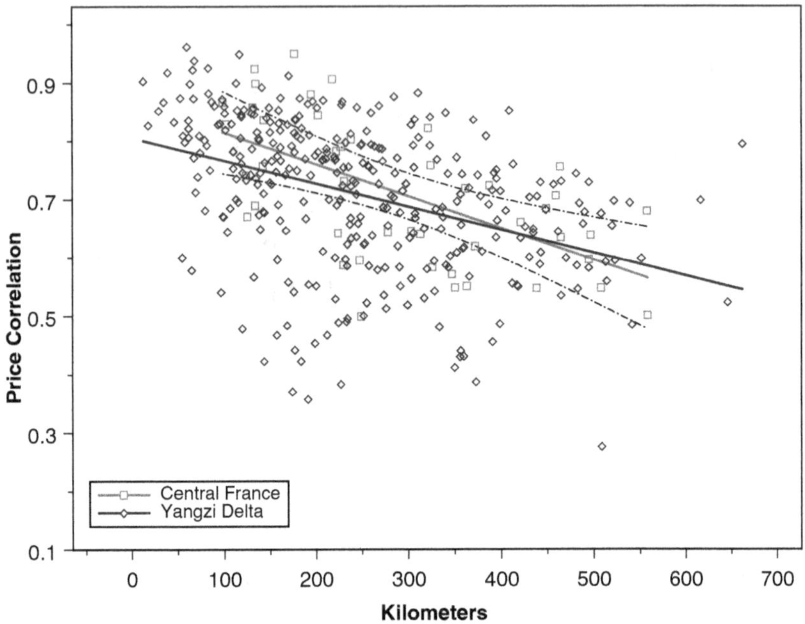

Figure 17.3 Price correlations of Yangzi Delta compared to France, 1770–94

Smithian framework, larger markets imply more specialization and enhanced learning by doing, especially before the advent of systematic applied scientific inquiry (Persson and Sharp 2015: chapter 2). More formally, Desmet and Parente (2012) argue that with larger markets, there arise higher demand elasticities. This leads to increased profits for larger firms, and potentially more innovation (Findlay and O'Rourke 2009: 344; Meissner 2014).

A third reason that trade could have a wider impact on the economy is that trade introduces new goods to a country. This possibility addresses the criticism that traditional static computation of gains from trade assumes domestic production can provide close enough substitutes for imports, if at a higher opportunity cost. Even if the volume of imports is not large, new goods could provide great benefits if the importing country cannot produce those goods, for example, for climatic or geological reasons (Ossa 2015). For Europe, such commodities included pepper, tea, cane sugar, silk, cotton, indigo, nutmegs or cloves, and certain furs in the period after 1500. Today, precious metals such as gold and silver, as well as oil, would be outstanding examples of trade based on geological endowments.

In Europe, new and more varieties of goods likely also promoted an 'industrious revolution', increasing work effort and market orientation in the population (de Vries 1994). In Asia, new goods may have had similar effects, but greater access to European goods among consumers was delayed until the mid-nineteenth century, when ports of trade in Japan as well as in China were forced open by Western navies. But even as Western powers took control of China's customs houses and tariff policy, and installed their own legal institutions in China, trade increased incrementally in the first decades. Only later, as trade expanded beyond Shanghai and to ports along the southeast coast and the trunk lines of the Yangzi River, did exports and imports increase not only in volume, but also in their diversity (Keller and Shiue forthcoming).

The patterns in the types of commodities traded with China suggests that trade, even when forced, produced increases in welfare for all trading partners. In addition, new goods introduced via trade could result in competition effects or innovation responses. For example, among the new goods imported to China in the nineteenth century were machines, for which domestic firms initially lacked the know-how, but over time learned to copy and reconstruct. Similarly, trade in porcelain, silk textiles, and other goods may lead to the establishment of new forms of manufacturing in foreign countries. To the extent that foreign goods, in and of themselves, embody a flow of technology, quality standards, or manufacturing techniques, the effects of trade are not limited to the static gains from trade analysis outlined above (Keller et al. 2017).

Conclusions

The traditional gains from trade that have been most studied are what can be called the static gains. Despite the positive correlation between trends in trade and growth, both empirically and in theory, the magnitude of the causal impact of trade on growth derived from static gains is not large relative to the gains reaped from industrialization. GDP gains from greater openness along these lines are too small to explain the emerging differences in per-capita GDP of the 1700–1870 period.

Such static gains are only one part of the story, however. Therefore, we discussed several possible extensions to current models and estimates, based on evidence suggesting a broader role for trade. Many of these extensions have a dynamic element, in which trade triggers something else that matters for growth or is part of a larger process of growth. This could occur, for example, if growth itself creates large increases in trade, or if trade interacts with another factor that matters for economic development. In this context, dynamic processes of learning, technology diffusion, and imitation of new goods might change the pathways by which trade ultimately affects domestic efficiency in the aggregate. This implies that much more than reductions in trade or transport costs are involved. In addition, openness of borders can generate incentives for migration, which can in turn transfer technologies across locations. Thus, migration in the eighteenth and early nineteenth century, although small compared to what happened after 1850 (de Zwart and van Zanden 2018; Volume II Chapter 17), was probably another important factor, as evidenced by the fact that once transport technologies enabled intercontinental trade in bulky food stuffs, large waves of migration led to the intensive cultivation of initially sparsely populated regions in North and South America, North and South East Asia and Oceania.

Thus far, dynamic gains have been challenging to capture in a definite way. However, reduced form estimates of trade and growth suggest these are quite important. While these dynamic processes can be grasped in principle through theory and descriptive evidence, tracing the relative importance and impact through causal links – and thus ultimately revising the breadth of the multiple influences of trade outlined above – establishes a promising research agenda for economic historians in the decades to come.

References

Acemoglu, D., Johnson, S. and Robinson, J. A. (2001). 'The Colonial Origins of Comparative Development: An Empirical Investigation', *American Economic Review*, 91(5), 1369–1401.

(2005). 'The Rise of Europe: Atlantic Trade, Institutional Change and Economic Growth', *American Economic Review*, 95(3), 546–579.

Allen, R. (2011). *Global Economic History: A Very Short Introduction*, Oxford University Press.

Bernhofen, D. M. and Brown, J. C. (2005). 'An Empirical Assessment of the Comparative Advantage Gains from Trade: Evidence from Japan', *American Economic Review*, 95(1), 208–225.

Bogart, D. (2014). 'The Transport Revolution in Industrializing Britain: A Survey', in Floud, R., Humphries, J. and Johnson, P. (eds.), *The Cambridge Economic History of Modern Britain, vol. 1: 1700–1870*, 4th ed., Cambridge University Press.

Chilosi, D. and Federico, G. (2015). 'Early Globalizations: The Integration of Asia in the World Economy, 1800–1938', *Explorations in Economic History*, 57, 1–18.

Chilosi, D., Murphy, T. E., Studer, R. and Tunçer, A. C. (2013). 'Europe's Many Integrations: Geography and Grain Markets, 1620–1913', *Explorations in Economic History*, 50, 46–68.

Costinot, A. and Rodriguez-Clare, A. (2014). 'Trade Theory with Numbers: Quantifying the Consequences of Globalization', in Gopinath, G., Helpman, E. and Rogoff, K. (eds.), *Handbook of International Economics*, vol. 4, Amsterdam: Elsevier, 197–261.

Desmet, K. and Parente, S. L. (2012). 'The Evolution of Markets and the Revolution of Industry: A Unified Theory of Growth', *Journal of Economic Growth*, 17(3), 205–234.

de Vries, J. (1994). 'The Industrial Revolution and the Industrious Revolution', *Journal of Economic History*, 54(2), 249–270.

de Zwart, P. and van Zanden, J. L. (2018). *The Origins of Globalization: World Trade and the Making of the Global Economy, 1500–1800*, Cambridge University Press.

Dixit, A. K. and Norman, V. D. (1980). *Theory of International Trade: A Dual, General Equilibrium Approach*, Cambridge University Press.

Dobado-González, R., García-Hiernaux, A. and Guerrero, D. E. (2015). 'West versus Far East: Early Globalization and the Great Divergence', *Cliometrica*, 9(2), 235–264.

Donaldson, D. (2018). 'Railroads of the Raj: Estimating the Impact of Transportation Infrastructure', *American Economic Review*, 108(4–5), 899–934.

Federico, G. (2012). 'How Much Do We Know About Market Integration in Europe?', *Economic History Review*, 65(2), 470–497.

Federico, G. and Tena-Junguito, A. (2016). 'World Trade, 1800–1938: A New Dataset', *EHES Working Papers in Economic History*, 93.

(2017). 'A Tale of Two Globalizations: Gains from Trade and Openness 1800–2010', *Review of World Economics*, 153, 601–626.

(2018). 'American Divergence: Lost Decades and Emancipation Collapse in Latin America and the Caribbean 1820–1870', *European Review of Economic History*, 22(2), 185–209.

Findlay, R. (1990). 'The "Triangular Trade" and the Atlantic Economy of the Eighteenth Century: A Simple General-Equilibrium Model', *Essays in International Finance, Princeton University*, 177.

Findlay, R. and O'Rourke, K. H. (2009). *Power and Plenty. Trade, War and the World Economy in the Second Millennium*, Princeton University Press.

Fogel, R. W. (1964). *Railroads and American Economic Growth: Essays in Econometric History*, Baltimore: Johns Hopkins University Press.

Frankel, J. and Romer, D. (1999). 'Does Trade Cause Growth?', *American Economic Review*, 89(3), 379–399.

Grossman, G. E. and Helpman, E. (1991). *Innovation and Growth in the Global Economy*, Cambridge, MA: MIT Press.

Harley, C. N. (1994). 'Foreign Trade: Comparative Advantage and Performance', in Floud, R. and McCloskey, D. (eds.), *The Economic History of Britain Since 1700, vol. 1: 1700–1860*, 2nd ed., Cambridge University Press, 300–331.

Head, K. and Mayer, T. (2014). 'Gravity Equations: Workhorse, Toolkit, and Cookbook', in Gopinath, G., Helpman, E. and Rogoff, K. (eds.), *Handbook of International Economics*, vol. 4, Amsterdam: Elsevier, 131–195.

Helpman, E. and Krugman, P. (1985). *Market Structure and Foreign Trade: Increasing Returns, Imperfect Competition, and the International Economy*, Cambridge, MA: MIT Press.

Jacks, D. S. (2009). 'On the Death of Distance and Borders: Evidence from the Nineteenth Century', *Economics Letters*, 105(3), 203–233.

Keller, W. and Shiue, C. H. (2014). 'Endogenous Formation of Free Trade Agreements: Evidence from the Zollverein's Impact on Market Integration', *Journal of Economic History*, 74(4), 1168–1204.

(2020). 'Market Integration and Institutional Change', *Review of World Economics*, 156, 251–285.

(forthcoming). 'Foreign Trade and Investment', Ch. 12, in Ma, D. and von Glahn, R. (eds.), *The Cambridge Economic History of China*, Vol. 2, Part 2, Cambridge University Press.

Keller, W., Li, B. and Shiue, C. H. (2011). 'China's Foreign Trade: Perspectives from the Past 150 Years', *The World Economy*, 34(6), 853–892.

Keller, W., Andres Santiago, J. and Shiue, C. H. (2017). 'China's Domestic Trade during the Treaty-Port Era', *Explorations in Economic History*, 63, 26–43.

Keller, W., Lampe, M. and Shiue, C. H. (2020). 'International Transactions: Real Trade and Factor Flows between 1700 and 1870', National Bureau of Economic Research Working Paper 26865.

Kelly, M. and Ó Gráda, C. (2019). 'Speed under Sail during the Early Industrial Revolution (*c.* 1750–1830)', *Economic History Review*, 72(2), 459–480.

Krugman, P. (1991). *Geography and Trade*, Cambridge, MA: MIT Press.

Lampe, M. and Sharp, P. (2019). 'Cliometric Approaches to International Trade', in Diebolt, C. and Haupert, M. (eds.), *Handbook of Cliometrics*, 2nd. ed., Heidelberg: Springer, link.springer.com/referenceworkentry/10.1007%2F978-3-642-40458-0_8-1 (accessed 12 October 2020).

Maddison, A. (2005). *Growth and Interaction in the World Economy: The Roots of Modernity*, Washington, DC: AEI Press.

Matsuyama, K. (1992). 'Agricultural Productivity, Comparative Advantage, and Economic Growth', *Journal of Economic Theory*, 58(2), 317–334.

McCloskey, D. (1994). '1780–1860, A Survey', in Floud, R. and McCloskey, D. N. (eds.), *The Economic History of Britain since 1700, vol. 1: 1700–1860*, Cambridge University Press, 300–331.

Meissner, C. M. (2014). 'Growth from Globalization? A View from the Very Long Run', in Aghion, P. and Durlauf, S. N. (eds.), *Handbook of Economic Growth*, vol 2, Amsterdam: Elsevier, 1033–1069.

Nunn, N. (2007). 'Relationship-Specificity, Incomplete Contracts and the Pattern of Trade', *Quarterly Journal of Economics*, 122(2), 569–600.

Nunn, N. and Trefler, D. (2014). 'Domestic Institutions as a Source of Comparative Advantage', in Gopinath, G., Helpman, E. and Rogoff, K. (eds.), *Handbook of International Economics*, vol. 4, Amsterdam: Elsevier, 263–315.

O'Brien, P. K. (1982). 'European Economic Development: The Contribution of the Periphery', *Economic History Review*, 35, 1–18.

O'Rourke, K. H. (2006). 'The Worldwide Economic Impact of the French Revolutionary and Napoleonic Wars, 1793–1815', *Journal of Global History*, 1(1), 123–149.

O'Rourke, K. H. and Williamson, J. G. (1999). *Globalization and History: The Evolution of a Nineteenth-Century Atlantic Economy*, Cambridge, MA: MIT Press.

O'Rourke, K. H., Prados de la Escosura, L. and Daudin, G. (2010). 'Trade and Empire', in Broadberry, S. and O'Rourke, K. H. (eds.), *The Cambridge Economic History of Modern Europe, vol. 1: 1700–1870*, Cambridge University Press, 96–121.

Ossa, R. (2015). 'Why Trade Matters After All', *Journal of International Economics*, 97(2), 266–277.

Pascali, L. (2017). 'The Wind of Change: Maritime Technology, Trade and Economic Development', *American Economic Review*, 107(9), 2821–2854.

Persson, K. G. and Sharp, P. (2015). *An Economic History of Europe: Knowledge, Institutions and Growth, 600 to the Present*, 2nd ed., Cambridge University Press.

Pomeranz, K. (2002). 'Political Economy and Ecology on the Eve of Industrialization: Europe, China, and the Global Conjuncture', *American Historical Review*, 107(2), 425–446.

Shiue, C. H. (2005). 'From Political Fragmentation Towards a Customs Union: Border Effects of the German Zollverein, 1815 to 1855', *European Review of Economic History*, 9 (2), 129–162.

Shiue, C. H. and Keller, W. (2007). 'Markets in China and Europe on the Eve of the Industrial Revolution', *American Economic Review*, 97(4), 1189–1216.

Solar, P. M. and Hens, L. (2016). 'Ship Speeds during the Industrial Revolution: East India Company Ships, 1770–1828', *European Review of Economic History*, 20(1), 66–78.

Steinwender, C. (2018). 'Real Effects of Information Frictions: When the States and the Kingdom Became United', *American Economic Review*, 108(3), 657–696.

Stolper, W. F. and Samuelson, P. A. (1941). 'Protection and Real Wages', *Review of Economic Studies*, 9(1), 58–73.

Studer, R. (2008). 'India and the Great Divergence: Assessing the Efficiency of Grain Markets in Eighteenth- and Nineteenth-Century India', *Journal of Economic History*, 68 (2), 393–437.

Tena-Junguito, A., Lampe, M. and Tâmega, F. (2012). 'How Much Trade Liberalization Was There in the World Before and After Cobden-Chevalier?', *Journal of Economic History*, 72(3), 708–740.

Thomas, R. P. and McCloskey, D. N. (1981). 'Overseas Trade and Empire 1700–1860', in Floud, R. and McCloskey, D. N. (eds.), *The Economic History of Britain since 1700, vol. 1: 1700–1860*, Cambridge University Press, 87–102.

Trefler, D. (1995). 'The Case of the Missing Trade and Other Mysteries', *American Economic Review*, 85(5), 1029–1046.

Wallerstein, I. (1974). *The Modern World System I: Capitalist Agriculture and the Origins of the European World Economy in the Sixteenth Century*, San Diego: Academic Press.

Zahedieh, N. (2014). 'Overseas Trade and Empire', in Floud, R., Humphries, J. and Johnson, P. (eds.), *The Cambridge Economic History of Modern Britain, vol. 1: 1700–1870*, Cambridge University Press, 392–420.

Appendix 17.1 Data sources for Table 17.1

Openness UK 1700 and 1760: Crafts (1985, p. 131). Trade Growth UK 1700–60, calculated from Bank of England, A Millennium of Macroeconomic Data, v. 3.1, 1760(1772)–1820 based on Cuenca Esteban 2001. Trade growth France 1716–80 from Daudin (2001: 166); 1787–1821 calculated from RICardo (ricardo.medialab.sciences-po.fr/#/); trade growth India 1700–60 and 1760–1820 refer to nominal values: 1700–60: East India Company exports from Chaudhury (1978: 508–10, value 1699–1701 compared to 1658–60 for Madras, Bengal, and Bombay), for Surat based on Swarmy (chapter I.5) and Das Gupta (1970: 383). East India Company export growth, total invoice value 1760/2–1819/21 of British imports from Madras, Bengal, and Bombay from Bowen (2007). Indonesia trade growth 1760s–1820s: sum for VOC pepper, coffee, and sugar exports as in table 6.4 in this volume, based on Reid (1997: 74). Export growth Mexico 1760–1820 based on Cuenca Esteban (2008: 349), i.e., private non-bullion exports from 'Indies' to Spain in current prices. Brazil export growth, 1800–30: Bértola and Ocampo (2012: 59); the same reference gives Mexican export growth 1800–30 as 0.5 per cent per year. Africa (slave trade): slaves exported per 1,000 Inhabitants. From chapter 10 in this volume. United States before 1800: Openness calculated from Mancall et al. (2006: 20, 26; 2008, online appendix), and Rosenbloom and Weiss (2014: 54), trade growth calculated from Mancall et al. (2006; 2008). US trade growth 1790–1820 from Irwin (2006: Ee366).

Bértola, L., and Ocampo, J. A. (2012). *The Economic Development of Latin America since Independence*, Oxford University Press.

Bowen, H. (2007), *East India Company: Trade and Domestic Financial Statistics, 1755–1838* [computer file]. Colchester: UK Data Archive [distributor]. SN: 5690, doi.org/10.5255/ukda-sn-5690-1 (accessed 9 November 2020).

Chaudhury, K. N. (1978). *The Trading World of Asia and the English East India Company 1660–1760*, Cambridge University Press.

Crafts, N. F. R. (1985). *British Economic Growth during the Industrial Revolution*, Oxford: Clarendon Press.

Cuenca Esteban, J. (2001). 'The British Balance of Payments, 1772–1820: India Transfers and War Finance', *Economic History Review*, 59(1), 58–86.

(2008). 'Statistics of Spain's Colonial Trade, 1747–1820: New Estimates and Comparisons with Great Britain', *Revista de Historia Económica – Journal of Iberian and Latin American Economic History*, 26, 323–354.

Das Gupta, A. (1970). 'Trade and Politics in Eighteenth Century India', reprinted in Alam, M. and Subrahmanyam, S. (eds.), (1998), *The Mughal State, 1526–1750*, Oxford University Press, 361–397.

Daudin, G. (2001). *Le role du commerce dans la croissance: une réflexion à partir de la France du XXVIIe siècle*, unpublished doctoral thesis, Université Paris I – Pantheón-Sorbonne.

Irwin, D. A. (2006). 'Exports and Imports of Merchandise, Gold, and Silver: 1790–2002', Table Ee362–375 in Carter, S. B., Gartner, S. S., Hains, M. R., Olmsted, A. L., Sutch, R. and Wright, G. (eds.), *Historical Statistics of the*

United States, Earliest Times to the Present: Millennial Edition, Cambridge University Press. dx.doi.org/10.1017/ISBN-9780511132971.Ee362-611 (accessed 13 October 2020).

Mancall, P. C., Rosenbloom, J. L. and Weiss, T. (2006). 'Exports and Slow Economic Growth in the Lower South Region, 1720–1800', National Bureau of Economic Research Working Paper 12045.

(2008). 'Commodity Exports, Invisible Exports and Terms of Trade for the Middle Colonies, 1720 to 1775', National Bureau of Economic Research Working Paper 14334.

Reid, A. (1997). 'A New Phase in Commercial Expansion in Southeast Asia, 1760–1850', in Reid, A. (ed.), *The Last Stand of Asian Autonomies: Responses to Modernity in the Diverse States of Southeast Asia and Korea, 1750–1900*, London: Macmillan, 57–81.

Rosenbloom, J. L. and Weiss, T. (2014). 'Economic Growth in the Mid-Atlantic Region: Conjectural Estimates for 1720 to 1800', *Explorations in Economic History*, 51, 41–59.

18

Monetary Systems and the Global Balance of Payments Adjustment in the Pre-Gold Standard Period, 1700–1870

RUI PEDRO ESTEVES AND PILAR NOGUES-MARCO

Introduction

In 1878 Yale professor Francis A. Walker famously coined the definition 'money is that money does'. In this chapter we describe the types of money and the functions that money fulfilled, both domestically and internationally, from the eighteenth to the nineteenth centuries. In the early modern world, monetary systems were based on commodity moneys. Two commodities dominated as currencies in this period: gold and silver. The overriding characteristic of commodity moneys is that they have a market value as a commodity and a legal value as money.

In the first section, we explain how commodity monetary systems worked and how they conditioned government policy, particularly in episodes of debasement for monetary reasons or fiscal reasons. In the eighteenth century, European bullion markets were already integrated and integration limited the range of policies that policymakers could apply. Countries could be bimetallic only if they coordinated their legal ratios. We pay special attention to the cases of England, the Dutch Republic, and France, the most relevant money markets at that time.

Commodity-money was crucial for the expansion of intercontinental trade. A steady flow of silver travelled from West to East, most of it taking the Atlantic routes and going through Europe before reaching East Asia. The second section describes the main international monetary flows in the early modern period and relates them to East-West trade balance adjustments and monetary systems in Asia.

Commodity-money was replaced by bills of exchange to transfer funds for long-distance trade and finance. In the third section, we describe the most relevant features of bills and the geography of monetary relations. We document the existence by the mid-eighteenth century of a multilateral payments system and the progressive enlargement of the bills-of-exchange network from a European scope to a worldwide scope by the time of the mid-nineteenth century.

The collapse of mercantilism and the intercontinental expansion of the bills of exchange influenced the global adjustment of the balance of payments. In the fourth section, we test empirically the specie-flow mechanism of balance-of-payments adjustment for the period between the end of mercantilism and the early liberalization of trade (1820s–1870s). To that effect, we calculate world effective exchange rates to distinguish between adjustments driven by changes in relative prices and by changes in nominal exchange rates.

Monetary Systems in Europe in the Pre-Gold Standard Period

Before the adoption of the gold standard as the international monetary system in the 1870s, monetary standards consisted of a variety of precious metals that served as money. Gold and silver were the commodities that performed the money functions in Europe throughout medieval times and into the modern era: store of wealth, means of payments and unit of account.[1] As a store of wealth, gold and silver were not perishable commodities and had minor wear-and-tear, so they could be easily stored.

As a means of payment, gold and silver had a high value-to-weight ratio so they were easily carried for transactions, and they were recognizable enough to be used among strangers. They were cast into coins of a value convenient for transactions. Because silver had a smaller value for a given weight, the joint circulation of gold and silver coins was advantageous because it provided means of payment for both large and small transactions.

1 One exception is the case of Sweden, which possessed the largest copper mine in Europe and established a copper standard in 1625. From that moment to 1776, full-bodied copper coins circulated together with gold and silver coins, forming a trimetallic monetary system. In 1777, the experiment ceased and a silver standard was reintroduced (Heckscher 1954; Edvinsson 2012). Outside Europe, we also find regions that developed monetary systems beyond gold and silver. In Asia, Indian and Chinese monetary systems included full-bodied copper coins circulating together with silver and gold. The second section explains the specificities of the Indian and Chinese monetary systems. In West Africa, cowrie shells circulated in local marketplace transactions. Cowries were mostly imported to Africa by European traders who paid for slaves with them. Cowries also served as a store of wealth and a unit of account until the second half of the nineteenth century, when the great cowrie inflation paved the way for their replacement by colonial currencies (Johnson 1970; Hogendorn and Johnson 1986).

On the one hand, merchants mostly used higher denominations for international payments. Gold coins such as the Florentine florin and the Venetian ducat were the most important means of payment inside Europe and between western Europe and the Levant in the Late Middle Ages (Spufford 1988: 177, 320–321). From the mid-sixteenth century, the steady expansion in the volume of international transactions encouraged the use of heavy silver coins for large payments (Cipolla 1989: 19–20). The best example is the Spanish-American piece of eight, which became the most common means of payment used in international transactions in America, Europe, and Asia (Cipolla 1996).

On the other hand, low silver denominations were used mainly for small daily transactions. European monetary authorities considered that exchange rates of coins in all denominations should reflect their relative metal contents. However, coins were minted freely. So keeping the coining of the different denominations appropriately aligned with the market conditions was difficult because coining money was more costly in small rather than in large denominations. As a consequence, from the thirteenth to the nineteenth century, intermittent shortages and recurrent debasements of the smaller coins occurred. To solve this 'big problem of small change', monetary authorities issued token coins for small transactions, that is, copper coins whose face value was higher than the metallic content. They were the precursor of modern fiat money (Cipolla 1956; Redish 2000; Sargent and Velde 2002).

Finally, as a unit of account, money was the standard of measurement (the *numéraire*). Transactions were expressed in units of account, although payments were naturally made subsequently in coins (means of payment). In Western Europe, the system of account established by Charlemagne survived during the Middle Ages and the early modern period until the introduction of the decimal system by Napoleon (and in the United Kingdom down to 1971). The standard of measure (unit of account) was the penny (*denarius*), together with its multiples, the shilling (*solidus*) of twelve pennies and the pound (*libra*) of twenty shillings (Shaw 1895; McCusker 1978; Fantacci 2008). The unit of account differed from the means of payment because it permitted the reconciliation of coins of different species into a sole monetary system. The monetary authority established the legal value of both gold and silver coins in terms of the money of account. For instance, the Royal Mint of England produced no coin equivalent to the 'sterling pound' until the Great Recoinage of 1816 when the accounting value of the coin sovereign was set at one pound sterling (McCusker 1978: 6). Before the nineteenth century, gold coins were struck in guineas and valued in pounds sterling, shillings, and pence. The value of the guinea was reduced from 22 shillings to 21 shillings and 6 pence in 1699, and again to 21 shillings in 1717 (Nogues-Marco 2013: 461–462).

As we have seen in the previous example, the accounting value of coins underwent alterations in the form of debasements and reinforcements.[2] Changes of the legal relationship between the unit of account and the means of payment responded to monetary or fiscal problems. Because precious metals were commodity-money, they had two values: the legal value defined by law and the market value defined by the market when gold and silver were traded as commodities. Alterations of value for monetary reasons occurred when the monetary authority had to adjust the legal value of coins to their market value. When the market price of gold to silver equalled the legal ratio, the standard was bimetallic; but if the market price was lower or higher than the legal ratio, the standard was monometallic de facto.[3] At the end of the seventeenth century, the most important European money markets, such as London or Amsterdam, had already liberalized the export of precious metals, so one 'international' (i.e. European) money market emerged and forced countries to coordinate legal ratios to preserve bimetallism.

The exception was England. It is commonly believed that Sir Isaac Newton, Master of the Mint, mistakenly overvalued gold at the Mint in 1717.[4] However, Nogues-Marco (2013) demonstrated that the London bimetallic ratio remained too high not because of Newton's 'mistake', but because Parliament did not alter the monetary standard of England, as Newton proposed, to adjust the legal ratio to the European market ratio. Parliament decided 'that no Alteration be made in the Standard of the Gold and Silver Coins of this Kingdom, in Fineness, Weight or Denomination'.[5] Therefore, England switched to a de facto gold standard in the eighteenth

2 Experiences of European debasements are analyzed in Miskimin (1964; 1984); Bordo (1986); Sussman (1993); Rolnick et al. (1996); Pamuk (2000); Redish (2000); Chilosi and Volckart (2010); Elgin et al. (2015).

3 The stability of bimetallism has generated an extensive body of literature. See Locke (2010 [1696]); Walras (1881); Laughlin (1885); Giffen (1892); Fisher (1894); Shaw (1895); Walker (1896); Darwin (1898); Willis (1901); Chen (1972); Garber (1986); Rolnick and Weber (1986); Friedman (1990); Redish (1990; 1995; 2000); Garber and Weisbrod (1992: chapter 8); Flandreau (1996; 1997; 2002; 2004); Oppers (1996, 2000); and Velde and Weber (2000).

4 Feavearyear (1931: 142–143); Jastram (1977: 12–13); Cooper (1987: 44–45); Redish (1990: 789–790); Kindleberger (1993: 60); Eichengreen (1996: 12).

5 *The History and Proceedings of the House of Lords*, 75–76, Parliamentary Papers.

century. No change was made in the legal value of money after 1717 and finally England adopted the gold standard de jure in 1816.

The accounting value of coins suffered alterations also for fiscal reasons. In this case, the monetary authority reduced the metal content of the coins by decreasing their weight or fineness, while maintaining their nominal value in terms of the unit of account. The reduction of the quantity of precious metal in each coin was collected as a minting tax denominated seigniorage. When the rulers found that their fiscal resources were constrained, they often exploited their mints to produce greater seigniorage revenues. This was especially true in times of war (Munro 2012: 6). Debasement for fiscal reasons provided a short-term source of revenue, but considerable debasement could lead to a loss of public confidence in the currency or result in a chaotic circulation.

This was the case in the Dutch Republic. The Dutch monetary system was decentralized, the Republic had multiple provincial mints rather than a national one. Ordinances made each province's mint output legal tender in the whole republic. If a province debased its coins to increase seigniorage, those debased coins would migrate to the other provinces. Decentralization caused monetary conditions to deteriorate. Large coins traded at a premium; old, clipped, and worn-out ones remained in circulation for a long time; foreign coins were introduced into circulation; and in the end the mints themselves were tempted to strike 'inferior' coins (Dehing and 'T Hart 1997: 39–41; de Vries and van der Woude 1997: 81–82; Polak 1998: 16–17, 63–68; Quinn and Roberds 2009; 2014).

Because of the monetary chaos, the Bank of Amsterdam (*Amsterdamsche Wisselbank*) was established in 1609 upon the request of several merchants who complained about confusion regarding currency. The bank acted as guarantor for the legal standard, eliminating uncertainty about the intrinsic value of coins and protecting creditors against debasement (Gillard 2004; Quinn and Roberds 2009; 2014). The bank received money on deposit, provided settlement through a giro system, and traded in coined money and bullion (Vilar 1974: 252; van der Wee 1977: 342, 346–347; Dehing and 'T Hart 1997: 46–47).

The bank's main policy objective was to stabilize the market price of its money relative to large-denomination 'trade coins' circulating among merchants in Amsterdam. The bank created bank money, denominated bank *guilder*, which was backed predominantly by trade coins, current *guilder*. Bank money almost always circulated at a premium (called the *agio*) to the current money (Quinn and Roberds 2016: 64). The Bank of Amsterdam stabilized bank money at a level compatible with market prices, preserving Amsterdam on an effective bimetallic standard (Nogues-Marco 2013). Bimetallism could collapse in one place, such as London, and succeed in another, such as Amsterdam. Indeed, Amsterdam bank currency, the bank *guilder*, became the European reserve currency until the bank became insolvent at the end of the eighteenth century and was liquidated after the Napoleonic period (Jonker 1996).

The French monetary system also suffered alterations of the accounting value of coins for fiscal reasons. An experiment undertaken between 1716 and 1720, known as John Law's 'system', is especially noteworthy. The system was a combination of a fiscal component (involving an operation in public finance) and a monetary component (involving fiat money). The state of French finances had been dismal due to the War of the Spanish Succession. Law's system was intended to be a radical restructuring of French public finances based on the development of two institutions. First, in 1716, he established a privately owned bank that issued banknotes. Originally, they were convertible into a specific number of coins of a given weight and fineness. But from the end of 1718, banknotes were denominated in units of account. Second, in 1717, Law created a trading company, whose shares were publicly traded and whose purpose shifted from colonial development and overseas trading to management of public funds. In order to refinance the national debt, the company doubled its equity and the new shares were sold in exchange for government bonds. From 1719 to 1720, the bank and the company merged and the company reimbursed the whole national debt. Gold and silver coins stopped being legal tender and banknotes became the sole currency. Finally, Law pegged the price of shares at a fixed price above their market level in banknotes, leading to a massive issue of banknotes in exchange for shares. The exchange rate on the *livre* began to fall and Law reduced the account value of banknotes instead of withdrawing them. Once the price of shares collapsed, in 1720, there was a bank run, and the inconvertible notes depreciated. From 1721 to 1723, a massive clean-up operation dismantled Law's system. Gold and silver were restored as currency and in 1724 an abrupt deflationary policy revalued the debt, returning France's debt burden to roughly the level at which it stood before Law. The first full-scale attempt to move from a commodity-money system to a permanent fiat currency in Europe had failed (Velde and Weber 2008).

During the eighteenth century, France consolidated as an outstanding money market in continental Europe and eventually replaced Amsterdam as the centre of bimetallism in the nineteenth century. Like Amsterdam in the eighteenth century, France successfully preserved an effective bimetallic standard. The French monetary system's attempt to fix the market ratio during the nineteenth century was successful because shocks to gold or silver supplies led to smooth arbitrage. For instance, during the Gold Rush after 1848, France imported gold and exported silver, but French circulation was large enough to buffer the shock (Flandreau 2004). French bimetallism in the mid-nineteenth century was, thus, another example of the stability of bimetallism. However, European monetary systems shifted from the bimetallic standard to the gold standard in the third quarter of the nineteenth century. Once the main countries pegged their currencies to gold, small countries had an incentive to adopt the gold standard to prevent their exchange rates from fluctuating against the gold world because the wider the exchange rate fluctuations, the greater the disruption to international trade and finance (Meissner 2005).

Overseas Silver Flows, West-East Balance-of-Trade Adjustments and Monetary Systems in Asia (1700–1800)

During the early modern period, intercontinental trade had a counterpart in a steady flow of precious metals travelling from West to East. Between 1500 and 1800, nearly 85 per cent of the world's silver and more than 70 per cent of the world's gold was produced in America and large amounts were systematically transferred from America to Asia (Barret 1990; TePaske 2010; Palma and Silva 2017; Freire Costa et al. forthcoming). There were several routes to transfer American precious metals to Asia, with Europe being the major transshipment region. First, western Europe imported grain, timber, and furs from the Baltic in exchange for wine, textiles, and precious metals. Then, the Baltic sold precious metals to the East in exchange for Persian silk and other luxury commodities from the Middle East. Second, the Levant route of European trade through the Mediterranean also resulted in an outflow of precious metals to purchase Eastern spices through the Red Sea and the Persian Gulf. Third, the Cape route, used by Europeans to purchase spices, silk, tea, and cotton textiles also generated a steady outflow of precious metals. Finally, American precious metals, mainly silver, reached Asia directly via Manila, where they were exchanged for silk and other luxury Chinese goods (Attman 1983; TePaske 1983; von Glahn 1996; De Vries 2003; Findlay and O'Rourke 2007).

Asia was the final destination of precious metal flows, but the trade imbalances paid with these flows did not correct even over the long run, despite the steady flow of bullion. How can we explain the persistence of these disequilibria? The traditional interpretation states that the inflow of bullion did not increase Asian prices even though these countries absorbed prodigious amounts of precious metals. This assumption is based on the logic of Hume's price-specie flow mechanism to adjust the balance of payments, that is, European persistent trade deficits happened because precious metal flows did not lead to a higher price level in Asia that would have reduced its exports and increased its imports. Scholars have considered that prices did not increase in Asia because precious metals were hoarded as a store of wealth or transformed into jewellery (Blitz 1967; Braudel 1979; Kindleberger 1989).

However, according to Chaudhuri (1982) the traditional explanation is speculative because it does not have empirical support since imported precious metal became money in India and was used as a means of payment in China (von Glahn 1996; Prakash 2005). An alternative explanation is that prices did not move up because the influx of precious metal into Asia was also accompanied by an expansion of the monetary sector at the expense of the barter and subsistence sector (Blitz 1967: 47; Habib 1982: 366; von Glahn 1996: 432; Prakash 2005: 15).

Flynn and Giráldez (2002; 2004) and Flynn (2012) have given a different explanation. According to these scholars, silver should not be considered as money but as a commodity. They argue that there was no imbalance of trade between Europe and Asia for which monetary resources had to flow in compensation. Silver flows were just the result of arbitrage that responded to profitability. Merchants simply purchased silver where it was cheap (Europe) and shipped it to where it was expensive (Asia). Arbitrage between Europe and Asia (China) had two phases, that is, one from the 1540s to the 1640s, by which time gold-silver bimetallic ratios had converged around the world, and a second phase, from around 1700 until the 1750s, when global silver prices had converged a second time. Similarly, Palma and Silva (2017) argue that the gold-silver price ratio was 6:1 in China and it was between 11:1 and 12:1 in Europe when the silver from America began to be available in Europe, which suggests large arbitrage gains, even under the prevailing transport technology and institutional settings.

The hypothesis of precious metal arbitrage has been recently tested by Nogues-Marco (2019), who collected data on the price of silver and gold in London and Asia (India and China) from 1664 to 1800 from the archive of the East India Company (EIC). Her results show that it was not profitable to export silver from London to Asia because the exchange rate was defined according to the silver arbitrated par, that is, the relative market price of silver between centres. There were episodes of arbitrage by which the EIC exported silver to China in exchange for gold for profit, but the vast majority of silver was exported without profit to pay for imports. Silver moved from Europe to Asia to compensate payments resulting from large and persistent trade disequilibria (Krishna 1924; Chaudhuri 1978; Prakash 1985; 1986).

The last interpretation is that the silver influx did not increase prices, but silver depreciated relative to copper (Braudel 1979 (vol. 1): 417; Cartier 1981; Flynn 1984: 409; Habib 1987: 141–142). The monetary system in India was trimetallic, composed of gold, silver, and copper coins. Indian authorities did not standardize the legal value of coins in different metals into a common unit of account as in European monetary systems. The exchange rate between gold-silver and silver-copper was determined by market conditions in India (Habib 1987: 157). Figure 18.1 shows the exchange rate between copper and silver for Agra and East Rajasthan from 1540 to 1750. We can observe the rupee (silver coin) depreciation in dams (copper coin) in the long run. In 1540, one rupee was exchanged for 48 dams; in 1583, the exchange rate was 1:40; in 1640, it was 1:28 and, in 1750, it had been reduced to 1:14. The depreciation of the copper price of silver was more intense from the early to the mid-seventeenth century than in

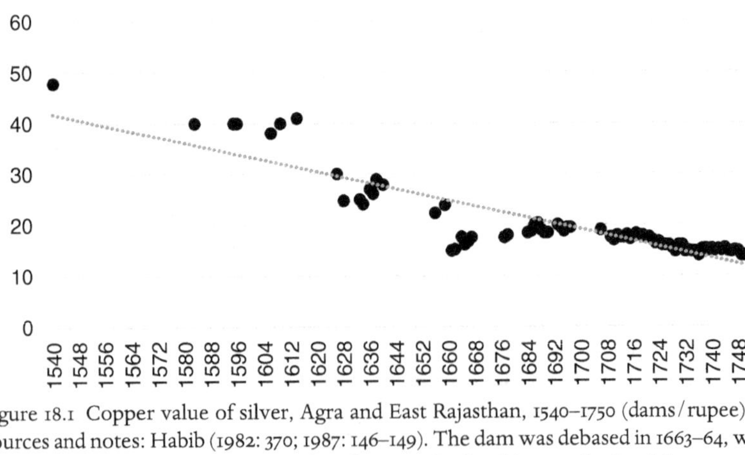

Figure 18.1 Copper value of silver, Agra and East Rajasthan, 1540–1750 (dams/rupee)
Sources and notes: Habib (1982: 370; 1987: 146–149). The dam was debased in 1663–64, when the weight of the lighter dam was reduced to two-thirds of the standard weight, according to Habib (1987: 140). In this figure, we expressed the price of silver in standard dams (copper coins of 323 grains) for the whole period (Habib 1987: 150).

the first half of the eighteenth century, when the Portuguese had lost their monopoly status as the Dutch and English penetrated the Indian Ocean.

Prices of Indian commodities could be expressed in copper or in silver as both were means of payment in India. At the end of the sixteenth century, prices were reported in copper, silver, or gold, depending on the commodity considered. For example, food grains, vegetables, *ghee* (clarified butter), milk, yoghurt, sweetmeats, spices, and Indian fruits were defined in copper. Sheep, goats, and foreign fruits were priced in silver. Cheaper textiles had prices in copper, but the more expensive in silver. The most expensive varieties of silk and cotton cloth were priced in gold (Habib 1987: 145). The influx of silver from Europe not only caused the value of silver in copper to depreciate, but also gradually displaced copper as the unit of account for some ordinary transactions. At the end of the seventeenth century, while copper continued as the most important currency medium, food grains were already priced in silver while *ghee* and *gur* (jaggery) were priced in copper (Habib 1987: 154). Figure 18.2 reports prices of wheat in silver and copper respectively. We can see that although copper prices did not rise, prices show a significant upward trend when they are measured in silver.[6]

The monetary system in China was de jure a copper monetary system, but de facto trimetallic. Gold and silver were not minted, but they circulated in the form of ingots that were used as means of payment by weight. Additionally, foreign silver coins, mainly Mexican pieces of eight, also circulated by weight (Cartier 1981: 456). Yan et al. (2018) have recently defined the Chinese monetary system as a multilayer system of currencies. On the one hand, silver currencies were influenced by the changes in international politics and the global economy. They circulated freely among major commercial centres, and their prices were synchronized with the international market. On the other hand, copper coins functioned as the primary form of currency in the landlocked rural areas, where the penetration of silver was very slow. Copper facilitated small transactions within regional boundaries. The state minted copper coins at fixed face value and strictly monopolized copper coinage in the official mints. By contrast, the state adopted a laissez-faire attitude towards the circulation and production of silver ingots, so that

6 These results are based on the price of wheat for Agra and the region of East Rajasthan. However, they might not extend to all commodities and centres. For example, Prakash (1994: 70–71) does not find a significant increase of the price of rice, wheat, *ghee*, and sugar in Bengal during the period 1657–1714, measured in silver (rupees/maund). Contrary to this result, Datta (2003: 444–445) shows a significant upward trend in the price of rice, *ghee*, and oil in Lower Bengal during the period 1700–1800, measured in silver (rupees/maund).

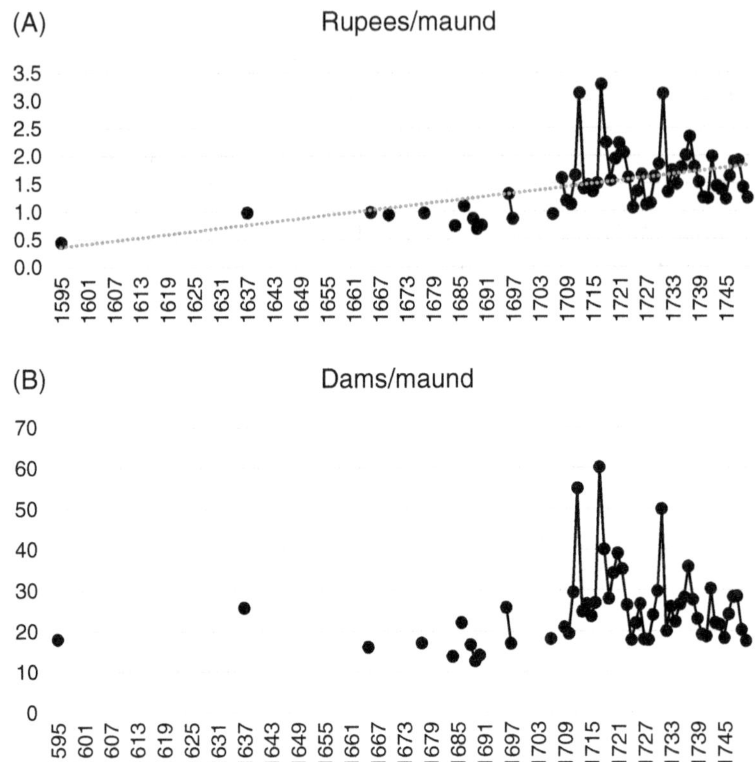

Figure 18.2 Price of wheat, Agra and East Rajasthan, 1595–1750
Sources and notes: Prices of wheat in Agra for 1595, 1673, and 1670 from Habib (1982: 373). Wheat flour has been converted to wheat taking into account the reduction of 10 per cent in weight when converting wheat to flour (Habib 1982: 373). We collected the price of wheat in East Rajasthan from 1665 to 1750 (single average of prices in Amber, Chatsu, Dausa, Lalsot, Bahatri, Malarna) from Nurul Hasan and Gupta (1967). Silver prices were transformed to copper prices using the exchange rate between rupees and dams (Figure 18.1). We use the maund of 40 seers (Gupta and Moosvi 1973: 185).

their melting and casting were mostly done by private agents. Using the changes in the exchange ratio between silver and copper as a price signal, the multilayered monetary system reduced the mutual impacts between the international market, urban areas, and rural places.

Figure 18.3 shows the exchange rate between copper currency (*cash*) and silver (*kuping taels*). The official exchange rate was fixed as one *tael* equal to 1,000 *cash*. The market exchange rate fluctuated according to the production of domestic copper mines, monetary debasements, and reinforcements in

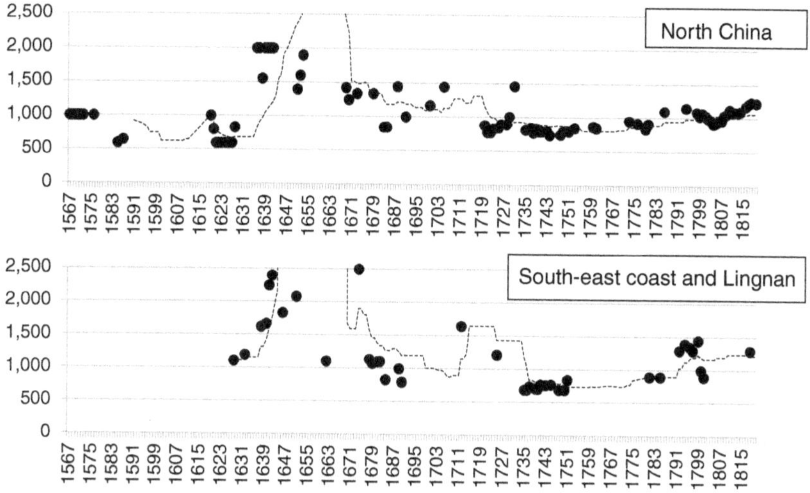

Figure 18.3 Copper value of silver, China, 1567–1820 (cash/tael silver)
Sources and notes: Vogel (1987: table 3). North China = Peking and Zhili Province and Ningjin (Zhili). The Ningjin series, which starts in 1798, is the most homogenous series, calculated from daily records of a store (Vogel 1987: 26; Allen et al. 2011: 34). Southeast Coast and Lingnan = Hubei, Hunan, and Jiangxi. The dotted line is the twenty-five-year moving average.

copper coins – as well as silver imports entering China as the result of a positive balance of trade (Vogel 1987). In the first half of the sixteenth century, the value of silver in copper depreciated more than 50 per cent (Cartier 1981: 457). The depreciation of silver continued in the second half of the sixteenth century, but this trend changed after 1600 because the Chinese state debased copper coins, so the copper value of silver rose despite the greater influx of silver (von Glahn 1996: 431; 2003: 191). Silver depreciated again in copper in the early eighteenth century. The exchange rate between both metals stabilized during the remainder of the century. Finally, at the end of the century, silver suffered an important appreciation in copper (Cartier 1981: 458; von Glahn 2003: 191).

The price of rice can be used as a proxy to measure inflation in China. Figure 18.4 shows the long run series of the price of rice measured in grams of silver. The longest series, which runs from 1500 to 1800, covers the whole of China. Because price trends probably varied across provinces, Figure 18.4 also plots two additional series for prices in the Yangtze Delta. The two sets of prices are highly correlated and there is evidence of a common upward trend in the price of rice for the whole period, from the early sixteenth to the late eighteenth centuries.

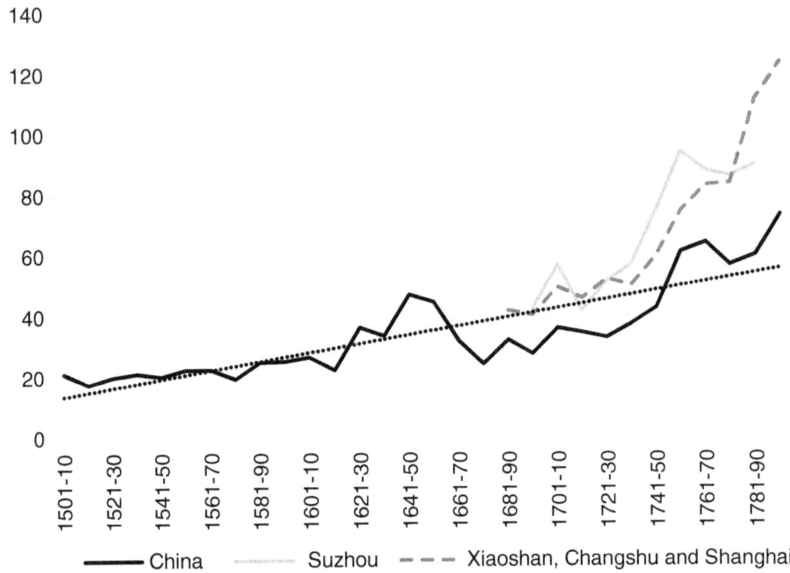

Figure 18.4 Price of rice, China, 1500–1800, decennial average (grams of silver/quintal)
Sources and notes: Data for China from Cartier (1981: 464) in *kuping taels* (37.3 grams [1.3 oz]) per quintal. This series averages rice prices in different locations across China in each year. Data for Suzhou, Xiaoshan, Changshu, and Shanghai were collected by Wang (1992) to represent rice prices in the Yangtze Delta. Because of the proximity between these locations, the two series are probably better interpreted as alternative sources for delta prices rather than independent price series. Wang (1992) reported data in *kuping taels* per *shi*. We use the equivalence 1 *shi* = 78.623 kg (173 lb) (Lemale 1875: 113).

To sum up, available evidence on prices in India and China shows that there is a positive relationship between silver influx and inflation when we express prices in grams of silver. However, European trade deficits with Asia persisted through the seventeenth and eighteenth centuries. Our explanation for this apparent violation of normal current account adjustment is based on market structure. In the mercantilist period, trade between Europe and Asia was conducted by European chartered companies (the English, Dutch, and French East India Companies) that controlled the volume of trade and prices of Asian imports in Europe to sustain high mark-ups for a very small number of commodities with low demand elasticities (Hauser 1936; Blitz 1967; Chaudhuri 1978; Bulbeck et al. 1998). In this way, chartered trade companies prevented price convergence and, as a consequence, sustained the Euro-Asian current account deficits that were cleared with silver flows.

The Development of the Global Foreign Exchange Market

Europe developed a foreign exchange market based on bills of exchange in the Middle Ages. A bill of exchange was a letter by which funds were transferred between distant cities. Four persons participated in the transaction: two at the city where the bill was drawn and two at the city where it was payable. They were, first, the drawee (deliverer, giver, remitter, or negotiator), the person who delivered the money; second, the drawer (taker) who received the money by exchange; third, the party who paid the money by virtue of the bill drawn on him, commonly termed the payer (accepter); and fourth, the person to whom the bill was made payable, called the payee (possessor or holder). Typically, the payer and the drawer would keep accounts with each other and could offset the payment of the bill with claims from other transactions so that only small net amounts would have to be occasionally settled (de Roover 1953; Einzig 1962; Neal 1990).

A bill was a safe and cheap financial instrument and thus became the most widely used instrument for international payments. The operation of exchange permitted not only the transfer of funds, but also the lending of money from the moment of the purchase of the bill to its payment. As a consequence, bills provided a useful tool to escape the regulation on interest rates. This regulation prevented interest rates from rising above a certain ceiling, which would constitute 'usury'. Unlike other financial instruments, which had a local circulation and were thus subject to the regulation of interest rates, bills of exchange escaped usury ceilings because the transaction took place between two distant cities. The price charged on bills of exchange was motivated, according to contemporary bankers, by the risks and efforts associated with overcoming the obstacles of foreign settlement. In practice, the price of bills was determined by the geographical distance as well as by time, so the interest rate was hidden by the exchange rate (Flandreau et al. 2009a; Nogues-Marco 2018).

International trade supported the emergence of a liquid market for bills of exchange in Europe, organized along lines defined by trading relations and provided the infrastructure for financial development. The adoption of the Joint Liability Rule (JLR) facilitated the expansion of bills beyond personal networks from the early seventeenth century because it provided high financial protection against non-payment as all parties involved in a bill transaction (the payer, all the endorsers, and the drawer) had a joint liability for the payment. As a consequence, the JLR played a major role in ameliorating fundamental information problems in long-distance trade and turned the bill of exchange into the most important transfer instrument in a period of imperfect international enforcement (de Roover 1953; Santarosa 2015).

The market for bills-of-exchange was restricted to Europe until the late eighteenth century. Flandreau et al. (2009b) mapped the bills-of-exchange connections between nearly eighty cities in the mid-eighteenth century. A high proportion of the cities (close to one half) were ports. There were typically several markets per country, except for the case of England, which stands out as the one large political entity with only one exchange centre in London. Locations were evenly scattered all over Europe with outreaches on the fringes of the Orient. There were no American, Asian, or African cities and only two cities in the Ottoman Empire – Constantinople and Smyrna. This European bias is the result of a structural characteristic of the foreign exchange network: European sources did not direct to non-European centres while non-European sources directed back to Europe. The global financial system of that period had a distinct European focus.[7]

Amsterdam, London, and Paris were the core of the system in the mid-eighteenth century. They were quoted in the vast majority of the cities (more than 60 per cent of the cities quoted London and Paris while 84 per cent quoted Amsterdam), implying that multilateral settlement using these centres as clearing centres was feasible by the mid-eighteenth century. Amsterdam, London, and Paris were already tightly integrated with one another by the mid-eighteenth century and enjoyed a high degree of liquidity (Neal 1990; Flandreau et al. 2009a).

The agglomeration of monetary links is shown in Figure 18.5, which plots the number of links that a particular market received by the mid-eighteenth century. About 20 per cent of links between cities were direct, 75 per cent had to pass through an intermediary centre, while only 7–8 per cent had two intermediaries. This reinforces the notion of an encompassing multilateral settlement system, with Amsterdam, London, Paris, and also Hamburg and Genoa as the main

7 Exchange contacts from London to North America and the British West Indies had already existed during the colonial era, in particular Boston from 1630 and Philadelphia probably from the 1730s to American independence in 1776, but bills drawn in London on the colonies were negotiated only occasionally, mostly during wartime. The exchange transactions of London on North America or the West Indian colonies were insignificant for the London merchants to be mentioned in the exchange rate quotations (Denzel 2010: 12–13, 406). The use of bills was limited because there seems to have been difficulty locating anyone in London with sufficient credit in the colonies to draw against. Instead, London merchants preferred to bring such credit home and ship specie (McCusker 1978: 122, 131–150).

Figure 18.5 Monetary agglomeration in the mid-eighteenth century
Source: Map redrawn from Flandreau et al. (2009b: 161).

connecting hubs. Therefore, the European system was a dense web with an area of intense financial linkages that stretched from an Amsterdam-London-Paris-Hamburg core and thinned out as it headed towards Italy.

The European network of bills of exchange expanded worldwide at the end of the eighteenth century and in the early nineteenth century. London started to quote Rio de Janeiro from the early nineteenth century, after the Brazilian ports had been opened to non-Portuguese trade. Quotations in London on New York and Philadelphia as well as on Buenos Aires and Mexico City existed by the 1840s (Denzel 2010: 9, 12).

Philadelphia was the first centre in North America that quoted Europe after American independence in 1776. Philadelphia quoted on London from 1783 and quoted regularly on Paris, Amsterdam, and Hamburg from 1794. New York superseded Philadelphia not only as the financial but also the general economic centre of the Atlantic coast in the USA, and started quoting London in 1794, as well as Amsterdam, Hamburg, and Paris from the early nineteenth century (Denzel 2010: 408, 117).

The slave trade expanded the use of bills of exchange in North America in the second half of the eighteenth century. Colonial planters bought and sold slaves through local factors and met their bills through crop sales. Agents transferred bills to ship captains, who handed them to British slave merchants, who then redeemed them, via other merchants, businessmen, and brokers, to secure their funds. The interconnections of merchants, factors, planters, and guarantors in the eighteenth-century British slave trade helped to foster greater financial integration in the transatlantic trading world (Morgan 2005).

Trade integrated Asian centres into the European bills-of-exchange network. To be sure, before this integration, domestic systems of bills of exchange already operated in both India and China. In India, *hundi* was the financial instrument developed to transfer money in the early modern period. However, even if the *hundi* was a transferable instrument, it did not include a JLR, which limited the expansion of the financial instrument beyond personal networks. This meant that in case of non-payment, the payee had to demand payment from the last person from whom he had bought the *hundi*; and so on, up the chain of endorsements until the original drawer (Habib 1971; Chaudhuri 2017). Similarly, *fu-tie* (also called *dui-tie*) was a commercial-finance instrument developed in North China in the eighteenth century to facilitate business transactions. Analogous to European bills of exchange, the receiver of a *fu-tie* was required to pay the bearer the designated amount of cash on behalf of the issuer. But this instrument was not personally registered and was thus payable to whoever possessed it, which also limited its expansion to personal networks (Qiao 2017). By the end of the eighteenth century, Asia had become integrated into the European network of bills of exchange. The East India Company had started issuing company's bills on the court of directors payable in London for trade with India and China, and company's bills payable on the government of Bengal (and, rarely, Bombay) for trade with China (Canton) (Greenberg 1951; Dermigny 1964; Marshall 1976; Nogues-Marco 2021).

The openness of trade to private merchants at the end of the mercantilist period facilitated the expansion of bills of exchange as transfer instruments between Asia and Europe during the first half of the nineteenth century. Contemporary merchant manuals listed quotations in London on Calcutta, Bombay, and Madras by the early nineteenth century and on Canton by the mid-nineteenth century. By the mid-nineteenth century, *The Economist* listed rates on Indian, South and East Asian as well as Australian centres. Regular quotations in Canton on Bombay started in 1827/31. Quotations in Shanghai on London started in 1848, on Canton in 1849/52, on Hong Kong in 1856, on Calcutta in 1850, and on Bombay in 1855 (Denzel 2010: 13, 511–512).

By the end of the nineteenth century, the bills-of-exchange market had achieved a worldwide scope. The core of the system was composed of three senior centres: London, Paris, and Berlin/Germany in descending order. The periphery – that is, countries quoted almost nowhere – comprised Latin American and Pacific Asian nations but also Canada and parts of Europe. Finally, there was a large group of centres between the two extremes. This group was formed by the United States, the north-western European centres (Netherlands, Belgium, and Switzerland), Austria-Hungary, Italy, Spain, and, to an extent, Russia (Flandreau and Jobst 2005: 989).

The Specie-Flow Mechanism and International Trade Adjustment (1820–70)

The Scottish philosopher David Hume articulated the first model of balance of payments adjustment in a letter to Montesquieu in 1749:

> If half the money in England were suddenly destroyed, labour and goods would suddenly become so cheap that there would suddenly follow a great quantity of exports which would attract to us the money of all our neighbours. If half the money which is in England were suddenly doubled, goods would suddenly become more expensive, imports would rise to the disadvantage of exports and our money would be spread among all our neighbours. (Hume 1955: 188–189).

The model came to be known as the price-specie flow mechanism and predicts that external adjustment will happen mostly through expenditure switching rather than expenditure reduction or increase: a country facing a current account deficit would adjust by losing gold, leading to a fall in relative prices that would reestablish its competitiveness with respect to its trade partners. The mechanism rests on two assumptions: an open capital account and flexible prices. While Hume repeatedly stated his belief in the flexibility of the prices of 'all labour and commodities', he conceded that barriers to trade in precious metals could prevent the adjustment of external imbalances:[8]

> in money, if the communication be cut off, by any material or physical impediment (for all laws alone are ineffectual), there may, in such a case, be a very great inequality of money (Hume 1955: 64).

Despite Hume's dismissal of the effectiveness of capital controls (legal barriers to trade in specie), practically all nations retained laws preventing the free export of monetary metals until the mid-nineteenth century, a policy consistent with the mercantilist doctrine of retaining precious metals at home that lived on in many countries until the dismemberment of mercantilism. Whether these were effective is an empirical question and we should be able to test it by decomposing the sources of real exchange rate variations. Real exchange rates (q) measure the ratio of domestic and foreign prices (p and $p^{\star}$), adjusted by the nominal exchange rates (e), i.e. $q = (p^{*}e)/p$. They are a measure of competitiveness. But since no country trades with just one partner, the relevant measure of competitiveness should take into account the actual trade networks of each nation. This is referred to as the *effective* exchange rate. For a given country i, we can define its nominal effective exchange rate (NEER) as the average of bilateral exchange rates (e_{ij}) weighted by the share of each of its j trade partner's in its exports (x_{ij}) and imports (m_{ij}):

$$NEER_i = \sum_j e_{ij}x_{ij} + \sum_j e_{ij}m_{ij}$$

Similarly, we can define a concept of real effective competitiveness as:

$$REER_i = \frac{1}{p_i}\sum_j e_{ij}p_j x_{ij} + \frac{1}{p_i}\sum_j e_{ij}p_j m_{ij}$$

where p_i and p_j are the domestic and foreign price levels, respectively. Computing the effective exchange rates offers several insights about the adjustment of international trade. First, it reveals which countries gained and lost competitiveness over time and whether those deviations were

8 In fact, Hume was aware that price adjustments might take a while to take effect, and acknowledged that changes in real income could occur in the short run as a consequence of external disequilibria (Murphy 2009).

related to external disequilibria. Second, it allows a distinction to be drawn between adjustment through relative prices (p_j/p_i), as envisaged by Hume, and adjustment through changes in nominal exchange rates. In a world in which all countries pegged their currencies to a commodity (gold or silver), nominal exchange rates should have been largely constant, at least so long as the market prices of gold and silver were successfully anchored, as previously mentioned. However, countries had frequently to abandon their pegs and adopt inconvertible currencies with floating exchange rates. As shown by Catão and Solomou (2005), even in the heyday of the classical gold standard (1870–1913), nominal exchange rate flexibility was instrumental in facilitating current account adjustment. Especially in the case of peripheral nations, external imbalances were corrected more through exchange rate fluctuations (e_{ij}) than price changes. This runs contrary to the predictions of Hume's model in that the flexibility of peripheral currencies also diminished the need for specie flows and price adjustment in the core European countries (Bloomfield 1959).

In this section we extend Catão and Solomou's (2005) analysis to the first seven decades of the nineteenth century to confirm how well Hume's price-specie flow applied in that earlier period. In so doing we draw on large new data sets of bilateral trade (Fouquin and Hugot 2016; Dedinger and Girard 2017), exchange rates (Denzel 2010) and prices (de Zwart 2015). The data covers a maximum of 54 countries and territories.

Figures 18.6 to 18.8 represent the evolution of nominal exchange rates after the Napoleonic Wars, separating between core and periphery nations, as well as between monetary regimes. To measure nominal exchange rates we use the pound sterling (GBP) as the *numéraire*. In all cases, there are substantial deviations between the nominal and the effective exchange rates, suggesting that competitiveness was very much a bilateral phenomenon: individual countries' effective exchange rates were influenced at least as much, if not more, by their trade partners' exchanges as by their own.[9] In general, nominal and effective exchange rates are closer for emerging or peripheral nations than for the core European nations (Figure 18.8), which accords with what we know about the stability of their monetary regimes in this period, namely, the greater prevalence of inconvertible currencies among peripheral countries. Core nations, on the other hand, witnessed moderate effective nominal appreciation as a counterpart.

9 Brazil and the USA are exceptions as most of their NEER variation is driven by their own nominal exchange rates (see Figure 18.6).

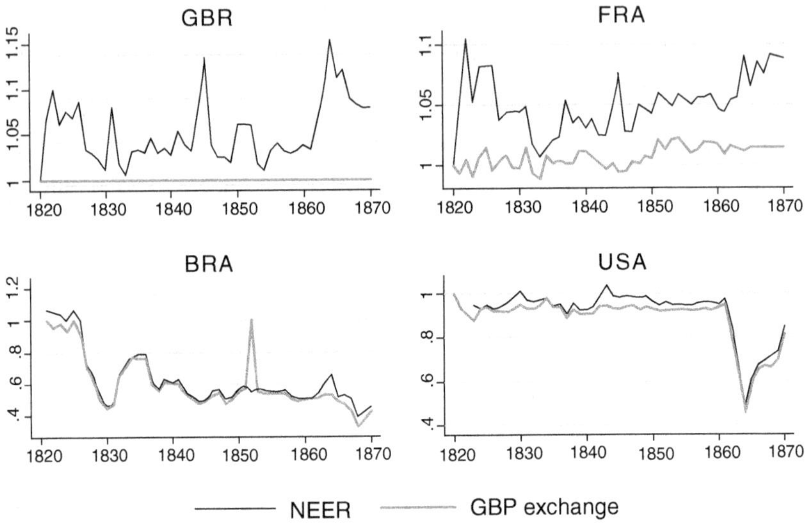

Figure 18.6 Nominal and effective exchange rates, 1820–70
Sources: see text. Values in deviation from parity with 1820=1.

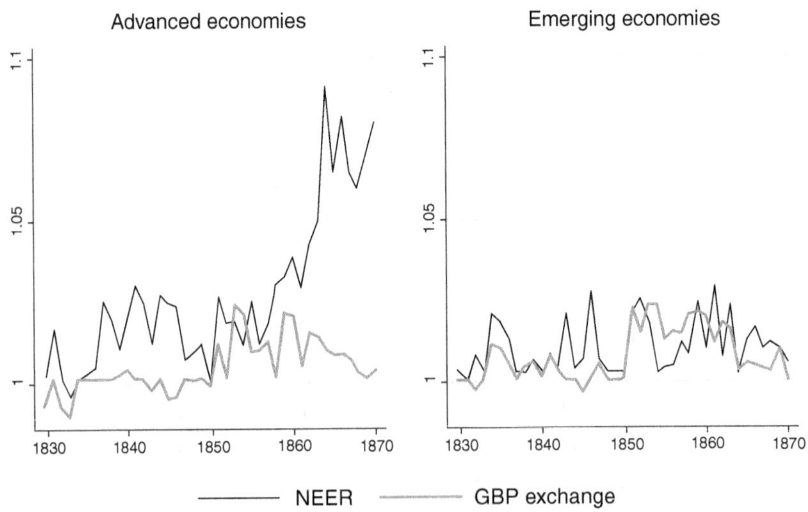

Figure 18.7 Nominal and effective exchange rates, 1820–70
Sources: see text. Values in deviation from parity with 1820=1.
Advanced economies = Britain, France, Germany (Zollverein), Belgium, and the Netherlands.

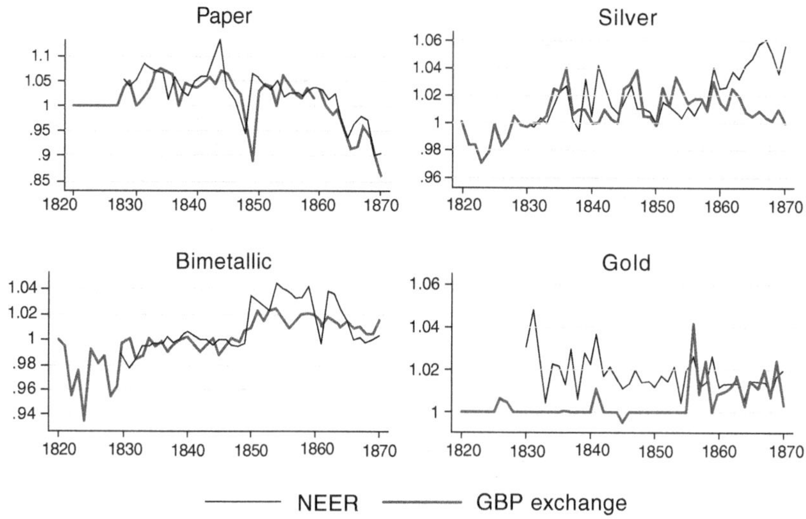

Figure 18.8 Nominal and effective exchange rates, by monetary regimes 1820–70
Sources: see text. Values in deviation from parity with 1820=1.

All in all, this evidence coincides with the findings of Catão and Solomou (2005) for the subsequent period. Table 18.1 summarizes the evidence by comparing the coefficients of variation of the two nominal measures of the exchange rate, divided by group of countries and monetary regime.[10] The majority of nominal exchange rate variations of advanced nations and nations on metallic pegs were driven by their trade partners. For these nations, the volatility of their effective exchange rates is always larger than their exchange against the *numéraire* (sterling). The opposite applied to peripheral nations and countries on inconvertible paper standards, where the ratio between the two was lower than one.

As a way of testing directly for David Hume's price-specie flow mechanism, we compute the real effective exchange rates and compare the fraction of their variance explained by nominal exchange rate (NEER) fluctuations with that due to relative price movements (PREL).[11] Table 18.1 summarizes this as a ratio between the variances of the two variables. In line with Catão and Solomou's (2005) work, we find that nations on

10 The table covers the period from 1830 only because of sparse price data to compute REERs before that date.

11 Formally, we do this by decomposing the variance of the log of REER: $\ln(\text{REER}) = \ln(\text{NEER}) + \ln(\text{PREL})$.

Table 18.1 Volatility of exchange rates, 1830–70

	Nations		Regimes			
	Advanced	Emerging	Paper	Silver	Bimetallic	Gold
GBP exchange	0.007	0.008	0.056	0.012	0.010	0.007
NEER	0.019	0.007	0.046	0.018	0.017	0.007
Ratio (NEER/GBP)	2.677	0.909	0.819	1.523	1.656	1.023
REER	0.072	0.037	0.072	0.053	0.041	0.208
PREL	0.066	0.030	0.081	0.040	0.036	0.214
Ratio (NEER/PREL)	0.265	0.197	0.633	0.337	0.422	0.036

Sources and notes: See text. Values in coefficient of variation = standard deviation/mean of each variable. PREL is the trade-adjusted relative price index (1830=1).

metallic pegs did not have much margin for nominal exchange rate adjustments. The most extreme case was nations on gold where the variance of their NEER was only 4 per cent of the variance of their relative prices. Contrary to the evidence post-1870, this was true even for nations on inconvertible monetary regimes, where the contribution of nominal exchange rate adjustments was still only 63 per cent as large as that of relative price adjustments.

In conclusion, notwithstanding the pervasiveness of barriers to exporting specie until the mid-nineteenth century, in practically all nations nominal rigidity did not stand in the way of real exchange rate adjustments, consistent with Hume's dismissal of the effectiveness of capital controls and his model of balance of payments adjustment.

Conclusion

From early on, precious metals were adopted as currency because their properties made them ideal to solve the triple functions of money – unit of account, means of payment, and store of value. However, these same properties made money a tempting target for bankrupted sovereigns, who resorted to debasements as a straightforward way of raising funds – straightforward but not painless, as the loss of metallic content of coins led inevitably to higher prices of goods and services in terms of the debased unit of account, in other words, inflation.

The fact that precious metals had value both as money and as commodities also limited what sovereigns could get away with because of arbitrage. An integrated European market for bullion from the eighteenth century onwards further constrained policy choices, so long as bullion flows were allowed.

In our story, commodity moneys eventually went global and helped convey intercontinental trade, particularly silver, that became the linchpin between America, Europe, and Asia. Since not all regions of the world used the same monetary commodities, this led to the rise of the foreign exchange market, initially for bullion and later for bills of exchange, a more efficient form of international currency. But money did not only fulfil a passive role of facilitating international trade: it also conditioned how trade imbalances were corrected. Consistent with David Hume's mid-eighteenth century model, we conclude that the widespread use of commodity moneys prevented an adjustment via exchange rates. The rebalancing act came mostly through domestic price corrections.

Many of the strands of early modern monetary history – monetization (debasement), inflation, FX market, monetary flows compensating for trade imbalances, and current account adjustment – sound remarkably relevant to today's world and that is not by chance. The history of money in the eighteenth and nineteenth centuries followed the rising trends of international trade and financial integration – what came to be known as 'globalization'.

References

Allen, R., Bassino, J.-P., Ma, D., Moll-Murate, C. and Van Zanden, J. L. (2011). 'Wages, Prices, and Living Standards in China, 1738–1925: In Comparison with Europe, Japan and India', *Economic History Review*, 64(S1), 8–38.

Attman, A. (1983). *Dutch Enterprise in the World Bullion Trade, 1550–1800*, Göteborg: Kungl. Vetenskaps – och Vitterhets – Samhället.

Barret, W. (1990). 'World Bullion Flows, 1450–1800', in Tracy, J. (ed.), *The Rise of Merchant Empires: Long-Distance Trade in the Early Modern World 1350–1750*, Cambridge University Press.

Blitz, R. C. (1967). 'Mercantilist Policies and the Pattern of World Trade, 1500–1750', *Journal of Economic History*, 27(1), 39–55.

Bloomfield, A. (1959). *Monetary Policy under the International Gold Standard, 1880–1914*, New York: Federal Reserve Bank of New York.

Bordo, M. (1986). 'Money, Deflation and Seigniorage in the Fifteenth Century: A Review Essay', *Journal of Monetary Economics*, 18, 337–346.

Braudel, F. (1979). *Civilisation matérielle, économie et capitalisme, XVe–XVIIIe siècle, vol 1: Les structures du quotidien*, Paris: Armand Colin.

Bulbeck, D., Reid, A., Tan, L. C. and Wu, Y. (1998). *Southeast Asian Exports since the 14th Century: Cloves, Pepper, Coffee and Sugar*, Leiden: KITLV Press.

Cartier, M. (1981). 'Les importations de métaux monétaires en Chine: essai sur la conjoncture chinoise', *Annales: Économies, sociétés, civilisations*, 36(3), 454–466.

Catão, L. and Solomou, S. (2005). 'Effective Exchange Rates and the Classical Gold Standard Adjustment', *American Economic Review*, 95, 1259–1275.

Chaudhuri, K. N. (1978). *The Trading World of Asia and the English East India Company, 1660–1760*, Cambridge University Press.

(1982). 'European Trade with India', in Raychaudhuri, T. and Habib, I. (eds.), *The Cambridge Economic History of India, vol. 1: c.1200–c.1750*, Cambridge University Press, 382–407.

Chaudhuri, S. (2017). 'No Ready Money? No Problem! The Role of Hundis (Bills of Exchange) in Early Modern India, c. 1600–1800', in Chaudhuri, S., *Trade, Politics, and Society: the Indian Milieu in the Early Modern Era*, New York: Routledge, chapter 3.

Chen, C. (1972). 'Bimetallism: Theory and Controversy in Perspective', *History of Political Economy*, 4(1), 89–122.

Chilosi, D. and Volckart, O. (2010). 'Good or Bad Money?: Debasement, Society and the State in the late Middle Ages', Economic History Working Papers, 140/10, Department of Economic History, London School of Economics and Political Science.

Cipolla, C. M. (1956). *Money, Prices and Civilization in the Mediterranean World, Fifth to Seventeenth Century*, New York: Gordian Press.

(1989). *Money in Sixteenth-Century Florence*. Berkeley: University of California Press.

(1996). *Conquistadores, pirati, mercatanti. La saga dell'argento spagnuolo*, Bologna: Societa Editrice Mulino.

Cooper, R. N. (1987). *The International Monetary System: Essays in World Economics*, Cambridge, MA: MIT Press.

Darwin, L. (1898). *Bimetallism: A Summary and Examination of the Arguments for and against a Bimetallic System of Currency*, New York: Appleton.

Datta, R. (2003). 'The Agrarian Economy and the Dynamics of Commercial Transactions', in Marshall, P. J. (ed.), *The Eighteenth Century in Indian History: Evolution or Revolution*, Oxford University Press, 405–555.

Dedinger, B. and Girard, P. (2017). 'Exploring Trade Globalization in the Long Run: The RICardo Project', *Historical Methods: A Journal of Quantitative and Interdisciplinary History*, 50(1), 30–48.

Dehing, P. and 'T Hart, M. (1997). 'Linking the Fortunes: Currency and Banking, 1550–1800', in 'T Hart, M., Jonker, J. and van Zanden, J. L., *A Financial History of the Netherlands*, Cambridge University Press, 37–63.

Denzel, M. A. (2010). *Handbook of World Exchange Rates, 1590–1914*, Farnham: Ashgate.

Dermigny, L. (1964). *La Chine et L'Occident: Le Commerce à Canton au XVIIIe siècle*, 3 volumes, Paris: S.E.V.P.E.N.

de Roover, R. A. (1953). *L'Evolution de la Lettre de Change, XIVe–XVIIIe siècles*, Paris: Armand Colin.

de Vries, J. (2003). 'Connecting Europe and Asia: a quantitative analysis of the Cape-route trade, 1497–1795', in Flynn, D. O., Giráldez, A. and von Glahn, R. (eds.), *Global Connections and Monetary History, 1470–1800*, Aldershot: Ashgate, 35–106.

de Vries, J. and van der Woude, A. (1997). *The First Modern Economy: Success, Failure, and Perseverance of the Dutch Economy, 1500–1815*, Cambridge University Press.

de Zwart, P. (2015). 'Inflation', IISH Dataverse, hdl.handle.net/10622/UJ3H1Q (accessed 15 October 2020).

Edvinsson, R. (2012). 'Early Modern Copper Money: Multiple Currencies and Trimetallism in Sweden 1624–1776', *European Review of Economic History*, 16(4), 408–429.

Eichengreen, B. (1996). *Globalizing Capital: A History of the International Monetary System*, Princeton University Press.

Einzig, P. (1962). *The History of Foreign Exchange*, London: Macmillan.

Elgin, C., Karaman, K. and Pamuk, S. (2015). 'Debasements in Europe and their Causes, 1500–1800', Centre for Economic Policy Research working paper, cepr.org/sites/default/files/Pamuk%20-%20oslo%20text%20June%202015.pdf (accessed 14 October 2020).

Fantacci, L. (2008). 'The Dual Currency System of Renaissance Europe', *Financial History Review*, 15(1), 55–72.

Feavearyear, A. E. (1931). *The Pound Sterling: A History of English Money*, Oxford: Clarendon Press.

Findlay, R. and O'Rourke, K. H. (2007). *Power and Plenty: Trade, War, and the World Economy in the Second Millennium*, Princeton University Press.

Fisher, I. (1894). 'The Mechanics of Bimetallism', *The Economic Journal*, 4(15), 527–537.

Flandreau, M. (1996). 'Adjusting the Gold Rush: Endogenous Bullion Points and the French Balance of Payments, 1846–1870', *Explorations in Economic History*, 33(4), 417–439.

(1997). 'As Good as Gold? Bimetallism in Equilibrium, 1850–1870', in Marcuzzo, M. C., Officer, L. H. and Rosselli, A. (eds.), *Monetary Standards and Exchange Rates*, London and New York: Routledge, 150–176.

(2002). '"Water Seeks a Level": Modelling Bimetallic Exchange Rates and the Bimetallic Band', *Journal of Money, Credit, and Banking*, 34(2), 491–519.

(2004). *The Glitter of Gold: France, Bimetallism, and the Emergence of the International Gold Standard, 1848–1873*, Oxford University Press.

Flandreau, F. and Jobst, C. (2005). 'The Ties that Divide: A Network Analysis of the International Monetary System, 1890–1910', *Journal of Economic History*, 65(4), 977–1007.

Flandreau, M., Galimard, C., Jobst, C. and Nogues-Marco, P. (2009a). 'The Bell Jar: Commercial Interest Rates between Two Revolutions, 1688–1789', in Atack, J. and Neal, L. (eds.), *The Origins and Developments of Financial Markets and Institutions from the Seventeenth Century to the Present*, Cambridge University Press, 161–208.

(2009b). 'Monetary Geography before the Industrial Revolution', *Cambridge Journal of Regions, Economy and Society*, 2(2), 149–171.

Flynn, D. O. (1984). 'Use and Misuse of the Quantity Theory of Money in Early Modern Historiography', in van Cauwenberghe, E. and Irsigler, F. (eds.), *Minting, Monetary Circulation and Exchange Rates*, Trier: Verlag Trierer Historische Forschungen, 383–417.

(2012). 'Precious Metals and Moneys, 1200–1800', in Caprio, G. (ed.), *Handbook of Key Global Financial Markets, Institutions, and Infrastructure, vol. 1*, Amsterdam: Elsevier, 220–230.

Flynn, D. and Giráldez, A. (2002). 'Cycles of Silver: Global Economy Unity through the Mid-18th Century', *Journal of World History*, 13, 391–428.

(2004). 'Path Dependence, Time Lags and the Birth of Globalization: A Critique of O'Rourke and Williamson', *European Review of Economic History*, 8, 81–108.

Fouquin, M. and Hugot, J. (2016). 'Two Centuries of Bilateral Trade and Gravity Data: 1827–2014', Centres d'Études Prospectives et Informations Internationales (CEPII) working paper 2016–14.

Freire Costa, L., Münch Miranda, S. and Nogues-Marco, P. (forthcoming). 'Early Modern Financial Development in the Iberian Peninsula', in Lains, P. (general ed.), *An Economic History of the Iberian Peninsula, 700–2000*, Cambridge University Press, part II, chapter 3.

Friedman, M. (1990). 'Bimetallism Revisited', *Journal of Economic Perspectives*, 4(4), 85–104.

Garber, P. M. (1986). 'Nominal Contracts in a Bimetallic Standard', *American Economic Review*, 76(5), 1012–1030.

Garber, P. M. and Weisbrod, S. R. (1992). *The Economics of Banking, Liquidity, and Money*, Lexington: D. C. Heath and Company.

Giffen, R. (1892). *The Case Against Bimetallism*, London: Bell.

Gillard, L. (2004). *La Banque d'Amsterdam et Le Florin Européen Au Temps De La République Néerlandaise (1610–1820)*, Paris: Éditions de l'École des Hautes Études en Sciences Sociales.

Greenberg, M. (1951). *British Trade and the Opening of China, 1800–42*, Cambridge University Press.

Gupta, S. P. and Moosvi, S. (1973). 'Weighted Price and Revenue-Rate Indices of Eastern Rajasthan (c. 1665–1750)', *Proceedings of the Indian History Congress*, 34(I), 298–302.

Habib, I. (1971). 'The System of Bills of Exchange ("Hundis") in the Mughal Empire', *Proceedings of the Indian History Congress*, 33, 290–303.

(1982). 'Monetary Systems and Prices', in Raychaudhuri, T. and Habib, I. (eds.), *The Cambridge Economic History of India, vol 1: c.1200–c.1750*, Cambridge University Press.

(1987). 'A System of Trimetallism in the Age of the "Price Revolution": Effects of the Silver Influx on the Mughal Monetary System', in Richards, J. F. (ed.), *The Imperial Monetary System of Mughal India*, Oxford University Press, 147–159.

Hauser, H. (1936). *Recherches et documents sur l'histoire des Prix en France de 1500 à 1800*, Paris: Les Presses Modernes-Imprimerie au Palais – Royal.

Heckscher, E. F. (1954). *An Economic History of Sweden*, Cambridge, MA: Harvard University Press.

Hogendorn, J. and Johnson, M. (1986). *The Shell Money of the Slave Trade*, Cambridge University Press.

Hume, D. (1955). *Writings on Economics*, ed. Rotwein, E., Madison: University of Wisconsin Press.

Jastram, R. W. (1977). *The Golden Constant: The English and American Experience, 1560–1976*, New York: John Wiley.

Johnson, M. (1970). 'The Cowrie Currencies of West Africa', *Journal of African History*, 11, 17–48.

Jonker, J. (1996). *Merchants, Bankers, Middlemen: The Amsterdam Money Market during the First Half of the 19th Century*, Amsterdam: Nederlandsch Economisch-Historisch Archief.

Kindleberger, C. P. (1989). *Spenders and Hoarders: The World Distribution of Spanish American Silver, 1550–1750*, Singapore: Institute of Southeast Asian Studies.
(1993). *A Financial History of Western Europe*, 2nd ed., Oxford University Press.
Krishna, B. (1924). *Commercial Relations between India and England (1601 to 1757)*, London: Routledge.
Laughlin, J. L. (1885). *The History of Bimetallism in the United States*, New York: D. Appleton and Co.
Lemale, A. (1875). *Monnaies, poids, mesures et usages commerciaux de tous les états du monde*, Paris: Hachette & Cie.
Locke, J. (2010 [1696]). *Further Considerations Concerning Raising the Value of Money*, Whitefish: Kessinger Publishing.
Marshall, P. J. (1976). *East Indian Fortunes. The British in Bengal in the Eighteenth Century*, Oxford: Clarendon Press.
McCusker, J. J. (1978). *Money and Exchange in Europe and America, 1600–1775: A Handbook*, London: Macmillan Press.
Meissner, C. (2005). 'A New World Order: Explaining the International Diffusion of the Gold Standard, 1870–1913', *Journal of International Economics*, 66(2), 385–406.
Miskimin, H. A. (1964). *Money, Prices and Foreign Exchange in Fourteenth Century France*, New Haven: Yale University Press.
(1984). *Money and Power in Fifteenth-Century France*, New Haven: Yale University Press.
Morgan, K. (2005). 'Remittance Procedures in the Eighteenth-Century British Slave Trade', *Business History Review*, 79(4), 715–749.
Munro, J. H. (ed.) (2012). *Money in the Pre-Industrial World: Bullion, Debasements and Coin Substitutes*, London: Pickering & Chatto.
Murphy, A. (2009). *Genesis of Macroeconomics: New Ideas from Sir William Petty to Henry Thornton*, Oxford University Press.
Neal, L. (1990). *The Rise of Financial Capitalism: International Capital Markets in the Age of Reason*, Cambridge University Press.
Nogues-Marco, P. (2013). 'Competing Bimetallic Ratios: Amsterdam, London and Bullion Arbitrage in mid-18th Century', *Journal of Economic History*, 73(2), 445–476.
(2018). 'Money Markets and Exchange Rates in Preindustrial Europe', in Battilossi, S., Cassis, Y. and Yago, K. (eds.), *Handbook of the History of Money and Currency*, Singapore: Springer.
(2019). 'Trade Imbalances or Specie Arbitrage? Anglo-Asian Bullion Flows in the Early Modern Period, 1664–1811', Centre for Economic Policy Research working paper 14582, portal.cepr.org/discussion-paper/14582 (accessed 9 November 2020).
(2021). 'Measuring Colonial Extraction. The East India Company's Rule and the Drain of Wealth, 1757–1858', *Capitalism: A Journal of History and Economics*, 2(1), 154–193.
Nurul Hasan, S. and Gupta, S. P. (1967). 'Prices of Food Grains in the Territories of Amber (c.1650–1750)', *Proceedings of the Indian History Congress*, 29(1), 345–368.
Oppers, S. (1996). 'Was the Worldwide Shift to Gold Inevitable? An Analysis of the End of Bimetallism', *Journal of Monetary Economics*, 37(1): 143–162.
(2000). 'A Model of the Bimetallic System', *Journal of Monetary Economics*, 46(2), 517–533.
Palma, N. and Silva, A. (2017). 'Spending a Windfall: American Precious Metals and Euro-Asian Trade 1531–1810', *GGDC Research Memorandum*, 165.
Pamuk, Ş. (2000). *A Monetary History of the Ottoman Empire*, Cambridge University Press.

Polak, M. S. (1998). *Historiografie En Economie Van De 'muntchaos': De Muntproductie Van De Republiek (1606–1795)*, Amsterdam: Nederlandsch Economisch-Historisch Archief.

Prakash, O. (1985). *The Dutch East India Company and the Economy of Bengal, 1630–1720*, Princeton University Press.

(1986). 'Precious Metal Flows in Asia and World Economic Integration in the 17th Century', in Fischer, W., McInnis, R. M. and Schneider, J. (eds.), *The Emergence of a World Economy, 1500–1914*, Wiesbaden: Franz Steiner Verlag, 83–96.

(1994). 'Precious Metal Flows, Coinage and Prices in India in the 17th and the Early 18th century', in Prakash, O. (ed.), *Precious Metals and Commerce: The Dutch East India Company in the Indian Ocean Trade*, Aldershot: Variorum.

(2005). 'The Great Divergence: Evidence from Eighteenth-Century India', LSE Working Paper (paper presented at the Seventh Global Economic History Network Conference at Istanbul).

Qiao, Z. (2017). '*The Rise of Shanxi Merchants: Empire, Institutions, and Social Change in Qing China, 1688–1850*', unpublished Ph.D. thesis, Department of History, Stanford University, September 2017.

Quinn, S. and Roberds, W. (2009). 'An Economic Explanation of the Early Bank of Amsterdam, Debasement, Bills of Exchange and the Emergence of the First Central Bank', in Atack, J. and Neal., L. (eds.), *The Origins and Development of Financial Markets and Institutions: From the Seventeenth Century to the Present*, Cambridge University Press, 32–70.

(2014). 'The Bank of Amsterdam through the Lens of Monetary Competition', in Bernholz, P. and Vaubel, R. (eds.), *Explaining Monetary and Financial Innovation*, Cham: Springer Press, 283–300.

(2016). 'Death of a Reserve Currency', *International Journal of Central Banking*, 12(4), 63–103.

Redish, A. (1990). 'The Evolution of the Gold Standard in England', *Journal of Economic History*, 50(4), 789–805.

(1995). 'The Persistence of Bimetallism in Nineteenth-Century France', *Economic History Review*, 48(4), 717–736.

(2000). *Bimetallism. An Economic and Historical Analysis*, Cambridge University Press.

Rolnick, A. and Weber, W. E. (1986). 'Gresham's Law or Gresham's Fallacy?', *Journal of Political Economy*, 94(1), 185–199.

Rolnick, A. J., Velde, F. R. and Warren, E. W. (1996). 'The Debasement Puzzle: An Essay on Medieval Monetary History', *Journal of Economic History*, 56(4), 789–808.

Santarosa, V. A. (2015). 'Financing Long-Distance Trade: The Joint Liability Rule and Bills of Exchange in Eighteenth-Century France', *Journal of Economic History*, 75(3), 690–719.

Sargent, T. J. and Velde, F. R. (2002). *The Big Problem of Small Change*, Princeton University Press.

Shaw, W. (1895). *The History of Currency: 1252–1894*, London: Wilsons & Milne.

Spufford, P. (1988). *Money and its Use in Medieval Europe*, Cambridge University Press.

Sussman, N. (1993). 'Debasements, Royal Revenues and Inflation in France during the Hundred Year's War, 1415–1422', *Journal of Economic History*, 53(1), 44–70.

TePaske, J. J. (1983). 'New World Silver, Castile and the Philippines 1590–1800', in Richards, J. F. (ed.), *Precious Metals in the Later Medieval and Early Modern Worlds*, Durham, NC: Carolina Academic Press, 424–446.

(2010). *A New World of Gold and Silver*, in Brown, K. W. (ed.), Leiden: E. J. Brill.

van der Wee, H. (1977). 'Monetary, Credit, and Banking Systems', in Rich, E. E. and Wilson, C. H. (eds.), *The Cambridge Economic History of Europe, vol.5: The Economic Organisation of Early Modern Europe*, Cambridge University Press, 290–392.

Velde, F. R. and Weber, W. E. (2000). 'A Model of Bimetallism', *Journal of Political Economy*, 108(6), 1210–1234.

(2008). *Government Equity and Money – John Law's System in 1720 France*, Princeton University Press.

Vilar, P. (1974). *Or et Monnaie dans l'Histoire*, Paris: Flammarion.

Vogel, H. U. (1987). 'Chinese Central Monetary Policy, 1644–1800', *Late Imperial China*, 8 (2), 1–52.

von Glahn, R. (1996). 'Myth and Reality of China's Seventeenth-Century Monetary Crisis', *Journal of Economic History*, 56, 429–454.

(2003). 'Money Use in China and Changing Patterns of Global Trade in Monetary Metals, 1500–1800', in Flynn, D. O., Giráldez, A. and von Glahn, R. (eds.), *Global Connections and Monetary History, 1470–1800*, Aldershot: Ashgate.

Walker, F. A. (1896). *International Bimetallism*, London: Macmillan.

Walras, L. (1881). *Théorique mathématique du bimétallisme*, Lausanne: Corbaz.

Wang, Y. C. (1992). 'Secular Trends of Rice Prices in the Yangzi Delta, 1638–1935', in Rawski, T. G. and Li, L. M. (eds.), *Chinese History in Economic Perspective*, University of California Press, 35–68.

Willis, H. P. (1901). *A History of the Latin Monetary Union: A Study of International Monetary Action*, University of Chicago Press.

Yan, H., Qiao, Z. and Xu, C. (2018). 'A Multi-Layer System and Its Features: Reconceptualizing the Monetary Regime of Late Qing and Modern China', *Frontiers of Economics in China*, 13(3), 437–457.

19

War and Empire, 1700–1870

PHILIP T. HOFFMAN AND TIRTHANKAR ROY

Although warfare is a constant in human history, it was transformed radically, first by gunpowder and then by the Industrial Revolution. After guns first appeared in China in the thirteenth century – they were small hand-held cannon – they swiftly spread throughout Eurasia. Thereafter gunpowder technology never ceased to improve. More powerful guns were soon sprouting on ships and punching through fortress walls, and musketeers replaced archers in armies. In reaction, military architects built forts that could resist an artillery barrage and hold off besieging armies, only to have generals devise tactics that succeeded against even the strongest forts. And with the Industrial Revolution, the advances in military technology only accelerated, as muskets gave way to rifles and then machine guns, sails yielded to steam power, and artillery grew more mobile and ever deadlier.

But guns did not just modify the technology of conducting warfare; they reshaped trade and politics and did so around the world. The consequences – from the Atlantic slave trade to the rise and fall of empires across the globe – were huge. In the sixteenth century, conquistadors toppled the Aztec and Inca empires, and the Ottoman Empire expanded. In the seventeenth and eighteenth, the Russian Empire reached across Asia, China marched west (Perdue 2005), more European colonies sprang up in the Americas, and Britain began to take over territory in India. The European conquests extended further in the nineteenth century (in Asia, Australia, and Africa, in particular), spurred on not just by improved military technology but also by railways, steamboats, and quinine, the remedy against the disease – malaria – that kept Westerners out of the African interior. By 1914, 84 per cent of the globe was under European control, either directly or as now-independent colonies dominated by Europeans (Headrick 1981; 2010; Hoffman 2015).

Traders extended their reach, too, particularly (though certainly not exclusively) those from Europe. They sailed to Asia and used force to muscle in on trade, erecting fortresses and warships to protect against hostile local powers and European competitors. They brought spices and silk back home and, later, cotton and tea. European slavers exchanged guns for African captives and then shipped millions of them to the Americas to toil growing sugar, coffee, tobacco, and eventually cotton. In the New World, European settlers mined silver and gold that paid for wars back home, and from Asia, they brought back silk, porcelain, tea, and cotton textiles. The Industrial Revolution then made Britain the world's dominant textile exporter, and by the end of the nineteenth century, shipping technology had progressed far enough (and tariffs dropped low enough) that the prices of bulk commodities such as wheat were now being set in world markets (O'Rourke and Williamson 1999).

Gunpowder also affected politics. The states that pushed gunpowder technology furthest were the ones that not only fought with it incessantly but also mobilized increasing amounts of tax revenue to buy the best guns, ships, and fortifications. By the eighteenth century, those states were in western Europe. Their fiscal capacity – their ability to tax and borrow – simply dwarfed that of states elsewhere in the world. Part of the difference, at least by the late nineteenth century, was higher income, for by then much of western Europe had begun to industrialize. But the rest of the difference derived from political changes that increased the state's ability to mobilize resources.

In what follows, we will examine those political changes and the reasons why they took place in western Europe. We will also seek to understand why western Europe ultimately took the lead in military technology over Asian or Middle Eastern states that had once stood at the forefront of the use of guns. We will also explore how the military technology and industrialization facilitated conquest and colonization.

But military technology and European politics were not the only driving forces behind the conquests and the evolution of warfare. Politics in Africa, Asia, and the Americas also had a major role to play, as did international trade. In Africa, the slave trade militarized indigenous politics and devastated both the local economy and society. In India, the disintegration of the Mughal Empire ushered in conflicts between local powers and European trading companies, in which the English East India Company and then Britain itself ultimately emerged as a victor for reasons that had more to do with Indian politics than with military technology. That, too, we will analyze, and at the conclusion we will sum up the benefits of empire and their broader costs, both for the colonizers and the colonized.

The Frequency and Cost of Warfare

Historians of warfare and empire ask whether there were differences between the great Eurasian empires of the 1600s and European colonial empires of the 1800s in the manner in which they raised armies and used them. One clue to this topic is the enormous size and diversity of the regions that the Eurasian empires managed. Inner Asian cavalry armies were instrumental in the making of empires in Eurasia between 1200 and 1600. From about 1650, the imperial states of Qing China and Mughal India needed to deal with 'unusually daunting challenges to stability and local penetration' (Lieberman 2008). Regions and frontiers were militarily and politically unstable zones, and attempts to integrate these zones into the imperial administrative system increased the risk of rebellion. While the threat was a shared one, the means of dealing with it differed – a variable combination of military threat and fiscal incentives, and perhaps crucially, policy towards the regions. Most writings on the survival and fall of the great Eurasian empires – Ottoman, Mughal, and Qing – emphasize their success or failure in incorporating the regions into a union.

While dealing with potentially restive regions, both Mughal and the Qing expanded, the Mughal in the seventeenth century, and the Qing especially in the eighteenth (Perdue 2005). Yet both grew weaker in the presence of a European threat in the late eighteenth or the early nineteenth century. The explanation of this reversal is open to debate. Regions figure in one approach. For example, in Mughal India, regional powers, which had been left in a semi-independent state, asserted independence, giving rise to 'centrifugal tendencies' that had been uneasily contained until then (Gommans 2002: 202). On the other hand, 'in China the limited role of interstate competition reduced pressures for improvements in military technology' (Lieberman 2008; see also Hoffman 2015; Andrade 2016). Another approach argues that '[t]he institutions that emerged in the West to help finance war and other state activities, overall had no Asian counterpart' (Vries 2002). The Ottoman Empire survived into the twentieth century despite losing crucial wars with external enemies and dealing with rebellions within, thanks to its comparatively greater success in co-opting regions, as well as openness to European technology and institutions (Pamuk 2004).

War was common in pre-Columbian America, in Africa, and throughout Eurasia. China spent just as much time fighting foreign enemies, for example, as did the bellicose powers of early modern Europe (Table 19.1). In addition, China faced numerous civil wars, rebellions, and battles against pirates. The

Table 19.1 Frequency of foreign wars in China and Europe, 1500–1799

Country	Percentage of time country is at war against foreign enemies, 1500–1799
China	56
France	52
England/Great Britain	53
Spain	81
Austrian Dominions	24

Source: Hoffman (2015: table 3.1).

Table 19.2 Central government annual tax revenue per capita

	China	Ottoman Empire	Russia	France	Spain	England	Dutch Republic
	Per-capita tax revenue (grams of silver)						
1650–99	7.0	11.8		46.0	35.8	45.1	
1700–49	7.2	15.5	6.4	46.6	41.6	93.5	161.1
1750–99	4.2	12.9	21.0	66.4	63.1	158.4	170.7
1800–49	3.4					303.8	
1850–99	7.0					344.1	
	Per-capita tax revenue (days of unskilled urban labour)						
1650–99		1.7		8.0	7.7	4.2	13.6
1700–49	2.26	2.6	6.4	6.7	4.6	8.9	24.1
1750–99	1.32	2.0	8.3	11.4	10.0	12.6	22.8
1800–49	1.23					17.2	
1850–99	1.99					19.4	

Source: Brandt et al. (2014).

table omits that sort of fighting unless foreign enemies were involved, and the omission was likely far more serious for China, meaning that it faced even more fighting than the table suggests (Andrade 2016).

What was different about Europe, however, was not the frequency of war; rather, it was the resources devoted to it. The states in western Europe could extract far more in resources than other major powers in Eurasia, at least those for which some quantitative evidence is available. The difference is large, whether we measure in silver or in days of labour (Table 19.2). Clearly, political leaders in the western European states had learned how to raise far more tax revenue than in other countries (Hoffman 2015).

The table does admittedly omit taxes that were collected and spent locally. Such local revenue was likely much larger in China and the Ottoman Empire than in western Europe (Huang 1974; Coşgel and Miceli 2005; Coşgel et al. 2009; Sng 2014; Monson and Scheidel 2015), although it need not have been under the central government's control. The table also omits labour and resources in kind that could be mobilized, such as serfs conscripted in Russia. That, too, would reduce the gap between western Europe and the other countries. But even so the difference is simply too big to disappear altogether. And in Europe, virtually all of the tax revenue was spent on warfare. There was no state-wide programme of famine relief, as in China, and expenditures on even the most elaborate palaces absorbed only a sliver of the state budget. Versailles, for example, consumed less than 2 per cent of Louis XIV's tax revenue (Hoffman 2015).

Western European states also led the way in borrowing to finance wars, which allowed the military expenses to be spread over time. That was no small achievement for states, many of which were still defaulting on their debt in the eighteenth century. Britain was particularly successful in making the transition, and it could soon tap a large liquid market for its bonds (Neal 1990).

Extensive borrowing and heavy taxes were made possible by political and constitutional changes. Making taxes the same across an entire state increased tax revenue, but in most of western Europe that sort of fiscal uniformity was not achieved until the Napoleonic period. Parliamentary control of taxation, spending, and borrowing also boosted taxes and facilitated borrowing, too, but that took until later in the nineteenth century (Dincecco 2009a; 2009b; 2011; Cox 2012). On both fronts, Britain was a century or more ahead of its neighbours, which (along with its high level of per capita income) help explain the high level of tax revenue it collected (Table 19.2). Similar representative institutions arrived even more slowly elsewhere in the world, which slowed the development of states' fiscal capacity and public debt markets.

The heavy spending on war in western Europe fuelled the improvements in gunpowder technology, whether it was deadlier guns and artillery, faster warships with more arms, or better tactics and fortifications. Each pound spent on war gave officers, troops, and suppliers a chance to learn what worked and what did not, both from their own experience and that of their enemies. This sort of learning by doing was easier in Europe than in much of the rest of Eurasia (India was perhaps an exception here) because distances between the contending powers were small, and the traffic in arms, tactics, and military personnel did not respect international borders. The learning by doing in turn advanced the military technology.

Other parts of the world eventually lagged behind. They fought less often, spent less money on war, relied on technologies other than gunpowder that were more effective against their enemies, or faced greater obstacles to learning while fighting. Western Europeans continued to push the gunpowder technology forward even after fighting within Europe subsided somewhat in the century after 1815. They could do so because they were still armed to the teeth and spending heavily on the military in what amounted to a cold war. They could also harness all the advances of the Industrial Revolution and apply them to weaponry (Hoffman 2015). That yielded rifles and rifled artillery, steam-powered gunboats, and eventually machine guns, which all proved important for fighting and conquests not just in Europe but in Africa and Asia as well (Headrick 1981; 2010).

Why then was Europe fragmented into small, hostile states? And why did political leaders spend so much on war? Why did one of the contending states not defeat the others and become a hegemon like Qing China or a megastate like the Ottoman or Mughal Empire? Simple arguments about geography (for instance, that Europe was more mountainous than China and that the mountains and Europe's irregular coastline favoured political splintering) do not stand up to scrutiny. But it might be possible to explain the smaller scale of states in Europe via more sophisticated analysis that takes into account the advantage the big states have in providing insurance or protective infrastructure in regions subject to widespread climate shocks. That might have been the case, for instance, in much of China and a reason why it was often unified. In Europe there is also arguably a role for a form of cultural evolution set in motion by the centuries of what we would now call warlord rule after the fall of the Roman Empire in the West. The evolution generated lasting political hostilities in Europe that made political unification difficult, and it favoured continued rule by leaders obsessed with war who spent all of their revenue on the military, in contrast, say, to Chinese emperors, who certainly fought wars but likely spent much more on famine relief (Will and Wong, 1991; Hoffman 2015).

Europe's political fragmentation, it has been argued, had economic consequences, too. Although the incessant warfare and the heavy spending on it did take a heavy toll on the economy (as we shall see), having multiple states did mean that one ruler's bad decision did not spell disaster for the entire continent (Jones 2003). It also meant that authorities would have a harder time stifling innovation, because people with new ideas could and did move around Europe (Mokyr 2017: 166–178). And the incessant warfare itself may have encouraged technical change by drawing early manufacturing into cities, where it could be protected by city walls. Instead of, say, having peasant women spin in the agricultural slack season, cloth makers would hire urban workers, whose wages would have to be higher to offset the cost of housing. The higher wages would incline the cloth makers to more capital-intensive technologies, and they might also find it easier to copy or share technological innovations if they were all grouped near one another in the city (Rosenthal and Bin Wong 2011).

The deadlier weapons that the warfare gave rise to were not used just in armies and navies. They were also employed by private entrepreneurs who launched most of the expeditions of conquest and of predation on trade. That was true of the conquistadors and the Portuguese explorers, who used violence to muscle in on trade, and it held for the Dutch and English East India companies. Chartered to profit from trade, the companies used force and supported Dutch and English foreign policy in Asian warfare against both local powers and European enemies. Such private use of military technology was not unknown outside Europe, as East Asian pirates like Coxinga make clear. But for a variety of reasons it was much easier in Europe, and that facilitated European conquest and settlement. And as military and transport technology improved, conquest of this sort became possible in more and more places in the eighteenth and nineteenth centuries.

Warfare, Trade, and Politics

But military technology alone, as we have stressed, cannot explain either the European conquests or the changes in warfare. Trade had a major role to play, in some cases a catalytic role, in aiding warfare and state formation, as we can see from what happened in Africa and South Asia.[1] In some cases, trade directly abetted conflicts, and in others, trade stoked conflicts indirectly by intensifying political and military competition among indigenous states.

1 Since the initial conquests in the Americas happened before 1700, we leave them out, but one could make a similar case for the expansion of the newly independent United States, for much of the impetus to incorporate new territory used military force and derived from growing international trade in goods such as slave-produced cotton (Hahn 2016).

Trade and Warfare in West Africa

European firearms were a major item of trade in many world regions from the late eighteenth century onwards. In West Africa, guns were included in payment for slaves, but rarely for other commodities, which 'indicates very strongly the connexion between firearms and the acquisition of slaves' (Inikori 1977: 351). The connection was an indirect one. Guns had a variety of uses besides that as an instrument of war. A common item of import, the African trade musket, was not suitable for warfare at all, being slow to load. But it was light in weight and easy to repair, making it usable in hunting. Wars could occur for reasons unrelated to the slave trade. Subject to these qualifications, the volume of trade and patterns of exchange show that guns had a growing use in raids, in wars that led to the acquisition of captives who were sold, and to deter such wars. No matter the nature of the link, the gun trade was an integral part of slave-gathering, and 'slave-gathering by its very nature provoked inter-territorial war', stimulating the gun trade (Inikori 1977: 351).

A similar circular causation worked for horses in regions that relied on cavalry more than the infantry (such as the Oyo kingdom in interior Nigeria). The foreign trade in firearms was more easily accessible by coastal states than the interior ones. Jack Goody suggested that firearms empowered states in the forested regions dependent on the infantry (such as the Asante and Dahomey), and comparatively speaking, weakened the West African savannah-based cavalry armies (Goody 1971). Although Goody drew precise implications on patterns of state formation based on this model, not all of these conjectures survived scrutiny. But an indirect connection between geography, technology, and political process has endured.

Africanists debate whether wars were fought to sustain the slave trade directly, or indirectly by adding to the pool of surplus war captives. The use of the term 'raid' for wars favours the former view, but this usage is questioned (Thornton 1999). In practice, slaves captured by raids and war captives were both common modes of supply, for example in Dahomey, and raids were conducted not necessarily by the state, but also by licensed private actors, giving rise to negotiations in the relationship between the merchants and the state (Law 1989). Wars or raids were common also for an institutional reason. Property right in land was relatively weak, even absent, whereas rights over people tended to be well defined. People, therefore, were relatively mobile, and forced mobilization was relatively common. 'Enslavement and transportation of people was easier than conquest' (Thornton 1999: 17).

Trade, in this way, led to a thorough 'militarization' of institutions and society, for example, in eighteenth-century Dahomey (Law 1986). Further into the interior, the Sokoto kingdom turned into 'a state whose political and economic forms were largely defined by perpetual warfare' (Roberts 1980). Wars produced unintended consequences for politics and regulation. The dependence of trade on wars and raids dislocated credit markets (Ojo 2008). Patrick Manning (1990: 84–85) and others have argued that slave raids depopulated vast semi-arid regions. The wars 'rendered precarious the security of the trade routes and scared away the long-distance trader' (Guézo 2010). And, therefore, strong states were necessary in the long run, both to sustain the trade and to procure supplies. In turn, political regulation led to substantial rents from the trade, which reinforced the warrior states (Evans and Richardson 1995).

Guns were a popular item of import also in eighteenth-century India, and as in West Africa, we again observe a growing connection between the demand for firearms and the rise of warrior states. But in the South Asian case, the contest was over land revenue rather than profits in the slave trade.

Trade, Warfare, and Empire in Eighteenth-Century India

From the mid-eighteenth century, the Mughal Empire (1526–*c*.1720), which ruled from the Indo-Gangetic Basin, started to disintegrate. The empire's military force consisted of contributory armies from the major provinces and allies. Contributions of the larger provinces like Awadh, Bengal, and Hyderabad became uncertain, while in southern and western India the empire faced rebellion and secession. The break-up of the empire unleashed a fierce competition for territorial revenues among the successor states, led to a series of wars and predatory raids, and forced the successor states to spend a very high proportion of their revenue on the military.

While this process engaged states in the Indo-Gangetic Basin and the Deccan Plateau, along the coasts, another battlefront opened between the British and the French East India companies. Anglo-French military competition in the wake of the War of the Austrian Succession (1740–48), and the Seven Years War (1756–63), spilled over into battles in India between the two merchant firms. Both entities had gunships and soldiers, or could command the help of home resources. Starting with the minor succession dispute in the state of Carnatic, in the major conflicts that unfolded in the second half of the century, the British and the French took opposite sides. Despite occasional reverses, the British emerged victorious in these battles. The Treaty of Paris in 1763 all but destroyed French imperial ambitions in India, though individually French commanders and mercenaries continued to resist British expansion.

In the course of these conflicts, the British company acquired full control over the revenues of Bengal, a process completed between 1757 and 1765. The major clusters of battles that saw the Company establish a powerful empire in India, beginning with Carnatic in the 1740s, through the Battle of Plassey in Bengal (1757), Buxar in north India (1763–64), and the Rohilla, Maratha, and Mysore wars, were fought with Indian allies. The Hyderabad state, for example, was a generally reliable ally of the British. When it acquired power in Bengal (1757–65), the British East India Company was still militarily weak in relation to the biggest forces of the times, the Marathas, the Afghans, Awadh, Hyderabad, and emergent Mysore. The British did not fight with all of them; they did not need to. More often, alliances of which the Company formed a member fought others. The Company had a few major reverses, but in the end prevailed in the most consequential battles. A formal empire began around 1784, when Parliament started to exercise oversight of Indian governance.

Although the eighteenth-century battles were fought by a merchant company, protection of trading interests was not necessarily the overriding motive behind them. The British Company surely knew that they would make some economic gains by capturing state power. So did some of the Indian capitalists who had a stake in overseas and coastal trades, and who saw their future interests better protected by the foreign merchants than by the feudal warlords (Bayly 1990: 204). And yet there was more than commercial interest at stake in these battles. After all, the London shareholders of the Company did not want these wars. The eighteenth-century foundation of a British Empire in South Asia cannot be understood in terms of the *demand* for a new kind of state, but needs to be read instead as the *supply* of a militarily stronger political order than the Indian states could provide at this time.

Where did the superior military capacity derive from? At least four theories are available to answer the question: military technology, credible alliance, fiscal effort, and design of the army.

Inspired by the Roberts-Parker's 'military revolution' approach, some historians contend that the Europeans were better equipped, technologically as well as strategically (Parker 1988; Barua 1994; Gordon 1998). The military revolution paradigm suggests that they were better equipped because they were inheritors of a European military revolution. Consistent with this view, the European merchant firms had an acknowledged superiority in sea warfare, while none of the Indian states had a navy worthy of the name. Against this view, the decisive battles in the eighteenth century were fought on land, and mainly with infantry soldiers. In land warfare, the Europeans did bring to India some useful knowledge relating to infantry formation, command structure, professionalized officer corps, flintlock guns, cannon of cast iron, and mobile artillery, but none of these made a decisive difference, and they were quickly copied by others. As the eighteenth century progressed, the Indian regimes were hiring so many European mercenaries and adopting European knowledge so readily that by the second half of the century a distinction cannot be drawn between European and Indian technologies.

Did technology, then, not matter at all in land warfare? Kaushik Roy (2005) suggests that it did, because the Europeans managed to *combine* much better than the Indians elements of new technology and 'certain indigenous military techniques and ... the natural, human and animal resources of India in warfare'.

In other explanations of the emergence of the British Empire in India, emphasis falls on institutions. Being European, an outsider, and a merchant firm might make the Company state more willing to make institutional experiments, enter credible commitments, and consider hybrid military strategies. Oak and Swamy (2012), for example, state that whereas alliances formed between rivals often failed due to limited trust, alliances formed by the Company were more secure due to greater trust. The source of that trust was parliamentary oversight of the Company's Indian governance, which began in 1772.

Roy (2013) considers that the fiscal innovations that sustained a standing army crucially helped the Company. Although in the mid-eighteenth century, the Company relied on alliances and mercenary soldiers just as many Indian regimes did, by 1820, a fundamental rupture had taken place. This rupture occurred in two connected ways: the Company fought using its own army and relied less on landlords and land grantees for the military purpose than did the Indian regimes; and the Company raised the efficiency and taxable power of land, thanks to its reduced dependence on landlords. When the Indian Mutiny began in 1857, about 350,000 military personnel received pay from the Company. They consisted of British and European infantry, cavalry, and artillery, and 'native infantry' regiments and battalions numbering more than 200,000 soldiers. The Mutiny broke out among the native infantry, and almost all of the cost was paid out of Indian revenues. Several of the prominent Indian states, as they fought more battles, relied more on mercenaries, gave away revenue rights, and shrunk in revenue earnings and the size of the army. The Company alone managed to raise its revenue as well as the size of the army while continuing the war effort over many decades.

Having a standing army created new problems. The army was diverse in ethnic terms. How to create a command structure that would override the diversity and not cause tensions was a challenge. In many historical examples of ethnically diverse armies diversity led to some form of decentralization – that is, soldiers followed their own commanders rather than the central command. The East India Company retained ethnic segmentation but created a uniform service with a single set of rules and a salary and pension system that bound the segments together. The Company also left the officer corps more or less European.

At the turn of the nineteenth century, the Napoleonic Wars (and in particular, Napoleon's domination of Spain) helped trigger the movement for independence that freed most of Latin America from Spanish and Portuguese control by the 1820s. If the Napoleonic Wars undermined Spain's and Portugal's American empires, they influenced the making of the British Empire in Asia in several ways. The battles of Marengo and Hohenlinden consolidated Napoleon's position in the Middle East. French control over the land route to India was a worry for the British. Although Napoleon did not seem to have an India strategy, the Company state in India feared the prospect of a rebellion in India with French help (Ingram 1984). The continental blockade in Europe and the Dutch blockade of south-east Asia disrupted the export trade from the Indian Ocean region. 'When these markets opened again, they received British-made goods' (Bayly 1985). In this way, India emerged as a strategic possession in this global war.

Until the mid-nineteenth century, the British and the French were marginally involved in the West African wars. Imperialism was still far away. The British were entrenched in India, but the wars that they needed to win to be able to rule were not 'imperialist' wars in the nineteenth-century British sense, if we define the British Empire mainly as a political construct existing to serve trade, industrialization, migration, and investment. A global or imperial economic interest was not palpably present in the Rohilla-Maratha-Mysore-Sikh conflicts. The European element was no more important in these wars than was the instability of Indian states. By contrast in the late nineteenth century, starting from the Great Indian Mutiny (1857–58), the empire fought to defend its economic geography. Similarly, in Africa, the British Empire formed, penetrated inland, and partitioned territories, to defend global imperial economic interest from the late nineteenth century onwards.

From Warfare to Imperialism in Africa

The end of the slave trade in nineteenth-century West Africa and the rise of 'legitimate commerce' – palm oil in Nigeria and the groundnut in Senegambia, for example – is thought to have introduced a new form of political instability, which aided the transition to British imperial rule in the region. African states that risked losing wealth due to the end of the slave trade resorted to warfare and plunder. The merchants and the peasants who had a stake in legitimate commerce would see their interests poorly protected by the existing political structure. Europeans shared their concerns, and were readier to interfere in politics to protect their trading profits. Hopkins (1968), a proponent of this view, would thus see a new type of capitalism as the catalyst in changing the nature of warfare, and eventually the breakdown of indigenous political structures and 'Partition' of Africa. From the perspective of the capitalists, the problem was not anarchy or statelessness, but fragmentation of political power, or the absence of the kind of centralized legislating states 'that foreign investors could readily identify as being suitable vehicles for development' (Hopkins 2009: 248).

Later readings of the commercial transition suggest that there was more continuity than disruption within African states (Law 2009). The end of the slave trade itself was a more gradual process than it may seem from this account. The persistence of local trade in slaves and the use of slaves in export crop production cushioned the effects of the end of overseas trade to some extent. Economic motivation was not always paramount in all imperialist wars. But there is little dispute that conflict between African states and coastal capitalists in the late nineteenth century made new state formations, ones in which Europeans would have a stake, more likely. In a similar fashion, contradictory interests of overseas trade and indigenous states contributed to wars, and the making of informal empires and zones of influence in the Middle East and China as well. Again, drawing on Hopkins (2009), Africa 'fits into an international pattern'.

The Indian Mutiny (1857–58) as an Imperialist War

The great Mutiny, which nearly ended British rule in South Asia, reveals the nature of the British imperial state more clearly than the turn-of-the-century wars fought by the Company's army against Indian states. It does so in two ways. First, the technological explanation for British superiority disappears, since the rebels had emerged from the same army that fought with them, leaving us with purely political and economic factors to explain outcomes. Second, the rebellion partly destroyed trade and commercial infrastructure, and threatened the existence of major commercial cities like Bombay and Calcutta. It threatened capitalism to a degree not experienced during earlier conflicts.

The extensive literature on the episode underplays the risks that capitalists faced during it. The scholarship recognizes that the Indian civilian population often supported the rebels because they had been under some form of economic pressure, such as industrial decline. This still leaves the role of business firms, bankers and merchants, undeveloped. Roy (2016) suggests that capitalist attitudes, whether in the war zone or outside it in the port cities, were shaped by attacks on private property and by the fraught relationship that developed between the rebel soldiers, rebel governments, and the wealthy townsmen in war zones. The rebels' fiscal basis was confined to the economies of a few cities. Increasingly cut off from trade and revenue flows, the war effort within the cities turned extortionate on the resident merchants. Outside the war zone, military control of the riparian trade highways gave the British access not only to the ports, but also to materiel procured from friendlier merchants located in the interior, and occasionally, a supply of loans from Indian bankers.

These propositions confirm that Indian capitalists saw the British Empire in a different light from the feudal chieftains, soldiers, and landlords. They saw it as a marketplace and as an institutional space favourable to their long-term interests and were willing to fight to protect the economic geography of the empire. In turn, by extending support, urban bankers and merchants shaped the course of the rebellion of 1857.

Costs and Benefits of Empire for the Colonizers and the Colonized

Were empires worth defending? For the Russian or Ottoman empires, for imperial China, the answer is unknown. But for the western European empires, the benefits and costs for the colonized people is a subject that has spilled a great deal of ink and that remains politically charged. We can offer a few propositions on which there is unlikely to be much controversy, particularly for South Asia. That is a large example, no doubt, but how typical remains to be studied. In India, the British Empire sought to protect trade and factor movements within the regions over which it had influence. Given its global ambitions, any assessment of its effects will need to distinguish between the empire as a state in India, that is, assess its record in producing public goods, and the empire as an agent protecting a global market.

That Indian capitalists based in the port cities made significant gains from the global marketplace cannot be gainsaid. Between 1800 and 1914, the volume of goods passing through Bombay, Madras, and Calcutta increased sixtyfold. With realistic estimates of national income growth, this extent of trade growth would mean a dramatic rise in the ratio of trade to income, possibly from 1–2 per cent in 1800 to more than 20 per cent in 1914. While there was some decline in employment in the artisanal industries in the nineteenth century, between 1860 and 1940, employment in factories increased from near-zero to 2 million (Gupta and Roy 2017). India – and Indian firms – led the contemporary developing world in two leading industries of the Industrial Revolution, cotton textiles and iron and steel. In 1910, 55 per cent of the cotton spindles outside Europe, North America, and Japan were installed in India. In 1935, 50 per cent of the steel produced outside Europe, North America, and Japan was made in India. At the time of independence in 1947, the port cities in India were homes to some of the best schools, colleges, hospitals, universities, banks, insurance companies, and learned societies available outside the Western world. A big part of that infrastructure had been created by the Indian merchants and industrialists. This was possible despite the high cost of credit and capital in India because Indian businesses benefited from trade or were able to access capital and labour from abroad. The government facilitated that process by maintaining open borders to both trade and factor market transactions, by enabling railway construction, and by creating a giant customs union within the empire.

But if we look at the record on public goods, the British Indian Empire did badly. It was a small government (tax-GDP ratio around 5 per cent almost throughout) and too conservative to grow bigger. It had to fund a massive army, which was employed to defend the empire as much as India's own borders. Many of the benefits of globalization remained confined to the cities, whereas between the cities and the agricultural interior there was widening inequality. That the minimalist state did not invest enough in the regions falling behind, and did not distribute opportunities more widely, was its decisive failure. The failure was compounded by the appalling record of colonial India in universal healthcare and education. British India spent less than 1 per cent of the money spent per head by the British government on social welfare (1930). Around 1950 India's illiteracy rate was one of the highest in the world. In terms of its infant mortality rate, India again belonged in a set of countries with exceptionally high child mortality in 1950.

A similar argument could be made about certain other colonies, although the evidence is as yet far from conclusive. In West Africa, for example, the French government spent little on its colonies, and it forced poor African taxpayers to foot 98 per cent of the bill for developing the colonies, including paying the elevated salaries of French colonial officials (Huillery 2014).

Beyond minimalist colonial states and lack of investment in human capital, there was also the onerous institutional legacy of conquest and colonialism. When the labour of slaves or indigenous workers could be exploited on a grand scale, inequality rose, and colonial institutions aimed above all else to protect elites from redistribution. As a result – it has been argued – the colonial institutions discouraged long run economic and political development, particularly in Africa, the Caribbean, and Latin America (Engerman and Sokoloff 1997; 2012; Acemoglu et al. 2001; 2002).[2] The slave trade may well have had similar devastating effects on long run growth by causing African states to collapse and aggravating ethnic fragmentation (Nunn 2008). But the reality may have been more complex than these arguments allow (Austin 2008), and in any case there remains the question of explaining why the bad institutions persisted after the end of colonialism.

What about the colonizers? Did they benefit from empire, at least in the case of Britain? If we judge from the years 1880–1912, Britain's colonial holdings around the world generated no excess returns, and the British Empire itself required a subsidy that ended up redistributing income from middle-class British taxpayers to the upper classes (Davis and Huttenback 1986).

If we move further back in the past, the evidence for some possible benefits from colonies and warfare may seem stronger, at least at first glance, for it has been argued that the Industrial Revolution itself was fuelled by warfare, colonial trade, and land-intensive colonial inputs (Pomeranz 2000) such as timber or, especially, cotton (Beckert 2015). The claims about cotton, however, are difficult to accept. North America only became a major supplier of Britain's raw cotton in the nineteenth century, long after the United States had become independent. And new sources of cotton supply could be tapped in many parts of the world. They did not depend on servile colonial peasants (although colonies often did grow cotton) or on slave labour either, as is clear

2 North American colonies in which native populations were small and free labour predominated escaped this institutional curse.

from the recovery of cotton production in the United States after the Civil War.

As for wars and colonial trade, Britain's military victories in the eighteenth century do seem to have raised English wages by giving Britain the lion's share of international trade (Findlay and O'Rourke 2007; Allen 2009). That finding can then be extended to an argument that the higher wages encouraged British inventors to find ways to substitute relatively cheap capital for expensive labour and hence to an explanation of why the Industrial Revolution was British. But this second part of the argument has been criticized. It is also hard to reconcile with the evidence mounted in favour of a very different explanation of why the Industrial Revolution was British, one that stresses useful knowledge and human capital – in particular, an abundant supply of mechanics and machine-makers in Britain (Kelly et al. 2014).

It seems, then, that colonial empires yielded few benefits for the average European, apart from sugar and other cheaper consumer goods produced by slaves and the mountains of silver mined with forced labour in the Americas. One could say the same for all the warfare in Europe. Although it may have spurred technological innovation in metalworking, it imposed huge costs on most Europeans. It interrupted trade, and battles on land drastically reduced agricultural productivity by destroying capital embodied in improvements to the soil such as land clearance (Hoffman 1996). The chief benefits from all the fighting in Europe – glory on the battlefield – accrued to the continent's kings and military leaders. Perhaps the only truly positive side to the military buildup in Europe came in the nineteenth century, thanks to the British navy: the end to the traffic in slaves, and the suppression of piracy, which contributed to the growth of free trade.

References

Acemoglu, D., Johnson, S. and Robinson, J. A. (2001). 'The Colonial Origins of Comparative Development: An Empirical Investigation', *American Economic Review*, 91, 1369–1401.

(2002). 'Reversal of Fortune: Geography and Institutions in the Making of the Modern World Income Distribution', *Quarterly Journal of Economics*, 117, 1231–1294.

Allen, R. C. (2009). *The British Industrial Revolution in Global Perspective*, Cambridge University Press.

Andrade, T. (2016). *The Gunpowder Age: China, Military Innovation, and the Rise of the West in World History*, Princeton University Press.

Austin, G. (2008). 'The "Reversal of Fortune" Thesis and the Compression of History: Perspectives from African and Comparative Economic History', *Journal of International Development*, 20, 996–1027.

Barua, P. (1994). 'Military Developments in India, 1750–1850', *Journal of Military History*, 58, 599.

Bayly, C. A. (1985). 'State and Economy in India over Seven Hundred Years', *Economic History Review*, 38, 583–596.

(1990). *Indian Society and the Making of the British Empire*, Cambridge University Press.

Beckert, S. (2015). *Empire of Cotton: A Global History*, New York: Vintage.

Brandt, L., Ma, D. and Rawski, T. G. (2014). 'From Divergence to Convergence: Reevaluating the History behind China's Economic Boom', *Journal of Economic Literature*, 52, 45–123.

Coşgel, M. M. and Miceli, T. J. (2005). 'Risk, Transaction Costs, and Tax Assignment: Government Finance in the Ottoman Empire', *Journal of Economic History*, 65, 806–821.

Coşgel, M. M., Miceli, T. and Ahmed, R. (2009). 'Law, State Power, and Taxation in Islamic History', *Journal of Economic Behavior and Organization*, 71, 704–717.

Cox, G. W. (2012). 'Was the Glorious Revolution a Constitutional Watershed?', *Journal of Economic History*, 72, 567–600.

Davis, L. E. and Huttenback, R. A. (1986). *Mammon and the Pursuit of Empire: The Political Economy of British Imperialism, 1860–1912*, Cambridge University Press.

Dincecco, M. (2009a). 'Fiscal Centralization, Limited Government, and Public Revenues in Europe, 1650–1913', *Journal of Economic History*, 69, 48–103.

(2009b). 'Political Regimes and Sovereign Credit Risk in Europe, 1750–1913', *European Review of Economic History*, 13, 31–63.

(2011). *Political Transformations and Public Finances: Europe, 1650–1913*, Cambridge University Press.

Engerman, S. L. and Sokoloff, K. L. (1997). 'Factor Endowments, Institutions, and Differential Paths of Growth Among New World Economies', in Haber, S. (ed.), *How Latin America Fell Behind*, Palo Alto: Stanford University Press, 260–304.

(2012). *Economic Development in the Americas since 1500*, Cambridge University Press.

Evans, E. W. and Richardson, D. (1995). 'Hunting for Rents: The Economics of Slaving in Pre-Colonial Africa', *Economic History Review*, 48, 665–686.

Findlay, R. and O'Rourke, K. H. (2007). *Power and Plenty: Trade, War, and the World Economy in the Second Millennium*, Princeton University Press.

Gommans, J. L. (2002). *Mughal Warfare: Indian Frontiers and Highroads to Empire, 1500–1700*, London and New York: Routledge.

Goody, J. (1971). *Technology, Tradition and the State in Pre-Colonial Africa*, Cambridge University Press.

Gordon, S. (1998). 'The Limited Adoption of European-Style Military Forces by Eighteenth Century Rulers in India', *Indian Economic and Social History Review*, 35, 229–245.

Guézo, A. (2010). 'The Impact of British Abolition on the States in the Hinterland of the Slave Coast', *Journal of the Historical Society of Nigeria*, 19, 132–156.

Gupta, B. and Roy, T. (2017). 'From Artisanal Production to Machine Tools: Industrialization in India over the Long Run', in O'Rourke, K. H. and

Williamson, J. G. (eds.), *The Spread of Modern Industry to the Periphery since 1871*, Oxford University Press, 229–255.

Hahn, S. (2016). *A Nation Without Borders: The United States and Its World in an Age of Civil Wars, 1830–1910*, New York: Penguin.

Headrick, D. R. (1981). *The Tools of Empire: Technology and European Imperialism in the Nineteenth Century*, Oxford University Press.

(2010). *Power over Peoples: Technology, Environments, and Western Imperialism, 1400 to the Present*, Princeton University Press.

Hoffman, P. T. (1996). *Growth in a Traditional Society: The French Countryside, 1450–1815*, Princeton University Press.

(2015). *Why Did Europe Conquer the World?*, Princeton University Press.

Hopkins, A. G. (1968). 'Economic Imperialism in West Africa: Lagos, 1880–92', *Economic History Review*, 21, 580–606.

(2009). 'The "New International Economic Order" in the Nineteenth Century: Britain's First Development Plan for Africa', in Law, R. (ed.), *From Slave Trade to 'Legitimate' Commerce: The Commercial Transition in Nineteenth-Century West Africa*, Cambridge University Press, 240–264.

Huang, R. (1974). *Taxation and Governmental Finance in Sixteenth-Century Ming China*, vol. 4, Cambridge University Press.

Huillery, E. (2014). 'The Black Man's Burden: The Cost of Colonization of French West Africa', *Journal of Economic History*, 74, 1–38.

Ingram, E. (1984). *In Defence of British India: Great Britain in the Middle East, 1775–1842*, London: Frank Cass.

Inikori, J. E. (1977). 'The Import of Firearms into West Africa, 1750–1807', *Journal of African History*, 18, 339–368.

Jones, E. (2003). *The European Miracle: Environments, Economies and Geopolitics in the History of Europe and Asia*, Cambridge University Press.

Kelly, M., Mokyr, J. and Ó Gráda, C. (2014). 'Precocious Albion: A New Interpretation of the British Industrial Revolution', *Annual Review of Economics*, 6, 363–389.

Law, R. (1986). 'Dahomey and the Slave Trade: Reflections on the Historiography of the Rise of Dahomey', *Journal of African History*, 27, 237–267.

(1989). 'Slave-Raiders and Middlemen, Monopolists and Free-Traders: The Supply of Slaves for the Atlantic Trade in Dahomey *c.*1715–1850', *Journal of African History*, 30, 45–68.

(2009). 'Introduction' in Law, R. (ed.), *From Slave Trade to 'Legitimate' Commerce: The Commercial Transition in Nineteenth-Century West Africa*, Cambridge University Press, 1–31.

Lieberman. V. (2008). 'The Qing Dynasty and Its Neighbors: Early Modern China in World History', *Social Science History*, 32, 281–304.

Manning, P. (1990). *Slavery and African Life: Occidental, Oriental, and African Slave Trades*, Cambridge University Press.

Mokyr, J. (2017). *A Culture of Growth*, Princeton University Press.

Monson, A. and Scheidel, W. (eds.) (2015). *Fiscal Regimes and the Political Economy of Premodern States*, Cambridge University Press.

Neal, L. (1990). *The Rise of Financial Capitalism: International Capital Markets in the Age of Reason*, Cambridge University Press.

Nunn, N. (2008). 'The Long-Term Effect of Africa's Slave Trades', *Quarterly Journal of Economics*, 123, 139–176.

Oak, M. and Swamy, A. V. (2012). 'Myopia or Strategic Behavior? Indian Regimes and the East India Company in Late Eighteenth-Century India', *Explorations in Economic History*, 49, 352–366.

Ojo, O. (2008). 'The Organization of the Atlantic Slave Trade in Yorubaland, *c.*1777 to *c.*1856', *International Journal of African Historical Studies*, 41, 77–100.

O'Rourke, K. H. and Williamson, J. G. (1999). *Globalization and History: The Evolution of a Nineteenth-Century Atlantic Economy*, Cambridge, MA: MIT Press.

Pamuk, Ş. (2004). 'Institutional Change and the Longevity of the Ottoman Empire, 1500–1800', *Journal of Interdisciplinary History*, 35, 225–247.

Parker, G. (1988). *The Military Revolution: Military Innovation and the Rise of the West 1500–1800*, Cambridge University Press.

Perdue, P. C. (2005). *China Marches West: the Qing Conquest of Central Eurasia*, Cambridge, MA: Harvard University Press.

Pomeranz, K. (2000). *The Great Divergence : China, Europe, and the Making of the Modern World Economy*, Princeton University Press.

Roberts, R. L. (1980). 'Production and Reproduction of Warrior States: Segu Bambara and Segu Tokolor, *c.*1712–1890', *International Journal of African Historical Studies*, 13, 389–419.

Rosenthal, J. L. and Bin Wong, R. (2011). *Before and Beyond Divergence*, Cambridge, MA: Harvard University Press.

Roy, K. (2005). 'Military Synthesis in South Asia: Armies, Warfare, and Indian Society, *c.*1740–1849', *Journal of Military History*, 69, 651–690.

Roy, T. (2013). 'Rethinking the Origins of British India: State Formation and Military-Fiscal Undertakings in an Eighteenth-Century World Region', *Modern Asian Studies*, 47, 1125–1156.

(2016). 'The Mutiny and the Merchants', *The Historical Journal*, 59, 393–416.

Sng, T. H. (2014). 'Size and Dynastic Decline: The Principal-Agent Problem in Late Imperial China, 1700–1850', *Explorations in Economic History*, 54, 107–127.

Thornton, J. (1999). *Warfare in Atlantic Africa 1500–1800*, London: UCL Press.

Vries, P. H. H. (2002). 'Governing Growth: A Comparative Analysis of the Role of the State in the Rise of the West', *Journal of World History*, 13, 67–138.

Will, P. E. and Wong, R. B. (1991). *Nourish the People*, Ann Arbor: University of Michigan Press.

Index

For EU product safety concerns, contact us at Calle de José Abascal, 56–1°, 28003 Madrid, Spain or eugpsr@cambridge.org.

www.ingramcontent.com/pod-product-compliance
Lightning Source LLC
LaVergne TN
LVHW052213200926
848481LV00001B/97

* 9 7 8 1 3 1 6 6 1 2 2 4 8 *